REBBE

ALSO BY JOSEPH TELUSHKIN

NONFICTION

The Nine Questions People Ask About Judaism (with Dennis Prager)

Why the Jews: The Reason for Antisemitism (with Dennis Prager)

Jewish Literacy: The Most Important Things to Know About the Jewish Religion, Its People, and Its History

Jewish Humor: What the Best Jewish Jokes Say About the Jews

Jewish Wisdom: Ethical, Spiritual, and Historical Lessons from the Great Works and Thinkers

Words That Hurt, Words That Heal: How to Use Words Wisely and Well

Biblical Literacy: The Most Important People, Events, and Ideas of the Hebrew Bible

The Book of Jewish Values: A Day-by-Day Guide to Ethical Living

The Golden Land: The Story of Jewish Immigration to America

The Ten Commandments of Character: Essential Advice for Living an Honorable, Ethical, Honest Life

Everything Is Possible: Life and Business Lessons from a Self-Made Billionaire and the Founder of Slim Fast by S. Daniel Abraham with Joseph Telushkin

A Code of Jewish Ethics, Volume 1: You Shall Be Holy

A Code of Jewish Ethics, Volume 2: Love Your Neighbor

Hillel: If Not Now, When?

FICTION

The Unorthodox Murder of Rabbi Wahl

The Final Analysis of Dr. Stark

An Eye for an Eye

Heaven's Witness (with Allen Estrin)

REBBE

THE LIFE

and TEACHINGS *of*

MENACHEM M. SCHNEERSON,

THE MOST INFLUENTIAL RABBI

in MODERN HISTORY

Joseph Telushkin

HARPER WAVE

An Imprint of HarperCollins*Publishers*

www.harperwave.com

HarperCollins books may be purchased for educational, business, or sales promotional use. For information, please e-mail the Special Markets Department at SPsales@harpercollins .com.

FIRST EDITION

Designed by Leah Carlson-Stanisic

The photographs in this book were provided by JEM's Living Archive and American Friends of Lubavitch.

Photographs by C. B. Halberstam, L. Y. Freidin, Y. Melamed, and Z. Schildkraut are copyrighted by Jewish Educational Media, Inc., and are used with permission from JEM. Cover photo: L. Y. Freidin.

Library of Congress Cataloging-in-Publication Data has been applied for.

ISBN: 978-0-06-231898-5

14 15 16 17 18 OV/RRD 10 9 8 7 6 5 4 3 2 1

To the blessed memory of Yitzchak Leib (Lyle) Federman,
and in honor of Chedva Federman

CONTENTS

Part Four: Life Lessons According to the Rebbe

Part Five: Uniting the Jews:
The Rebbe's Approach to a Fractured People

Part Six: Judaism Confronts Modernity:
Controversial Views of the Rebbe

Part Seven: The Rebbe and His Family

Part Eight: "It Is the Books That Were Victorious"

Part Nine: The World of Messianism

Part Ten: Leadership After Life

Part Eleven: The Life of Rabbi Menachem Mendel Schneerson

PREFACE

I entered into the writing of this book with a high regard for the Rebbe (why else devote years of one's life to focusing on another person's life and teachings), and after five years of research and writing I came out with an even higher one. Much, I know, has been said of the Rebbe, both true and untrue, both highly adulatory and highly critical, and thus I pursued my subject with much scrutiny and with open eyes. Along the way, I learned that one can have great admiration for a person with whom one has profound disagreements. To cite just two: unlike the Rebbe, I believe that it is very worthwhile for Israel under certain conditions to make territorial compromises with the Palestinians, just as I believe it was right for her to do so with Egypt, a position the Rebbe believed would put lives at risk (see chapter 19), and that I believe saved lives. Also, I was an ardent member of the Student Struggle for Soviet Jewry and supporter of anti-Soviet demonstrations during the 1960s and 1970s (a time of severe antisemitism by the Soviet government), at a time when the Rebbe was convinced that such demonstrations were harming Russian Jews, and that only "quiet diplomacy" could improve their situation. In the course of researching this book I learned things I hadn't known, that the Rebbe, despite his fervent opposition to demonstrations, was a more nuanced and practical thinker on the issue of how to help Russian Jews than many people—I being one of them—realized. True, he opposed anti-Soviet demonstrations, but on the quiet, out of earshot of the Russians (and in addition to the secret work he was spearheading to maintain Jewish life inside Russia), he found ways to cooperate with people who supported them—and I believe that the actions taken by both sides greatly helped the Jews of Russia (see chapter 21). In general, I was struck again and again by the nuanced nature of the Rebbe's thinking. Thus, to no one's surprise, the Rebbe thought that Reform and Conservative Judaism were wrongheaded in their approach to Judaism, but when a Reform rabbi asked him if he should leave his congregation, the Rebbe told him, "You're a soldier on the front" (the sort of response he might well have given one of his *shluchim* [emissaries]), and told the man that not only should he not leave his congregation but that he should challenge his congregants to do more, and even challenge him, the Rebbe, to do more as well (see page 224).

Perhaps the most unanticipated result of the researching and writing of this book is the profound impact it has had on my life. Given that the Rebbe transformed so many people's lives, it is perhaps not surprising that he has impacted the life of this biographer as well. In many ways. Most significantly, the Rebbe's innate optimism and his focus on the use of optimistic language has changed me, I hope forever. I was first struck when I learned of the Rebbe's refusal to use the word "*beit cholim,*" the Hebrew term for "hospital," a word that literally means "house of the sick," and which the Rebbe felt demoralized people (see the term he proposed instead; page 110). I immediately realized he was right. Similarly, because of the Rebbe, I have stopped using the word "deadline," substituting instead "due date," the first term—which is so widely used—connoting the end of life and the second, life's beginning. Does this change seem minor and petty? Maybe minor, but certainly not petty. There are few things we use more often than words, and the types of verbal changes the Rebbe recommended, which invariably involved seeking out encouraging words, have in turn changed me. My wife, Dvorah, often commented that whenever I spent the day researching at 770 Eastern Parkway, the generic address for the Chabad movement's Brooklyn headquarters, I came home in an uplifted, invigorated mood. That is because Lubavitchers as a group are upbeat, a result in large part of the influence exerted upon them by the Rebbe and his teachings, even now, almost twenty years since his death. If one can make a generalization about so large a group of people as Lubavitcher Chasidim, one generalization I feel comfortable in making is that Lubavitchers exude a warm calm and optimism, they avoid negative language, and the mood they convey is contagious. I am a happier and more spiritual person as a result of writing this book—and I would like to believe more generous and less judgmental of others. All of these things would not have occurred if not for the fact that my life was consumed in learning the details of the life and thinking of the Seventh Rebbe of Chabad.

Similarly, the Rebbe's insistence that anything worth doing should be done now and not delayed (see chapter 10), even in instances in which most of us would delay, has repeatedly caused me to act in a more forthright and direct manner. If a difficult phone call has to be made or a difficult issue confronted, I am now more likely than in the past to not procrastinate but to do so right away; I am not yet sure if I have the guts to also do so even in the middle of the night, as the Rebbe sometimes advocated (see page 148).

The Rebbe's impact on my life has grown strong, and I suspect will grow stronger, in a whole host of spiritual, ethical, and ritual ways over the coming years. It is difficult to be exposed to the teachings of such a man and not be affected in some fundamental ways. I hope and expect that these impacts will long endure.

I was well aware of the Rebbe as a significant figure before researching and writing this book but have come to appreciate over these past years the magnitude of his achievements. Rabbi Menachem Mendel Schneerson assumed leadership of a relatively small movement of Lubavitcher Chasidim in 1951, and he turned Chabad into the most dynamic and geographically diverse religious movement in Jewish life; furthermore, his influence extended well beyond his movement. The outgoing chief rabbi of Great Britain, Lord Jonathan Sacks, described well the enormity of the Rebbe's accomplishments: "Among the very greatest Jewish leaders of the past, there were some who transformed communities. There were others who raised up many disciples; there were yet others who left us codes and commentaries which will be studied for all time. But there have been few in the entire history of one of the oldest peoples in the world who in one lifetime made their influence felt throughout the entire Jewish world. . . . The Rebbe was one of the immortals."

Early on in my work on this book, I met Ben Federman, a highly successful young businessman, with a fascinating background. His father was a man of great kindness, a computer whiz who loved nature, and whose family is involved in the movie and entertainment industry. His mother, a social worker, hails from an old Lubavitch family, while her father was an early Maccabiah champion weight lifter. Ben himself is an army veteran, a U.S. history buff, and an innovative-entrepreneur. We bonded at a dinner over our mutual interest in Civil War history, as well as our curiosity to discover more about the Rebbe's personality and a desire to reach a greater understanding of who he was. Ben subsequently granted me the great gift of time by making it possible for me to devote the years necessary to bring this book to fruition. I am grateful, as well as honored, to dedicate this volume to Ben Federman's parents.

One of the great joys of working on this book was knowing the immense gratification both my father, Shlomo Telushkin, of blessed memory, and my grandfather, Rabbi Nissen Telushkin, of blessed memory, would have in knowing that their son and grandson was writing a book about a man whom they so esteemed. My grandfather was long ensconced in the world of Chabad, had a close relationship with both the Rebbe and his father-in-law, the Frierdiker (previous) Rebbe, and is indeed buried only a few feet away from the *Ohel*, where the two Rebbes are interred. My father served as the accountant to the Rebbe and to his father-in-law as well. He held this position from shortly after the arrival of the Frierdiker Rebbe in the United States, and was very proud of this connection. When people had a private meeting with the Rebbe, it was known as a *yechidus*. My father had an annual *yechidus* with the Rebbe on or just before April 15, when the Rebbe would sign his tax return, and my father, in turn, would have the chance to speak to and consult with the Rebbe about various personal, professional, and familial matters going on in his life. I myself didn't get married until deep into my thirties, and I remember the happiness my father had when he brought home one day from 770 a bottle of vodka given to him by the Rebbe, which he told my father was to be opened at a *simcha* (a joyous occasion) for me. A couple of years later, when a book I had written was about to be published, I jokingly asked my father if we could open the bottle at a launch party for the book. My father said, "This is not the *simcha* the Rebbe meant." Indeed, the bottle was opened at my wedding. When my father was in his mid-seventies, and started to give up some of his clients, he always made it clear that he would work as Chabad's accountant as long as he had the strength; that this would be the last client he would ever give up.

As positive as my associations with Lubavitch were, while growing up and for many years after, I was not at all closely involved in these parts of my father's and grandfather's lives. Lubavitch, for much of my life, was something always dear to me, but often from a distance, and not actively on my radar. In some ways, therefore, these past years of researching and writing have not only acquainted me with the Rebbe in a way I had not previously known, but brought me to a deeper and more intimate knowledge of both my father and grandfather, of the spiritual paths they trod, and of the very special role Rabbi Menachem Mendel Schneerson played in their lives. In the course of researching and writing this book, I have come to understand them better, to grow closer to them (even though my grandfather died in 1970 and my father in 1987), and I regard this as a sacred gift.

Sometimes, as I commuted to the Chabad offices in Crown Heights to do my research, it felt as if I were visiting my father as well; so many Chabadniks shared with me recollections of seeing my father working there. The sense of satisfaction increased when my daughter Shira spent three months in the early stages of this project helping me research and define the areas of the Rebbe's life that I wished to explore, and as my son, Benjamin (BenTzion), interned in the summer at Chabad.org, the Chabad website that attracted thirty-seven million visitors last year.

As a believer in an afterlife, I sense my father and grandfather are aware their son and grandson has been chronicling the life and teachings of the Rebbe, and that this has been a source of great satisfaction to them. This thought, which obviously I can't prove but which I strongly believe, is very precious to me. More precious than rubies, as the Bible would say.

AUTHOR'S NOTE

In addition to years of immersion in letters, recordings, and other numerous documents, much of the material in this book also derives from people's encounters with the Rebbe, and their recollections of what he told them. When citing statements the Rebbe made to others, I put his words in quotation marks, though I acknowledge that what is being cited are people's recollections of what he said, and while I only cite statements that I am confident represent the gist of his words, I also acknowledge that, given the frailty of human memory, it is likely that these citations are often not the Rebbe's exact words. Similarly, quotes from the Rebbe's Yiddish speeches and Hebrew correspondence have been translated (as my Yiddish is weak, I consulted with others), and any mistranslations or errors in conveying intent or nuance are mine alone.

While biographies generally set down their subject's story in chronological order, starting with birth, the Rebbe's greatest and most enduring legacies stemmed from the multitude of his ideas and religious campaigns. As these were the activities that most concretely defined the Rebbe's life, I have elected, therefore, not to write his story sequentially, but to describe, rather, issue by issue how the Rebbe took a small movement and turned it into a worldwide force. However, in the final chapter of the book, I have included an extensive timeline that brings together in chronological order the tapestry of the Rebbe's life, and includes a variety of incidents, many of them not discussed earlier in the book. I encourage you to read it thoughtfully.

Lastly, but importantly, when I refer to the Creator, I spell it as "God," yet when citing from the writings of the Rebbe, God is written as "G-d," as the Rebbe did. The same goes for certain other Jewish and Yiddish words in this book, for which there is a glossary at the end.

Part One

·⟨══⟩·

LEADERSHIP

of the

REBBE

Chapter 1

·❦·

A REBBE FOR THE NEW WORLD

In 1994, a few months after his passing, Rabbi Menachem Mendel Schneerson, the Lubavitcher Rebbe, was posthumously awarded the Congressional Gold Medal, the highest award granted by the American government to a civilian (he is the only rabbi, and only the second clergyman, to have received this honor).[1] The rarely awarded Gold Medal is designated for those "who have performed an achievement that has an impact on American history and culture that is likely to be recognized ... long after the achievement." At the award ceremony, African American congressman John Lewis, the civil rights legend and cosponsor of the award, noted that perhaps the only issue on which he and Speaker of the House Newt Gingrich agreed was the importance of bestowing this medal on the Lubavitcher Rebbe. Congressman Lewis, citing his awe at the Rebbe's accomplishments, expressed his sorrow that neither he, nor his mentor, the Reverend Martin Luther King Jr., had ever met the Rebbe. Gingrich, yet another cosponsor, spoke not just of the Rebbe's integrity but of his respect for the Rebbe's representatives whom he had met in Washington. Gingrich described his good feeling at being approached by one of the Rebbe's emissaries, someone "not in the right Gucci shoes [and] not in the right Italian suit, who doesn't ask you to increase their profit margin, but instead says, 'For the good of the world, this is something noble and idealistic that should be [done].'" And that's why, Gingrich concluded, he felt so celebratory that day.

Nor was it only Lewis and Gingrich who felt this admiration for the Rebbe. President Ronald Reagan, upon receiving letters from the Rebbe, would take them upstairs from the Oval Office to his residence and personally draft his responses.[2] In an April 1982 letter, the president cited words from a proclamation for a National Day of Reflection he was about to issue honoring the Rebbe's eightieth birthday: "Your work stands as a reminder to us all that knowledge is an unworthy goal unless it is accompanied by moral and spiritual wisdom and understanding." When a National Scroll of Honor signed by President Reagan was awarded to the Rebbe, every single member of the House of Representatives and Senate signed it as well.

By 1990, when Peggy Noonan, the longtime White House speechwriter, published *What I Saw at the Revolution*, her best-selling political memoir, the Rebbe had become a widely acknowledged cultural reference. When speculating in the book's final pages about moral issues that Noonan, of Irish-Catholic descent, felt were better addressed by religious rather than political leaders, she specified three, "the Archbishop of Canterbury, the Lubavitcher Rebbe, and the Pope."[3]

By the Rebbe's later years, and continuing after his death, his impact had become far-reaching in a manner dissimilar from any other modern rabbinic figure. In 2013, on the night preceding his election to the Senate, Democratic candidate Cory Booker, an African American Christian, went to the *Ohel*, the site of the Rebbe's grave, to pray. It was done in a private manner, no journalists were present, and the visit only came to public attention after the election. As Booker has often made clear, he regards the Rebbe as one of his foremost teachers.

Rabbi Menachem Mendel Schneerson, the Seventh Lubavitcher Rebbe,[4] was, inarguably, the most well known rabbi since Moses Maimonides (Rambam). Hundreds of prominent rabbinic figures have lived in the intervening eight hundred years, but how many can be named before an audience of Jews from the United States, Israel, France, or the former Soviet Union (the four largest Jewish communities in the world today), without the speaker needing to add a sentence or two explaining who the person was?[5]

The Rebbe is widely recognized in all the Jewish denominations and in all the countries just mentioned. And beyond. Visitors to Morocco have long reported seeing two pictures hanging in Moroccan Jewish homes, one of the Moroccan king and one of the Rebbe.[6] Just a few days ago I saw a picture of the Rebbe in my local barbershop; the owner and senior barber is from Uzbekistan.

There is also no shortage of non-Jews who know of and feel connected to the Rebbe. In effect, he has become a global ambassador for Judaism. In 1989, Uruguayan presidential candidate Luis Alberto Lacalle, a religious Catholic, came to Crown Heights, Brooklyn, for what proved to be a brief but highly significant meeting with the Rebbe. What Lacalle was pursuing was a blessing from the Rebbe, whom he regarded and continues to regard as a holy man. In an interview more than a decade later, Lacalle, who went on to serve as Uruguay's president, spoke of how moved he was when the Rebbe gave him a dollar—one of several thousand people to whom he gave a dollar that day—and asked him to give it to charity. "I give it to you," Lacalle recalls the Rebbe telling him, "to remember to do works of good."[7]

Lech Walesa, the Polish labor leader who helped lead his country to democracy and later served as Poland's president, has long carried in his wallet a dollar from the Rebbe that was given to him by an American-Jewish businessman, David Chase. When Walesa visited the Museum of the Diaspora in Tel Aviv and saw a picture of the Rebbe, he asked Chase, who was accompanying him: "Is this my Rebbe? The one who gave me the dollar?"[8] When told that it was, Walesa bowed from the waist toward the Rebbe in a gesture of respect. The museum's curator, who had overheard Walesa's exchange with Chase, was stunned. "What is he doing?" he asked Chase. "Is the president of Poland bowing to the Rebbe?" "Right," Chase responded. "He's showing his respect to the Rebbe."[9]

Four years ago, a full sixteen years after the Rebbe's death, Rabbi Yehuda Krinsky, a secretary to the Rebbe, was at the Atlanta airport when he was stopped by a young African American man of about twenty: "Did anyone ever tell you that you look like the Lubavitcher Rebbe?" the man asked.[10] Krinsky soon learned that the man had watched the Rebbe on television.

This, too, was an unusual feature of Rabbi Menachem Mendel Schneerson. How many rabbis of any background routinely broadcast

speeches on television, not sound bites, but full-fledged talks? The
Rebbe's subjects encompassed not only lessons from the Torah and from
Chasidic thought but insights on the space race and the moon landing
(see page 181), energy independence, and the attempted assassination
of President Reagan.[11] In the heyday of Chabad broadcasts, 770 Eastern
Parkway, the movement's headquarters in Brooklyn, commonly received several hundred letters a day addressed to the Rebbe, the majority from Jews but many from non-Jews as well. This was among the
largest number of private letters being delivered to any address in the
New York area.

But the Rebbe's popularity and legacy were not without controversy.
Indeed, he expressed his views fearlessly, even when they were not
popular. His views on Israeli security and his opposition to any territorial compromise by Israel sparked both support and intense opposition
and, on one noted occasion, kept a leading prime ministerial candidate
from becoming Israel's leader. His stern opposition to public demonstrations against the Soviet Union's oppression of Russia's Jews, focusing
instead on "behind-the-scenes diplomacy" to sustain Soviet Jewry and
facilitate their release, put him at odds with the overwhelming majority
of American, European, and Israeli Jewish leaders who thought demonstrations to be an indispensable and very necessary option. On more
than one occasion he butted heads with leaders from both the Jewish
religious left and right, and while he was determined to engage Jews
from across the spectrum of observance, many Reform, Conservative,
and *haredi* leaders as well voiced opposition to his outreach ideas, and
found others of his policies alienating. And, of course, in the last years
of his life, while many of his followers believed he would soon be revealed as the Messiah, this notion was overwhelmingly rejected and
sometimes ridiculed by others. Notwithstanding these controversies,
no one can deny the immense and reverberating worldwide impact of
Rabbi Menachem Mendel Schneerson both during his lifetime and no
less forcefully since.

What was it about the Rebbe that caused *Yediot Achronot*, Israel's then
largest-circulation newspaper, to devote twenty pages to the Rebbe on
the day following his death, the type of coverage normally reserved for a

sitting head of state? What was it about him that caused *Newsweek*, which rarely had occasion to write of the Chasidic world, to label the Rebbe "the most influential Jew in the world"?

It would seem that two factors in particular account for the Rebbe's extraordinary impact: first, his innovative ideas on how to reach Jews (later non-Jews as well), and second, the army of *shluchim*, the emissaries, he nurtured to carry out his ideas and his vision, eventually in well over a thousand cities.

For American Jews, even those who maintained no synagogue affiliation and had no involvement with their local Jewish community, an exposure to Judaism might well have come from being approached by a young bearded man on the street, and asked, "Are you Jewish?" If the listener was male and responded yes, he was escorted to a nearby van, a Mitzvah Mobile, and encouraged to wrap tefillin on his arm and on his head—tefillin are two small black boxes with leather straps attached to them in which are inserted texts ordaining, among other commandments, a love of God.[12] Over the years, the number of men who had this experience reached into the hundreds of thousands. The same question, "Are you Jewish?," was also addressed to women; those who answered yes were offered candles and candlesticks and asked to light and make the blessing over the candles on Friday before sundown in honor of the Sabbath.

For the Rebbe, asking Jewish women (starting with girls aged three and older) to make the blessing over the candles was only the beginning. Jewish tradition wanted them to do it right, at the specified time, for that, too, is ordained in Jewish law, which forbids lighting a fire after the Sabbath begins (Exodus 35:3). Thus, a small ad started to appear in the *New York Times* every Friday in which "Jewish women" were informed as to the time candles should be lit that day. It was the only ad the *Times* ran regularly on its front page. Many traditional Jews routinely checked the Friday paper to know when Shabbat started, since it varies from week to week, based on when the sun sets.

No less than this outreach to the broad Jewish community, what equally characterized the Rebbe was his ability to always remain focused on individuals. I know of no other leader of his stature who remained so accessible to all those who wanted to meet with him. For the first thirty years of his leadership, he would meet with visitors three and then two nights a week, at which time people would pose personal and religious questions to him. The meetings would commence at 8:00 p.m. and last till 2:00 or 3:00 a.m., sometimes until dawn. Rabbi Uri Kaploun recalls a private meeting with the Rebbe (*yechidus*) that concluded at 2:45 a.m. and notes that he was the forty-third person the Rebbe saw that evening— and that was not the last meeting of the night. Visitors from abroad appreciated that they needed no translator to speak to the Rebbe. He was fluent in English, Yiddish, Hebrew, Russian, German, and French (he had studied at universities in the last three languages, earning a degree in engineering) and was known to understand visitors who spoke to him in Spanish and Italian.

As he neared his eighties, he stopped conducting all-night meetings but soon started Sunday Dollars. Each Sunday, for several hours, he would dispense a blessing and a dollar (to be donated to charity) to thousands of people who waited in line to have a brief encounter with him.

Miriam Fellig, the sole survivor of a family destroyed in the Holocaust, was one of those who came to meet with the Rebbe. It was shortly after her marriage, and she was distraught at being alone in the world. "[You have] no one?" the Rebbe asked her. "No," she answered, "just my husband; no one else." She confided that the thought of becoming a mother frightened her, as she had no mother or family members to offer her guidance and help. Fellig soon made clear the one thing she did want was for the Rebbe to adopt her, making her in essence part of his family—and he did. As she recalled decades later, the Rebbe took out a little black book from his pocket, marked down her and her husband's names, extended to her a blessing for happiness, and made sure that they stayed in touch on a regular basis.[13]

It is told—and this account might well be apocryphal—that when Henry Ward Beecher, among the most prominent and admired clergymen in nineteenth-century America, was approached by his sister, Harriet Beecher Stowe (the author of *Uncle Tom's Cabin*), to become involved in the case of an individual who needed assistance, the already overworked preacher demurred, "Harriet, Harriet, I am too busy. I can no longer become involved in cases of individuals." To which his sister is said to have responded, "Even God is not that busy."

The Rebbe, and this is not apocryphal, tried to make sure to always find time. In June 1986, my father, Shlomo Telushkin—who had been the accountant both for the Rebbe and for the Previous Rebbe, since Chabad had come to the United States more than forty years earlier— suffered a serious stroke, one from which he never fully recovered. For several days he lay in a hospital bed in a coma, and I was with him when he awoke.

During those days, we received calls twice daily from the Rebbe's office asking about my father's condition. "The Rebbe wants to know," we were told. A few days later, I received a call from Rabbi Yehuda Krinsky, the Rebbe's secretary. He told me that an accounting issue had come up and the Rebbe had said, "Ask Shlomo."

"But you know how sick and disoriented my father is," I protested.

"We reminded the Rebbe of that," Krinsky answered. "He, of course, remembered, but he insisted that we ask your father."

I immediately went back to my father's room and posed the question to him. He looked at me, puzzled, and said the answer was obvious and told it to me.

At that moment, I realized what the Rebbe had done. He had made a calculation and asked my father a question that he knew my father would be able to answer. Sitting in his Brooklyn office at 770 Eastern Parkway, dealing with macro issues confronting Jews and the world, he had the moral imagination to feel the pain of one individual, my father, lying in a hospital bed, partially paralyzed, and wondering if he would ever again be productive. And so the Rebbe asked him a question, and by doing so he reminded my father that he was still needed and could still be of service.

Of his innovative campaigns to reach out both to communities and to individuals, perhaps the foremost and most innovative idea the Rebbe preached was the love of every Jew and, as we shall see, the broad love of humanity.

The preceding words sound neither innovative nor revolutionary. "Love your neighbor as yourself," the basis of the Golden Rule, is the Torah's most famous verse (Leviticus 19:18), and two of Judaism's best-known rabbis, Hillel and Akiva, regarded it as Judaism's most fundamental law.[14]

With such emphasis on the centrality of love of neighbor, it would seem that interpersonal love was always a uniformly treasured and practiced part of Judaism. Only it wasn't. The Talmud attributes the first-century Roman destruction of Judea and the Great Temple in Jerusalem, perhaps the greatest catastrophe in Jewish life prior to the Holocaust, to *sinat chinam*, causeless hatred, inside the Jewish community, a hatred that made it impossible for the Jews to unite and fight as one force against their Roman oppressors.[15]

This pattern of infighting has characterized and harmed the Jewish community ever since. In thirteenth-century France, it was a group of rabbis, not antisemites, who turned over Maimonides's writings, which they regarded as containing heretical ideas, to the Dominican-headed Inquisition to be burned.[16] Just as the Romans took advantage of Jewish infighting to decimate Judea, killing some million Jews in the process and selling hundreds of thousands of others into slavery, the Dominicans took advantage of this "gift" given them by these French rabbis and, seven years later, started to burn the Talmud as well.

In the eighteenth century, Rabbi Elijah, the Gaon of Vilna, among the greatest Jewish scholars in Jewish history, so despised the newly emerging Chasidic movement, which he regarded as heretical, that he refused to meet with its representatives who wished to assuage his concerns, and instead he issued a ban of excommunication against the Chasidim, forbidding Jews from conducting business with or marrying them. In addition, he declared of one of its leaders in his hometown of Vilna, "If it was in my hands, I would [do] to him what Elijah did to the false prophets of Ba'al"; in short, kill him, as Elijah led the Israelites in massacring 450 idolatrous priests (see I Kings 18:19, 40).[17] After the Gaon's death, one of his admirers made a false accusation of treason against the founder of Chabad, Rabbi Shneur Zalman of Liadi, in an attempt to have the rabbi executed by the czar's government.

The Rebbe came with a different message, one that he preached non-stop for over forty years: Love your fellow, and not just those who agree with you.

As the Rebbe intuited, while all Jews are familiar with the command-ment "Love your neighbor as yourself," it seems that virtually everyone, even some otherwise very great figures, has reasons and rationales to justify why it doesn't apply to those with whom they disagree.

As Rebbe, Menachem Mendel Schneerson introduced what was in effect a new standard in Jewish life, an *unconditional* love and respect for all Jews, regardless of their denominational affiliation or non-affiliation. Love all Jews, he preached, because they are your brothers or sisters, and just as you don't look for excuses not to love your sibling, don't look for reasons not to love other Jews.

This refusal to judge others based on their observance of Jewish laws, particularly ritual ones, was, and still is, a radical idea. Indeed, one prominent Orthodox rabbi, who was a devoted supporter of the Rebbe, had one complaint against him, that he allowed Reform and Conser-vative rabbis to attend public events at Chabad (see chapter 16). When he raised his objection to the Rebbe, it was dismissed; all Jews were, and continue to be, fully welcome at Chabad events.

The Rebbe's openness was not just a tactic, as some opponents of Chabad suspected, to augment financial support or to stimulate goodwill for Chabad, but represented what the Rebbe really felt. The young rabbi Israel Meir Lau (later, Israel's chief rabbi) recalls that when he came to meet with the Rebbe and proudly explained that he was involved in *kiruv rechokim*, bringing back to Judaism lost Jews who had strayed far away, the Rebbe immediately corrected his inherently judg-mental language: "We cannot label anyone as being 'far.' Who are we to determine who is far and who is near? They are all close to God."

One year, shortly after Rosh Hashanah, George Rohr, the prominent New York philanthropist and supporter of Chabad, was understandably proud and excited to tell the Rebbe of the beginners' service he had conducted at Manhattan's Kehilat Jeshurun synagogue: "The Rebbe will be pleased to know that we had 180 people for Rosh Hashanah services who came to us with no Jewish background." The Rebbe did not react. Rohr, thinking that the Rebbe had not heard what he had said, repeated his words, this time in a louder voice. "We had 180 people for Rosh Hashanah services with no Jewish background." The Rebbe gently challenged him for his choice of words: "No Jewish background? Tell them that they have the background of Abraham, Isaac, and Jacob, Sarah, Rebecca, Rachel, and Leah."[18]

The belief in the brotherhood of all Jews, not just those who live like oneself, led to another remarkable innovation: the Rebbe's willingness to send his followers out into the world. The Lubavitch movement now has Chabad Houses in forty-eight American states (only Mississippi and South Dakota are without permanent Chabad representation) and in some eighty countries (a number that might well be higher by the time this book is published), run by over four thousand Chabad couples. The *shluchim* (emissaries), as these couples are known, go to countries as Jewishly remote as the Congo and Cambodia (in 2010, my friend Dennis Prager and his wife spent Shabbat at the Chabad House in Phnom Penh, Cambodia, along with fourteen other Jews from some ten countries) and to cities with small Jewish communities such as Jackson Hole, Wyoming (Prager has come to define "remote" as referring to a city that doesn't have a Chabad presence). And, of course, there are the Chabad Passover Seders, the most famous of which in Kathmandu drew eleven hundred participants in 2012, the large majority of them young Israeli backpackers trekking through Nepal.[19] Meanwhile, over eighteen hundred Jews attended Seders in six Thai cities: Bangkok, Chiang Mai, Ko Samui, Phuket, Koh Phangang, and Pattaya. It is fair to assume that few people outside of Thailand can name any cities in that country aside from Bangkok, yet the Seder in Koh Phangang alone drew five hundred attendees.

What was particularly notable about the Rebbe's willingness to dispatch disciples far away from the Lubavitch community in Brooklyn was his openness to sending them to communities that were largely nonreligious in character, where the arriving Chabad couple would have few, sometimes no, peers, and where their children's friends would come from homes that did not keep kosher and in which their children could not eat. This was challenging and problematic in two ways. First, the family would likely feel isolated and lonely in so nonreligious an environment, and second, their children might be influenced by their peers and move away from traditional Jewish life.

In this regard, the Rebbe was fearless. The Rebbe wanted to take Judaism into the world, without being stymied by the fear that contact with nonobservant Jews or with non-Jews would diminish the observance of his emissaries and lessen their religious convictions. The prevalent attitude in the most traditional Jewish circles is to avoid, to the extent possible, the outside world and the Jews who inhabit it, a mind-set that is reflected in a Talmudic story:

"Rabbi Yossi ben Kisma said: 'I was once walking on the road when a man met me and greeted me, and I returned his greeting.'

"Said he to me, 'Rabbi, from what place are you?'

"I told him: 'From a great city of scholars and scribes am I.'

"He said to me: 'Rabbi, would you be willing to live with us in our place [and serve as our rabbi and teacher]? I would then give you a million gold denarii and precious stones and pearls.'

"I answered him: 'Were you to give me all the silver and gold and precious stones and pearls in the world, I would live nowhere but in a place of Torah'" (*Ethics of the Fathers* 6:9).

This was precisely the sort of attitude the Rebbe rejected.[20] True, he wanted his followers to first spend years of immersion in a yeshiva and to experience a full involvement in Jewish learning and in traditional Jewish life. But then, if there was a city devoid of Torah knowledge, they should go there. For the first time in Jewish history, a campaign was launched to reach every Jew and every Jewish community in the world. The Rebbe set a new standard with this campaign. As the former British chief rabbi Jonathan Sacks has expressed it: "If the Nazis searched out every Jew in hate, the Rebbe wished to search out every Jew in love."

But it wasn't only Jews whom the Rebbe loved, and non-Jews came to know that. One dramatic and little-known incident involved the Rebbe and Congresswoman Shirley Chisholm. In 1968, Chisholm became the first black woman elected to Congress. A powerful figure in her own right, Chisholm lacked the power to stop senior, and influential, southern Democratic congressmen, many of whom in those days were racists, from assigning her to the Agriculture Committee, an intentionally absurd appointment for a representative from Brooklyn. One New York newspaper headlined the affront: "A Tree Grows in Brooklyn?"

Chisholm, who wanted to work on education and labor issues, was both frustrated and furious.

She soon received a phone call from the office of one of her constituents. "The Lubavitcher Rebbe would like to meet with you." Representative Chisholm came to 770.

The Rebbe said, "I know you're very upset."

Chisholm acknowledged both being upset and feeling insulted. "What should I do?"

The Rebbe said: "What a blessing God has given you. This country has so much surplus food and there are so many hungry people and you can use this gift that God's given you to feed hungry people. Find a creative way to do it."

A short time later, on her first day in Congress, Chisholm met Robert Dole, the Kansas congressman who had just been elected to the Senate; Dole spoke to Chisholm and expressed great concern regarding the plight of midwestern farmers who were producing more food than they could sell and were losing money on their crops. Working with Dole and on her own, in an effort that eventually benefited millions of poor people and farmers, Chisholm greatly expanded the food stamp program. In 1973, the Agriculture and Consumer Protection Act ordered that food stamps be made available "in every jurisdiction in the United States."[21] Chisholm played an even more critical role in the creation of the Special Supplemental Nutrition Program for Women, Infants, and Children (WIC), which mandated food supplements for high-risk pregnant women and for young children at nutritional risk. Chisholm led the battle in the House, and Dole and Hubert Humphrey did so in the Senate; today some eight million people receive WIC benefits each month.

David Luchins, a twenty-year veteran of New York senator Daniel Patrick Moynihan's staff, heard Chisholm relate the story of her meeting with the Rebbe and her work on behalf of food stamps and WIC at a 1983 retirement breakfast in her honor. As she said that morning, "A rabbi who is an optimist taught me that what you think is a challenge is a gift from God." And, she then added, "If poor babies have milk and poor children have food, it's because this rabbi in Crown Heights had vision."

In 1951, when Rabbi Menachem Mendel Schneerson became the leader of Chabad, the then small movement was headquartered in one neighborhood of one borough in New York City and was not well known beyond it. During his four decades of leadership, he turned Chabad into the most dynamic and geographically diverse religious movement in Jewish history. Even more remarkably, though Chabad has remained leaderless since his death, basing itself on principles of leadership that he set in motion, it has far more than doubled in size. How one man came to do this is the story to which we now turn.

Chapter 2

1950–1951

Rabbi Menachem Mendel Schneerson Becomes Rebbe

"Everything now depends on us."

Prior to becoming Rebbe, Menachem Mendel Schneerson was also known in Chabad by the acronym Ramash, the contraction for Rabbi Menachem Mendel Schneerson. In this chapter, these two names—Ramash and Menachem Mendel—are used interchangeably. Subsequent to his death in 1950, the Sixth Rebbe (Rabbi Yosef Yitzchak Schneersohn) became known as the Frierdiker Rebbe (Previous Rebbe).

In the case of Menachem Mendel Schneerson, the Seventh Rebbe of Chabad, the desire for leadership does not seem to have come naturally. Though the numerous accounts of private audiences (*yechidus*, plural *yechidusen*) he conducted during his more than forty years as Rebbe reveal that he was very capable of interacting in an easy manner with people, one senses that this was more of an acquired trait than a natural inclination. He was, by all accounts, certainly during his earlier years, an inward, somewhat introverted person who craved time for learning[1] and who seems to have also craved a devoted and decidedly private life with his wife, Chaya Mushka. As he once wrote, "I have no pleasure in communal activity."[2]

But as shall soon become apparent, despite a year of resistance following the death of his father-in-law, the Sixth Rebbe (on the tenth of Shevat; January 28, 1950), Menachem Mendel would eventually be persuaded by Chabad to become their Rebbe. One also senses that although the Frierdiker Rebbe never explicitly pointed to his successor (for reasons we will discuss later), his clear preference was for Menachem Mendel.

In the weeks following the Frierdiker Rebbe's death, it appeared that Menachem Mendel had not given much thought to the possibility of his becoming Rebbe. Yet logically, that efforts would be made to have him become the next Rebbe could not have come to him as a complete surprise. The Frierdiker Rebbe had three daughters and no sons. Chabad, like all Chasidic courts, had a tradition of hereditary leadership, and had there been a son, the mantle of Rebbe would likely, though not necessarily, have fallen on him.[3]

However, the Sixth Rebbe was the first Rebbe to have no male children and Lubavitchers had assumed that when the time came, the position would devolve upon one of the Rebbe's sons-in-law. The Sixth Rebbe's youngest daughter, Sheina, and her husband, Rabbi Menachem Mendel Horenstein, were caught in Poland when World War II began, and both perished in Treblinka in 1942 (see page 380).

The two sons-in-law who succeeded in making it to America with their wives were Rabbi Shmaryahu Gourary, who was married to the Rebbe's oldest daughter, Chana, and Rabbi Menachem Mendel Schneerson, who was married to the Rebbe's middle daughter, Chaya Mushka.

It is clear that both Chana Gourary and her husband, Shmaryahu, hoped that when the time would come for a new Rebbe, it would be him. Rabbi Gourary had been a student at Yeshiva Tomchei Temimim and wed the Frierdiker Rebbe's eldest daughter in 1921. From that point on, Gourary worked for his father-in-law (except for a period in 1935–1936 when he lived in Palestine and opened a business). He played a key role within the movement, running the network of Tomchei Temimim yeshivot, a position previously held by the Frierdiker Rebbe himself.

Chaya Mushka, though only two years younger than her sister, did not marry until a full seven years later, and when she did—and despite the singularly grand nature of the wedding celebration and the very public pride the Sixth Rebbe took in his new son-in-law[4]—her sister probably assumed that her brother-in-law would not be interested in the position of Rebbe. Unlike Chana's husband, whose public identity was enmeshed with Chabad institutional life, Chaya Mushka and her husband spent the large majority of the next twelve years in Berlin and Paris, where Rabbi Menachem Mendel had extended years of secular studies. Menachem Mendel's manner of dress (he usually wore gray suits, not traditional rabbinic garb) and his shy manner[5] could have only strengthened Chana's hope that it would be her husband, Shmaryahu, who would one day head the Chasidic movement. One also suspects that throughout the 1930s the Gourarys hoped that Menachem Mendel would earn his living as an engineer and would make intellectual, but not leadership, contributions to the movement. It would seem that not only Chana and Shmaryahu Gourary hoped so, but quite likely the young Rabbi Schneerson and his wife did as well.

But there is also another part to this story, one that has been over-looked in a number of accounts of the Rebbe's life. Perusing the de-tailed journals Menachem Mendel kept during his years in Berlin and Paris—the journals were found in his office after his death and have since been published under the title *Reshimot*—one finds much new information about his life in this period.[6] Of particular interest, Me-nachem Mendel recorded hundreds of conversations he had with his father-in-law in which the Frierdiker Rebbe passed on to him oral tra-ditions he had heard from his father, some of which dated back to the Alter Rebbe (Chabad's founder) and were passed along from Rebbe to Rebbe.[7] Another striking feature of the *Reshimot* are Menachem Men-del's recording of his own Torah thoughts and analysis, documented by thousands of sources drawn from the Talmud, halacha (Jewish law), and kabbalah.[8] In addition, he spent an average of four months a year at the Chabad court, including the Hebrew month of Tishrei, when the High Holidays and Sukkot occur, and Nisan, during which Passover is observed.[9] At his father-in-law's request, he conducted *far-brengens*, joyous hours-long gatherings characterized by a mix of lec-tures teaching lessons in Torah and concepts in Chasidic philosophy (Chasidus), interspersed with the singing of soulful Chasidic melo-dies.[10] During these years of university study, he was appointed by the Frierdiker Rebbe to key roles in the movement; he also wrote a commentary on the *Tanya*, the basic philosophic treatise of Chabad, and edited and prepared his father-in-law's Torah writings for publication.[11] There were periods in 1937 and 1938 when he served as one of the Rebbe's personal secretaries, a position previously held by the Frierdiker Rebbe for *his* father, the Fifth Rebbe.[12] Less known is that Menachem Mendel also conducted a variety of clandestine activities for his father-in-law, most notably coordinating a complex transatlantic banking arrangement to move funds from America to help the beleaguered Jews in Stalinist Russia.[13]

Even when not working in the realm of Judaica and Jewish communal affairs, Menachem Mendel was anything but a typical university student: He immersed himself in the *mikveh* (ritual bath) daily, fasted often (including certain religiously designated Mondays and Thursdays; see page 554), and, at his father-in-law's request, put on four pairs of tefillin each morning (there are variations among them, representing various views among medieval Jewish scholars).[14]

In 1940, after Germany's invasion of France, Menachem Mendel and his wife fled Paris and eventually escaped from Europe, arriving in the United States a year later, where they joined the Frierdiker Rebbe and the Gourarys at the movement's new headquarters at 770 Eastern Parkway, in Brooklyn's Crown Heights neighborhood (the Frierdiker Rebbe had arrived fifteen months earlier). Menachem Mendel and Chaya Mushka took up residence a few blocks away, on New York Avenue and later on President Street.

Within a short time, Rabbi Menachem Mendel started to work at the vocation he had prepared for in university, engineering, and took a position at the Brooklyn Navy Yard. But his close proximity to Chabad headquarters enabled his father-in-law to indulge in what was a long-held hope to bring his erudite son-in-law into the full day-to-day orbit of running the Chabad institutions. He appointed Menachem Mendel to head the three major new Chabad institutions: Merkos L'inynei Chinuch, founded to promote Jewish education among young people through schools and youth groups; Machne Israel, intended to foster Torah study and kind acts among the Jewish people; and Kehot, the movement's publishing house. At his father-in-law's request, Menachem Mendel would hold monthly *farbrengens* with the Chasidim.

"Without having to say so, the wishes of the Frierdiker Rebbe became clear."

Throughout the 1940s, we find no discussion of possible successors to the Frierdiker Rebbe. There were several reasons for this. In Jewish tradition, it is considered unseemly, to say the least, to discuss a religious group's future leadership while the current leader is alive and leading the movement. In addition, it seems that many Lubavitchers were nurturing the hope that the Frierdiker Rebbe would either be revealed as the Messiah or would usher in the Messiah, and there would be no need for a Seventh Rebbe because the world would soon be redeemed. The Frierdiker Rebbe himself hoped and expected that he would live to witness the coming of the Messiah and the redemption of the Jewish people and the world.[15] This is perhaps just one reason he never explicitly stated whom he wished to succeed him in the event of his death; in addition, Chabad Rebbes did not generally say who they hoped their successor would be.

In any case, there never had been a specified pattern of succession in Chabad. The Alter Rebbe, for example, was succeeded by his oldest son, Rabbi DovBer, while DovBer, who had several sons, was succeeded by his son-in-law and nephew, the Tzemach Tzedek. The Tzemach Tzedek, in turn, was succeeded by the youngest of his seven sons, Shmuel.[16] The one consistent pattern in Chabad was that every Rebbe was a direct descendant of the Alter Rebbe (which Rabbi Gourary was not).

Although the Frierdiker Rebbe never specifically vocalized his preference for Menachem Mendel, he made it evident in other ways. Most important, it is clear that the Frierdiker Rebbe had a higher regard for the intellectual and spiritual capabilities of his younger son-in-law than his older. This becomes obvious when examining the manner in which he refers to them in his correspondence. In one letter, he describes Rabbi Gourary, known in Chabad circles as Rashag (an acronym for Rabbi Shmaryahu Gourary), as deeply loyal to Chabad, concerned with the honor and well-being of the yeshiva students, and a man of intellectual sophistication, one "who can understand a matter to its full depth."[17]

This is indeed a complimentary description, but it doesn't come close to the sorts of honorific descriptions he bestowed on Menachem Mendel. Thus, there is one term he consistently applies to his younger son-in-law, *Gaon* (the Hebrew word for "genius"), which he rarely applied to Rabbi Gourary. On some occasions, he calls Menachem Mendel *ha-Gaon ha-Amiti*, "the true genius," more frequently *ha-Rav ha-Gaon ha-Chasid*, "the genius and pious rabbi." In yet other letters, he speaks of "my son-in-law, Rabbi Shmaryahu Gourary and my son-in-law the genius and pious Rabbi Menachem Mendel Schneerson."[18]

The Frierdiker Rebbe was not a tactless person, yet his willingness to restrict the use of terms "genius" and "pious" to only one son-in-law, even when writing in a context in which both men were being mentioned, is a clear indication of the higher regard he had for Rabbi Menachem Mendel's intellectual and spiritual capacities.

It was not only in the context of his letters that the Frierdiker Rebbe took note of his younger son-in-law's unusual intellectual gifts. At the time of the marriage of Menachem Mendel to Chaya Mushka, he described his new son-in-law to others as follows: "I have given my daughter to a man who is totally fluent in the Babylonian and Jerusalem Talmuds and knowledgeable in the entire writings of the *rishonim* and *acharonim* [the classic and modern commentators on the Talmud], and much, much more. At four o'clock in the morning, he has either not yet gone to sleep, or has already awoken."

However, as significant as intellectual and spiritual qualities are, they are, of course, not the sole determinants of who should be a Rebbe. After all, a Rebbe is meant to be a pastoral leader and community organizer as well. It is therefore important to record other indications of the Frierdiker Rebbe's particularly high regard for his younger son-in-law and his preference for him as a successor.

Some two years before the Frierdiker Rebbe's death, Professor Abraham Luchins, an Orthodox Jew and a renowned Gestalt psychologist, presented the Rebbe with a scholarly article he had recently written. The Frierdiker Rebbe, whose knowledge of English was limited, suggested that he bring the article instead to his son-in-law, Menachem Mendel: "Show it to him. You'll be asking him all your questions soon."[19]

Rabbi Shlomo Aharon Kazarnowsky told of an even more intriguing episode. During the 1940s, Kazarnowsky used to travel to various cities in the United States on behalf of the Frierdiker Rebbe, where he would make contact with the local Jewish communities. Once, before departing on a trip to Chicago, he went to the Sixth Rebbe to discuss strategy for the trip and how to carry out his assignment. After advising him of what he should do, the Frierdiker Rebbe directed him to go downstairs to the office of his son-in-law, Ramash, and ask his opinion also. Kazarnowsky did so, soliciting Menachem Mendel's advice without revealing to him that he already consulted with his father-in-law about the matter. After hearing Kazarnowsky's question, Ramash offered him an entirely different opinion from the one offered by his father-in-law. When Kazarnowsky went back and informed the Frierdiker Rebbe of the different advice tendered by his son-in-law, the Frierdiker Rebbe nodded in approval: "*Ah, a deah rechava. Gor anderesh! Tu vos er zogt*" ("Ah, a broad mind, totally different. Do as he has said").[20]

While such examples are not definitive proof of the Frierdiker Rebbe's preference for a successor, they are highly suggestive, particularly since we know of no anecdotes in which he is depicted as expressing a preference for Rabbi Gourary.

In addition, there might have been another factor that made Menachem Mendel a more attractive candidate to head the movement in the United States (though, ironically, this factor might have been a detriment in Poland): his extensive university education. Among the less worldly Chasidim of Poland and Russia, the Rebbe's secular studies might have caused some Chasidim to question his fitness to lead the movement (it was perhaps to counter such objections that the Frierdiker Rebbe underwrote the expenses of his university education). In the United States, a university degree in engineering, along with fluency in English (although the Rebbe's Eastern European accent always remained strong, his vocabulary was rich), made him a figure with a potential appeal beyond Chabad, and one suspects that this thought also occurred to his father-in-law. Furthermore, it was not simply that the Rebbe knew English, it's that he quickly acquired knowledge of American culture and of ways in which this knowledge could be utilized to excite young American Jews' curiosity about Judaism. The young artist Michel Schwartz recalls being called in by Menachem Mendel to discuss the Chabad children's magazine *Talks and Tales* and his thoughts as to how to broaden its appeal. Menachem Mendel mentioned to Schwartz an idea he had for a cartoon character about whom adventure stories could be written with moral lessons and told him, *"Ess zol oys'zehn vee Dick Tracy"* ([the cartoon strip] should look like Dick Tracy); Tracy, a crime fighter, was the most famous comic strip hero of the time and a pop hero among American youth of all ages. Schwartz recalls being startled at receiving such advice from a man whom he knew to be the son-in-law of the Sixth Rebbe.

While there is no direct connection between studying engineering and knowing about Dick Tracy, they both represent a type of worldliness that was not common in the world of Chasidic leadership, Chabad or not.

Such an episode reflects a mind-set, and what many Chasidim sensed was that the mind-set of Menachem Mendel Schneerson was peculiarly congenial to the United States, something that the Frierdiker Rebbe— who understood that his movement's future followers were going to be drawn from the United States and no longer from Belarus and Poland— must have felt as well.

Still, the question remains: Why then did he not make his preference public and do so in a direct manner?

The reason may have had to do with issues of family relations and diplomacy. In addition to the great amount of care the Frierdiker Rebbe received from his trusted nurse, known as Shvester Manya [Rosen], who had come to the United States with him in 1940, Chana Gourary and her husband lived in the same building with the Frierdiker Rebbe, and an enormous measure of daily care for the sickly Rebbe was attended to by Chana. Hadassah Carlebach, a family cousin, recalls that Chana begged off attending Hadassah's wedding, explaining that she did not want to leave her father even for one evening. Chana told her cousin that she wanted to be present in the apartment so that she could turn him and tend to his needs.

Given the close nature of the Frierdiker Rebbe's relationship with his daughter Chana, he likely dreaded the pain that would be inflicted on her if he made known a wish that her brother-in-law and not her husband be his successor. He may have feared to hurt his daughter, and possibly feared to provoke her anger or to provoke the innumerable sorts of endless conversations and arguments that might have ensued had he expressed a preference for his successor being a man other than her husband.[21]

While the Frierdiker Rebbe gave no explicit instructions, the information we do have—particularly the way he wrote of Ramash and Rashag when referring to them in tandem—supports the conclusion that he felt Ramash to be the preferable successor, and that he believed Ramash's superior talents to be sufficiently obvious to others as well. Even his wife, Nechama Dina, who maintained a very close relationship with both Rashag and her daughter Chana, and was concerned that Rashag be treated by the Chasidim with great respect, also seems to have understood that Ramash was the most fitting person to succeed her husband (she told a group of Chabad elders during that period: "I know that you will certainly be crowning the holy Ramash to become the Rebbe and leader of Chabad. I agree with this with all my heart").[22]

The Events Following the Death of the Sixth Rebbe, Yosef Yitzchak Schneersohn [23]

Rabbi Zalman Schachter-Shalomi, widely known as Reb Zalman, was in his mid-twenties when the Sixth Rebbe died. The shock in the community was palpable, though in truth the Rebbe had long been in very ill health. He was sixty-nine, which is not old, but he suffered from multiple sclerosis, had had a stroke and a heart attack, and in his final years spoke in a low, often garbled voice that was hard to follow. His death occurred on a Shabbat morning, and Reb Zalman, who was serving as a rabbi in Massachusetts, learned of the death only after Shabbat

(Orthodox Jews do not use the telephone on Shabbat). He immediately set out by car for Brooklyn. At 770 the following morning, he found himself in the midst of a group of Lubavitchers outside the room where the *tahara* (ritual washing) of the deceased Rebbe's body was taking place. Standing outside the room as well were the Rebbe's two sons-in-law, Rabbis Schneerson and Gourary. On a number of occasions that morning, Reb Zalman recalls, the door of the *tahara* room opened, and someone would come out with a halachic query, a legal question concerning the proper carrying out of some aspect of the ritual cleansing.[24] What struck Reb Zalman was that in each instance the question was directed to Menachem Mendel Schneerson, not to both men, although his brother-in-law was standing alongside him. Clearly, Reb Zalman thought, he was deemed by the elders to be the superior rabbinic authority.

That at moments of such critical import people were turning to Ramash was a clear indication to Reb Zalman that Mendel Schneerson would be the successor to his father-in-law as Rebbe.[25]

What is it indeed that defines a Rebbe? The word itself means simply "rabbi," and refers to the head of a Chasidic group. As a general rule, the relationship of Chasidim to their Rebbe is far more intense than the relationship that exists between most Jews and their synagogue rabbi. While rabbis are usually, but not only, consulted on specifically religious issues, Chasidim will go to their Rebbe to consult on all issues, including matters of faith and issues of Jewish law, but also on business, marital, and health issues; they will seek guidance not only on child-rearing and their children's education, but also on undertaking a new job or finding spouses for their children.

Chasidim trust a Rebbe's advice on such a variety of issues because they feel a Rebbe, in addition to having wisdom, has achieved a spiritual level of *bittul ha-yesh*, a nullification of his personal will. Such a person, one who can negate his own ego before God, and who can negate his own ego in the presence of others, becomes a pure vessel for transmitting God's wisdom. A Rebbe must also set an example of living a life completely in accordance with the *Shulchan Aruch*, the Code of Jewish Law, an attribute that very much characterized Menachem Mendel Schneerson, who was punctilious in the fulfillment of Jewish law. In addition, and as

Rabbi Zalman Posner, a contemporary Chasidic philosopher, expresses it: "The Chasid is certain that the Rebbe is selfless enough to tell him not what the Rebbe might personally prefer, but only what the Torah would have the Rebbe say." [26]

Combined with this nullification of personal ego, Chasidim trust in the Rebbe's unconditional love and concern for them. Rabbi Posner recalls the experience of a friend, a devoted Chasid, whose son had chosen to follow a different lifestyle. At a meeting some time later with the Rebbe, the Rebbe commented, without the father having raised the subject: "Ask your son if he thinks of me at least as often as I think of [him]." [27]

Is what I have written here true of all Chasidic Rebbes? Not at all. But it is certainly what some people were starting to sense, even early on and even before he assumed the leadership role, about Menachem Mendel Schneerson. Thus, Rabbi Yitzchak Dubov, a highly distinguished Chabad rabbi in Manchester, England, was in New York for his son's wedding when the Frierdiker Rebbe died. In a letter written several years later, he describes how "I saw with my own eyes the attachment of the young men and the Yeshiva students to [Ramash] . . . they practically made me their emissary to speak to [him] regarding his nomination." Knowing that he would have to return to England very soon, Dubov approached Menachem Mendel only three days after the Frierdiker Rebbe's death, urging him to accept the position of Rebbe. Menachem Mendel protested vehemently: "The Rebbe lives." Dubov persisted, arguing that although the deceased Rebbe was still living in a spiritual sense, the movement now needed, as it had always needed, a flesh-and-blood leader. Menachem Mendel questioned whether he was in any event qualified for such a role. In a tone reminiscent of Moses's response when God revealed himself at the burning bush and commanded Moses to take the Jewish people out of slavery—"Who am I that I should go to Pharaoh and lead the Israelites out of Egypt?" (Exodus 3:11)—Menachem Mendel now said to Dubov, "What do you suppose? That Mendel Schneerson is a Rebbe?" [28]

In spite of Menachem Mendel's objections, Dubov was by no means dissuaded. Upon his return to England, he contacted two other leading Chabad rabbis, Bentzion Shemtov and Sender Nemtzov, and the three initiated the writing of a communal letter of *hitkashrut* (attachment), in which the signatories bound themselves to Menachem Mendel Schneerson as their Rebbe. They sent the signed letter, dated February 19, 1950, to Ramash, and shortly thereafter Menachem Mendel wrote to Rabbi Nemtzov, "Surely . . . Rabbi Dubov has conveyed what I told him in this regard when he was here." [29]

Despite such protestations, the movement to pressure Menachem Mendel Schneerson to accept the position gathered steam in other countries as well. In Israel, on the thirtieth day after the Rebbe's death, the senior figures in Chabad convened a meeting "to deliberate matters regarding the progression of the community of the Chasidim of Chabad." In the aftermath of the meeting, a letter was dispatched to the organized leadership in the United States: "Ramash, may he live for long and good years, is from the offspring of the dynasty, a direct descendant [of the Alter Rebbe]. Therefore, it is fitting to urge him that he should succeed the Rebbe." [30] Among the signatories were Rabbis Nachum Sosonkin, Avraham Chen, and Shlomo Yosef Zevin, the founding editor of the *Encyclopedia Talmudit*, one of the great works of twentieth-century Jewish scholarship. [31]

In addition to establishing Ramash's superior lineage (hinging support on lineage might itself have been a strategy to minimize any sense of insult to Rabbi Gourary), Rabbi Shmuel Zalmanov, editor of the yeshiva periodical *Hatamim*, wrote an extraordinarily laudatory letter speaking of Ramash's "wondrous" wide-ranging knowledge of all Jewish religious sources, his piety, his humility, and his devotion to his father-in-law. Ramash is the one who can "continue the golden chain of Chabad leadership." The arguments on behalf of Menachem Mendel could not have been more emphatic. [32]

From an examination of the events of that year, it would seem no coincidence that the campaign to persuade Menachem Mendel was at first most forcefully pursued outside the United States, and certainly not in Crown Heights. There, in addition to Menachem Mendel constantly discouraging the elders from pushing him to become Rebbe, fears of offending and provoking the Gourarys, who coveted the position, caused many Chasidim to hold back on expressing their preference, at least in public. Recognizing this himself, Rabbi Dubov wrote a letter to his colleagues in July 1950, six months after the Frierdiker Rebbe's death: "In my opinion, all the Chasidim outside of America must crown him with the title of Rebbe, and then the objective would be achieved automatically, despite the fact that he does not want it. My consideration is that the Chasidim [in the United States] are not able to do anything." [33] Dubov makes explicit his belief that the reason the U.S. Chasidim are "not able to do anything" is out of fear of offending Rabbi Gourary. Dubov, who regarded Ramash as the new Rebbe ("I already call him Rebbe"), considered Rabbi Gourary's opposition to be shortsighted: "If he would act appropriately, he would also be respected" (by which he presumably meant that Rabbi Gourary would maintain his high position in the movement). [34]

Around the same time, Rabbi Schachter-Shalomi returned to New York to pray at the grave of the Frierdiker Rebbe. As he recalls: "When I came back to 770, I washed my hands because I was coming from a cemetery. The Rebbe [Menachem Mendel Schneerson] saw me coming in. This was only a short time after his father-in-law's death so, of course, he was not yet the Rebbe. As a matter of fact, he was wearing a gray suit. And, seeing me wash my hands before entering the building, he realized where I was coming from. And he said to me, '*Halevai*, what you prayed for, you should get.'

"And I answered, 'If people don't interfere.'

"The Rebbe said to me, 'What do you mean by that?'

"I answered. 'I prayed for three things. That we should have a Rebbe, that you should be the Rebbe, [35] and that you should be blessed with children.'

"At that point, he took my hand and we both were weeping. A moment later, he said, 'But we already have a Rebbe. What difference does it make in which world he is?'

"I answered, 'Why did the *Ribbono shel Olam* [Master of the Universe] bury Moshe [Moses] in a place that was anonymous, where no one would know where his body was? [Deuteronomy 34:6] It was so that Joshua would not be able to send people to Moshe's grave.'

"Again, we both wept, and then he said to me, '*S'vet zein gut*, Reb Zalman' ['It will be good, Reb Zalman']."[36]

Yet another factor in Menachem Mendel's reluctance to assume leadership was quite possibly the need to focus so much of his time and energy on the plethora of responsibilities associated with being a Rebbe. We know how assiduous a scholar Menachem Mendel was, and he may have foreseen that his duties as Rebbe would pull him away from his learning. Indeed, the hours he would later devote to meeting with people at *yechidusen*, maintaining a massive correspondence, and supervising Chabad activities throughout the world were exacting. He was already intimately acquainted with some of the organization's more demanding issues, particularly those involving its finances. Throughout its history, Chabad had often lived in penurious circumstances. Menachem Mendel was well aware of this; the lack of sufficient funds in the late 1920s to make a festive wedding seems to have been one of the factors delaying his marriage to Chaya Mushka.[37] Now, twenty years later, and after having spent the first half of those years studying in the more serene academic world and the more recent years heavily involved in the movement's finances, Menachem Mendel may well have been discouraged at the thought of assuming responsibility for the movement's considerable financial burdens. Just how severe the organization's poverty must have been jumps out when one reads a letter in which Menachem Mendel writes a rabbi thanking him for a $10 check the rabbi had forwarded to the organization from a Mr. Chaim Yosef.

In the same letter in which the $10 gift is mentioned, Menachem Mendel writes with uncharacteristic sharpness: "It is not understandable why you . . . as a good friend have not taken a more active participatory role in our efforts, such as arranging appeals in your congregation and the like. Must we knock on the gates of your heart every day?"[38]

Menachem Mendel makes no effort to hide the strain under which he is working: "The tremendous [financial] stress that exists in directing the vast plan of activities called for by my father-in-law, the Rebbe, defies description." [39]

The truth is that although Menachem Mendel might have fervently hoped that the movement could continue as it was (" . . . we already have a Rebbe. What difference does it make in which world he is?"), Chabad wanted to ensure the future of the movement, and in their eyes Ramash was the one leader who could secure that future. The biblical verse, "The sun rises, the sun sets" (Ecclesiastes 1:5) was long understood in Chabad as meaning that the subsequent Rebbe is already present at the time of his predecessor's death, but it was possible that an interval could lapse until the successor would be officially named (as had been the case with some of the previous Chabad Rebbes' successions). Among those Chasidim who had a view on the subject, an overwhelming majority hoped to see Menachem Mendel Schneerson emerge as the new Rebbe.[40] Their only concern was that he be willing to accept the position.

A humorous anecdote circulated in Chabad circles at the time. To the question, "Who appointed Menachem Mendel Schneerson and not Shmaryahu Gourary as the successor?," the answer offered was, "The non-Jewish postal worker who delivered the mail to 770." One day, as the man was bringing in the mail, he saw a number of yeshiva students engaged in an intense discussion. When he asked them what they were talking about, one of the students explained they were speaking about the future of the movement in light of the Sixth Rebbe's death. The mailman said he was sure the next Rebbe would be Rabbi Schneerson. Taken aback by the man's quick and assured response, a student asked him why he said so. The man pointed to Menachem Mendel's office and said, "Because he gets much more mail than Rabbi Gourary."

As noted, the groundswell of support for Menachem Mendel was first openly expressed by Chasidim outside the United States—most notably in England, Australia, Israel, and even the DP camp in Pocking, Germany. Many of them began sending letters to him—including letters urging him to accept the position and signed by large numbers of people addressing him as Rebbe.[41] The elders of the movement reasoned that this show of support from Chasidim throughout the world would also make it easier for the Chasidim in Brooklyn, where Rabbi Gourary was a figure with power, to act as well.

All of this was occurring against the backdrop of Menachem Mendel maintaining his noncandidacy. Months after his father-in-law's death, he continued to appear daily at his office in 770 in his trademark gray suit, not the garb of a Chasidic Rebbe.[42] He continued to fend off all requests that he become Rebbe. Yet the campaign did not diminish. It sometimes seemed as if his disavowal of the desire to be Rebbe only strengthened his supporters' certainty that he was the right candidate.[43]

Menachem Mendel was capable, on occasion, of regarding the whole matter with a certain amount of humor and detachment. Esther Goldman reports that when her brother Shalom went in to see Ramash to discuss a certain matter, he brought with him his four-year-old son. Ramash extended his hand to the child, but the boy, overcome with shyness, turned away, whereupon he commented, "He is also playing politics."[44]

But as months passed, certain signs emerged that indicated a growing openness to the possibility of Ramash becoming Rebbe. Thus, by September 1950, four months before the *yahrtzeit* (anniversary) of the Frierdiker Rebbe's death, and the time at which it was commonly assumed a successor would emerge, Menachem Mendel changed his daily attire from a short jacket to the traditional long, black rabbinical garb (he had always dressed in rabbinic attire for Shabbat and holidays). Then, on Simchat Torah, he was called up to the Torah for an aliyah in a manner that betokened great honor: "*Adoneinu, Moreinu, ve-Rabbeinu*" ("Our Master, Our Teacher, Our Rabbi"). The acronym of these three words, "Admor," is reserved for a Rebbe and suggests how clear the matter of succession was in the minds of so many Chabadniks.[45] He accepted the call to go up and bless the Torah.

Rabbi Leibel Posner recalls a point at which he returned to Brooklyn from an out-of-town trip. Menachem Mendel, seeing him, extended his hand, but Posner kept his hands at his side (out of respect; unlike the case with royalty, a Chabad Chasid will not shake hands with a Rebbe even if the Rebbe extends his hand first). The Rebbe smiled and, speaking in a warm manner, told Posner he was acting like an *akshan*, a stubborn person.

Posner recalled in an interview, though, that "never again did he give me his hand." This, too, likely reflected a greater willingness on Menachem Mendel's part to accept the position, as some months earlier he had complained that people had stopped shaking his hand.

In brief, one thing seems clear: Menachem Mendel Schneerson did not covet the position of Rebbe. Still, at some point, as yet undefined, it must have dawned on him, and likely on Rebbetzin Chaya Mushka as well, that whether he wanted it or not, he would likely be drafted for the position—and would not in good conscience be able to say no.

His loyalty to Chabad and to his father-in-law precluded his doing so. The Rebbe, I believe, understood, or came to understand during the course of 1950, that Chabad's future viability depended on his becoming the movement's leader. He must have perceived that the movement—which had lost so many of its adherents in the Holocaust, with many others still trapped behind the Iron Curtain—was now a relatively small movement centered in one borough of New York City (with small outposts elsewhere) and that it was in danger of going under or becoming so small as to be insignificant. In addition, we know that his wife, Chaya Mushka, also joined in the effort to persuade her husband to accept the position, telling him, in effect: "If you don't become Rebbe, thirty years of my father's life will have gone to waste." [46]

This concern about the movement's future survival and viability was revealed not in any subsequent public utterances of the Rebbe but, strangely enough, in an interview with a Reform rabbi, Herbert Weiner. Weiner talked with the Rebbe at length on two occasions in 1955 and 1956 in connection with an article on Chabad Weiner was writing for *Commentary* magazine. In the context of answering a question posed by Weiner as to how the Rebbe could assume responsibility for giving advice to his Chasidim not only on religious matters but on medical and business issues as well, the Rebbe offered a response that clearly related to his decision to assume the leadership position five years earlier: "To begin with, it is always pleasant to run away from responsibility. But what if running might destroy the congregation, and suppose they put the key in your pocket and walk away? What can you do then . . . ?" [47]

At some point during the year following the Frierdiker Rebbe's death, it seems Rabbi Menachem Mendel Schneerson came to believe that while it might be preferable for him on a personal level not to be Rebbe, his refusal to accept the position could, as he said to Weiner, "destroy the congregation," or certainly weaken it greatly.[48]

Menachem Mendel Schneerson must have known on some level that he was delaying the inevitable. But still, he did try to delay. Rabbi Yosef Weinberg recalls that he threatened at one point to run away if the Chasidim did not stop pressuring him to accept the role of leader. When they continued beseeching him, Menachem Mendel told them that he had never received instructions from his father-in-law to take over the leadership. Upon hearing this, the elder Chasidim went to the *Ohel*, the gravesite of the Frierdiker Rebbe, and prayed that Ramash would accept the position of Rebbe. This was the last time Menachem Mendel used this argument.

Nevertheless, shortly after his father-in-law's death, Menachem Mendel started answering questions posed by Chasidim and others and meeting with them in *yechidusen*; sometimes, though, he seemed ambivalent about doing so.[49] According to one account, when a Chasid once approached him for a *yechidus*, Menachem Mendel tried to fend off the man: "You want to come to someone who wears a short jacket for *yechidus*? That's not a Rebbe." The Chasid replied: "I don't come for the jacket, I come for the Rebbe."[50]

The Dawn of a New Era: Rabbi Menachem Mendel Schneerson Becomes Rebbe

Until the very last day, hours before the *farbrengen* convened to commemorate the Sixth Rebbe's first *yahrtzeit*, it was still not definite if Menachem Mendel was going to accept the position. The *farbrengen* was scheduled for the tenth of Shevat (January 16, 1951), and that morning Chasidim, many of whom had come to New York for the *yahrtzeit farbrengen*, circulated a public letter (*pan klali*), which was read aloud at the yeshiva. It was a plea, addressed to all Chasidim, both those in the vicinity and those far away, to entreat the soul of the deceased Rabbi Yosef Yitzchak to intercede from the other side and influence Menachem Mendel Schneerson to become their leader. After the public reading, the letter was brought to Menachem Mendel; at first, he refused to read it. Then, when he finally did, he started to sob. Amidst the tears, he finally made it clear that, yes, he would accept the role of Rebbe, but "you [the Chasidim]," he added, "must help me."[51]

That night, a large crowd gathered in the yeshiva's *Beit Midrash* (study hall); among them were non-Lubavitchers as well; during the preceding month, reports in Jewish newspapers implied that "Ramash" was going to formally accept the position of Rebbe that night.[52]

At almost 10:00 p.m., after spending much of the day in study, prayer, and a visit to the grave of his father-in-law where he read letters from Chasidim across the globe acknowledging him as Rebbe, Ramash entered the synagogue.

Two places had been prepared for him. One was the spot where he usually sat at a *farbrengen*, in the middle of a table and surrounded by other Chasidim; another seat was prepared at the head table, at a place set aside for a Rebbe, and alongside where Menachem Mendel used to sit on those occasions when his father-in-law asked him to speak.

As Menachem Mendel walked in, flanked by men who had been Chasidim of the Fifth and Sixth Rebbes, the Chasidim scrutinized him carefully. Where would he go? He proceeded to the head of the table.

Over the course of the next two and three-quarter hours, Menachem Mendel spoke five times, most of the speeches quite short. His physical appearance was vibrant and energetic as he expounded upon themes that soon came to define his years as leader: an extraordinary emphasis on the love of fellow Jews and how they should be approached; a commitment to bring Judaism and its teachings to every Jewish community, no matter how remote; and a commitment to follow in the footsteps of Abraham, the first Jew, and make known the teachings of monotheism to non-Jews, to the whole world.

At one point, Menachem Mendel recalled an incident that had happened ten years earlier: "When the [Sixth] Rebbe arrived in America, he quoted the words of the Sages (*Genesis Rabbah* 48:14): 'When you come to a town, follow its customs.' Here in America people like to hear a statement, a declaration that is novel and preferably groundbreaking."

He then proceeded to offer an insight into the relationship among God, the Jewish people, and the Torah that was revolutionary in its implications. While his style was understated, there was no mistaking that the words that followed—with their distinctive focus on the love of one's fellow—were historic.

Rabbi Schneerson quoted the kabbalistic teaching that "the three loves—love of God, love of Torah, and love of one's fellow—are one."

"Loving God alone is not enough," he then continued. "Without love of Torah and love of one's fellow Jew, the love of God . . . will not endure. On the other hand, where love of one's fellow Jew exists, this will eventually bring also a love of Torah and a love of God." What the new about-to-become Rebbe was conveying was this: If a Jew loves God but lacks love for his fellow Jews, that in itself indicates that there is something lacking in his love of God. On the other hand, if a Jew loves people, is concerned with "providing bread for the hungry and water for the thirsty," that person can be brought to a love of God and Torah as well.

The Rebbe's emphasis on the centrality of the command to love one's fellow was striking in its formulation: "for just as we were exiled from our land because of practicing the opposite of the love of fellow Jews [a euphemism for Jewish infighting], it is precisely through love of one's fellow that the Redemption will come speedily, quite literally in our own days."

Dramatic as the contents of the speech were, with its call for universal outreach, it was still delivered in the style of what Lubavitchers call a *sicha*, a conventional speech. The Chasidim were impressed, but something was missing.

Suddenly, an eighty-year-old Chasid from Manchester, England, Rabbi Avraham Sender Nemtzov, jumped up and publicly addressed Ramash: "The people request that the Rebbe say a *ma'amar*. *Sichos* are good, but the people request a *ma'amar*. . . . The Rebbe should say Chasidus."

Silence filled the room as all eyes turned to Ramash.

The *ma'amar* is a very specific style of speech; it is usually preceded by the singing of a contemplative wordless melody (*niggun*) and all those present stand during its delivery. The *ma'amar* itself starts with a biblical verse, cites many distinctive Chasidic teachings, involves an in-depth analysis of a religious issue, and usually expounds upon various kabbalistic teachings.

The etiquette of a *ma'amar* is distinctive as well. The Rebbe generally keeps his eyes closed while delivering the talk and holds a handkerchief in his hands, guaranteeing, according to Chabad custom, that he remain grounded even while speaking of the most heavenly matters. The tempo of the speech is also unique, delivered with a special singsong melody.

Most important, a *ma'amar* is given only by a Rebbe. Thus, in asking for such a talk, Rabbi Nemtzov was imploring Ramash to now take the final step (equivalent to an elected presidential candidate taking the oath of office) and formally assume the movement's leadership.

A short silence ensued, during which Ramash opened the pamphlet containing his father-in-law's last *ma'amar*, the one he had prepared for study on the day that turned out to be the day of his death. Ramash had recently republished the *ma'amar* and, in the weeks preceding the *yahrtzeit*, written letters to Chasidim worldwide asking them to prepare for the *yahrtzeit* by carefully studying this *ma'amar*, internalizing its message, and having it read aloud in their communities. Ramash now began to read aloud the first passage ("*Bah-tee Le-Gani*" ["I have come into my garden"]; Song of Songs 5:1) as if all he was doing was just teaching aloud the Frierdiker Rebbe's *ma'amar*.

In a soft, almost tremulous voice—the Rebbe's emotions can be detected in the tape recording of the speech[53]—the Rebbe's lengthy, tear-soaked discourse unfolded. Slowly but surely the elucidation of the Frierdiker Rebbe's *ma'amar* turned into a completely new and innovative talk, all presented as if it was there all along, embedded in his father-in-law's words.

The theme of the *ma'amar* was a Midrashic passage that describes the reason and purpose of creation: "God desired to have a *dirah b'tachtonim*" (a dwelling place on earth; literally "in the lower realms").

Initially, the Rebbe explained, at the time of creation, a sense of God's presence was manifestly apparent on earth. Later, as a result of various sins and evils, starting with Adam and Eve eating from the forbidden fruit, the Godly presence was exiled and was no longer nearly as accessible.

But then, the Midrash relates, along came seven righteous people, starting with Abraham and continuing through Moses, who, through their acts of extreme goodness, succeeded level by level in drawing the Godly presence back down until it finally reached earth.

While each of the first six figures drew the divine presence back into this world level by level, it was Moses, the seventh in the cycle, whose actions finally brought about God's reentry into this physical world, a reentry exemplified by God's giving Moses the Torah on Mount Sinai.

How was Moses able to accomplish what his six predecessors, among them Abraham, Isaac, and Jacob, had not? Was he so much greater than those who preceded him?

The Rebbe answered this by analyzing the words of another Midrashic passage, "All sevenths are beloved," and noted again that Moses was seventh in this cycle. What the Midrash is suggesting is that the main advantage, the very "beloved" nature of the seventh, is a result of nothing more than his being "seventh from the first." It was the grace of being the seventh of these men, all of them righteous, that empowered Moses to accomplish what the others before him could not: to manifestly restore the divine presence to earth.

In short, the greatness of the seventh derives not from an innate superiority but from his being seventh from the first; thus, when examining the seventh, one recognizes as well the uniqueness and greatness of the first. The seventh reflects the first. And who, after all, was the first in the cycle that culminated with Moses? Abraham, the patriarch of the Jewish people.

Soon, the Rebbe began to weep. At first, the cry was like a whisper, as if coming from far away. But then the cries deepened, permeated by heavy sighs; it seemed as if he would have trouble continuing. But he resumed. Now, he explained, as Chabad was entering its seventh generation from the Alter Rebbe, Chasidim must understand that the "beloved" nature of being the seventh generation of Chabad Chasidim comes with great responsibility. It is the responsibility of all those present, and for Chasidim throughout the world, to transform the world, to make it a place that God can call home.

"Our sages tell us that each person must say to himself, 'When will my actions be like those of Abraham, Isaac, and Jacob?' " The Rebbe then continued: "We need to know that the entire specialness of the seventh is . . . to finish the mission of the first [Abraham], to urge the entire world to proclaim the name of one God.

"This is what is demanded of each one of us, the seventh generation. Although our being the seventh generation is not by our choice, nor a result of our deeds, and perhaps to some degree even against our wishes, nevertheless, all sevenths are beloved. Our work is to complete the full manifestation of the Godly presence throughout this earthly world."

Twice during the forty-five-minute-long *ma'amar*, the Rebbe stopped to lead everyone in singing favorite *niggunim* of each of his predecessors. In addition, he invoked each of the previous six Rebbes twice during the course of his talk, once expounding on their kabbalistic teachings concerning the divine manifestation, and the second time while reflecting on specific instances in which they had each performed acts of kindness to others.

"The Alter Rebbe, for example, once interrupted his prayers in order to go and chop wood, cook a soup, and feed it to a woman who had just given birth, because there was nobody else home to do so." In the case of the Third Rebbe, he spoke of an incident when the Rebbe had gone out of his way to lend money to a person in need, a simple person, and made sure to do so before, not after, he prayed, so as not to delay the help to the poor person at all. The Fourth Rebbe cut short a needed stay in a healing spa to travel to a distant city, for the sake of influencing one young man to return to Judaism.

Obviously, the Rebbe did not refer to himself or to incidents from his life at this point, but this focus on individuals was a trademark feature of his as well. Just a little over twenty-four hours earlier, the phone had rung in the Merkos office, and the only one present, Moshe Groner, answered. It was Menachem Mendel calling, and he asked if Groner could come to his home. When Groner arrived, Menachem Mendel told him that he needed to visit an elderly man in a nearby home (Groner later realized that Menachem Mendel's presence was necessary to ensure that the man be given proper medical treatment). The visit, though, would take up the time necessary to locate all the references he needed for the speech he was to give the following evening. He showed Groner some books, handed him a note containing various texts he wished to review, and asked Groner to insert bookmarks at the appropriate pages. He then left to assist the sick man.[54] The following night, as the *farbrengen* unfolded, Groner recognized many of the references he had looked up the night before.

The Rebbe now spoke in a manner that anticipated the work that was later to be done by the *shluchim* whom he dispatched throughout the United States and the world: "One must go to a place where nothing is known of Godliness, nothing is known of Judaism, nothing is even known of the Hebrew alphabet, and while there, put one's own self aside and ensure that the other calls out to God! . . . Indeed, if one wants to ensure his own connection to God, he must make sure that the other person not only becomes familiar with but actually calls out to God!" It was not enough, it was never enough, to simply practice Judaism by oneself or in an already religiously observant community; one has to bring others to embrace God as well.

After expressing deep pain over the loss of the Frierdiker Rebbe—and echoing the Jewish belief that all deceased will be resurrected doing Messianic times—he concluded the *ma'amar* by saying, "May we merit to see the Rebbe [meaning his deceased father-in-law] here in this world in a physical body, in this earthly domain," concluding with, "and he will redeem us."[55]

Each Rebbe along with his generation, the new Rebbe explained in a later *sicha* that evening, accomplished one step more and went one step further than his predecessor. But the task, to make the world a dwelling place for God, was still not complete. It would be up to the seventh generation, the people there with him, to complete the divine mission.

Throughout the talk, many times, the Rebbe softly wept; often, many seconds would go by until he composed himself. Then he would resume speaking, returning to his central theme: the obligation of every Chasid, every Jew, to carry out God's mission on earth, and to do so with overflowing love. This is what would set the stage for God to redeem the world. Be my partners, the Rebbe beseeched those present. We're in this together, for this is the responsibility of every member of the Jewish people.

"Everything now depends on us."

Part Two

·⟨═╳═⟩·

On

BEING

a

REBBE

Chapter 3

CONNECTING TO INDIVIDUALS

The Experience of Yechidus *(One-on-One Meetings)*

Private meetings, *yechidus* (plural, *yechidusen*), between a Rebbe and a Chasid were present in Chabad from the beginning. In the early years of the movement, people would come to see the Alter Rebbe, the first Chabad Rebbe, primarily to consult on spiritual matters. With the passage of time, followers started seeking his advice and blessings on a wide range of issues, particularly matters involving livelihood and finances, health, and issues concerning children and marriage.

People first started scheduling meetings with the Rebbe on a regular basis in 1950, in the months following his father-in-law's death, and before he had assumed the leadership role. *Yechidusen* were scheduled three nights a week, commencing at 8:00 p.m. and lasting till the early hours of the morning, sometimes until dawn. In the early years of the Rebbe's leadership, *yechidusen* were generally arranged on short notice. By the mid-1950s, they were being scheduled a month or more in advance, and by the early 1970s it was not uncommon for such meetings to be set up a full half-year in advance.

Chasidim, who regarded the *yechidus* as a spiritual encounter, practiced a special protocol for such meetings. In preparation, they would immerse themselves in a *mikveh* (ritual bath), spend the day in prayer and study, and put on freshly laundered clothes (some would even acquire new garments). At the meeting, they would not shake hands with the Rebbe—it was considered inappropriate at all times to touch the Rebbe—and they would not sit in his presence.

Non-Lubavitchers and, on occasion, non-Jews as well came to see the Rebbe; indeed, the Rebbe received far more such visitors than any of his predecessors, and for them the atmosphere was more relaxed. The Rebbe would extend his hand to visitors, and he encouraged them to sit. The confusion experienced by some visitors who had been warned in advance by Lubavitchers about proper protocol at such meetings could sometimes lead to comical situations. Zalmon Jaffe of London recalled that before his first meeting with the Rebbe he had been prepared for the event by the *shliach* (emissary) in London, Rabbi Bentzion Shemtov. "I took particular note of his instructions such as, 'Real Chasidim don't shake hands with the Rebbe . . . don't sit down, and so forth. . . .' Upon entering the Rebbe's sanctum we were startled and amazed to see the Rebbe actually stand up and come forward to greet us, with his hand outstretched. 'Oh,' said I, 'I am sorry, but Rabbi Shemtov said I must not shake hands with the Rebbe.' 'Never mind,' answered the Rebbe, smiling, and with a lovely twinkle in his eye. 'We won't tell Rabbi Shemtov.' He shook hands with me. He then invited us to sit down. 'Oh dear, no,' said I, horrified. 'Rabbi Shemtov told me that on no account must I sit down.' The Rebbe laughed it off and said, 'After the third time, I will see about you standing during *yechidus*.'" A genuine devotee of the Rebbe, Jaffe, over the coming three and a half decades, ended up crossing the Atlantic to visit the Rebbe seventy times and met with him at 120 *yechidusen*.

The range of people who came to meet with the Rebbe was vast and the meetings consequential. When Robert Kennedy came to 770 in 1964, his encounter with the Rebbe was far more than a photo op for Kennedy, who was then running for the Senate from New York. He and the Rebbe had a substantive discussion focusing on the problem of increasing numbers of teenagers on drugs, and on government funding for religious schools—at least for secular studies—which the Rebbe favored. Kennedy did not support such aid, even though, as he told the Rebbe, he was a committed Catholic who had eight children. The Rebbe interjected, "Yes, but I have two hundred thousand children."[1]

The meeting with Kennedy was a singular occurrence, while the encounters between the Rebbe and Elie Wiesel were far more numerous.

Wiesel's recollections of his *yechidusen* convey with raw power the emotional impact such meetings had on attendees: "I know of no one who left the Rebbe without being deeply affected, if not changed by the encounter.... Time in his presence begins running at a different pace.... In his presence, you come closer in touch with your inner center of gravity. Whenever I would see the Rebbe, he touched the depths in me. That was true of everyone who came to see the Rebbe. Somehow, when the person left, he or she felt that they had lived deeper and ... on a higher level."

In later years, and shortly before he turned eighty, the Rebbe, for reasons of health and on doctor's orders, stopped meeting with people in private. Once this decision was reached, it was enforced almost without exception (except perhaps for matters that the Rebbe regarded as emergencies). The Rebbe's attitude was that if he couldn't meet with everyone, and just met with some, those with whom he didn't meet would feel slighted. Thus, in expressing his "profound regrets" at turning down a request for a meeting with Governor Thomas Kean of New Jersey, he explained in a letter dated February 22, 1985, to David Kotok, Kean's friend who had served as the conduit to arrange the meeting, "I am bound by [a] basic tenet of our Torah which requires us to be extra careful in showing respect to *all*, including those who are less privileged in terms of stature and the like, and they would be embarrassed if they had the feeling that they have been discriminated against."

Scattered throughout this book are numerous references to various *yechidusen* with many people. To give a more detailed sense of what transpired at these meetings, and the different ways in which the Rebbe reached out to people, here are the recollections of four individuals: Dr. Yitzchak (Irving) Block, at the time a young philosophy student at Harvard; Israeli diplomat Yehuda Avner; Harvey Swados, an American novelist, short-story writer, and essayist; and Mrs. Chana Sharfstein, whose father, Rabbi Yaakov Yisrael Zuber, was murdered when she was a teenager and for whom the Rebbe became a lifelong father figure and adviser.

Yitzchak Block:
The Man to Whom the Rebbe Said "No"

*"IF YOU FIND SOMEONE WITH MORE FEAR OF GOD (YIRAT SHAMAYIM)
THAN YOU, YOU CAN GIVE THE JOB TO HIM."*

When the young Irving (now known as Yitzchak) Block set up an appointment for a private meeting with the Rebbe, Rabbi Chaim Hodakov, the Rebbe's chief of staff, scheduled it for Thursday at ten. At the time, Block was staying at an apartment in upper Manhattan, a considerable distance from the Lubavitch headquarters in Brooklyn. Thursday morning, Block made sure to set out early, allowing himself a full hour and a half, and was relieved when he arrived early for his appointment in Crown Heights. Yet when he presented himself at the Rebbe's office, he was greeted with puzzled stares and the question, "What are you doing here?"

Block in turn was puzzled by this odd response. He walked over to Rabbi Hodakov. "I have a ten o'clock meeting with the Rebbe."

"Ten o'clock at night," Rabbi Hodakov answered.

Everyone in Rabbi Hodakov's world knew that the Rebbe's private meetings were held at night, information so obvious to Chabad insiders that no one thought to clarify this for Block (the Rebbe once explained to the *New York Times* reporter Israel Shenker that after 8:00 p.m., it is difficult to reach people at work, so time is available for visitors).[2] Equally obvious, it would never have occurred to Block, raised in Nashville, that an appointment scheduled for ten o'clock could mean anything but 10:00 a.m.

One feature that made the *yechidus* experience so memorable for participants was precisely this feature. You didn't meet with the Lubavitcher Rebbe at 10:00 a.m. or at 1:00 or 3:00 in the afternoon, the way other meetings were scheduled. You met with the Rebbe, if you were lucky enough to get an early appointment, at 8:00 or 9:00 p.m., or more likely at 2:00 or 3:00 in the morning. You saw the Rebbe when the rest of the world was asleep.

Those of non-Chabad background sometimes bristled at these unusual times. When Yehuda Avner set out to schedule an appointment for Yitzchak Rabin, then Israel's ambassador to the United States, Rabin told him, "Don't let them make it at a *sha'ah meshugga* [crazy hour]." Indeed, the Rebbe acceded to Rabin's request and met him during the afternoon.

But for many people, part of the mystique of encountering the Rebbe was the lateness of the hour.

The meeting with Block was eventually rescheduled, and it inaugurated a long relationship with the young man, who was then a graduate student at Harvard. Block had recently spent some weeks at 770 learning in the yeshiva, and his Hebrew and Aramaic textual skills were still quite rudimentary. But it was not Talmud that the Rebbe wished to speak to him about at that first meeting; rather, it was his university studies.

At the time, Block, who was studying for an MA in philosophy, was immersed in the study of the great Greek thinkers, Plato in particular. And that's the direction in which the Rebbe led the discussion. Only Block didn't realize at first to whom the Rebbe was referring, because it was a man named Platon about whom the Rebbe started talking. It finally struck him that Platon is how the name of the Greek philosopher is written in Greek, though in English his name is always pronounced as Plato. It's not that the *n* is silent in English; it isn't written at all.

This was Block's first surprise of the day. The man seated in front of him, dressed in the garb of a Rebbe, obviously knew about Plato, or Platon, from the original Greek and pronounced his name as it was supposed to be pronounced.

But the Rebbe's next comments are what really staggered Block. In the circles in which Block moved at Harvard, Plato was regarded with the highest respect, representing the epitome of high culture and civilization. But the Rebbe had a different take on Plato's writings: He spoke of Platonic philosophy as cruel. "That's the word he used, 'cruel,'" Block recalled in an interview decades later. What upset the Rebbe in particular was Plato's social philosophy, his advocacy of the abolition of the nuclear family and his belief that children should be taken away from their parents. Plato claimed that parents influence children to be egotistical, and it would be better if children were raised without knowledge of their parents, as wards of the state.

For Judaism, the family was central, as expressed in the Fifth Commandment; for Plato, the family was destructive.

Although everything Block heard that day about Plato was accessible to anyone who read through his writings, this critique was new to the young philosophy student. He had never heard it offered at Vanderbilt or Harvard, the two universities where he had studied. Yet, as he sat there, he realized it was unarguable (it was clearly expressed in Plato's writings, though academics ignored it) and that the implications were immense and far-reaching. In addition to the obvious ills that resulted from alienating children from their parents, an attack on the family was also the source of totalitarian ideologies. Once you raise a generation of children to be more loyal to the state than to their families, there is no limit to what you can demand of them. In the Soviet Union, as the Rebbe, who had lived under Communist rule, knew, the government glorified children who informed on their parents and sometimes brought about the imprisonment—or worse—of their parents for making anti-Communist remarks or showing opposition to the state. Raise people to not feel love or loyalty to their parents, and it will not be easy for them to feel love or loyalty to anyone else—only to the state.

The cruelty of Plato's thinking, the Rebbe emphasized that day, was not just in breaking up the family unit. It was in depriving children of parental love. For it is the parents, not the state and its functionaries, who have a genuine love for their children. And depriving children of this love, which is their due, was perhaps Plato's greatest cruelty.

Block recalled that a few years later, a philosopher with respected academic credentials stunned the world of philosophy by writing about these aspects of Plato's writings. In the book, he depicted Plato's social philosophy as "cruel." Block remembered being struck by the philosopher's use of this term, the same word used by the Rebbe. The book caused a furor, but what really impressed Block was that "nobody ever refuted it in any way." However, as Block recalled, all that this professionally trained philosopher, a man who devoted his whole life to philosophy, had done was "to say the same thing that the Rebbe told me years earlier."

It is perhaps no surprise that shortly thereafter Block became an Aristotelian, no longer a devotee of Plato, and has remained so for his entire academic career.

At this same meeting, when Block asked the Rebbe if he should remain at Harvard, the Rebbe emphatically told him, "You should stay there."[3]

Over the coming years, it became apparent that the Rebbe's enthusiasm for Block's academic pursuits at Harvard was even greater than Block's own. On several occasions, Block faltered in his studies, once early in his graduate career, another time when he was at a far more advanced level. Both times, he conveyed his wish to the Rebbe to leave Harvard and to learn full-time at the Lubavitch yeshiva. On one occasion, he actually left Harvard for the yeshiva and announced to his friends and to the rabbinic teachers there that he was back to stay. Everyone at Lubavitch was overjoyed except for one. "I think that you will regret that you gave up your profession" was the Rebbe's response. Block was shocked and upset, but nonetheless, "I got back on the bus and went back to Harvard."

Block eventually completed his PhD and subsequently became a faculty member at the University of Western Ontario in the Canadian city of London. There was a small Jewish community in London and a few Jewish faculty members at the university. Soon, Block was asked to run the Hillel on campus. After a few years of doing so, it became clear to him that it was consuming much of his time—"hundreds and hundreds of hours," as he put it—and he wasn't enjoying it. Furthermore, the university administration was unhappy with the amount of time he was diverting to Hillel. Block asked for a *yechidus* with the Rebbe and told him: "I want to resign because I'm having too much political *tzoros* [headaches; literally "sorrows"]. What do I need it for?" he lamented. The Rebbe said to him: "If you can find someone with more fear of God (*yiras shamayim*) than you have, you can give it to him."

The Jewish population in London, Ontario, was small, the job remained overly demanding, and Block never found a replacement. No surprise.

The Rebbe said no to Block's repeated requests to leave Harvard, no to his request to resign his position at Hillel, and a particularly emphatic no to his request to study for rabbinical ordination (see page 347), but it was part of the wonder of the Rebbe that Block always felt loved and respected by him. While still a young man, he was once sitting on a bench, waiting his turn for a *yechidus*, when a couple came out from their meeting with the Rebbe and glanced at him. One said to the other, "That's the one the Rebbe was talking about." He wondered what they might have heard, and soon learned that the Rebbe had told them that sitting right outside his office was a great philosopher. At the time, Block had not yet published any philosophic writings and was still a graduate student. After hearing such praise, how upset could Block be by the Rebbe's "no's"?

Block also knew of another talent of the Rebbe, the ability to find the quick word, the flash of insight that could inspire an otherwise dejected soul. In this case, it was Block's mother who needed the inspiration. Mrs. Block had been widowed at a young age; throughout Block's years in Crown Heights, the Rebbe would often ask him about his mother, who continued to live in Nashville. Having heard so much from her son about his meetings with the Rebbe, she came to New York and told her son that she wanted to meet the Rebbe. Block was able to arrange for a *yechidus*, and she told him not to accompany her; she wanted to go in alone. After the meeting, she told him what she had discussed with the Rebbe, that she had two sisters, both married, but that she was alone. "And on Friday nights when I light the Shabbat candles, I'm all by myself, and I feel very lonely."

Block was embarrassed at his mother's words, feeling that this was an inappropriate emotion with which to approach the Rebbe, particularly at a first encounter. But the Rebbe, it turned out, didn't feel that way at all. He simply told her, "You don't have to feel lonely. *Der Aibershter is ale mol mit dir*" ("God is with you all the time").

Block recalls: "My mother came out and she was calm." Later, whenever he asked his mother how she was and how she was feeling, she would answer, "Come on, now, God is always with me." Indeed, she told her son that from the point at which the Rebbe told her these words, she was not lonely in the same way anymore.

The Rebbe knew what the elderly Mrs. Block needed to hear and to know. And he sensed what the Jewish people needed from Yitzchak Block, that he become a Harvard-trained philosopher and a God-fearing person. In the United States of the 1950s that was a rare and needed combination, and the Rebbe knew that even before Yitzchak Block did.[4]

Yehuda Avner

"I HAVE GIVEN YOU THE MATCH. ONLY YOU CAN LIGHT YOUR OWN CANDLE."

While the Rebbe always encouraged those whom he met to become more involved in their Jewish activities, even if they already were, he rarely encouraged non-Chabad visitors to become Lubavitchers. Thus, throughout the 1960s and beyond, Rabbi Shlomo Riskin, one of the most effective exponents of Modern Orthodoxy in the United States (he moved to Israel in 1983), visited the Rebbe on several occasions and regarded him as the *manhig ha-dor*, the [spiritual] leader of the Jewish people in his generation. On several occasions, the Rebbe responded to Riskin's queries on highly sensitive issues, blessed him, and in one instance even asked a major favor of him (see pages 293–94). What the Rebbe never asked of Riskin, though, was to become a Lubavitcher, although Riskin acknowledges that had the Rebbe done so, he would have complied.

Yet, for reasons known perhaps only to the Rebbe, there were very rare instances in which the Rebbe did make such a request.[5] One of the few such cases involved Yehuda Avner, a British-born Jew who made aliyah (moved to Israel) as a young man, and who had the distinction of serving four Israeli prime ministers, Levi Eshkol and Golda Meir as a speechwriter, and Yitzchak Rabin and Menachem Begin as a personal adviser. Avner developed close relations with Rabin and Begin, and he accompanied both of them on visits to the Rebbe. While the Rebbe's remarks on those occasions were primarily directed to Begin and Rabin, respectively, a warm relationship between the Rebbe and the religiously observant Avner was established as well.

In 1977, Begin, who had recently been elected as Israel's prime minister, had Avner accompany him to meet with the Rebbe shortly before he went to Washington for a meeting with President Jimmy Carter. These talks were regarded as particularly significant, since Carter was anxious for Israel to compromise and be more forthcoming in its approach to the Palestinians and to her Arab neighbors. For the president, this involved Israel being willing to cede the land, or at least a great deal of it, that Israel had won in the 1967 Six-Day War.[6] This the Rebbe firmly opposed, believing that any land ceded by Israel in exchange for peace would lead to further concessions, would not culminate in a lasting peace, and would put Jewish lives at risk.

That day, when Begin arrived at the Chabad headquarters, a reporter asked him: "Mr. Begin, why have you come to see the Rebbe? Surely, you being the newly elected prime minister of Israel, he should be coming to see you?"[7]

"I have come tonight to our great master and teacher, the Rabbi," Begin responded, pausing for a moment, "to ask for and get from him his blessing before I go to Washington to meet with President Carter for the important talks we are going to hold. Rabbi Schneerson is a great man in Israel, all of us respect him, all of us accept his judgment.[8] He is a great lover of the House of Israel. He has shown his deep sentiment and love for our children, and his blessings are very important to me."

The meeting that ensued between Begin and the Rebbe went very well, and before it concluded, Begin made it clear that he had every intention of keeping the Rebbe in the loop during this delicate time. He therefore informed the Rebbe that when the White House talks concluded, he would dispatch Avner back to 770 to provide the Rebbe with a full summary of his conversations with Carter.

When Avner returned a few days later, he met with the Rebbe alone for four hours, during which he offered him an extended review of the prime minister's meeting with President Carter, Secretary of State Cyrus Vance, and National Security Adviser Zbigniew Brzezinski. Throughout the meeting, Avner explained, Begin made it clear that he had no intention of ceding Judea and Samaria, the lands known as the West Bank, to the Palestine Liberation Organization, whose national charter at that time called for Israel's destruction. These lands, Begin argued, were part of Eretz Yisrael, the Jewish homeland.

To the argument that Israel should halt settlements there in the interim, Begin responded by taking out a paper from his inside pocket. He started to read aloud from it: "Mr. President, here in the United States of America, there are eleven places named Hebron, five places named Shiloh, four places named Bethel, and six places named Bethlehem."

"Indeed, there are," Carter acknowledged. "Within twenty miles of my home [Plains, Georgia], there is a Bethel and a Shiloh."

"May I be permitted to visit them one day?" Begin asked.

"Of course. With pleasure! There are three good Baptist churches there."

"In that case," Begin joked, "I shall bring along our chief rabbi to protect me." Everyone laughed, and then Begin continued: "Allow me to put to you a hypothetical question. Imagine one day that the governors of the states in which these Hebrons and Shilohs and Bethels and Bethlehems were located were to issue a decree declaring that any citizen of the United States was free to settle in any one of these places except for one category—the Jews. Jews are forbidden to build homes in the Shilohs and the Hebrons and the Bethels and the Bethlehems of America—so it should be decreed." At that point, Begin threw up his hands and let out an exaggerated sigh. "Oh dear! Everybody is welcome to settle in any of these cities whose names derive from the Book of Books except for the People of the Book. Good women and men everywhere would cry from the rooftops—'Scandalous! Discrimination! Bigotry!' Am I not right?"

Carter, who seemed to have sensed the direction in which Begin was heading, responded in a dry voice, "Hypothetically."

Begin stood ready now to clinch his argument against all the forces calling upon Israel to stop Jews from settling in the West Bank: "So how can you expect me—a Jewish prime minister of the Jewish state, who heads a cabinet of fifteen Jews—to forbid my fellow Jews from acquiring a piece of land and building a home in the *original* Shiloh, in the *original* Beth El, in the *original* Bethlehem, and in the *original* Hebron from where our Jewish forefathers *originally* came? Would that not be scandalous?"

Needless to say, Carter was not convinced by this and Begin's other arguments, and told him that continuing settlement activities might close off all hopes of negotiations and peace. But the Rebbe, after hearing Avner's summation of the discussions, was highly impressed by Begin's performance. He conveyed to Avner a message to be communicated to the prime minister, congratulating him on safeguarding the integrity of Israel while avoiding a confrontation with the United States. "This is true Jewish statesmanship . . . without pretense or apology. Continue to be strong and of good courage."

Only then, after all matters involving Begin's discussions in Washington and the Rebbe's concerns with Israeli security had been discussed, did the Rebbe choose to both broaden and personalize the discussion. With a "surprisingly sweet smile," the Rebbe asked Avner, "Now tell me, Reb Yehuda, you visit us so often yet you are not a Lubavitcher. Why?"

Avner was totally taken aback. True, he had already met with the Rebbe five or six times and had long served as an unofficial liaison between several prime ministers and the Rebbe. True, too, the Rebbe knew that Avner was already an observant Jew, so that what he was asking of him did not involve a full change in lifestyle. Still, he was stunned at the directness of the question.

Avner, as he related in an interview, had a very high regard for the Rebbe,[9] but he had no particular inclination to become a Chasid. Yet he also did not wish to insult the Rebbe. Swallowing hard, he said, "Maybe it is because I have met so many people who ascribe to the Rebbe powers which the Rebbe does not ascribe to himself." Avner found his voice trailing at the final words.

The Rebbe's blue eyes seemed to shift into something between "solemnity and sadness," as he said, *"Yesh k'nireh anashim ha-zekukim l'kobayim"* ["There evidently are people who are in need of crutches"]. There was no tone of contempt for such people in the Rebbe's voice, only compassion.

Suddenly, the Rebbe started to meditate aloud, as he offered perhaps the clearest exposition he ever expressed on how he saw his role in Jewish life.

"Reb Yehuda, let me tell you what I try to do. Imagine you're looking at a candle. What you are really seeing is a mere lump of wax with a thread down its middle. So when do the thread and the wax become a candle? Or, in other words, when do they fulfill the purpose for which they were created? When you put a flame to the thread, then the wax and the thread become a candle."

The Rebbe's voice now shifted into the chanting cadence in which the Talmud is studied: "The wax is the body and the wick [the thread] is the soul. Bring the flame of Torah to the soul; then the body will fulfill the purpose for which it was created. And that, Reb Yehuda, is what I try to do—to ignite the soul of every Jew with the fire of Torah, with the passion of our traditions, and with the sanctity of our heritage, so that each individual will fulfill the real purpose for which he or she was created."

At this point it was 2:00 a.m., and the buzzer on the Rebbe's desk was sounding every few minutes, a reminder that there were still visitors outside awaiting their turns for an audience. As the staggered and subdued Avner rose to bid his farewell, the Rebbe escorted him to the door. Avner then posed his final question of the evening: "Has the Rebbe lit my candle?"

"No," the Rebbe said, clasping Avner's hand and sending him out with one final thought: "I have given you the match. Only you can light your own candle." [10]

Harvey Swados

"Now that you have interviewed me, I'd like to interview you. Unless you have any objections?"

Harvey Swados (1920–1972) was a highly regarded American novelist and nonfiction writer, known for his naturalistic style. He is widely recognized for several works, among them *Standing Fast* and his classic, *On the Line*, a collection of stories set in an auto plant.

Swados's *yechidus* with the Rebbe took place in 1964; his wife, Bette, accompanied him.[11]

The Rebbe's most striking physical characteristic, the one most often commented upon, particularly by those who met him in *yechidus*, were his eyes; in Swados's case, he recalled how "the pale blue eyes remain fixed upon [me] with an unblinking directness that could be disconcerting." [12]

Of course, Swados, himself a keen possessor of a fine novelist's eye, noticed far more details about the Rebbe than just his eyes. After his *yechidus*, he peppered his recollection of his encounter with just the sorts of details that illuminate what it was like to meet Menachem Mendel Schneerson in private. Among the first things that struck Swados was the Rebbe's workspace: "[His] office was as bleak as the rest of the dingy building,[13] the bare venetian blinds drawn against the beating snow outside, the walls bare also, and with nothing on his desk but a pad and a telephone. The Rebbe sat very still, attending to my queries with his head bent forward so that his broad brimmed hat shaded his face, which appeared deceptively ruddy. He is a strikingly handsome man, whose almost classically regular features are not at all obscured by a graying beard which is full but not bushy."

Swados, then in his early forties, was on something of a quest, not searching for background material for a new book but seeking truths that he could incorporate into his own life. A short time earlier, he had met with the Satmar Rebbe (the leader of a large Hungarian Chasidic group in Brooklyn's Williamsburg neighborhood), and some of the things he had heard at that meeting disturbed him, particularly the Satmar Rebbe's insistence that the Holocaust was a punishment of the Jews for their sins. Only very great sins, the Satmar Rebbe stated, could account for the six million victims' gruesome end. Even today, almost seventy years since the Holocaust ended, such a theology would profoundly trouble the large majority of Jews, but hearing these words then, less than twenty years after the Holocaust, in a world in which many survivors were themselves still in their thirties and forties, was particularly disturbing to Swados (and disturbing as well to the Rebbe; see page 144).

But on this evening, it was not Holocaust theology that Swados was most intent on discussing. Rather, there was another Holocaust-related issue that he found even more pressing on that day. Three years earlier, Israel had publicly tried Adolf Eichmann, the Nazi official in charge of the Jews' annihilation. Filled with detailed testimony from survivors, the Eichmann trial had turned into a seminal event in Jewish life, fully acquainting Jews and interested non-Jews with what Jews had experienced inside the Nazi ghettos and inside the work camps and death camps.

In the aftermath of the trial, Hannah Arendt, the well-known political philosopher who had covered the trial for the *New Yorker,* published a book of her reflections on the trial, titled *Eichmann in Jerusalem: A Report on the Banality of Evil.* In it, Arendt leveled charges against the European Jewish leadership, accusing the local *Judenraete* (the Jewish councils appointed by the Nazis to be their liaisons to the Jewish community) of having acquiesced to the Nazis' most terrible demands. When the Nazis ordered the *Judenraete* to supply Jews for deportation, they did so, fearing that if they didn't cooperate, the Germans would murder even more Jews.

Now, Swados began his discussion by asking the Rebbe his opinion of the behavior of the *Judenraete* and of the German masses as well. The Rebbe's animus toward the Germany of the Hitler era was well-known and of course not surprising.[14] But unlike the Satmar Rebbe, who spoke of the Holocaust as a response in large part to Jewish sinfulness, the Rebbe "made no reference to abstractions, whether theological or philosophical. He pointed instead to political realities, to the incredible difficulties in maintaining one's faith under a totalitarian regime."

The Rebbe started speaking about the persecution then being undergone by Jews in the Soviet Union and asked rhetorically, "How much more difficult do you suppose it was to keep hold of one's integrity under the crushing weight of the German tyrants, who were so much more efficient than the Russians? No," he said firmly, "the miracle was that there was any resistance at all, that there was any organization at all, that there was any leadership at all."

This sort of sober political analysis was clearly not the direction Swados had expected his conversation with a Chasidic Rebbe to take. Was it the Rebbe's opinion, therefore, Swados found himself asking, that the tragedy was not a unique visitation upon the Jewish people and that it could happen again?

"Morgen in der fruh," the Rebbe replied without hesitation, "Tomorrow morning." This was a particularly disconcerting statement from the Rebbe because of his long-standing belief that the Holocaust would never repeat itself. However, that latter belief was always expressed in a theological context. The Rebbe was convinced that God would never again allow such an attack against the Jewish people. But as his conversation with Swados was not about theology, but rather about history and human nature, the Rebbe was making more of a commonsense observation. According to the Rebbe, a society that does not inculcate in its citizens belief in a God who demands righteous and moral behavior could, if it has the military might to do so, carry out genocide against any ethnic group.

"Why [are you] so certain that so terrible a horror could occur again?" Swados asked the Rebbe.

Swados reported what happened next: "The Rebbe launched into an analysis of the German atrocities in a rhetoric that shifted eloquently and unswervingly, often in the same sentence, from English (for my benefit) to Yiddish (for nuance and precision). He did not speak mystically, nor did he harp on the German national character and its supposed affinity for Jew-hatred.

"Rather, he insisted upon the Germans' obedience to authority and their unquestioning carrying out of orders—even the most bestial—as a cultural-historical phenomenon that was the product of many generations of deliberate inculcation."

The conversation continued a few minutes longer, then Swados, conscious of how many people were waiting outside to see the Rebbe, started to prepare for the meeting's end. He thanked the Rebbe and half rose to leave, when the Rebbe restrained him with a motion of his hand.

"Now that you have interviewed me, I'd like to interview you. Unless you have any objections?"

"Please," Swados said, "go right ahead."

The Rebbe grinned. "But I am afraid that I won't be as diplomatic with you as you have been with me."

As Swados later recalled: "After a few questions about my background, he asked me about the subject matter of my books. When I protested that it was no easy thing to sum up, in a sentence or two, books that had taken me years to write, he retorted, 'Surely I can expect a better summation from you than from anyone else.' He seemed particularly interested in my description of *On the Line*, a book in which I had attempted, by means of a series of fictional portraits of auto assembly workers, to demonstrate the impact of their work on their lives.

" 'What conclusions did you come to?'

"The question nettled me. It struck me as obtuse, coming from a man of such subtle perception.

" 'Did you suggest,' he persisted, 'that the unhappy workers, the exploited workers, the workers chained to their machines, should revolt?'

" 'Of course not. It would have been unrealistic.'

" 'What relation would you say that your book bears to the early work of Upton Sinclair?'

"I was flabbergasted. Here I was, sitting in the study of a scholar of mystic lore on a wintry night, and discussing not Chabad Hasidism . . . but proletarian literature! 'Why,' I said, 'I would hope that it is less narrowly propagandistic than Sinclair's. I was trying to capture a mood of frustration rather than one of revolution.'

"Suddenly, I realized that he had led me to the answer that he was seeking—and what was more, with his next query, I realized how many steps ahead he was of my faltering mind: 'You could not conscientiously recommend revolution for your unhappy workers in a free country, or see it as a practical perspective for their readers. Then how could one demand it from those who were being crushed by the Nazis?' "

The *yechidus* now shifted from the macro issue of the Holocaust and the discussion of totalitarianism to the micro, Swados's own life. The Rebbe started by challenging the novelist to think in terms of his own

obligations as a writer and a Jew: "After all, you have certain responsibilities which the ordinary man does not; your words affect not just your
own family and friends but thousands of readers."

"I'm not sure what those responsibilities are," Swados responded.

"First, there is the responsibility to understand the past. . . . Suppose
I ask how you explain the past, the survival of Judaism over three mil-
lennia."

"Well," Swados answered, "the negative force of persecution has
certainly driven people together who might otherwise disintegrate."
Swados went on to argue that if antisemitism disappeared, Jewishness
might well be weakened or destroyed.

To this the Rebbe responded: "Do you really think that only a negative force unites the little tailor in Melbourne and the Rothschild in
Paris?"

"I wouldn't deny the positive aspects of Judaism."

The Rebbe jumped on Swados's concession: "Then suppose that scientific inquiry and historical research led you to conclude that factors
which you might regard as irrational have contributed to the continuity
of Judaism. Wouldn't you feel logically bound to acknowledge the power
of the irrational, even though you declined to embrace it?"

"Hypnotized by the elegance" of the Rebbe's argument, as Swados put
it, he assented. But the Rebbe was not finished with his challenge. "You
must have a certain talent, a gift for expressing yourself so that thousands are swayed by what you write. Where does that talent come from?"

"Partly from hard work. From practice, from study."

"Naturally. But is it unscientific to suggest that you might owe some
of it to your forebears? You did not spring from nothing."

"I recognize that in the genes, the chromosomes . . ."

"If you wish. The point is, isn't it, that something has been transmitted to you by your father, your grandfather, your great-grandfather,
down through the ages? And that you owe them a debt, a debt which you
have the responsibility to try to repay."

By this point, Swados found himself sweating heavily, his hands
tightly clenched, as were those of his wife. The Rebbe, however, sat relaxed, waiting for the writer's response.

"Are you suggesting, Rebbe," Swados finally said, "that I should reexamine my writing or my personal code and my private life?"

"Doesn't one relate to the other? Doesn't one imply the other?"

"That's a complicated question."

"Yes," the Rebbe responded amiably, "it certainly is." He paused, then reminded Swados of what he had said earlier. "I warned you that I wouldn't be diplomatic, didn't I?"

At the meeting's end, when Swados thanked the Rebbe for being so generous with his time, the Rebbe waved aside the complimentary words. "We'll see what your writing turns out like in the time ahead."

At first, Swados thought that the Rebbe might be referring to something that he would write about the meeting, but he immediately realized that that was wrong. "Few things could matter less to him. For he is a man quite without vanity, and what he was expressing was the hope that my work would go well, certainly better than before." The Rebbe then extended a *bracha* (blessing) to the Swadoses and their children.

Minutes later, standing outside in the howling snow, Swados found himself surrounded by Chasidim who wanted to know what had transpired in the hour-and-a-half-long meeting. The author, profoundly moved, did not want to try to sum up so intense a conversation in a few words, although he offered a few impressions.

"Tell me," demanded one Chasid, beaming at the realization of how taken Swados seemed to have been with the Rebbe, "what kind of impression did the Rebbe make on you? I know it's cold, but just tell me in one word."

Swados surprised himself by his own definition of what had struck him most about the Rebbe, and it was not the intellectual rigor of the discussion or all the personal challenges posed by the Rebbe: "If I had to choose one word to characterize him, I guess I would choose the word 'kindly.' " [15]

The Many *Yechidusen* of Chana Sharfstein

"IT'S THE SMALL ACTS THAT YOU DO ON A DAILY BASIS THAT TURN TWO
PEOPLE FROM A 'YOU AND I' INTO AN 'US.'"

Chana Sharfstein was a daughter of Rabbi Yaakov Yisrael and Zlata Zuber, a family with deep ties to Chabad. Her parents, Russian-born Jews, were sent by the Frierdiker Rebbe to Stockholm, where her father served as the community's chief rabbi. One of her early childhood memories was of meeting the Frierdiker Rebbe during a ten-day layover he made in the Swedish capital when he was fleeing from Nazi-occupied Poland to the United States. Now in her seventies, Sharfstein still recalls her timidity when the Frierdiker Rebbe asked her name; the young girl answered in a low voice, and the Rebbe blessed her.[16]

Later, in 1946, when Ramash (who was not to become Rebbe for almost five more years) was trying to extricate his mother from Russia, one of the people he wrote to ask for help was Rabbi Zuber, Chana's father.[17]

Rabbi Zuber, a religious scholar, had long hoped to leave Sweden for a more intensely Jewish environment, one better suited for raising his family. In 1946, he was offered the position of rosh yeshiva (head of the school) at the Chabad yeshiva Tomchei Temimim in Brooklyn. He was set to take the job when the yeshiva's former head, who had been presumed to have been killed in the Holocaust, reappeared, and Rabbi Zuber relinquished the post. Then, in 1948, a rabbinic position opened in Boston, and he moved there with his wife and two of his four children, of whom Chana was the youngest. After occupying two pulpits, Rabbi Zuber became dean of the Lubavitch yeshiva in Boston.

Then, on December 31 (New Year's Eve), 1952, tragedy struck. That evening, muggers attacked Rabbi Zuber and beat him so severely that he died. The assailants were never caught. This man had survived Stalin only to be murdered in the safe haven of the United States. For Chana's mother, living now without a support system in a new country whose language she barely knew, the loss was one from which she never recovered.

The Rebbe sent representatives from Brooklyn to the funeral and reached out to the family. A few months later, in the spring, Chana Sharfstein, then in her late teens, went with her mother to New York for a *yechidus* and established an immediate rapport with the Rebbe: "He seemed so human, so warm. I immediately felt at ease." What struck her as well was the Rebbe's appearance: "His most expressive feature were his eyes, looking directly at you." Deprived at so vulnerable an age of a father with whom she had been very close, for Chana this encounter with the Rebbe was particularly significant.

After first speaking at some length with Rebbetzin Zlata Zuber about her late husband, her daily activities, her difficulties, and her plans for the future, the Rebbe turned his attention to the young woman, asking her about her studies and her interests. He wanted to know why she was attending college, an activity that he generally discouraged for members of the Chabad community (see chapter 24). When Sharfstein answered that she wanted to be a teacher, the Rebbe asked if it was necessary to go to college to become a teacher.

"I want to be a really good teacher," Sharfstein answered, explaining that she was taking courses in both psychology and education. The Rebbe smiled and asked her to "be sure to use your talents for your people." Sharfstein subsequently became a principal of the Bais Rivka primary school, though during her long career in education she taught in public schools as well.

Throughout the meeting, the young Sharfstein found herself responding with ease. "I knew he was listening carefully . . . he seemed so genuinely interested in everything I said." As she told me in 2013, almost sixty years later, "the Rebbe's body language, looking at me without moving, made it evident that he was totally focused on what I was saying." She recalls leaving the meeting feeling as if the Rebbe were someone she had known her whole life, even closer, a family member: "Indeed, that is how I felt."

Some months later, Sharfstein was back in New York and returned to see the Rebbe. When she entered his office, she was carrying a tape recorder, the old type of recorder in use in the 1950s, with spinning reels of tape. As she set it up, the Rebbe asked her not to tape anything. He explained that when a person has a tape recorder, his or her attention becomes directed to the machine, and the person is constantly checking to see if the tape is moving, how far it has moved, whether it's coming to the end, and whether the tape needs to be changed. "If you use the tape recorder," the Rebbe warned, "you're not going to be listening to me intently, and I want you to listen to what I say and to be involved in what I say, so don't use a tape recorder."

The Rebbe clearly knew his agenda for this meeting, and the conversation quickly turned in a personal direction. At a certain point, he asked Sharfstein if she felt ready to get married. Sharfstein told him that she had begun dating—in Chasidic circles, young men and women date only for the purpose of marriage—and the Rebbe asked her about a specific young man. She recalls being taken aback and thinking to herself, *That's interesting that he should ask about somebody that I had met.* Sharfstein told the Rebbe that she had met the young man he mentioned, that he was clearly a fine person, but not for her.

The Rebbe said all right, and then mentioned another name, and again it was someone to whom Sharfstein had been introduced. Here, too, the young man was very nice but not for her.

Then the Rebbe mentioned a third name, and a fourth, "and I became really uncomfortable then. How did the Rebbe choose all the names of young men (*bachurim*) that I had met? I was just absolutely overwhelmed that he should mention people that I had actually met." Only later did she learn that prior to going out with a girl, each *bachur* in Chabad would write to the Rebbe to inquire if the girl seemed suitable for him, and so the Rebbe, who obviously had responded in each case that Chana Zuber was suitable, had a very precise idea of all the people with whom she had gone out. But even taking all this into account, Sharfstein still remained staggered at the Rebbe's recall. After all, he "was [already] a world leader at this time, and to keep track of each person and who had been dating whom, it's really mind-boggling."

After exhausting the list of the men whom Sharfstein had met, the Rebbe smiled broadly and asked if there was someone she had in mind whom she would like to meet. Sharfstein's mind drifted to a well-known singer of Chasidic songs, a man of considerable charisma who excited the young people who attended his concerts. The singer used to remove his jacket while performing and fling it off, and then fling off his tie as well. Sharfstein mentioned to the Rebbe that she would like to meet him.

The Rebbe chuckled but shook his head. "That's not for you." And then he offered Sharfstein an explanation of love that she has been sharing with people ever since. The Rebbe began by recalling that Sharfstein had mentioned at their earlier meeting that she was an avid reader, and he now asked what kinds of books she preferred to read. She answered that she loved to read novels. The Rebbe responded that as novels are fiction, what you read in them is not necessarily what happens in real life. It's not as if two people meet and there is a sudden, blinding storm of passion. That's not what love or life is, or should be, about. Rather, he said, two people meet and there might be a glimmer of understanding, like a tiny flame. And then, as these people decide to build a home together, and raise a family, and go through the everyday activities and daily tribulations of life, this little flame grows even brighter and develops into a much bigger flame until these two people, who started out as virtual strangers, become intertwined to such a point that neither of them can think of life without the other. This is what true love is about, the Rebbe told Sharfstein. "It's the small acts that you do on a daily basis that turn two people from a 'you and I' into an 'us.' "

Sharfstein still recalls the huge smile on her face when she walked out of the Rebbe's office: "The Rebbe knew how to communicate with a dreamy young girl. He knew what to say and how to say it. His words, spoken from the heart, reverberated within my heart."

Not long after, Sharfstein met and married Rabbi Mottel Sharfstein and began a family. But then again, tragedy. Within just five years of her father's death, Chana's mother, Rebbetzin Zuber, had a stroke. It was just a few days before Passover, and she was visiting Sharfstein in Brooklyn and helping her prepare for the holiday. The date of her mother's stroke was the eleventh of Nisan, the Rebbe's birthday, and a day the Rebbe used to spend at the *Ohel*, his father-in-law's gravesite and during which—particularly in those pre–cell phone days—he was pretty much incommunicado. Throughout the day, Sharfstein kept calling the

Chabad office at 770, informing the people there of her mother's condition and asking for a *bracha*, a blessing, from the Rebbe. But she kept getting the same response: "He is still at the *Ohel.*" It was only many hours later, when the Rebbe returned from the cemetery, that she received a call from the office telling her that the Rebbe wanted to know how her mother was faring. It was too late; Rebbetzin Zuber was no longer alive.

The following months were very hard. A young woman still in her twenties, Sharfstein had lost both her parents and her mother-in-law as well; in addition, her father-in-law had died even before she had met her husband: "I had never envisioned that in America my children would grow up without grandparents, just like me, but I had grown up in the Hitler era." A sense of tragedy and great longing for her mother sent her into a period of emotional turmoil, during which she wrote a sorrowful letter to the Rebbe explaining what she was going through. She received no answer, and this devastated her.

A few months later, Sharfstein requested a *yechidus* at which she told the Rebbe of the great emotional pain she was still experiencing and asked for guidance on how to deal with her grief. The Rebbe's face exuded concern, but he explained that all he had to say on the subject he had set down in the letter he had written her months earlier.

"What letter?" the astonished Chana asked.

The Rebbe became quite distraught. He had written her, he knew, and he summoned Rabbi Groner, who shortly thereafter located a copy of the letter that had been sent. What had happened was that Chana and her family had moved some months earlier within Crown Heights, and the address to which the Rebbe's letter had been sent was the family's old one; unfortunately, the letter had never been forwarded. And so the Rebbe now told her the contents of the letter and then had a copy of the original sent to her.

The letter begins with a statement of three of the Rebbe's most fundamental theological convictions: God is infinite, God is incomprehensible, and God is actively involved in the world. This last point is crucial, since there have been many people, deists, who believe that God created the world but then left it to its own devices. However, this is not the Jewish view since, "if this were the case, there would be no place for prayer and appeals to God's mercy." Rather, God "is the continuous Master of the world, Who is constantly watching over it and taking care of everything and every individual."

But if God is "taking care of everything," why then would He allow such awful things to happen, such as the death of Rebbetzin Zuber? There is a divine answer, the Rebbe asserts, but one inaccessible to human beings—and this should not surprise us: "Obviously, it is impossible for a human being whose intellect . . . is limited, to understand the ways of God." For while it is true that there are many things people do learn during the course of a lifetime, "clearly God's ways and reasons cannot fully be understood by created beings, for there is an infinite gap between the Creator and the created."

Therefore, while it is beyond human capabilities to know why tragedies happen, what God has made known through the Torah "is that all that God does is for the good of man, whether the person concerned understands it or not." That we cannot understand God's ways might be frustrating but should not be startling, "as it would be rather surprising if [a person] did understand the infinite ways and reasons of God."

The Rebbe's reasoning is reminiscent of one of the enduring insights—its original author is unknown—of medieval Jewish philosophy, *lu yidativ, hayeetiv,* "If I knew God, I'd be God." Only God can understand all of God's ways; indeed, a God Whose ways could be *fully* understood by a human being would be on the same level as human beings, no higher. Therefore, all that believers can be sure of is that what God does is for their good. Thus, while faith will not grant us an understanding of why bad things happen to good people, our belief that what happens to us and our loved ones is what God has willed provides a human being, even when suffering loss, with a great measure of consolation.

The Rebbe then proceeded to offer an additional and, in some ways, more comprehensive consolation, the notion that death of the physical body does not mean the total annihilation of the deceased: "All believers in God believe also in the survival of the soul. Actually, this principle has even been discovered in the physical world, where science now holds, as an absolute truth, that nothing in the world can be physically destroyed. How much more so in the spiritual world, especially in the case of the soul, which in no way can be affected by the death and disintegration of the physical body. . . . *The truth is that when the physical body ceases to function, the soul continues its existence,* not only as before, but even *on a higher level, inasmuch as it is no longer handicapped by the restraints to its physical frame"* (emphasis added).

At the *yechidus* with Sharfstein, the Rebbe emphasized these points in an even more concrete manner than in the letter: "If you take a piece of paper and you burn it with a match, ashes are going to [remain]. It's not going to be totally destroyed, something will remain. It will be in a different shape or form but something will remain of it. And the same thing is with the human being. . . . Something that exists cannot be totally destroyed." Furthermore, "when you love a person . . . you love what the person is, you love the person's [character traits], you like his character, his personality. And those are the things that cannot be destroyed."

This belief in the soul's enduring existence and elevation is a mainstay of Chabad teaching. Thus, the Rebbe, who spent hundreds and hundreds of hours at his father-in-law's gravesite, clearly believed, in line with the Zohar, that his father-in-law was even more accessible now that his essence had become pure spirit. Similarly, now that Rebbetzin Zuber had been liberated from her body, Chana could more easily access her.

The Rebbe then addressed the most immediate pain people feel when a loved one—a parent, a spouse, or a child—dies. Usually, the sorrow is most deeply experienced because we can no longer touch, hold, hug, or converse with the deceased. All this is a very real cause of ongoing pain, particularly if the primary expression of our relationship was with the dead person's physical body. But if the most important attachment we have with those we love is to the quality of the person's soul, "including such spiritual things as character, kindness, goodness, all of which are attributes of the soul, and not of the body," the devastation will not be as acute. Furthermore, if our relationship with the dead person was solely physical, then we can do nothing for the person once he or she has died. On the other hand, the focus on the spiritual enables us to "bring joy and benefit to the soul [of] one's parents [for example] . . . even after they are physically no longer here."

In brief, and as distinct from the expression "Death ends a life but not a relationship," the Rebbe's view in essence was that "Death ends neither a relationship nor a life."[18] Even after the body dies, "the relationship continues [because the soul is still alive. Therefore] we know that when we do good, we bring joy to our loved ones."

Some years later, when Sharfstein was studying for an MA in education at Brooklyn College, she took a course in urban sociology. The course focused in part on the survival of minority groups within urban environments largely inhabited by other groups. Sharfstein chose to write her term paper on the Lubavitch movement and titled it "A Minority Within a Minority," referring both to the status of the Jews as a minority within American society and to Chabad as a minority within the Jewish community. She was pleased when the heavily researched paper was given an A.

At a *yechidus* a short time later, Sharfstein brought the paper to the Rebbe, who started to read it in her presence. Thinking back, it would seem, to his own university years, he immediately asked why the paper had no footnotes. Sharfstein explained that while the earlier norm had been to insert footnotes at the bottom of each page (the "foot" of the page, so to speak), more recently it had become the practice to list the footnotes at the end of the essay.

The paper focused on the community Chabad had established in Crown Heights; it also contained a considerable amount of material about the Rebbe, as his leadership was an indispensable element in Chabad's growth. Sharfstein remembers growing anxious as the Rebbe turned to a page on which she related an anecdote about him. A young man who was about to be sent to fight in the Korean War (1950–1953) had gone to the Rebbe for a *bracha*, and the Rebbe had advised him that during this period—when he would be far away from home and traditional Jewish life—he should make every effort to observe as many *mitzvot* as he could. Some time later, the young man was encamped with his company and, as the soldiers were preparing to have lunch, he broke away for a few moments to walk to a nearby stream where he could wash his hands before making the *ha-motzi* blessing (Jewish law dictates a ritual washing of one's hands before making the blessing over bread). In the few minutes it took him to walk to the water and return, a shell hit his company and all of the soldiers were killed. Sharfstein had mentioned this story as an example of the sort of advice the Rebbe offered his Chasidim and the dramatic lifesaving effect it had.

The story had irritated her professor, who jotted down on the side of the sheet his belief that such an anecdote proved nothing, that he had a friend in Korea who had dismounted from a tank and during the few minutes he was away, the tank was blown up and the people inside killed. The professor's tone was sarcastic, and he made clear his belief that there was no reason to attribute any of this to anything but pure dumb luck.

Sharfstein, her eyes focused on the Rebbe perusing her paper, remembers thinking, "I hope he doesn't get to that page. I hope he doesn't notice it." Then the Rebbe stopped for a minute. Not surprisingly, he had noticed the professor's response, as his handwritten comments filled half a page. After he read through the professor's words, the Rebbe shook his head calmly and said in a low voice, "*Nu, an apikores*" ("So what? A nonbeliever.").[19] Sharfstein recalls: "He just dismissed it like that, not a big deal."

The Rebbe continued scanning the paper and then, before Sharfstein left, asked if he could keep it so that he could read it more thoroughly. At this time (1972), little had been written about Chabad, and the Rebbe was eager to see how Sharfstein had represented the community. A short time later, she received her paper back along with emendations on several of its pages. These are particularly significant, as they offer insight into the Rebbe's mind and his priorities.

For example, in describing the role of music within Chabad, Sharfstein wrote: "It is felt that singing can lift the soul, help one overcome troubles, and provide comfort. . . . Many Lubavitcher songs consist of only a melody, for the words are of lesser importance in supplying the mood. There is a strain of sadness in the music, reminiscent of the hard life of the Chasid."

The Rebbe suggested deleting "the hard life of a Chasid" and substituting "the hardships of life." The point to be conveyed was not the disheartening thought that the Chasid's life is particularly hard but that there are hardships in life, period. "A small change in words," Sharfstein comments, but one that conveys a very different sensibility.

In explaining Chabad's hesitations about post–high school secular education, Sharfstein had written, "[The Rebbe has stated that] college means exposure to certain circles and activities which conflict with faith and values. He therefore believes that a college education should be postponed until the person's character is crystallized and he can withstand all the alien forces."

The Rebbe circled the words "should be postponed" and substituted "should not be considered," so that the last sentence now reads, "a college education should not be considered until the person's character is crystallized . . ." As Sharfstein understood the Rebbe's intention: "When something is postponed, it is on one's mind, very much in one's definite future plans. It is put on temporary hold, yet the plan is 'on.' 'Should not be considered,' on the other hand, means total removal from one's thoughts." Not necessarily forever, but at least "until the person's character is crystallized and he can withstand all the alien forces." Emanating from the Rebbe's desire to de-emphasize secular education, he also asked Sharfstein to delete the references she made in the paper to his university degree in electrical engineering and to his wife's university-level study of architecture. He obviously did not wish to convey to his followers the belief that a person needs a university education to be a complete human being.

Some changes the Rebbe suggested to Sharfstein seemed to emanate out of a desire that a cult of personality not develop around him (see pages 497–98). Thus, Sharfstein had written that "the Lubavitcher Rebbe regards himself as the Spiritual Shepherd of all Israel in his generation. He feels responsible for the spiritual and physical welfare of all Jews." All this talk of the Rebbe regarding himself as the "Spiritual Shepherd" was deleted, and in its place the Rebbe set for himself a more modest agenda: "The Rebbe's interests and activities encompass the spiritual and physical welfare of all Jews."

The Rebbe's well-known sensitivity to individuals' feelings came through in yet one additional edit, in which Sharfstein had been discussing the "Released Time" public school program during which Lubavitchers were allowed to take children out of public schools for an hour of instruction in Jewish studies. Sharfstein noted that the program, which was national in scope, "was conducted by volunteers from Lubavitch in New York, Boston, and many other cities." The Rebbe deleted the reference to New York and Boston and simply wrote "many cities." His reasoning was obvious, though not one that would have occurred to most people: "In specifically mentioning some [cities] by name, others may feel slighted or left out. Rather than hurting someone's feelings through omission, it is preferable to not single out anyone or any city, and thus give equal honor to all."

What is noteworthy are the number of insights and priorities dear to the Rebbe that were communicated in his editing of this one research paper: his concern that the life of a Chasid not be regarded as a hardship, either by Chasidim themselves or by others; that a person should not think of postponing college education when he or she completes high school, but simply not consider college at all in that period of one's life; his desire to de-emphasize his accomplishments and to eliminate idolization of him; thus, he didn't want to be regarded as a "prophet" or a "Spiritual Shepherd," a term that brings to mind the opening verse of the most famous Psalm: "The Lord is my shepherd" (23:1). He clearly did not want to be confused with the Divine shepherd, and his unusual and trademark sensitivity to not making any individuals or communities feel overlooked.

What is perhaps most unusual about all these edits is the context in which they were offered. It was not as if Sharfstein had brought him the draft of an article that would soon be appearing in a large-circulation magazine or newspaper. Rather, here was a term paper written by a student for a graduate course in a local university. The Rebbe had no reason to assume that the paper would be read by a broad audience, yet he edited it as one can imagine a parent—and perhaps only a parent—reviewing the work of a child. And one thing is clear: Chana Sharfstein was not the only person for whom the Rebbe performed such a service (see Susan Handelman's recollections on pages 215–17).

Finally, we come to Sharfstein and the Rebbe during a later stage in his life, the time when he no longer conducted *yechidusen* with individuals. In those last years, people could have brief encounters with the Rebbe at "Dollars" (the attendees could express a sentence or two), the Sunday mornings and afternoons at which the Rebbe would stand at the table in front of his office and hand out a dollar and a *bracha* to the several thousand people who would routinely come. The Rebbe was then in his late eighties and would remain on his feet for the many hours it took to hand out the bills and offer a blessing.

Sharfstein was a frequent attendee at these gatherings, and she was able to inform the Rebbe that she had started organizing tours to her native Sweden and elsewhere in Scandinavia, at which she would expose people to the natural beauty of these countries and to the largely unknown Jewish life there (few Jews, when they hear "Sweden," have any Jewish associations whatsoever). Sharfstein would frequently come to "Dollars" to solicit the Rebbe's *bracha* on behalf of her beloved sister-in-law, Sarah Zuber, who had a fatal bout with cancer. She recalls one encounter with the Rebbe when her sister-in-law's condition was rapidly deteriorating: "I was brokenhearted that Sunday . . . as I walked through the aisles toward the Rebbe. And finally I was there, right in front of him, and I could no longer . . . choke back my anguished sobs." She asked for a *bracha* for Sara bas Henia (Sara, the daughter of Henia). The Rebbe offered a warm blessing, gave Sharfstein a dollar, and she started off.

Suddenly, someone grabbed her arm and told her, "Go back to the Rebbe. He wants to see you." She turned around and saw that the line had halted and the Rebbe was looking at her, waiting for her to return. She walked back, and the Rebbe smiled at her, handed her another dollar, and said, "Nu, so when are you leaving for Scandinavia?" She told him the date, and he gave her a warm *bracha* for the tour. "I continued on my way. I must have looked quite strange, tears still streaming down my cheeks yet with a smile on my face."

As Sharfstein recalled years later: "That was the Rebbe. During a moment of total despair he was able to renew hope. In the midst of tragedy, he was making me aware that there are [still] tasks to be accomplished, projects to be continued." [20]

Chapter 4

THE TEN CAMPAIGNS

Taking Judaism into the World

"AMERICAN JEWS CANNOT BE TOLD TO DO ANYTHING,
BUT THEY CAN BE TAUGHT TO DO EVERYTHING."
—*The Rebbe in conversation with Herman Wouk*

On June 30, 1958, at a *farbrengen* celebrating what would have been the Frierdiker Rebbe's seventy-eighth birthday (12 Tammuz), the Rebbe proclaimed his *U'faratzta* campaign, which in many ways has defined Chabad to the Jewish world ever since. The word "*u'faratzta*" occurs only once in the Torah,[1] when God appears to Jacob in a dream during a very difficult period in his life and assures him that "your descendants shall be as [numerous as] the dust of the earth; *u'faratzta*—you shall spread out to the west and to the east, to the north and to the south.... Remember, I am with you; I will protect you wherever you go" (Genesis 28:14–15).

The *U'faratzta* campaign highlighted and reinvigorated what had been a central theme in his first *ma'amar* in 1951, when he assumed leadership of the movement and told those assembled there that night: "One must go to a place where nothing is known of Godliness, nothing is known of Judaism, nothing is even known of the Hebrew alphabet, and while there put one's own self aside and ensure that the other calls out to God." Over the coming years, he repeatedly made clear his goal: that Chasidim disseminate knowledge of Judaism to the entire Jewish world, even to its most remote corners. He intended this mission to be accomplished by emissaries (*shluchim*), couples who would move into a community and encourage the Jews there to lead more active Jewish lives. The *shluchim* were expected to remain permanently in the communities to which they were dispatched, thereby earning the long-term trust and friendship of the Jewish residents—the prerequisite traits for bringing people to a trust *in* and love *of* Judaism.

The dispatching of such emissaries—an issue he had discussed with his father-in-law—had been something that the Rebbe had thought about even before assuming the movement's leadership. In 1950, just three days following the completion of shiva, the seven-day mourning period for his father-in-law, Ramash communicated his father-in-law's earlier decision to send Rabbi Michoel and Taibel Lipsker to serve as *shluchim* to the Jewish community of Morocco, where they eventually established seventy Jewish schools throughout the country.

During his early years of leadership, he made a number of additional such appointments. As in the case of the Lipskers, most went smoothly. Yet periodically, the Rebbe encountered dismay and even resistance when he asked a couple to move away from Brooklyn or their hometown. Today, the sending out of Chabad emissaries throughout the world is acknowledged as the Rebbe's most revolutionary and perhaps enduring achievement, yet at its inception the idea provoked much hesitation. The *shluchim* themselves were generally newly married couples in their early twenties, and there were parents (and sometimes the young couple themselves) who were less than thrilled about their children permanently relocating to cities that more often than not had small populations of observant Jews.[2]

In 1952, a year after becoming Chabad's leader, the Rebbe undertook to send a newly married couple to serve as *shluchim* in Brazil. Unlike the Lipskers, in this case the bride and her parents, all three Lubavitchers, were very unhappy with the Rebbe's request. The father, who held a key position for the movement in Israel, couldn't comprehend the idea of his daughter and son-in-law moving to a country with little Jewish infrastructure in place, and he wrote to the Rebbe to express his unhappiness.

We possess no copy of the father's letter, but the basic content of what he said is clear from the Rebbe's response (when the letter was published, the Rebbe, as was his custom, omitted all names). The father, clearly pleased about the marriage, wrote that the family's "happy event was [now] disturbed" by the news that the couple were to be sent abroad. It seems apparent from the Rebbe's response that the father made no effort to disguise his displeasure at what the Rebbe had done.

The Rebbe was in no way apologetic. He wrote in his capacity as a leader, in a sense as a military general who understood the need to deploy his troops where they were most needed, to "a place where your son-in-law and your daughter can fully utilize their potential." The Rebbe acknowledged that moving to a foreign and largely nonobservant Jewish community requires a certain measure of self-sacrifice (*mesirut nefesh*), but he then posed a rhetorical question intended to overwhelm any further opposition. To paraphrase: "If one can't expect such self-sacrifice from a graduate of our yeshiva, one who is a child as well of such a graduate and who is married to the daughter of such a graduate, if even from such people one can't ask for a measure of self-sacrifice, then upon whom can one rely?"

The Rebbe proceeded to offer both a carrot and a stick. Thus, he assured the father—knowing that the letter would be read by his daughter as well—that the couple would flourish in every meaningful manner by undertaking such a mission: "The vastness of the good fortune that will result if they accept this offer, including good fortune in a physical sense, is obvious to me." On the other hand—and the Rebbe stated this as a fact, not a threat—refusing such a mission would cut the couple off from the work of the Previous Rebbe (who had died just two years earlier), and, by implication, from the Rebbe himself.

Although he expressed "shock" that an offer to spread "the light of Torah and Chasidus" to unknowledgeable Jews could lead to the parents feeling that their happiness had been "disturbed," he also set down, near the letter's end, his trademark conclusion: "As stated above, I am not giving an order, Heaven forbid. This is only a suggestion."

On occasion, the Rebbe's responses could be more curt, and his annoyance more apparent. To a mother who wrote of her displeasure at his intention to send out her son and his wife as emissaries, he responded: "I was surprised because when I spoke to your son and daughter-in-law

I was under the impression that he was my soldier, and I could give him an assignment in——[the city's name is omitted from the published version of the letter] but it has now become apparent that before he agrees he has to first hear what his mother says and what the family says. This is obviously not the way a soldier operates, to ask [and set] conditions concerning how long, and to then go ask his family what they think. I am therefore retracting my offer."

The Rebbe ends the letter by expressing his hope for both the woman and her family to be blessed by God with everything good.[3]

We know of several other similar instances of designated *shluchim* who resisted going to their assigned places, and we also know of the Rebbe's disappointment that more couples did not volunteer to be sent as emissaries without having to be asked. At some point, it seems to have become apparent to him that before he could succeed in sending out substantial numbers of *shluchim* to outlying communities, he would first need to educate the Chabad community itself, men and women alike, on the importance of such a mission. During the 1950s, the concept of outreach was largely unknown.

Such is the background for the *U'faratzta* campaign, and over the coming years, the Rebbe would repeatedly emphasize the theme of spreading Judaism to Jews throughout the world[4] (a theme that went back, as noted, to his first speech as Rebbe; see page 39). On one occasion in 1962 he offered his followers a striking image for the mission with which he was entrusting them: "In the old days there was a person in every town who would light the streetlamps with a flame he carried at the end of a long pole. . . . Sometimes, however, the lamps were not easily accessible. . . . There were lamps in forsaken places. Someone had to light those lamps, too, so that they would fulfill their purpose and light up the paths of others. Today, too, someone must be willing to forgo his or her conveniences and reach out to light even those forsaken lamps."

The word *"u'faratzta"* soon became Chabad's motto for the teaching and spreading of Judaism. On one noted occasion (March 2, 1961), the immediate impetus for the Rebbe's appeal to Lubavitchers to become emissaries was a speech delivered the previous day by President

John F. Kennedy announcing the establishment of the Peace Corps, a government-financed program to send American volunteers to share their expertise, particularly in education, agriculture, and health, with citizens of developing countries.

In Kennedy's announcement, he challenged Americans, especially young people, to join this program, and he made no effort to downplay the difficult change in lifestyle this would entail: "It will not be easy. None of the men and women will be paid a salary. They will live at the same level as the citizens of the country which they're sent to, doing the same work, eating the same food, speaking the same language." The speech electrified the nation and dominated the news.

A day later, at a large Purim *farbrengen* in Crown Heights, the Rebbe made an explicit and highly complimentary reference to Kennedy's speech. Then, reminding those present of the *U'faratzta* campaign started three years earlier, he continued, in a manner both reminiscent of the president and yet more challenging and confrontational: "Don't convince yourselves that you can live off the 'fat of the land,'[5] in the radius of these few blocks. Here, you have radio and television . . . you can shower twice a day, there's no worry about [obtaining] kosher milk and kosher bread—[and so you think] you'll just serve God [comfortably] here." But, the Rebbe reminded his listeners, outside the confines of Crown Heights there was, spiritually speaking, an undeveloped, even desolate, land, "filled with Jews who don't even know they are lacking."[6]

Consistent with the Rebbe's desire that his followers not see themselves as superior to those who are nonobservant and unknowledgeable, the Rebbe reminded his listeners that it was only through God's kindness and not their own merit ("We did nothing to deserve or earn it") that they received the gift of a Torah upbringing. But so many Jews throughout the world have not received this gift. And so, he asked of those present, "Give up a few years, whatever it takes, and go out to the Jew who is in such need that he doesn't even know that he lacks anything." He then blessed those who heeded his call that "as many years as the work requires, God will grant you, and from your own years nothing will be diminished."

Though there was an upbeat, encouraging tone to his message, the Rebbe could not refrain from expressing his frustration that he had been issuing such appeals for years ("asking one way, another way, a third way"), and "I've heard every excuse there is just to avoid leaving this place." He accused many of his followers of adopting the mind-set, *Let someone else worry about the Jews who are not involved in Jewish life. It's not my job.*

But this attitude is wrong, for "what will be then with the Jews in those countries?" Rather, he maintained, Lubavitchers should be guided by the words of Israel Baal Shem Tov, Chasidism's eighteenth-century founder, who taught that "we are obligated to love a Jew who is across the globe even if we've never met him." And then, in a remarkable return to the challenge offered a day earlier in Washington, the Rebbe expressed the hope that now that the new, highly popular president had spoken, his words would motivate even some of the Rebbe's followers in Crown Heights to spread out across the globe with a message of love and commitment to *Yiddishkeit* (Jewish living). God—the Rebbe was in essence saying—is sending us through the words of the American president a reminder of what we must do.[7]

Finally, the Rebbe acknowledged, in yet one more comment reminiscent of Kennedy's, that he could not guarantee a high salary. One thing, though, he would guarantee: "You will go as an emissary of God." In addition, embarking on such a mission would help bring redemption to the world: "For if the exile was brought about through unfounded hatred, we will bring the redemption through unbounded love." (The Rebbe was referring here to the well-known Talmudic teaching that the Second Temple was destroyed in 70 CE because of causeless hatred that prevailed in the Jewish community [*Yoma* 9b] and his belief that if "causeless hatred" can lead to so grievous a catastrophe, causeless and boundless love can bring about unending good.)

Sending *shluchim* out into the world greatly accelerated the process of Chabad outreach (and eventually influenced other Jewish groups to start their own programs of outreach). What moved it even further were the various *mivtza'im* (campaigns) to increase observance of the commandments. The Rebbe believed that for a Jew largely uninvolved in the performance of the commandments, the journey to God begins with the performance of a single mitzvah. Over the coming decades, this belief manifested in a plethora of ways. The extensive menorah-lighting campaign, for example, increased awareness of Chanukah and also made the holiday more widely known in the non-Jewish world (see pages 261–70). Each campaign focused on a specific commandment—often one that had been largely ignored outside the Orthodox world (such as the wearing of tefillin by men)—and the goal was to bring it to the attention of the broader community.

The first campaign to increase the number of Jewish men putting on tefillin was initiated just before the 1967 Six-Day War, but starting in 1974 this, and all the campaigns, was given a great boost. That year, parked Ryder trucks started to appear in Manhattan with their back doors rolled up, and young men with beards and black hats stood inside and outside, asking passersby: "Excuse me, are you Jewish?" Men who responded in the affirmative were invited to come inside and put on tefillin. The invitee would roll up his shirtsleeve and a young Chasid would bind the tefillin around his arm and on his head and instruct the person to recite the appropriate blessing. A poster taped to the trucks proclaimed: "Mitzvot on the Spot for People on the Go." Among its other virtues, the regular donning of tefillin ensured that the person who did so daily would put himself in touch with something higher, with God. Women who answered that they were Jewish were offered a free kit containing a small tin candleholder, candles, and a small brochure explaining how to carry out the ritual of candlelighting on Shabbat.

This early Mitzvah Tank (also known as Mitzvah Mobile) campaign, in which hundreds of thousands of people were asked, "Are you Jewish?" and invited to participate in performing a mitzvah, was responsible for bringing Chabad to the attention of more people than any previous activity of the Rebbe. More important, from the Rebbe's perspective, it brought tefillin and Shabbat candles to the attention of American Jews who had never thought of performing these rituals. As one Chabad account of the Mitzvah Tanks explained the Rebbe's thinking: "If a large part of American Jewry had ceased coming to *Shul* [synagogue] each morning to don tefillin and pray, the Rebbe was going to bring tefillin to them."[8]

The Mitzvah Tank campaign also highlighted the Rebbe's belief that the performance of any mitzvah in and of itself, and even when performed by a person who is otherwise nonobservant (such as a Jew who puts on tefillin in a Mitzvah Tank and then goes off to eat an un-kosher meal), has value. This belief was highly atypical in the Orthodox world of the 1960s and 1970s, although because of the Rebbe's precedent, it is not as atypical today.

As noted, the Rebbe also initiated the *Neshek* campaign, in which all Jewish girls and women, three years and older, were encouraged to start lighting candles on late Friday afternoons (no later than eighteen minutes before sunset) to usher in the Sabbath.[9] Chabad placed ads in newspapers depicting women lighting candles.

While the Rebbe usually supported Jews following the religious cus-toms practiced by their parents,[10] on the issue of Shabbat candles he generally advocated that all women carry out such lightings. When a woman wrote him that it was her family's custom that young women not light candles (in many Jewish families, girls do not light candles before marriage, in others before bat mitzvah [age twelve]), and that her doing so would go against her family's custom, the Rebbe, who seemed to be acquainted with the woman's family, answered: "It was the custom of the women in your family once and for many generations not to read newspapers, not to study secular subjects, not to put on makeup and more. Are you so careful to follow your family's custom also in those areas?"[11]

The ten campaigns initiated by the Rebbe, and through which Chabad exerted its influence throughout the world were:

1. Tefillin.

2. *Neshek*—the Shabbat candle campaign.

On one occasion, the Rebbe spoke of an incident that had been brought to his attention that illustrated how this one practice, the light-ing of a candle by a child, had transformed an entire family.

There was a family in Israel, the Rebbe related, whose five- or six-year-old daughter had heard one Friday morning about the importance of the Shabbat candles and that even a young girl can light them. When she came home that day, she told her mother what she had heard and of her desire to light Shabbat candles. The mother, who was Jewishly un-knowledgeable, said that she did not know of such a custom and would not allow her daughter to introduce new acts into the home. The young girl became upset and eventually even a bit hysterical. She kept beseeching her mother to simply let her light a candle, and finally the mother heeded her request.

With great excitement, the girl set a candlestick on the dinner table and lit the candle by herself. Some other girls had told her that a Shabbat candle should not be touched once it is lit; she therefore went around warning her family not to move the candle.

When the mother and father realized that the candle lighting was not disruptive, they allowed the girl to light a candle the following week without fuss.

After a few weeks of Friday-night candlelightings, one of the parents concluded that it was not appropriate to have the TV turned on while the candles were burning. Soon, also, the phone was not answered while the candles were burning. A short time later, the mother started to feel awkward about the contrasting patterns of behavior in the house. A neighbor might walk in and see a Shabbat candle being lit by her excited daughter while she, the mother, was dressed in informal weekday clothes; it would seem out of place. One Friday evening, the mother decided to light Shabbat candles as well. After she did so for a few weeks and recited the blessing affirming that this was a holy day, she found that she could not bring herself to turn the oven on and off to heat up supper anymore. This soon had an effect on how the family acted on Saturday as well. "Thanks to one girl's desire to light the Shabbat candles," the Rebbe noted, "the entire family started keeping Shabbat."

3. *Chinuch*—the campaign for Jewish education, "to see that not one boy or girl is left without a genuine Torah-true education." The Rebbe noted that it was the custom in the United States to launch new programs "with a storm of excitement, publicity in the media, formation of committees." He asked that this be the way the education campaign be launched as well, though not simply because this is the way things are customarily done in the United States but because educating our children is what the Torah wants us to do.

In a December 1974 letter to Mordechai Shoel Landow, a Miami Beach–based philanthropist who had helped create the local Jewish school, the Rebbe addressed the philanthropist's anxiety over the school's rapidly growing deficit. The Rebbe explained that the "financial deficit is surely of secondary importance" in comparison with the far more significant statistic, the growing number of students. In explaining why the school must never consider turning away students, even though facing very real financial pressure, what emerges is the Rebbe's total commitment to the importance of reaching out to every individual: "a deficit in terms of students, namely if even one boy (or girl) is turned away, can be an irretrievable loss, for that boy (or girl) may become a casualty of the pernicious forces of assimilation, whereas a financial deficit can always be made good, if not today then tomorrow, or the day after, with God's help. Here, too, a successful American businessman like yourself knows very well what the real score is." [12]

In short, a dollar lost can be replaced, but a child lost may never be retrieved.

4. Kashrut—to increase observance of kashrut. The Rebbe offered to reimburse 50 percent of the expenses incurred by a person in making his or her house kosher (for example, through the purchase of new dishes, pots, and silverware). When people would request assistance in making their homes kosher, Chabad *shluchim* would come over, blowtorch the oven, and boil plates, pots, and cutlery that could be *kashered* (made kosher; items that are porous cannot be made kosher). The process of *kashering* a kitchen generally takes a minimum of two hours and, depending on the number of items that need to be made kosher, can last up to six hours, on occasion even more.

Each year, the most well known act of *kashering* a kitchen (making a kitchen kosher) occurs when Rabbi Levi Shemtov *kashers* the White House kitchen in preparation for the annual Chanukah party there hosted by the president.

Chabad *shluchim* also endeavor to make kosher food available to Jews who observe the dietary laws but who are in places in which kosher food is difficult to obtain. It is through Chabad Houses that Jews visiting China, Singapore, Thailand, the Democratic Republic of the Congo, Ecuador, and dozens of other countries are able to find a kosher facility at which to eat.

At a public address in 2013, former senator Joseph Lieberman, the Democratic vice presidential nominee in 2000, and an observant Jew, reported that during the 2000 presidential campaign, the Secret Service enforced a policy of high-level security and kept the identity of the hotels at which he was staying strictly secret. The policy, Lieberman noted, seemed to work quite effectively and people really didn't know at which hotel he was. Yet, to Lieberman's astonishment, in virtually every city to which he traveled, when he arrived at the hotel there was a kosher meal waiting for him from the local Chabad *shliach*.[13]

5. *Tzedaka*—to increase the giving of charity. In addition to donating to charitable causes, people were encouraged to have charity boxes (*pushkas*) in their homes, into which they were asked to make daily deposits. While the amount of money people put into the boxes was small (most people inserted coins) compared to checks made out to charities, the presence of a *pushka* in a house is a constant reminder of the need to fulfill the mitzvah of charitable giving.

The Rebbe also encouraged mothers and daughters to deposit money into *pushkas* before lighting Shabbat candles. Because Jewish law prohibits handling money on the Sabbath, this ensured that a person's final act of the week was to give charity. While the Rebbe obviously wanted people to give substantial sums and not just coins, he knew that the daily giving of charity affected a person's character and made him or her more generous.

Eight hundred years earlier, Maimonides, of whom the Rebbe was a lifetime student, had noted in his commentary on the *Ethics of the Fathers* 3:18 that when a donor gives a person in need a thousand gold coins all at once, it does not increase within the donor the trait of generosity as much as if he dispensed the same number of coins one at a time to different needy recipients. The very act of giving habitually, rather than sporadically and impulsively, converts generosity into an innate part of a person's character.

In a similar manner, the Talmud records that Rabbi Elazar gave a coin every weekday to charity before praying (*Bava Batra* 10a), and the Code of Jewish Law (*Shulchan Aruch*) standardized this idea: "It is good to give charity before praying" (*Orach Chaim* 92:10). While this tradition is known to Jews who attend daily services (a member of the congregation circulates with a charity box), the Rebbe's promoting of *pushkas* as part of the *Tzedaka* campaign was intended to bring the tradition of daily giving into the lives of Jews who might not attend daily services.

6. Mezuzah—a call to Jews to post a mezuzah on the doorposts of their homes. The Torah ordains the commandment of mezuzah: "And you shall inscribe them [these words from the Torah] upon the door-posts [mezuzot] of your house and upon your gates" (Deuteronomy 11:20). Jewish law ordains that mezuzot be installed on the doorposts of Jewish homes and on the doorposts of the rooms inside the house. Inside each mezuzah is a small scroll that contains the biblical verse ordaining the mezuzah. The Talmud teaches that God will guard those inside a house on which a mezuzah is affixed (*Avodah Zarah* 11a). The Rebbe was known to advise people who were undergoing difficulties to check the mezuzot on their doorposts to make sure that they were handwritten by a scribe, as Jewish law requires (some stores sell mezuzot with printed texts inside), and that the texts were accurate.

Strangely, the Mezuzah campaign at one point became a source of some controversy. In March 1974, Palestinians terrorists took 115 hos-tages at an Israeli high school in the town of Maalot. Israeli troops were called in, in an effort to save the students, but the terrorists murdered twenty-five people before being killed themselves. At a speech a short time later, the Rebbe noted that an inspection of the high school build-ing revealed there to have been twenty-five unkosher mezuzahs posted on the doorposts, and he asked that Jews be very careful to carry out this mitzvah and to make sure that they did so with kosher (properly pre-pared) mezuzahs. The Rebbe's statement, with its seeming implication that God inflicted cruel suffering upon individuals for inadvertently hanging unkosher mezuzot, outraged many people.

In truth, the Rebbe consistently avoided attributing an individual's suffering to a ritual violation (who are we to know why God allows an event to occur?; see pages 143–44) and rather insisted that a mezu-zah be regarded as a protective helmet. Though there are soldiers who wear helmets who are killed, and others who don't and yet emerge from battle unscathed, nonetheless, if a soldier wears a helmet he is less likely to be killed by gunfire. The mezuzah, the Rebbe insisted, is like a protective helmet, and not a guarantee; in consequence, he continued to ask people in vulnerable situations to check that their mezuzahs (and tefillin as well) were in order and that the written texts were valid. This reasoning, though, still affronted many people. As one person expressed it to me, "The notion of a mezuzah as a protective helmet seems absurd if not offensive. After all, during the Holocaust, many observant Jews had mezuzahs on their doors, and it didn't help them when their homes were raided by the Nazis or their collaborators."

When a man who had suffered a robbery asked the Rebbe if he should check his mezuzahs, the Rebbe told him to first check the locks on his doors.

Over the decades since this campaign was launched, Chabad *shluchim* have been responsible for substantially increasing the number of Jews who put mezuzahs on their doorposts, sometimes in places not associated in people's minds with Jewishness. A July 4, 2013, Associated Press article reported that Chabad *shliach* Rabbi Chaim Bruk has been crisscrossing the huge state of Montana in a campaign to influence Jews to carry out this mitzvah (the whole state of Montana, which is almost fifteen times the size of Israel, is estimated to have only 1,350 Jews, though Bruk thinks the number might be closer to 3,000). During the first weeks of the campaign, Bruk, traveling from the city of Whitefish in the north (a city that does indeed sound ethnically Jewish) to Dillon in the south, put up thirty mezuzahs. Installing a mezuzah on one's front door, the Rebbe realized, involved a Jew's willingness to make a public and permanent declaration about his or her Jewishness; in addition, it is also a relatively easy mitzvah to perform. "Our motto's been baby steps," Rabbi Bruk, who was not yet bar mitzvah, thirteen, when the Rebbe died, told reporter Matt Volz, "[our goal is] to make people comfortable with their traditional Jewish lifestyle. . . . I'm young, I'm thirty-one, I've got a long life ahead of me, God willing, and I hope to get to every house."

7. Family Purity—a call to observe the laws of *taharat mishpacha* (family purity), which mandate that husbands and wives refrain from a sexual and physical relationship during the woman's period (Leviticus 18:19 and

20:18) and for one week afterward. At the end of this week, women go to the *mikveh* (ritual bath). Subsequent to the woman's immersion (*tevila*) at the *mikveh*, she is considered to be renewed like a bride to her husband, and it is an obligation for the couple to resume marital relations when the woman returns from the *mikveh*. Unlike the widely known laws of Shabbat and kashrut, the laws of family purity are virtually unknown to non-Orthodox Jews, and it was the Rebbe's goal to renew knowledge and observance of these laws among the broader Jewish population.

As a result of this campaign, several hundred *mikvehs* have been built throughout the world, often alongside Chabad Houses. And the Rebbe's concern about this issue influenced people outside the orbit of Chabad as well. When the Rebbe learned that Rabbi Dov Zlotnick, a Jewish Theological Seminary graduate, had delivered a powerful sermon on the subject of *mikveh*, he encouraged him to have the sermon published. It subsequently appeared in a collection of the best sermons given that year, and Zlotnick learned that a Conservative congregation in Canada was so influenced by this sermon that its members ended up contributing to building a *mikveh* in its city.

8. Torah Study—The previously mentioned *Chinuch* campaign was geared toward providing a Jewish education for youth, while the Torah Study campaign intended to involve Jews of all ages in the daily study of Torah. The Rebbe specifically asked people to set aside a designated time each day for Jewish learning. Lubavitcher Chasidim were already in the practice of studying daily, starting with a section from the weekly Torah portion, several chapters of Psalms, and a section of the *Tanya*, the movement's philosophic treatise. In later years, the Rebbe also requested men, women, and children to study three chapters daily from Maimonides's fourteen-volume code of Jewish law, the *Mishneh Torah*, and to complete it once each year (for those who would not, or could not, do three chapters daily, the Rebbe asked that they study a chapter each day and to complete the cycle in three years). The Rebbe himself also followed this course of study.

When a man mailed to 770 a photograph of the Rebbe, which he asked the Rebbe to autograph so that he could thereby feel a closer connection to him, the Rebbe responded that the best way to establish a close connection between the two of them was for the man to start following the Chabad daily study cycle. That way, the man and the Rebbe would connect every day as they studied the same texts.

9. To Acquire Torah Books—The goal of this campaign was to make sure that every Jewish home contained Jewish books, specifically, religious books. At a minimum, the Rebbe's wish was to guarantee that each Jewish family possessed a Torah, a siddur (prayer book), and *Tehillim* (the book of Psalms).

10. *Ahavat Yisrael*—Love of all Jews, not just those, for example, whose religious practices and ideologies are similar to one's own; see chapter 5 for examples of how the Rebbe intended this commandment to be carried out.

More campaigns than just these ten were launched,[14] but the "army" of *shluchim* created by the Rebbe, and the efforts they make to bring Jews to the observance of these commandments, remains the backbone of Chabad's influence in the Jewish world. At a time when *mitzvot* such as tefillin and *mikveh* were largely unknown outside of the most traditional Jewish circles, these campaigns brought Jewish pride and very important Jewish precepts into public consciousness. To this day, if you meet a Jewish man who grew up in a nonobservant household and who today puts on tefillin (at least on occasion) or a Jewish woman from a similar background who lights Sabbath candles, it is more likely than not that the initial factor responsible for his or her transformation was an exposure to one of the troops in "the Rebbe's army" (the title of Sue Fishkoff's book), and quite possibly to being stopped on the street by a Lubavitcher Chasid and asked, "Excuse me, are you Jewish?" In large part and as a result of these campaigns, the word "*mitzvah*" has become widely known beyond traditional circles, tefillin are widely perceived as something more than a strange piece of paraphernalia for a bar mitzvah boy, and Shabbat candles are no longer confined for many to the category of "something Grandma lit." They have all become viable possibilities, even for Jews who have no intention of becoming Orthodox.

As the Rebbe intuited, there are many Jews who in their hearts do wish to become more involved but who on their own won't do so; they simply need to be asked; they simply need to know how much they are wanted.

Part Three

·⟨✦W✦⟩·

SEVEN

VIRTUES

Chapter 5

LOVE YOUR NEIGHBOR

The Focus on the Individual

"HOW CAN YOU SAY YOU'RE HIS FRIEND IF YOU
DON'T KNOW IF HIS FINANCIAL SITUATION IS IN ORDER?"

An emotional highlight of the first Chasidic discourse (*ma'amar*) Rabbi Menachem Mendel Schneerson delivered on the night he became Rebbe in January 1951 was his telling of an incident in which the Alter Rebbe, Chabad's founder, left his synagogue in the middle of a prayer service to chop wood and cook soup for a woman who had just given birth and had no one to attend to her.

The story was powerful—the image of a Rebbe removing his *tallit* in the middle of services and leaving the synagogue to perform an act of kindness is hard to forget—but also perplexing. Given that the woman had just given birth, why indeed was she alone? Even if she was unmarried (a far less common occurrence two hundred years ago), was there no one else, a parent, a sister, a cousin, a friend, someone who could help her?

Years later, also at a public speech, the Rebbe offered more background to the story, adding information that made the Alter Rebbe's behavior seem even more unusual.[1] All the actions he performed that day, including chopping wood and cooking a meal, took place on Yom Kippur, the holiest of Jewish holidays, and a day on which such activities are normally—and strictly—forbidden by Jewish law. The reason the new mother was alone now became clear as well; her family members were apparently so anxious to attend the Yom Kippur service that they left her alone, assuming that the woman would be all right resting by herself with the baby for a few hours.

That day, the Alter Rebbe, having somehow learned that the new mother was alone, was suddenly overwhelmed with the certainty that the woman required someone to attend to her needs immediately; it might well be a matter of life and death. And since no one else was taking care of her, he concluded that he should be the one to do so.[2]

The Rebbe acknowledged that telling the hundreds of people present that evening the complete story would create a sensation. He also acknowledged that his intention was to do so, and to make people aware that *ahavat Yisrael*, love of one's fellow, is not just one mitzvah among many *mitzvot*, but that it supersedes all others. He could well imagine that the people hearing him that day, and at some point facing such a situation in their own lives, would react by trying to find another person, perhaps a Gentile, who is not bound by the laws of Yom Kippur, to carry out such acts. He therefore asked his followers to consider whether they regarded themselves as greater than the Alter Rebbe, and if they didn't (and he made it clear that he didn't think any of those present, including himself, were), then they should realize that this incident and the precedent it established should apply to them as well. He wanted every listener to personalize the mitzvah. A Jew should never consider performing a kindness for another as beneath him- or herself or somehow less consequential than other religious acts, such as praying on Yom Kippur or studying Torah. Obviously these acts are of great significance, but if a kindness is required, particularly a great kindness, and certainly if a life is at stake and you are the only one who can help, then that should be your priority.[3]

Rabbi Tzvi Hersh Weinreb has wisely commented that if there is one commandment the Rebbe has bequeathed to the Jewish world, it is this one: to love one's fellow. Other Jewish groups, both now and in the past, have placed their greatest stress on other commandments. The Gaon of Vilna, perhaps the most influential rabbinic figure in the non-Chasidic world during the last three centuries, thought that the study of Torah was Judaism's most fundamental requirement. In his commentary on the book of Proverbs, he describes a hero (*ish chayyil*; literally "man of valor") as one who devotes himself to performing commandments and to the study of Torah to the exclusion of all else, "even though in his own house there is no food and clothing, and his sons . . . cry out to him, 'Bring us food so that we can live, [bring us] some livelihood.' But," the Gaon continues, "he pays no attention to them at all . . . for he has denied all love except that of God and of the Torah" (commentary to Proverbs 23:30).

The Alter Rebbe had a very different set of priorities. Perhaps the most famous of the stories told about him, and one that the Rebbe liked to relate, was of a time when he lived on the ground floor of a two-story home in Liadi; his son, who succeeded him and became the Mitteler Rebbe, lived on the second floor.

One night, the Mitteler Rebbe's infant fell out of his cradle and began to cry. The boy's father did not hear the baby's sobs. The Alter Rebbe was also studying; nonetheless, he heard the crying and ran upstairs to comfort the baby. After quieting the infant down, he went over to his son. "How could you ignore the crying child?" he challenged him.

The Mitteler Rebbe explained that he had been so absorbed in his studies that he hadn't heard the cries. His father was unimpressed with this excuse: "You should never be so engrossed in your studies that you fail to hear the cry of a child."

The behavior described in these activities is rooted in the most famous law in the Torah, "Love your neighbor as yourself" (Leviticus 19:18). The Torah's command is not "Love humanity as you love yourself" but rather "Love your neighbor . . ." The Torah recognizes that it is often harder to love our neighbor, the flesh-and-blood person who lives near us and whose faults and annoying characteristics we are well aware of, than to love mankind, consisting of people whom we have never met and never will meet. It is wise to be guided by the words of Israel Baal Shem Tov (1700–1760), the founder of Chasidism: "Just as we love ourselves despite the faults we know we have, so we should love our fellows despite the faults we see in them."

One innovative insight of the Rebbe concerning love was that the affection and honor that others receive from us will, in turn, influence them to become more loving and decent to others. Harvard law professor Alan Dershowitz recalls his great annoyance when he learned that North Carolina senator Jesse Helms had been honored at a celebration of the Rebbe's eightieth birthday. Dershowitz characterized Helms as no friend of Israel or of the Jewish people. He wrote a letter to the Rebbe in which he expressed his annoyance. As he later recalled, "[The Rebbe] wrote me back one of the most beautiful responses. He said 'you honor not only to influence the past but to influence the future.' He then wrote, 'Watch Senator Jesse Helms and see whether or not our decision was a correct one.'" Within a year of that honor, Dershowitz reported, Helms had become one of Israel's strongest supporters in the Senate and, as chairman of the Foreign Relations Committee, one of its most important.

Of course, most of the Rebbe's displays of love and concern for others were carried out in far more private settings. What follows are six representative examples of moral imagination exercised by the Rebbe, incidents in which he used the full resources of his heart and intellect to find a way to help others in the manner that would most benefit them— and that would make them feel loved.

"What Do You Mean That You Feel My Pain?"

Rabbi Shmuel Kaplan has served for over thirty-five years as the senior *shliach* in Maryland, and today he supervises some twenty Chabad institutions there, along with a yeshiva in Baltimore. But one of the remarkable events of Kaplan's life occurred when he was still living in Brooklyn, a recently married young man, learning at the Chabad Kollel (an institute for the advanced study of Talmud and rabbinic literature). One day, Kaplan was summoned by Rabbi Chaim Hodakov, the Rebbe's personal secretary, who told him of a special mission the Rebbe had for him. This mission, Hodakov emphasized, was to take priority over any other responsibilities he had, and any time he needed to take off from his studies, he should.

The case involved a seventeen-year-old girl who was having extreme emotional difficulties, involving issues of rebellion and serious doubts about faith and religious practice, "the typical kinds of things that you find among teenagers, but in this case quite severe and for some reason,

I can't tell you why, the Rebbe took an extraordinary interest in helping this girl through this stage in her life."

Kaplan was assigned to remain accessible to the young woman at all times, and over the following three or four months he devoted as much as 30 percent of his time, sometimes even more, to working with the girl on her issues. Whenever he had any question as to how to proceed, he would turn to Rabbi Hodakov, who would either answer him on the spot or consult with the Rebbe and quickly get back to him.

The young woman herself would often write to the Rebbe and would then share and review with the young rabbi the responses she received. Kaplan was amazed at the speed with which the Rebbe responded to the girl's letters, sometimes within hours, never longer than a day. One exchange of letters remains vivid to Kaplan. The young woman had written an extended letter to the Rebbe, describing the continuing emotional turmoil and constant anguish she was experiencing. The Rebbe, in turn, responded that he felt her pain.

Somehow, this response did not assuage the young woman—perhaps she felt the Rebbe was being condescending. "I don't believe you," she wrote back. "How can you feel my pain? You're not going through what I'm going through. What do you mean to write me that you feel my pain?"

This time the Rebbe responded within two hours.[4] "When you will merit to grow up and marry and, G-d willing, have a child, the nature of things are that in the first year, toward the end of the first year, a child begins to teethe and teething is a painful process and the child cries as a result. And the mother feels that pain as if it were her own. *Kach ani margish tza'arah*" ("That is how I feel your pain"). (Throughout this book, when quoting directly from the Rebbe's writings, I follow his practice of spelling God as G-d.)

Kaplan recalls the impact of these words. The girl felt that there was a person who actually did feel what she was going through, and who did truly want to help her; it was from that point on that the young woman's life slowly started to turn around.

To this day, Kaplan remains staggered that the Rebbe—a man who was known to often receive hundreds of letters a day—placed himself in this situation with such intensity, "answering the girl's letters back and forth . . . and doing so within a day, and sometimes within hours."[5]

Helping People, Including Those Who Didn't Like Him, to Earn a Livelihood

When the Rebbe turned seventy in 1972, he issued a call for the Chabad movement to establish seventy-one new institutions over the coming year, the seventy-first of his life (see page 497). Bobby Vogel, a successful London diamond dealer, decided to seize upon the Rebbe's idea and open a trade school to teach the diamond business to Orthodox men and women who had attended yeshivot but who lacked professional skills. By training people in skills such as diamond cutting, Vogel hoped to provide them with a means to support themselves and their families.

Yet, when Vogel spoke of his plan to the Rebbe, he was stunned when the Rebbe told him that the school should in no way be part of the campaign to establish seventy-one new institutions or even be referred to as a part of Chabad. When Vogel asked why, the Rebbe explained that if there was, for example, a young Satmar Chasid in London seeking job training, he would likely be hesitant—because of widespread negative feelings in Satmar toward Chabad (see pages 542–43)—to walk into a school that was identified as a Chabad institution. The Rebbe, therefore, urged Vogel to start the school, which he did, but to avoid using the Chabad name.[6]

Moral Imagination: Take Great Care Not to Embarrass Others

Rabbi Sholom Lipskar of Miami Beach founded the Aleph Institute, a Chabad organization devoted to working with Jewish prisoners, and which endeavors to keep them connected to both their families and their religion. In 1985, Lipskar negotiated an experimental program with the federal Bureau of Prisons to take twenty carefully screened prisoners out of prison for several days, during which time they would be trained in prayers, the study of Jewish texts, and various spiritual behaviors that could be helpful to them in their restricted prison environment. That Sabbath, Lipskar brought the men to the Rebbe's weekly Shabbat afternoon speech and *farbrengen,* and he arranged to have a large table set aside so that the men could be seated together. The Rebbe heard of Lipskar's intention. Shortly before his speech was due to begin, he sent down a message to advise Lipskar *not* to seat the men together. He explained that the large majority of men in attendance would have beards and black hats, while the prisoners would be clean-shaven and dressed in Western clothes; therefore, if the prisoners were all seated in one group, it would provoke curiosity. People would come over to their table and ask them who they were, what sort of group they were, and where they came from. While the questions would be well intentioned, the men would be compelled to identify themselves as prisoners. Therefore, to avoid embarrassing them, the Rebbe asked Lipskar "to put them at various places around the room."[7]

When the Rebbe Didn't Avert His Face

As a rule, when praying in the small synagogue upstairs where he faced the public, the Rebbe tried to keep his face somewhat hidden. Whether it was just to enable him to focus more intently on his own prayers, or to make sure that the Chasidim, who were in awe of him, were not monitoring his facial expressions instead of attending to their own prayers, is uncertain, but the covering of his face during prayers was known to all within Chabad.[8] Yet, there were days, rare in number, when he did not do so. There was a certain Israeli man (for obvious reason, his name has been omitted) who periodically showed up at Chabad and who came to the Rebbe's minyan to pray. His face was grotesquely disfigured, most likely from a terrorist attack or an army wound; people often went to great lengths to avoid looking at him. When this man prayed in the Rebbe's synagogue, the Rebbe made no effort to cover his face; he did not want this man or any of those present to think that he found it distasteful to look at him.

The disfigured gentleman himself spoke of the Rebbe's behavior and the reason for it to a Lubavitcher who begged his forgiveness for having mocked his appearance eighteen years earlier when the Lubavitcher was a child of eleven. The disfigured man twice refused to grant forgiveness (mocking another person is a grievous sin in Judaism). He finally did so, but only after adding this reproof: "You regard yourself as a follower of the Lubavitcher Rebbe, and yet you acted toward me with such cruelty. So let me tell you something about the character of the man whom you claim to follow." He then related the above story about how the Rebbe never covered his face while praying in his presence. After relating the story, he granted the Chasid full forgiveness on condition that he deliver periodic speeches on the importance of treating the handicapped with compassion and never mocking them. The Chasid, who was interviewed for this book, has now given this lecture several times, and the disfigured gentleman now greets him with hugs when they meet.

The Responsibilities of Friendship

In the mid-1960s, Rabbi Zalman Schachter-Shalomi drifted away from his involvement with Chabad and started seeking a somewhat different spiritual path. Some years later, the Rebbe asked the *shliach* Rabbi Avraham Shemtov, who lived in Philadelphia, as did Schachter-Shalomi at the time, if the two men knew each other.

Shemtov answered that he did know him and that they were friends.

"And how is he is doing with *parnassah* [livelihood]?" In other words, is he earning a satisfactory living?

Rabbi Shemtov, who told me this story, was not in ongoing contact with Schachter-Shalomi at that time and answered, "I don't know."

The Rebbe said, "How can you say you're his friend if you don't know if his financial situation is in order?" [9]

Bringing Joy to a Very Poor Bride and Groom

From 1941, when he came to America, until 1963, the Rebbe would often attend or officiate at weddings held at 770, in an outdoor area only a few yards from his office (all Chabad weddings are done, when possible, under the open sky). He stopped this practice in 1963 due to the large number of newlywed couples within Chabad, but he was still able to hear the ceremony, even while sitting at his desk. When the Rebbe once heard a chuppah (marriage ceremony; literally the "wedding canopy") ending without the traditional burst of music, he summoned his secretary Rabbi Leibel Groner and asked him the reason. Groner explained that the newly married couple couldn't afford to hire a musician. The Rebbe instructed Groner to immediately arrange for a musician to come for the remainder of the wedding celebration. He told Groner that he would pay for the musician but asked him to make sure that the couple did not know who had arranged it.

Chapter 6

CREATING FEARLESSNESS, CREATING LEADERS

"A GOOD LEADER CREATES FOLLOWERS.
A GREAT LEADER CREATES LEADERS."
—*Rabbi Lord Jonathan Sacks,
former chief rabbi of Great Britain and the Commonwealth*

One common assumption about the Rebbe is that he craved followers. The origin of this belief is obvious; he had an enormous number of followers, and their devotion to him was quite absolute. But what he seemed to want most from his followers was for them to become leaders. To achieve that, he pushed them to become *less*, not *more*, reliant on him. When Leibel Groner posed a halachic (legal) query to him, the Rebbe refused to answer. "You're a rabbi just like me," he told Groner. "You study the sources and you decide." Rabbi Groner went home, examined the issue, and reached a conclusion. When he told the Rebbe of the conclusion he had reached, the Rebbe smiled and told Groner that that was the conclusion he would have reached as well.[1]

Some Chasidim pushed back at this approach. Louise Hager once wrote the Rebbe a question on an important personal matter, and he responded that she should make the decision herself. Hager, who had a close relationship to the Rebbetzin, called her from London to complain, "That's not good enough. This is a very big step in our lives. I can't take the responsibility. I need a yes or no."

The Rebbetzin applauded her bravado. "Bravo! Bravo!" she called out. But she also refused to call her husband. "If my husband said you can make the decision, *you* can make the decision," she now told her. End of issue.²

On one occasion, the Rebbe responded in a tongue-in-cheek but equally decisive manner to Rabbi Moshe Yitzchak Hecht, the Chabad *shli-ach* in New Haven. The year was 1974, and Hecht was feeling overwhelmed by a variety of issues. He wrote to the Rebbe and laid all of his professional and spiritual problems on the Rebbe's lap, appealing to him to "help, and do it all." Instead of acceding to Hecht's request, or even expressing sympathy for his sense of dejection, the Rebbe took the discussion in an altogether different direction: "I have already done as you have suggested, and I sent [to New Haven] Rabbi Moshe Yitzchak Hecht. It is apparent from your letters, both this and the previous one, that you don't yet know him, and you don't know the strengths that were given to him. You should at least try to get to know him now, and then everything will immediately change; the mood, the trust in God, the daily joy, etc."

Directing a person to face and deal with an issue himself was a technique the Rebbe also practiced with some non-Lubavitchers as well, that is, if he thought the person capable of reaching a solution on his own. Perhaps the most remarkable such episode involved a young man of thirty, Tzvi Hersh Weinreb, who, at the time, was already trained both as a rabbi and a psychologist. Shortly after Weinreb married, he and his wife lived for several years in Crown Heights, and though he never met the Rebbe, during that period he attended a number of *farbrengens* at 770.

A few years later, the couple moved to Silver Spring, Maryland, and Weinreb went into overdrive. He completed a doctorate in psychology, worked in the local public school system, and offered a number of Talmud classes for the Jewish community.

In the midst of his great busyness, Weinreb confronted an early midlife crisis. The immediate impetus was his difficulty in deciding on a career choice: psychology, education, or the rabbinate. At the same time, he found himself plagued by some religious doubts and challenges. The combination of career and other uncertainties threw him into a bit of a depression.

Weinreb shared his unhappiness with several close friends, one of whom, a Chabad Chasid, told him to go speak to the Rebbe. In February 1971, Weinreb called the Rebbe's office to see if he could arrange an appointment. The call was answered by a secretary, whom Weinreb later deduced was Rabbi Chaim Mordechai Hodakov. Hodakov started asking him questions to ascertain the purpose of the call, when Weinreb heard a voice in the background—which he recognized from those earlier *farbrengens*—asking in Yiddish, "Who's calling?"

At that point, Weinreb was anxious to maintain his anonymity—particularly if he did not end up meeting with the Rebbe. He replied, "A Jew from Maryland." Hodakov repeated the response aloud, and Weinreb then told Hodakov that he had several questions he wished to discuss with the Rebbe, involving both career decisions and matters of faith.

As Weinreb elaborated on some of the issues, Hodakov repeated and paraphrased his words; the Rebbe, it appeared, was following the discussion.

But then, even before Weinreb could pin down a date for a meeting, he heard the Rebbe call out in the background, "Tell him that there is a Jew who lives in Maryland that he can speak to. *Der Yid hayst Weinreb* (His name is Weinreb)."

Hodakov said to him, "Did you hear what the Rebbe said?"

Weinreb had heard and was in shock. As he had carefully avoided saying his name (this was many years before caller ID), he assumed that he had probably misheard the Rebbe. So he told Hodakov no, he had not heard what the Rebbe said.

Rabbi Hodakov repeated the Rebbe's words: "Tell him that there is a Jew who lives in Maryland that he can speak to. His name is Weinreb."

Weinreb said, "But my name is Weinreb."

Now it was Rabbi Hodakov's turn to be shocked. But not the Rebbe. When Hodakov repeated aloud what Weinreb had said, the Rebbe simply responded, "*Oib azoi*. If that is the case, then he should know that sometimes a person needs to speak to himself."

Weinreb thanked Rabbi Hodakov and the Rebbe and the call ended.

For Weinreb, the Rebbe's message proved to be transformative. As he understood it, what the Rebbe was telling him was this: "You're not a kid, you're a man. You are thirty years old, you are a father, you are a teacher of Torah. You have to have more self-confidence. Don't be so dependent on others. Trust yourself."

Until that point in his life, Weinreb recalls, he had never been a risk taker and invariably procrastinated when it came to making decisions. But after that conversation, he became decisive. In addition, Weinreb, a trained psychologist, knew himself well enough to realize that if the Rebbe had simply instructed him as to the choices he should make, he might have had a natural resistance to being told what to do, even if it was the Rebbe who was telling him. "I think the Rebbe had the insight to know that it was better if I heard the answer from myself than if I heard it from him."

Rabbi Weinreb still has no idea how the Rebbe knew to say, "There's a Jew that lives in Maryland that he can speak to. His name is Weinreb." Had he heard about Weinreb's work in the Silver Spring Jewish community from one of the Lubavitchers, or other Jews in the city, or was the information conveyed to him in a supernatural way, which is what Weinreb is inclined to think.

Some months later, when he was in Brooklyn visiting his in-laws, Weinreb went to a *farbrengen* at 770, at the end of which some of those present came over to the Rebbe for a blessing. Weinreb waited his turn and then said to the Rebbe, "My name is Weinreb and I'm from Maryland." To this day, one of Rabbi Weinreb's most precious memories is the warm smile of recognition the Rebbe gave him.

Tzvi Hersh Weinreb went on to have a highly distinguished professional career, which included serving as the executive vice president of the Orthodox Union and as the editor in chief of the *Koren Talmud*, the English-language translation of the *Steinsaltz Talmud*. And to this day, whenever he faces difficult decisions in life, the first thing he does is read through some of the Rebbe's teachings in order to connect again with the Rebbe. And then, he explains, "I follow the advice he gave me, to talk to myself. Before you go asking others [what to do], first listen to what you have to say about it—sometimes your own advice is the best advice."[3]

The Rebbe's emphasis on pushing individuals to assume responsibility and to do more than that of which they might think themselves capable is most strikingly apparent in his encounters, both at *yechidus* and through correspondence, with Jonathan Sacks, which began when Sacks was a university student. It was 1968, and Sacks, raised in an Orthodox home and studying philosophy at Cambridge University, was going through a period of religious doubt and questioning. That summer, while traveling around the United States, he heard several references made to the Rebbe, but when he told a Lubavitcher Chasid that he was interested in meeting with the Rebbe, the man laughed: "There are thousands of people who want to see the Rebbe. Every moment of his day is full."

Sacks persisted and left the Chasid his aunt's phone number in Los Angeles. "I will be there in three weeks' time," he told him. "If you can arrange a meeting, please let me know."

Three weeks later, the call came: "The Rebbe can see you this Thursday night." Lacking the money for a cross-country flight, Sacks boarded a Greyhound bus in Los Angeles for an exhausting three-day trip to New York.

At the meeting, what first struck Sacks was the Rebbe's understated, nonaggressive manner. For a good while, the Rebbe listened and responded patiently to Sacks's philosophical queries and concerns, always acting "as if the most important person in the room was me." But then, having taken his measure of the young man, the Rebbe suddenly turned the conversation around. The interviewee became the interviewer. "Things are going wrong," the Rebbe had said to him. "Are you willing to be one of those who helps to put them right?"

The young man was taken aback. He had gone into the meeting to ask questions, not answer them. Furthermore, at that early, somewhat uncertain stage of his life, his intention was to become an economist, a lawyer, or an academic. He certainly did not see himself as a leader, though that was the role the Rebbe was now telling him to assume; at one point, the Rebbe even challenged him as to what he was doing to strengthen Jewish life at Cambridge.

The Rebbe's insistent manner made a profound impact on Sacks: "I had been told that the Rebbe was a man with thousands of followers. After I met him, I understood that the opposite was the case. A good leader creates followers. A great leader creates leaders. More than the Rebbe was a leader, he created leadership in others."

Years later, under the impetus of the Rebbe's questions, Sacks undertook to resume his Jewish studies at the Etz Chaim Yeshiva and at Jews' College, both in London. With the Rebbe's encouragement, he eventually became a rabbi, then principal of the Jews' College rabbinical seminary. From 1991 to 2013, he served as chief rabbi of Great Britain and the Commonwealth. A prolific writer, Rabbi Sacks called one of his seminal works, *To Heal a Fractured World*, a "part-payment of a debt I incurred to a great Jewish leader many years ago."[4]

Were the meetings described in this chapter characteristic of all the Rebbe's encounters? By no means. The Rebbe was eminently capable of offering people concrete and specific advice (thirty volumes of the Rebbe's letters have been published so far, much of the correspondence comprised of advice offered by him in response to questions sent him), and while he often added the thought that the recipients should follow his advice only if they agreed with it, and not simply because he said it, he was also aware that many Chasidim would indeed do something simply because he suggested it. Despite his non-insistence that people follow his advice, the Rebbe was confident in what he did suggest to people. To one man who had ignored his advice and regretted it, he wrote: "I received your letter. Apparently, what I had written previously was not acted upon, and now there are complaints that things have not turned out right. Since this has already happened, what good would it do for me to start lecturing? Perhaps, though, this can serve as a lesson for the future. Either one doesn't ask or, if one does ask, it would be best for the questioner to follow the advice."[5]

That's why the above episodes are so significant; in each, with the exception of the encounter with Jonathan Sacks, he refused to make a suggestion.

Why the Rebbe did so in all these cases and not in others, we cannot know for sure. But one can venture a guess: What he saw in these instances was that the individuals consulting him were at an important crossroad in their lives, one that could influence their future development. If the Rebbe wished to create leaders, and clearly he did, he first needed to make sure that people who have leadership potential take control of their own lives. Had he told Rabbi Groner the ruling, he would have removed from him a feeling of self-sufficiency; similarly in the cases of Mrs. Hager and Rabbis Hecht and Weinreb. There might well be other occasions during which he would choose to offer these people advice, but he knew that the decisions they were now confronting were decisions they needed to make on their own; their growth as individuals depended on their doing so. And, as can be seen in the case of Weinreb, the challenge to "speak to himself" altered his life.

Followers can be turned into leaders only by leaders who want to do so. In sending out *shluchim*, the Rebbe knew that for them to impact the communities into which they were sent, their own leadership skills had to be cultivated. That is one reason he refrained from being overly specific in telling *shluchim* how to behave when they arrived in a community.

When Rabbi Nachman Sudak was sent to London in 1959 and asked the Rebbe what he was to do there, the Rebbe replied that "there are thousands of things to do in London."[6] As Sudak was going to be the one on the ground, the Rebbe wanted him to understand that he was the one most qualified to figure out what it was that the London Jewish community was most in need of and which of those "thousands" of possibilities to pursue. Also, the Rebbe, well aware of the high regard in which his followers held him, probably feared that if he offered tangible suggestions to *shluchim* as to what they should do, it would effectively undermine their ability to react spontaneously and creatively. When Rabbi Moshe Feller went out as a *shliach* to Minneapolis in 1962, Feller did in fact covet precise advice. The Rebbe wouldn't offer it: "In general, I cannot give you specific instructions, but you should be flexible." And this enabled Feller to be so. I don't know if the Rebbe would have suggested that if Sandy Koufax happened to come play in Minneapolis for the World Series, Feller should go over to his hotel and encourage him to put on tefillin. But Feller, a great baseball fan, did do so, and because of his grounding in sports, he also knew that Koufax was left-handed and therefore would need the far less common tefillin made for left-handed people. All this was Feller acting on his own, becoming his own leader even as he remained the Rebbe's emissary.[7]

The fact that the Rebbe was willing to send out young people, usually in their early to mid-twenties, with an instruction to be "flexible" or an acknowledgment that in London there are "thousands of things" one could do, underscored to *shluchim* how much the Rebbe trusted them. The Rebbe made his esteem for his emissaries apparent in other ways as well. When he became too busy to continue performing weddings, the sole exception was for couples setting out to serve as *shluchim*. According to one report, the only books on his desk at the time of his stroke, aside from his prayer book, was a four-volume set—which he had commissioned—with photos of all the *shluchim* and their children.

Just before Rabbi Berel and Batsheva Shemtov went off in 1958 as *shluchim* to Detroit a week after they were married, they went in to speak to the Rebbe. The Rebbe learned that they would be traveling by train and had been booked in coach. He immediately arranged for the young couple to be upgraded to sleeper accommodations. Being newly married, he told them, "You should be treated like a king and queen." One could still sense the glow of satisfaction from this gesture when Rabbi Shemtov recounted this incident in 2013, some fifty-five years after the event.[8]

And it was not just adults whose leadership potential the Rebbe was seeking to develop. He wanted the process to start early (certainly by bar and bat mitzvah, perhaps earlier), at an age when parents and children alike generally see themselves as fully under their parents' control. Yitzchak Meir Gourary was granted a *yechidus* when he was fourteen; he arrived at the Rebbe's office with his father, Rabbi Zalman Gourary, one of the movement's leading figures. The Rebbe gently asked the young man, "Why have you come here with your father? You have to be your own man [mensch] now, you have to take care of yourself . . . and not rely on your father." From that point on, Gourary reports, when his father would raise an issue with the Rebbe regarding his son, the Rebbe would say, "Let him [Yitzchak] come in and talk about it himself."[9]

Zev Katz, then a teenager, recalls the summer he got his first paid job. At summer's end, his father told him that it would be appropriate to send one's first earnings to the Rebbe to be distributed for charitable purposes. The father sent the money to the Rebbe along with a letter explaining that this money represented his son's first income. The check was immediately returned, along with a note from the Rebbe telling the elder Katz that as the money was earned by Zev, the money belonged to him and that Zev alone should be the one to decide what to do with it.[10]

Sixteen-year-old Esther Gourary (Yitzchak's sister) was of a somewhat shy disposition, and she was quite nervous when the Rebbe insisted that, while on a trip to France, she address the students at a girls' seminary in Paris. The young woman had not done public speaking before, but the Rebbe insisted she could and should. And she did.[11] Several decades later, the no-longer-shy Esther [now Sternberg] emerged as the leader of the *Neshek* campaign, the Chabad-initiated drive that influenced tens of thousands of Jewish women to start lighting Shabbat candles (see page 81).

Leadership in Chabad was developed in a variety of ways, sometimes as a by-product of other activities. The Tefillin campaign, for example, was not created to develop leadership skills, but for many of its participants it did. Thus, a friend of mine, a Conservative rabbi, asked a Chabad rabbinic colleague in his community how he was so comfortable soliciting substantial contributions from people whom he had only recently met, while my friend, who had lived in the community far longer, found it much harder to do so. The Lubavitcher answered, "When you're trained from the age of fifteen to go out into the street and stop passersby and say, 'Excuse me, are you Jewish?' and then ask these strangers to put on tefillin, you very quickly learn to overcome your inhibitions."

The rabbi's comment was incisive and by no means self-evident. In addition to common sense and a sense of mission, the trait a leader most needs is a lack of fear. Many people of extraordinary capabilities are held back by fear, fear of challenging others, fear of rejection, fear of being laughed at or of appearing to be naive or foolish.

The gift the Rebbe gave his followers—which enabled them to touch and challenge people two and three times their age, with far more secular knowledge and professional attainments—was the belief that they were on a mission for something higher than themselves. To serve God. And that God would not have sent them on such a mission unless He believed in them. And the Rebbe would not have sent them unless he believed in them. And by carrying out their personal missions, these *shluchim* became leaders. They became visionaries, they became proactive. They became fearless.

Chapter 7

OPTIMISM AND THE CAREFUL CHOOSING OF WORDS

"Rabbi Joshua ben Levi said: 'A person should never utter an
ugly word. The Torah adds on eight letters just to avoid
using an ugly word.'"
—Pesachim 3a

While most people think of words as intangible (a child accused of
humiliating another might defend himself by saying, "I didn't
do anything, I just said something"), the Jewish tradition sees words
as things (*dvarim*),[1] and thus as very tangible. The third verse of the
Torah records, "And God said, 'Let there be light' and there was light"
(Genesis 1:3). Like God, human beings also create with words. Lest one
think that this is simply a hyperbolic statement, consider that every
one of us has at some point read a novel and been so moved by the fate
of a character in the book that we felt emotions of love, compassion,
anger, and hate, and sometimes were moved to tears—even though the
characters whose fate so moved us never lived. Rather, a writer took a
blank piece of paper, or looked at a blank screen, and through words
alone was able to elicit our deepest emotions.

If words are so powerful, then we must be very careful how we use
them. But most of us aren't. Even many strictly observant Jews who are
vigilant about only putting kosher food into their mouths are far less
careful about the words that come out of them. Jews who sometimes
eat unkosher food are often described as nonreligious because of their

inconsistent observance of Judaism's ritual laws, but seldom, if ever, does one hear a ritually observant Jew described as nonreligious because of his or her violations of the laws of *lashon hara* (see Leviticus 19:16), which forbid speaking ill of another.[2]

In contrast, the Rebbe, both in his public lectures and in his private interactions, emphasized that extraordinary attention must be paid to the words we use.

It is hard to know if his caution with words was an acquired trait or one that he always possessed, but five years of research into his life reveal the extraordinary care he took both to avoid using negative words and to avoid speaking negatively of others. A perusal of forty years of the Rebbe's public lectures reveals that he did not criticize people by name (see chapter 9).

I first became aware of the Rebbe's tendency to avoid using negative language when learning that he never used the term "*beit cholim*," Hebrew for "hospital." I was puzzled. What word could he have used, I wondered, as I am unfamiliar with any other term in Hebrew for "hospital."

It turned out that the Rebbe was troubled by "*beit cholim*" because it means, literally, "house of the sick," clearly a discouraging term.[3]

The term the Rebbe therefore created was "*beit refuah*," a house of healing.[4]

At that point, I was reminded of a conversation I had had with my mother, Helen Telushkin, perhaps forty years earlier. My mother was commenting on the fact that when she was growing up, there were several hospitals in New York City called "Home for the Incurables." It was only as a middle-aged adult that she had come to realize how awful it must have been for a person to be told that he or she was being sent to the "Home for the Incurables."[5]

In the term "house of healing," and in other expressions he coined, what becomes apparent is that the Rebbe's opinion on how to use words represented an innovative way of thinking and an anticipation, in part, and by several decades, of the discipline known as "positive psychology." The nature of the Rebbe's thinking on this issue was communicated in a letter to Professor Mordechai Shani, director of the Sheba Medical Center at Tel Hashomer in Israel. In it, he made reference to an earlier conversation he had had with Shani and a colleague in which he had strongly urged the men to call the hospital a *beit refuah* instead of a *beit cholim*. He then made two points: "Even though . . . this would seem to represent only a semantic change, the term *beit refuah* brings encouragement to the sick; [in addition], it also represents more accurately the goal of the institution . . . which is to bring about a complete healing. Therefore, why call it by a word that doesn't suit its intentions?"

An incident from 1976 indicates that the Rebbe's thinking concerning the sick and disabled and how they should be described went well beyond creating a new Hebrew word for hospitals. That year, the Rebbe arranged to meet with a group of disabled Israeli war veterans who had been brought to the United States by the Israeli Ministry of Defense; the group included men who had been badly wounded during Israel's wars (most recently, the 1973 Yom Kippur War) and in army mishaps. All had suffered severe injuries, some were crippled, and all were maimed.

Referring to the fact that such people are designated in Israel as *nechei Tzahal*, "handicapped of the Israel Defense Forces," the Rebbe addressed the men as follows: "If a person has been deprived of a limb or a faculty, this itself indicates that G-d has also given him special powers to overcome the limitations this entails, and to surpass [in other areas] the achievements of ordinary people. You are not disabled or handicapped, but special and unique as you possess potentials that the rest of us do not. I therefore suggest"—the Rebbe then interspersed with a smile— "of course it is none of my business, but Jews are famous for voicing opinions on matters that do not concern them—that you should no longer be referred to as 'disabled veterans' but as 'exceptional veterans' [*metzuyanim*], which more aptly describes what is unique about you.

"Therefore," the Rebbe concluded, "I would be honored to shake every one of your hands, for the great honor you have given me for visiting me." He then walked over and spent time in conversation with each and every veteran, grasping their hands in his.[6]

To gauge the striking nature of the language the Rebbe used, it is necessary to set this incident within its historical context. At the time this meeting happened, and even more so in the preceding decades, it was common to describe physical and other handicaps in terms that easily could demoralize the people being spoken of. An American soldier who had lost both hands in World War II recalled an army doctor—practicing a version of what is known as "tough love"—telling him and other badly wounded and soon-to-be-released soldiers: "This year you're a hero. Next year you'll be a disabled veteran. After that, you're a cripple."[7] Contrast that with the Rebbe's approach, "You're exceptional."

Throughout history, it hasn't only been physically handicapped people who have suffered from being labeled with harsh words. In the 1950s and 1960s, it was still common to use words such as "moron," "idiot," and "retarded"—all supposedly technical and scientific terms—as expressions with which to taunt others. Children with mental deficiencies were dismissed as "retarded" and spoken of as part of one undifferentiated group, as if all people with this label could be fully defined by this word and this word alone. In those days, no one would have thought to refer to a child with lowered capabilities in some areas as a "child with special needs." Thus, few people thought of such children as "special" in any way; rather, they were commonly regarded as burdens to be endured. Here, too, the Rebbe's approach was to avoid labeling people with a single word such as "retarded" that, in effect, defined and limited them. When asked to send a message to a Jewish communal conference "On Issues and Needs of Jewish Retarded," the Rebbe noted his objection to that final word: "I prefer to use some term such as 'special' people, not simply as a euphemism, but because it would more accurately reflect their situation, especially in view of the fact that in many cases the retardation is limited to the capacity to absorb and assimilate knowledge, while in other areas they may be quite normal or even above average."[8]

When a father, Cantor Joseph Malovany, spoke to the Rebbe about his autistic son who was residing in an institution, the Rebbe reminded the understandably upset father that the fact that a person is autistic, suffering from a disorder that severely limits one's ability to interact with others, "doesn't mean that [autistic people] don't relate to anyone. To people they don't relate, but to God they relate as well as everyone else, and [sometimes] even more so. While they're not busy with people,

they're busy with God." This more positive take on this difficult disorder caused Malovany to recall his success in training his son to say a
blessing. He then also noted that his son had learned to perform other
religious rituals and they were very precious to him. The Rebbe urged
Cantor Malovany to go further and to put a charity box in his son's
room. "It would benefit your son to deposit charity," the Rebbe said,
"and when people visit him he will remind them that they must give
charity." Few other people would have thought to turn an autistic child
into a collector for charity.[9]

For the Rebbe, the desire to choose positive words was so deeply ingrained that he hesitated to use words like "evil" even when describing
something that was. He did not wish to have negative words or words
that had negative associations cross his lips. Instead, to refer to something bad he would use an expression such as *hefech ha-tov* ("the opposite
of good"); to refer to something foolish, he would say *hefech ha-seichel* ("the
opposite of intelligent"); to refer to death, he would say *hefech ha-chayyim*
("the opposite of life"); to refer to something unholy he would say *hefech
ha-kedushah* ("the opposite of holiness").[10] In a usage that sounds almost
humorous, he would often speak of a bad person, a *rasha*, as "one who is
not a tzaddik" ("one who is not a highly righteous person").

The Rebbe's search for nonnegative language went well beyond
anything that traditional Jewish texts might have intended. He apparently believed that words with bad connotations could trigger harmful
associations in even the most innocent of contexts. He avoided the word
"undertake" lest it trigger an association with the word "undertaker."
And not surprisingly, no matter how great the pressure to finish a
project, he never referred to the due date as a "deadline."[11] Once the word
"deadline" is removed from one's vocabulary, one possible alternative
is "due date," the forbidden expression connoting death and "due date"
connoting birth.

The Rebbe's avoidance of anything with potentially negative associations was consistent, and often unexpected and surprising. The most
famous of Maimonides's Thirteen Principles of the Jewish Faith is the
twelfth, "I believe in the coming of the Messiah, and even though he
may tarry, I shall wait for him on any day he comes." Audiotapes from

farbrengens document that when this song was sung, the Rebbe would clearly enunciate the opening words, "I believe in the coming of the Messiah," but he would not sing "and even though he may tarry." He would hum along but would not say these words. Apparently, his hope was that the Messiah would come immediately, and not tarry; therefore, why acknowledge in advance the expectation that he might delay? Rather, if something good is going to happen, let's at least hope it will happen now.

The Rebbe seems to have instinctively sought out the good even in contexts that contained more negative news than positive. When told that if he continued working so hard after his heart attack, there was a 60 percent chance he would have another heart attack, the Rebbe chose to focus on the implied assurance that there was a 40 percent chance that he wouldn't. That this was a long-standing trait of his is suggested by an incident that happened in 1928, when he was still in his twenties. The saddest day on the Jewish calendar is Tisha Be'Av, the fast day that commemorates the day on which both Temples were destroyed (586 BCE and 70 CE). Most Jews, when mentioning Tisha Be'Av to less knowledgeable Jews or to non-Jews, almost reflexively remark that it is "the saddest day in the Jewish calendar." I was therefore taken aback to see a letter the soon-to-be-married Menachem Mendel Schneerson wrote to his future mother-in-law, Rebbetzin Nechama Dina, a few months before the wedding, in which he dated the letter "*Erev* [the day before] Tisha Be'Av, the birthday of the righteous Messiah." While there is a midrash that teaches that the Messiah will be born on Tisha Be'Av, one rarely hears another try to mitigate the sadness of the day by mentioning this teaching when referring to the upcoming fast day.

The Rebbe's avoidance of unhappy terms did not only apply to words, but also to events. To this day, Chabad remains the one large Jewish group in which little emphasis is placed on the Holocaust, both in terms of erecting memorials and sponsoring events about it. The Rebbe opposed such a focus from early on. In 1952, when his cousin, Yitzchak Schneerson, wrote of his involvement in Paris in the creation of the Tomb of the Unknown Jewish Martyr to memorialize victims of the Holocaust, the Rebbe expressed a polite, but forceful, demurral.

"Forgive me if my view is not in accordance with yours." He then explained, "Now, at a time when there are hundreds of thousands of living martyrs, not 'unknown' by any stretch, who live in abject need for physical bread, and many more in need of spiritual sustenance, the main impediment to meeting their needs is simply lack of funds. Therefore, whenever funds can be procured, this immediately creates a dilemma: Should the monies be used to erect a stone [memoriam] in a large square in Paris, to remind passersby of the millions of Jews who died sanctifying God's Name, or should these monies sustain the living who are starving, either literally or figuratively, to hear the word of God? The solution to [your] dilemma is, I believe, not in doubt." [12] The Rebbe's lack of emphasis on the building of Holocaust memorials was certainly not dictated by indifference. His life, like the life of virtually every twentieth-century Jew who grew up in Eastern, Central, and much of Western Europe, was devastated by the Holocaust. His brother DovBer was murdered by the Nazis, as were his sister- and brother-in-law, Sheina and Menachem Mendel Horenstein. And, of course, a large percentage of followers of Chabad were murdered between 1941 and 1945, along with millions of other Jews. In a letter to a child of Holocaust survivors, a man plagued by issues of religious doubt, the Rebbe writes a strong letter affirming his faith and then adds as a postscript: "Needless to say, the above may be accepted intellectually . . . and one may perhaps say, 'Well, it is easy for one who is not emotionally involved to give an "intellectual explanation." ' So, I ought to perhaps add that I too lost in the Holocaust very close and dear relatives such as a grandmother, brother, cousins, and others (God should avenge their blood). But life, according to God's command, must go on, and the sign of life is growth and creativity."

In Chabad outreach, and in the Rebbe's speeches throughout the postwar years, the emphasis was never on the Holocaust, but on *simcha shel mitzvah*, the joy of doing a mitzvah. This probably had to do both with the Rebbe's naturally optimistic inclination and with a strategic assessment that the Holocaust does not ultimately provide a positive motivation for Jews to go on leading Jewish lives.[13] By the last decades of the twentieth century and the early years of the twenty-first, the percentage of American Jews willing to intermarry and to raise their children without a Jewish identity had climbed steeply. The Rebbe intuited, one senses, that a focus on the Holocaust was not an effective way to stimulate Jews to want to lead Jewish lives; indeed, on purely rational grounds it could cause many Jews to want to assimilate and thereby avoid such a fate for themselves and, even more so, for their children (in addition, and not surprisingly, it leads many people to questions about God, causing either disbelief in God or anger at Him).[14] Underlying the Rebbe's campaigns to teach Jews to observe commandments was his assumption that if a Jew enjoys studying Torah, putting on tefillin, lighting Shabbat candles, praying to God, and performing acts of charity and kindness, five of the activities most commonly promoted by Chabad, he or she will want to lead a Jewish life.[15] But if a Jew does not experience Judaism on a meaningful basis, to ask him or her to perpetuate the Jewish people in essence to spite Hitler will not guarantee Jewish survival or a healthy Jewish psyche.

The de-emphasis on the Holocaust in Chabad outreach and education is striking, simply because it so distinguishes Chabad from the rest of contemporary Jewry. Even in terms of perpetuating the memory of the six million, the Rebbe felt it wiser to focus attention *not* on how they met their tragic deaths but on how so many of them lived their lives.

All of this is of a piece with the Rebbe's optimistic philosophy, a philosophy that had been articulated a century earlier by the Third Rebbe, the Tzemach Tzedek, the man for whom Menachem Mendel Schneerson was named. A noted aphorism of the Tzemach Tzedek, and one that the Rebbe repeated over and over, was "Think good and it will be good" (*tracht gut un vet zein gut*).

In this, the Tzemach Tzedek and the Rebbe were in conflict with a mind-set still common in the Jewish community. A story that has long circulated in Chabad tells of a man who complained to the Rebbe that his children were assimilating. The man started to meditate aloud, in a somewhat self-pitying manner: "What have I done wrong? Why are they straying from the path I taught them?" He then sighed. "*S'iz shver tzu zein a Yid*," he continued, citing an old Yiddish expression, whose English translation—"It's hard to be a Jew"—is well known even to many Jews who don't know Yiddish.

At this point, the Rebbe asked the man if he often expressed himself in this way, and the man acknowledged that in stressful times, of which there are many, he did often cite this Yiddish saying.

The Rebbe responded: "Then that is the message your children hear, and that is the impression of Judaism they have." The Rebbe then continued. "There is another Yiddish saying, '*S'iz gut tzu zein a Yid.*' 'It is good to be a Jew.' Switch your refrain and you will notice a difference in your children's appreciation for their heritage."

Chapter 8

"I'M ALSO TIRED. SO WHAT?"

The Rebbe's Work Ethic

"At four o'clock in the morning, he has either not yet gone to sleep, or has already awoken."
—*Frierdiker Rebbe speaking of his son-in-law, Rabbi Menachem Mendel Schneerson*

"He would sweep through a one- or two-page letter with extraordinary speed. . . . Then putting that letter down and taking another one up, the Rebbe simultaneously dictated his response to the first letter point by point. . . . Thus, while [I] the secretary was racing against time, taking notes . . . the Rebbe was already [reading and] poised to reply to the next letter."
—*Dr. Nissen Mindel, longtime secretary to the Rebbe*[1]

Unlike the above account, some of the details recounted in hagiographic biographies and oral recollections of the Rebbe are fantastical, more in the nature of urban legends than sober facts. One devotee of the Rebbe insists that during his years of university study in France, Menachem Mendel Schneerson amassed nine PhDs, a feat that would indeed be unprecedented in human history. There is neither evidence to support this assertion nor any listing of the supposed nine disciplines in which the Rebbe acquired such degrees, or a record of the book-length dissertations he would have had to have written.

While it is widely known that the Rebbe was an exceptionally fast reader, many have exaggerated this claim. A 2003 wide-eyed account of the Rebbe informs us that a visitor brought the Rebbe a fifteen-page letter that the Rebbe read in twenty seconds, and then discussed it in detail (equivalent to reading a three-hundred-page book in under seven minutes); in fact, "the Rebbe had not overlooked a single detail in the letter." The Rebbe's intellect was such, the same author relates, that he needed no advisers or aides but carried the entire burden of responsibility for all decisions on his own shoulders, offering unequivocal answers to all questions "on the spot."[2]

One approaches such claims with obvious skepticism, yet there are other remarkable claims made about the Rebbe that were offered by people who seem less prone to exaggeration. One relates to the Rebbe's extraordinary work ethic, a commitment that went back to his early years. Yona Kessa, who long served in the Israeli Knesset (1949–1965), most of the time representing the secular Mapai Party but who, as a young man, lived in Yekaterinoslav, remembers visiting the Schneerson household often: "I was witness to the Rebbe's diligence in Torah study. Whenever I found him, I always found him learning in a standing position, never sitting down. I remember, as well, that already then, he was well versed in physics and mathematics. I even remember that although he was an autodidact, he would be visited by students and even professors to consult with him on problems of physics and mathematics; apparently, already then, he had an incredible combination of knowledge."[3]

What this reminiscence reveals, of course, is not only the Rebbe's early interest in acquiring secular knowledge but also his incredible capacity for intellectual work. And while many religious figures from Yekaterinoslav had recollections of the long hours of study in which the young Schneerson would engage, there is no reason why Kessa would be inclined to concoct such an anecdote.

While the accomplishments of youth can and often have been exaggerated,[4] the greatest proof of the Rebbe's work ethic was provided in the public sphere, during his forty years as Chabad's leader, at a time when his work schedule was witnessed by hundreds of people. For the entirety of his *nesiut* (leadership), the Rebbe did not take any vacations or, for that matter, days off, at least none that his secretaries are aware of.[5] Americans think in terms of a five-day workweek, eight hours of work a day, with vacations generally lasting from two to four weeks a year. Self-employed people often push themselves harder, perhaps working ten hours a day, sometimes six days a week. The Rebbe's schedule was of a different dimension. He was at his office on a daily basis, Sunday through Friday. On Shabbat, of course, he engaged in none of the activities forbidden on that day (such as writing or dictating letters), but he taught, often for many hours, at the *farbrengens* that he held an average of twice a month on the Sabbath (after the Rebbetzin's death, on every Shabbat) and other Jewish holidays. Teams of *chozrim*, trained to recall with great precision the Rebbe's words, would gather when the Sabbath or holidays ended to write down, as faithfully as possible, the lectures the Rebbe had delivered (the Rebbe would later review and edit some of the transcripts). More than two hundred volumes of these lectures have been published, evidence that even on this one supposed day of rest, the Rebbe was not resting. To cite just one example: In February 1971, the Rebbe conducted a Saturday-evening *farbrengen* that lasted till the early-morning hours. While the event was interspersed with singing, the Rebbe's several talks that night lasted approximately five hours. That same day, starting at about 1:30 p.m., the Rebbe had conducted an afternoon *farbrengen*, during which he spoke for about three hours.

On weekdays, his hours were irregular and very long. Rabbi Herbert Weiner, who interviewed the Rebbe twice in the mid-1950s, recalls his surprise at learning that the thrice-weekly *yechidusen* (the Rebbe's private meetings with people) could run into the early hours of the morning; 3:00 a.m. was quite a regular hour for finishing, and on occasion the visits lasted till dawn or later. Weiner asked Rabbi Hodakov, the Rebbe's chief of staff, if the Rebbe slept during the day after these meetings. Hodakov raised his brows at such a thought: "During the day, the Rebbe is busy directing the activities of the Lubavitcher movement in every part of the world."[6] This involved both macro and micro issues, for example, determining the communities to which Chabad *shluchim* should be sent and answering individuals' requests for advice from throughout the world.

"When then does the Rebbe sleep?" Weiner asked, a question that elicited from Hodakov an enigmatic smile and a shrug.

There were yeshiva students who used to stand near the Rebbe's house on President Street and witnessed lights going on and off on different floors throughout the night. Such behavior is consistent with the fact that the Rebbe, when leaving 770 at the end of his workday, generally took with him a satchel filled with correspondence and other matters requiring attention. Rabbi Krinsky recalls that he would generally return to his office the following morning with much of the work attended to. Also, as the Rebbe did not have many opportunities to continue his Talmudic, Chasidic, and kabbalistic studies during the day, it is assumed that he did so at night.

My grandfather, Rabbi Nissen Telushkin, who was twenty-two years older than the Rebbe, once helped organize a delegation of Chabad notables in the 1960s to meet with him and urge him to slow down, work shorter hours, take vacations, and not spend hours at the *Ohel* during freezing weather (to this last comment, the Rebbe responded, "I too need a Rebbe"). The Rebbe greeted them politely and with warmth. But did his behavior alter? Not at all.

"Ich bin oichet meed. Is vos?"—*"I'm also tired. So what?"*

Rabbi Herbert Bomzer, an Orthodox rabbi of non-Lubavitch background, met with the Rebbe on several occasions. Bomzer had become involved in the matter of conversions to Judaism, an issue very significant to the Rebbe, who wanted to ensure that only strictly halachic, in effect Orthodox, conversions be accepted as valid, both in Israel and throughout the world. After involving himself in this issue, Bomzer soon found himself the recipient of up to twenty phone calls a week, many from people who had previously been converted by non-Orthodox rabbis and who now wished to undergo Orthodox conversions. The amount of time Bomzer spent with each potential candidate was considerable, and all this came in addition to his pulpit responsibilities, his teaching schedule, his organizational commitments, and his family responsibilities. He sought out a meeting with the Rebbe to discuss this problem: "*Ich bin meed*, I'm tired," he told the Rebbe, and he explained just how overwhelming his commitments were.

The Rebbe answered: "*Ich bin oichet meed. Is vos?*"—"I'm also tired. So what?" So forty years of unending nights and no vacations did take their toll. But "so what?"[7]

Rabbi Zev Segal, a community activist, encountered a similar, though subtly different, response. After a long career in the rabbinate, Segal went to work for the Memorial Foundation for Jewish Culture. Once, as he was getting ready to depart on an overseas mission, he received a call from Rabbi Hodakov, with a request from the Rebbe that he fulfill a certain assignment. Segal agreed to do so, although he eventually found the task requested by the Rebbe to be much more difficult than he had anticipated, and even a bit dangerous.

When he returned, he said, "I came back and gave the Rebbe a report and I concluded that the Rebbe should know that this was not an easy task for me. It was, rather, very difficult. The Rebbe looked at me quizzically and said, 'Rabbi Segal, since when did you make a contract with the Almighty for an easy life?'"[8]

At a speech delivered after the Rebbe's death, Segal explained how this one, seemingly throw-away line, uttered in fewer than ten seconds, permanently affected him. Even though a task will not be easy, each of us must do what we know we were put on earth to do.

The Rebbe had a rather singular philosophy as to how to prioritize one's work when it started to seem overwhelming. The following advice, which he offered to Rabbi Adin Steinsaltz, is perhaps not the advice that he would have offered to everyone else.[9] After all, Steinsaltz is one of the most accomplished and tireless Jewish scholars of modern times, the translator of the entire Talmud into modern Hebrew (along with an extensive commentary), the creator of a network of schools and educational institutions in Israel and the former Soviet Union, and the author of some sixty books. *Time* famously hailed him as a "once-in-a-millennium scholar." Yet the nature of the advice extended by the Rebbe to Steinsaltz gives us an insight into how the Rebbe dealt with the ever-greater demands made of him as well. Steinsaltz spoke of this incident at a speech delivered at the John F. Kennedy Library in Boston, marking the tenth *yahrtzeit* (anniversary) of the Rebbe's death:

> *Years ago, I wrote a letter to the Rebbe. I tried to describe what I was doing, tried to explain that one project I'm involved with is enough work to occupy me all day, every day.*
>
> *There was also a second project, which was also enough to fill my entire day.*
>
> *And then there was a third undertaking, which was a full day's work.*
>
> *I told the Rebbe that I find it hard to carry on with them all and that every day is more difficult than the one before because there is just so much. So what should my priorities be? What should I cut out? This is the letter I wrote.*
>
> *So he responded—this is practically the last letter I received from the Rebbe: "Continue all these things that you are doing and add more to all of them."*
>
> *He demanded these things. How can I explain? You know the famous story about the farmer who comes to the rabbi complaining about his small house so full of children. It's unbearable. So the rabbi tells him to take a goat into his house, a noisy, smelly, dirty goat. Very soon the farmer comes back to the rabbi. "Every problem I had is [now] worse," he cries. The rabbi tells him to take the goat out. So he takes the goat out of his house and soon he's back to tell the rabbi what a big wonderful house he now has.*
>
> *A very old story, but what the Rebbe said was similar and yet quite different. When people complained about how hard their work was, he would give them more to do. When they complained how terrible that was, he would give them even more.*
>
> *He told them to add the goat, and then he'd give them the camel too to put in their house! That was the way he worked all the time. Whenever people complained about their inability to cope or the hard time they endured, he would suggest, "Take on something more."*

Steinsaltz believed that the Rebbe wanted to do nothing less than change the very nature of human nature, the "very way the human being operates. He wanted to change people's nature into something different, something that could accomplish more than had previously been expected of human beings: '*The first person that the Rebbe tried this experiment on was himself*' " [10] (emphasis added).

Despite this extraordinary demand from Rabbi Steinsaltz—and I believe from many *shluchim* as well—the Rebbe was capable of moderating his demands from others, if only by a little. At a meeting with David Chase, a well-known businessman and longtime Chabad supporter, the Rebbe urged him to work hard but not too hard. As he explained, a human being is constituted like an engine, a motor. If one underutilizes the engine it becomes sluggish, but if one overuses it, it burns out: "Always try to get it into a 90 percent level of efficiency. But don't overdo it, and don't drop to 60 percent."

Did he apply this advice to himself? I suspect not.

Why? One theory: Since it is clear that the Rebbe was driven from the moment he assumed leadership of Chabad to help set the stage for the future coming Redemption (see pages 39–40), it makes sense that he could not be satisfied with doing a job that was in any way incomplete or imperfect; perhaps the last step in the process would be the step necessary to usher in the Messiah.

The English language encourages us to think that imposing a very heavy burden can lead to catastrophe; we are all familiar with the expression "the straw that broke the camel's back." The Rebbe, it would seem, at least when considering himself and his *shluchim*, thought differently, that the extra bit of effort might be exactly what is necessary to bring about the world's redemption. Only a person with a compelling sense of mission would write, as the Rebbe wrote to Hindy Lew on her birthday, that if a person has the capability to bring a hundred people close to God, and brings only ninety-nine, he or she has not fulfilled their obligation.[11]

Success with Time *(Hatzlacha B'zman)*

The Rebbe's substantial achievements emanated in large part not only from the long hours he put in at work, but from his ability to utilize time in an unusually productive manner. In a 1970 *sicha* the Rebbe related that he learned this trait from his father-in-law, the Frierdiker Rebbe. He was with the Frierdiker Rebbe in Leningrad (this was in the period before he and Chaya Mushka were married but he already had a close relationship with his future father-in-law), and the Frierdiker Rebbe was preparing to leave within the hour on a trip to Moscow. The Frierdiker Rebbe knew that the Soviet secret police, who routinely monitored him, tracked his movements even more vigilantly when he traveled, as they were aware that the goal of his trips was to spread *Yiddishkeit*, Jewish commitment—exactly what the Communist government was interested in eradicating. Menachem Mendel himself was quite concerned about this trip, yet when he entered the Frierdiker Rebbe's room, he was taken aback: The Rebbe "was sitting totally calmly . . . and he was doing whatever [work] he was involved in at that moment."

The young Menachem Mendel expressed his amazement that at a time of such tension, the Frierdiker Rebbe could sit there calmly and with full concentration attend to whatever task he was performing.

This, the Rebbe now related, is when his father-in-law taught him the secret of "success with time," a technique that the Frierdiker Rebbe had learned from his father, the Rebbe Rashab: The first prerequisite for fulfilling one's responsibilities is to fully grasp that a person can never add to the amount of time in the day or the night. Since time is finite, the only way we can carry out all that we need to do is to utilize whatever time we do have to its full capacity; this means giving our entire focus, our full concentration, to whatever we are doing at that moment. Therefore, while working on one task, "we must regard anything else we have done before and anything that we are planning to do later as totally insignificant."

In this case, though the Sixth Rebbe would be going within the hour to the train station and would soon find himself followed and possibly harassed by the secret police (he was subsequently arrested, though not on this trip; see pages 458–59), there was nothing to be gained by transferring his attention to what he would be doing in another hour. This is why, he explained to Menachem Mendel, he could now sit in his room and focus on the task in front of him. "He had no other distracting concerns, not from the past and not from the future.

"To utilize this moment fully," the Rebbe now explained, "that is what it means to have *hatzlacha b'zman*, success with time." [12]

"The worker is enjoined not to deprive the employer of the benefits of his work by frittering away his time, a little here, a little there."

—MAIMONIDES, "LAWS OF HIRING" 13:7

Jacob Hanoka, a young scientist who had wanted to leave graduate school and to study at the Chabad yeshiva, and whom the Rebbe discouraged from doing so, received a letter from the Rebbe shortly after he completed his PhD, urging him to pursue a professional career (see page 349). The Rebbe then added on some more advice: When Hanoka did start working, it was important that he give his employer an honest, full day's work. Hanoka showed the letter to Rabbi Nissen Mangel, who told him how important this value was in Jewish ethics and, therefore, to the Rebbe.

Mangel related to Hanoka the story of the rabbinic sage Abba Hilkiah, a saintly man whose prayers for rain were solicited by the rabbis when there was a drought. Once, when such prayers were needed, two rabbis went to seek his help. They found him hoeing in the field "and greeted him, but he took no notice of them." Later, after Abba Hilkiah and his wife had offered a prayer for rain and rain had fallen, the rabbis asked him to explain his earlier, seemingly rude, behavior. He answered: "I was a laborer hired by the day, and I said to myself [that since I am being paid for the day], let me not interrupt [my work] even for a moment" (*Ta'anit* 23b).

In a similar manner, Maimonides ruled in his code of Jewish law, the *Mishneh Torah*: "The worker is enjoined not to deprive the employer of the benefit of his work by frittering away his time, a little here, a little there. . . . Indeed, the worker must be very punctilious in the matter of time" ("Laws of Hiring," 13:7). Few workers, Jewish or non-Jewish, are conscious of this. But from Judaism's perspective, "just as theft of money is theft, so is theft of time" (*Mesillat Yesharim* [*The Path of the Just*], chapter 11), and Mangel wanted to emphasize to Hanoka how serious this matter is.

A different insight of the Rebbe concerning the interplay of ethics and ritual was conveyed in a discussion with his physician, Dr. Ira Weiss. Weiss, an observant Jew and a cardiologist who started treating the Rebbe after his 1977 heart attack, often found himself running late, both because of his commitment to spending sufficient, unrushed, time with his patients, and because of a propensity to tardiness. In consequence, Weiss sometimes found himself reciting Mincha, the afternoon prayer, late and he felt uncomfortable about doing so. He asked the Rebbe about this, and the Rebbe told him (the following is a summary, not a verbatim account): "In a case like this, where your obligations are first to your patients, and where making them wait can cause them physical or emotional harm . . . you are not entitled to delay them any further. You have to finish your work with them first, and God will understand the delay in your Mincha. You don't have to make any apologies for a late Mincha."

By offering Weiss concrete guidance as to how to behave, the Rebbe also freed him from unnecessary feelings of guilt for not praying at the specified hour. But even that was not enough; the Rebbe wanted to make sure that Weiss did not feel that he was in any way doing something wrong. And so he confided to Weiss that he, too, encountered a similar problem in his work. On those afternoons when he visited the *Ohel*, the site of his father-in-law's grave, he would often spend many hours reading through dozens, even hundreds, of letters, offering prayers on behalf of those soliciting a *bracha*, and formulating responses to the letter writers: "To him," Dr. Weiss comments, "it was a very serious matter; it was like seeing patients, only it was through the letters." As a result, the Rebbe, too, would sometimes have to start Mincha late. Obviously, sharing with Weiss this highly personal detail from his own life further reassured the doctor about his own behavior.

Still, there was more. Even as the Rebbe explained to Weiss those instances in which he was permitted to pray late, he also emphasized that this behavior should not lead him to become lax and indifferent—when there was no pressing reason—to praying at the right time. Indeed, as a rule, that is exactly what he should do: pray on time. But not always. There is a human dimension to one's responsibilities to God: "You should always be attentive to the time of Mincha except when it makes someone delayed or causes them to suffer."

"I'm very sorry, Mr. Weingarten, but I don't understand that word, 'retirement.' It's not in my vocabulary."

The most famous figure in the Torah, the man whose personality dominates the last four of the Torah's five books, is Moses. At the end of his life, Moses was forcibly retired from his leadership role by God, not because of a lack of strength but because God did not want him to lead the Israelite people into the land of Israel. Moses's age at the time of retirement was 120, and the Torah emphasizes that he was still vigorous (Deuteronomy 34:8).

For the Rebbe, Moses's work ethic might well have been a model: Don't retire, certainly not voluntarily. The Rebbe clearly had no intention of doing so—at close to ninety, he was still standing every Sunday for many hours, handing out dollar bills to be distributed to charity—and he did not think it appropriate for others to retire either. The American government might deem a retirement age of sixty-five suitable, but the Rebbe firmly disagreed. When he turned seventy, his birthday request was that over the coming year, the seventy-first year of his life, seventy-one new Chabad institutions be established.

In similar manner, the Rebbe told Frank Lautenberg that even as he, the Rebbe, was getting older, he took on more and more responsibilities. "I'm over seventy. I belong in an old age home," he said, laughing, "but I'm not going there. I'm continuing." Lautenberg himself went on to become a senator from New Jersey and served in the Senate until his death at age eighty-nine.

The Rebbe's opposition to retirement became even more pronounced when he was advising rabbis. In 1980, when the sixty-seven-year-old rabbi David Hollander confided to the Rebbe his intention to retire from the rabbinate, the Rebbe answered: "I am older than you [the Rebbe was then seventy-eight] and I'm assuming other burdens. By what right are you prepared to leave this job? You have to stay in the rabbinate [*rabbanus*] for life." [13] Hollander, whose pulpit had declined greatly in the preceding years, took over another congregation and remained there for more than twenty years.

But, of course, it was not just rabbis whom the Rebbe pushed to remain creative. When Freddy Hager and his father-in-law met with the Rebbe, and the latter told him that now that he had turned seventy, he wanted to sell his business and retire, the Rebbe answered, "I'm very sorry, Mr. Weingarten, but I don't understand that word, 'retirement.' It's not in my vocabulary." [14]

At some level, it would seem that the Rebbe equated retirement with death. Certainly in the case of Moses, death followed "retirement" almost immediately. Rabbi Avraham Shemtov, one of the movement's most distinguished elders, recalls the Rebbe's response to Rabbi Herbert Weiner, who expressed a wish to retire. "How can a person even think of retiring from life?" [15]

The Rebbe's Tragic Retirement

This last sentiment only magnifies the sense of tragedy of the last year and a half of the Rebbe's life, when a stroke stilled his voice forever, and he could no longer counsel those in need, go to the *Ohel*, or offer directives to the movement. He was reduced to shaking or nodding his head, and being pressured on occasion, as when making an appearance before audiences, some of whose members were screaming for him to reveal himself as the Messiah.

Adam le-amal yulad, "Man was born for hard toil," the Bible declares (Job 5:7), a verse the Talmud understands as applying to "the toil of Torah study" (Sanhedrin 99b). The Talmudic commentator Maharsha writes that the goal of such toil is "to learn Torah in order to teach it." And, of course, the verse in its simple meaning (*peshat*) also applies to other, more general types of work. In addition to not being able to engage in learning, one wonders what it was like for the Rebbe when he could no longer respond with anything more than a shaking or nodding of the head to the hundreds of letters sent to him daily, or give blessings to those waiting on line to receive a dollar, or offer policy guidance to the Jewish world.

Much attention was devoted in that last period by those who wished to ascertain whether the Rebbe was trying to signal or in some way make known that he was the Messiah. Far more likely, the Rebbe, who was mute, was immensely frustrated. He could no longer do the work for which he lived. Retirement had been forced upon him by his stroke. But it was not followed by a quick death—as in the case of Moses—but rather by more than two years of muteness. What was he thinking? We don't know, but the thought of what this man who fought so strenuously against retirement for himself and for others went through is heartrending.

Chapter 9

EXPRESSING DISAGREEMENT
WITHOUT BEING DISAGREEABLE

"I don't speak about people, I speak about opinions."

We often hear the phrase, "It's not personal." But often, perhaps more often than not, disagreements do become personal. For example, in theory, since differences of opinion between political liberals and conservatives, and among Reform, Conservative, and Orthodox Jews, are over matters of policy and beliefs, they need not result in personal ill will among those holding opposing views or advocating different policies. As a Hebrew expression puts it: *Halevai*, if only that were true. For the Rebbe, though, it was true.

It is hard to know if his ability to oppose a view with which he disagreed while maintaining affection for the person who held it was a natural or an acquired trait. It is possible that the development of this attribute derived, at least in part, from his own life experience. We know, for example, that the Rebbe continued to maintain an affectionate and loving relationship with his cousin, Avraham Shlonsky (his next-door neighbor and classmate while growing up), even after Shlonsky—who became a renowned Israeli poet—adopted secular ideologies and became religiously nonobservant. During a 1968 trip by the poet to Brooklyn, the Rebbe tried to influence Shlonsky to become more observant. At one point, though, he said to him, "You and I both have a deep-seated belief in God. I express it through following Torah and mitzvot, while you express it through your poetry" (*Ma'ariv*, March 25, 1977). Shlonsky would send his books of poetry to the Rebbe.[1]

However, the Shlonsky example might not be conclusive. The phenomenon of individuals maintaining loving feelings toward family members with whom they have strong ideological disagreements is a known one. What seems to have been unusual in the case of the Rebbe is that he regarded all Jews as family—and the affection that many people can maintain for family members with whom they have profound disagreements he could maintain for many thousands of people.

One of those was Shimon Peres, Israel's president. One might well have thought that Peres would bear a certain level of animosity, or at least annoyance, toward the Rebbe; it was Menachem Mendel Schneerson's earlier opposition to Peres's foreign policy that cost Peres, on one well-known occasion, the prime ministership (see pages 284–85; Peres did serve as prime minister on two other occasions). When President Peres was interviewed for this book, he spoke very warmly of the Rebbe.[2] He had no critical recollections about the Rebbe whatsoever, an attitude reflected in the public letter he issued several days after the Rebbe's death: "The legacy that he bequeathed was a love of Jews as they were, and the constant search to find that which unified him with others."

Peres was likely reciprocating the warmth shown him by the Rebbe. In addition to several meetings, the two maintained a periodic correspondence. In one letter, Peres shared with the Rebbe news about the upcoming unity government he was then crafting in Israel. And, in a 1985 letter from the Rebbe, he reminded Peres of a meeting the two men had had at 770, during which Peres proudly confided to the Rebbe that his parents had sought a blessing for children from a Chasidic Rebbe and, in the aftermath of the blessing, he was born.[3] In the letter, the Rebbe also recalled that when the two of them had gotten into a discussion about Israel's pressing security needs, Peres had responded with a traditional Yiddish affirmation of faith, "*Der Aibershter vet helfen*" ("God will help").

It is no secret that the Rebbe and Peres had very different and potentially divisive views on what policies Israel should adopt (in negotiations with the Palestinians, for example, the Rebbe opposed territorial compromises, which Peres favored; hence the Rebbe's concerns about his becoming prime minister), but what is equally clear is the level of respect and affection they maintained for each other.[4]

Another person with whom the Rebbe had equally strong and differing views on the Palestinian-Israeli conflict was President Jimmy
Carter. On the one hand, the Rebbe could not but be appreciative of the
president for declaring a National Education Day in the United States, a
project dear to the Rebbe's heart—and arranging for it to be observed
on the Rebbe's birthday. On the other hand, the Rebbe felt that the pressure the president exerted on Israeli prime minister Menachem Begin
led to Israel signing a peace treaty that bestowed irrevocable assets such
as land and oil fields to Egypt; the Rebbe believed the treaty might in the
end result in Jewish lives being lost (see chapter 20). Yet, when Carter
finished his term of office, and it was during a low point of popularity
for him, the Rebbe made known in a public talk that he regarded much
of the criticism being directed at the outgoing president as unfair. He
particularly decried the "disturbing trend" that when a president loses
an election, "people seem to forget any good that he may have done."
The Rebbe speculated that perhaps because a defeated president is now
deprived of power, people no longer seem to care about speaking ill
of him; he can no longer grant them favors or inflict upon them any
harm. The Rebbe believed Carter's "outstanding achievement was the
prevention of war," wars that could have led to the deaths and sufferings
of millions of people, both in the United States and abroad.

Even as the Rebbe acknowledged his gratitude, he also expressed his
ongoing reservations about policies advocated by Carter: "The above
acknowledgment is in no way to be construed as a retraction from
my previous stand concerning the Camp David accords. I reiterate as
strongly as possible that it was, and remains, a disaster and peril for Jews
and for the rest of the world. But the President's part in the accords was
no doubt motivated by the hope that it would bring peace, and for this
he is to be commended. But the fact remains that the only thing that
has been achieved is that one side has made numerous concessions. . . .
Such concessions merely prompt demands for further concessions, creating an even greater danger to peace. [But] to return to our main point,
notwithstanding any errors made, we are enjoined to express gratitude
where credit is due. This is a man who, among his achievements, safeguarded the well-being of millions of Americans."

What further fortified the Rebbe in his affection for those with whom he had differing views was a carefully cultivated consciousness of the areas in which he and his opponents agreed.[5] To a rabbi who expressed deep disagreement with him over a certain religious issue, the Rebbe noted that even if they disagreed on this matter, there still remained 612 issues on which they could work together—a reminder to the letter's recipient that they were two allies having a disagreement, not two opponents having a feud (the number 612 was of course a figurative reference to the Torah's 613 commandments, minus one). In this instance, he also reminded Rabbi Shmuel Lew, who had ongoing dealings with the same rabbi, "how positive a person this man and his family were, and how they can be forces for good [so] let's look [therefore] for the unifying force." For Lew, the Rebbe's approach became a general directive for how to conduct his life: "Look always for that which you have in common with the other person and build that up." This was a good way, Lew came to understand, to avoid alienating potential allies and avoid living an existence filled with needless enmity.

The "Who is a Jew?" issue—in which the Rebbe insisted on Israel only recognizing what he regarded as fully halachic, in effect only Orthodox, conversions to Judaism as valid—was one of those issues that provoked considerable opposition to the Rebbe, and one on which he found himself in periodic opposition with the Israeli minister of the interior, Yosef Burg (who was himself an Orthodox Jew). The Rebbe felt that Burg was permitting compromises on what he felt must be a non-compromisable issue. At a meeting with Bernie Rader, the Rebbe, in an uncharacteristic manner, screamed out at one point, "Why does he allow people who are not Jewish to be written down as being Jewish?" Yet, at this very moment of great annoyance, the Rebbe drew back and then, in typical Rebbe style, he said, "But it's also true that he is a Jew who prays three times a day." For Rader this was vintage Rebbe: "He always finished up by saying something nice about a person." And not just a general platitude about the person being nice, but a specific detail ("prays three times a day") that served to remind the Rebbe (and Rader) of areas in which he and Burg were united.

Yet another Israeli figure with whom the Rebbe had a fundamental disagreement over an issue he regarded to be of overriding importance was Moshe Dayan, Israel's renowned general. In Dayan's later years, when he served as Prime Minister Menachem Begin's foreign minister, Dayan played a critical role in convincing Begin that Israel could safely give back the entire Sinai, the land conquered from Egypt in the Six-Day War, in return for a peace agreement with Egypt.[6] The Rebbe, as noted, believed that this policy was putting Jewish lives at risk.

Nor was this the only time that the Rebbe felt Dayan was profoundly wrong on an issue of life-and-death significance. Years earlier, the Rebbe felt that Dayan, then serving as Israel's defense minister, had sacrificed the lives of hundreds of Israeli soldiers in the opening days of the 1973 Yom Kippur War by his wrongheaded opposition (in conjunction with Prime Minister Golda Meir) to launching a preemptive military strike against Syria and Egypt whom Israel had just learned was about to mount an attack against Israel (see page 562).

Dayan led a decidedly secular life, and when he died, in 1981, it was apparent that his sons, with whom he had a shaky and, in his later years, an embittered relationship, were not going to say Kaddish, the memorial prayer for the dead, which Jewish tradition dictates that children recite daily for eleven months after the death of a parent.[7]

Despite his passionate opposition to policies of Dayan that he felt caused lives to be lost, the Rebbe also was aware that this war hero had repeatedly played a major role in saving lives. During Israel's 1948 War of Independence, Dayan commanded the defense of the Jordan Valley and then of Jerusalem. He headed Israel's army during the invasion of Sinai in 1956 and led it to a brilliant victory. Within days of his appointment as minister of defense in 1967, he ordered the preemptive strike against Israel's enemies, which destroyed the air forces of Egypt and Syria in one day.[8]

And so, upon learning of Dayan's death, the Rebbe arranged for a Chabad Chasid to recite Kaddish at three services a day for eleven months on behalf of Moshe Dayan. Though Dayan had many admirers in Israel, both for his military achievements and from the circles that supported the peace treaty with Egypt, no other individual or group arranged for the ongoing religious commemoration of his death.

Not Speaking Critically of Others' Motives

M oshe Dayan carried out policies that the Rebbe opposed, but there was never an expression of direct opposition by Dayan to the Rebbe that we know of. On the other hand, the Satmar Rebbe had much to criticize about Chabad and Rabbi Menachem Mendel Schneerson, including the Rebbe's sympathetic view of the State of Israel. Much of this opposition surfaced after the Six-Day War, during which, the Rebbe argued, God had performed miracles on Israel's behalf. The Satmar Rebbe responded that if any miracles had been performed, they emanated from Satan, who was trying to seduce people away from the service of God.

In the war's aftermath, the Rebbe stationed Lubavitchers at the Western Wall to encourage visitors to put on tefillin. In contrast, the Satmar Rebbe opposed encouraging nonobservant Jews to put on tefillin, feeling that they were not spiritually worthy of doing so.[9] He also opposed his followers visiting the Western Wall lest it cause them to feel a sense of gratitude to the State of Israel and its soldiers for capturing it during the Six-Day War.

In 1964, three years before the war, the writer Harvey Swados met with the Rebbe to discuss a large variety of issues (see pages 51–61). One topic he inquired about was the Rebbe's opinion of the Satmar Rebbe, Yoel Teitelbaum, and, in particular, of his fierce, and already well-known, opposition to the State of Israel. The Rebbe refused to be drawn into needless controversy and *lashon hara* (speaking ill of others): "Why should I comment about the relationship between a man in Williamsburg whom I do not know [well] and the State of Israel, which I have never visited?"

Even when the Rebbe felt compelled to comment in a critical manner about another person, he restricted his criticism to a precise area of disagreement and did not attack the other's motives. In the 1950s, when Rabbi Herbert Weiner was discussing religious thought in Israel and mentioned the late rabbi Abraham Isaac Kook—a passionate pro-Zionist and sort of a polar ideological opposite of the Satmar Rebbe—the Rebbe nodded slightly but said nothing. Sensing that the silence might have

been a way of expressing disapproval without violating the commandment against speaking ill of others (Leviticus 19:16), Weiner asked the
Rebbe directly if he did not share his admiration for Kook. Though Rabbi
Kook was widely known as a man of exemplary character, the Rebbe
had some profound disagreements with Kook, particularly, but not only,
with his espousal of Zionism as a Jewish religious value.

In response to Weiner's query, the Rebbe shook his head gently.
"He tried to mix too much together. Philosophy, law, mysticism—
there were too many paradoxes in his teachings. A leader should not
confuse the mind too much."[10] The criticism was directed to aspects of
the person's teachings but not to the person himself.

Similarly, at his 1964 meeting, Harvey Swados initiated a discussion
with the Rebbe about Martin Buber, the twentieth century's most
famous Jewish philosopher. Although not a religiously observant Jew,
Buber was fascinated by the world of Chasidism and constructed much
of his philosophy around his understanding of the movement and
its leaders.

Through his two-volume *Tales of the Hasidim*, Buber brought the largely
unknown world of Chasidism to the attention of many Jews, Christians,
and secular intellectuals as well.[11] Yet Buber's overriding emphasis on
the importance of the individual's spontaneous responses to various life
situations put him at odds with traditional Jews who, justifiably, felt that
in his depiction of Chasidim he ignored a very central aspect of Judaism,
halacha, the Jewish legal system that legislates very precise modes of
daily behavior. Buber found little room in his life or philosophy for
responses that were not spontaneous or personal.[12] He felt that Judaism's
comprehensive system of ritual laws stifled spontaneity and forced its
practitioners to imitate other holy men's actions. Consequently, religious Jews were uncomfortable with the impression generated by Buber
that Chasidism as a philosophy could be divorced from its roots in strict
Jewish Orthodoxy.[13]

Swados recounts that he raised the issue of Buber with the Rebbe,
specifically because Buber was so renowned for his retelling of Chasidic
tales and had brought Chasidism to the attention of more people throughout the world than the Chasidim themselves had done. The Rebbe

expressed his concerns about Buber's representations of Chasidim without critiquing Buber personally: "The Buber version of our Chasidic tales can be compared to reproductions of works of art. One gets a sense of what a great painting is like from a print, but one cannot apprehend the painting from the print any more than one can apprehend a great sculpture from a plastic copy. In terms of their value, it is true that some people are stirred by reproductions and copies to seek out the original and discover the secrets of its greatness. Most, however, are inclined to take simple satisfaction in the delusion that they have been given a painless revelation of artistic profundity. To the extent that Buber leads people to think that they are getting a genuine understanding of Chasidism without having to learn from the source, his influence is not constructive." [14]

Because Swados's question specifically solicited the Rebbe's opinion of Buber's work, the Rebbe inevitably referred to Buber by name in expressing his disagreement. But his criticism was restricted to Buber's philosophy, which he felt misrepresented Chasidism, and not directed to the person himself. In any case, this comment to Swados about Buber was the exception (the Rebbe did not criticize Buber in public).

Yet another way in which the Rebbe kept disagreements from becoming personal was by almost always refraining from naming those with whom he disagreed. No matter how controversial the issue, and how passionately he felt about it, he found a way to express his views, particularly in public, without citing by name the person with whom he disagreed, and often without indicating even indirectly who he was. The Rebbe gave a critique of the Soviet Jewry protest movement and made the effort to convince one of its unnamed leaders to cancel a demonstration. The man refused and, in the Rebbe's view, this refusal led to a hundred Jewish families being denied exit visas. As sharply as he expressed his disapproval at a 1971 *farbrengen*, he commented in passing that the man was "a fine Jew." The unnamed man turned out to be Nehemiah Levanon, who long worked in Israeli intelligence. His identity became known only when he wrote in his memoir of his encounter and dispute with the Rebbe over this issue. [15]

What was achieved by the Rebbe's refraining from criticizing people by name? The clearest result was that he kept attention focused on the issue and didn't let the disagreement deteriorate into a personal dispute. In consequence, his relations with those with whom he strongly disagreed were never ruptured. In the case of Levanon, when an issue arose on which he could work with him (setting up underground yeshivot and Hebrew classes in Russia), he was able to pick up a telephone and call him (see page 293). The devotion to civil discourse and not questioning another's motives were not only in consonance with the Rebbe's notion of love of others, they were what enabled him to work with people with whom he had profound disagreements, and enabled them to work with him.

The episode with Levanon illustrates the extent to which the Rebbe regarded those with whom he disagreed as ideological opponents, not personal foes. Such behavior is uncommon; one characteristic feature of Jewish religious and political life, and American political life as well, is the demonizing of one's opponents. Thus, two of Israel's great leaders were its founding prime minister, David Ben-Gurion, and Menachem Begin, who became prime minister in 1977. The two fought over many issues and had a particularly contentious confrontation in 1952 on whether Israel should accept reparations from Germany (Ben-Gurion favored and Begin opposed doing so). During that clash, Begin at one point addressed Ben-Gurion as if he were the leader of a Nazi-like state: "I know that you will drag me to the concentration camps. Today, you arrested hundreds [of anti-reparation demonstrators]. Tomorrow, you may arrest thousands. No matter, they will go, they will sit in prison. We will sit there with them. If necessary, we will be killed with them." Ben-Gurion felt the same way about Begin, and in a letter to the Israeli poet Haim Gouri some years later—at the time, the underlying issue was once again relations with Germany—Ben-Gurion wrote that "Begin is clearly a Hitlerist type, a racist" and predicted that if he were to ever become prime minister of Israel, he "would rule as Hitler ruled Germany." [16]

The Rebbe's language could be very strong on matters of ideology (in the aftermath of the Egyptian-Israeli peace treaty, he wrote that no government official has the right "to sign away the very security of the people and the country he represents, nor the security of the next generation and subsequent generations"), but one looks in vain for his attacks becoming personal. Rabbi Michoel Seligson, who authored a 1,600-page index to all the Rebbe's public orations (*sichos*), claims that he has not come across instances in which the Rebbe identified a person whom he was criticizing by name: "I don't speak about people, I speak about opinions," the Rebbe liked to say. This was an essential characteristic of his approach to those with whom he disagreed, and one he influenced his *shluchim* to emulate.

"You will just build a wall between you and them, an impenetrable wall."

In the 1960s, Rabbi Tzvi Greenwald, an Israeli educator and lecturer, started offering talks on Judaism before members of nonreligious kibbutzim and other secular audiences in Israel. In certain segments of the Orthodox world, he started hearing criticism for being too easygoing and tolerant in his approach to nonreligious Jews. Rather, he was told, he should be rebuking these people for their lack of observance, in conformity with the Torah command, "Rebuke, yes you shall rebuke your fellow" (Leviticus 19:17).

Eventually, in 1967, Rabbi Greenwald raised the question to the Rebbe of whether he should adopt a more critical and confrontational manner in his lectures before nonobservant audiences.

Though Greenwald had written the Rebbe a lengthy letter about many different matters, the Rebbe went straight to his last few lines posing the question, and answered: "That which you write, that people are suggesting you give these audiences *mussar* (criticism), what will you accomplish? You will just build a wall between you and them, an impenetrable wall. You're there not to tell them who they are, they know who they are, but to tell them what you have to give to them." [17]

The Rebbe's advice to Greenwald was reminiscent of a comment he made to the novelist Herman Wouk concerning those who were highly critical of American Jewry because of their generally low level of religious observance. The Rebbe said he was actually optimistic about American Jews: "The American-Jewish community is wonderful. While you cannot tell them to do anything, you can *teach* them to do everything."

In short, if winning an argument means prevailing over your opponent's arguments, then there are arguments that can be won. If it means influencing your opponent to change his or her mind, then arguments rarely are won. Therefore, if the Rebbe couldn't persuade another of his position on a given issue, he was content to drop that issue for the time being and focus on areas in which he and the other did agree, or on issues in which the other person could be influenced. It sounds commonsensical, but then, common sense is not so common.

An Alternative Approach to That of the Rebbe

During the Rebbe's later years, one of the most influential *haredi* (the most traditional Orthodox) rabbis in Israel was Rabbi Elazar Shach (1899–2001), the long-term president of the Moetzes Gedolei HaTorah, the ranking body of the *haredi* political party, Agudat Yisrael. Rabbi Shach had a very different attitude from the Rebbe's, one that was far more confrontational in its approach toward nonobservant Jews in particular, but also toward religious Jews with whom he disagreed (Lubavitch being the most noted such group).

Among Rabbi Shach's well-known positions was his certainty that the Holocaust was a divine punishment for Jewish sinfulness or, as he phrased it: "God kept count of each and every sin, in a running count over hundreds of years, until the count amounted to six million Jews, and that is how the Holocaust occurred. So must a Jew believe, and if a Jew does not completely believe this, he is a heretic, and if we do not accept this as a punishment, then it is as if we don't believe in the Holy One, blessed be He." He then continued, "After exterminating the six million, He began counting again. We don't know where the count is up to now, maybe a year or two, but when it is full, God will punish again. This is how it is and no one can deny this. It is forbidden to say that this is not so." [18]

Unsurprisingly—and though Rabbi Shach was known to be a compassionate person in his personal dealings with others—he often came across in his public pronouncements as quite angry with irreligious Jews (certainly with irreligious Jewish leaders); after all, if one believes that a lack of religious observance leads to Jews undergoing a Holocaust, how can one not feel fury at those Jews whose nonobservance provokes God's ire?

Rabbi Shach's most famous speech was delivered during the 1990 political campaign in Israel, when he expressed his opposition to religious parties entering into a coalition with the Labor Party. In the speech, Shach singled out the secular Israeli kibbutzim for particular condemnation, speaking of kibbutz members as those who "rear rabbits and pigs," "who do not know what Yom Kippur is," and "who have no concept of Judaism." Speaking before ten thousand supporters at an Israeli basketball stadium, and before tens of thousands of viewers on television, Rabbi Shach called out rhetorically, "Can these people be called Jews?" The Rebbe responded to this speech four days later.[19]

But were secular Israelis, the ones who heard their Jewishness called into question, moved to reconsider their irreligiosity by Rabbi Shach's words? His supporters were certain they would be. *Yated Neeman*, the *haredi* newspaper that considered itself under Rabbi Shach's spiritual guidance, was ecstatic at the immense publicity that the speech generated: "We are certain that following the massive media coverage in Israel and around the world, the main message of the [speech] will succeed in penetrating the hearts of all mankind: 'God is the Lord. Blessed be His Name for ever and ever.'"

The response turned out to be quite different from what the newspaper predicted. Instead of support for Rabbi Shach, there was anguished and furious condemnation, emanating as much from hurt as anger, from Israel's non-*haredi* populace. A cartoonist in *Haaretz*, a secular and widely read Israeli newspaper, depicted Rabbi Shach standing on a podium in the middle of a military cemetery, surrounded by graves of kibbutz youth killed in Israel's wars. The rabbi is shown pointing at the tombstones as he calls out the line from his speech: "Can these people be called Jews?" Israel's president Chaim Herzog, the son of the late Israeli chief rabbi Isaac Halevi Herzog, and himself a former general, asked in a radio broadcast "if this nation knows how much it owes to the kibbutzniks, with their work-calloused hands and weather-beaten faces. When I stand at the graves of our war dead, who fought and sacrificed without any thought for political or religious differences, I ask myself whether we should seek their posthumous forgiveness."

Degel Hatorah, the political party Rabbi Shach established (this was during a period when he had broken away from Agudat Yisrael, one reason being that its party newspaper had run ads placed by Chabad), responded to Herzog's words with the demand that he resign for the criminal offense he had committed by "sowing dissent between one section of the populace and another." Rabbi Shach himself, in a speech delivered a year later, warned Herzog that he would be "punished [presumably by God] for his defense of the kibbutzim and their pig-eating."[20]

If Rabbi Shach's intention was to strengthen opposition to the Labor Party among *haredi* Jews, he might well have succeeded (Rabbi Shach was deeply venerated and influential in the *haredi* world, and when he died well over a hundred thousand people attended his funeral). But if his intention was also to cause secular Israelis to reconsider their worldview, his speech seems to have backfired.

Given the divergent nature of Rabbi Shach's and the Rebbe's approaches to non-Orthodox Jews, it is perhaps not surprising that Rabbi Shach had a less than warm view of the Rebbe. Though he had long condemned Chabad in public talks (focusing on, among other things, the campaign to teach the "Seven Noahide Laws" to non-Jews, on the campaign to organize study of Rambam among Jews, and even the Rebbe's organizing of children's parades on Lag B'Omer), what seemed particularly to fuel his ire against the movement was the claim that started to circulate among many Chabad Chasidim in the 1980s, particularly in the last years of the Rebbe's life, that the Rebbe was the Messiah, a claim that the Rebbe himself never made (see chapter 28). On at least one occasion, he described the Rebbe as "the madman who sits in New York and drives the whole world crazy."[21]

In characteristic fashion, the Rebbe never responded to Rabbi Shach by name, though he did offer a full speech in repudiation of his comment that the Jews who were murdered in the Holocaust were being punished for both their and their ancestors' sins. In the Rebbe's words, "as regards the awful events of the last generation [i.e., the Holocaust], it is clear and obvious (*barur ve-pashut*) that they did not come as punishment." [22] He returned to this issue again: "To say that those very people were deserving of what transpired, that it was a punishment for their sins, heaven forbid, is unthinkable. There is absolutely no explanation or understanding for the Holocaust. . . . Certainly not the explanation of a judgment and punishment. No scales of judgment could ever condemn a people to such horrors."

Instead of speaking of the supposed sins of the six million (and their ancestors), the Rebbe spoke of each of the Holocaust victims as martyrs who had died *al kiddush Hashem*, "in sanctification of God's Name." [23] Why, then, did God permit the Holocaust? As the Rebbe once answered a correspondent who challenged him with this question: "The only answer we can give is 'Only God knows.' " [24]

Furthermore, the Rebbe emphasized that evil sometimes reflects rather the ability of evil human beings to misuse their free will. Commenting on the promise offered in Deuteronomy 32:43, "For He [God] will avenge the blood of his servants," the Rebbe noted that the very wording of the Torah verse suggests that the death of these "servants" is against God's will; that is why He will avenge it. In a comment that serves as a response to the view that God was counting the Jewish people's sins, the Rebbe said, "God forbid that one should picture God as a cruel king who punishes His people for their disobedience and then waits until it mounts again to the point at which it is fitting to punish them again." [25] Rather, in the Rebbe's view, God should be depicted not as "the Master of punishment" but as "the Master of mercy." [26]

Chapter 10

ANYTHING WORTH DOING IS
WORTH DOING NOW

"If not now, when?"
—*Hillel, Ethics of the Fathers 1:14*

Bernie Rader, a devoted follower of Chabad from London, was on a business trip to Detroit. One evening, the family who was hosting him invited guests, and soon the main subject of discussion was Judaism. One guest started directing many questions to Rader, specifically concerning tefillin (phylacteries, the black boxes containing verses from the Torah that Jewish men are instructed to put on their head and arm each morning). The questions were quite technical in nature and revealed the questioner's familiarity with the subject: "Why must tefillin be black?" "Why must they be square and not round?" By the time the gathering broke up, it was after one in the morning and Rader couldn't resist asking the man about his great interest in tefillin, not the sort of subject that normally dominates a social get-together. The man denied any particular interest in the subject and even noted that he didn't put tefillin on. With the innate zeal of a Chabadnik, Rader responded, "You should."

Instead of responding to Rader directly, the man started to talk about the fact that while all the other guests were now going home, he was heading to work. A baker, he began his workday in the middle of the night and worked until the afternoon. "But if you feel it's so important for me to put on tefillin," he told Rader, "and if you'd like to be at my bakery at six thirty in the morning when there is a gap between one load of baking and another, and you bring tefillin, I'll put them on."

Rader took the baker up on his offer, and early that morning, standing amidst sacks of flour, the man put on Rader's tefillin. It became immediately apparent that the baker had donned tefillin consistently at some point in his life; he knew exactly how to put them on—for one who has never done so, just learning how to wind the straps around the fingers of one's hand is a process—and the appropriate blessings to make.

When the baker finished praying, Rader asked him, "You know what to do, so why don't you do it regularly?" The man responded that he didn't regard wearing tefillin as a priority and, in any case, he didn't own a pair. Yet, he added, if Rader provided him with a pair, he would put them on regularly. Rader told the man that when he returned on a follow-up trip to Detroit in six weeks, he would be happy to bring a pair of tefillin as a gift (this was a generous offer, as tefillin are expensive; today, a pair can cost many hundreds of dollars, sometimes more).

The following day, Rader flew to New York. He brought a letter to the Rebbe's office in which he wrote about his business dealings in Detroit (the Rebbe had asked to be informed) and in which he mentioned, in passing, the curious incident with the baker and the tefillin. He also told the Rebbe how happy he was that he would be returning the following evening, on Thursday, to London, where, for the first time, his whole family, including all of his children and grandchildren, would spend Shabbat together.

Early the following morning, Rabbi Leibel Groner, the Rebbe's secretary, saw Rader and handed him the Rebbe's response to his letter. Concerning his business dealings, the Rebbe offered him a *bracha* (blessing) that all would proceed well. Regarding the incident with the tefillin, the Rebbe wrote, "Do you think it's right that a Jew who put on tefillin yesterday for perhaps the first time in twenty years should wait six weeks for you to bring him a pair of tefillin? You should buy the tefillin today." Then the Rebbe, aware now of Rader's long-anticipated weekend plans, went even further: "If you can get the tefillin to the man in Detroit so that he can put them on today, do so, but if not, you yourself should go back to Detroit today and put the tefillin on with him, even if this means you won't get to be home with your family for Shabbat." Furthermore, "When this person sees how much it means to you that he has these tefillin straightaway, this mitzvah will have special importance to him."

Rader was taken aback by the Rebbe's response. He immediately set out to buy a pair of tefillin in the surrounding Crown Heights neighborhood. The only pair he found[1] was far more expensive than he had anticipated, but he bought it, then drove immediately to LaGuardia Airport and arranged to have the tefillin travel with the next flight to Detroit. At the same time, he arranged for his host from two nights earlier to meet the plane and bring the tefillin to the baker. After he received word later that afternoon that the baker had received and had put on the tefillin, he informed the Rebbe of what had been accomplished; only then did he set out to join his family for Shabbat in London.

Six weeks later, as Rader had promised, he was back in Detroit, where he made sure to be in touch with the baker. "Do you put on tefillin regularly now?" he asked the man.

The baker explained, "I don't put them on in the morning because I'm busy in the bakery, but I put them on in the afternoon when I get home [in general, tefillin are supposed to be worn at the morning Shacharit service, but they are allowed to be worn anytime before dark]. One day, I was caught in a traffic holdup and I could see that I wasn't going to get home in time [once it becomes dark, it is forbidden to put on tefillin], so I ditched the car and I went home on foot; because it was so important to you that I should put on tefillin, I wasn't going to miss it."[2]

If Rader had acted according to his original plan and brought the tefillin six weeks later, his behavior would have unintentionally conveyed to the baker that it's all right not to wear tefillin for an additional six weeks (much as if a doctor gives a patient a prescription for medication that the doctor regards as very important, yet tells him, "If you don't fill the prescription now, you can fill it when you come back for your next appointment in six weeks"). The man might even have decided that it would be okay to wait another year or two before wearing them or, alternatively, that it is all right to put them on sporadically (maybe today, maybe once again next week, or maybe in six weeks).

It was Rader's understandable willingness to wait six weeks (how many of us would have thought to act any differently?) that struck the Rebbe as so counter to Jewish teachings—*mitzvah ha-ba le-yadcha*, if a mitzvah falls into your hand, seize upon it (*Mechilta, Bo*).

In the case of Rabbi Shabsi Katz, the Rebbe's concern that an opportunity be seized immediately caused him to push the rabbi to do something almost every one of us would be exceedingly uncomfortable doing. When Katz, a rabbi in Pretoria, and the head Jewish chaplain for South Africa's Department of Prisons, came to visit the Rebbe in December 1978, the Rebbe started discussing with him the situation of Jewish prisoners in South Africa, many of whom were incarcerated for political offenses. Katz explained that conditions there were harsher than in the United States, and that the only holidays on which Jews were excused from labor were Passover, Rosh Hashanah, and Yom Kippur; on the first two, the rabbi was also permitted to bring the prisoners food parcels.

"What about Chanukah?" the Rebbe asked. "Are they permitted to light Chanukah candles?" When Rabbi Katz told him that they weren't, the Rebbe started to speak of how important it was for a person in jail to be able to light a Chanukah menorah: "Do you realize how much a little bit of light would mean to a person incarcerated in a dark cell, how important it would be if he could light the candles? Can't you arrange for the prisoners to light Chanukah candles?"

Impressed by the Rebbe's words, Rabbi Katz promised that when he returned to South Africa, he would start negotiating with General Sephton, the religious director of prisons, to ensure that during the following Chanukah, Jewish prisoners would be permitted to light candles.

"What about this Chanukah?" the Rebbe asked him.

Katz was taken aback, as it was now only a day before the holiday. He explained that because he was in New York, thousands of miles away from Pretoria, there was nothing he could do. The Rebbe did not agree. He told Katz that as soon as their meeting ended, he could use one of the telephones in the outer office to make any calls that were necessary.

"It is the middle of the night in South Africa," Katz explained. How could the Rebbe expect him to call the general at three or four in the morning?

The Rebbe answered that now would be precisely the right time to call. When the general, who was also an ordained minister in the Dutch Reformed Church, saw that the matter was so important to Katz that he was calling him in the middle of the night, he would be impressed by the matter's urgency.

As soon as Katz left the Rebbe's office, one of the secretaries escorted him to a small nearby office, showed him the phones, and told him to make any calls he needed.

First, Rabbi Katz called his secretary in Pretoria and asked her to find the home phone number for General Sephton, call him, and tell him that he would soon be getting an international call from the United States. When he called Sephton a few minutes later, the general was prepared for the call, though obviously he was more than a little curious about the nature of this matter that was so important that it had motivated Rabbi Katz, whom he knew quite well, to call him at such an hour. Katz explained that he had just been meeting with a rabbi who was one of the leaders of the Jewish people, and who had expressed tremendous concern about the Jews in South Africa's prisons. He explained how important it was that they be allowed to light Chanukah candles and that doing so would bring them light and hope.

To Rabbi Katz's surprise and relief, General Sephton answered that he understood from the call—coming from overseas in the middle of the night—how urgent the matter was, and he promised that he would go into his office in the morning and telex all the prison facilities in South Africa and instruct them to make it possible for Jewish prisoners to light Chanukah candles.

The following morning, when the Rebbe came to 770, Rabbi Katz was waiting for him in the foyer and had the pleasure of telling him how successfully the mission had gone. The Rebbe smiled broadly, then told Katz he wanted to see him again in a short while. This time, when he entered the Rebbe's office, the Rebbe explained that in New York, the state with the largest Jewish population, Jewish prisoners were not allowed to light Chanukah candles: "I would like you to try to do something about that," the Rebbe told him.

For the second time within twenty-four hours, Rabbi Katz was taken aback. First of all, it was now December 24 and Chanukah would be starting in a few hours. Second, unlike South Africa where he knew the people to contact, in New York he had no connections to the prison system. Where would he even start?

The Rebbe told him to go to Rabbi J. J. Hecht's office. Rabbi Hecht already had some knowledge of the matter and would know to whom to direct him. Hecht gave him a name and contact information and Katz called the official in charge. He reached the man at an office Christmas party. Unsurprisingly, the official was a bit taken aback to get a call at such a time but, as was the case with the prison official in South Africa, he quickly concluded that if this rabbi was calling him at so inconvenient a time, just prior to the major Christian holiday of the year, the issue should be taken seriously. When Katz explained that he had been able to work out the matter with the prison official in South Africa—a country that was known to be quite repressive—the official concluded that he could do so in New York as well.[3]

Sure enough, Rabbi Katz had the pleasure of telling the Rebbe yet again that his mission had succeeded, and the Rebbe gave him a special, beautifully bound edition of the *Tanya* for his son (when Rabbi Katz said he didn't want a gift for what he had done, the Rebbe said, "I don't want to owe debts"); he also gave him two English-language books about Chabad, one for General Sephton and one for Sephton's wife.

Upon his return to South Africa, and within twenty minutes of his calling General Sephton and telling him of the gift he was holding for him, Sephton was at Katz's house: "When I heard that your rabbi, sitting there in Brooklyn in America, was thinking about me [and the prisoners] here in Pretoria, I felt I had to get to your house as quickly as possible to collect these books."[4]

The Rebbe issued a similar sort of challenge to Frank Lautenberg, the future New Jersey senator, who was then serving as the national chairman of the United Jewish Appeal (UJA). At a meeting between the two men (which Lautenberg taped), the discussion between Lautenberg and the Rebbe touched on many issues, among them financial support for Jewish schools and aid for Jews in other countries. The Rebbe pressed Lautenberg to bring about certain changes in both these areas, and Lautenberg assured him that he would start working on the matter the following day.

"If you start tonight, you will change it," the Rebbe responded.

"It's not a process we can do overnight."

"How do you know?" the Rebbe said.

"How do I know?" Lautenberg responded rhetorically, and gave a small laugh.

The Rebbe didn't back down. "At least give yourself the benefit of the doubt. Try to do it overnight, and I am certain you will see results."

"How do you do it overnight?" Lautenberg asked.

"You have a secretary, you phone her tonight [even] in the middle of the night, and tell her you have a new instruction page [to be included with your proposals]."[5]

Unlike the case with Rabbi Katz, we do not know whether Lautenberg followed through on the Rebbe's suggestion. What is clear, though, is that whether it was a question of a day, a few hours, or even minutes, the Rebbe pushed to see that if a task could be accomplished, it be accomplished as soon as possible.

Esther Sternberg, who ran the Shabbat candle campaign, recalls an incident that began only twenty minutes before Shabbat, when she received a phone call from the Rebbe's office saying that the Rebbe had just read a letter from the father of a young girl in Bowie, Maryland, who wanted his daughter to start lighting Shabbat candles. The Rebbe requested that Sternberg be contacted and see to it that the girl light candles that Shabbat.

As Mrs. Sternberg recalls: "I immediately called the *shliach* in the town nearest the girl, hoping that he could rush candles to her in time, but he told me that there would be no way for him to reach the girl's home before sunset; Bowie was two hours away. I then called the girl's home and spoke to her mother. I asked if she had any candles in the house. She answered that, indeed, she had candles that she used for formal dinner parties. I asked her to give a candle to her daughter to light for Shabbat. I then asked the mother if she, too, would light. She said that she had no objections but that she had no idea how to do it. If I could instruct her over the phone, then she and her daughter would both light candles together." Mrs. Sternberg instructed the mother on the procedure, and the woman wrote down the transliteration of the blessing word for word.

The following Friday, close to candlelighting time, Sternberg received another call from the Rebbe's secretary. "The Rebbe wants to know, 'What's happening with the girl in Bowie, Maryland?'" Mrs. Sternberg was glad to report that the girl and her mother had both lit candles the previous week and had told Sternberg that they had received the candleholders she had since sent and would use them that night.

But Sternberg had more to report. During a second conversation with the mother, Mrs. Sternberg also asked the woman if her daughter had friends who would like candleholders. The mother said that there were several Jewish girls in town who she was sure would be interested; also, she could think of some women in her *chavurah* (a group of friends who study and practice Judaism together), and several other friends as well. Mrs. Sternberg ended up sending more than forty candleholders to Bowie.[6]

All this happened because a father had written a letter to the Rebbe, and the Rebbe, checking his watch, saw that there were still twenty minutes that could be utilized. The matter didn't have to wait until the following Friday; the change could be initiated that very day.

These sorts of incidents involving the Rebbe conveyed a mind-set to those who regarded themselves as his disciples, and profoundly influenced their perception of what they were capable of. Rabbi Moshe Bryski, a Chabad *shliach* in Southern California's Canejo Valley for more than twenty-five years, recalls his first Rosh Hashanah there, leading what was then a very small congregation. When the service ended, he explained to the participants the ritual of *Tashlich*, the ceremony in which Jews symbolically rid themselves of their sins by throwing them into the sea (the ceremony, therefore, is performed near a body of water). He invited those who wished to carry out this tradition to walk with him to a nearby lake. En route, one of the walkers pointed out a shortcut the group could take through the parking lot of a condominium complex. As they proceeded, Rabbi Bryski saw an elderly woman coming toward them using a walker. When she saw the group she became excited and started calling out, *"Gut Yom Tov! Gut Yom Tov!"* ("Good Holiday!"), the traditional greeting on Jewish holidays. The woman explained that a few weeks earlier, she had surgery on one of her legs, and this was the first Rosh Hashanah in her life that she had been unable to go to services. She had been crying the whole day because she couldn't be in shul (synagogue). Now, for the first time since the surgery, she was able to get out of bed and take a few steps outside. "And who does she bump into?" Rabbi Bryski thought, "A walking shul." Bryski spoke to the woman for a few minutes, wished her a complete recovery, and expressed the hope that soon she would surely be well enough to come to shul.

A few minutes later, as he was standing at the lake preparing to cast his sins into the water, Bryski felt a sudden feeling of heaviness, a sense that he had been presented with a wonderful opportunity and had failed miserably: "What had happened was that a woman had cried out to God, 'Master of the Universe, I didn't hear the shofar today, and it's the first time in my life that I wasn't in shul on Rosh Hashanah and I feel terrible.'"

Rabbi Bryski remembered the thoughts that coursed through his mind. God had given this woman the strength to get out bed for the first time in weeks and, in effect, told her, "Take your walker and go out, and I will arrange for a *shliach* of the Lubavitcher Rebbe to walk by at that precise moment—and even if he starts going a different way, I'll make sure that someone convinces him to take a shortcut that crosses right where you are walking." And surely, Rabbi Bryski thought, it must have occurred to the Almighty that a *shliach* of the Rebbe will be carrying a shofar with him on Rosh Hashanah, just in case he encounters a Jew who hadn't heard the shofar blown that day. But that hadn't happened. The emissary of the Rebbe—the despairing Bryski thought—forgot to take a shofar with him.

On the way home from *Tashlich,* Bryski and his small congregation went the same route to see if the woman was still there, but she wasn't. "I couldn't sleep that night, thinking of how I had failed the Rebbe, had failed this woman, had failed God."

The next day, the second day of the holiday, he recounted the episode in his shul and asked for volunteers to help him find the woman so he could blow the shofar for her. When services were finished, the group returned to the same area and started going door to door, asking everyone, "Do you by any chance know this woman who walks with a walker?" It took an hour of knocking on doors until someone realized who Bryski was talking about and pointed him in the direction of one condo.

He knocked on the door, and when a man answered, Rabbi Bryski said to him, "I know this is an odd question, but does your wife use a walker? Did she have surgery a few weeks ago?" It turned out that he was at the right house. When he explained to the man that he had messed up the preceding day but that he had now come to blow the shofar for the man's wife, the man slammed the door in his face. He knocked again, assured the man that it would take but a few minutes, and that he was not asking for any money. This time the man yelled at him, "Go away!" and slammed the door again.

Bryski, now feeling very dejected, started to walk away, but then he heard the woman calling out to him from the condo's back patio. "Rabbi, please don't go." She told him that he should come back and she would make sure that her husband let him in. This time, the man opened the door, but before Bryski could say a word, he ran down the hall. The woman, understanding the oddity of her husband's behavior, explained to Bryski that her husband was furious with religious Jews because their son had become Orthodox and was now refusing to eat in their house. "He's angry," she said, "and he let it out on you." Bryski explained that God had listened to her prayers so that she could hear the shofar; he then went and invited the husband to come listen to the shofar blowing as well. He assured the man that tomorrow—the holiday would be ending that night—he would contact the son and find a way to arrange for the boy to be able to eat in his parents' house (for one thing, by providing the parents with a new toaster oven and microwave that would only be used for kosher food). Eventually the man agreed, and then he arranged for Bryski to go with him to retrieve his brother so that he, too, could hear the shofar.

The holiday ended and, after some negotiations, Rabbi Bryski was able to make peace between the son and his father and to bring the family together in harmony.

But of course, all of this would not have happened had Bryski made only the initial effort after *Tashlich* to find the woman and then given up, assuring himself that the woman would eventually recover and perhaps show up at his synagogue at some future date. I suspect that that is how the large majority of us would have acted (that is, make a single effort and then give up), and that likely is how Bryski himself would have behaved if the Rebbe hadn't modeled for him and for all *shluchim* a different form of behavior—that if something is worth doing, you do it now and don't stop trying, even if it is highly inconvenient and even if it seems unlikely that you will succeed (even after finding the woman's apartment, he still had to deal with her husband, who twice slammed a door in his face). Had Bryski acted as most of us would have, the woman would not have heard the shofar, nor would her husband and brother-in-law, and no less important, the relationship between the man and his son would likely have deteriorated further.

Chapter 11

JUDAISM'S MISSION TO THE WORLD

"We are not two sides. We are one side.
We are one people living in one city under
one administration and under one God."

In 1990, Geoffrey and James Davis, two African American community activists in Brooklyn (James Davis later became a New York
City councilman), founded an organization, Love Yourself: Stop the
Violence, with the goal of increasing self-esteem and lowering violence
in American life, particularly within the black community.

In a 2012 interview, Geoffrey Davis revealed that the initial inspiration
for much of his work, and even his organization's name, was the Rebbe:
"Our whole life career-wise was because of a lot of the teachings that he
taught us." As Davis related, he and his brother grew up on Brooklyn
Avenue, a block from the Rebbe's house. The two boys used to play ball
in the street, and the Rebbe, walking home from synagogue, would
often stop to chat with them: "We embraced him because he embraced
us," Davis remarks of their frequent informal conversations. He recalled
one incident in particular when he was about twelve, and he and his
brother were arguing over a ball game. The dispute was growing heated
and at that moment the Rebbe walked by. After telling them to behave,
he immediately added words that Davis insists forever changed his and
his brother's life: "Love your brother as you love yourself. And love yourself as you love your brother, because you're one, so love yourself."[1]

At the time these encounters occurred, starting in the mid-1970s,
neither brother knew just who this man was, only that he was "a nice

friendly man" who always spoke to them warmly and used to give each boy a dollar. They eventually learned that he was the "Grand Rebbe" of Chabad, and some fifteen years later, when they founded the organization Love Yourself: Stop the Violence, it was the Rebbe's words that framed their goal: "We have his picture hanging in our house not because he was a Grand Rebbe, but because he was our friend, somebody who took a liking to two children. He didn't look like us, but he opened the door for us to communicate and to embrace all human beings."

Is this story unusual? It would be nice to say that it isn't, but this tale of a prominent rabbi befriending and deeply influencing two non-Jewish children is not a common one. Yet it represents the sort of world the Rebbe wanted to help shape. His love of Jews, intense as it was, did not come at the expense of others. Indeed, when dealing with correspondence, the Rebbe usually responded first to letters addressed to him by non-Jews: "My Chasidim will understand the delay; others might feel slighted."[2] In a remarkable and infrequently commented-upon encounter with David Dinkins, New York City's first black mayor, the Rebbe told Mayor Dinkins: "I hope that in the near future, the 'melting pot' [of America] will be so active that it will not be necessary to underline every time [when speaking of others], 'They are Negro,' or 'They are White,' or 'They are Hispanic,' because *they* are no different. All of them are created by the same God and created for the same purpose, to add to all good things around them."[3]

Not surprisingly, the Rebbe's embracing attitude and behavior influenced those around him. We have related elsewhere how the Rebbe requested, as a birthday present for himself, that David Chase pray daily, and Chase agreed to do so. Some time later, Chase, a successful businessman and philanthropist, was vacationing on his yacht. Each morning he would ask the captain in which direction—north, south, east, west—the boat was heading. After several days of such questions, the captain, a man named Dick Winters, asked Chase, "Are you studying navigation? Are you trying to learn how to run a boat?" Chase answered no. The reason he needed to know the ship's direction was that each morning he prayed, and the Jewish tradition is to face east, in the direction of Jerusalem, while praying. He told Winters: "I don't want to start up facing east and wind up facing south because the ship is turning."

The captain asked Chase how much time he needed for his prayers. Chase told him twenty minutes, and Winters assured him that during those twenty minutes he would not change course. That way, Chase could face east without trepidation.

A few days later, on Sunday morning, the boat pulled into Block Island and Winters came to Chase with a request to leave the boat for an hour or two. Chase answered yes and asked the captain where he was going. "I would like to go to church," Winters answered. "You pray to your God every morning, and you're making me feel guilty that I don't follow my faith. So I want to go to church and say my prayers."

At his next visit to 770, Chase told the Rebbe about this incident.[4] The Rebbe, to quote Chase, "got a big kick out of it," and the businessman learned that the Rebbe shortly thereafter spoke of this event at a public lecture; he wanted his Chasidim to know that their behavior could encourage non-Jews, not just Jews, to come closer to God.[5]

Bringing non-Jews closer to God was not a goal that would have occurred to, let alone preoccupy, many Jewish leaders. Indeed, throughout the Jewish people's millennia-long history in exile, they generally did little to make known their religious teachings to the non-Jewish world. As a rule, Jews encountered so much hostility in the societies in which they lived that their primary hope was simply that the non-Jewish world would leave them alone. And so the Jewish people generally made no effort to discuss the notion of God and His demands of human beings with non-Jews. Therefore, when the Rebbe launched his campaign in 1980 to bring knowledge of the *sheva mitzvot b'nai Noach* (the Seven Noahide Laws) to the non-Jewish world, many Jews, particularly in the Orthodox world, were surprised and some were upset.

Indeed, if going out into the world with religious teachings was a value, they wanted to know, why do we not find efforts by earlier Chabad Rebbes, scholars such as the Alter Rebbe, the Tzemach Tzedek, and the Rebbe's own father-in-law, the Frierdiker Rebbe, to educate non-Jews about God's expectations of them?[6] The Rebbe's response was that his program did not represent a change in ideology but a recognition of a change in historical circumstances. God, he asserted, has always wanted Jews to reach out to the non-Jewish world—He is, after all, the God of all humankind, not just of the Jews—but until now there was no opportunity to do so; the environments in which Jews lived were too hostile. In czarist Russia where Chabad originated, the government orchestrated pogroms against the Jews and sometimes organized campaigns to convert Jews to Russian Orthodoxy. In such a society, there was no openness on the part of non-Jews to Jewish teachings. And in Communist Russia, the successor government to the czars, the government's decades-long campaign to wipe out Judaism (and other religions as well) would have made any Jewish effort at educating non-Jews about God a suicide mission.

But America, the Rebbe concluded, was different.[7] A nation of high ideals—the Rebbe routinely referred to the United States as a "government of kindness" (*malchut shel chesed*)—he saw America as perhaps the first society in which there was a hope of carrying out Judaism's universal mission: not to make the whole world Jewish but to bring the world, starting with the United States, to a full awareness of One God, Who demands of human beings moral behavior. The Rebbe was deeply impressed by the fact that the country's currency carried the words "In God we trust," and he was struck as well by yet another of America's foundational principles, *e pluribus unum* ("from many, one"). At yet another meeting with Mayor Dinkins, during a tense period following anti-Jewish rioting in Crown Heights in which a Jewish man, Yankel Rosenbaum, had been murdered in the aftermath of a car accident in which a black child, Gavin Cato, had been killed, the Rebbe expressed the hope that the mayor would be able to bring peace to the city. "To both sides," Dinkins responded. The Rebbe replied, "We are not two sides. We are one side. We are one people living in one city under one administration and under one God. May God protect the police and all the people of the city."[8] For the Rebbe, and he emphasized this on different occasions, "From many, one" and "In God we trust" were the bedrock of the United States' power and specialness.

This is why the Rebbe reacted with such concern and upset when the Supreme Court outlawed all prayers and any acknowledgment of God in the country's public schools; the United States, he feared, would be in danger of great moral deterioration if the next generation was not raised with a belief in a God before Whom each individual was responsible (see chapter 19).

The Rebbe's vision of how to safeguard the values that defined America and all moral societies was best articulated in a speech prepared for presentation at the United Nations on October 21, 1987, by Dr. Nissen Mindel, the Rebbe's secretary, and the man in charge of all of the Rebbe's English-language correspondence (unfortunately, in the end, the UN speech did not take place). Mindel based the draft of the speech on the Rebbe's teachings, and the speech itself was edited by the Rebbe (all citations are drawn from a copy of the speech that contains the Rebbe's handwritten emendations).

Early in the text of the speech, Mindel raised the issue of ongoing problems of lawlessness and violence throughout the world and then posed the question: "Is there perhaps a basic universal moral code that would be acceptable to all nations, all of humankind?"

There was indeed such a code: "We are talking about a G-d-given moral code which has served as the foundation of human society from its very inception . . . the Seven Noahide Laws," the ordinances that Jewish tradition teaches that God gave to Noah and his children in the aftermath of the biblically recorded flood ("children of Noah" is the rabbinic term for non-Jews; "children of Abraham" is the rabbinic term for Jews): "These [seven laws] were to serve as the minimum set of Divine injunctions for all mankind in order that [the world] not degenerate into a [place of lawlessness and violence].

"The Seven Laws of the Children of Noah:

1. Prohibition of idolatry
2. Prohibition of blasphemy
3. Prohibition of homicide
4. Prohibition of incest
5. Prohibition of robbery
6. Prohibition of eating the limb of a living animal
7. Institution of courts of justice (*Sanhedrin* 56a, based on Genesis 9).[9]

The text continues, "The Jewish people were assigned the task and the obligation of disseminating and promoting the Seven Noahide Laws in their immediate society and in the world at large."

Mindel's draft of the speech made reference several times to the "Gentile world" and the obligation of the Jews to bring God's teachings to them. The Rebbe repeatedly crossed out the word "Gentile"; he was not interested in this context in emphasizing a Jewish/Gentile dichotomy but in establishing that God's message is directed to all humanity.

Similarly, the fundamental factor motivating the launching of the 1980 Seven Noahide Laws (*Sheva Mitzvot*) campaign was to make God and his ethical demands known to the world. When Jews are spoken of as "the Chosen People," the Rebbe believed, it is this mission—to bring knowledge of God into the world—for which they were chosen. (Whether or not one believes that the Jews were in fact chosen by God for this mission, it is historically undeniable that it is through the Jews that the concept of One God became known to humankind.)

Making God and His moral demands of human beings known to non-Jews was regarded by the Rebbe as equal in significance to promoting knowledge and practice of the commandments (*mitzvot*) among Jews, a universalist position that one does not find, to say the least, echoed widely in traditional Jewish circles.[10]

Perhaps the cause with which the Rebbe became most associated in the American mind was his emphasis on education. In the late 1970s, the Rebbe's *shliach* Rabbi Avraham Shemtov joined the Rebbe's campaign to help establish the Department of Education as a separate cabinet-level position (until then, education was subsumed into the Department of Health, Education, and Welfare), which President Carter subsequently did. In honor of the Rebbe's involvement in this cause, the president declared the Rebbe's seventy-sixth birthday in 1978 as the first Education Day U.S.A. Since then, Education Day U.S.A., commemorated on the Rebbe's birthday, has become a part of the American calendar, and has been signed into effect every year by the president.

In the Rebbe's thank-you letter to President Ronald Reagan for declaring the 1987 Education Day U.S.A., the Rebbe noted that the proclamation itself, issued by the American government, spoke of "the historical tradition of ethical values and principles which have been the bedrock of society from the dawn of civilization when they were known as 'The Seven Noahide Laws.' " [11]

The Rebbe's role in the focus on education was acknowledged in a talk given in honor of the third anniversary of his death by Richard Riley, then serving as secretary of education under President Bill Clinton. In speaking of the creation of the Department of Education, Riley noted that the Rebbe helped "make it happen. *So I owe my job to him*" (emphasis added).

But the truth is, while the Rebbe prized intellectual achievements, the education in which he was most interested was moral education. Having attended university in Germany in the late 1920s and early 1930s, he knew firsthand that academic excellence in and of itself is no predictor of moral behavior: "For it is precisely the nation which had excelled itself in the exact sciences, the humanities, and even in philosophy and ethics, that turned out to be the most depraved nation in the world" (see page 258).

The Rebbe wanted education, and not fear of police or of incarceration, to foster morality. As he emphasized in the speech composed for the UN: "Respect for law and order will not be instilled by fear of punishment, especially when the delinquent juvenile or adult may feel that he can outsmart the cop and the judge. What will make a human being a better and more decent person is awareness that there is 'an eye that sees and an ear that hears,' an awareness of always being present in the presence of a Supreme Being—our Heavenly Father who cares how every one of his children conducts himself or herself, and before whom every one of us will have to account for our every action, word, and thought."

Part Four

·❦·

LIFE LESSONS

According to the

REBBE

·(⟨⟩)·

Chapter 12

"IT IS A COMMANDMENT
TO TELL THE STORY"

The Rebbe and Journalism

"Do you have a right to withhold that which you know?"

In 1972, the veteran journalist Gershon Jacobson was considering starting a new Yiddish newspaper (*Der Tog Morgen Zhurnal* had recently closed) and he went to consult with the Rebbe. When Jacobson expressed concern because "people say Yiddish is dying," the Rebbe responded: "They said the same thing fifty years ago, and they'll say it fifty years from now." Encouraged, Jacobson asked if he should proceed with such an undertaking, and the Rebbe responded, "Absolutely." He even came up with the name *Algemeiner Journal*, a "Journal of General Interest."

Jacobson liked the title and asked, "Should we then call it the *Algemeiner Vochin Journal* [*Algemeiner Weekly Journal*]?" The Rebbe answered, "Why limit it? It's weekly now, maybe . . . ?"

Jacobson should not have been surprised by the Rebbe's encouragement. An omnivorously curious person, newspapers had long mattered to the Rebbe, as vehicles for both acquiring knowledge and disseminating it. There are people who lived in Crown Heights in the 1940s who recall seeing him heading for the subway station in the morning, carrying four newspapers, the *New York Times*, the Yiddish *Der Tog Morgen Zhurnal*, a newspaper in French, and another in Russian (the newsstand special ordered these last two for him).

The fact that he was reading newspapers in four languages suggests not only the Rebbe's unusual linguistic abilities but also bears testimony to his lifelong belief in the importance of having a wide variety of sources for acquiring information. His nephew, Barry Gourary, recalls seeing the Rebbe carefully reading newspapers during the time the young Gourary—who was then six—spent in Berlin in 1929 and 1930: "I remember observing that my uncle was an avid reader of . . . many daily newspapers. He was very interested in politics. He was also fascinated with military strategy. This was one of the areas that was always of interest to him." [1] The intimate knowledge of military matters was a feature of the Rebbe frequently commented upon by Israeli political and military leaders who met with him. When Yitzchak Rabin, then serving as Israel's ambassador to the United States, but formerly chief of staff of the Israel Defense Forces (IDF), emerged from a *yechidus* with the Rebbe, he commented to his adviser, Yehuda Avner, "That man knows more about what's going on in Israel than most of the members of our Knesset put together."

Once he became Rebbe, the burdens of responsibility diminished his time for newspapers, and soon he was largely confined to reading articles that were sent to him by others around the world or that had been cut out and given to him by his office staff and his wife; it was the Rebbetzin in particular who brought to his attention articles from newspapers and magazines in languages other than English. His recall of what he read remained acute. Rabbi Asher Zeilingold, a Chabad rabbi sent by the Rebbe to a congregation in Minnesota, used to send the Rebbe pages from the local St. Paul newspaper that contained articles dealing with synagogue activities. Once, Rabbi Zeilingold sent a question to the Rebbe that had been posed to him by a local Jew. The man had a beard but had been told by his employer that he needed to cut it off; the company did not want bearded employees. The man sought guidance from Rabbi Zeilingold as to what he should do, and the rabbi forwarded the question to the Rebbe.

The Rebbe recalled a photograph he had seen on one of the newspaper pages Zeilingold sent to him of the mayor of St. Paul, George Latimer, wearing a beard. As beards were quite uncommon then in

American society, a bearded mayor presumably made an impression on the Rebbe. Nonetheless, how many people would notice and remember such a detail? The Rebbe wrote back that the man should tell his boss that if it was okay for the mayor to wear a beard purely for pleasure, it should be okay for him to wear a beard for religious reasons. The appeal succeeded.[2]

Newspapers were also recognized by the Rebbe as an important vehicle for disseminating knowledge. Rabbi Hirsch Chitrik, a wealthy Chabad businessman, was once summoned by the Rebbe, who told him of a newspaper with Conservative Jewish leanings that was suffering financial setbacks and was in danger of closing. He asked Chitrik to find out how much money the publication needed, and he, the Rebbe, would supply it (though he did not wish his involvement to become known). Chitrik was shocked. Why was the Rebbe concerned with supporting a Conservative-leaning paper, given that its views on matters of Jewish law and thought were so at variance with those of the Rebbe? The Rebbe told him that each week the publication supplied the right time at which people were supposed to light Shabbat candles; if the paper ceased to publish, those who relied on it would no longer have easy access to such information.

Similarly, when speaking to Jacobson, the Rebbe mentioned in passing the role newspapers could play in educating Jews who might not otherwise be reached. He told Jacobson of an incident from the 1930s, when his father-in-law, the Frierdiker Rebbe, lived in Warsaw. "He said to me that I should go find a newspaper that will publish his talks. So I came back with a list of three or four newspapers and my father-in-law said, 'In all of Warsaw there are only three or four Jewish newspapers?' "[3]

"I answered, 'No, but these are the religious ones.'

"And the [Frierdiker] Rebbe said to me, 'If I want to reach only religious Jews, we could put these writings in every *shtiebel* and shul in Warsaw. I want to reach Jews who don't go to synagogue.' "

The Rebbe told Jacobson that he eventually found a Socialist-leaning paper that was willing to publish his father-in-law's talks.

But the Rebbe didn't penetrate only the world of Yiddish newspapers. Rabbi Joseph Soloveitchik spoke with great admiration of Chabad's impact on the American press: "In the past, when a Jewish issue came up, the major newspapers such as the *New York Times* would only cite the viewpoints of representatives of Reform Judaism. Orthodoxy did not exist for them. Nowadays, the Lubavitch movement has placed Orthodoxy in these newspapers, and on the radio and television" (interview in *Ma'ariv*, October 28, 1977).

Jacobson soon went ahead with his decision to begin the *Algemeiner Journal*. In time, as the newspaper became known and its influence grew, a local Crown Heights rabbi suggested to him that a group of rabbis check over the weekly paper in advance to make sure the content was appropriate.

"Did anyone ask the Rebbe about this?" Jacobson inquired.

The rabbi said: "We think this is what the Rebbe would want."

Jacobson went in to ask the Rebbe, telling him that some people wanted to set up a kind of rabbinic supervision bureau to determine what should and shouldn't be put into the paper.

The Rebbe smiled: "And what will you do if these rabbis decide that the newspaper should be closed down?"

Jacobson said: "So what's the Rebbe's opinion?"

The Rebbe lifted his hands in a way that was clearly dismissive of the other rabbi's message to Jacobson. "What do rabbis have to do with a newspaper? A rabbi should *pasken* [rule] that a Jew should be learning Torah all day, and every second that's free is *bittul Torah* [wasted time that should be spent studying Torah]. So how are rabbis going to issue a ruling regarding a newspaper when they should be telling a person not to read newspapers but to study Torah? Newspapers are for people who don't listen to rabbis or who don't ask rabbis. And when you put into the paper a few words of Torah, you will be reaching such people."

To make certain he was clear about the Rebbe's attitude toward the direction the *Algemeiner Journal* should take, Jacobson asked if the paper should establish a formal affiliation with Lubavitch.

This, the Rebbe opposed: "A Lubavitch newspaper is a contradiction in terms. You have to look at everything in terms of its mission. The mission of Lubavitch is to help people access their Jewishness [*Yiddishkeit*]. The mission of a newspaper is to have more readers and be a successful media outlet. A newspaper has its goals and Lubavitch has its goals. As far as your editorial positions are concerned, that's your decision."

These thoughts in particular were refreshing and liberating. Newspapers and magazines published under Orthodox auspices generally adhere to a very restricted editorial line, more or less identical with the beliefs of the publisher or the organization supporting the publication. However, because the *Algemeiner Journal* had no organizational affiliation, Jacobson could follow his instincts and keep the paper open to opinions with which he—and the Rebbe as well—disagreed.

On one occasion, he feared he had gone too far. At a *farbrengen* during a period of tension in the Middle East, the Rebbe spoke of the grave situation facing the region and, of course, Israel. "The world is shaking," he said, and if rabbis would decide to issue a call for a half-day fast, he wouldn't oppose it (Chabad traditionally opposes fasting other than on those days designated by Jewish law). Soon thereafter the Union of Orthodox Rabbis declared such a fast. An *Algemeiner* correspondent, Shlomo Shamir, a religious Jew from a Gerer Chasidic background, wrote a column attacking the rabbis for their action. "Why All of a Sudden a Fast?" he headlined the piece. The substance of the column was that the situation in Israel was the same as it had been in recent months, and it made no sense to suddenly declare a fast as if some grave danger were facing the country.

At a *farbrengen* a few days later, on December 15, 1979, the Rebbe spoke critically of Shamir's column (in keeping with the Rebbe's practice of not expressing criticism in personal terms, he didn't mention Shamir by name) and expressed his distress that a journalist from a religious background should write in so dismissive a manner of Jews undertaking a religious fast in the face of the current situation. The Rebbe explained why he, unlike Shamir, did feel the situation now was so serious. A short time earlier, an organized group of young Iranians, clearly operating with government approval, had occupied the American embassy and taken over fifty American hostages. The Rebbe reasoned that if such acts were being carried out by Iran against the United States, the strongest country in the world, it meant that a great escalation of evil was occurring in the Middle East, and the gravity of the situation is what prompted him to support a fast.

Gershon Jacobson felt bad and told the Rebbe that he wanted to apologize for publishing an article that caused so much aggravation (Shamir himself, after hearing the Rebbe's reasoning for supporting such a fast, wrote a letter to him apologizing for the tone of his article).

The Rebbe assured Jacobson that he had done nothing for which he needed to apologize. "You have to do your job, I have to do my job. You're a newspaper. You're not supposed to be censoring opinions. What I'm saying is what I have to do."

What's most apparent from this episode was the open-mindedness of the Rebbe. He wasn't trying to stop other people from expressing their views, but at the same time, if someone said something with which he didn't agree, he felt he was as entitled as anyone else to say what he did think and why he disagreed. According to Simon Jacobson, Gershon's son—the current publisher of the *Algemeiner Journal* and author of *Toward a Meaningful Life: The Wisdom of the Rebbe Menachem Mendel Schneerson*—this incident helped shape his future thinking: "I learned from this episode that a person can totally disagree with another opinion without feeling that the other opinion has to be silenced. Confidence in your idea means that you don't have to make other people wrong for you to be right. Unfortunately, there are many people, among them many religious people, who don't have this attitude." Jacobson noted his appreciation that he learned this strong belief in tolerance and the need for a free press from the Rebbe and that he learned it at an early age.

The Rebbe's opposition to censorship was reflected in another encounter with Gershon Jacobson. The two men were talking about a variety of issues in the Jewish world when the Rebbe suddenly asked him, "You're a journalist, so if you'd like you can interview me." Jacobson was startled because the Rebbe almost never gave interviews to journalists. "Can I ask anything?" Jacobson wanted to know, or were there some topics to be regarded as off-limits. The Rebbe said, "An interview's an interview. You don't censor an interview" (for the Rebbe's response to Jacobson's first question, see pages 202–3).

Jacobson not only published journalists such as Shlomo Shamir, a religious Jew with views moderately to the left of the Rebbe, but he also published, on an ongoing basis, columns by Nathan Yellin-Mor, a decidedly nonreligious Jew and a man who held views on the far left. In his early years, Yellin-Mor had been one of the three leaders of Lehi, the pre-state organization that carried out anti-British violence to force the British out of Palestine. After Israel became a state in 1948, Lehi's two other leaders, Yitzhak Shamir, a future prime minister of Israel, and Israel Eldad, became ardent Israeli nationalists and proponents of right-wing ideologies. In contrast, Yellin-Mor emerged in the 1950s as a very early supporter of negotiations with the Palestinians over the creation of a Palestinian state alongside Israel. As the Palestinian leadership then uniformly opposed Israel's right to exist as a state, his political views were shared only by those on the far left. Although Jacobson strongly disagreed with Yellin-Mor's views on both political and religious issues, he admired him for several things, among them his courage, his clear vision of what he advocated, and his considerable writing abilities in Yiddish. Therefore, he concluded that it was worthwhile for his newspaper to give Yellin-Mor a forum. In turn, Jacobson would, on occasion, forcefully and critically respond to Yellin-Mor's articles in his own columns, and these controversies, he believed, generated interest in the paper and good discussions: "My father was a believer that you let someone speak and then argue the point. You know, we Jews are smart people; we don't have to be afraid to hear another opinion."

On one occasion in 1976, Yellin-Mor was visiting the United States and Jacobson suggested that he come with him to see the Rebbe. He asked Yellin-Mor to come on the night immediately following the Jewish holiday of Shavuot when it was the Rebbe's custom to give all visitors a *kos shel bracha*, a cup of wine, along with a blessing.

Jacobson introduced Yellin-Mor to the Rebbe. The Rebbe smiled at the journalist and told him, "I read your column every week."

Yellin-Mor was taken aback. He, who had little dealings with rabbis, certainly did not expect to receive such recognition from a Chasidic Rebbe. The Rebbe then continued: "God blessed you with the ability to write, so you should continue using your talent and use it to the fullest, and continue to write and God should bless you that you should be successful."

The journalist, well aware of the content of the articles that the Rebbe had read, was startled. He asked: "Does the Rebbe agree with what I write?"

The Rebbe answered: "Not everything one reads does one have to agree with. You have to continue writing and, hopefully, as you continue writing you'll come closer to *emet* [truth] as you evolve and become a better writer."

It was clear to Jacobson from the expression on Yellin-Mor's face that he had been touched by the Rebbe's words. But the Rebbe was not finished: "Tell me," he asked the journalist, "how are things by you with Torah and *mitzvot* [observance of the commandments]?"

Yellin-Mor later told Jacobson the mixture of thoughts that went through his mind when the Rebbe posed this question. On the one hand, he didn't want to respond with some formulaic religious expression, such as *Baruch Hashem* ("Blessed is God"), and thereby pretend to a greater piety than he possessed. But he also didn't want to say the truth, that he hardly observed Jewish ritual laws. Instead, he answered ambiguously, *"A Yid tracht* ['A Jew thinks']."

The Rebbe did not back off. "But Judaism is not about thinking, it's about doing."

Yellin-Mor responded, "Well, at least I'm in the category of the man in the story they tell about Rabbi Levi Yitzchak of Berditshev."

Without specifying the story, Yellin-Mor was alluding to a Chasidic tale told about Rabbi Levi Yitzchak of Berditshev, who was renowned for his love of the Jewish people and his willingness to find merit in even the most flagrant sinners among them. Once, Reb Lev Yitzchak met a Jew who was smoking on the Sabbath, a clear and serious violation of Jewish law. Reb Levi Yitzchak asked the man, "Perhaps you forgot that it is Shabbes [the Sabbath] today."

"No, Rebbe," the man replied. "I know it is Shabbes."

"Perhaps you just lit up a cigarette automatically, without thinking about it, and didn't even realize you were smoking?"

"Rebbe, how can a person not know that he is smoking?"

Reb Levi Yitzchak wouldn't give up. "Perhaps you forgot that it is forbidden to smoke on Shabbes?"

"I know that it is forbidden to smoke on Shabbes."

At this point, Reb Levi Yitzchak turned his eyes upward and called out, "Master of the Universe, how wonderful are your people Israel. This Jew simply won't tell a lie. In what other people can you find such scrupulous honesty?"

The Rebbe smiled at Yellin-Mor's response and then, without missing a beat, said to him, "The difference is that Rabbi Levi Yitzchak was seeking merit for another person. You're seeking merit for yourself."

A year later, Gershon Jacobson received two articles in the mail from Yellin-Mor, accompanied by a note from the writer that he had been diagnosed with terminal cancer and did not have long to live. He asked that these articles be published posthumously. He died on February 19, 1980. After his death Jacobson published the articles. Both were, in a sense, obituaries for himself, the first an overview of his life. The other, a recounting of just one episode in Yellin-Mor's life, was starkly written: "Right now, dear reader, as you're reading this article, I am being judged by the Heavenly Court, the *Beit Din shel Ma'alah*, and I'm sure they have a whole list of sins I have committed, and I don't have much with which to defend myself. However I do have this story I want to share . . ."—here he related the encounter with the Rebbe. He then wrote, "And the Rebbe did say that I have a power to write, and I should use it. I don't know if they are going to give me equal time up there to defend myself, but I know that whatever happens down on earth is read up there, so that's why I wanted this article to be published while I was standing before the Heavenly Court so that they'll see this story. Because the story is that I did try to use my writing in the best way I could, and the Rebbe acknowledged that. This is my *zechut*, my merit.

"And I acknowledge that the Rebbe made an important point that in Judaism action is the paramount thing. And certainly one should not use words to justify one's own self-interest."

When Jacobson was preparing to go to Rome to cover Vatican II, the 1962 conclave of the Catholic Church convened by Pope John XXIII, the Rebbe advised him to read extensively about the Vatican and to make a concentrated effort to learn about a variety of Church practices so that he would be a far more informed and trusted journalist. One example the Rebbe offered was being familiar with the secret behind-the-scenes proceedings of choosing a new pope. This sort of wide-ranging knowledge, the Rebbe told him, would gain him access and credibility with the people in the Vatican with whom he needed to speak and would also encourage them to speak to him in a more forthcoming manner.

But perhaps nothing so forcefully demonstrated to Jacobson the high regard in which the Rebbe held good journalism as his annual presentation of matzah to the journalist before the Passover Seder, along with the blessing, *mitzvah l'saper*: "It's a commandment to tell the story." The Rebbe was of course quoting the well-known injunction recorded in the Haggadah: "It's a commandment to tell the story of the going forth from Egypt throughout the night,"[4] but Jacobson understood the Rebbe as saying: "Your job is to tell the story of what's happening in the world. Understand that what you are doing is a mitzvah, a commandment to tell the news and to tell the truth, and to give people an accurate and comprehensive understanding of what's going on in the world."

The Rebbe's respect for journalism when done well was underscored in a *yechidus* with Moshe Ishon, who had previously worked as a reporter for the Israeli newspaper *HaTzofe*, published by Mizrachi, the religious Zionist party; now, though, he was serving as a representative for Israel's Jewish Agency in New York. Ishon came to the Rebbe seeking advice: He had been offered two jobs, either an elevation in his position with the Jewish Agency or to become the editor in chief of *HaTzofe*. Which should he take?

To the Rebbe, the answer was so obvious that it required no further discussion: "The newspaper, of course." He pointed to the variety of newspapers on his desk, among which was *HaTzofe*. "You see that I value journalism, because it fulfills a very important mission; it influences, it creates public opinion. If the journalist understands the mission he has, he has the power to sway public opinion and to influence the public to approach a subject properly."

Ishon followed the Rebbe's advice and served as *HaTzofe*'s editor in chief for sixteen years.[5]

When speaking to journalists, the Rebbe liked to focus on the great good they could do. In a warm but brief encounter with the *New York Times* correspondent Ari Goldman, the Rebbe asked him to remember to "report good news." It is in the nature of newspapers to be disproportionately filled with troubling news and unpleasant events. But that is not the whole picture—even though readers may sometimes think it is—and Goldman told me that the Rebbe's advice influenced him to think more in terms of also reporting things that were going right, not just those that were going wrong. In a similar manner, when a reporter from the *Daily News* met the Rebbe, the Rebbe blessed her that she should seek out and report good news daily.

The Rebbe was not being naive, and he certainly was willing to read his share of unhappy news. When Yehoshua Saguy, director of AMAN, Israeli military intelligence, met with the Rebbe, he was staggered—as Yitzchak Rabin had been—that the Rebbe was "very acquainted" with all matters, including minor ones, going on between Israel and the Arab states. What particularly struck Saguy was that while he himself knew of all these things, it was because he spent ten hours a day reading newspapers and intelligence reports, whereas the Rebbe seemed to have acquired his detailed knowledge by means that Saguy could not comprehend.[6]

Another journalist, Herbert Brin, described in detail his 1954 meeting with the Rebbe, a meeting that was remarkable, particularly because it lasted six hours and was with a man whom the Rebbe had never previously met. Brin had made a decision a short time earlier to leave the *Los Angeles Times*, where he had been a successful feature writer, and start a Los Angeles–based Jewish newspaper. His motivation was a sense of guilt for not having previously done more for the Jewish community, particularly during the years of the Holocaust. As Brin explained to the Rebbe, he had always been a proud Jew, but not a knowledgeable or observant one. During 1938 and 1939, he had worked as a secret informant for the Anti-Defamation League. Because Brin did not have what are thought of as classical Jewish looks—he was six foot one, with blue eyes and blond hair—he was assigned to infiltrate the Nazi Party in Chicago and provide the ADL with information about every move the party was planning. His information helped Jewish groups to surprise the Nazis at demonstrations and at other events, and break them up.

Speaking of the meeting with the Rebbe many years later, Brin recalled that he assumed he would be coming in to get a blessing from a rabbi and the whole meeting would probably last no more than one or two minutes. In preparation, though, Brin, feeling somewhat insecure about his new undertaking, went into the Rebbe's office with a question: "Do I have a right to act as an editor and write editorials for a Jewish newspaper, when I know so little of *Yiddishkeit*, when I can't even *daven* [pray]? What right do I have to serve as the editor of a Jewish newspaper? Maybe I'm in the wrong field."

Before relating the Rebbe's response, it is worth recalling a directive of the Rebbe that motivated the Chabad philanthropist Sami Rohr to start offering a weekly Torah class: "If all you know is *alef-beis*, then teach *beis* to someone who knows only *alef*" ["if all you know are the letters *a* and *b*, then teach *b* to someone who only knows *a*"]. Rohr knew far more than *alef* and *beis*, but until he learned of the Rebbe's encouraging and demanding words, he felt that he lacked sufficient knowledge to teach others.

In this instance, the Rebbe tried to reassure Brin concerning his lack of knowledge and told him a Chasidic story, well known among religious Jews but unknown to Brin, about a young shepherd boy who entered the synagogue where the Baal Shem Tov, the founder of Chasidism, was praying. It was Yom Kippur and worshippers were reciting the prayers when one congregant, seeing this young boy standing in the synagogue balcony with nothing in his hands, went upstairs and handed him a prayer book. But the boy couldn't read. He stood there silently while the others prayed, and finally, frustrated that he could not participate in the service, he started to engage in the one activity he knew he could do well and offer to God; he started to imitate the crowing of a hen (when telling this story in public, the Rebbe would repeat the sound, *kukeriku*, several times).

The other participants turned around in shock and fury. Who crows in a synagogue on Yom Kippur, the holiest day of the Jewish year? A number of men advanced toward the balcony to throw the boy out of the synagogue. But the Baal Shem Tov stopped them. "Until now, our prayers have been blocked from reaching heaven. And then this young boy came in here and offered God a gift from his heart, the gift of so artfully imitating animal sounds, and it broke though heaven and carried all our prayers with it."

Brin was moved but not convinced: "I don't whistle in balconies. I've got to know that I'm doing the right thing."

The Rebbe stood up from his chair, walked toward Brin, and reached into his pocket. "How much is a subscription to your newspaper?"

"Three dollars and fifty cents."

The Rebbe took out three dollar bills and two quarters and told Brin, "I want a subscription."

After giving Brin the money, the Rebbe looked him square in the eye and said, "Obviously, you're a learned man. You've read a great deal. Do you have a right to withhold that which you know?"[7]

Chapter 13

CHESS, THIEVES,
ASTRONAUTS, AND ATOMS

"Every thing is by Divine Providence. . . . Every single
thing a person sees or hears is an instruction to him in his
conduct and service of God."
—*Israel Baal Shem Tov in a statement
frequently quoted by the Rebbe*

Judaism has an ancient tradition going back to both the Bible and
the Talmud of learning ethical and spiritual lessons from the
animal world: "Go to the ant, you sluggard," the book of Proverbs
advises indolent people. "Study its ways and learn . . . it lays up its
stores during the summer, and gathers in its food at the harvest"
(Proverbs 6:6–8).[1] Many centuries later, the Talmud noted moral
virtues to be derived from a variety of creatures: "If the Torah
had not been given, we could have learned modesty from the cat,
honesty from the ant, chastity from the dove, and good manners
from the rooster, who first coaxes, then mates" (*Eruvin* 100b). Rashi,
the eleventh-century Talmud commentator, explains that the cat
covers its excrement, ants do not steal from each other, and the dove
is monogamous.

An innovation of the Rebbe lay in expanding the search for
spiritual and ethical lessons to the worlds of business, science, the
professions, and even recreational activities such as baseball and
board games.

Chess

"PROTECTING THE KING AND ATTACKING THE PIECES THAT THREATEN
THE KING'S DOMINION IS THE GOAL OF ALL THE OTHER PIECES."

Chess has exerted a centuries-long fascination and attraction for Jews; we
find references to the game in Jewish literature as early as the tenth century.
In Maimonides's commentary on the Mishnah, he is a bit critical of the game,
particularly when it is played for money.[2] In contrast, two medieval European
rabbinic scholars, Judah ha-Hasid, author of *Sefer Chasidim* (*The Book of the Pious*),
and Menachem ha-Meiri, express passing, if casual, approval of the game.

In the nineteenth and twentieth centuries, many European Jews
emerged as leading players in the world of international chess, and the
game became a popular pastime in the Jewish community. Unlike card
games, which were often viewed in religious circles as constituting a
waste of time (and worse, when played for money), chess, because of its
intellectual demands and its ability to help develop logical and strategic
thinking, often was viewed sympathetically, even approvingly.

One of the most famous pictures of the Rebbe and his father-in-law—
certainly the most famous informal shot—is of the two men playing
chess. The photograph was taken in 1935 at the Perchtolsdorf Sanatorium
outside Vienna, where the Frierdiker Rebbe was recuperating from
a period of illness. The chess play had come about in response to the
advice of physicians that the Frierdiker Rebbe should, during his stay at
the sanatorium, avoid intellectual strain. The Rebbe later explained that
"after the first game, the [Frierdiker] Rebbe felt that I didn't play properly,
so we played a second game." Apparently, the Frierdiker Rebbe had felt
that his son-in-law, out of deference, had played a weaker game than he
could have, and he now wanted him to play for real. A second game was
played, and this time the Frierdiker Rebbe was satisfied with his son-in-
law's play and declared him victorious. One senses from this account that
the Rebbe outplayed his father-in-law and the Frierdiker Rebbe conceded
the game before checkmate had been declared. Perhaps he feared that his
son-in-law would deem it disrespectful to say checkmate and defeat him.

Though it is not known how often the Rebbe played chess—we do know that he also played with his grandnephew when the boy visited with him at his home—the Rebbe spoke about chess and its lessons for life at a 1949 *farbrengen*, less than two years before his elevation to the movement's leadership. The talk was occasioned by the appearance of Samuel Reshevsky as an attendee at the *farbrengen*. Born in 1911 to a family of Gerer Chasidim in Poland, Reshevsky was a chess prodigy who had been competing in and winning chess tournaments since the age of eight. He and his family moved to the United States in 1920, and over the coming years he won both the U.S. Chess Championship and the Open Championship, becoming the most noted American chess player prior to Bobby Fischer. Throughout his life, Reshevsky was an observant Jew and refrained from playing in tournaments on Shabbat.

Seeing Reshevsky at the *farbrengen*, the soon-to-be Rebbe started to expound on spiritual lessons conveyed by chess. The game itself, he noted, is a game of hierarchies. The king represents God, and is therefore the most valuable piece on the board. Protecting the king and attacking the pieces that threaten the king's dominion is the *goal* of all the other pieces.

The officers—the two rooks, bishops, and knights—represent the world of angels. Like angels, these pieces are imbued with distinct powers; they can move several squares at a time, some in straight lines, others in diagonal ones.

On the front line, and at the lowest rung, are the eight pawns, which represent the human soul as it is encapsulated in a physical body. As distinct from the officers who can move both forward and backward, the pawns can only move forward; also, unlike the officers, they can only move one square at a time (except on the opening move). Thus, the pawns, like human beings, must work within the limits of the natural universe, performing simple actions that are not glamorous. However, once a pawn completes its step-by-step progression and reaches the other side of the board, it can be promoted to a higher level, even to attain the level of queen. This is in contrast to the rook, the bishop, and the knight, who can only move in the way they have been assigned, no matter how many times they reach the other side of the board.

Angels, Jewish tradition teaches, have an advantage over human beings; they have greater power. But they also have a disadvantage; they can never change, upgrade, or improve themselves. Pawns can do so, but not, so to speak, in this lifetime, *only* when they have reached the "other side."

Pawns offer a lesson in humility as well. They remind us that no matter how elevated they become, the one piece they can never become is the king, for there is only one king: God, the King of Kings.[3]

The Disciplined Life of Astronauts

"THE ASTRONAUTS ALSO LIVE IN A DEMOCRATIC SOCIETY. YET EVERY SINGLE ACT THEY PERFORM MUST BE CARRIED OUT IN AGREEMENT WITH INSTRUCTIONS AND PLANS WORKED OUT BY A HIGHER AUTHORITY."

Within the past half century, one of the events that most fired people's imagination and happy excitement was the successful 1969 landing on the moon by the astronauts of the Apollo spacecraft. At the Shabbat *farbrengen* following the lunar landing, it was perhaps inevitable that the Rebbe would mention so momentous an event, but his take on this historic occurrence was decidedly different from the observations that most commentators were making:

"The imagination of the entire world has been excited by the Apollo flight to the moon. Around the globe, their preparation and progress have been followed with keen interest. . . . We know what and when the astronauts are going to eat, when they are going to sleep, and [when they] are permitted to exercise. Everyone understands the respective role of the astronauts and of the Ground Control directors [who oversee the mission]. No one dreams of asking: 'Why are the astronauts under the direction of Ground Control?' No one questions the need for detailed plans about what to eat, and when to eat and sleep. What would the world say about an astronaut who . . . decides that he is a mature adult who knows better than mission control? Everyone agrees that the success of the Apollo flights depends on mutual responsibility and submission to strict discipline. . . . Each of us as Jews," the Rebbe continued, alluding to Judaism's numerous ritual and other directives, "has also been sent on a mission, here on earth, for seventy or eighty years of our life. . . . We are told what to eat and what not to eat, what to study, how to speak, how to behave ourselves with respect to our companions and with respect to the 'Mission Director,' and in general we are given a carefully worked-out program designed specifically to help us complete our mission successfully." [4]

Regarding the argument commonly offered by Jews who do not observe Jewish ritual laws that they live in a democratic society and should be free to act as they wish, the Rebbe countered, "The astronauts also live in a democratic society, yet every single act they perform, even the most trivial, must be carried out in agreement with instructions, and plans worked out by a higher authority. If these instructions are followed, the mission has a probability of success. But if the instructions are disregarded or disobeyed, the very mission—and even human lives—is endangered."

"If they tell you there is wisdom among the Gentiles, believe it," counsels the Midrash (*Midrash Rabbah*, Lamentations 2:17). In this case, the Rebbe discerned in the disciplined lifestyle of the astronauts lessons with which Jews—particularly the sort who would not instinctively accept the demands of the Torah—could inspire themselves to be more observant of God's laws.

Bookkeeping and Accounting

"THE BOOKKEEPING IS WRONG IF A DIFFERENCE IS ONE SHILLING OR ONE HUNDRED POUNDS. SO TOO WITH *MITZVOT* . . . THE GREAT OR THE SMALL. IF ANY ARE NEGLECTED, THE ACCOUNT WILL NOT BALANCE."

Between 1965 and 1981, Peter Kalms had nine extended private meetings (*yechidusen*) with the Rebbe. At each meeting, Kalms would enter the Rebbe's office with a small notepad and "accepting the Rebbe's invitation to sit, would scribble key words and phrases during the conversation." Upon leaving the Rebbe's room, Kalms would head immediately to a quiet corner of the building and for several hours (on one occasion, all night) would write down his recollection of the complete dialogue, "using the Rebbe's own words."[5]

Toward the end of his first *yechidus* (June 1, 1965), the Rebbe asked Kalms if he intended to continue working as an accountant: "I responded strongly that I did not believe that this was the right course for me." The Rebbe did not respond immediately to this statement but instead suggested a program of Torah study for Kalms to start pursuing in addition to his work. Then, as the meeting was concluding, he turned back to the world of bookkeeping and accounting and conveyed a valuable spiritual teaching that could be garnered from them, whether or not Kalms left that type of work.

"You should be aware of the importance of bookkeeping in Jewish thought. It is necessary to balance the right side of the ledger exactly with the left. The bookkeeping is wrong if a difference is one shilling or one hundred pounds. So, too, with the *mitzvot*, all 613, the great or the small. If any are neglected, the account will not balance."[6]

Learning from a Thief

"ALL CHARACTER TRAITS, EVEN THOSE THAT ARE NOT GOOD, OR ARE
EVEN EVIL . . . CAN BE USED [AS A LESSON] IN SERVING GOD."

—RABBI YOSEF YITZCHAK SCHNEERSOHN,
THE FRIERDIKER REBBE, AS CITED BY THE REBBE

The Talmud teaches that the very first question human beings are asked after they die and come before the heavenly court is, "Did you carry out your business dealings honestly?" (*Shabbat* 31a). That one can learn lessons in spiritual growth from an honest businessman comes as no surprise. But the extent to which the Rebbe and, in this case, the Frierdiker Rebbe, as well as previous Chasidic masters, were willing to cast their net to learn how to serve God, is made most apparent in a Chasidic teaching cited in *Hayom Yom*, the Rebbe's first book (1943), in which he arranged daily teachings selected from the writings of the Frierdiker Rebbe, his father-in-law.

For the third of Iyar (which falls in the spring, shortly after Passover), the Rebbe cites the following passage from a letter written by his father-in-law.[7]

"All character traits, even those that are not good, or are even evil in name and description, can be used [as a lesson] in serving God according to the Torah.

"In this vein, the saintly Rabbi Meshullam Zusya of Hanipoli [usually referred to as Reb Zusha] learned several approaches to Divine service by pondering on the work ethic, so to speak, of a thief:

1.   A thief is modest.
2.   He is prepared to endanger himself.
3.   The minutest details are as important to him as greater considerations.
4.   He labors with great exertion.
5.   He works quickly.
6.   He exhibits trust and hope.
7.   If he fails the first time, he tries again and again."

A Brief Commentary

What does it mean to say that a thief is modest? It means that he makes an effort *not* to call attention to himself. Many people want their goodness to become widely known and recognized. While this might be an understandable desire of the ego, we can learn from the thief to do our work without seeking public recognition, something a thief definitely does not want.

The other traits mentioned in this passage are, relatively speaking, self-explanatory but still challenging. A thief is prepared to endanger himself for something dishonest. Are we willing to put ourselves at risk to do something good?

The thief is concerned about seemingly minor details, for such particulars can lead to his capture (for example, neglecting to wear gloves and leaving behind fingerprints). Are we as concerned about seemingly less important, supposedly "minor," laws as we are about the more well-known commandments?

The thief "labors with great exertion." Do we work as tirelessly at doing good as the thief works at doing evil?

The thief works quickly. When we want to make money, many of us are willing to pursue opportunities immediately. But do we do so with the same avidity and speed when we consider a spiritual matter? Or if a question arises of helping someone in the community, do we act with the same speed as if it were a question of making money for ourselves?

A thief remains hopeful and optimistic. In any area of life a person will be inspired to work day after day only if he trusts that, at the end, there will be success. This, too, can be learned from a thief.

Finally, when a thief fails, he doesn't lose hope but tries again and again. Chasidic tradition tells of the late-eighteenth-century Rebbe, Moshe Leib of Sassov, who was on a mission to ransom Jews in debtors' prison. He was having little success in collecting the amount needed and grew discouraged, concluding that it would be better to go home and focus instead on his own learning and praying. While preparing his bags for the journey back, he heard of a Jew who had stolen some clothing and had been severely beaten and thrown in jail. Reb Moshe Leib sought out the judge and succeeded in getting the man released to his custody.

When they left the jail, Reb Moshe Leib said to the thief, "After the beating they gave you, I hope you'll learn to never do anything like this again."

The thief responded: "Why not? I didn't succeed this time, but I may well succeed the next."

Reb Moshe Leib thought to himself, "If that's the case, then I must keep trying at my job, too."

Baseball

"YOU CAN BE EITHER A FAN OR A PLAYER. BE A PLAYER."

Shimshon Stock's father was friendly with the Rebbe, and Stock himself knew the Rebbe from the time before he assumed the movement's leadership. He recalls an incident around 1951 when Stock was walking with a man and his son, both devoted Brooklyn Dodgers fans, who were en route to a game at nearby Ebbets Field.

Suddenly, Stock saw the Rebbe walking toward them, and he introduced the men to him. The Rebbe immediately started to talk to the pair, particularly the son, about baseball. The boy, assuming that the Rebbe was quite uninformed about baseball, mentioned in passing that when the team that one favors is either winning or losing by a large margin, many spectators leave the game without bothering to wait for the end.

"Do the ball players leave?" asked the Rebbe

"Of course not," the young man said. "They are not allowed to leave. They stay to the end and keep trying to win."

The Rebbe smiled at the young man. "This is the lesson in Judaism I want to teach you. When you pray, when you put on tefillin, you're playing with the team. You're not just a spectator; you're in the game. [You're not a fan who can leave the game early.] You can be either a fan or a player. Be a player."

In the following story as well, baseball provides the context for the Rebbe to extract a moral lesson, in this case by showing a young man how he can triumph over his negative inclination, what is known in Hebrew as the *yetzer ha-ra*.[8]

As Yossi ben Eliezer recalls: "I accompanied my grandfather to a private audience with the Rebbe a month prior to my bar mitzvah. After speaking with my grandfather, the Rebbe turned to me and asked: 'Which sport do you like most?'

"In shock at the Rebbe's question, I replied, 'Baseball.'

"The Rebbe continued, 'Do you like to play when there are two teams or just one?'

" 'Rabbi, you cannot play baseball with just one team.'

" 'Why not?' the Rebbe asked, his face serious.

"I explained patiently, 'Rabbi, the whole game is to see who will triumph. Therefore, there must be two opposing teams.'

" 'And who usually wins?' the Rebbe asked.

" 'The one who plays better.' I smiled.

"The Rebbe continued. 'Do you ever play baseball with your friends?'

" 'Sure.'

" 'Do you ever go to see professional games?'

" 'Sure I do' "

" 'Why is it not enough to just play with your friends?'

" 'Rabbi, I'm just playing kids' play with my friends. But at a professional game, it's for real.'

" 'Yosef,' the Rebbe addressed me, 'in your heart there is a large baseball "field." The two teams are your evil inclination and your good inclination. Up to now they played "amateur." From now on, they are playing "professionally"; it is for real. You have to make sure that you are always victorious over your negative tendencies. Remember, like in baseball, the one who plays better wins. If you want, you will always be triumphant.' "

The Atom

"WE HAVE SEEN HOW THE ENERGY CONCEALED WITHIN THE MINUTEST . . . PARTICLES CAN DESTROY AN ENTIRE CITY. . . . WITHIN EVERY TINY BIT OF MATTER, GOD HAS INFUSED A TREMENDOUS AMOUNT OF POWER."

Reform rabbi Herbert Weiner spent a year studying the Lubavitch movement in the mid-1950s, and his account of the experience,[9] including two extended *yechidusen* with the Rebbe, remains among the best accounts of the Rebbe during his early years of leadership. During this period, Weiner also spent some time studying in the Lubavitcher yeshiva where he was assigned a teenage study partner, Avraham

Shemtov, who later emerged as an elder and leader of the movement. The young Shemtov, a religious firebrand, saw it as a personal mission to persuade Weiner of the illogic of his liberal, non-Orthodox position.[10] At one point, Weiner, who was growing irritated by the young man's repeated challenges, asked him if the fact that "so many intelligent people were unable to see the logic of Orthodoxy did not make him wonder about the absolute certainty of his own convictions." Instead of being daunted by Weiner's challenge, the young man said quickly, "Ah-hah, but Abraham, too, was alone. And we now know from the atom bomb how much power there is in the little."[11]

I suspect that this argument was not original to Avraham Shemtov but derived from an argument offered by the Rebbe in the years following the August 1945 bombings of Hiroshima and Nagasaki. As the Rebbe expressed it: "We have seen in our time how the energy concealed within the minutest subatomic particles can destroy an entire city and millions of inhabitants. This is possible because within every tiny bit of matter, God has infused a tremendous amount of power. If this is true with negative activities such as warfare, it is true regarding a person's spiritual potential as well. Through the proper use of the power locked within a person's divine soul, an individual can have an immeasurable effect on himself and on the entire world."[12]

"Have we not all one Father?" the biblical prophet Malachi wrote. "Did not one God create us?" (2:10). The Rebbe discerned this lesson too: "Where we once believed the world to be made up of a multitude of different elements, through examining substances at the sub-atomic level we find that they are all built of the same matter. This demonstrates the tremendous unity of creation."

Chapter 14

GOING TO THE POOLROOM WITH THE REBBE'S BLESSINGS, AND GRATITUDE WITHOUT END

"What does the Lubavitcher Rebbe want from me?"
—*Egyptian president Hosni Mubarak*

Hundreds of stories circulate about the Rebbe—sometimes the same basic story with numerous variations—but many are anonymous and thus impossible to verify. What follows are a variety of authenticated incidents that do not fit into any of the earlier chapters and reveal additional aspects of the Rebbe.

Love, Marriage, and Deciding on a Partner

Rabbi Leibel Groner approached the Rebbe seeking guidance. He had been introduced to a young woman; they had met several times and had compatible values and good feelings for each other, and now he wanted to know whether he should become engaged or, as he put it, "finish the *shidduch.*"

The Rebbe did not offer Groner the sort of definitive response he was seeking: "When it comes to a marriage, not I can help you, not your father can help you, not your mother can help you, not your *seichel* [your intellectual faculties] can help you. The only thing that can help you is your heart. If you feel for her, go ahead. If you don't, do not."

Groner's heart told him yes, and the marriage took place shortly thereafter. When relating this story in 2008, more than fifty years after his wedding, Rabbi Groner mentioned that he had heard of a somewhat similar incident in which the Frierdiker Rebbe was asked by a young man if he should marry a woman whom he had recently met and who he knew had good *midot* (character traits). The Frierdiker Rebbe asked him, "Are you attracted to her?" The young man answered, "I don't know."

"You don't know?" the Frierdiker Rebbe said. "Then go look for someone else."

The *shidduch* system common in the Orthodox world opposes people dating unless it's for purposes of finding a mate and encourages its adherents to go out only with a man or woman to whom they have been formally introduced. That way, it is guaranteed that the person one is meeting comes from an appropriate family and has religiously similar views. Non-Orthodox Jews commonly assume that in the Orthodox world, and certainly in what they think of as the ultra-Orthodox world, considerations of the heart are dismissed as minor or even insignificant.

This was certainly not the Rebbe's thinking. A young woman, Yehudis Fishman, who was not from a Chabad background, succeeded in meeting with the Rebbe at a time when she was in a quandary. She had been introduced to a young man who by all measures seemed to be a suitable match, but she remained uncertain if he was, in her words, "my soul mate."

The Rebbe's first question to her was an obvious one. "Do you like this man?"

Fishman replied, "I have *stam ahavat Yisrael*" (the basic love for a fellow Jew commanded in the Torah; see Leviticus 19:18).

The Rebbe gave Fishman a large grin even as he offered her advice that clearly suggested the relationship should be terminated: "For a husband, one must have more than the plain, basic love of a fellow Jew."

One person whom the Rebbe did push to get married was Elie Wiesel, the world-famous Holocaust survivor, writer, and winner of the 1986 Nobel Peace Prize. Wiesel had a long-standing relationship with the Rebbe, and he is generally private about the contents of their meetings, but one detail of their encounters that he is open to discussing is that the Rebbe used to scold him—Wiesel was then in his late thirties—citing the biblical verse: "It is not good for man to be alone" (Genesis 2:18). Wiesel recalls a long letter he received from the Rebbe dealing with a variety of theological issues, including what was for Wiesel, a survivor of Auschwitz, a most pressing matter: "Is it possible to believe without believing in God?" Suddenly, the Rebbe's letter shifted gears, as he wrote that he wanted to ask Wiesel a question that "has nothing to do with theology. Why don't you get married?"

Wiesel responded that indeed his reluctance to get married had a great deal to do with theology. The Holocaust, as he recounted in his memoir, *And the Sea Is Never Full*, had "convinced him" that "a cruel and indifferent world did not deserve our children." It was Marion, his future wife, who persuaded him that by refusing to have children, he was giving "the killers one more victory." The long line from which he sprang, Marion argued, must not end with him.

On the day of Wiesel's wedding, the largest and most beautiful bouquet of flowers that he received came from the Rebbe. And when his and Marion's son, Elisha, was born, the Rebbe dispatched emissaries to the *brit milah* (the circumcision), bringing him a note from the Rebbe in which he wrote that his heart and soul were overflowing with joy.

Gratitude Without End

The Rebbe maintained a lifelong feeling of gratitude to Rabbi Shneur Zalman Vilenkin, his teacher from the age of seven and a half to eleven, and the man of whom he said, "He put me on my feet [in Jewish learning]." When Rabbi Vilenkin first came to the United States and visited the Rebbe's office in Brooklyn, the Rebbe stood in his honor and refused to sit down until Vilenkin sat. Rabbi Vilenkin, in turn, refused to sit in the presence of the man he accepted as *his* Rebbe, so the two remained standing for their hour-long meeting. The second time they met, Vilenkin again refused to sit, so the Rebbe said to him, "[More than] forty years ago, we sat together at one volume of the Talmud. Let us sit together now as well." Rabbi Vilenkin consented and the two men sat down. On other occasions, when the Rebbe would see Rabbi Vilenkin entering the hall to hear one of his public lectures, he would rise in his honor and not sit back down until he saw that his teacher was seated.

In 1963, when Rabbi Vilenkin died, the Rebbe paid for his burial and for the erection of a *matzevah* (gravestone). He asked the rabbi's children to each pay only a dollar so that they could participate in the mitzvah of honoring their father, but he wanted to pay the rest himself.[1]

A little over a week after his mother, Rebbetzin Chana Schneerson, died (in September 1964), the Rebbe made sure that a *lulav* and *etrog* (consisting of a frond from a date palm tree along with leaves from a willow tree [*aravah*] and a myrtle tree [*hadas*], and a fruit known as a citron, both of which are used in the Sukkot ritual) were provided to Mrs. Wiener, the woman who had cared for his mother. Each Sukkot, the Rebbe used to provide his mother with a *lulav* and *etrog*, and he knew that Mrs. Wiener would also recite the blessing over them. Now that his mother was dead, he was concerned that Mrs. Wiener might not have access to a *lulav* and *etrog* because they—specifically the *etrog*—can be quite expensive. Rabbi Meir Harlig recalls the Rebbe's insistence on seeing that the articles were brought to the elderly woman right away: "I'm going to wait here until I see somebody get into a car to go to Mrs. Wiener's house to deliver the *lulav* and *etrog*."[2]

No Gifts

When Dr. Elliot Udell, a podiatrist, first came to 770 to meet his new patient, he told the Rebbe that he was honored to treat him and would not accept payment. The Rebbe told the doctor that such an arrangement was unacceptable: "I'm giving you a check for your services, and I expect you to cash it."

Still, when Udell left the Rebbe's office, he told Rabbi Groner that he felt it was improper for him to take money from the Rebbe. Groner told him: "If you don't cash the check, the Rebbe will never allow you to come here again."

Dr. Udell deposited the check.

A Reason Not to Accept Gifts

A devoted admirer of the Rebbe from England, Zalmon Jaffe, told Rebbetzin Schneerson of his desire to present her husband with an elegant silver wine decanter. The Rebbe wrote Jaffe a warm response ("I must take [your kind] thought for the deed") yet refused the gift. Then, perhaps feeling that so blunt a refusal might sound curt, he added, "But one reason, if it will satisfy you, is that I do not wish to make a distinction between me and those surrounding me" (letter of February 23, 1982). For a similar reason, the Rebbe explained, he did not keep his *etrog* in a silver container over Sukkot; since not all people can afford so ornate an object, doing so might make those who had little more than a simple cardboard box in which to hold their *etrog* feel diminished, even humiliated.[3]

When the Rebbe Did Ask for a Gift

As reluctant as the Rebbe was to accept gifts, we know of several incidents when he solicited birthday gifts, though the gifts were never personal.[4] One such request was made on his seventy-ninth birthday (11 Nisan 1981) and the person solicited was David Chase, a businessman who was a generous contributor to Chabad. The Rebbe wrote Chase: "Although it is not customary or proper to ask for a birthday gift, but considering our special relationship, I venture to do so, being confident that you will treat it in the proper spirit. The birthday gift that I have in mind, which I would consider an honor as well as a great pleasure, is that you devote a quarter of an hour of your time every weekday morning and dedicate it for the sacred purpose of putting on tefillin, with the appropriate prayers that go with it, such as *Sh'ma* and the like. The words need not necessarily be recited in Hebrew. If you can manage this in ten minutes, I am prepared to forgo five minutes and let it be only ten minutes. . . . I trust that you put on tefillin every morning in any case, and the reason I am asking the above is only that you should make it a definite point on your calendar, to make sure that your preoccupation with your personal business . . . [will] not distract you even once to overlook the putting on of tefillin. And this will be my reward."[5]

At the time, Chase, a successful businessman, was serving as chairman of the board of the New Jersey–based Chabad Rabbinical College of America. It was the Rebbe's practice to automatically send a copy of all letters he sent Chase to Rabbi Moshe Herson, the yeshiva's dean. On this occasion, however, the Rebbe, not wishing to pressure or embarrass Chase, noted that he was not sending a copy to Rabbi Herson, as the letter was of a personal nature.

Chase began to be punctilious in his practice of morning prayers, a practice that eventually caused him to influence by example several non-Jews with whom he was in contact to become more prayerful, a detail that brought the Rebbe great pleasure (see pages 157–58).

Honesty

The Rebbe would sometimes ask his secretary Rabbi Yehuda Krinsky to buy objects that the movement needed. Once, when the Rebbe looked at the receipt for a purchase that had been made, he noticed that no sales tax had been charged. He asked why, and Rabbi Krinsky explained that because Merkos L'inyonei Chinuch, the movement's educational wing, was a tax-deductible concern, it was exempt from the requirement to pay sales tax. "But this was not bought for Merkos," the Rebbe told him. "It was bought for my own personal use." He then reimbursed Rabbi Krinsky for the purchase and asked that if it was not too much of an imposition, could he please return to the store and pay the applicable sales tax.[6]

When the Rebbe gave money to be distributed to charity, he would regularly remind recipients from foreign countries that the money had to be exchanged legally. And, of course, he often reminded people to give far more than the one dollar he was giving them.

"Why don't you have a birthday cake?"

In the entire Bible only one birthday is recorded—that of Pharaoh (Genesis 40:20). Unlike the American tradition, in which the lives of great leaders are commemorated on or around their birthdays (Washington's birthday, Lincoln's birthday, Martin Luther King Day),[7] Jewish tradition has long put its emphasis on the day of death (*yahrtzeit*), perhaps because it is only when a person dies that we can know if he or she led a worthwhile life; at the time of birth, we know nothing.

This distinctive Jewish emphasis is reflected in the Chabad-published book *Days of Chabad*, a retelling of the movement's history and of its leading figures through the dates on which significant events occurred. There are twenty events recorded for Tishrei, the first month in the Jewish calendar. Thirteen are *yahrtzeits*; none is a birthday (there are several birthdays recorded elsewhere in the book, but far fewer than the number of *yahrtzeits*).

An innovative practice of the Rebbe was the institution of the oft-ignored birthday (a few selected birthdays, such as the day of the bar mitzvah, were always commemorated in Jewish life) as a day of celebration and introspection. Rabbi Yehuda Krinsky has the following recollection:

> In 1951, soon after the Rebbe became Rebbe, we learned that the Rebbe had a high regard for the significance of birthdays. Anyone who had a birthday coming up could arrange to go into yechidus. The Rebbe would give a bracha; he'd spend 30 seconds or a minute, maybe two minutes, depending if the Rebbe asked you a question or anything.
>
> Later, I had a little personal experience with the Rebbe on one of my birthdays. It was in the 1980s. My birthday is the same date as the Rebbe's wedding anniversary,[8] and the Rebbe used go to the Ohel [where his father-in-law was buried] every year on his anniversary. One year, we came back from the Ohel, and later I drove the Rebbe home. I parked the car and went around to open the door for him. As he was walking out of the car, he said, "If I'm not mistaken, isn't it your birthday today?"
>
> I said, "Yes."
>
> He said, "Did they prepare a birthday cake for you?" I didn't think that anybody had; we didn't have that custom since I was a little kid. But the Rebbe was wondering, "How come you don't have a birthday cake?"

I heard clearly what he said, and [when] I came home my wife baked a cake, and she called the family together. We all made a l'chaim (toast), and the next morning when I picked the Rebbe up he said, "Did you have a birthday cake last night?" Since that time, in our family it became a custom.

For the Rebbe, Rabbi Krinsky explained, a birthday was not just a day of celebration. "On one's birthday, the Rebbe believed that each person should be secluded for a certain part of the day, do a *cheshbon ha-nefesh* [soul-searching] and engage in introspection. The custom also is to take on a resolution for the coming year, to do something that you didn't do in the past year, something a little bit additional in your observance or in your studies, your *Yiddishkeit*." (Characteristic examples are taking upon oneself an extra study session, or giving more charity, but, in truth, of course, it could be any act involving ethical and/or spiritual self-improvement, and kindness to others.)[9]

Going to the Poolroom with the Rebbe's Blessing

Dr. Ira Weiss, the Rebbe and Rebbetzin's cardiologist, recalls that when his father had a severe stroke, the Rebbe took a great interest in how his father was doing. At one point, he asked Weiss: "What are you doing to help your father feel better about his condition? He cannot talk, he cannot read, he cannot move his right side . . . he's totally dependent on your mother's care and your care. So what do you do to make him a little happier?"

Weiss explained that he visited his father almost daily, and that on Sundays he took his father out to a restaurant, and his father liked that.

The Rebbe did not seem satisfied with the response. "Do you do anything that's really fun for him?"

Weiss answered: "Well, it's hard to do that when a person can't read or talk."

"But what are the things that make him have fun?" the Rebbe pressed. Weiss explained that when his father was healthy, what he really enjoyed doing was going to a poolroom, playing cards there with his friends, and talking about the horse races. Weiss was a bit embarrassed: "I didn't want to bring this up because you're the Rebbe and to tell you about my father like this . . . but this is how he grew up. This is what he knows."

The Rebbe took it all in stride. "Well, why don't you take him to the poolroom, and maybe on Sundays you could bring him there to see his old friends and at least watch the card games being played and hear about the horse races?"

From then on, Weiss recalled, "We spent every Sunday at the poolroom, where he would sit for a couple of hours just to hear the usual drill of things that you would not hear in the synagogue."

Years later, Weiss remained impressed by the Rebbe's unexpected response. "He really considered every case individually. He asked me a brilliant question [about my father]: 'What are the things that make him have fun?' " [10]

The Rebbe's "Baby"

Diane Abrams recalls: "We would go regularly to 770 Eastern Parkway for special occasions such as for the receiving of a piece of honey cake [*lekach*] on Hoshana Rabbah [the last day of Sukkot]. On this holiday, there would be lines around the block with people from all over the world waiting patiently for the Rebbe to hand them a piece of cake as he stood in his sukkah. Our first child, Rachel, was ten years old at the time and we [my husband, Robert, was then serving as New York State attorney general] desperately were hoping for another child. We had even gone to an expert doctor who said that I had less than a 5 percent chance to have another child due to my age, which was forty-eight at the time. However, we told no one about our hopes and prayers. To our great shock and surprise, when the Rebbe handed us the *lekach* that day, he said out of the blue: 'I give you a *bracha* for an addition to your family within the next year.' We were stunned, amazed. I kept this *bracha* very much in mind after that meeting, and approximately six weeks later, I found out that I was pregnant with my second child. Great was our happiness. . . . We named her Binyamina for Bob's father, and she is known as Becky.

"When we came back the next year on Hoshana Rabbah, we brought Becky with us. As soon as the Rebbe saw me holding the baby in my arms, he smiled and said, 'I see you have brought the addition to the family with you.' We have always wondered. How did he remember the precise words of the previous year after having seen thousands and thousands of people? That is still a mystery.

"When we thanked him for his blessing, he said to us, 'Don't thank me.' And then he pointed up to the heavens.

"We found out that Becky became known in Crown Heights as 'the Rebbe's baby.' " [11]

A *Yechidus* That Changed a Life, and Then Another

Rabbi Shmuley Boteach, one of today's widest-selling and prolific writers on Judaism, recalls: "At the time of my bar mitzvah, the principal Lubavitch figure in my life was Shneur Zalman Fellig, a young rabbinical student who exerted spiritual influence on me, and was my surrogate older brother. . . . He somehow finagled a meeting between myself and the Rebbe. . . . I met the Rebbe at 3:00 a.m., in his tiny Brooklyn office, while hundreds waited outside for their private meetings. I had been told that I would have only a few moments with him, so I prepared a long letter detailing the negative effects of my parents' divorce on me, how I had become a cynic, and how my life at school consisted of teasing the girls and playing practical jokes on the teachers, while my life at home consisted mostly of fighting with my siblings and watching television.

"I was moved by the Rebbe's slow reading of my letter, occasionally marking passages with a short yellow pencil. When he finished, he looked up at me and I saw in his piercing blue eyes a sea of infinite kindness. He said to me: 'You are too young to be a cynic, especially since you will grow to be a source of *nachas*, inspiration, joy, and pride to your family, your school, and the entire Jewish people.' He then asked me to write to him and to inform him of the progress I was making in achieving these goals, and he said that he would write to me, too, a promise he kept. . . . I felt filled with hope for the first time in my life." [12]

Boteach recalls leaving the meeting with the feeling that it was a matter "of deep concern" to the Rebbe that Boteach do something with his life to aid humanity. Less than a decade later, while still in his early twenties, Boteach, by then an ordained rabbi, founded the L'Chaim Society at Oxford University, an organization that brought the teachings of Judaism to thousands of students, both Jews and non-Jews. Among those whom Boteach touched was Cory Booker, at the time a visiting Rhodes Scholar at Oxford. Over the years, the friendship between the African American Booker, a Christian, and the young rabbi grew very close. Boteach exposed Booker to the teachings of both Jewish texts and of the Rebbe, inciting an interest in Jewish thought that has remained with Booker ever since (he even shared a *dvar Torah*—a lesson from the Torah—when he delivered the 2012 commencement address at Yale College). Booker went on to become the mayor of Newark, New Jersey, and today serves as a New Jersey senator. Boteach, in turn, is now one of the foremost writers of books about Judaism—particularly on what Jewish teachings can offer both Jews and non-Jews—in the United States (see page 4 on Booker's visit to the Rebbe's grave on the night preceding his election to the Senate).

"We Cannot Abandon Any Ship"

In the 1960s, Rabbi Marvin (Moshe) Tokayer served as a U.S. Air Force chaplain in Japan, and subsequently returned to the United States. A graduate of the Jewish Theological Seminary, Tokayer took a position as the associate rabbi at a congregation in Great Neck, New York. Some time later, when Tokayer became engaged, a Lubavitcher Chasid whom he had befriended suggested that the soon-to-be-married couple go to the Rebbe for a blessing. Tokayer, who already had a brief but warm association with the Rebbe, complied. Some years earlier, while a college student at Yeshiva University, he had met with the Rebbe to discuss questions he had about Jewish thought. He had been very taken with the Rebbe who, in addition to a wide-ranging intellect, had "the most intriguing and beautiful eyes I had ever seen. . . . I felt he understood me more than I understood myself."

Only now, when he came in for what he assumed would be a brief encounter, the Rebbe giving him and his fiancée a blessing for their marriage, the Rebbe politely greeted him, then said words that seemed to make no sense at all: "It is enough that you were working with the dead, now you need to work with the living." The utterly confused Tokayer had no idea what the Rebbe was alluding to. "Rebbe, I don't understand."

The Rebbe ignored his response: "Enough working with the dead, now you need to work with the living."

When Tokayer again expressed his confusion, the Rebbe mentioned a newspaper article he had read some time earlier that spoke of Tokayer, during his years as a chaplain, discovering a Jewish cemetery in Nagasaki. "Why are you wasting your time looking for cemeteries? There are living people in Japan. Japan is a growing country and they need a rabbi."

True, Tokayer knew, there was no rabbi servicing the small Jewish community in Japan, but he was not interested, and his wife even less so. The young rabbi tried to steer the conversation in other directions, but the Rebbe wouldn't let go. When Tokayer noted that in any case he didn't speak Japanese, the Rebbe pointed out that he knew English, Hebrew, and Yiddish—three languages that would serve him well in dealing with most of the Jews there, few if any of whom were actually Japanese. In addition, the Rebbe thought that Tokayer's college education would serve him well. "I think you should go there."

Again Tokayer said no, and the Rebbe tried yet another tack: "When I send someone to be my emissary, it's a one-way ticket, they don't come back. But you, you do not have to stay there forever."

Tokayer understood how unusual this situation was. The Rebbe clearly was distraught that there was no rabbi in Japan, and that he had no one appropriate in his community to send there. Why else, Tokayer understood, would he ask a graduate of the Jewish Theological Seminary to assume this responsibility?

Tokayer again declined, but eventually circumstances conspired against him, including three invitations, each one increasingly urgent, from the president of the Japanese Jewish community. Finally, he and his wife decided to go for two years, to have a bit of an adventure; in the end, they stayed for many years.

Before leaving to assume his new position, Tokayer returned to 770. The Rebbe, well aware that Tokayer, though highly traditional, had received his rabbinical training at the Conservative seminary, asked him to whom he would turn when difficult questions of Jewish law arose. The Rebbe offered either himself or Rabbi Moshe Feinstein, the preeminent decisor of Jewish law, as resources. Tokayer said that because of the Rebbe's very extensive responsibilities, it would probably be best if he called upon Rabbi Feinstein. The Rebbe arranged to introduce Rabbi Tokayer to Reb Moshe.

Today, the Far East is dotted with small Jewish communities and many rabbis, most of them from Chabad. But that was not the case then, and Tokayer has never forgotten the Rebbe's words: "We cannot abandon any ship. No community should be abandoned."

Tzaddikim Without Tefillin

Rebbetzin Chaya Mushka Schneerson shared in her husband's love and warm appreciation of the good acts performed by Jews who were not conventionally religious. She was known to refer to the individuals involved in Bricha, the underground organization whose members helped Jews escape from Russia and Eastern Europe in the years immediately following World War II, as "tzaddikim without tefillin" (saints who don't put on tefillin). The weekday wearing of tefillin is among the most fundamental commandments observed by Jewish men, and the term "tzaddik" is, as a rule, reserved for only the most pious of Jews. That the Rebbetzin applied this high appellation to ritually non-observant but exceedingly self-sacrificing and heroic Jews is reminiscent of her husband's contention that the Israeli soldiers who fought in the Six-Day War acquired greater religious merit than those who sat and studied Torah during this period (see page 288).[13]

Why Moses Looked to See if There Were Witnesses

Gershon Jacobson was a longtime journalist and founder of the *Algemeiner Journal* (see page 165). On one occasion when meeting with the Rebbe, the Rebbe suddenly said to him, "You're a journalist, so if you'd like, you can interview me."

As the Rebbe rarely granted interviews, Jacobson was taken aback. But then he asked, "One of the questions people are asking is why the Rebbe takes on causes that seemingly are impossible or that no one else is touching on." To this day, Gershon's son, Simon, is not sure whether his father was alluding to any specific cause, but he suspects it was the conflict in Israel over "Who is a Jew?" (see pages 493–94).

Instead of responding directly, the Rebbe turned to an episode in the Torah: "The first story the Torah tells us about Moses's heroism was when he went out of Pharaoh's palace [where he had been raised] and saw an Egyptian hitting a Jewish slave. The Torah then adds on a very odd phrase: 'And he looked this way and that, and he saw that there was no man about, and he struck down the Egyptian'" (Exodus 2:12). The Rebbe then asked, "Why does the Torah feel it's so important for us to know that Moses was being so cautious? Some commentaries say it was because he didn't want anyone to see what he was doing. But is this really so important, that Moses of all things cared so much about saving his own skin? And the fact is, his act was seen" (see Exodus 2:14). "Rather," the Rebbe suggested, "what happened was this: 'Moses saw that a Jew was being hurt. He looked around to see if anyone cared; instead, he saw "there was no man," no one was standing up and protesting. When no one else is doing something, Moses comes and does what he has to do."

"At this point, the Rebbe stopped," Simon Jacobson remembers his father telling him. "But my father understood what he was saying: 'The causes I take upon myself are because I see that no one else is taking them upon themselves; they're ignoring it. That's precisely why I become involved.'"

"You didn't ask"

P eter Kalms, the faithful chronicler of nine *yechidusen* with the Rebbe (*Guidance from the Rebbe*), is a well-to-do British businessman who invested in a number of different ventures, one of which involved the buying and selling of old maps, as well as autographed letters by famous people. In a 1981 *yechidus*, he explained to the Rebbe that the business, which he had earlier informed the Rebbe he was entering, was not succeeding as he had hoped.

To Kalms's considerable surprise, the Rebbe commented that he had thought that Kalms should not go into this business as he did not think that there was a real future in the modern technological age for "old maps and antiquities." In addition, "this is not your field."

Kalms wondered why the Rebbe hadn't said something earlier, and the Rebbe answered, "You didn't ask."

The Rebbe then proceeded to explain to Kalms that his father-in-law, the Frierdiker Rebbe, had long ago advised him: "If a person doesn't ask your advice, you should not give it." [14]

"How many mothers did Moshe Rabbeinu have?"

W hen Rabbi Chaim Gutnick of Australia told the Rebbe of a class for women on the laws of family purity (*taharat ha-mishpacha*) that he had helped arrange and complained that only one woman had come to the class, the Rebbe responded, "How many mothers did Moshe Rabbeinu have?"

"There is no such thing as a small Jew"

In 1982, Rabbi Moshe Kotlarsky, who today directs development for the global network of *shluchim*, was asked by Rabbi Chaim Hodakov, the Rebbe's chief of staff, to visit the small Jewish community on the Caribbean island of Curaçao, and deliver a speech about Judaism there. One of those who attended Kotlarsky's talk was a man named Chaim Yosef Groisman, who seemed startled that a representative of Chabad had come to his hometown. Decades earlier, Groisman's grandmother had told him that if he ever encountered a difficult, seemingly insurmountable problem, the person to whom he should turn was the Lubavitcher Rebbe. Now, indeed, Groisman had a problem, and a representative of the Rebbe had come to Curaçao. Groisman consulted with Rabbi Kotlarsky, who was able to assist him. Shortly thereafter he wrote Kotlarsky a warm letter thanking him, and asked him "to tell the Rebbe that a small Jew from Curaçao felt that the Rebbe . . . touched my soul."

Rabbi Kotlarsky sent a copy of the letter to the Rebbe, who was moved by Groisman's heartfelt thanks, though distressed by one aspect of the man's warm regards: "I must take exception to your referring to yourself as 'a small Jew from Curaçao,'" he wrote to Groisman. "Every Jew, man or woman, has a soul which is part of Godliness above, as explained in the *Tanya*. Thus, there is no such thing as 'a small Jew,' and a Jew must never underestimate his or her tremendous potential."

Helping to Sculpt a Young Soul

R abbi Moshe Kotlarsky grew up in the 1950s in the then relatively small Lubavitch community in Crown Heights. Kotlarsky recalls how children would vie for the chance to hold the door open for the Rebbe as he would come and go from 770, and thereby receive a greeting from him. Once a month, on those Saturday nights on which the *kiddush levana* prayer (blessing the new moon) was recited outdoors under the sky, a child would hold the door for the Rebbe and get a greeting or a *bracha* from him on his way back inside. What made this occasion particularly auspicious was the chance to get three blessings from the Rebbe at the same time: a *yasher koach* (a congratulatory greeting and thank-you for holding the door), a *gut vokh* (a blessing for a good week, as in Jewish tradition the new week begins when Shabbat concludes), and a *gut chodesh*, a greeting for the upcoming month. Rabbi Kotlarsky remembers one Saturday night when, as a child of only six or seven, he proudly held the door as the Rebbe stepped outside to recite the *kiddush levana* prayer. The young Kotlarsky stood by the door, watching the Rebbe reciting the prayer, as he eagerly anticipated the Rebbe coming back and offering the three greetings. Instead, when the Rebbe returned he said to the young boy with a gentle smile, "Did you bless the moon or were you busy holding the door?" The answer was self-evident, and the Rebbe continued. "First, *bentch levana* [say the prayer for the new moon] and then come to my office." Kotlarsky immediately stepped outside to recite the prayer. When he finished, he came back in, and knocked on the Rebbe's door, and the Rebbe gave him the three blessings.

To this day, Rabbi Kotlarsky reflects on how the Rebbe's handling of the situation taught him an important lesson. He brought the young boy to a right action not through reproof, but rather by simply pointing out what needed to be done, and by doing so in a gentle way. Once the boy had done what he needed to, the Rebbe gladly offered the three greetings he knew the child coveted.

Stamp Collecting

R abbi Binyamin Klein, the Rebbe's secretary, recalls an instance
  when a couple came to the Rebbe, along with their young daughter. At one point, the Rebbe turned to the girl and asked her if she
had a hobby. "Stamp collecting," the girl replied. The Rebbe opened
his drawer, took out some recent letters he had received, and tore off
and gave the girl some foreign stamps. For an extended period after the
meeting, Klein relates, the Rebbe continued to remove stamps from
incoming mail and had his secretaries send them to the young girl.

The Blessing from a Bat Mitzvah Girl

S hulamit Saxon, an eleven-year-old girl in Crown Heights, was due to
  celebrate her bat mitzvah in September 1983. In anticipation of the
special day, she wrote a letter to the Rebbe, asking for his blessing that
she have a good year. But she also had the impulse to give the Rebbe a
blessing and not just ask for one.

Although the Rebbe and Rebbetzin were then in their early eighties,
she felt the best thing she could wish for them was that they be granted
children of their own. Aware of the sensitivity of the issue, she wanted to
be certain that the Rebbe, who was known to personally open all letters
addressed to him, would be the only one to see her message. And so, in
addition to writing the Rebbe a standard sort of letter informing him
of her upcoming bat mitzvah, she added a one-line blessing, written in
Hebrew letters but employing a code.

The code she used was a simple one, but one that would be deci-
phered only if the letter was read carefully, and by someone who had
some talent in deciphering codes. She substituted each letter with the
one that followed it. For example, instead of writing an *aleph*, she wrote
a *bet*, the Hebrew equivalent of, for example, substituting a *b* for an *a* and
a *c* for a *b*.

So instead of writing, "I bless the Rebbe that he have children," she wrote this thought in code, "J cmftt uif Sfccf uibu if ibwf dijmesfo" (the preceding is presented as if she had written the Rebbe in English, though her letter was in Hebrew).

A few weeks later, she received a letter from the Rebbe with the standard message he would send to all girls about to celebrate their bat mitzvah, blessing her that she lead the life of a worthy Jewish woman, and serve as a good example for the rest of the community. But then, at the letter's bottom, the Rebbe added a line, responding to the young girl in the same code in which she had written him. As the Rebbe expressed it, "Uibol zpv gps uif cmfttjoh," meaning "Thank you for the blessing."

Accepting Responsibility

Rabbi Jonathan Sacks recalls an early meeting with the Rebbe, when he, Sacks, said in passing, "I found myself in a situation . . ." The Rebbe stopped him and told Sacks that the expression "I found myself in a situation" was both inaccurate and an evasion of responsibility; one should say, rather, "I placed myself in a situation." And the Rebbe continued, "If you can place yourself in one situation, then you can place yourself in another situation."

Sacks notes that since then he has "never been able again to make that excuse . . . and believe it."

"If You Give Over Your Will, You Become a Robot. God Doesn't Want That."

Rabbi Zalman Schachter-Shalomi was teaching Jewish studies in Winnipeg, Canada, at the University of Manitoba. He started to feel restless and asked the Rebbe if he could move to Mumbai, India, and take over a congregation there. The Rebbe did not think this was a good idea and said no. Some time later, Reb Zalman sent the Rebbe another proposal: that he open up a Lubavitch center on Wall Street (this was several decades before Chabad's great expansion). The Rebbe vetoed this idea, which could cost a considerable amount of money to launch, as well.

By now Reb Zalman was upset and angry and decided to come to Brooklyn and confront the Rebbe in person. "Why was the Rebbe keeping me in Winnipeg when I could do greater things in the world?" he remembers thinking. Yet, a few hours later when he saw the Rebbe at the evening *ma'ariv* service shortly before their meeting, the Rebbe was coughing badly and looked exhausted. Reb Zalman was filled with compassion. He knew that the Rebbe worked very long hours and made himself available to everyone who had a need. His anger and sense of rebellion melted away, and when he went in for his *yechidus*, he simply asked the Rebbe: "Since you've said no to this and no to that, here's my feeling. You program me. You call the shots, and I'll jump where you tell me to go."

The Rebbe looked at Reb Zalman a long while and shook his head. "What you're describing is *hefech ha-chayyim* [the opposite of life, i.e., death]. If you give over your will, you become a robot. God doesn't want that."

Egyptian President Hosni Mubarak: "What Does the Lubavitcher Rebbe Want from Me?"

The Israeli journalist Yisroel Katzover made eleven trips to Egypt during the years President Hosni Mubarak was in power. On one of those occasions, Mubarak had just spent some time meeting with a number of Israeli journalists and then asked Katzover, whom he knew to be a religious Jew, to stay behind. To the journalist's shock, the president said, "I have a question for you. Can you explain to me: What does the Lubavitcher Rebbe want from me?" Katzover was taken aback. "To what is the president referring?" he asked. Mubarak said: "He speaks out against the peace treaty with us. He sees us as a threat in the future. Why does he do this? What does he have against me?" Mubarak's questions prompted a half-hour conversation between the two men, in which Katzover tried to explain the Rebbe's hesitations about the peace treaty and culminated in Katzover suggesting that on Mubarak's next visit to New York he meet with the Rebbe. No such meeting ever occurred, but two decades later the fact that the Egyptian leader was so familiar with who the Rebbe was—and that he was so concerned with the Rebbe's opposition to the peace treaty—astounded, and continues to astound, Katzover.[15]

"What is a Rebbe good for?"

When Rabbi Zalman Schachter-Shalomi was Hillel director at the University of Manitoba in Winnipeg, Canada, he brought a group of students to meet with the Rebbe in Brooklyn. At the conclusion of the Rebbe's opening remarks, one of the students, intending to be blunt rather than disrespectful, asked him: "What's a Rebbe good for?" To this day, Reb Zalman remembers his feelings at that moment: "I could have sunk through the floor in embarrassment." However, the Rebbe didn't seem offended at all and responded to the query directly:

"I can't speak about myself, but I can tell you about my own Rebbe [his father-in-law]. For me, my Rebbe was the geologist of the soul. You see, there are so many treasures in the earth. There is gold, there is silver, and there are diamonds. But if you don't know where to dig, you'll only find dirt and rocks and mud. The Rebbe can tell you where to dig, and what to dig for, but the digging you must do yourself."[16]

Part Five

·(⚭)·

UNITING

the

JEWS

The Rebbe's Approach to a Fractured People

Chapter 15

·(⁓⁓⁓⁓)·

"THERE ALSO NEEDS TO BE A GIRL"

Women, Judaism, and the Twentieth Century

Dvorah Leah, daughter of the Alter Rebbe, died at age twenty-six. It is widely accepted in Chabad that she took upon herself such a fate so as to spare her father, then sick, from a premature death. The *Sefer ha-Toldot Admur ha-Zaken* (*The Biography of the Alter Rebbe*) relates that on the eve of Rosh Hashanah, just after the afternoon Mincha service, she entered the small synagogue where her family prayed and found other members of her family, along with her father's closest disciples, reciting Psalms.

She approached the Ark, opened it, and declared in the presence of the Torah scrolls: "I call all of you to witness that I, Dvorah Leah, daughter of Sterna, hereby pledge upon the holy Torah scrolls—in full and complete awareness of my actions, and with the most solemn and binding vows—to take the place of my father, Rabbi Shneur Zalman ben Rivka, so that he may live and not die."

This act was done without her father's knowledge, and later that evening, when he tried to offer her the customary New Year's blessing, she cut him off before he could finish. She then offered him the traditional blessing, "Father, be inscribed and sealed for a good year," then added, "Say nothing more, Father," thereby stopping him from completing his blessing to her.

On the second day of Rosh Hashanah, Dvorah Leah took ill, and she died a day later, on the third of Tishrei, 5553 (1792). Her dying wish, it is said, was that her father personally educate her son, a young child not yet three. The Alter Rebbe promised to do so, and declared, "Your son Menachem is a comfort to me [the name "Menachem" means "one who comforts"]; he will be a comfort to you and to all Israel." This son, Menachem Mendel, grew up to be the Third Rebbe, and the forebearer and namesake of the Seventh Rebbe.[1]

In traditional Orthodox circles, there has always been a recognition of righteous women as models, going back to the Matriarchs. On Friday evenings, fathers bless their daughters: "May God make you like Sarah, Rachel, Rebecca, and Leah." However, as a rule, the Bible's central female figures are known because of who their husbands were. Sarah, though regarded as a great spiritual model—God tells Abraham, "Whatever Sarah tells you to do, do as she says" (Genesis 21:12)—nonetheless is best known for being Abraham's wife, as Rachel is for being married to Jacob.

However, three biblical women are known for their own accomplishments: the prophetess Deborah, who served as a judge and as a leader of the community in Israel's earliest days (book of Judges, chapters 4–5); Ruth, a Moabite woman who joins the Jewish people and from whom the Messiah will descend (book of Ruth); and Esther, the Jewish princess who thwarts Haman's genocidal attempt to wipe out the Jewish people. Esther worked closely in conjunction with her cousin Mordechai but, as the Rebbe pointed out on many occasions, the scroll named for these events in ancient Persia is "Esther," not "Esther and Mordechai."

Despite these striking examples, the focus in Jewish life has long been directed to male figures and to the virtual exclusion of female ones. This phenomenon developed and accelerated in postbiblical, post-Talmudic Jewish life. Thus, while there are few people who know the names of the Patriarchs and not those of their wives, or the name of Moses and not the name of his sister, Miriam, we find that all knowledgeable Jews know the names of the two greatest rabbinic figures of the medieval world, Rashi and Maimonides, but no one, scholars included, know the names of their wives, or of almost any other medieval Jewish women, for that matter.

Similarly, in the history of Chasidism, stories are told about many dozens of different Chasidic Rebbes, but few about great female Chasidim. When such stories are related, they often focus on the self-sacrificial manner in which these women enabled their husbands, or children, or, as in the above story about Dvorah Leah, their father, to fulfill their spiritual destinies. Women were traditionally thought of as enablers of men (or of their children) rather than as great figures in their own right.

The Rebbe was concerned to see this change, and he understood that it could be initiated only by first changing people's perceptions and expectations, particularly those of younger people, including younger women. Therefore, if until now males were perceived as being the only ones in the forefront of Jewish life, then women had to start being seen as playing a more public role, a transformation that involved overturning traditional expectations.

Susan Handelman, a professor of English at Bar-Ilan University, has noted the quiet revolution engineered with the Rebbe's encouragement in the children's magazine *The Moshiach Times,* which Chabad began publishing in 1981. The journal was the publication of the Chabad youth group, Tzivos Hashem (Soldiers of Hashem), and was tied in with Chabad's campaign to encourage people to perform acts of goodness to hasten the coming of the Messiah. One of the primary *mitzvot* the magazine focused on was *ahavat Yisrael,* the love of all Jews. In line with this, the artist who designed the magazine's first cover depicted a group of boys dancing together, each holding a letter of the word *"Yisrael."* Standing one level above the boys, four dancing girls were depicted, each holding a letter of the Hebrew word *"ahavat"* ("love of"). When the cover's prototype was examined by the movement's staff, one expressed consternation at the depiction of girls and boys dancing on the same page, which seemed to him inappropriate, even immodest. Other staff members argued that since the Tzivos Hashem organization had both boys and girls as members, the cover was appropriate. It was decided to seek the Rebbe's guidance and he quickly made it known that he thought the cover was fine.[2]

The second issue was due to come out shortly before Purim, and a cover was designed showing a boy and a girl in Purim costumes blowing bubbles, each alongside a caption depicting the various *mitzvot* and activities associated with the holiday. Again, an objection was raised: Unlike the first cover, the boy and girl were not separated but standing next to each other. Once again, the cover was submitted to the Rebbe, who returned it with a check, indicating his approval.

A month later was Passover, and this time the proposed cover consisted of a boy looking at a stamp album, with each of the fifteen stamps in the album depicting one of the fifteen stages of the Passover Seder. The nature of the rather busy drawing seemed to allow no room for an additional figure in the picture. By now, however, it seemed customary to seek the Rebbe's approval for the cover, and it was sent to him. A reply quickly followed: *Tzarich li'hiyot gam na'arah* ("There also needs to be a girl"). The artist redesigned the cover so that it included the faces of a boy and a girl sitting near each other, looking into the album together.

Some months later, a cover was designed showing a boy on one corner of the page coming home from summer camp carrying his summer equipment and walking into his bedroom, which contained holy objects, such as a *tzedakah* (charity) box, a *Chumash* (the Torah), and a prayer book. A moving picture, but the Rebbe was not satisfied. For one thing, he wanted the boy's tzitzit (ritual fringes) to be showing. And, as could now be anticipated, "There must be a girl in another corner." The picture was redrawn to show the boy entering a common room, in which a girl, presumably his sister, is playing.

"There also needs to be a girl"; "There must be a girl in another corner," the Rebbe had written. These might seem to be minor innovations, but they weren't. When Handelman first spoke of these four covers at an academic conference, she feared that she would call into question her own credentials as a literary scholar; others might find the issue too trivial to speak of in an academic setting. When her lecture concluded, she saw another member of the university faculty rushing toward her, and she prepared herself for a possible onslaught. Instead, the woman expressed tremendous enthusiasm. "I grew up in Bnai Akiva [the Modern Orthodox youth movement in Israel]," she told Handelman, "and I never saw a girl on the cover of any of our magazines."

The attitudinal change suggested by these magazine covers was dwarfed by the change the Rebbe brought about in upgrading the status of *shluchot*, the women who serve with their husbands as emissaries. People commonly err when they speak of some four thousand–plus Chabad *shluchim* currently serving throughout the world. The number four thousand does not represent individuals but rather the number of couples serving on *shlichut*; alternatively, and more accurately, one can speak of eight thousand *shluchim*.

In all denominational movements of Judaism, rabbis' wives are known as rebbetzins, but the term is an honorific one (in Reform, Conservative, Jewish Renewal, and Reconstructionist Judaism, all of which ordain women, there is no title for the spouse of a female rabbi). Some rebbetzins choose to be active participants in their spouses' work; others don't. Rebbetzins are certainly not perceived as having defined responsibilities simply by virtue of being married to a rabbi. The case of Chabad is different. To cite one example, Rabbi Nisson and Rochel Pinson were sent to Tunisia in 1952 as *shluchim*. Since Rabbi Pinson's death in 2007, Rebbetzin Pinson has continued to direct Chabad activities in the country.

Similarly, while all rabbinical organizations have annual or periodic conventions at which rabbis come together, it is inconceivable that there would be a specific convention organized for rebbetzins. In Chabad, specifically because the *shluchot* are perceived as full work partners with their husbands, a convention of *shluchot* is convened each year in February, and some three thousand women attend (the gathering does not occur at the same time as the annual November convention for men, one reason presumably being that during the time the husbands attend their convention, their spouses are in charge of the Chabad Houses). Did such a status for *shluchot* exist prior to the Rebbe? No. The wives of rabbis were treated with respect, but they were not perceived as full-fledged partners. This was the Rebbe's innovation, and it was he who suggested the annual convention for *shluchot*.

On Women Dancing with the Torah

"Not only may you do it [next year], you *must* do it."
—Speaking to Rabbi Shlomo Riskin about a special Simchat Torah service for women that Rabbi Riskin had recently instituted

When Rabbi Shlomo Riskin became rabbi at Lincoln Square Synagogue in Manhattan, he instituted intensive courses in Jewish study for women as well as for men. On the Jewish holiday of Shemini Atzeret, eight women who had spent the past year or more studying the Bible and the Talmud knocked on the door of Riskin's apartment. The rabbi invited them in, but this was clearly not a social visit: "We've come with a serious question," Riskin recalls them saying. "Tomorrow evening ushers in Simchat Torah, when every male, even a male child, gets called up to the Torah and is offered the opportunity to dance with the Torah. Every male is filled with such joy of Torah . . . but only the males, not us, the females. Why can't we read from the Torah and dance with the Torah? . . . Didn't God call out his Sinaitic Revelation both [to the men and the women]? Why aren't we adult learned women as privileged as a male child?"[3]

Rabbi Riskin promised to answer their query the next day and stayed up the entire night, poring over the Talmud, the codes of Jewish law, and the rabbinic responsa that addressed related issues. He knew, of course, that the prevailing tradition in Orthodox synagogues was that only men carry the Torah or even touch it. But what quickly became apparent to him during that night of study is that while *custom* excluded women from any physical contact with the Torah, there was no actual legal ban on their doing so. Therefore, the following morning he ruled that there could be a women's service at which women could both read from the Torah (without the blessings that Jewish law mandates for men) and dance with it.

Immediately after the holiday concluded, the same group of women returned to his house to tell him what an ecstatic experience they had, how women from the ages of fifteen to seventy-five had wept with joy at being allowed to be in such close proximity to the Torah for the first time. Riskin was overjoyed. "And then all hell broke loose."

A prominent rabbinic scholar, whose congregation was in close proximity to Riskin's, announced that if Lincoln Square Synagogue had allowed women to perform *hakafot* (dance cycles around the synagogue while carrying the Torah), and also read from the Torah, then it could no longer be regarded as an Orthodox synagogue.

Riskin was devastated. He felt that what he had achieved at his congregation that Simchat Torah was a "historically significant religious experience," and now his very rabbinic credentials were being challenged. He consulted with his foremost teacher, Rabbi Joseph Soloveitchik, who assured him that though it was not the prevailing custom in Jewish communities, Jewish law permitted what he had done.

Then Riskin went to see the Rebbe. He wanted to hear his response to the situation, though he had no reason to assume that the Rebbe would approve of what he had done. Certainly at 770, there was no special service for women to dance with Torah scrolls, nor did such services occur at any of the services conducted by Lubavitcher *shluchim* throughout the world. The meeting that ensued turned out to be the longest meeting with the Rebbe that Riskin had ever had, lasting almost two hours. The conversation ranged over many issues involving women and Jewish law, during which the Rebbe said that the greatest challenge to Orthodoxy in this century is the place of the Orthodox woman. He told Riskin that he had revived the custom (*minhag*) of young girls lighting Shabbat candles because he wanted girls, no less than boys, to feel that they are as much "children of God" (*bnot Hashem*; literally, "daughters of God") as boys, and he thought that that was especially important at this point in history. He also spoke in glowing terms of the importance of Torah study for women, and he was proud to tell Riskin that, with his encouragement, Rabbi Yitzchak Groner, the Rebbe's *shliach* in Australia, offered a weekly Talmud class for women, which included *rishonim* (the medieval commentators who are normally studied only by advanced Talmud students), a fact that greatly and pleasantly surprised Riskin. The Rebbe, whose mind was constantly focused on hastening the Messiah's coming, suggested that one sign of the Messianic Days (*yemot ha-Moshiach*) is that women, like men, would be studying Judaism's holy texts.

Together with the Rebbe, Riskin reviewed the main legal sources concerning the issue of women and Torah scrolls. While it was clear that, according to Jewish law, there was no problem with women holding or reading from a Torah scroll, it was equally clear that a custom had developed in Jewish life (cited by Rabbi Moshe Isserles, the sixteenth-century Polish sage known as the Rama, whose rulings form part of the *Shulchan Aruch*) that women not touch the Torah during their menstrual period. This in turn expanded into a custom that women never touch the Torah at all (and not even enter the synagogue to look at the Torah scroll during their menstrual period). The Rama conceded that women not touching the Torah was only a custom—albeit one very widely practiced—and not binding Jewish law. On the other hand, in the Orthodox world, custom sometimes acquires the virtual status of law.

Finally, after Riskin explained to the Rebbe the sort of women who were coming to his synagogue—many of whom were highly intellectual and from largely nonobservant backgrounds, and who had been drawn into Jewish practice largely through their attraction to Torah study—and that some of them would leave Orthodox life if they were forbidden the innovation Riskin had made, the Rebbe said to him: "Not only may you do it, you *must* do it." [4]

Riskin left the meeting feeling that he had received tremendous confirmation for what he had done, though he understood from a letter that the Rebbe wrote him shortly afterward that he was extending his approval to Riskin's synagogue and was not "speaking general policy." Thus, Riskin did not feel that he had the right to cite the Rebbe as having offered a blanket approval for women to conduct *hakafot* on Simchat Torah, especially not for movements like Chabad itself that had preexisting customs in place. One might argue, though, that such approval could perhaps be extended to a congregation like Lincoln Square Synagogue, many of whose members were growing in observance, and which included women highly committed to Torah study who were accustomed to working in the secular world in positions alongside men, and who would find alienating any policies that restricted their access to the Torah scroll. Obviously, the women at Rabbi Riskin's synagogue were not anti-Orthodox, but what they refused to accept were restrictions on their contact with the Torah scroll. And the Rebbe, whose own communities practiced a different standard of behavior, clearly supported Riskin's efforts not to impose such restrictions on his community.

Chapter 16

·◦⟨═══⟩◦·

REFORM JEWS, CONSERVATIVE JEWS, AND THE REBBE'S OPEN DOOR

"YOU SHOULD SAY TO ME, 'SCHNEERSON, LOOK OUT YOUR WINDOW AND SEE WHAT YOU STILL HAVE TO DO.'"

Learning from Reform and Conservative Jews

In a speech that the Rebbe gave in July 1958, he made reference to a controversy going on within the Orthodox world and, without being specific, criticized the tendency among many observant Jews to be more mindful of opinions of lay leaders than of rabbis. The Rebbe made it clear that in the matter under discussion, it would be best to have two or three rabbis clarify what should be done, rather than have the decision made by lay leaders.

The late rabbi Zvi Hirsh Gansbourg (1928–2006), who wrote a detailed summary of this *sicha* in his diary, recorded that the Rebbe's talk then veered off in an unexpected direction: "The Rebbe stated that with regard to this [issue of not entrusting authority to lay leaders in matters that should be decided by rabbis], we can learn from the positive qualities found among Conservative and Reform Jews. He said: 'The laws regarding [such movements] are stated in Rambam[1] [i.e., that many of their religious views and practices are illegitimate], however, the Mishnah instructs us, 'Who is wise? He who learns from every person' (*Ethics of the Fathers* 4:1). Among the positive qualities he then mentioned were:

- not speaking during the reading of the Torah or during the cantor's repetition of the prayers;

• not raising money through projects that are unbecoming to the synagogue, for example, bingo or card games;

• in religious matters, the Rabbi's ruling is the determining factor, and the lay leaders do not become involved." [2]

How the Rebbe knew these things, we do not know. He spoke of the decorum at non-Orthodox services, but of one thing we can be quite sure: He never attended such a service. On the other hand, the information concerning not permitting bingo or card games in synagogues as fund-raisers had been widely publicized in the press.

In drawing out the positive lessons described above, the Rebbe could simply have spoken of these three points as desired characteristics. There was no need for him to point to Reform and Conservative Jews as the ones practicing these virtues.

Why did he do so?

As the Rebbe's opposition to Reform and Conservative theology was well known, it is possible that he, in line with his love for fellow Jews, did not want it to appear that he opposed everything Reform and Conservative Jews did. One way to fulfill the commandment of "Love your neighbor," when dealing with a neighbor who has traits you don't love or admire, is to focus on those traits that you do. One can think of few other Orthodox leaders who went out of their way to specify, particularly in public, lessons that Orthodox Jews should learn from their Reform and Conservative brethren.

Advising a Reform Rabbi Who Asked If He Should Leave His Pulpit

There have long been Orthodox Jews, some highly devoted to the Rebbe, such as the late rabbi David Hollander, who would have preferred that Jews in America have but two alternatives: Orthodoxy or nothing. This attitude was apparently animated by the belief that

Reform and Conservative Judaism represent "nothing" in terms of spirituality and commitment to Judaism, and therefore beguile people into thinking they are practicing Judaism when they are not.

Rabbi Hollander criticized the Rebbe for permitting students at the Conservative movement's Jewish Theological Seminary to attend events at Chabad; he thought it inappropriate for them to be there and, on occasion, when he would see a Conservative rabbi attending a *farbrengen*, he would leave.[3]

This kind of attitude was utterly alien to the Rebbe: The thought of making Jews of any denomination feel unwelcome at Chabad was totally opposed to the Rebbe's notions concerning love of one's fellow. Even so, he strenuously opposed both the ideologies and practices of Conservative and Reform Judaism. Conservative Judaism introduced changes into Jewish law such as permitting people to drive to synagogue on the Sabbath, while the Reform movement had long declared the observance of Jewish ritual laws, such as the laws of keeping kosher, to no longer be binding.

To the Rebbe such changes falsified Judaism. That is one reason he opposed Orthodox rabbis joining rabbinical organizations such as local boards of rabbis, since membership in such organizations might convey the impression that all ideological expressions of Judaism are equally valid. But he also encouraged Orthodox rabbis to maintain friendly relations with non-Orthodox rabbis and to study with them if they were interested. He explained his position on non-Orthodox movements to a Reform rabbi in the mid-1950s: "The great fault of Conservative and Reform Judaism is not that they compromise, but that they sanctify the compromise . . . and leave no possibility for return." The Rebbe went on to say that while Chabad encouraged Jews to observe as many of the commandments as they could be influenced to observe, even if only a few, it insisted that Jewish tradition be identified with Orthodox Judaism. Otherwise, a Jew who wished to repent and return to Judaism would not know what it was to which he should return.[4]

On one occasion, Rabbi Zalman Schachter-Shalomi encouraged his friend, Rabbi Dudley Weinberg, a Reform rabbi in Milwaukee, to meet with the Rebbe. Weinberg found himself very taken with the Rebbe's charisma and understanding of Judaism (the *yechidus* lasted more than three hours). At one point, as he told Schachter-Shalomi, he asked the Rebbe, "Should I stop serving my Reform congregation?" "You should continue," the Rebbe told him. "You're a soldier on the front." Weinberg later confided to Rabbi Yisroel Shmotkin, the Chabad *shliach* in Milwaukee: "The Rebbe just had to point with his finger and I would have been out of there." But the Rebbe didn't point with his finger, and Weinberg—a soldier on the front—continued at his synagogue. And just as the Rebbe challenged Weinberg to do more, he then told the Reform rabbi that he should challenge him as well: "You should say to me, 'Schneerson, look out your window and see what you still have to do.'"

The Rebbe similarly advised Dov Zlotnick, a halachically observant Jew and a prize student of Professor Saul Lieberman (the great Talmud scholar at the Jewish Theological Seminary), to continue working at the congregation where he was serving. Subsequent to receiving ordination at JTS, Zlotnick became the spiritual leader of a Conservative synagogue in Swampscott, Massachusetts. He helped the congregation institute a daily minyan, influenced many members to start putting on tefillin, and intensified the Jewish education offered to the synagogue's children.

Zlotnick would use the money he received for officiating at funerals, weddings, and bar mitzvahs to buy tefillin for members of the congregation who as yet were not putting on tefillin. He and his wife, Alice, loved the warmth of the community and the city's physical beauty (their house was just a few blocks from the ocean). After he occupied the pulpit for only two years, the congregation offered him a lifetime contract, a highly unusual and powerful vote of confidence. Zlotnick cared deeply for his congregants but also was greatly tempted to return to the Jewish Theological Seminary, where he had been offered the opportunity to teach.

His father-in-law was upset that Zlotnick seemed inclined to accept the position at the Seminary: "What do you want to leave this beautiful place for?" he challenged his son-in-law. Rabbi Zlotnick knew what his father-in-law was thinking: *Why leave a loyal congregation, a beautiful neighborhood, and a well-paying job, in exchange for an academic position that offered none of these advantages?*

The two men decided to consult with the Rebbe. Alice Zlotnick recalls the report of the *yechidus* that she received from both her husband and her father.[5] Dov Zlotnick explained to the Rebbe why he wanted to leave the pulpit while his father-in-law explained why he wanted him to stay. The Rebbe thought for a moment, then said to the young Zlotnick: "Dov, are you smarter than Moshe Rabbeinu [our teacher Moses]?" Alice Zlotnick recalls her husband being "taken aback"; he had no idea what the Rebbe meant. But then the Rebbe continued: "Moses listened to his father-in-law."

The Rebbe was alluding to a well-known passage in the Torah, in which Jethro, Moses's father-in-law, comes to visit Moses in the desert. The relationship between the two men is warm; Moses bows when he sees Jethro, kisses him, and ushers his father-in-law into his tent. Jethro, in turn, expresses his admiration for the God of Israel, to Whom he offers a sacrifice. But one thing bothers Jethro on his visit; his son-in-law spends his entire day adjudicating conflicts between feuding Israelites and offering people advice. "Why do you act alone?" he challenges Moses.

Moses defends his behavior, arguing that his personal involvement is necessary to make known God's teachings (Exodus 18:15–16). But Jethro is not convinced: "The thing you are doing is not right." If Moses continues acting as he does, he will wear himself out, and then he will be of no use to anyone.

Jethro devises a strategy by which Moses will appoint a hierarchy of judges who will be able to rule on the large majority of cases, so that only the most difficult cases will be brought before Moses; that way, neither Moses nor the people who now wait long hours to speak to him will be wearied. Moses "heeded his father-in-law, and did just as he had said" (Exodus 18:24), which is what the Rebbe was now suggesting that Dov Zlotnick do.

In this instance, Zlotnick chose not to follow the Rebbe's advice and returned to New York to teach at the Seminary. However, he remained devoted to the Rebbe and continued to consult with him.

In trying to generalize from these last instances about the Rebbe's attitude to non-Orthodox denominations, one might think that the Rebbe's advice to Rabbis Weinberg and Zlotnick might have been restricted to rabbis, "soldier[s] on the front," as he expressed it. But a conversation many years later between the Rebbe and Frank Lautenberg, the future senator from New Jersey and at the time a national Jewish leader, reveals that similar advice also was directed, at least on occasion, to lay people. At this encounter, Lautenberg, in making the case for American Jews directing much of their philanthropy to Israel, offered a bleak assessment of Jewish life in America: "We must give money to Israel because there is no future to Judaism in America."

The Rebbe demurred: "Through observance of Torah and *mitzvot*, there will be a future in America."

"Correct," Lautenberg conceded.

The Rebbe continued: "If you agree, let me ask: In which movement is there more *mitzvot*, Conservative or Reform?"

Assuming that he was anticipating the direction of the Rebbe's argument, Lautenberg responded: "It would have to be the Orthodox."

"But I am asking between Reform and Conservative."

"Conservative," answered Lautenberg.

"So you should move to Conservative," the Rebbe said.

The Rebbe wanted Lautenberg, a Reform Jew, to observe more than he was then observing, even if it was not within an Orthodox setting. Never satisfied with an individual remaining behaviorally static, the Rebbe assured the senator that the next time they met, he would urge Lautenberg to grow still more in his observance.

The extent to which the Rebbe hoped that individuals would move toward greater observance and acceptance of Orthodox practice is reflected in his final conversation with Rabbi Herbert Weiner, which took place several decades after their initial encounter in the mid-1950s. During the preceding years, Weiner had gone to the Rebbe several times to receive a *bracha*. This time he reminded the Rebbe of the book he had written, *9½ Mystics*, and the Rebbe responded: "Nine and a half is a good number, but it's not enough. It should be ten, whole and complete. I want you to announce in the very synagogue where you have operated that you are an Orthodox Jew, and that you have always been an Orthodox Jew, even though you have served as a rabbi in a Reform temple, and I would like you to publicly announce it."

Weiner was startled by the request. Not sure how to respond, he placed his hand on his chest and said, "I put your words on my heart."

Several years later, Weiner was honored by his congregation on his seventy-fifth birthday and for his forty years as rabbi: "I said to myself, here I am standing at the pulpit. I said, 'I have something to announce.' I told about the Rebbe, and what he had said to me, and so forth. So I said, 'Even though I have served in a Reform pulpit, in my heart I have always been Orthodox, and I am fulfilling the request of the Rebbe.'"

Weiner had assumed that his statement would elicit some reaction—at least an "Oh really?" or a "Why?" Instead, to his considerable surprise, the celebration continued but no one responded to what he had said. No response at all.

"Later on, during the party, people made speeches and were reminiscing," Weiner recalled. One very nice former president got up and said, 'Oh yes, Rabbi, about that announcement. We always knew you are an Orthodox Jew. It is all right, we always knew that.'"[6]

The Rebbe never lost sight of his goal of influencing Jews to accept the totality of Jewish law, but he also never lost sight of the fact that many were not ready to do so. Yet, because of his belief that each commandment a person observes has value in itself (for example, a woman's lighting Shabbat candles is intrinsically significant even if she does not observe other Sabbath laws), he wanted to see every Jew—Orthodox, Conservative, Reform, or unaffiliated—do one more mitzvah; one could never know which act performed by which person could be the one that would bring the person to a sense of personal redemption and the world to its ultimate redemption. In this regard, he was deeply influenced by a passage in Maimonides's *Mishneh Torah*, one that he quoted often:

"Throughout the year, a person should always regard himself as if he were equally balanced between innocence and guilt, and should regard the whole of humankind as if it were [also] equally balanced between innocence and guilt. Therefore, if he performs one sin, he tips his balance and that of the entire world to the side of guilt and brings destruction upon himself [and, by implication, to the world]. [On the other hand,] if he performs one mitzvah, he tips his balance and that of the entire world to the side of merit and brings deliverance and salvation to himself and others" (Laws of Repentance 3:4).[7]

Chapter 17

NO ONE IS BEYOND THE POSSIBILITY OF REPENTANCE

"YOU SHOULD TELL HIM THAT HE SHOULD STILL REPENT,
HE STILL HAS A CHANCE."

T he Rebbe's openness to Jews of all backgrounds, including non-observant and alienated, is one of his best-known features; largely through his influence, it is also one of the characteristics most commonly associated with Chabad. That *the Rebbe placed no restrictions whatsoever* on those whom he thought could be welcomed back into the Jewish community is less well known and is reflected in a startling conversation he had with Israel Singer, the longtime secretary general of the World Jewish Congress, when they were discussing a recent visit Singer had made to the Soviet Union:[1]

"I remember the shock the Rebbe was in when I told him that I had met a member from the Politburo [the executive committee of the Communist Party in the Soviet Union] who was Jewish; his name was Lazar Kaganovich.

"'He must be an *alter Yid* [old Jew],' the Rebbe said."

Kaganovich, who had joined the Politburo in 1930, had been ousted from all leadership roles in 1957 and, as he had not been heard from since, was generally assumed to be dead. Singer told the Rebbe that Kaganovich was in his nineties. The editor of a Communist Yiddish newspaper had brought Singer to Kaganovich's apartment.

The Rebbe absorbed the information. "Is Kaganovich doing *teshuvah* [repenting]?" the Rebbe finally asked.

Singer answered that he didn't think so, and that judging by the very nice apartment in which he lived, it seemed as if he was still a person highly respected by the Communist Party.

The Rebbe then said that Kaganovich was a "big *rasha*" (an evil person) but added, "But you never know, maybe he'll repent. When you go back the next time, you should tell him he should still do *teshuvah*, he still has a chance."

In the normal course of events, nothing about this exchange should seem surprising. The Rebbe hears of an elderly Jew, a lifelong Communist now in his nineties, and encourages Singer to seek to influence the man to accept God and Judaism and repent for the bad things he has done. That, after all, is what one would expect a Rebbe to do.

The difference is this. Lazar Kaganovich was among the horrific mass murderers of the twentieth century, a century already known for its large number of tyrannical killers. It is likely that Kaganovich brought about the deaths of more people than any other Jew in history.

Kaganovich had the unique "distinction" of being the one Jew who always remained on close terms with the highly antisemitic Soviet dictator Josef Stalin. It was Kaganovich whom Stalin called upon to enforce the policy of forced starvation of *kulaks* (relatively well-off peasants) in Ukraine, a policy that resulted in the deaths by killing and starvation of an estimated six million people.

An effective administrator, Kaganovich also headed the construction of the subway system in Moscow. It is unknown how many overworked and maltreated laborers died in the extremely rushed process of building the underground rail system (in addition to those executed for making critical remarks about Kaganovich's employment practices). Stalin rewarded Kaganovich by naming the subway system the Kaganovich Subway.

Robert Conquest, the foremost historian of Stalin's years of terror, portrayed Kaganovich as "a brilliant administrator. A clear mind and a powerful will went with a total lack of the restraints of humanity. . . . There was no . . . pity at all in his make-up. . . . He took the extreme line that the Party's interests justified everything." Referring on more than one occasion to the murders of millions of people carried out under his and Stalin's direction, and to the realization that many of those killed must have been innocent even by Kaganovich's standards, Kaganovich explained that there were bound to be occasional mistakes: "When the forest is cut down, the chips fly."

Basic to Kaganovich's philosophy was that a Communist must be ready to sacrifice himself for the party: "Yes, ready to sacrifice not only his life, but his self-respect and sensitivity." [2]

There is a concept in Yiddish known as the *pintele Yid*, the "spark of Jewishness." This Yiddish phrase presumes that even in the most alienated of Jews there is a spark of Jewish feeling and, as is the case with any spark, it can be ignited into a fire.

In the case of Kaganovich, one would have to look with a powerful microscope to find any trace of such a "spark." When his wife criticized him for enforcing an antisemitic policy ("Have you no sense, no compassion, no feelings for one of your own?"), he told her not to bother him with such pleas: "Stalin is my god. Do you hear me? Hear me good."

On yet another occasion, and by his own admission, Kaganovich didn't defend his brother, Mikhail, when Stalin told him that he suspected Mikhail of being a Nazi spy planted by Hitler to form a puppet government after the Nazis captured Moscow. In later years, Kaganovich explained with brotherly pride that he provided Mikhail with a gun so that he could kill himself and be spared torture. Kaganovich was well aware of what happened to people arrested and charged with crimes by Stalin. He himself had long been one of those responsible for dealing with Stalin's unfortunate victims. [3]

That the Rebbe expressed his desire to influence Kaganovich to repent reflects his unbending conviction that "the gates of repentance" are never closed—even to the most evil people. In this instance, there was little, if anything, Kaganovich could do to undo his acts of evil (the most basic prerequisite for full repentance), both because he had been responsible for the irrevocable crime of killing so many people and because he, in any case, had been stripped of all powers. The Rebbe might also have been thinking that having someone of Kaganovich's great notoriety acknowledge the terrible wrongs he had done would make a profound impression on many people. As regards Kaganovich himself, perhaps the Rebbe was also thinking of the Talmudic teaching that just before a person who commits a capital crime is executed, he is instructed "to confess the sin [for which you are going to be put to death] and all your other sins . . . because one who confesses [and repents of the evil he has done] has a share in the World-to-Come" (Mishnah *Sanhedrin* 6:2).

As this incident makes clear, the Rebbe believed that one should never fully give up on any human being.

Despite the Rebbe's wishes, Kaganovich never repented—or, if he did, he does not seem to have made it known to anyone—and defended his behavior under Stalin until the end of his life.[4]

In another instance, the Rebbe encouraged outreach to a man who had long expressed antagonism about his Jewish background and who subsequently evolved into a vicious antisemite, Bobby Fischer. Fischer remains well known to this day as perhaps the greatest chess genius in history. He was also Jewish according to Jewish law, having been born in 1943 to a Jewish mother, Regina Wender Fischer, and a non-Jewish father, Hans-Gerhard Fischer.[5]

As far as can be ascertained, Fischer received no training in Judaism from his mother (his father divorced her when the young Fischer was two and played no role in his son's upbringing), and Fischer did not seem ever to have thought of himself as a Jew. He did, however, emerge at a very young age as a brilliant chess player and, at fifteen and a half, became the youngest grandmaster and the youngest candidate for the World Championship until that time. In 1972, he won the World Championship from the Russian Boris Spassky in Reykjavik, Iceland, in what remains the most widely watched chess championship in history.

A few years later, the Rebbe turned to the great Jewish chess master, Samuel Reshevsky, with a request. The Rebbe had always retained a particular affection and admiration for Reshevsky, an observant Jew who often competed in American and international tournaments and who made it a condition of his participation that he not play on Shabbat (for more on Reshevsky, see pages 180–81). After a warm note congratulating Reshevsky on a recent tournament win, the Rebbe added on this postscript:

The following lines may appear strange, but I consider it my duty not to miss the
opportunity to bring it to your attention. You surely are familiar with the life story of
Bobby Fischer, of whom nothing has been heard in quite some time [this was during
a period in which Fischer had become highly reclusive].

   Unfortunately, he did not have the proper Jewish education, which is probably
the reason for his being so alienated from the Jewish way of life or the Jewish people.
However, being a Jew, he should be helped by whomever possible. I am writing to you
about this, since you are probably better informed about him than many other persons,
and perhaps you may find some way in which he could be brought back to the Jewish
fold, either through your personal efforts, or in some other way.

According to one account, Reshevsky reached out to the chess genius
after receiving the Rebbe's request, and he had an extended meeting
with him; unfortunately, Fischer was not at all open to affirming his
Jewishness. A short time later (1984), Fischer wrote to the editors of the
Encyclopedia Judaica, demanding that they remove the entry about him
in the encyclopedia's sixth volume and accused them of "fraudulently
misrepresenting me to be a Jew . . . to promote your religion."

While Kaganovich's acts of evil seem to have resulted from a free will
decision by a sane man to advance Communism, Stalin, and himself,
with no concern for the number of people he murdered in the process,
Fischer's subsequent evil behavior was likely occasioned in large part
by severe mental illness. Whatever the reason, Fischer soon started to
utilize his prominence to try to harm the Jewish people, most notably
by asserting again and again that the Holocaust was a lie concocted by
Jews. His lifework, he announced, was not to be a great chess player but
rather to "expose the Jews for the criminals they are . . . the murderers
they are." He expressed a particular wish to bring about the destruction
of America's Jews, arguing that the United States is "controlled by dirty
hook-nosed, circumcised Jew bastards."

In 1999, Fischer gave a call-in interview to a Budapest radio station
in which he claimed that he was the "victim of an international Jewish
conspiracy." Among the books visitors reported seeing in Fischer's
house were Hitler's *Mein Kampf* and *The Protocols of the Elders of Zion*, a forged
document that alleged that the world is under the domination of Jews,

and a work that the Nazis used as justification for their genocide against the Jews.[6]

In the aftermath of 9/11, Fischer wrote a public letter to Osama bin Laden—architect of the murderous attack on New York and Washington in which almost three thousand Americans were murdered—and assured him that "you should know that I share your hatred of the murderous bandit-state of Israel, and its chief backer, the Jew-controlled USA."

Years earlier, the Rebbe had made an effort to bring this alienated, self-hating Jew back from the abyss. Such an effort, if successful, would have spared the Jewish people much pain, as it would have spared the disturbed and hate-filled Bobby Fischer much pain as well—if he had been able to recognize, as some mentally disturbed people can, that he was in need of help.

Again, what is striking, as in the case of Lazar Kaganovich, is the extent to which the Rebbe believed that no one was beyond repentance, that everyone should at least be approached and urged, in the words of the Psalms, "to turn from evil and do good" (Psalms 34:15, 37:27).

That this tactic yielded no fruit in the cases of Kaganovich and Fischer tells us something about them. That such an approach was urged by the Rebbe tells us something very different about him.

Chapter 18

·❦·

DIFFERENCES THAT DON'T AFFECT A FRIENDSHIP

The Rebbe and the Rav

WHEN SOMEONE WROTE IN A LETTER TO THE REBBE THAT
HE UNDERSTOOD THAT HE AND RABBI JOSEPH SOLOVEITCHIK
"WERE GOOD FRIENDS [DURING THEIR YEARS IN BERLIN],"
THE REBBE CIRCLED THE SENTENCE AND WROTE ON THE PAGE,
"MUCH MORE THAN IS KNOWN."

In theory, the word "*rav*" (the Hebrew word for "rabbi") refers to any rabbi, and the word "Rebbe" to a teacher of Judaism's holy texts and to any leader of a Chasidic dynasty. But in the last part of the twentieth century, the terms came to be associated, respectively, with two men: Rabbi Joseph Baer Soloveitchik, who offered the most advanced class (*shiur*) in Talmud at Yeshiva University's Rabbi Isaac Elchanan Theological Seminary, and Rabbi Menachem Mendel Schneerson. Throughout the Orthodox world, the Modern Orthodox world in particular, when people spoke of "the Rav," the reference invariably was to Rabbi Soloveitchik, as in "I studied with the Rav," or "The Rav teaches that . . ." Similarly, when people spoke of "the Rebbe," they were most often—unless they were Chasidic followers of a different Rebbe—referring to Rabbi Schneerson, the Lubavitcher Rebbe.[1] With the passage of time, the designation of "the Rebbe" for Rabbi Schneerson reached well beyond the Orthodox world, and the term became widely used throughout the Jewish world and beyond.[2]

These titles became so linked to these two men that it is easy to over-look how unusual such designations are. For example, if a contemporary American writer mentioned that he was writing a book on "the president" (unless he was referring to the incumbent), he would immediately feel the need to clarify the president about whom he was writing. No American president is held in higher esteem than Abraham Lincoln, but when one speaks of "the president" ("Over a hundred years ago, the president declared . . ."), no one assumes that the person is talking of Lincoln. On the other hand, we have good reason to believe that even a century from now, when people speak of "the Rav" and "the Rebbe," they will be referring to Rabbis Soloveitchik and Schneerson, respectively.

While it is not surprising that these two men knew each other (one assumes that rabbinic figures of such stature would have had some contact), what is surprising is *where* they met—not at a yeshiva or at a gathering of rabbinic sages, but in Berlin as university students in the 1920s.

The pursuit of such studies was not what either of their families had anticipated for them. While the Rebbe's father seemed comfortable with his son gaining a certain amount of secular education, his soon-to-be father-in-law was by no means supportive of yeshiva students attending university (though he did subsequently financially support his son-in-law's secular education). In Rabbi Soloveitchik's family, too, there was opposition to secular studies, particularly advanced secular studies.[3]

"My name is Menachem Mendel Schneerson, and I'm here to study. I don't know anybody here, or hardly anybody in the city."

Rabbi Soloveitchik arrived in Berlin in 1926, when he was twenty-three. Two years later, when the young Menachem Mendel Schneerson came to the same city, Soloveitchik seems to have been among the first people he sought out. "I was in Berlin studying at the university," Soloveitchik recalled, "and I had a small apartment and I was taking a nap in the afternoon. And you know, sometimes, even when you're sleeping, you have a sixth sense that somebody is in the room, and I opened my eyes and I saw this man standing there over my bed, and I sort of reacted and said, 'Who are you?' and he said, 'My name is Menachem

Mendel Schneerson and I'm here to study. I don't know anybody here,
or hardly anybody in the city. I heard you were here. I know of your
name and I came to introduce myself." The Rav explained that from
that point on, he introduced the young Schneerson to various people
and places in Berlin.[4]

Rabbi Herbert Bomzer recalls hearing an additional detail from Rabbi
Soloveitchik about this first encounter.[5] It seems that at that meeting,
the young Rabbi Schneerson stood by the bedside of Soloveitchik for
quite a long while, and when Rabbi Soloveitchik woke up and asked
him, "Why didn't you wake me?" Rabbi Schneerson answered, "You
don't wake up a sleeping *sefer* Torah" (Torah scroll).

With the passage of more than eighty years, it is impossible to ascertain how much time the two men spent together in Berlin.[6] Many recall
hearing the Rav speak of knowing the future Rebbe in Berlin, among
them Julius Berman and Rabbis Sholem Kowalsky, Shlomo Riskin, Menachem Genack, Herbert Bomzer, and Moshe Berger. However, it should
be noted that Professor Haym Soloveitchik, the Rav's son, has stated that
his father told him that the young Menachem Mendel Schneerson had
been pointed out to him in Berlin as the son-in-law of the Lubavitcher
Rebbe, but that they had no personal contact. In addition to the above-
named figures, Rebbetzin Chaya Mushka Schneerson, in a deposition in
the 1985 library case (the legal dispute discussed in chapter 27 over ownership of the Frierdiker Rebbe's library), made reference to her knowing
Rabbi Soloveitchik in Berlin, while her father, the Frierdiker Rebbe, wrote
that, in addition to meeting Soloveitchik in Germany, he had heard great
things about him from his son-in-law.[7] What appears is that a permanent affection between them was established there. More than forty years
later, Rabbi Soloveitchik sent a greeting to the Rebbe on his seventieth
birthday and signed his letter with *chibbah gedolah* (great affection).[8] In a
similar manner, when a volume of articles honoring Rabbi Soloveitchik on his many years as rosh yeshiva at Yeshiva University was being
compiled, a letter was sent to the Rebbe that asked him to contribute an
article, "especially since they [the Rav and the Rebbe] were good friends
[in Berlin]." The Rebbe circled this sentence and wrote on the page, "*harbeh
yoter me-mah she-atem yodim*" ("much more than you realize").

"It is my hope that the great, excellent, and renowned Gaon, Rabbi Joseph Baer Soloveitchik, will be selected to sit on his father's chair as the rosh yeshiva of RIETS [the Rabbi Isaac Elchanan Theological Seminary of Yeshiva University]."
                    —Rabbi Yosef Yitschak Schneersohn, the Frierdiker Rebbe

Yet despite the expression of such affectionate sentiments, once the two men left Germany the contact between them became very infrequent. Rabbi Soloveitchik was the first to come to the United States, arriving in 1932 and settling shortly thereafter in Boston. Three years later, he traveled to Palestine, where he was a candidate to become the chief rabbi of Tel Aviv. He did not receive the position, and though he later became a fervent supporter of Mizrachi, the international organization of religious Zionists, he never again visited Israel.

After this experience, Rabbi Soloveitchik returned to Boston, where he started teaching an advanced Talmud class and, in conjunction with his wife, Tonya, established Maimonides, a coeducational, highly regarded Jewish day school.[9]

During this period, Rabbi Soloveitchik's father, Reb Moshe, was offering the highest Talmud class at Yeshiva University. When Reb Moshe died in January 1941, there was a strong movement to have the position assigned to his eldest son, Joseph,[10] though there was also strong opposition to doing so. While the reasons for the opposition do not seem fully clear, one concern apparently was the fear that Rabbi Soloveitchik would advocate the positions of the more religiously right-wing Union of Orthodox Rabbis. In any case, the opposition was sufficiently strong that Rabbi Soloveitchik's appointment could by no means be taken for granted. There was much support for him among the school's faculty and rabbinical students, and a petition among the students supporting his candidacy was presented to Samuel Levy, chairman of the yeshiva's board of directors. Soon, the agitation on behalf of the Rav acquired support from an unexpected source, in the form of a letter written by the Frierdiker Rebbe, Yosef Yitzchak Schneersohn, who had just recently come to the United States. The Frierdiker Rebbe wrote: "It is my hope that the great, excellent, and renowned Gaon, Rabbi Joseph Dov Soloveitchik, will be selected to sit on his father's chair as the rosh yeshiva of the Rabbi Isaac Elchanan Theological Seminary. It is only fitting and proper that he inherit this position. He will bring abundant blessings to the yeshiva after the recent loss of its two heads [the school's president, Dr. Bernard Revel, had died two months earlier]. The eminent Gaon has the ability to restore the school's former glory, and through him solace will be attained."

From what is known, at least one member of the YU board, Mr. Abraham Mazer, was deeply devoted to the Frierdiker Rebbe and highly influenced by a phone call he received from him in support of Rabbi Soloveitchik being appointed to this position, and he seems to have played an active role in helping him secure the position.[11]

"The Rebbe has a peirush *[insight] for every [comment of] Rashi in the Talmud."*
—RABBI JOSEPH B. SOLOVEITCHIK

From the time of his arrival in the United States in 1941, and during the ensuing four decades, we know of only a few instances in which the two men met, of at least one phone call (there might well have been more) between them, and of a few letters.

The first meeting known to have occurred after the Rebbe assumed his position happened in 1964 when Rebbetzin Chana Schneerson, the Rebbe's mother, died.[12] Rabbi Soloveitchik came from Manhattan's Washington Heights to pay a shiva visit to the Rebbe in Brooklyn. Among those who accompanied him that day was Rabbi Shlomo Riskin, then a student of the Rav and today the chief rabbi of Efrat, Israel. The visit lasted two hours, an unusually long time for a condolence call. When Rabbi Soloveitchik arrived, everyone stood up in respect, among them the Rebbe (mourners do not normally rise for visitors, no matter how distinguished).[13]

The two men soon became engrossed in a highly detailed discussion of the Jewish laws of mourning (during the week of mourning, it is forbidden for mourners to engage in Jewish studies about any other topic). One issue that was discussed was a theoretical one, whether a *kohen* (priest) who is an *onain* (one who has lost an immediate family member who has not yet been buried; until the burial occurs, the *onain* is freed from observing positive commandments, such as prayer) is permitted to eat of the priestly portion known as *terumah*. Witnesses recall that the discussion was somewhat hard to follow. Talmudic quotations were started but not completed; there was no need to do so, as each rabbi knew exactly the citation to which the other was alluding.

Riskin still has very clear recollections of Rabbi Soloveitchik's comments on the car ride back: "You know," he said, "the Rebbe is a very great *manhig* [leader], but what people don't know is how great his learning is. He has an explanation [*peirush*] for every [comment of] Rashi in the Talmud." Riskin was struck by the Rav's compliment, knowing how high his standards were and how sparing he normally was in praise of others' learning. Riskin also was struck by the obvious warmth—a sense of electricity, as he described it—between the two men: "The Rav wasn't a very demonstrative person; he didn't have that kind of relationship with many people." [14]

Rabbi Sholem Kowalsky, who was driving the Rav that day, recalls Rabbi Soloveitchik reminiscing in the car about the Rebbe's years in Berlin, and how impressed he was by the fact that the Rebbe always carried the key to the *mikveh* (the ritual bath) in his pocket when he attended lectures at the university. "At about two or three o'clock every afternoon when he left the university he would go straight to the *mikveh*. No one was aware of this custom, and I only learned about it by chance. On another occasion, I offered the Rebbe a drink. The Rebbe refused. When I started pressuring him, I understood that he was fasting that day. It was Monday, and the Rebbe was fasting.[15] Imagine that," Rabbi Soloveitchik said, "a Berlin student immersed in secular studies maintaining the custom of *mikveh* and fasting. The Rebbe behaved like a Jew from Warsaw or from Russia. Berlin made absolutely no impression upon him at all."

As was the case with Rabbi Riskin, Rabbi Kowalsky recalls the Rav's commenting on the Rebbe's learning as well, and how particularly impressed he was by the Rebbe's "*gevaldig* [astounding] memory."

In 1966 and 1967, Rabbi Soloveitchik, in a span of just a few months, lost his brother, Shmuel; his mother, Pesha; and then his wife, Tonya. Rabbi Fabian Schonfeld was present during the time the Rav was observing shiva for his mother. The phone rang and Schonfeld picked it up. It was Rabbi Hodakov: "The Rebbe would like to speak with Rav Soloveitchik," he said. Schonfeld passed the phone to the Rav. From that point on, he could only hear the Rav's side of the conversation, and something started to sound a little puzzling, particularly the Rav's statement, "Well, if you are doing this, then it's allowed."

Later, Schonfeld asked Rabbi Soloveitchik what had prompted this response. The Rav explained: "He said to me, 'I want to be *menachem avel* [make a condolence call; literally, "comfort the mourner"] and I think it is permitted to do so on the phone." Traditionally, comforting the mourner is done in person, and it was to this comment that the Rav responded, "Well, if you are doing this, then it's allowed."

In 1971, when the Rebbe's mother-in-law, Nechama Dina Schneersohn, died, Rabbi Kowalsky took the Rav to pay a shiva visit to the Rebbetzin and her sister, Rebbetzin Chana Gourary. The Rav of course knew Rebbetzin Chaya Mushka from their time together in Berlin. On this occasion, the Rebbe and his brother-in-law, Rabbi Shmaryahu Gourary, came into the room to greet Rabbi Soloveitchik.

The best known of the men's several encounters in America was the least private, Rabbi Soloveitchik's attendance at the giant *farbrengen* celebrating the thirtieth anniversary of the Rebbe's assuming the leadership of Chabad. Though an invitation to the Rav to attend had been extended by Rabbi Avraham Shemtov, it appears that, at first, the Rav was reluctant to come (among other reasons, he was already not in the best of health). Rabbi Hershel Schachter, a prominent leader in the Jewish community and a close disciple of the Rav, kept urging him to attend. Finally, the Rav agreed, but only after setting down a number of conditions: "Number one, I cannot stand, because by the Rebbe everyone stands there, and there are no open chairs. They have to give me a chair. [Rabbi Soloveitchik was then in his late seventies.] Number two, I cannot be called upon to speak. Number three, I have to feel comfortable to leave whenever I want to." [16]

The conditions were immediately accepted. Apparently, the Rav's initial intention was to come for a short period, but once there, he became engrossed and remained for several hours. Rabbi Schachter recalled asking the Rav right after they left, "Nu, what do you say about the

Rebbe?" Rabbi Soloveitchik answered in Yiddish: "*Er iz a Gaon. Er iz a Gadol. Er iz a manhig b'Yisra'el.*" ["He is a genius. He is a great man. He is a leader."][17]

When Rabbi Fabian Schonfeld later spoke to Rabbi Soloveitchik about his impressions of the *farbrengen*, he offered a different observation. "I'll tell you," he said. "I am considered to be a good public speaker. If I have to speak for five minutes, I prepare sometimes an hour or two—maybe a whole day—what to say in those five minutes. And I never say it by heart. I always have notes to be sure I am saying what I want to say. I come to the Rebbe and he's sitting there and speaking for hours and hours without a shred of a paper in front of him, and he quotes midrashim, and the Zohar, and Gemaras that are familiar to me, but he quotes without hesitation and without looking at any kind of notes. This I would never be able to do." For a long time after the event, Rabbi Schonfeld remembers, the Rav would speak about the marvelous memory the Rebbe had, and his ability to transmit his thoughts to thousands of people without consulting a piece of paper.[18]

In addition to an extraordinary memory, a distinguishing characteristic of the Rebbe's teachings was his ability to draw out practical, day-to-day implications from almost all Jewish texts. Even while discussing the most esoteric mystical concepts, or seemingly abstract legal regulations, he would strive to derive an insight as to how this teaching could be utilized to improve one's character or yield a lesson regarding a person's responsibility to the world at large.

Another distinctive feature of the Rebbe's understanding of Jewish sources was his refusal to acknowledge any wall between the legal and the mystical, considering them to be two sides of the same coin of Torah; he would often incorporate both in the same teaching, demonstrating how they complemented each other. To the Rebbe, the five books of the Torah and the whole genre of the Oral Law (Talmud and Midrash) were *one big tapestry* of unity. Where only a short while before there might have been dissonance—between various interpretations or methodologies or genres, between the abstract and the practical, between man and God—by the time the Rebbe finished his teaching there was a sense of harmony, of unity. As Rabbi Jonathan Sacks expressed it, "To hear or read a *sicha* of the Lubavitcher Rebbe is to undertake a journey. We are challenged and forced to move: where we stand at the end is not where we were at the beginning."[19]

Differences That Don't Affect a Friendship

"WHAT DO YOU THINK THE REBBE DOES WHEN THERE IS A FAMILY WHOM
HE HIMSELF THINKS OUGHT TO ADOPT CHILDREN?"

—RABBI JOSEPH B. SOLOVEITCHIK

As this section highlights a number of areas in which the Rav and the
Rebbe held differing views—differences that sometimes helped define
Lubavitch and Modern Orthodoxy for years to come—it is important to
mention that they obviously had many areas of agreement. To cite three
examples: Both were opposed to interfaith dialogue between Jewish
leaders and representatives of other faiths.[20] The Rebbe, as is known,
supported nondenominational prayers in public schools, believing that
the acceptance of monotheism was crucial for a society's moral development, and the Rav felt it appropriate for members of different religions
to discuss what could be done to address moral and social inequities. But
interfaith dialogue—having Jews and Christians, for example, meet to
discuss such issues as why Jews don't believe that Jesus was the Messiah
or any specifically religious issues (as opposed to issues of social responsibility, for example, matters involving civil rights issues)—was regarded
by both men as strictly forbidden. Such a stance became somewhat controversial when Pope John XXIII, regarded, along with Pope John Paul II,
as the friendliest pope toward the Jews in history, convened an Ecumenical Council in the early 1960s to make certain changes within the
Catholic Church. The Church wanted to formally engage the Jewish
leadership in discussing issues due to be raised at the council that were
relevant to Jews.[21] This, both the Rebbe and Rabbi Soloveitchik opposed.
From the Rav's perspective, the most significant concern—rooted in the
long and often unhappy history of Catholic-Jewish relations—was that
the Catholic expectation would be evangelical in return; he also feared
that the Jewish participants might be expected to engage in reciprocal
theological compromise.

In a letter written in June 1962 to Dr. Solomon Gaon, a rabbi and
leader of Sephardic Jewry, Rabbi Soloveitchik forcefully expressed his
opposition to Jewish participation in such dialogue and then suddenly,

at the letter's end, cited the Rebbe's similar view: "Rabbi [Menachem Mendel] Schneerson of Lubavitch has commented that the Ecumenical Council is a strictly Catholic wedding, and it would be undignified if we were to crash the party. Unfortunately, Jewish political leaders in America possess neither a sense of dignity nor an awareness of Jewish historical continuity."

In truth, the comment about "crash[ing] the party" does not sound like the type of language the Rebbe would use (nor have I been able to locate such a reference), but the fact that the Rav concluded this highly significant letter by citing the view of the Rebbe suggests, again, the depth of respect that existed between the two men.[22]

Also, the Rav recognized that Chabad and Modern Orthodoxy share a strong inclination to reach out to nonobservant Jews. In a 1977 interview with the Israeli newspaper *Ma'ariv*, Rabbi Soloveitchik lauded Chabad's "keen sense of the historic reality. They are practical in their approach. Chabad opens up centers on the main college campuses. . . . While many other [right-wing] Orthodox Jews disavow these male and female students who study at these universities, Chabad reaches out to them. In this respect, there is much in common with my approach and that of Chabad. We both recognize that there is a large world of male and female Jews out there who do not belong to our camp. Yet many do possess some feeling for Judaism. We must ignite this spark into a full appreciation for Torah."[23] (See as well page 567, regarding the circumstance in which both Rabbis Schneerson and Soloveitchik agreed as to when a Jew should not make aliyah [move to Israel.])

College Studies

One remarkable feature of the relationship between the Rebbe and the Rav was the extent to which their differences of opinion on several significant issues in no way affected the affection and high regard they had for each other. For example, while the Rebbe opposed his disciples attending college, particularly during their late teens and early

twenties (see chapter 24), Rabbi Soloveitchik vigorously approved of individuals pursuing a post–high school secular education and wanted
such studies to be offered, along with Jewish studies, on a high level. He
believed that the success of Yeshiva University was largely contingent
on its college studies, not just its yeshiva, being esteemed. When Rabbi
Dr. Norman Lamm assumed the school's presidency in 1976, he came
to consult with Rabbi Soloveitchik, whom he regarded as his mentor.
Lamm asked him, "What do you think should be the first goal I set for
myself?" To Lamm's surprise, the Rav answered, "Improve the college."[24]

Rabbi Aaron Rakeffet-Rothkoff, author of the two-volume *The Rav: The
World of Rabbi Joseph B. Soloveitchik*, and a student at YU starting in the mid-
1950s, recalls an incident that he witnessed. He befriended a young man,
Chaim Gold, the grandson of Rabbi Zev Gold, the longtime president of
the American Mizrachi movement, the organization of religious Zionists. Rabbi Gold had died a short time earlier, as had his son, Rabbi Moshe
Gold, Chaim's father. The young Gold had now come to study at YU.

The students at the YU College attended Jewish studies classes in
the morning and early afternoon and commenced their college classes
at 3:00 p.m. On a number of occasions, Rakeffet noticed that Chaim
Gold continued learning Talmud during the college hours. In response
to Rakeffet's puzzled inquiries, Gold explained that though he had attended some college classes the previous year, he now wanted to devote
all his time and intellectual efforts to Talmud and would decide at a later
point whether or not to attend college. Rakeffet, who was a close disciple
of the Rav, mentioned Gold's comment to Rabbi Soloveitchik. The Rav
asked Rakeffet to bring Chaim Gold to see him. Fifty years later, Rakeffet recalled not the exact words, but the clear gist of what Soloveitchik
said to him: "Chaim, I am responsible for you. Your father has passed
away. Our sages declare that the *beit din* (members of the rabbinic court)
are the parents of orphans (*Gittin* 37a). Since you have no father, I am
responsible for you. I was told that you do not wish to continue your
college education. Let me tell you something: Our sages stated that 'it is
good to combine Torah study with *derech eretz*' (*Ethics of the Fathers* 2:2). I am
not certain what the exact translation of *derech eretz* should be [it is generally rendered, depending on context, as "proper manners," "worldly

matters," and sometimes "an occupation"]. However, I am positive that, nowadays, it means that one has to go to college. Listen to me, go up-stairs, and register for the new semester," which Chaim Gold did.

From Rabbi Soloveitchik's perspective, securing a BA was not always enough, *particularly* in the case of rabbis. At a 1960s dinner honoring the newly ordained rabbis at Yeshiva University, Shlomo Riskin, one of those being honored, was seated next to Rabbi Soloveitchik. The Rav offered him several pieces of advice, the last of which was: "Get a PhD. I want you to know that I believe no one's education is complete without a PhD."[25] This is the very opposite of the advice one could imagine the Rebbe offering a newly ordained rabbi.

Rabbi Soloveitchik's embrace of university education was but one area in which he and the Rebbe held diverging views.

Public Demonstration on Behalf of Soviet Jews

Rabbi Riskin recalls that as a young man, he went to consult with the Rav about becoming involved in demonstrations on behalf of the suffering Jewish community inside the Soviet Union. It was well known that much of American Jewry's Orthodox religious leadership, most no-tably the Rebbe and Rabbi Pinchas Teitz, opposed demonstrations; they believed that such activities would endanger the welfare of the Jews in Russia as well as what they then were accomplishing—such as bringing in prayer books for the remaining synagogues, *matzot* for Passover, and sustaining whatever limited religious activities would be permitted; in addition, Chabad was maintaining an ongoing, and totally illegal, system of underground Jewish education. As noted, the Rebbe felt that much worse things would result from the demonstrations and that the people providing religious leadership inside Russia might well be arrested. Other Jews, among them the young activists who formed the Student Struggle for Soviet Jewry under the leadership of Yaakov Birnbaum and Glenn Richter, felt that public demonstrations were crucial if there was ever to be any significant improvement in the condition of Russian Jews.

Riskin recalls the Rav's surprised reaction when he asked him his view as to which path he should follow. "I don't understand why you are asking me. You have to ask a top Sovietologist." Decades later, Riskin claims that the Rav's response that day permanently affected his whole philosophy of halacha (Jewish law). When one is dealing with matters that are not the kind of legal issues discussed in the Talmud but that have to do with historical trends and ramifications, one should consult with the experts in those fields (it should be emphasized that when the Rebbe expressed his public opposition to such demonstrations, he was basing it on his extensive knowledge and understanding of what was going on inside the Soviet Union, not on his rabbinic credentials). Riskin consulted with Professor Erich Goldhagen, a leading Sovietologist who taught at Harvard University. When Riskin reported back the results of his research—Goldhagen thought such demonstrations might well be beneficial—the Rav gave his blessings for activist demonstrations.[26]

Return of Territories in Israel in Exchange for Peace with the Arab World

The belief that the decision on whether to demonstrate on behalf of Soviet Jews should be based more on experts' recommendations than rabbis' also shaped the Rav's views on the sensitive issue of whether Israel should be willing to vacate any of the lands captured in the Six-Day War (1967) in return for a peace agreement with an Arab country or countries. In this case, too, there was *in theory* no disagreement between the Rav's and the Rebbe's positions, but there was a disagreement about facts. The Rebbe always held that his opposition to returning even one inch of land was based on his belief that no reliable peace agreements could be established with any of Israel's Arab neighbors, and that relinquishing any land whatsoever would endanger Jewish lives. In addition, he opposed Israel ever making any territorial concessions simply to avoid tension with the United States.

Rabbi Soloveitchik by no means accepted these positions as a given. Shortly after the Six-Day War, he offered this analysis concerning the possibility of exchanging land for peace: "I don't need [as a rabbi] to rule whether we should give the West Bank back to the Arabs or not give the West Bank to the Arabs; we rabbis should not be involved in decisions regarding the safety and security of the population. . . . And if the government were to rule that the safety of the population requires that specific territories must be returned . . . their decision is the deciding factor." In a 1975 interview with the Israeli newspaper *Ma'ariv*, he spelled out this position even more concretely: "When one is required to feed an ill person on Yom Kippur, it is done upon the advice of [medical] experts. In the areas of territory, policy, and endangerment of life, the experts are the chief of staff and the leadership of the Israel Defense Forces, and the government of Israel. If they would conclude that it is possible to compromise over territory, without threatening the life of the *yishuv* [Jewish community] and the existence of the state, we should rely upon them."

While the Rav makes no reference in this interview to the Rebbe and his opposition to returning any land whatsoever, he does offer this comment: "Many write and publicize letters calling for [the government] not to compromise on even one centimeter. They do not take into account that through lack of compromise, we may, God forbid, pay a heavy price in blood."

In an interview with *Ma'ariv* two years later, the Rav emphasized the importance of not alienating the United States in a manner that clearly put him at odds with the thinking of the Rebbe on this very issue: "I am in favor of a more conciliatory approach with America, even if this requires us [to hold on to] less territory, in the context, of course, of careful protection of the security of Israel. . . . No one in history has ever received all that he wanted [in a negotiation]." [27]

As noted, in theory the Rebbe and the Rav did not disagree. The Rebbe, too, felt that the decision on whether or not to return land should be based on the policy that would least endanger Jewish lives. But because he believed that any return of land would do just that, and because Rabbi Soloveitchik did not believe so, their positions were in effect opposite.

On Adoption

Jewish law has very strict regulations restricting physical contact between members of the opposite sex. It dictates that a man and a woman not married to each other are not to be secluded in a room, while another law prohibits an unmarried couple from engaging in physical contact (among the very Orthodox, men and women do not shake hands). Of course, these laws do not apply to immediate family members, most obviously to one's parents, siblings, spouse, and children.

However, a problem arises in the case of adopted children. Since such children are not the biological offspring of their adoptive parents, the Rebbe, in line with most other decisors of Jewish law, concluded that once a girl becomes bat mitzvah (at the age of twelve) and a boy bar mitzvah (at the age of thirteen), all laws of separation of the sexes apply, most notably *yichud* (the prohibition of being alone in a room) and *negiah* (the prohibition of physical contact). For example, a woman would be prohibited from hugging or kissing her adopted son once he turned thirteen, and a man would be forbidden to be alone in a room with his adopted daughter once she turned twelve. Not surprisingly, the Rebbe was known to generally discourage adoption.

In the early 1980s, Rabbi Saul Berman was discussing the issue of adoption in Jewish law with Rabbi Soloveitchik, who, in contrast to the Rebbe, believed that "the functional parent-child relationship" was sufficient to eliminate the problem of *yichud* and of *negiah*, despite the absence of biological relationship. Berman noted the contrasting position of the Rebbe, who took the traditional approach.

"As we spoke further of the [disagreement between the two men's positions], the Rav asked me, 'What do you think the Rebbe does when there is a family in his community whom he himself thinks ought to adopt children?' I had no answer. The Rav broke into a broad smile and said, 'Then he sends them to me to give the ruling [*pasken* the *she'elah*].' "

Berman recalls his own pleasure and amazement at Soloveitchik's comment: "What an extraordinary picture the Rav provided us with, of two giants, understanding that their opposite positions were both "the words of the living God" (*Eruvin* 13b) who were able to use the position they personally rejected to serve the emotional needs of people for whom they cared as a shepherd cares for his flock."[28]

"When you have a bonding, it is not a question of how often you meet."

What is remarkable is not that the Rebbe and the Rav had some very marked differences of opinion, but that their esteem and affection for each other was unaffected by these differences. We all understand in theory that we should be able to love and respect those with whom we disagree, but few of us can do so. Often, people end up concluding that there is something deficient either in the intelligence or character of those with whom they disagree. Quite characteristically, this is what liberals and conservatives commonly think of each other, that their opponent has something wrong either with his head or his heart.

The Rebbe and the Rav provide an altogether different model of how to regard those with whom we disagree. For one thing, we know it was characteristic of the Rebbe, even—perhaps particularly—when dealing with others with whom he had disagreements, to focus on their areas of agreement; in the case of the Rebbe and the Rav, a passionate love of God, Torah, and the Jewish people. Therefore, even when they reached different conclusions about some action that needed to be taken in one of these areas, the two didn't lose sight of the fact that they were being guided by the same intense love.

When Shlomo Riskin initially consulted with the Rebbe, the first words the Rebbe, who knew that Riskin was a student of Rabbi Soloveitchik, said to him were, "You have a wonderful rebbe and you should always listen to everything he says."

The admiration was mutual. When Kehot (the Chabad publishing house), under the prodding and direction of the Rebbe, compiled a new book on Maimonides, a monumental work citing all the references upon which Maimonides had based his legal rulings, the Rebbe dispatched Rabbi Avraham Shemtov with a copy to be hand-delivered to Rabbi Soloveitchik. Soloveitchik was a lifetime devotee and student of Maimonides, and when Rabbi Shemtov explained to him what the book consisted of, the Rav "grabbed the book out of my hand, and he grabbed onto it as if he had discovered a treasure that he had lost or that he was looking for. He started to turn the pages as if he was looking for something special in different places. He looked here, looked there, skipped, and looked back and forth." Highly impressed with what he saw, the Rav looked at Shemtov and said, "Now there will be a new Rambam" (Maimonides).

Rabbi Aharon Lichtenstein, Rabbi Soloveitchik's son-in-law and a major rabbinic scholar, has commented that the Rav's great respect for the Rebbe emanated from both his appreciation of the Rebbe's learning, particularly his mastery of Chasidus, and his leadership and ability "to marshal an army of sorts dispersed throughout the four corners of the globe and yet united as if they were all together." And of course the Rav's admiration went back to their days in Berlin, to his appreciation of how the Rebbe maintained piety in an atmosphere that was anything but pious. Rabbi Moshe Berger recalls the Rav speaking of the intellectual mastery that enabled the Rebbe to simultaneously understand and fully follow a lecture in philosophy while studying a religious text (see page 338).

A final question remains: If these two men so liked and admired each other, why did they make so little effort to remain in direct contact? An average of one or two meetings every ten years, several of which involved shiva visits, hardly suggests a deep-seated friendship (though we do know of instances in which messages were exchanged between them).

Here we are in the realm of speculation. One possibility is that although the deep differences of opinion between them—for example, the Rav's ardent approval of university studies and his passionate espousal of Zionism—did not detract from their admiration for each other because each trusted in the authenticity and intellectual honesty of the other, but still it can be hard to spend large amounts of time with someone with whom you have such fundamental disagreements. Sometimes, it is easier to retain affection and respect when you see each other infrequently.

Another explanation for why maintaining continuous contact was not a fundamental priority for either man was suggested by Julius

Berman (a student of the Rav and a former chairman of the Conference of Presidents of Major American Jewish Organizations), and based on an explanation offered to him by Rabbi Soloveitchik himself. One day, while sharing with Berman his recollection of that first time he and the Rebbe met, the Rav suddenly broke off his recollections "and started generalizing about the whole concept of friendship. He said, some people feel friendship is a question of how many times do you meet with somebody, how many times do you go out with somebody, and the more frequent the contact reflects [the depth of the] friendship." The Rav dismissed this idea. "No, a friendship is a bonding, and when you have a bonding, it is not a question of how often you meet, or anything of that sort. There was a bonding there."

That bond, despite the differences, is what always remained.

Part Six

·(⊰⊱)·

JUDAISM

CONFRONTS

MODERNITY

Controversial Views of the Rebbe

Chapter 19

UNITED STATES

Prayers in the Schools, Menorahs in the Streets

"Under existing conditions in this country, a daily prayer in the public schools is for a vast number of boys and girls the only opportunity for cultivating . . . an awareness [of God]."

Almighty God, we acknowledge our dependence upon Thee, and we beg Thy blessings upon us, our parents, our teachers, and our country."

This twenty-two-word prayer, composed in 1951 by the New York Board of Regents and recommended for daily use in New York State public schools, provoked debate not only in New York but also throughout the country. The debate culminated in a legal suit, *Engel v. Vitale*, which came before the Supreme Court in the early 1960s. In anticipation of the justices' deliberations as to whether such a prayer should be allowed in the country's public schools, twenty-two state governments signed an amicus curiae brief urging the Court to uphold the prayer's permissibility.[1]

Public opposition to the prayer came largely, though by no means exclusively, from the organized Jewish community; secular organizations such as the American Civil Liberties Union, which had a disproportionately high percentage of Jewish members, were heavily involved in this battle as well. A brief urging the Court to outlaw all such prayers in public schools was submitted by the Synagogue Council of America, a national organization representing rabbis in the different denominations,[2] and the National Jewish Community Relations Council,[3] representing

Jewish communities throughout the United States. The brief's essential
argument was that although the New York State prayer did not advocate
a specific religion—it spoke rather of "Almighty God"—it still violated
the First Amendment, which ordains that "Congress shall make no law
respecting an establishment of religion." Although this constitutional
provision is popularly understood as meaning that Congress is forbidden to establish a state religion (in the way that the Church of England
is that country's state religion), the Jewish organizations argued that a
prayer promoting an "acknowledgment of dependence upon God and
the invocation of His blessings" constitutes a preference for theistic religions that affirm a personal God, over nontheistic religions, such as
Buddhism, which do not. Thus, although the prayer was not religiously
specific (as it would be, for example, if it spoke of Jesus), it still promoted
very specific religious ideas, notably "the existence of a personal God who
can and will respond to prayer and grant the blessings prayed for." In the
view of these organizations, such a prayer has no place in a public school.
The government, they argued, is obliged not only to be neutral among
competing faiths (e.g., not to favor Protestantism over Catholicism, or
any form of Christianity over Judaism) "but also between religion and
non-religion." The state, quite simply, has no business participating in
any way in religious affairs. The signatories emphasized that their opposition to prayer in public schools had nothing to do with opposition to
religion. Indeed, they had submitted this brief "on behalf of the coordinating bodies of 70 Jewish organizations, including the national bodies
representing congregations and rabbis of Orthodox, Conservative, and
Reform Judaism. The thousands of rabbis and congregations who have
authorized submission of this brief can hardly be characterized as being
on the side of those who oppose religion." [4]

In the end, in a historic decision (1962), the Supreme Court ruled
6–1 that all prayers should be forbidden in public schools. (The newly
appointed justice Byron White took no part in the case and therefore did
not vote, while Justice Felix Frankfurter had suffered a cerebral stroke
and was forced to retire from the bench before the decision could be announced.) Although the ruling acknowledged that the New York Board
of Regents' prayer did not promote any one religion, still it promoted

those religions that recognize "Almighty God," and therefore violated the First Amendment clause banning the establishment of any religion.

The ruling was widely hailed throughout the American Jewish community, many of whose older members recalled a time when readings from the New Testament were commonly conducted in public schools. The fact that the New York State prayer was decidedly nondenominational had not allayed the common Jewish fear that any opening in the wall between religion and state could eventually lead to the favoring of Christianity over other religions.

The most noted leader within the Jewish community who stood out almost alone in opposition to this commonly enunciated Jewish position was the Rebbe. Shortly after the ruling, the Rebbe argued that all legal means should be employed to obtain a reversal of the Court decision.[5] His passionate feelings on this issue received wide attention (see, for example, the *New York Times*, November 27, 1962), and many were surprised by the intensity of his response. One might have thought that the school prayer issue would have little resonance for him. After all, Lubavitcher Chasidim do not send their children to public schools but rather to Jewish day schools that start each morning with an extended prayer service. Those Jews who do attend public schools generally come from less traditional and often nonobservant backgrounds. To the Rebbe, though, this was precisely the point. The Jews who attend public schools often come from homes in which prayers are rarely, and in some cases never, recited. Yet, daily prayer is a requirement of Jewish law. Ideally, the prayers that are to be recited are those in the siddur (prayer book). But even if these prayers are not said, there is a great value in reciting any prayer addressed to God. Thus, reciting the "Almighty God" prayer composed by the Board of Regents fulfilled the requirement for some sort of prayer and, equally important, brought God into the daily life of Jewish children being raised in households where God might be infrequently discussed or invoked.

The Rebbe's support for prayers in public schools, and for public advocacy of a belief in God, also was influenced by other factors, most notably his early years in the aggressively atheistic and murderous Soviet Union, and his own later experience of living in Germany during the rise of

Hitler and the Nazis (yet another antireligious ideology). From the Rebbe's perspective, school prayers had important spiritual and moral ramifications and benefits for both Jews and non-Jews.[6] The same year, 1964, in which he issued a public letter in support of prayer in public schools, he also wrote a letter to Professor Velvel Greene of the University of Minnesota, the concluding paragraph of which underscored the importance of linking God and ethics: "If in a previous generation there were people who doubted the need of Divine authority for common morality and ethics, [and who believed instead] that human reason is sufficient authority for morality and ethics, our present generation has, unfortunately, in a most devastating and tragic way, refuted this mistaken notion. For it is precisely the nation which had excelled itself in the exact sciences, the humanities, and even in philosophy and ethics, that turned out to be the most depraved nation in the world. . . . Anyone who knows how insignificant was the minority of Germans who opposed the Hitler regime, realizes that the German cult was not something which was practiced by a few individuals, but had [been] embraced [by] the vast majority of the nation, who considered itself the 'super race.'"[7]

Two years after the Supreme Court ruling, the Rebbe was asked whether he had reconsidered his position. He hadn't, except to note that time had "reinforce[d] my conviction of the vital need that the children in the public schools should be allowed to begin their day with the recitation of a nondenominational prayer, acknowledging the existence of a Creator and Master of the Universe, and our dependence upon Him."[8]

In their brief to the Court, Jewish groups had specifically noted their opposition to mandating any sort of prayer acknowledging "dependence upon [a personal] God." But belief in a "personal God" before Whom all people are accountable is exactly what the Rebbe believed was required. What Jewish and non-Jewish children alike need—adults, too, for that matter—is understanding that "the world in which they live is not a jungle, where brute force, cunning, and unbridled passion rule supreme, but that it has a [Supreme Being] Who . . . takes a 'personal interest' in the affairs of each and every individual, and to Him everyone is accountable for [his or her] daily conduct."

The Rebbe went on to make reference to the rising rates of juvenile delinquency, noting that even if the government had sufficient police to keep an eye on every out-of-line child, that would not deter all crime. Further, even if marshaling so extensive a police force were possible, "this would not be the right way to remedy the situation. The remedy lies in removing the cause, not in merely treating its symptoms." And how was this to be done? "It is necessary to engrave upon the child's mind the idea that any wrongdoing is an offense against the divine authority and order."

Regarding the argument that the appropriate places for prayers are "houses of prayer" (synagogues and churches), the Rebbe noted that attendance at such services is not high, "both in regard to the number of worshippers and the frequency of their visits." Thus, "shifting the responsibility to the house of prayer will not correct the problem."

In his view, therefore, the problem of inculcating children with awareness of an "Eye that sees and an Ear that hears" cannot be solved through houses of worship alone, just as a criminal mentality cannot be eliminated through law enforcement agencies alone: "The crux of the problem lies in the success or failure of bringing up children to an awareness of a Supreme Authority, who is not only to be feared but also loved. Under existing conditions in this country, a daily prayer in the public schools is for a vast number of boys and girls the only opportunity of cultivating such an awareness."

The Rebbe offered a second argument as well, one intended to counter the overwhelming Jewish and liberal opposition to school prayers. Much of this opposition, whether it was stated explicitly or not, was rooted in a fear of Christianity. The concern was that any breakdown in the separation of church and state would lead to some form of Christian domination in the United States; after all, the large majority of Americans are Christians. For Jews, such a thought inevitably triggered the frightening recollection of the Jewish historical experience in medieval Europe during which a highly intolerant Christianity was the established state religion, and Jews suffered severe discrimination and persecution. For many Jews, therefore, an utterly secular America seemed preferable to one in which there was a state preference for religion in any form whatsoever.

To the Rebbe, such thinking was illogical, an example of people responding with a once-valid solution to an altogether new problem: "Suppose a person was ill at one time and doctors prescribed a certain medication and treatment. Suppose that years later, the same person became ill again, but with an entirely different, in fact quite *contrary*, malady. Would it be reasonable to recommend the same medication and treatment as formerly? . . . In medieval times, the world suffered from an 'excess' of religious zeal and intolerance. In our day, the world is suffering from an excessive indifference to religion, or even from a growing materialism and atheism." In other words, what is appropriate in an age of religious intolerance is less religion in the public sphere, what is appropriate in an age of indifference to religion is more religion.

But having acknowledged that, the Rebbe was not insensitive to Jewish fears of Christian domination, and the solution he proposed was a commonsensical one. Rather than respond to worries about Christian ascendancy by forbidding all prayers, he advocated that "a provision be made which would require the unanimous approval by the representatives of [different] religious denominations before a particular nondenominational prayer is introduced into the school."

In addition, and as a safeguard, it was only nondenominational prayers that the Rebbe endorsed, as such prayers united people in a feeling of responsibility before God. However, he strongly opposed Bible readings, since this could lead to readings drawn from religious texts that would make members of other religious groups uncomfortable.

For the organized Jewish communal leadership in the early 1960s, support for prayer and the affirmation of God in U.S. public schools was in itself a somewhat heretical notion, one it was happy to see outlawed by the Supreme Court. But the Rebbe stood steadfast in his opposition, though his arguments did not prevail.

Over the coming years, the Rebbe appears to have grown convinced that—at least for the foreseeable future—the Supreme Court was not going to allow such a prayer to be recited in public schools. In characteristic fashion, rather than give up entirely on the idea of bringing God into the classroom, the Rebbe sought out an alternative; in this case, becoming a supporter of a daily "moment of silence." The idea was that each school day would begin with a moment of quiet meditation. Such a moment, the Rebbe argued, would not compromise "the neutrality of the state, for this is not prayer, but silence."

He urged that the "moment" be instituted at the beginning of each day, thereby emphasizing its significance. There was a practical reason as well; if it came later in the day, many students would simply spend the minute reviewing something from the class period they had just concluded. However, if a child began the school day with such a moment, there would be a much greater likelihood that he or she would devote these sixty seconds, or at least part of them, to thinking about the big issues in life, devotion to parents, a general commitment to wanting to do good, "and belief in the Creator and the Ruler of the Universe."

Anticipating the objections secularists and other opponents of school prayers would offer to such a moment, the Rebbe then added that since each person has free will to think about whatever he or she wants, without suggestions from teachers, such a moment "does not represent an incursion of the state into the free exercise of religion by the individual."[9]

This cause, too, has, as of yet, failed to fully clear court-based opposition. The next time, however, that the Rebbe undertook to support religion in the public square, he was no longer on the losing side.[10]

The Lighting of Menorahs in the Public Square

"I AM FULLY CERTAIN THAT NONE OF THOSE WHO PARTICIPATED IN OR WITNESSED THE KINDLING OF A CHANUKAH LAMP IN A PUBLIC PLACE . . . FELT THAT HIS OR HER LOYALTY TO THE CONSTITUTION OF THE U.S.A. HAD BEEN . . . COMPROMISED."

Chabad's well-known focus on the public celebration of Chanukah started in the mid-1970s and was likely influenced, at least in part, by an unusual feature of contemporary American-Jewish life: In the United States, Chanukah is the third most widely observed Jewish holiday (after

Passover and Yom Kippur), although in Jewish law it is less significant than the biblically based Sabbath, Sukkot, and Shavuot (Chanukah is a postbiblical holiday).[11]

Because of Chanukah's proximity to Christmas, many Jewish parents in the United States and other Western countries observe it with special attention so that their children not feel deprived when they witness their Christian peers celebrating Christmas. Thus, many parents have turned the holiday, in part, into a Jewish form of the most widely observed Christian holiday. For example, Jewish children are given daily gifts throughout the holiday. By turning Chanukah into a fun-filled occasion, parents hope that their children will not feel they are missing out on Christmas trees and gifts "brought" by Santa Claus. And while this focus on gifts is certainly not an ideal religious response, it is, Jewishly speaking, preferable to the common alternative of bringing Christmas into Jewish homes. American-Jewish historian Jenna Weissman Joselit has documented that as recently as the 1960s, almost 40 percent of Chicago Jews "decorated their homes with Christmas trees."[12]

The close proximity of the two holidays impacted Jewish behavior on a year-to-year basis. For many years, my father, Shlomo Telushkin was the accountant for a Jewish company that produced Chanukah candles and decorations. He told me that the closer Chanukah fell to Christmas (under the Jewish calendar, which is lunar, Chanukah can start anywhere from late November to late December), the more business the company did.

With so many American Jews aware of Chanukah, whether they observed it or not, there was no way the Rebbe and Chabad *shluchim* would forgo the opportunity to reach out to Jews on this holiday.

The public lighting of a giant menorah originated in 1974 at the foot of Philadelphia's Liberty Bell, and was organized by the veteran Chabad *shliach* Rabbi Avraham Shemtov. A year later, Chabad *shliach* Rabbi Chaim Drizin in San Francisco lit a twenty-two-foot lamp in Union Square. The practice quickly spread, and in 1979, President Jimmy Carter ended a hundred days of self-imposed seclusion over the Iran hostage crisis by leaving the White House to light the Chabad menorah in front of the White House with Rabbi Shemtov.

In those first years, some Jews expressed unhappiness about this entrance of Jewish observance into public places, but no *legal* challenges were mounted. The foreshadowing of the many courtroom battles that would soon ensue was first anticipated in a remarkable 1978 exchange of letters between the Rebbe and Rabbi Joseph Glaser, the longtime head of the Central Conference of American Rabbis (CCAR), the organization of Reform rabbis.[13]

Rabbi Glaser initiated the first two letters. Their tone was respectful but demanding, and the issue addressed in both instances was Chabad's placement of menorahs on public property. Glaser's first letter (April 25, 1978) was written in a rather legalistic tone and opens rather curiously. (In a third letter, he noted that he had graduated law school before entering the rabbinate.) Though the lighting of public menorahs had been going on at that point since 1974, Glaser wrote as if he had only just heard about it:

> *It has come to my attention that Lubavitcher Chasidim are erecting Hanukkiot and holding religious services in connection therewith on public property in various locations throughout the United States.*
>
> *This is as much a violation of the constitutional principle of separation of church and state as is the erection of Christmas trees and crèches depicting the birth of Jesus.[14] It weakens our hand when we protest this intrusion of Christian doctrine into the public life of American citizens and thus, it is really not worth the value received.*

The relatively brief letter then shifted into a warmer tone:

> *I would very much appreciate the opportunity to meet with you to discuss the matter further, and also to indulge a desire I have had for a long time to know you personally. I feel that we have many common interests, and want to explore them with you.*
> *My warmest good wishes for the remainder of the Pesach season.[15]*
> *Shalom*
>
> *Rabbi Joseph B. Glaser*

On May 31, Rabbi Glaser wrote again, this time after receiving a call from the Rebbe's office asking him to further delineate his views for the

Rebbe's "consideration and response." On this occasion, Glaser set out to establish more of a common ground between Reform Judaism and Chabad, both of whose members do not necessarily think that the two groups have much in common: [16]

> As believing Jews, Lubavitcher Chasidim, Reform Jews, and others share the conviction that the mitzvah of kindling Hanukkiot should be fulfilled by all Jews. Likewise, that the lights should be placed in the windows or even outside of Jewish homes and synagogue "to proclaim the miracle" is a practice we encourage. All that we question is the necessity and desirability of holding this or similar religious ceremonies on public property.

In a further effort to establish common ground, Glaser offered a rationale rooted in Jewish law (halacha) for his position: Since the obligation to light Chanukah candles is fulfilled when the menorah is lit on Jewish property, there is "no halachic necessity for doing so on public property." Glaser insisted, therefore, that in addition to being unnecessary, such an act also is undesirable. Jewish comfort in the United States has resulted in large part from the constitutionally guaranteed separation of church and state. This has enabled Jews and other supporters of separation to prevent "Christmas displays, crèches especially, on public property, and [to prevent] prayer-periods in public schools." If Jews do not want to be exposed to Christian observances that they find "offensive"—in Glaser's words—then it is equally wrong for them to carry out Jewish religious rituals in the public square. Glaser further argued that continuing confrontations between Jews who disagreed with the celebration of menorah lightings on public property "serves no positive Jewish purpose, and indeed is counter-productive."

Near the letter's conclusion, we find the first indication that legal efforts to stop the Menorah Campaign might soon follow: "I must tell you in all candor that we continue to receive complaints about this particular Chabad practice, and thus I have no doubt that the disputations will continue and possibly even end up in court."

Glaser concludes his letter with an appeal to the Rebbe, in his role as leader, "to direct a cessation of *Hanukkiot* lightings or other religious observances on public property."

The Rebbe's response was dated barely a week later, 3 Sivan 5738 (June 8, 1978). It is written in a respectful tone, though he addresses Glaser, who signed his correspondence as *Rabbi* Joseph Glaser, as "Dr. Glaser," perhaps out of resistance to recognizing Glaser's rabbinic credentials, although by no means is this clear. To cite just one example, the Rebbe seemed very comfortable in addressing the prominent Reform clergyman Herbert Weiner as "Rabbi."

As the Rebbe saw it, Rabbi Glaser's critique was rooted in two objections: Chabad's behavior violates the principle of separation of church and state and also is counterproductive. He addressed the latter issue first:

> *Had I received your letter years ago, when this practice started, I would have had a more difficult task of defending it, for the simple reason that the expected positive results were then a matter of conjecture. But now, after the practice and the results have been observed for a number of years, my task is an easy one, since the general acclaim and beneficial results have far exceeded our expectations. The fact is that countless Jews in all parts of the country have been impressed and inspired by the spirit of Chanukah which has been brought to them, to many for the first time.*

Regarding Glaser's argument that any good gained from the public lightings could be achieved equally by lightings inside Jewish homes or at synagogues, the Rebbe noted that the actual experience of lighting candles in public places achieved its success specifically in "reaching out to Jews who *could not otherwise* have been reached, either because some of them are unaffiliated with any synagogue or, though loosely affiliated,[17] always thought that religious practices . . . do not relate to the personal everyday life of the individual. It was precisely through kindling the Chanukah Lamp in public places during 'ordinary' weekdays . . . that it was brought home to them that true Judaism is practiced daily, and that no Jew should feel abashed about it" (emphasis in original letter).

The Rebbe here might well have been tactfully alluding to the fact that though the Reform movement strongly encourages its adherents to light Chanukah candles, many members of Reform synagogues do not do so, certainly not for all eight days of the holiday. And, of course,

there are many Jews—about half or more of the American-Jewish community at any given time—who maintain no synagogue affiliation at
all and who, in the absence of these public lightings, will likely have no
exposure to Chanukah.

Regarding the constitutional question, the Rebbe's tone turned
slightly patronizing: "I can most assuredly allay your apprehension on
this score. I am fully certain that none of those who participated in or
witnessed the kindling of a Chanukah Lamp in a public place (and in all
cases permission was *readily* granted by the authorities) felt that his or her
loyalty to the Constitution of the U.S.A. had been weakened or compromised thereby . . . seeing that the U.S. Congress opens [its daily sessions]
with a religious invocation . . . and surely the U.S. Congress, comprising
each and every state of the Union, is *the* place where the Constitution of
the U.S.A. should be most rigidly upheld."

The Rebbe then seized upon the issue of those opposed to the public
lightings of menorahs as a springboard to discuss an issue that apparently
concerned him even more: the widespread opposition of many Jews, Rabbi
Glaser among them, who "thwart" every effort to secure government aid
to enable Jewish day schools and yeshivot to cover the costs of their secular
studies and other nonreligious needs (such as school lunches): "Be it noted
that money that would have been received in such aid carries the motto,
'In God we trust.' It is lamentable that as a result of this attitude [opposi-
tion to public funding of religious schools], thousands of Jewish children
have been *deprived* of their right to Jewish education."

Just as one suspects that Rabbi Glaser was quite aware that his earlier
appeal to the Rebbe to direct his *shluchim* to cease public candlelightings
would be rejected, the Rebbe now made an appeal to Glaser that, one
suspects, he understood would go unheeded as well, though he framed
his request in a respectful and friendly manner: "I am encouraged to
take advantage of this unexpected exchange of correspondence between
us to express my ardent hope that you will use your influence to put
an end to the *destructive* fight against state aid to parochial schools, at
any rate insofar as the secular department is concerned, so as to enable
Jewish Day Schools and Yeshivot to open their doors to the maximum
number of students."

The Rebbe concluded his letter with a blessing to Glaser for an inspiring Shavuot, the holiday that celebrates the giving of the Torah, and which would be observed in three days' time.

However, this was not the end of the correspondence. Rabbi Glaser was spending the summer at Oxford University researching Anglo-American and Jewish laws concerning self-incrimination, and he wanted the Rebbe to know that he was engaged in scholarly Jewish study. Just as he wanted "to assure you, dear Rebbe, that I believe in, worship and commune with God as deeply, as fervently, and as intensively as you do, and cherish and work for the perpetuation of Judaism as much and as indefatigably." Indeed, it was in light of the intensity of his commitment that he again urged the Rebbe to reconsider his positions.

The issue of governmental support for religious schools was one that deeply pained him, Glaser explained. He wanted to strengthen Jewish education but, for the reasons he had already offered, he ardently opposed government aid to parochial schools. He now introduced an additional argument, that such aid would, in the end, be catastrophic for the schools themselves: "The moment the camel gets its nose under the tent, the inhabitants thereof are in trouble. . . . The government will end up intervening in matters theological, and in the moral areas where religion must have full sway and unimpeded conscience."

Oddly, Rabbi Glaser's line of argument was reminiscent of certain ultra-Orthodox anti-Zionist groups in Israel who refuse all government aid to their schools, arguing that the government will then try to impose its views on them.

The rest of Rabbi Glaser's letter is a basic restatement and expansion of his views. He expresses his unhappiness that the U.S. Congress "lamentably begins its sessions with a religious invocation." Also, the insertion of the words "under God" in the Pledge of Allegiance pains Glaser. He points out that this addition to the Pledge came about only in the 1950s, during the administration of President Eisenhower, "whose understanding of the American process and constitutional principles was probably the least of all the presidents of the United States from George Washington to the present."

Finally, Glaser returns to the issue of the Chanukah menorahs, this time introducing a previously unstated argument. The Rebbe seems to believe, Glaser notes, that there is some "intrinsic value" in having Jews attend a public lighting and blessing of the Chanukah candles. But since "ultimately the survival of Judaism depends on the home," it is *there* that the menorah should be lit. Having people observing the ceremony in public constitutes a "flamboyant religious exercise instead of a sacred home ritual."[18]

All true, perhaps, but the response one can imagine the Rebbe offering (he did not answer this letter) is that the alternative to people attending public lightings of Chanukah menorahs is not that they will light candles at home, but that they will not light them at all. In addition, as the Rebbe had earlier argued, it is certain, based on reports Chabad had received, that because of these public lightings, some spectators, perhaps many, had already started to light candles at home.

Rabbi Glaser and the Rebbe's letters and responses were primarily shaped by different concerns. For Rabbi Glaser, the most significant consideration was that American Jews have succeeded very well in an America in which religion and state are totally separate. Given that Jews are a small percentage of the population, it is best to keep things that way; otherwise, the Jewish situation could deteriorate rapidly: "The wall of separation between religion and state is like a dike: the slightest breach is a dangerous portent of a torrent to follow." However, Glaser's position was not dictated solely by this pragmatic consideration; for him, it was a matter of principle that the government involve itself in no way, financial or otherwise, in a religious ritual, even if all that was involved was permitting the ritual to be carried out on public grounds.

For the Rebbe, influenced yet again by his notions of love of all Jews, what was paramount was reaching Jews who were not being exposed to Judaism, in this instance offering them as a point of entry the joyous "festival of lights." The Rebbe also wanted to show the non-Jewish world— and through them, nonobservant Jews as well—an image of Jews who were willing to be very public about their religious commitment.

Over the following years, the public lighting of menorahs continued to grow. Professor Jonathan Sarna of Brandeis University has noted that since President Carter's participation in the Chabad menorah lighting, "Every president has recognized Chanukah with a special menorah-lighting ceremony, and limited his Christmas message to those who actually observe the holiday." [19] In 1982, when President Ronald Reagan participated in the candlelighting ceremony at Lafayette Park, he referred to the menorah, erected by Chabad, as "the National Menorah," thereby, as historian Dr. Joshua Eli Plaut has noted, "equating its lighting with the National Christmas tree lighting." Five years later, the largest menorah lighting of all occurred at the Sun Life Stadium in Miami, when Chabad *shliach* Rabbi Raphael Tennenhaus lit a menorah in front of seventy thousand people. That same year, 1987, the Rebbe transformed the campaign into an international one, pushing for public candlelightings throughout the world. Twenty-five years later, I attended a menorah lighting on a main street in Geneva, Switzerland, along with some four hundred other Jews, and which was witnessed by many non-Jews as well. "God gave each of us a soul, which is a candle that He gives us to illuminate our surroundings with His light," the Rebbe taught at a 1990 worldwide Chanukah satellite linkup. "We must not only illuminate the *inside* of homes, but also the outside, and the world at large."

Even as the public lightings of menorahs continued to grow from year to year, so, too, did the legal challenges of which Rabbi Glaser had warned the Rebbe. The most significant case occurred in Pittsburgh, and the legal battle provoked there was so fierce that it eventually ended up before the Pennsylvania Supreme Court (Allegheny County, 1989). The case addressed both the menorah and the Christian crèche. Over a period of some years, the city of Pittsburgh had permitted the Holy Name Society, a Catholic group, to place a crèche, depicting Jesus, Joseph, and Mary, on the Grand Staircase inside the Allegheny County courthouse. Alongside the crèche was a Latin banner proclaiming "Glory to God in the Highest." The Chabad menorah in Pittsburgh was no less public (it was eighteen feet high) but, unlike the crèche, it was placed outside, near the city-county building, where it stood alongside a forty-five-foot-high Christmas tree (the menorah was owned by Chabad, but the city stored and erected it each year). In 1986, the American Civil Liberties Union (ACLU) sued to stop the city from displaying both, arguing that the crèche and the menorah alike violated the Establishment Clause of the First Amendment. A lower court initially decided that Pittsburgh was within its right to display them, but then a higher court ruled that it was forbidden. In 1989, the case reached the U.S. Supreme Court, which issued a split decision, outlawing the placement of the crèche but permitting the displaying of the menorah alongside the Christmas tree. The court's reasoning was as follows: Because the crèche was positioned inside the Allegheny County courthouse, "the principle or primary effect" of the display was to advance religion, indeed a specific religion (and to do so inside a courthouse), but the case of the menorah that the city placed near a Christmas tree was not seen as *endorsing* the Jewish or Christian faith, just recognizing their status in U.S. society.

Subsequent to the Supreme Court ruling, challenges to the menorah lightings continued sporadically but started to diminish. At the same time, the acceptance of Chanukah within the United States continued to expand. In 1993, President Bill Clinton hosted Jewish schoolchildren for a candlelighting in the Oval Office, and eight years later, George W. Bush became the first president to host a Chanukah party at the White House; during the party, he himself lit the *shamash*, the central candle, which is then used to light the other candles.[20]

Today, several thousand public menorah lightings under Chabad auspices take place throughout the world each year. An increasing number of non-Chabad and non-Orthodox groups carry out such lightings as well.

"Go out into the courtyard into the public domain," the Rebbe continued on that same Chanukah night, "and create light which illuminates the entire outside world."[21]

Chapter 20

ISRAEL

Territorial Compromises Won't Bring Peace

"I AM COMPLETELY AND UNEQUIVOCALLY OPPOSED TO SURRENDER
OF ANY OF THE LIBERATED AREAS CURRENTLY UNDER NEGOTIA-
TION. . . . THIS HAS NOTHING TO DO WITH THE SANCTITY OF ERETZ
YISRAEL, BUT SOLELY WITH THE RULE OF *PIKUACH NEFESH* [WHICH
PROHIBITS TAKING AN ACTION THAT NEEDLESSLY ENDANGERS LIFE]."

May 1967, the month before the Six-Day War, was among the most
frightening months in Jewish history; June 1967, among the
happiest.[1] The Six-Day War, fought June 5–10, was a conflict that Israel
desperately wanted to avoid. But by the time it ended, the Jewish state
was almost four times as large as it previously had been, and it was in
possession of Judaism's holiest sites.

Israel struck the first blow on June 5, 1967, but the stage had been set earlier by Gamal Abdel Nasser, Egypt's president. In May, Nasser, apparently
believing that the Arab states had finally achieved military superiority over
Israel, entered into a process of brinksmanship with the Jewish state, repeatedly announcing his intention to exterminate the "Zionist entity." On
May 22, in violation of international agreements, he declared the Straits of
Tiran closed to all Israeli ships and to any foreign ships carrying strategic
materials to the Jewish state. Under international law, such an attempt at
economic strangulation constituted legal grounds to declare war (casus
belli), but Israel did not do so. Unfortunately, this restraint apparently fed
Nasser's conviction that Israel knew herself to be weaker than the Arabs.

On the following day, the Rebbe sent a telegram to the Chabad community in Israel. Strongly encouraging them in the face of the fear that
was spreading in Israel, he wrote, "You have merited to be amongst
thousands of Jews in the Holy Land, the land which God's eyes are constantly watching (Deuteronomy 11:12). Certainly, the Lord of Israel will
not slumber or sleep. . . . I am anticipating hearing good news quickly."[2]

This proved to be the first of many such letters and public pronouncements the Rebbe issued over the coming weeks. The sense of insecurity
and isolation in Israel was sufficiently great that the Rebbe's encouraging words were featured in at least six Israeli newspapers, spanning
the ideological divide from *HaTzofe*, the organ of the religious Mizrachi
Party, to *Al Hamishmar*, the newspaper of the militantly secular Mapam
Party. In all the papers, the articles carried virtually identical headlines:
"Lubavitcher Rebbe Sends Letter of Encouragement" (May 25, 1967).[3]

In the meantime, however, the political and military situation continued to deteriorate. Egypt and Syria had already agreed to combine their
armies in the coming war against Israel, and now Nasser flew to Jordan
to sign a military agreement with King Hussein as well. The three largest
Arab nations bordering Israel had now forged an alliance to destroy it.

In the last week of May, the rhetoric emanating out of the Arab world
grew increasingly ferocious. On May 27, Nasser declared, "Our basic objective will be the destruction of Israel." Four days later, Iraq's president,
Abdel Rahman Aref, announced: "Our goal is clear—to wipe Israel off
the map."

World Jewry felt ever more despondent. Each day seemed to bring
more bad news. Arab governments broadcast their readiness to send
troops to join in the war, and Iraq announced that its army was preparing to move troops into Jordan. In a country in which a large portion of
the population was comprised of survivors of the Holocaust, it felt as if
another Holocaust might be imminent. In Israel itself, rabbinic figures,
anticipating the possibility of horrific losses, prepared for the prospect
of turning parks into giant cemeteries that could hold twenty-five thousand or more bodies.[4] Many foreign-born Jews used their non-Israeli
passports to leave Israel for safer dwellings elsewhere. The Rebbe instructed his followers not to do so. Throughout the terrifying three

weeks that preceded the war, the Rebbe proclaimed again and again that Israel would emerge from the upcoming conflict with a great victory. When a group of yeshiva students inquired as to whether they should leave Israel, he told them to "continue learning with diligence" and to remain where they were.[5] He also advised that they "help with the war efforts."[6] He gave the same advice to parents with children in Israel. And he instructed one frightened questioner: "Do not be afraid or frighten others" (in the Torah, one reason frightened soldiers were exempted from fighting was the concern that they would cause the other soldiers to panic as well [Deuteronomy 20:8]). These words of advice were well publicized in the media, sometimes on the front page, and stood in stark contrast with the words of doom so many others were expressing.

Perhaps the most significant speech of encouragement was the one the Rebbe delivered on May 28, at the 1967 Crown Heights Lag B'Omer parade, only a week before the war began. Addressing more than twenty thousand people, the Rebbe spoke forcefully and passionately about the expected conflict in Israel. Without hesitation, he predicted yet again: "God is guarding Israel and . . . the people of Israel will emerge from the current situation with a remarkable victory."[7]

In Israel, a taped version of the Rebbe's speech was broadcast on national radio, with simultaneous translation from Yiddish to Hebrew. The large-circulation *Yediot Achronot* headlined an account of the speech, "God Is Already Protecting the Holy Land and Salvation Is Near." The news article spoke of the Rebbe's displeasure with the overwrought atmosphere engulfing much of the country: "I am displeased with the exaggerations being disseminated and the panicking of the citizens in Israel."

Five days later, on June 5, with General Moshe Dayan, hero of the 1956 Sinai War, serving as the newly appointed minister of defense, Israel launched an extraordinary preemptive strike. In a few hours, its planes destroyed the entire Egyptian air force. Anxious not to fight on additional fronts, Israel asked United Nations intermediaries to plead with King Hussein not to join the war. But Jordan's monarch, convinced that Egypt would win, didn't want to miss out on the spoils.

From positions in the Jordanian-controlled West Bank, Jordanian artillery opened fire on Jerusalem, Tel Aviv, and several Israeli airfields.

At the same time, Hussein appealed on Radio Amman to "kill the Jews" wherever they could be found, with one's hands, nails, and anything else. Israel immediately fought back, and soon Jordan's air force was also destroyed.

Over the coming days, Israel, now with unchallenged air superiority, took possession of the entire Sinai Peninsula, and, in two days of brutal fighting (June 6–7), took control of the West Bank, which Jordan had occupied since 1948. For Jews, this victory was the emotional highlight of the war, for it meant that the Old City of Jerusalem and the Western Wall (*Kotel*) were again in Jewish hands. Yet Israel also suffered heavy losses in the battle for Jerusalem, in part because it refused to use artillery in the Old City out of a commitment to preserve the holy sites of all the religions represented there. In many ways, an even more difficult battle was the Six-Day War's last one, the one fought on the Golan Heights, then held by Syria. Here, Israeli soldiers literally had an uphill battle. Since Israel's founding in 1948, Syrian soldiers on the Heights had fired down on Israeli kibbutzim and settlements. By June 10, however, Israel's army had secured the Heights.

The war itself, though it lasted only six days, claimed the lives of 679 Israelis, a painfully high price for a country as small as Israel.[8] Despite these very painful deaths and injuries suffered by Israeli soldiers, the country, and the whole Jewish world, were euphoric on June 10. Two weeks earlier, many Jews had feared that Israel faced destruction; now, Israel was universally recognized as the greatest military power in the Middle East.

Ever since, the pre-1967 borders have been referred to as "the Green Line" because the armistice maps drawn up after Israel's War of Independence had colored Israel's borders in green. The lands conquered from Jordan became widely known as the West Bank (of the Jordan River), though Jews—particularly those who wish to retain these lands— commonly refer to them by their biblical names, Judea and Samaria.

Of all the parts of this book, it is the next part that I write with the greatest sense of caution. Logically, this should not be the case, as it is based on a spring 1968 *yechidus* with the Rebbe at which I was present, the only one I had. But I was in no way the main visitor at that meeting; I was only nineteen at the time, and actually tagging along with my grandfather, Rabbi Nissen Telushkin, a major rabbinical scholar and a man who had a very warm relationship with the Rebbe (and who was about to leave on a trip to Israel), and my father, Shlomo Telushkin,[9] who served as accountant both to the Rebbe, and earlier to the Frierdiker Rebbe.

The problem for me was that the *yechidus* was conducted in Yiddish. Unfortunately, my Yiddish is very weak and so, throughout the meeting, my father would whisper to me a brief summary of what the Rebbe was saying (at the end, the Rebbe spoke to me briefly in Hebrew and gave me a *bracha*, as I was to be spending the following year at a yeshiva in Israel). This meeting, held less than a year after the Six-Day War, touched on several issues relating to Israel, specifically the new lands brought under Israeli control and matters of security. What follows are my recollections of what the Rebbe said that day, as confirmed by later discussions with my father.

The Rebbe expressed unhappiness over the fact that many Israeli soldiers had died in the battle for Jerusalem because of the great and, in the Rebbe's view, excessive care that had been taken not to in any way damage buildings in the Old City that are regarded as holy. I recall him saying something to the effect that even capturing the *Kotel ha-Ma'aravi* (Western Wall) was not worth losing one innocent Israeli soldier's life, and the fact that needless deaths were brought about to safeguard religious sites, many of them sites holy to other people, struck him as very wrong. Lives are worth more than buildings, any buildings.

Regarding the tremendous demographic shift that had occurred in Israel (Arabs now constituted 40 percent of those living under Israeli rule versus 15 percent before the war), the Rebbe felt that this was a result of a tremendous error made by the Israeli military at the time Judea and Samaria were captured. From what I recall, he basically said: "When Israel took control of Judea and Samaria, her soldiers should have said to the Arabs living there. 'You made it known that had you conquered us, you would have killed us, man, woman, and child. We are not like you. We will not kill you, but you cannot expect us to let people who wish to kill us continue to live among us.'"

In the Rebbe's view, Israel should have told the Arabs to leave and go across the border into Jordan. I remember him saying something to the effect that, during the war, following those awful days in which Arab leaders had been issuing repeated death threats against Israel and its citizens, the world could have accepted such an action; it would have struck people as understandable self-defense, and the Arabs would have been relieved that the Israelis did not do to them what they would have done to the Israelis.[10] But once the war ended, Israel lost the opportunity to rid itself of enemies who wished to destroy her. Outside of wartime itself, such behavior by Israel, forcing Arabs out of Judea and Samaria, would not be possible.[11]

In the years ahead, what the Rebbe continued to oppose—with great passion and certainty—was Israel's giving back any of the lands conquered in 1967. For one thing, the Rebbe never tired of quoting the promise God made to Abraham: "For all the land that you see I give to you and to your descendants forever" (Genesis 13:15). Therefore, holding on to the land God gave the Jewish people was an imperative. More significant, though, from the Rebbe's perspective, giving back such lands would not in any case end the conflict and bring peace, since it was not Israel's conquest of the lands that began the conflict in the first place. Most important, the Rebbe argued again and again that Israel's conceding land would not only not bring peace, but would instead actually endanger Israel's survival and put the lives of innocent civilians at risk.[12] For years, this was a theoretical issue because there was, in any case, no one to whom to give the lands. On September 1, 1967, three months after the war ended, the leadership of the entire Arab world met in Khartoum, Sudan, and issued "The Three No's": "No peace with Israel, no negotiations with Israel, no recognition of Israel." Since the only motive for Israel to hand back any of the territories was to secure peace and recognition, the rejection of the possibility of peace by the entire Arab world effectively ended any such action by Israel.

But all this changed in 1977, when Egyptian president Anwar Sadat announced that he was willing to go to the Israeli Knesset to talk to the Israelis about peace and the return of the territories. Many people suspected Sadat's words might be mere rhetoric, but when Israeli prime minister Menachem Begin extended an official invitation to him, Sadat immediately accepted and arrived in Israel in November 1977. In his speech to the Knesset, Sadat offered Israel peace in exchange for land. But it wasn't only the Egyptian territories lost in the Six-Day War that Sadat wished to see restored. He himself was negotiating on behalf of Egypt, but if there was to be a real peace, he told the Knesset, Israel must withdraw to its pre-1967 borders and grant the Palestinians a homeland. In effect, Sadat shifted the responsibility for the Palestinian people's fate into the hands of the Israelis.

In September 1978, U.S. president Jimmy Carter hosted both Begin and Sadat at Camp David, outside Washington, DC. During thirteen torturous days of negotiations, Begin agreed to return all Egyptian lands conquered in 1967. In the final accords, the perennially thorny issue of the Old City of Jerusalem was sidestepped, and Begin agreed to negotiate the issue of Palestinian autonomy on the West Bank. In return, Sadat announced full recognition of Israel, including trade relations and an exchange of ambassadors.

The peace treaty negotiated between Israel and Egypt required the approval of the Israeli Knesset, and there were many Israelis and Jews throughout the world—though they turned out to be a distinct minority—who thought that Israel's relinquishing the Sinai was a grave mistake. Among them was the Rebbe, who argued that returning conquered land would certainly not strengthen Israel's security; in addition to losing territory that could serve as an important buffer in case of war, the Rebbe felt that Israel's succumbing to pressure would subject her to ever greater and continuing demands for the return of yet more land.[13] Not only would doing so not ensure Israel's security, it could earn her contempt from those, including the United States, who would come to believe that Israel could be pressured into acting against her own best interests.[14] Yet another point the Rebbe would often make, and this is not widely known, was that he felt that Israel's not conceding territories would save Arab lives as well, lives that would be needlessly lost in conflict;[15] in every Israeli/Arab war far more Arabs than Jews have been killed.

The Rebbe always insisted that his opposition to returning land was not just a personal view, but represented the opinion of Israel's military and security officials as well.[16] He did, however, also say that if Israel's security officials concluded that Israel would be safer from a *purely* security perspective if it returned certain territories, then it should do so.[17]

Yehuda Avner recollects that the Rebbe made known to him, during and even before the negotiations, his strong opposition to the agreement with Egypt, and he wanted Avner to transmit his views to Prime Minister Begin. When I asked Avner how the prime minister reacted when he did, he told me that when Begin, who was eminently capable of being confrontational, did not want to respond to something or did not want to enter into a debate (and he certainly did not want to debate the Rebbe for whom he had great admiration; see page 52), he had a way of just ignoring the issue. In this case, after Avner told Begin what the Rebbe felt, Begin responded with one word in Yiddish, *"Azoi"* ("So be it"), and dropped the discussion.

The Knesset eventually approved the agreement negotiated by Begin and Sadat by a vote of 84–19, with 17 abstentions.

However, this issue was so fundamental to the Rebbe (the treaty with Egypt constituted the first time Israel was handing back lands conquered in the Six-Day War) that he seized upon many opportunities to make his beliefs known, in one case in a letter to the editor in the Los Angeles–based *B'nai B'rith Messenger*. Befitting his rabbinic status, the Rebbe did not simply offer political arguments but opened with a comment on the first two words of the newspaper's name, *B'nai B'rith*, Hebrew for "children of the covenant." He noted that the first person to accept the covenant (*brit*) was the patriarch Abraham, to whom God promised: "Unto your seed, I have given this land . . . and I will give unto your seed, and to your seed after you, the land of your sojourn, all the land of Canaan, for an everlasting possession" (Genesis 15:18 and 17:7–8).

How sad, the Rebbe argued, that some Jews were now willing, "for the sake of peace or rather the illusion of peace," to surrender portions of the land "in the ill-conceived belief that our enemies would thereby be appeased." In the Rebbe's view, surrendering to such pressure would quickly invite ever greater pressure to give up more and more of the lands Israel had captured in 1967 and, in the end, undermine the country's security.

The Rebbe explained that he had opposed the negotiations with Egypt from the beginning, viewing it as a negotiation in which one party, Israel, "gives all, and the other party [Egypt] takes all. For what Israel gave to Egypt was tangible vital resources, including territory, airfields, [and] oil wells," while Egypt "gives in return no more than promises." True, Egypt offered an exchange of ambassadors and the normalization of relations, but the problem is that what Israel gave Egypt was given irrevocably and made the country both poorer and less secure, while what Egypt promised Israel in return "could be revoked at any moment under one pretext or another."

In one regard in particular, the Rebbe's judgment, although controversial, was based on an undeniable truth. In the years following the 1967 war, Israel had discovered and developed a large oil field in southern Sinai that had been supplying a large part of Israel's energy needs, but which it had been obligated to return to Egypt. Israel was now spending billions of dollars to procure oil that it formerly had been pumping for free.

Remarkably enough, one of those who seemed to agree with the Rebbe's analysis was Anwar Sadat. An October 19, 1980, article in the *New York Times* reported that Sadat declared, one presumes with a smile, to his colleagues, "Poor Menachem; he has his problems. I got back 90 percent of the Sinai and the Alma oil fields, and what has Menachem got? A piece of paper."

The Rebbe, in his letter to the *B'nai B'rith Messenger*, then posed a highly provocative question: "Now that we have a Camp David agreement signed, sealed and delivered . . . would it be legally and morally right to abrogate it unilaterally?"

The Rebbe's answer: Yes. For one thing, the Egyptians, he argued, had broken many of the pledges under the agreement: for example, by reporting to the PLO[18] (which at the time was still committed to terrorism against, and to the destruction of, Israel) on the ongoing negotiations with Israel, which it was forbidden to do. This alone, he felt, freed Israel from any legal or moral obligation to abide by the treaty's provisions. Even worse, the Rebbe noted, people were forgetting that years earlier, in the aftermath of a 1970 negotiation and agreement involving Israel, Egypt, and the United States, the Egyptians had almost immediately violated their commitments by placing missiles in the agreed-upon military-free zones and providing an air defense umbrella over the Suez Canal, setting the stage for it to be crossed by the Egyptian army, which it did three years later in the Yom Kippur War.[19]

The Rebbe's second objection was more fundamental, as he challenged the right of the government of Israel to have entered into such negotiations. By the Rebbe's reasoning, the Camp David agreement jeopardized the security of Israel, and no government official, even if elected in a democratic election, has the right "to sign away the very security of the people and the country he represents, nor the security of the next generation and subsequent generations." In such a case, the Rebbe insisted, "no signature, or even ratification [the treaty had been ratified by the Knesset], can be binding."

The Rebbe's letter stopped short of advocating that individual Israelis take the law into their own hands and find ways to abrogate the treaty, but he urged people to come to the realization that never again should Israel "give away any part of our tiny land . . . since the retention of every last inch of it is a matter of vital security for the three and a half million Jews, men, women and children, as well as for our Jewish people as a whole."[20]

For the rest of his life, the Rebbe always made a point of emphasizing that his opposition to Israel withdrawing from any of the lands it had won in the Six-Day War was rooted not in the sanctity of the land but solely on his conviction that such withdrawal would lead to Jewish lives being lost. The issue for him, therefore, was *pikuach nefesh* (the saving of endangered lives), which overrides all of Jewish law with but three exceptions.[21]

In this regard, the Rebbe quoted time and time again a ruling of the *Shulchan Aruch* (the Code of Jewish Law), based on a passage in the Talmud that he regarded as a mandate forbidding Israel from ceding even one inch of its land.

"When non-Jews besiege a Jewish city . . . if they come [with the intention] to take lives, or even if it is not clear why they have come [or they are simply making preparations to come], we go forth against them with weapons and desecrate the Sabbath in order to resist them. If the siege is on a city close to the border, then, even if they have only come for the sake of pillaging straw and stubble, we must desecrate the Shabbat because of them, [for] if we do not prevent their coming they may conquer the city; and from there the rest of the land will be easy for them to conquer, since a city on the border opens up the whole country before them" [22] (*Shulchan Aruch, Orach Chaim* 329:6).[23]

Although the Rebbe's views were not always acceptable to Israel's leadership, his opinions were reckoned with in the highest echelons of government. Ariel Sharon was known to quote the Rebbe's opinions on military matters (particularly the Rebbe's critique of the Bar-Lev Line years before the Yom Kippur War; see pages 289–90). When Prime Minister Begin visited the Rebbe before meeting President Carter in Washington, he told a group of journalists who questioned him about his going to 770: "Rabbi Schneerson is [considered] a great man in Israel. All of us respect him, all of us accept his judgment." General Mordechai Piron, who served as the Israeli army's chief rabbi from 1969 to 1980, has recently disclosed that during the Yom Kippur War and its immediate aftermath, he and Defense Minister Moshe Dayan would carefully review messages sent them by the Rebbe: "Whenever a new message would arrive from the Rebbe, we would sit together, we would pay close attention to it, to determine the Rebbe's intention." [24]

The most prominent Orthodox rabbi to oppose the Rebbe's view and to advocate territorial compromise by the Israeli government was Immanuel Jakobovits, chief rabbi of the United Kingdom. Rabbi Jakobovits rooted his call for compromise in two main premises:

- such a policy would save lives, since it would end the state of war between Israel and the Arab world;
- the Palestinians deserved a homeland, and Israel should offer them one.

The Rebbe clearly thought otherwise. He did not think that concessions could end the state of war, since, as noted, the Arabs had threatened and murdered Jews before any Israeli conquest.

In a series of forcefully argued letters between the two men (written between November 1980 and February 1982), the Rebbe outlined the reason for his disagreement with the positions taken by Rabbi Jakobovits. While it is accurate to say that he disagreed with Jakobovits's entire approach, the argument he most fundamentally rejected was the contention that territorial compromise by Israel would save lives; the Rebbe was certain that the opposite would be the case: "I am completely and unequivocally opposed to the surrender of any of the liberated areas currently under negotiation, such as Judea and Samaria, and the Golan, for the simple reason, and only reason, that surrendering any part of them would contravene a clear *psak din* [legal ruling] in the *Shulchan Aruch* [the ruling cited above]. I have repeatedly emphasized that this ruling [on which I base my opinion] has nothing to do with the sanctity of Eretz Yisrael . . . but solely with the rule of *pikuach nefesh*."[25] That is why he opposed giving the Palestinians a homeland on the lands that Israel had conquered from them; the PLO charter, he noted, called for the destruction of the Jewish state. Why, therefore, give them land from which they could launch murderous attacks against Israel?[26]

The Rebbe continued: "Should there be a question whether the risk does in fact create a situation of endangerment of life, then, as in the case of illness where a medical authority is consulted, the authority to make a judgment is vested in the military experts. If military experts decide that there is a danger to life, there can be no other overriding considerations, since *pikuach nefesh* overrides everything else. Should the military experts declare that while there is such a risk, yet [the risk] should be taken for some other reason, such as political considerations [goodwill of the non-Jewish world], this would clearly be contrary to the *psak din*, for the legal ruling requires that [endangerment of life], not political expediency, should be the decisive factor."

The Rebbe reasoned that no military expert, Jewish or non-Jewish, believes that giving up any part of the conquered areas will *enhance* the defensibility of Israel's borders. Some military experts, however, were willing to take a chance for political, not security, reasons, in order to improve Israel's international image or not to antagonize the United States (it should also be noted that some of those who took a more dovish position argued that reaching a peace agreement with one or more Arab states, even if it necessitated territorial compromise, would make war less likely and thereby lead to fewer people being killed). In the Rebbe's view, overconcern with Israel's image and fear of antagonizing the United States had already cost Israel dearly, as illustrated by the Yom Kippur War of 1973.[27]

Although people today often assume that Egypt and Syria's joint attack on Israel that Yom Kippur came as a complete shock, it has long been known that Israeli military intelligence was aware of the upcoming attack half a day before, and informed Israeli prime minister Golda Meir and the heads of the army of what was about to happen. Clearly, the Rebbe reasoned, Israel should have mounted a preemptive attack, as it had done in 1967. But it didn't do so because Israel's political leadership feared that launching such an attack, or even starting "a general mobilization, before the Egyptians actually crossed the border, would mean [Israel] being branded as the aggressor, and would jeopardize Israel's relations with the U.S.A."[28] This decision, the Rebbe wrote Jakobovits, "was contrary to the ruling of the *Shulchan Aruch*, as pointed out above. The tragic results of that decision bore out the validity of the *Shulchan Aruch*'s position (as if it were necessary) for many lives were needlessly sacrificed, and the situation came close to a total disaster, but for God's mercies. Suffice it to mention that the then Prime Minister later admitted that all [the rest of] her life she would be haunted by that tragic decision."[29]

One issue the two men did not really address in their letters was the danger to the Jewish character of the country if and when—which is still very possible—the Arab population under Israeli rule would come to equal, and eventually exceed, the Jewish population. It was fear of the growing Arab population that the hawkish right-wing prime minister Ariel Sharon cited when he decided upon a unilateral withdrawal by Israel from Gaza in 2005.[30] As he declared before the Knesset on October 25, 2004, explaining this decision: "We do not wish to control millions of Palestinians who double in number in each generation. A democratic Israel will not be able to withstand such a thing."

Even without the large number of Arabs in Gaza, the large Arab population in the West Bank (Judea and Samaria), and the implications for Israel of having Arabs comprise so large a percentage of people living under Israeli rule continues to worry Israel's political leadership and is the reason that even right-wing prime minister Benjamin Netanyahu has come to support the creation of a Palestinian state, though he obviously wishes to keep it smaller in size than the state demanded by the Palestinians. Given the continuously growing Palestinian population, it is hard to know what the Rebbe would say about how Jewish law would rule in such a situation. As he concluded in the last of his letters to Jakobovits, "When it comes to a question of endangerment of life . . . God Himself ordained that in addition to the strict observance of Torah and Mitzvos, and absolute *bitachon* [trust] in Him, a Jew is required to do what is necessary in the natural order of things."

Thus, the question remains: What today is necessary "in the natural order of things"?

This question notwithstanding, the Rebbe's passionate opposition to territorial compromise continued unabated, and in 1990, two years before the stroke that silenced him ever after, the entire Jewish world outside of Chabad became aware of just how much this issue mattered to him.[31]

That year, Secretary of State James Baker started to pressure the government of Prime Minister Yitzhak Shamir to enter into direct negotiations with a Palestinian delegation that included Palestinians whom Israel had deported from the West Bank, as well as Palestinians residing in East Jerusalem (which Israel had incorporated into her borders in 1967), and whom Israel knew would insist on redividing the now unified Jerusalem. Shamir refused to accede to the pressure, but Shimon Peres, head of the Labor Party, sided with the American position and threatened to leave the national unity government if Shamir did not accept Baker's proposal. While all this was going on, Labor courted several religious parties, including Agudat Yisrael, in an effort to see if they could establish a new government. It soon appeared that Peres would have the votes to do so, and a no-confidence vote was introduced against Shamir's government. It passed by a vote of 60–55—the only such vote to ever succeed in the Knesset—and the government fell. At that point, Israeli president Chaim Herzog invited Peres to form a new government, and Peres succeeded in gathering the support of sixty-one members of the Knesset, one more than necessary to form a government. A vote was set for April 11, 1990, at which time the new government was to be approved. The Rebbe had long made it known that Chabad had a nonpartisan approach; he did not mix into politics, and he did not endorse any particular political party over another[32] (throughout Israel's history, the sole exception was the 1988 election, when the Rebbe supported Agudat Yisrael). Yet, two Knesset members of Agudat Yisrael, Eliezer Mizrahi and Avraham Verdiger—aware of the Rebbe's concerns that a more dovish government would adopt policies that would endanger Israeli security by making territorial concessions—refused to go along with the agreement their party had enacted. The Rebbe did not approach the two men directly and did not ask them to vote against the formation of the new government. Mizrahi and Verdiger were in a bind. They could not in good conscience vote against the new government, as Agudat Yisrael had committed itself and all its members to support Peres's government, and the two men were bound by party discipline. Instead, on the day of the vote, the two men simply could not be found; they remained incommunicado. With the support of only fifty-nine Knesset members, instead of sixty-one, Peres's government could not come into power, and some weeks later Shamir was able to craft together a new government.

That it was the Rebbe, residing in Brooklyn, who had effectively blocked Peres's campaign for the prime ministership became widely known in Israel and throughout the world (there were newspaper articles and much other media discussion). Many Israelis, particularly those whose views were dovish, were infuriated that an overseas rabbi could determine the course of Israeli politics (much as many Americans would feel infuriated if a religious leader from France, for example, determined who would serve as America's president, or which party would control

Congress). Other Israelis were either bemused, amused, or somewhat in awe of the Rebbe's power. But whether one supported or opposed the Rebbe's action, one thing was clear: He had influence and he had power.[33]

A short time later, Rabbi Israel Meir Lau, then serving as chief rabbi of Tel Aviv, was in the United States and had a brief meeting with the Rebbe during Dollars (the Sunday gatherings at which several thousand people briefly met the Rebbe and were each given a dollar to give to charity). The Rebbe told Rabbi Lau to take care of the various issues that were confronting him in his rabbinical work in Tel Aviv, and to do so quickly, for within less than two years "you will be moving to Jerusalem as Israel's chief rabbi." The statement was so unexpected and unanticipated that Lau did not know what to make of it. A few minutes later, he saw Uri Savir, the Israeli consul general for New York, who was there at 770 with New York City mayor David Dinkins. Savir had already heard from others present what the Rebbe had said, and he greeted Rabbi Lau with good humor and a certain sense of ceremony: "Mazal Tov, Chief Rabbi of Israel." Lau asked Savir if he actually took this statement seriously, and Savir answered: "If this man who sits here [in Brooklyn] can determine who will be the Prime Minister in Israel—Peres or Shamir—he can certainly determine who will be the next Chief Rabbi."[34]

The Rebbe and the Israel Defense Forces

In addition to taking a keen interest in Israel's political strategies, and remaining in ongoing contact with the country's highest officials, including prime ministers and presidents, the Rebbe had a particular concern with the strength and well-being of the Israeli army (IDF); he regularly met and corresponded with many of the country's top military officers.

One dramatic, but by no means unique, example: In 1986, Major General Yossi Ben-Hanan, a recipient of Israel's Medal of Courage for his valor during the Yom Kippur War, was asked by the IDF's chief of staff, General Moshe Levi, to serve as commander of the Armored Corps.

Ben-Hanan, who had already served in the IDF for over two decades, was hesitant to accept the position. He had been gearing up to leave the army, his wife was expecting a child, and he knew that this new job would be all-consuming. He told Levi that he would require time to consider the offer; he needed "to consult with others," is how he put it. Ben-Hanan traveled to America a few weeks later and went to 770. It was a Sunday and the Rebbe was dispensing dollars. A legendary war hero— Ben-Hanan's photograph had once adorned the cover of *Life* magazine— Ben-Hanan was escorted to the head of the line. After telling the Rebbe his dilemma, the Rebbe strongly encouraged Ben-Hanan to continue in the IDF and to utilize his strengths "to protect and preserve the sanctity of the land, of the people and of the Torah." The meeting ended with the Rebbe offering Ben-Hanan his blessing that he be successful in his new task, not by winning battles but "through averting the need of battle."

Ben-Hanan returned to Israel where he told a very pleased Moshe Levi that he would be accepting the new position; Levi, though, was curious to know with whom he had consulted. Ben-Hanan did not answer Levi directly, but even though Ben-Hanan, by his own acknowledgment, was largely a nonobservant Jew, the chief of staff continued to question him and eventually deduced who Ben-Hanan's secret adviser was: "Don't tell me that you went to America and asked the Lubavitcher Rebbe!" he exclaimed. Levi was aware that over the years other generals in the IDF (including Ariel Sharon) had done just that.[35] Ben-Hanan acknowledged that this was the case and that it was the Rebbe who encouraged him to take the position. "What?" came Levi's shocked response. "You go to the Lubavitcher Rebbe to ask him what to answer me. I'm the chief of staff! I ask you something, and then you tell me that you need to think [about it and then you go] to seek advice [from] a rabbi who's never been in Israel . . . and that he's the one who gave you the advice!"

Ben-Hanan was not intimidated by Levi's annoyed tone. "Until when will you be chief of staff?" he asked his commander.

"Seven more months," Levi responded.

"And until when will the Rebbe serve?" Ben-Hanan countered rhetorically.

Ben-Hanan accepted the position and went on to become the longest-serving commander of the Armored Corps in Israel's history.[36]

The Rebbe's respect extended to all of Israel's soldiers, people whom he believed saved and safeguarded lives on a daily basis. In the aftermath of the Six-Day War, he spoke of the soldiers' bravery and of "the advantage and greatness of those who go out to war [to protect the Jewish people] over those who study Torah." [37] He expressed similar sentiments after the Yom Kippur War [38] (three years after the war, he also arranged a special and private meeting with soldiers who had been badly wounded in Israel's battles; see page 111), and after the victory at Entebbe in 1976, he spoke at length of the great bravery of the soldiers who risked their lives to save the lives of others (all the soldiers who participated in the Entebbe rescue had volunteered for the mission).

He was as interested in the soldiers' families as in the soldiers themselves. Shortly after the Six-Day War, the Rebbe instructed his followers in Israel to arrange care for the orphans and widows of Israel's fallen soldiers. [39] He later wrote of the importance of such work: "Their fathers . . . are looking down from heaven; they would like to see their families and children being cared for. The greatest thing for the fallen soldiers is to be certain that their children will grow up to be good people."

Subsequently, and in conjunction with the Rebbe's request, Shifra Morozov, a Lubavitcher Chasid, whose husband, David, an Israeli soldier, had been killed in the Six-Day War, began arranging bar mitzvah celebrations under Chabad auspices for the orphans of Israel's heroes. Each year since, as many as four thousand people have gathered in Kfar Chabad, where a special celebration takes place for the tens of orphans turning thirteen that year. Until his stroke, the Rebbe would send each young man a personal letter offering his own best wishes and a pair of tefillin.

The Rebbe's interest in the soldiers and their families extended beyond religious matters. Brigadier General Ran Pecker, commander of the Tel Nof Air Base, relates that when he came to 770 to meet the Rebbe, he was "unprepared" for the comprehensive nature of the Rebbe's knowledge and interests; as he later put it, he did not expect to sit with a Torah scholar and discuss "the strategic value of the air force in a complex war" or "why Ariel Sharon did this and did not do that," or "whether military families should live inside the army bases" (the Rebbe felt that being raised in such an environment, surrounded by tanks and weapons, could be injurious to a young child's emotional well-being). Pecker recalls the Rebbe discussing with genuine concern the living conditions of the soldiers' families, and he thought that they should live off base.

Similarly, Noach Blasbalg recalls bringing an Israeli soldier with him into a *yechidus* with the Rebbe, during which the Rebbe focused much of his attention on the soldier and tried to learn all that he could about the daily lives of the troops. He questioned the soldier about what the men did in their free time. Did they read, and if so, what did they read, and, for that matter, did they smoke? The Rebbe then shifted into less expected terrain: "What type of machine gun do they use?" When the soldier answered, "The Thompson" (the American-made submachine gun originally created during the Prohibition era), the Rebbe asked why they weren't using the more advanced Swedish model: "The Thompson only shoots such-and-such numbers of bullets per minute, whereas the Swedish guns shoot many more." [40]

Sometimes, the Rebbe's suggestions were even more pointed. One noted example concerns the Bar-Lev Line, which had been established after the Six-Day War by Israeli chief of staff General Haim Bar-Lev and which consisted of a series of fortifications, each several kilometers behind the other, intended to protect Israel in case of Egyptian attack. The Rebbe was convinced that the Bar-Lev Line was a blunder and that it would be much safer to concentrate Israel's forces in one place, and thereby be in a far stronger position to repulse an Egyptian attack. Ariel Sharon recalled a letter he received from the Rebbe in 1969: "I was the commander of the southern front which included Sinai, and the front along the Suez Canal, where we were facing the Egyptians and the Soviets [who were arming them]. The Rebbe sent me a letter describing the disaster that will happen to the Jewish people, and the tragedy that the Bar-Lev Line will bring." [41] There was no rabbinic component to the letter, Sharon recalled; rather, the Rebbe analyzed as a "military expert" (these are Sharon's words) what might ensue if the Bar-Lev Line was not replaced. As a matter of fact, Sharon continued, that is exactly what happened four years later when Egypt attacked Israel on Yom Kippur 1973 and many hundreds of Israeli soldiers were killed, as the Egyptians

broke through the several Bar-Lev Line fortifications. Years later, in discussing the Yom Kippur War and the crushing Egyptian attack across
the Suez, Sharon acknowledged that, "as a matter of fact," what the
Rebbe predicted, happened. "It was a tragedy." [42]

The trust many Israelis felt for the Rebbe was widespread and extended to several of the country's other leaders as well. Addressing the
UN General Assembly in 2011, one of the highlights of Prime Minister
Benjamin Netanyahu's speech was his recollection of an encounter he
had with the Rebbe in 1984, shortly after he was appointed Israel's ambassador to the UN. The Rebbe, acknowledging the widespread hostility
to the Jewish state that Netanyahu would soon be encountering, advised him: "You will be serving in a house of many lies. Remember that
even in the darkest place, the light of a single candle can be seen far and
wide." [43] Building on the Rebbe's insight and on the ongoing animosity toward Israel even twenty-seven years later, Netanyahu resumed:
"Today I hope that the light of truth will shine if only for a few minutes
in a hall that has for too long been a place of darkness for my country."

As unusual and as provocative as were both the Rebbe's and Netanyahu's words, what was equally striking was that it was the Lubavitcher
Rebbe whom Netanyahu chose to cite before this international body.

Unlike this widely publicized UN speech, often the incidents concerning the Rebbe and Israel's leaders were known to only a few people. On
April 23, 1990, the phone rang in the office of Rabbi Binyamin Klein, the
Rebbe's secretary, who often served as the conduit between Israeli officials
and the Rebbe. On the other end of the line was Elyakim Rubenstein,
cabinet secretary and later Israel's attorney general. He told Klein that
Prime Minister Shamir wished to speak with him. Shamir himself was a
rather secular Jew and had never met the Rebbe in person. Now Shamir
got on the phone and asked Klein to inform the Rebbe that Israeli intelligence had learned of some imminent attacks that were being prepared
by terrorists. The news was alarming, and Klein was not sure in which direction the conversation was heading. But the purpose of the call, it soon
transpired, was simple and straightforward. The prime minister of Israel,
head of one of the great armies and intelligence services in the world, was
calling to ask the Rebbe for a *bracha* (blessing) that the attacks be foiled.

Chapter 21

SOVIET JEWRY

Public Demonstrations Will Hurt Russian Jews

"THE KEY IS QUIET DIPLOMACY."

Two of the hottest political issues in the American Jewish community in the late 1960s and 1970s was how best to pressure the Soviet Union to allow Soviet Jews to leave Russia and how to combat the Soviet Union's antisemitic policies, which made it difficult and dangerous for Russian Jews, young Jews in particular, to practice or study Judaism. Groups such as SSSJ (Student Struggle for Soviet Jewry), the National Conference on Soviet Jewry, the Greater New York Conference on Soviet Jewry, and the Union of Councils for Soviet Jews advocated and organized large public demonstrations directed against the Soviet government and its leadership. On the other side, the Rebbe, who it was known maintained an active educational underground in the Soviet Union, publicly opposed such demonstrations, arguing that they caused harm to Russian Jews, leading to harassment and even imprisonment of committed Jews. He stated that, based on his knowledge, the demonstrations were anything but helpful to the plight of Soviet Jewry, and he advocated behind-the-scenes "quiet diplomacy" as the most effective tool to help Russia's Jews.

At a February 1971 *farbrengen*, the Rebbe devoted two of his talks, which lasted about an hour and a half, to expressing, in the strongest language he had used until that time, his opposition to demonstrations on behalf of Russian Jews. Several times during the talks that evening, the Rebbe challenged those who disagreed with this position with great emotion and pathos: "Tell the truth. Can they show that the demonstrations have led to even one Jew being allowed to leave the Soviet Union?" He referred several times to an incident that had happened some time earlier. A large group of Jews, some hundred families, had been scheduled to be allowed to leave Russia. To ensure that their visas were not canceled, the Rebbe had pleaded that a large demonstration planned for just before Passover be called off or at least postponed. The Rebbe did not name the person to whom he had directed his plea but emphasized that he had personally met with an individual who had the power to have such a rally canceled, and he urged that, at the very least, it be postponed until just before Shavuot, which falls almost two months after Passover, and by which time the families would have been allowed to leave. But the party to whom the Rebbe conveyed his urgent message refused his request and, indeed, the families who had been scheduled to be released were still languishing inside Russia, as a result, he believed, of the demonstrations.[1]

The Rebbe's support for "quiet diplomacy" and opposition to public demonstrations for Soviet Jewry had long been known, but it was never expressed in public with such specific arguments and details.

Even after the *farbrengen*, one thing that still remained unknown was with whom the Rebbe had been in touch. Who was the person who had the power to cancel a demonstration supported by a large variety of American Jewish organizations? And with what arguments did the person respond to the Rebbe's arguments and appeals? No more details were forthcoming from the Rebbe at the *farbrengen* or later.

Some years after this talk, Nehemiah Levanon, an Israeli who had worked at the Israeli embassy in Washington, DC, wrote his memoirs (*Code Name: Nativ*; the book is in Hebrew), in which he included a chapter about the Rebbe. Levanon, whose background was in Israeli intelligence, had long worked on behalf of the Israeli government. One of his major responsibilities was coordinating activities in the West on behalf of Russian Jewry, part of Israel's campaign to get the Jews out of the Soviet Union and bring them to Israel. While American Jews involved in the Soviet Jewry movement assumed that Levanon was an Israeli diplomat in charge of the Soviet desk in Washington, in fact he was an agent in the Mossad, Israel's national intelligence agency, who reported directly to the leadership of the Mossad and to Prime Minister Golda Meir. We know now from his account that he was the person to whom the Rebbe turned in his effort to call off this demonstration.

Levanon writes of the Rebbe with great respect, but he also recalls the sharp argument the two men had over the Rebbe's insistence that demonstrations were harmful to Russian Jews. The meeting ended with Levanon refusing to adhere to the Rebbe's request to cause the demonstration to be canceled, though he did promise to pass on the Rebbe's request to his superiors in Jerusalem.

One might have thought that Levanon's refusal of the Rebbe's request would have led, at the least, to a decided tension in the two men's relationship, and perhaps to a rupture. But such was not the case (significantly, and characteristically, when the Rebbe alluded to his meeting with Levanon at the *farbrengen*, he said of him, "He is a fine Jew"). Some months later, the Rebbe had Rabbi Hodakov, his chief of staff, invite Rabbi Shlomo Riskin to meet with him. Riskin had previously met with the Rebbe on a number of occasions, but this was their only meeting, Riskin recalls, initiated at the Rebbe's request. Though Riskin was among the founders of the Student Struggle for Soviet Jewry, the most widely known of the American groups organizing protest rallies on behalf of Russian Jews, the Rebbe did not try to dissuade him from engaging in such activities. This is in itself surprising given that Riskin made no secret of his great admiration for the Rebbe, a man whom he regarded as *manhig ha-dor*, the leader of the generation. One can assume that such an appeal by the Rebbe would have at least been seriously considered by Riskin. But this was not why the Rebbe had summoned him. Rather, it was to ask Riskin if he would be willing to undertake a secret mission on his behalf, to help organize four underground yeshivot in the Soviet Union. Riskin immediately assented. Then, to his amazement—Riskin later recounted that he felt as if he were in a scene from a James Bond film—the Rebbe opened a drawer in his desk and pulled out a telephone. He dialed, and when the phone was answered, the Rebbe said, "Nehemiah, Riskin *maskim*" ("Nehemiah, Riskin agrees").

The Rebbe then handed the phone over to Riskin, who a few seconds later found himself speaking to Nehemiah Levanon, the very man who rejected the Rebbe's insistent request to help cancel or postpone the demonstration.

Levanon asked Riskin if he would also be willing to help set up underground *ulpanim*, classes in Hebrew (the study of Hebrew outside of government supervision was also forbidden in the Soviet Union) while on his trip to the Soviet Union, and Riskin agreed to do so as well.

The Rebbe's willingness to direct Riskin to Levanon suggests as well his strategic ability to always keep in mind the big picture. There were ways, he recognized, in which Levanon and Riskin—who he felt were wrong, even dangerously misguided on the issue of demonstrations—could nonetheless help Russian Jews in other areas.

After leaving the Rebbe's office, Riskin found himself entrusted to a handler, a man assigned to prepare him for his trip. Over the coming days, Riskin was given many names and addresses to learn by heart, and he was also given a pair of shoes with false heels into which wads of money had been inserted. Riskin was instructed to go to the Leningrad (today St. Petersburg) *mikveh* and to leave the shoes in the changing room when he went inside to immerse himself. When Riskin returned from the *mikveh*, the money had been withdrawn. It was used, Riskin learned, to provide basic necessities for observant Jews in Leningrad who had lost their jobs and had become unemployable because of their refusal to work on Shabbat.

This story of Riskin at the Leningrad *mikveh* reflects the depth of the Rebbe's connections inside Russia. How did the person who opened the heel of Riskin's shoe (who had earlier introduced himself to Riskin as Michael) know that an American Jew would be arriving at the *mikveh* on such and such a date and at such and such a time with money hidden in his shoes? This incident took place in the early 1970s, well before the advent of cell phones and personal computers. How was such information transmitted? To this day, Riskin does not know, but what he does recall is that "Wherever I went [in the Soviet Union], they knew that I was coming; true in Moscow, true in Leningrad, true in Riga, and true in Vilna."

There is, I believe, another dimension to the Rebbe's repeated, and decidedly vehement, opposition to demonstrations on behalf of Russian Jews. The Rebbe, based on information and impressions gleaned from personal contacts—and as he made clear to all those with whom he discussed this issue—had an insider's knowledge of the Soviet leadership and of what they were capable. He also knew that the Russian leadership was very familiar with who he was and that the contents of his public speeches would become known to Soviet authorities. If the Rebbe supported anti-Soviet demonstrations in his speeches, Jews in Russia might well suffer, and I suspect (and this is my personal belief and not based on the Rebbe's public pronouncements) he also feared that the Russians might well wreak revenge against his followers in particular. Behind the scenes, the Rebbe was willing to work with pro-demonstration groups; such activities would not become known to the Soviets. But his sense of obligation to the Jews in Russia precluded him from going public with his criticism of the government.

What was the source of the Rebbe's fear of what the Soviets might do to the Jews under their governance? The young Menachem Mendel Schneerson was a teenager in Yekaterinoslav (now Dnepropetrovsk) when the Communists took control in Russia, and he was well aware from his own and his family's experiences of the depth of their ruthlessness and hatred of religion, Judaism in particular (see pages 456–57); his father had resisted the Communists and they eventually jailed him and then exiled him to a remote town in Kazakhstan where he suffered terribly (see page 457). That was decades earlier, but from the ongoing meetings the Rebbe held with people who either had lived in or visited the Soviet Union, he knew that the antisemitism had continued. He also knew of the intricate spy systems that the Communists had introduced and still maintained, in which informers were inserted into every organization. Or almost every. The late Yaakov Herzog, director of the prime minister's office in Israel, reported that an American State Department official had once told him that the Soviets had succeeded in infiltrating informers into every religious and political group in Russia, with the exception of "some Jewish sect headquartered and headed by a rabbi in Brooklyn."

Aware, therefore, of how carefully the Soviets tracked all information and details about their society, it appears to me likely that the Rebbe assumed that when he spoke against anti-Soviet demonstrations, and against engaging in any activities intended to publicly pressure and embarrass the Russians, he knew that his words would reach well beyond the thousand or more people present at the *farbrengen*. Most obviously, his opposition would become known in the broader Jewish community. But what likely mattered even more to the Rebbe was that it would become known to the Soviet government.

The Rebbe wished, it appears, for the Russian government to know that any demonstrations were in express opposition to his will, and that therefore the government should take no punitive actions against those whom they might otherwise target for harassment. The Rebbe did not want Jews in Russia blamed for provoking anti-Soviet demonstrations, and he wanted to protect all Russian Jews, including his followers, from such accusations.

Significantly, though, his commitment to helping all Russian Jews accounts as well for his willingness to work with people who did support demonstrations. His opposition to demonstrations was public; his cooperation with such people was private. He tried, when he felt he could, to halt or postpone anti-Soviet demonstrations.[2] On one occasion, he told Rabbi Israel Miller, president of the Conference of Presidents of Major American Jewish Organizations and an active proponent of protest demonstrations, "If you're going ahead with the demonstration, make sure it gets onto the front page of the *New York Times*." Equally important, he tried to work behind the scenes with groups supporting demonstrations in areas in which the lives of Russian Jews could be helped. The Mossad, it is known, helped Chabad bring into Russia religious materials such as Jewish calendars and Jewish religious texts. This was done as well by the Student Struggle for Soviet Jewry, many of whose members went on missions to meet with dissident Jews inside Russia. Glenn Richter, the longtime number two person at SSSJ, told me that they "worked a great deal with Chabad in getting their material into the USSR." One of those who supported demonstrations and who stayed in ongoing touch with the Rebbe was Malcolm Hoenlein, the founding executive director of the Greater New York Conference on Soviet Jewry, and the chairman, since 1986, of the Conference of Presidents of Major American Jewish Organizations.

The Rebbe's commitment to promoting Jewish identity inside Russia was so deep that he was happy to encourage the reading of books of which he would normally disapprove. At a meeting with Israel Singer of the World Jewish Congress, he asked Singer what kinds of books Jews inside the Soviet Union were reading. Singer mentioned Leon Uris's novel *Exodus*. An international bestseller published in 1959, *Exodus* presented in the form of historical fiction the story of how the State of Israel came into being. The narrative mixed in prominent historical figures along with fictional characters, and impassioned love stories against the background of historical events. *Exodus* was an avowedly secular, pro-Zionist work; religion played little role in the book. Yet when Singer informed the Rebbe of how profoundly significant this work was in promoting Jewish pride among Soviet Jews (it played a similar role in the United States as well),[3] the Rebbe was excited. Singer told the Rebbe of one man who informed him that he had been the four hundredth reader of a copy of the book, which had been brought in by an American couple who had visited Russia. The Rebbe told Singer, "We must get more such copies of the book into the country." As Singer recalls: "He didn't tell me only to bring in siddurim [prayer books]; he didn't tell me only to bring in *Chumashim* [the Torah], he told me if this strengthens people, then we have to bring more of this book, that that is a good thing."[4]

It is hard to think of other Chasidic Rebbes who would have encouraged the reading of the novel *Exodus*.

Despite all the barriers erected by the Soviet government, the Rebbe always maintained a connection with the Jews behind the Iron Curtain, both through clandestine contact with Chasidim, and also with others—sometimes far removed from the world of Chasidus—who had occasion to be in Russia and to be in communication with the Jews there. Thus, Aryeh "Lova" Eliav was a left-of-center Israeli politician and member of the Knesset. From 1958 until 1960, he served as the first secretary of the Israeli consulate in Moscow, and in 1965 became Israel's deputy minister of immigrant absorption. That year, Eliav, who had just

published his account of Russian-Jewish life, *Between Hammer and Sickle*, visited New York and asked to meet the Rebbe. As he later recalled: "I was
interested to meet him, and I knew he was also interested to meet me.
Who could have known as much as I did of the work that Chabad was
doing in Russia—we in the consulate may have not known everything,
but we did know of the Rebbe's clandestine work in the Soviet Union."[5]

Eliav has many recollections of his *yechidus*, extending from 11:00 p.m.
to 6:00 a.m. Pretty much the entire seven hours were devoted to a discussion of Jewish life inside Russia. By the time the meeting ended, Eliav
recalled, "I realized that the Rebbe knew much more about me and
my work than I could have imagined." He described how the Rebbe
"cross-examined" him while going to great lengths not to share any
new information that Eliav himself didn't already know; the Rebbe was
known to keep his own sources secret. Yet the range of his knowledge
of day-to-day life inside Russia, a country the Rebbe had left in 1928,
staggered Eliav: "I realized that I had no new secrets to share with him
as he already knew [the basics of] everything that was happening there;
what he wanted from me were details."

The Rebbe thrived on details, for it was through details, not general assessments, that he could most accurately determine the needs
of Soviet Jews—and strive to fulfill them. To procure information and
to provide help to Russia's Jews, he would dispatch people to visit the
Soviet Union posing as tourists (this was later done as well by the Soviet
Jewry protest organizations and by the Israeli government). In a 1957
letter, at a time when tourism to Russia was uncommon, we find him
reminding a man who was making a return trip to bring with him, as he
had done previously, Jewish books, "which you should leave at the synagogue."[6] The Rebbe would also entrust visitors to Russia with extra pairs
of tefillin and tell them to leave them behind with Jews who needed
them. Though most Jews wear only one type of tefillin, the people sent
in by Chabad practiced a variety of stratagems by which to bring in extra
tefillin, for example, informing the officials examining their bags that
all of the tefillin were for their personal use and that different types of
tefillin were needed for different days of the week. When dealing with
thieves and with oppressors, Jewish law does not obligate one to be

truthful. Professor Velvel Greene recalls Rabbi Shmuel Lew emptying out his wife's mascara case and filling it up with the special ink necessary for writing mezuzot and Torah scrolls. Nor was it just religious items that the Rebbe wanted people to bring in with them. That same year as well, the Rebbe asked a Chasid who was going to Russia to bring with him a variety of medications that could not be procured there.[7]

In 1971, during the heyday of the Communist regime, the journalist Gershon Jacobson, a Russian native, paid a weeklong visit there. He later told of how the Rebbe prepared him for his trip, advising him on the minutest details. Make up your bed in the morning, the Rebbe advised, particularly if it had become messy overnight. Otherwise, the maid who cleans your room will report to an official that you had slept very fitfully, and this indication of your nervousness might ignite suspicion against you and cause you to be carefully shadowed.[8]

The Rebbe also asked Jacobson to be in touch with him as soon as he came back. The *yechidus* they had, as in the case of Eliav, lasted from eleven at night till six in the morning. The first thing Jacobson did upon entering the Rebbe's office was to give him handwritten letters that Jews had entrusted him to bring to the Rebbe. He handed the Rebbe the whole pile, some 150 letters. Though all were intended for Menachem Mendel Schneerson, none of them addressed him as Rebbe or used his name; it would have been dangerous for the Russian Jews to do so, in case the letters were confiscated by Soviet authorities. Instead they wrote, *Tiere zeyde* (Dear grandfather) or *Tiere feter* (Dear uncle). When the Rebbe would respond to these letters, he did so through emissaries who would hand deliver them; he would sign his letters as *Zeyde Mendel* (Grandfather Mendel), and sometimes *dyedushka* (the Russian word for "grandfather").

Now, as the Rebbe took the letters, he handled them very gently, "cradling them like children," Jacobson recalled, and opened a few and started reading. The Rebbe started crying intensely, and Jacobson, embarrassed to be witnessing so intimate a scene, started to edge himself out of the room. With a hand gesture, the Rebbe signaled him to stay and then proceeded to spend the rest of the night grilling Jacobson on every aspect of his trip. As was the case with Eliav, what the Rebbe was in search of was details, the details that would enable him and Chabad to help, in the most concrete manner possible, more Jews, often one by one by one.

Professor Velvel Greene was dispatched by the Rebbe to Russia in 1981 with a decidedly limited agenda. The Rebbe wanted Greene to meet with three scientists, two in Moscow, one in Leningrad, who, the Rebbe had learned, "were prepared to become more religiously observant, but who were stymied in their advancement by one problem, the so-called contradiction between science and Torah." The Rebbe asked Greene, a distinguished scientist at the University of Minnesota, to go to Russia, meet with these men, and show them that there is no contradiction between being a scientist and following the Torah. Greene did so, though, to his frustration, one of the men was unavailable during his visit. Today, all three of the scientists live in Israel and lead religiously observant lives. Till the end of his life, Greene remained staggered by this whole incident, that the Rebbe, residing in Brooklyn, reached out to him in Minnesota, because he was worried about three professors in Russia who needed help to advance in their Jewish commitments.[9]

In the mid-1960s, Rabbi Israel Miller went to Russia with a delegation of American rabbis and spoke at the main synagogue in Moscow. The speech received a lot of publicity and was even reported on the front page of the *New York Times*. Upon his return, Rabbi Miller was invited to 770 for a meeting with the Rebbe. During their conversation, and after Miller described in detail the terrible situation of the Jews whom he had met, he mentioned to the Rebbe that he had been taken to a warehouse where he saw several rooms with unused Torah scrolls lying desolate. This so bothered Rabbi Miller—"I can't sleep at night"—and he confided to the Rebbe his intention to find a way to get the Torahs out and brought to the United States and Israel where they could be used. The Rebbe's response was both surprising and reassuring. "Don't remove the *sifrei Torah* [Torah scrolls] from Russia. The day will soon come when they will be used again there."[10]

Today, several decades since the Soviet Jewry movement, it seems clear that there were gains achieved both by behind-the-scenes quiet diplomatic efforts on behalf of Soviet Jews, and by public pressuring and demonstrations. The Rebbe identified with those who urged "quiet diplomacy" and in doing so was able to play an important, sometimes crucial, role—far greater than is generally known—in influencing the release of large numbers of Jews.

The late Republican senator from Nevada Jacob Hecht, universally known by his nickname, "Chic," was elected in 1982. Two years later, he was taken by his brother Martin and nephew Chaim to meet the Rebbe at a *farbrengen*. During their brief encounter, Hecht told the Rebbe of how his own mother had fled Russia decades earlier to escape death at the hands of the Cossacks. The Rebbe, in turn, told Hecht: "Your top priority [in addition, presumably, to his other senatorial responsibilities] should be to get the Jews out of Russia. . . . The key," he added, "is quiet diplomacy."

A short time later, Hecht was able to supply a crucial vote on a bill that mattered greatly to President Ronald Reagan. When Reagan expressed gratitude to Hecht for his support, the senator asked if he might bring up a concern of his. After spending a moment or two telling the president how his mother had succeeded in getting out of Russia so many years earlier, and that it was only by the grace of God that he himself was now standing on the floor of the U.S. Senate, he asked the president to place increased emphasis on the release of tens of thousands of Russian Jews at the upcoming Reykjavik, Iceland, summit conference with Soviet president Mikhail Gorbachev: "Those who are allowed to leave the Soviet Union, Mr. President, should not be just elderly, but children, teenagers, doctors, and scientists. All should be allowed the basic human right of freedom." The president, in turn, expressed his concern for Soviet Jews and his desire to aid Hecht and the Jewish community in this objective.

A short time later, Hecht found himself to be the president's final appointment before his departure to Iceland. He presented Reagan with a list of twelve hundred Soviet Jews who had applied to emigrate from Russia but had been unable to procure visas, and he expressed the hope that getting these people out would be a start, and would eventually culminate in many more Jews being permitted to leave. At the conference, Reagan gave the list of twelve hundred names to Gorbachev and emphasized how important this issue was to him. Within a few weeks, people on the list started to be released, and by the end of the 1980s and early 1990s, the number of Russian Jews allowed to leave swelled into the hundreds of thousands.[11]

Some years later, after Reagan left office and Hecht had been appointed ambassador to the Bahamas, the former president and his wife went there on vacation, and they invited Ambassador and Mrs. Hecht to a cocktail reception. Hecht offered his thanks to the president for helping to get Jews out of the Soviet Union and asked why he had never mentioned the act in public (particularly as it might have marshaled support for him in the Jewish community, which is largely Democratic). Mrs. Reagan told Hecht that when the president had made his plea to let the Jews on this list leave, Gorbachev told him that there were many people around him in the Kremlin leadership who did not want to let the Jews emigrate, and if Reagan publicized Gorbachev's concession, the exodus would stop. And so, Mrs. Reagan now said, President Reagan needed to use "quiet diplomacy" with Gorbachev.

"Quiet diplomacy," Hecht later recalled, were the very words the Rebbe had earlier addressed to him.[12]

Writing in 2004 of his involvement both with the Rebbe and with President Reagan, Senator Hecht, who died in 2006, referred to his work in helping get Jews out of Russia "*as the most important story of my life. It is the story of the wisdom of the Rebbe*" (emphasis added).[13]

President Reagan himself epitomized the two sides of the conflict over how to deal with the Soviet Union, employing "quiet diplomacy," when he deemed it appropriate, and a far more confrontational approach when he thought that it was needed. Indeed, in the same month in which Reagan employed a somewhat conciliatory approach with Russian ambassador Anatoly Dobrynin (see page 566), he also referred to the Soviet Union, in a widely cited speech, as the "evil empire."

Natan Sharansky, the best known of the Soviet Jewish dissidents and a man long committed to public demonstrations on behalf of Soviet Jews (he himself served nine years in Soviet prisons and credits demonstrations in the West with helping to get him released), has written of a meeting

The Rebbe at two and a half. Menachem Mendel Schneerson was born in southern Ukraine, in the city of Nikolayev, in 1902. This is the earliest extant photo of him, taken in 1904.

The Rebbe's passport photo. Though he went with his parents' blessings, after leaving Russia in 1927, he never saw his father again, and didn't see his mother for almost twenty years.

Rebbetzin Chaya Mushka Schneerson at a wedding in 1948. Although she was the daughter of a Rebbe and the wife of a Rebbe, Rebbetzin Chaya Mushka never flaunted her position, identifying herself over the phone simply as "Mrs. Schneerson from President Street" to storekeepers and others.

February 1935: The Rebbe standing alongside his father-in-law at Perchtoldsdorf Sanatorium, in Vienna, where the Frierdiker Rebbe was recuperating. The Frierdiker Rebbe suffered from a variety of illnesses and relied on the advice of his son-in-law Menachem Mendel concerning his treatment. When doctors advised him to go to this sanatorium, he wrote his son-in-law, "I would like to know if you can join me; it is essential that you be there, since you know fully the opinions of the specialists in Berlin."

The Rebbe playing chess with his father-in-law during a stay at the Perchtoldsdorf Sanatorium in 1937. The chess playing had come about in response to the advice of physicians that the Frierdiker Rebbe should, during his stay at the sanatorium, avoid intellectual strain. Years later, at a *farbrengen* in 1949, the soon-to-be Rebbe spoke about chess and its lessons for life, and extrapolated a number of lessons from chess that could be applied to service to God.

Rabbi Menachem Mendel Schneerson officiating at the wedding of Velvel and Ray Schildkraut, September 1948. When Menachem Mendel became Rebbe, it was common for Chasidim to seek his guidance regarding the finding of a spouse. Once, when a young man asked him if he should become engaged to a girl he was dating, the Rebbe responded, "When it comes to a marriage, not I can help you, not your father can help you, not your mother can help you, not your *seichel* [intellect] can help you. The only thing that can help you is your heart. If you feel for her, go ahead. If you don't, do not."

Surrounded by Chasidim at the wedding of Leibel and Tirtza Esther Posner, on February 6, 1951, twenty days after becoming Rebbe.

Rabbi Menachem Mendel Schneerson in the Luxembourg Gardens in Paris, circa 1933. Between 1933 and 1940, the Schneersons lived in Paris, where Menachem Mendel continued his university studies. Years later, the Rebbe showed this picture to a French journalist and related that after he had given a poor man a donation he paused for a moment to meditate "on what's mentioned in the holy books; that when you come to a new place and you meet a poor man, it awakens in you the feeling that the *Shechina* [Divine Presence] is in exile and the need for the Final Redemption."

An extraordinary variety of people sought advice and blessings from the Rebbe. A man greets the Rebbe and happily receives a blessing and a dollar to be given to charity. "When two people meet, it should bring benefit to a third," the Rebbe quoted his father-in-law as saying.

The Rebbe offering a piece of honey cake and a New Year's greeting to a New York City police officer in 1987.

Bob Dylan at 770 Eastern Parkway. In 1992, on the occasion of the fourth *yahrtzeit* of his wife, Chaya Mushka, the Rebbe distributed to several thousand men, women, and children a booklet of Chasidic discourses, along with a five-dollar bill to be given to charity. One of those who came that evening was the singer-songwriter Bob Dylan. As he did on several other visits, Dylan would come in the most modest attire, often with a hood, in order not to become a focus of attention.

In *yechidus*, listening intently to a visitor. The Rebbe's willingness to listen and empathize became legendary. Novelist Harvey Swados recalled the "pale blue eyes that remained fixed upon me with an unblinking directness," while communal leader Gordon Zacks recalled that the Rebbe "looked at me in such a penetrating way that I felt like I was being X-rayed."

At a 1964 meeting with Robert F. Kennedy, running at that time for the U.S. Senate, representing New York; seated beside Kennedy are Franklin Delano Roosevelt Jr. and New York's former governor Averell Harriman. Kennedy's hour-long discussion with the Rebbe focused on the problem of teenagers on drugs, and on government aid for religious schools—at least for secular studies. Kennedy noted that he opposed such aid even though he was a committed Catholic with eight children (he later had three more), all of whom were or would be in Catholic schools. The Rebbe was not dissuaded. "But I have two hundred thousand children!" he reportedly exclaimed.

A *farbrengen* in 1987. Though neither Rabbi Menachem Mendel nor Chaya Mushka Schneerson ever spoke about their childlessness in public, it can be assumed that it was one of the great sorrows of their lives, especially in light of how much each of them loved and doted on children. Photos of the *farbrengens* routinely show elders of the movement sitting behind the Rebbe, but the Rebbe also arranged to have children at his side at every gathering.

That the Rebbe's warm feelings toward children were reciprocated is apparent in this second photograph, taken in 1987, in which we see the pleasure of two young girls upon being greeted by the Rebbe. Handing out dollars to boys and girls, to be distributed to charity, was something he would often do either when arriving at or leaving his office.

U.S. senator Joseph Lieberman receiving a dollar from the Rebbe, to be distributed to charity. Subsequent to his 1988 election to the Senate from Connecticut, the last stop Lieberman made before flying to Washington for his swearing-in was a visit to the Rebbe, at his residence at 1304 President Street, to receive a blessing.

While he publicly opposed demonstrations on behalf of Soviet Jewry, the Rebbe would work behind the scenes with those movements and political figures who supported them. Here the Rebbe meets with Senator Henry Jackson, a co-sponsor of the Jackson-Vanik Amendment, intended to exert great pressure on the Soviets, and New York governor Hugh Carey.

Senator Jacob Javits of New York, introducing his grandson to the Rebbe.

Facing the public during daily services, the Rebbe would cover his face slightly, to focus more intently on his prayers. Surprisingly, there were some occasions when he did not. A certain Israeli man, whose face had been grotesquely disfigured, periodically showed up at 770, and out of concern for his comfort and their own, people would avoid looking at him directly. However, the Rebbe did not want this man or anyone present to think that he found it distasteful to look at him.

The Rebbe at the *Ohel* of the Frierdiker Rebbe, 1979. During his years of leadership, the Rebbe would often visit his father-in-law's grave, where he would stand for many hours reading from the sacks of letters sent to him and praying for their petitioners. When the Rebbe passed away, he was interred beside his father-in-law. Today, people of many backgrounds visit the *Ohel*. Thousands of written prayers on pieces of paper, which people either bring themselves or send by fax and e-mail, cover the grave like snow.

After prayers on the final day of the Jewish year in 1977, and just a few hours before Rosh Hashanah, the Rebbe, in *tallit* and tefillin, recites aloud the annulment of vows, ushering in the Jewish New Year.

The Rebbe greeting Israeli president Zalman Shazar. Upon arriving in the United States, Shazar, who regarded himself as a Chabad Chasid, upset Prime Minister Golda Meir by going to meet with the Rebbe. The prime minister felt that the dignity of the State of Israel dictated that the Rebbe travel to visit Israel's president, and not vice versa. Shazar disagreed, and continued to go to Brooklyn throughout the decade of his presidency; he and the Rebbe would secrete themselves for hours at a time, discussing matters of state.

On Prime Minister Menachem Begin's first visit to the United States after his 1977 electoral victory, he came to meet with the Rebbe prior to a meeting in Washington with President Jimmy Carter. To a newspaper reporter who queried Begin about the reason and timing of his visit, Begin responded: "I have come tonight to our great master and teacher to ask for and get from him his blessing before I go to Washington to meet with President Carter for the important talks we are going to hold. . . . His blessings are very important to me."

Israeli ambassador to Washington, and future prime minister, Yitzchak Rabin in a joyful dance in the foyer of 770 Eastern Parkway in 1972, after meeting with the Rebbe. Leaving the meeting, Rabin turned to his adviser Yehuda Avner and told him, "That man knows more about Israeli security than most of our Knesset put together."

Benjamin Netanyahu, recently appointed as Israel's ambassador to the UN, and Israel's future prime minister, comes to Brooklyn to meet the Rebbe in 1987. The Rebbe, referring to the widespread hostility toward Israel at the UN, encouraged the young ambassador to represent Israel forcefully: "You will be serving in a house of many lies. Remember that even in the darkest place, the light of a single candle can be seen far and wide."

Ariel Sharon, the legendary Israeli soldier and future prime minister, meets the Rebbe in 1989. On one visit, Sharon challenged the Rebbe over why he did not act like a commanding officer who marches ahead of his troops and move to Israel. The Rebbe resisted Sharon's challenge, arguing that there are times when it is forbidden for the commanding officer to go first, as in the case of a captain on an endangered boat. No Jewish leader in today's world, he told Sharon, should leave his or her community as long as there are those whose survival as Jews might well depend on them.

At a *farbrengen* honoring the Rebbe on his seventieth birthday, he asks Chasidim for a birthday gift, the establishment of seventy-one new institutions of outreach. The request is fulfilled. At the same time, in a *New York Times* interview, the Rebbe is asked about his willingness to offer advice on so many issues aside from religion, such as business affairs and even medicine. The Rebbe responds, "I am not afraid to answer that I don't know. [But] if I know, then I have no right not to answer. When someone comes to you for help and you can help him to the best of your knowledge, and you refuse him this help, you become a cause of his suffering."

New York mayor David Dinkins. Following anti-Jewish rioting in Crown Heights, in 1991, the Rebbe expressed his hope that the mayor would be able to bring peace to the city. "To both sides," Dinkins responded. The Rebbe replied, "We are not two sides. We are one side. We are one people living in one city under one administration and under one God. May God protect the police and all the people of the city."

The Rebbe with the Sephardi and Ashkenazi chief rabbis of Israel, Rabbis Mordechai Eliyahu and Avraham Shapira (left) in 1989. Throughout the Rebbe's four decades of leadership, many of Israel's religious leaders, representing a wide variety of religious and political viewpoints, came to visit and consult with him.

Israel Meir Lau, later Israel's chief rabbi, proudly explained in a 1991 meeting with the Rebbe that as a young man he had been involved in bringing back Jews who had strayed far from Judaism. The Rebbe immediately corrected Lau's choice of words, "We cannot label anyone as being 'far.' Who are we to determine who is far and who is near? They are all close to God."

Left: Two of the major campaigns the Rebbe initiated focused on encouraging Jewish males over the age of thirteen to put on tefillin and Jewish females over the age of three to light Shabbat candles. Here, future Israeli president Shimon Peres, assisted by Chabad Chassid Rabbi Meir Zeiler, has put on tefillin and is reciting the *Sh'ma.*

Right: President Jimmy Carter, standing beside Rabbi Avraham Shemtov, participates in the lighting of Chabad's Chanukah menorah in front of the White House. Several thousand public lightings of menorahs now take place annually throughout the United States and in the eighty countries in which Chabad is represented. (*Jimmy Carter Presidential Library*)

President Bill Clinton, standing beside Rabbi Avraham Shemtov, depositing dollars sent to him by the Rebbe in a charity box. The Rebbe encouraged all people to place charity boxes in their homes and offices and make regular contributions into them of their own funds, to help increase their sensitivity to the needs of others.

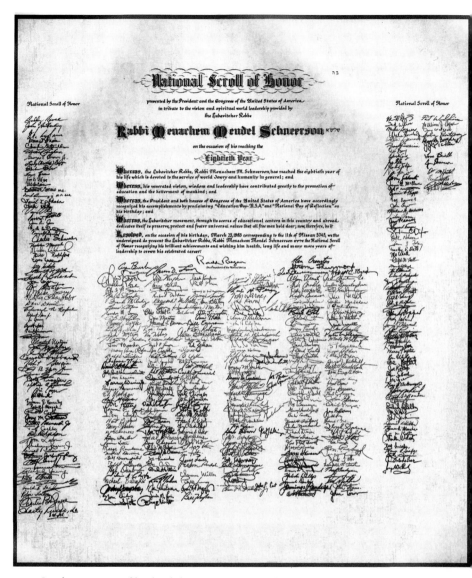

On the occasion of his birthday, 11 Nissan 5743 (corresponding to March 25, 1983), as the Rebbe entered his eighty-first year, a National Scroll of Honor was presented to him. The scroll speaks of the Rebbe's having "reached the eightieth year of his life, which is devoted to the service of world Jewry and humanity in general. . . . [His] vision, wisdom and leadership have contributed greatly to the promotion of education and the betterment of mankind." The historic document was signed by President Ronald Reagan, Vice President George Bush, and every senator and representative.

In 1976, a group of severely wounded soldiers, known in Israel as *nechei Tzahal*, "handicapped of the Israel Defense Force," came to meet with the Rebbe. In addressing the army veterans, the Rebbe told them that if a person has been deprived of a limb or another faculty, God gives that person some special powers "to surpass [in other areas] the achievements of ordinary people." The Rebbe told the soldiers, "You are special and unique as you possess potentials that the rest of us do not. I therefore suggest that you should no longer be referred to as 'disabled veterans,' but as 'exceptional veterans' [*metzu- yanim*], which more aptly describes what is unique about you."

Diane Abrams, with her two daughters, greets the Rebbe in 1988. Standing beside the Rebbe is his secretary, Rabbi Yehuda Krinsky. On one occasion, when Diane Abrams and her husband, Bob, New York State's attorney general, were meeting with the Rebbe, Diane, who created the first university-level course on "Women and the Law," which she offered at NYU Law School, was silent. When Bob sought the Rebbe's guidance on a particular issue, the Rebbe turned to Diane and said with a smile, "So, what about you? We are in the period of women's liberation. You must have a view. What's your opinion on the issue?"

The Rebbe and Rabbi Joseph Soloveitchik greeting each other in 1980 at the celebration of the Rebbe's beginning his thirtieth year as Chabad's leader. While it is not surprising that two rabbinic leaders of such stature knew each other, what is surprising is how they met, as university students in Berlin in the 1920s. On one occasion, when someone wrote in a letter to the Rebbe that he understood that he and Rabbi Soloveitchik "were good friends [in Berlin]," the Rebbe circled the sentence and wrote on the page, "Much more than is known."

he had with Reagan at the White House in September 1987. Reagan was scheduled to have a summit meeting a few months later with Gorbachev, and Sharansky asked the president what he thought of the idea of having a massive rally of several hundred thousand people on behalf of Soviet Jews during the summit. Sharansky was seeking the president's approval because "some Jewish leaders, concerned that if the rally were held, Jews would be accused of undermining a renewed hope for peace between the superpowers, had expressed reservations about such a frontal challenge to the new Soviet leader." Reagan's response was immediate: "Do you think I am interested in a friendship with the Soviets if they continue to keep their people in? You do what you believe is right." [14]

The Rebbe's dispute with the pro-demonstration activists in the United States did not derive from a differing assessment between the two sides on the nature of the Soviet Union. Both sides were in full agreement on the evil and antisemitic nature of the regime. The issue that divided them was what would be the most effective way to secure freedom for the Jews—public confrontations with the Soviets or behind-the-scenes diplomacy—or perhaps, as seems most probable, the pursuit of both, having different people doing different things, the Rebbe in effect being the "good cop" and the demonstrators the "bad cop."

The Rebbe therefore cultivated a public strategy (never to publicly antagonize the Soviet Union) and a private strategy (to find areas in which he could cooperate even with those who opposed his public strategy). His goals, though, remained constant: to get Jews out of Russia and to create an environment in which those Jews who remained could lead Jewish lives. Opposing demonstrations and opposing legislation directed against the Soviet Union (such as the Jackson-Vanik amendment, which blocked trade benefits to the Russians unless they allowed free emigration) could deflect Soviet antagonism away from Jews inside Russia. But despite his public pronouncements, at a private meeting with New York senator Daniel Patrick Moynihan the Rebbe could make it clear that he would be very happy to see Jackson-Vanik passed, or at least to have it used as a bargaining chip with the Russians in exchange for serious Soviet concessions.[15]

Open Secret: Chabad and Its Work for
Jews Inside the Soviet Union

When Menachem Mendel Schneerson assumed the leadership of Chabad in 1951, the Soviet Union was ruled by the totalitarian antisemite Josef Stalin, and the future of its Jewish community was bleak. It soon seemed bleaker. In 1953, Stalin started making preparations to exile the country's entire Jewish community, over three million in number, to Siberia. Like the biblical villain Haman, Stalin died shortly before he could carry out his plot. Nevertheless, during the following years, Russian Jews remained cut off from the rest of world Jewry. Yet, throughout the long decades of Communist rule, even preceding the Seventh Rebbe, Chabad maintained an underground network of schools, passing on a knowledge of Torah, Talmud, even *Tanya* to segments, albeit small segments, of the Jewish community. Professor Dov Zlotnick of the Jewish Theological Seminary, who served as executor of the estate of the Seminary's greatest Talmud scholar, Professor Saul Lieberman, related that "the only serious bequest that Lieberman made other than to his family members was to Lubavitch." Lieberman explained to Zlotnick that when he got out of Russia in 1927, "the only people who were really involved in Jewish education in Russia were the Lubavitcher Chasidim."

The situation remained the same during the following decades. Rabbi Israel Meir Lau (see page 286) recalls a 1965 symposium he attended in Tel Aviv under the aegis of the Israeli Labor Party. One of the speakers was Yitzhak Gruenbaum, Israel's first minister of the interior, and a deeply committed secular Jew. Lau was therefore startled when Gruenbaum declared before an audience of some two hundred: "Should the day arrive when the iron curtain is raised, and the Soviet Union opens its doors to citizens of the State of Israel, if we go there and find [even] one person who declares that he is a Jew, it will be thanks to one man who lives in Brooklyn, the Lubavitcher Rebbe." [16]

Chapter 22

·(⟫⟩)·

WHEN IT IS WRONG
TO MAKE ALIYAH

"I PERSONALLY SUPPORT ALIYAH, AND I'VE SOMETIMES INSTRUCTED
FAMILIES TO MAKE ALIYAH, BUT WE MUSTN'T JUST ELIMINATE A
JEWISH COMMUNITY."

The terms one generally hears people using when describing a *yechidus* with the Rebbe involve words such as "inspiring," "moving," and "transformative." One does not expect to hear a person who has emerged from a *yechidus* describe the experience as "traumatic." Yet that is exactly how Peter Kalms described his 1971 encounter with the Rebbe, the third of nine such meetings he had.

In anticipation of the meeting, Kalms, a committed supporter of Chabad in England, sent the Rebbe a six-page memorandum, in which he explained his desire to move to Israel. Kalms marshaled every argument he could think of—personal, financial, moral, and familial—for his decision. When he and his wife, Esti, entered the *yechidus*, he was fully confident that the Rebbe would bless his undertaking. How could he not? Is it not praiseworthy—particularly for a Jew from an affluent Western country—to leave the Diaspora and make aliyah?

As Kalms soon learned, not necessarily.

After some initial polite conversation—Kalms had brought the Rebbe a rare nineteenth-century Yiddish book printed in Russia, for which the Rebbe was grateful—the Rebbe turned his attention to the letter.

"Do you want a *bracha* [a blessing]," the Rebbe asked, "or my opinion, and to discuss the whole matter?"[1]

Kalms looked in the direction of his wife but could not attract her attention.

"It is not a closed matter," he told the Rebbe.

"If you ask, you must be prepared for an answer which can be 'No.' "

"Yes," Kalms said, "we really want to hear your advice."

The Rebbe turned to Mrs. Kalms. "Also for you?"

"Yes."

"In every way, this would not be beneficial," the Rebbe said, and then proceeded to outline two reasons in particular why he thought such a move would be detrimental, starting with the matter of Kalms's livelihood; it was known that Israel's Socialist-leaning economy made it very difficult for businessmen to prosper—and Kalms was a successful businessman. However, the more fundamental reason for the Rebbe's opposition was that Kalms would no longer be able to carry out the philanthropic and communal activities he was doing on behalf of the Jewish community in England. In Israel, he would become just one of some two million Jews living in a society largely controlled by the Socialist Labor Party, then in power: "In London, you are one of the leaders and in a position to influence two hundred thousand Jews; you are completely free and not answerable to anybody." Furthermore, Kalms's reach from England extended beyond that country's borders: "If you speak as a businessman from England, it will have meaning for the Jewish community in Australia or Canada."

The Rebbe went on to discuss other subjects during the rest of the *yechidus*, but when Kalms left the meeting, he was troubled. He wanted to move to Israel, and the Rebbe seemed to have abruptly eliminated this as a possibility. Kalms couldn't sleep that night and drafted a four-page letter, reemphasizing to the Rebbe his strong feelings about living in Israel and outlining the things he felt he could achieve there. In the morning, he brought his letter to the Rebbe's office. It was Friday, so he knew he would not hear back immediately. The following night, at midnight, a few hours after Shabbat had finished, the Rebbe's response was brought to him:

"Another important reason [for your not making aliyah] is that each and every one of us has been mobilized by Divine Providence to wage the battle for *Yiddishkeit* in a specific place, and it is not for a military man to forsake his post and all the military personnel around him, and the cities . . . which he is to defend, because he has found another place where the battle is easier. Especially if he is an officer over . . . hundreds or thousands [in other words, a leader in his society; see Exodus 18:25]. . . . This is simple to understand."[2]

Had Kalms been familiar with the Rebbe's earlier pronouncements on aliyah when undertaken by Jewish leaders, he would have been far less surprised by the Rebbe's response to his memorandum. The Rebbe's views, as he expressed them to Kalms, were repeated by him on several other occasions, both prior to and following this *yechidus* (Kalms did indeed remain in England).

Among the fullest expositions of his views on this matter was conveyed in a 1981 letter to members of the South African Jewish leadership who had requested a clarification of the Rebbe's ideas concerning aliyah. The Rebbe began his letter, which he did not want to be construed as a general opposition to Israel or to living in Israel, by noting several immigrant communities in Israel that Chabad had established. He mentioned a Chabad village comprised of immigrants from behind the Iron Curtain and the settling of Russian Jews in the southern city of Kiryat Malachi as well as in neighborhoods in Jerusalem and Safed. The Rebbe then pointed out three factors a potential immigrant should consider before moving to Israel, their focus being not only on what is good for the would-be immigrant but also on what is beneficial for the citizens of Israel and for the Jewish people in general. Therefore, a person contemplating aliyah should ask himself the following (this is a summary of what the Rebbe said, not his exact words): Will I be able to contribute toward the development of the country? Will I be able to integrate into the economy, and not add to the excessive burden already placed on it?

Finally, even if these conditions are met, one additional consideration must be taken into account: "The gain of a new immigrant . . . should be weighed against the loss that [his or her] emigration from their present country will cause to the local Jewish community. If the person happens to be a leader in his community, and his departure would seriously affect the well-being of the community, spiritually, economically, or politically, thereby [among other things] weakening that community's support for Eretz Yisrael, the gain would clearly be more than offset by the loss. We have seen this happen time and again, when the leaders of a community have been persuaded to make aliyah, with the inevitable result that the community dwindled rapidly, physically and spiritually. In a small community, the departure of a single influential member, whether a rabbi or a layman, can make all the difference."

The Rebbe cited as an example the large-scale emigration of Jews from Morocco, starting in the 1950s and accelerating in the early 1960s. When the aliyah from Morocco started, it began with a campaign directed toward the community's spiritual leaders, "despite my warnings, behind the scenes, of the disastrous consequences of despoiling the local communities of their leadership. The basic argument was that 'the leaders must show the way; the flock will follow.' What happened was that the leaders did, by and large, make aliyah, but the local communities became largely demoralized. In the end, [many] Moroccan Jews emigrated, not to the land of Israel [even though a large number did in fact go there], but to France, to be exposed to forces of assimilation they had not met before."[3]

On Not Leaving a Community in Which Your Presence Matters

The attitude the Rebbe expressed concerning leaders not leaving their communities to go to Israel was consistent with his long-standing opposition to leaders leaving a Jewish community because of personal or, in the case of aliyah, ideological inclinations. For example, the Rebbe made known his strong feelings, rooted in legal rulings in the *Shulchan Aruch*, that it was forbidden for Jews to move out of a Jewish neighborhood, even if the neighborhood was experiencing a rise in crime. Large-scale departures would lead to the further decline of the Jewish community, thereby exposing those Jews too poor to move to increased danger—and the Rebbe considered this strictly forbidden (see pages 491–92).

Professor Velvel Greene was at the University of Minnesota in Minneapolis, but when he was invited to accept a professorship in a more prestigious university in a larger city—a position that greatly appealed to him—he sought the Rebbe's counsel, and the Rebbe strongly advised Professor Greene against leaving Minneapolis.[4]

Similarly, when Rabbi Avraham Popack wanted to leave Barre, Vermont, in the 1940s and relocate to New York so that his children and family could live in a vibrant religious community, the Frierdiker Rebbe instructed him not to do so. "You are the only *shomer Shabbat* Jew there. If you leave, who will they [the small Jewish community in Barre] turn to?" Rabbi Popack's son, Shmuel Isaac, recalls that his father finally influenced one Jew in the community (there were a total of seventeen Jewish families living in Barre and nearby Montpelier) to start observing Shabbat, whereupon the Frierdiker Rebbe relented, and the family moved to Crown Heights.[5]

The Rebbe wanted Jews living in communities to which *shluchim* came to feel confident that the couple was there to stay. This was a striking commitment for a young couple to make, particularly when the community to which they were dispatched was small. Among all denominations of Judaism—Reform, Reconstructionist, Conservative, and Orthodox—it is assumed that newly ordained rabbis will accept a small congregation in a small city as their first pulpit and, after they gain experience, try to move to a larger congregation in a larger city. In contrast, Chabad couples are known to come into a community and make it clear that they are there to stay; they are not going to leave. There have even been instances where among the first purchases a new couple has made is a plot at the local Jewish cemetery—a particularly powerful act with which to signify to the community their intention to remain there.

The Rebbe and Aliyah from the Communist-Ruled Soviet Union

As is apparent, the Kalmses' case was one of many in which the Rebbe advised a person or family against leaving a community in which they were active, and it was by no means the most unusual. In this case, after all, the Rebbe's opposition to Kalms making aliyah did not subject him and his family to economic, political, or religious hardship. In other cases, it did. To the Rebbe, the notion of fulfilling your mission in the place where you live was so fundamental that he applied it on many occasions even to religious Jews living in the Soviet Union, in an environment where the practice of Judaism was often punished by the government.

Starting in the late 1960s, and escalating in the 1970s, an increasing number of Jews inside Russia started to discover their long-dormant Jewish identities, and many agitated with the government for permission to emigrate to Israel. The Rebbe usually supported the desire of such people to do so (see the incident involving Senator Chic Hecht on page 301) and even established institutions in Israel to help the absorption. However, there was one group whose wish to make aliyah the Rebbe consistently opposed: those who could teach and influence others Jewishly—the very people who were probably the most desirous of making aliyah. "I believe you know," the Rebbe remarked on another occasion to Peter Kalms, "that I have not let people [referring to more knowledgeable Jews] leave Russia. Anyone [of them] who is in Israel did not ask me. Activists are [acting] opposite to our interests if they go and take away the leadership, leaving the body without a head. Ten *shochtim* [ritual slaughterers], ten rabbis, ten *mohalim* [those who carry out circumcisions] all had the desire to leave, and were helped by everyone [to leave. Such a person] is saving [his] own soul at the expense of hundreds! It will not affect him or his *Yiddishkeit* to stay another ten years, but hundreds were influenced by him and his beard in the streets![6] It is a *churban* [destruction] to *Yiddishkeit* to let the activists go from the Soviet Union." In another instance he remarked, "The leader of the community in

Odessa was allowed to go to Israel, and the people there won't know [now] whom to ask when Yom Kippur falls. . . ."[7]

To say that it would not affect a religiously observant activist to remain another ten years in the Soviet Union was a reflection of the Rebbe's view that problems such as government harassment, economic poverty, and a lack of schools and peers for one's children were prices that had to be borne if remaining in Soviet Russia—or any place where one lived—enabled one to educate otherwise ignorant Jews in the teachings and practices of Judaism.

The Rebbe's reasoning was reminiscent of the covenant (*brit*) initiated by has father-in-law. In it, the Frierdiker Rebbe joined with nine of his leading, most knowledgeable and devoted followers, to take responsibility for synagogues, *mikvehs*, and most important, Jewish schools throughout the Stalinist-ruled Soviet Union. The participants in the covenant committed themselves to doing so "until the[ir] last drop of blood." In the end, most of these disciples spent years in Soviet prisons. Some, among them Rabbi Bentzion Shemtov, were able to escape decades later, after World War II, while others were put to death, or perished in prison, their names unknown to the world at large.

All of this was in line with the Rebbe's, and his father-in-law's, vision of *ahavat Yisrael*, love of all Jews, and his belief that often one had to make sacrifices—and, in the case of activist Jews in the Soviet Union, very heavy sacrifices—to practice such love. Such sacrifices are known in the Jewish tradition as *kiddush Hashem* (sanctifying God's name) and, as the Rebbe and these holy disciples knew, the survival of Judaism sometimes depends on people willing to risk everything, including their lives.

The Rebbe, the Mossad, and the Jews of Tunisia

At the end of the 1982 Lebanon War between Israel and the Palestine Liberation Organization, the PLO was forced to leave Lebanon and set up command in Tunisia. The Mossad, Israel's intelligence service, concluded that the PLO's relocation to Tunisia would put the country's five-thousand-member Jewish community in peril. At the Mossad's behest, the Israeli government concluded that the time had come to evacuate Tunisia's Jews to Israel. Efraim Halevy of the Mossad (in later years, Halevy headed both the Mossad and the Israeli National Security Council) recalls that Israel started sending people into Tunisia to work with the local Jewish community and prepare them to make aliyah. However, the Israeli agents soon encountered a problem; many of the Jews were strongly resistant to leaving the country.

Halevy learned that the person most aggressively encouraging Jews to remain in Tunisia was Rabbi Nisson Pinson, the longtime Chabad *shliach* there. In contradistinction to the Israeli agents, Rabbi Pinson assured the Jews that they were not in danger. Realizing that Pinson's authority flowed from the Lubavitcher Rebbe, Halevy concluded that he "needed to see the Rebbe to explain the situation to him, so that he'd understand and encourage the Jews to leave."

Halevy asked Israeli consul general Naphtali Lavie to arrange a meeting for him with the Rebbe. He flew to New York and the two-hour encounter took place, as was characteristic of so many of the Rebbe's meetings, in the middle of the night. Halevy explained to the Rebbe why the Mossad, internationally famous for its intelligence gathering, thought the Jews of Tunisia needed to be evacuated immediately. The Rebbe acknowledged that it was he who gave the instruction via Rabbi Pinson for Jews not to leave the country and explained that this directive was based on his own intelligence-gathering network, which consisted of a variety of sources, among them contacts he had inside the U.S. government. Despite the PLO's presence in Tunisia, the Rebbe's investigation led him to conclude that the government, which had long protected the Jews there, would continue to do so, and there was no special danger facing the community at that time.

While the government was committed to protecting Jews from attack, and during times of unrest would station armed guards to protect the synagogues, life for Rabbi Pinson and Jews living in the decidedly nondemocratic and Muslim Tunisia was far from pleasant. Rebbetzin Rochel Pinson reported to the Rebbe that there were periods during which not only was their telephone tapped, but taping devices were surreptitiously installed in their homes so that their private conversations could be listened to. Nonetheless, as long as the Rebbe felt that the government was committed to protecting the Jewish community, he did not wish the Pinsons to leave, certainly not as long as several thousand Jews remained in Tunisia and were in need of the services, such as Jewish schools, that Chabad provided. So deeply did the Pinsons feel their commitment to the community that subsequent to Rabbi Pinson's death in 2007, Rebbetzin Pinson, herself well into her eighties, remained in Tunisia and continues to lead the community.

Halevy disagreed with the Rebbe's view concerning the community's safety (although the Tunisian-Jewish community has since declined in numbers to about one thousand, it did not suffer persecution even after Israel's 1985 bombing of the PLO base in Tunis), but he was struck by what he described—he spoke about this encounter in 2009—as the Rebbe's "tremendous knowledge in the area of intelligence and intelligence gathering. He had connections with the White House and the State Department. He had connections in other places in the world with the powers that be. It was obvious that here was a man of the larger world, not just of a small Chasidic court."

Almost thirty years later, Halevy recalled perhaps the most important words the Rebbe said to him that night: "I believe we must sustain, to the extent possible, every Jewish community around the world. I recognize the role of the State of Israel—I personally support aliyah, and I've sometimes instructed families to make aliyah—but we mustn't just eliminate a Jewish community."[8]

The Rebbe, Nachmanides, and the Mitzvah to Live in Israel

As a rule, religious Zionists believe aliyah to be the highest of values, the great mitzvah of our time. In support of this position, they frequently cite the words of Nachmanides (also known as Ramban), the thirteenth-century Jewish scholar and philosopher, who, in his enumeration of the Torah's 613 commandments, includes living in Israel as one of them. The Talmud teaches that if one partner in a marriage (either the husband or wife) insists on making aliyah, they can demand that their partner go with them; refusal is grounds for divorce (*Ketubot* 110b).

The Rebbe himself never visited Israel, most likely because he questioned whether a Jew, having arrived in Israel, is permitted to leave. Others conjecture that it was not a halachic issue at all. Rather, the Rebbe, who used to visit his father-in-law's grave often—and who would remain there for hours at a time, reading over the hundreds of letters seeking his advice—did not wish to be so far away, even for a short period, so as to make visits to the *Ohel* impossible. In any case, when people challenged him to make such a visit—and he was asked about this often—he would answer to the effect, "The issue is not going, it's leaving from there afterward." Despite this seemingly resolute comment, it is clear that he did not believe that there was a categorical prohibition on visiting Israel and then leaving; rather, this seems to have been a stringency he took upon himself (his father-in-law, the Frierdiker Rebbe, went to Israel for a two-week visit in 1929). But he did see an outer limit to such visits. He frequently told those about to visit Israel that if they stayed for more than thirty days, they were forbidden by Jewish law to leave. I myself heard the Rebbe discuss this issue with my grandfather Rabbi Nissen Telushkin before he visited Israel in 1968, and when the Rebbe sent a delegation of Lubavitchers to Israel in the aftermath of a murderous terrorist attack in 1956, with the purpose of encouraging the community there, he instructed them to make sure to leave Israel before thirty days had elapsed.

Nonetheless, the Rebbe, punctilious observer of the commandments that he was, followed the ruling of Maimonides who, unlike Nachmanides, did not believe that making aliyah was a commandment of the Torah. In other words, if you did not live in Israel, you were not required to move there.

It is clear, though, that the Rebbe had some ambivalence about this position. At one of the several meetings he had over the years with General Ariel Sharon (later Israel's prime minister), the two men were discussing the need for Jews to observe Jewish laws and the

Rebbe emphasized that he, too, had areas in which he still needed to achieve, offering, as an example, the fact that he did not live in Israel. On another occasion, though, this time after the Yom Kippur War, Sharon challenged him forcefully on the issue of making aliyah, asking the Rebbe why he did not act like a commanding officer who marches ahead of his troops and move to Israel. If the Rebbe did so, Sharon believed, many Jews—most immediately tens of thousands of his followers—would follow him to the Holy Land.

The Rebbe resisted Sharon's challenge, noting that there are instances when it is forbidden for the commanding officer to go first, as in the case of a captain on an endangered ship. The captain is the last person to leave the ship, doing so after everyone else has been evacuated safely. Only then is he permitted to save himself. The Rebbe felt that he, and his *shluchim* as well, and indeed all people holding leadership roles in Jewish life, should see themselves as captains of a ship whose passengers' survival as Jews is endangered by assimilation; no Jewish leader, in his view, should leave his or her community as long as there still are people there whose survival as Jews might well depend on them.

This position of the Rebbe placed some distance between himself and the pro-Zionist rabbinic establishment. These rabbis, epitomized in the figure of Chief Rabbi Isaac Hacohen Kook, saw aliyah not only as a commandment but as a preeminent one. The Rebbe thought differently.[9] As high a value as aliyah is, bringing Jews to God and Jewish commitment is yet higher. If there is no conflict between the two, one is free to make aliyah; indeed, it is a very good thing to do. However, when a conflict exists, the obligation of a Jew, a soldier in God's army, is not to go AWOL.

Chapter 23

THE REVOLVING SUN, EVOLUTION, AND THE AGE OF THE WORLD

A Dissenting View

"I STUDIED SCIENCE ON THE UNIVERSITY LEVEL FROM 1928 TO 1932 IN BERLIN, AND FROM 1934 TO 1938 IN PARIS, AND I HAVE TRIED TO FOLLOW SCIENTIFIC DEVELOPMENTS IN CERTAIN AREAS EVER SINCE."

Science cannot a priori challenge religion . . . for science can never speak in terms of absolute truth. The best proof for this is that many scientific theories of the past that had been accepted as ultimate truth have been swept away absolutely and categorically.

The Rebbe never believed that science and religion were at odds; he saw them both as truth. As he once said to a group of students: "Science cannot contradict religion. Religion is true and science is true, therefore there cannot be any contradiction." Nothing illustrates this more concretely than his decision to spend eight years of his life at universities, where the majority of his studies focused on science.

It therefore bothered the Rebbe that for many Jews, and non-Jews as well, the study of science distanced them from religion. A disproportionately high percentage of the Rebbe's correspondence with academics focused on issues of science and his insistence that the teachings of the Bible and Jewish tradition were totally compatible with the teachings of science, even if they were not always compatible with the theories offered by many scientists.

Another issue that bothered the Rebbe was that over the preceding century many Jewish thinkers had adopted what he regarded as an apologetic approach, reinterpreting traditional Jewish beliefs so that verses from the Torah would not appear to be contradicting the emerging teachings of science. He was dismayed that many observant Jewish scientists and some very traditional rabbis were willing to interpret Genesis in a nonliteral way, so that it would be consistent with recent scientific claims.

The Rebbe's approach on the so-called science versus religion issue was rooted in a different assumption, that if there appeared to be a contradiction between science and Torah, it was likely science, not Torah, that needed to be revisited. Given that the literal understanding of the Creation account in Genesis had been the traditional Jewish view for thousands of years, this is what guided the Rebbe. His desire was more ambitious than to apologetically "prove" that the Torah did not contradict science. He wanted to show that scientific theories themselves need not be interpreted as contradicting the traditional account of Genesis.

That the Sun Goes Around the Earth

One of the more unusual correspondences in which the Rebbe engaged, dated September 16, 1968, came about as a result of a letter received by a rabbi from a man whom he was trying to influence to become more religiously observant. The man was resistant, in part because of the rabbi's insistence on a literal understanding of a Talmudic text (*Pesachim* 94b) that suggests that the sun revolves around the earth. That the rabbi insisted that this was not just his personal belief, but that it also represented the view of the Lubavitcher Rebbe, inflamed the man. How could the Rebbe, a man with university training and for whom he had great respect, deny something so obvious? When the rabbi reiterated yet again that this was the Rebbe's view, the man put in writing a remarkable offer, but only if a specific condition was met:

> *If the Rebbe will make a public statement [that] . . . since the Talmud says that the sun revolves around the earth, it is therefore his firm belief that the sun does indeed revolve around the earth, I will [then]:*
>
> *a) personally observe the laws of* taharat mishpacha *(family purity),[1] tefillin, and Shabbat; and*
>
> *b) influence my friends and colleagues to do the same.*
>
> *It is, however, more than obvious to me that the Rebbe will not in any way make such a ridiculous statement, because*
>
> *a) he does not wish to be labeled as a fool,*
>
> *b) he himself is not as foolish as some of his ardent but hypnotized followers.*
>
> *[Therefore], I predict with no hesitation that I will not hear any more about this matter from you or from the Rebbe.*

The man, certain that he had put the matter to rest, soon found himself the recipient of two letters from the Rebbe. As the man had made his performing the commandments contingent on the Rebbe making a public statement regarding this issue, the Rebbe responded to this challenge first: "It is my firm belief that the sun revolves around the earth, as I have also declared publicly on various occasions and in discussions with professors specializing in this field of science. In view of the above, I have no objection, of course, if you wish to make this view known to whomever you choose." In a postscript, the Rebbe added: "When I spoke on the subject publicly, I gave a clear and detailed explanation why this view is in no conflict at all with contemporary science. I emphasized, however, that I was speaking of modern and contemporary science, as it differs from Ptolemaic and medieval science [in which] conflicting views were held on this subject. Modern science, on the other hand, having rejected both systems, has reached conclusions which present no problem to one holding to the belief that the sun revolves around the earth." And then, a gentle reminder to the man: "It is surely unnecessary to add, though I am adding it for the record, that I take for granted that you will keep your commitments with regard to the practical aspects of your letter."[2]

Having disposed of what the Rebbe regarded as the most pressing matter, a person's observance of the commandments, he proceeded to a second letter, one in which he clarified in far greater detail why he did not accept the prevailing assumptions about the earth's rotation. As the Rebbe explained, the universal acceptance of the theory of relativity as the basis of modern science has made it impossible for proponents either of geocentrism (the belief in the earth as the center of the universe) or of heliocentrism (the belief that the sun is the gravitational center of the solar system) to prove their position. Rather, "One of the conclusions of the theory of relativity is that when there are two systems, or planets, in motion relative to each other—such as the sun and the earth in our case—either view, namely the sun rotating around the earth, or the earth rotating around the sun, has equal validity." Furthermore, even if some phenomena cannot be adequately explained according to one of these views, that doesn't disqualify the view, because similar difficulties will arise "if the opposite view is accepted."

Then, the Rebbe continues: "The scientific conclusion that both views have equal validity is the result not of any inadequacy of available scientific data, or of technological development (measuring instruments, etc.), in which case it could be expected that further scientific and technological advancement might clear up the matter eventually and decide in favor of one or the other view. On the contrary, the conclusion of contemporary science is that regardless of any future scientific advancement, the question as to which is our planetary center, the sun or the earth, must forever remain unresolved, since both views will always have the same scientific validity."[3]

The Rebbe presented a similar argument in a letter to the biologist and epidemiologist Velvel Greene: "Modern science is now convinced that when two systems are in motion relative to one another, it [can] never be ascertained, from the scientific viewpoint, as to which is in motion and which is at rest, or whether both are in motion."

In the same letter, the Rebbe reiterated his long-standing belief "that all scientific conclusions necessarily belong in the realm of probability, not certainty." He expressed his great frustration that so many scientists refuse to acknowledge this, and instead speak of their scientific theories with a certainty that is simply not justified; worse, they treat those who disagree with them with contempt: "I once asked a professor of science why he did not tell his students that from the viewpoint of the relativity theory the Ptolemaic system [that the sun revolves around the earth] could claim just as much validity as the Copernican [that the earth revolves around the sun]. He answered candidly that if he did that, he would lose his standing in the academic world, since he would be at variance with the prevalent legacy from the nineteenth century. I countered, 'What about the moral issue?' The answer was silence." [4]

That Evolution Is a Theory That Cannot Be Proven and That the World Is Less Than Six Thousand Years Old

One of the few personal memories the Rebbe shared publicly was of a conversation that took place while he was a child in *cheder* (elementary school) between some of his childhood friends and their teacher, a rabbi. The topic of discussion: Darwin's theory of evolution.

"One of us said [to the teacher] that there are those who disagree with the Torah which tells us that G-d created man. As the verse says 'Let us make man in our form, according to our likeness,' and then G-d 'blew into man the soul of life,' creating Adam and Eve and their descendants. . . . Instead, they believe that first a cell came into being, from which a fish developed, followed by animals, from which developed a monkey, and eventually man came into being." As the Rebbe recalled, "The entire theory [of evolution] was discussed."

He then went on to relate how the teacher, after hearing the young Menachem Mendel offer a critique of the theory of evolution to a fellow student who was inclined to accept it, called out to him and said, "Mendel! Why must you debate him? Why does it bother you? If he prefers this lineage, let him trace his roots to a monkey. . . . Why must you argue with him?" [5]

Despite his teacher's admonition, the Rebbe was not comfortable and did not feel he could simply ignore the arguments of those people, many of them highly educated, who did accept evolution. We know of at least one instance during his university years in Paris when he sought out an opportunity to speak before an academic audience to whom he presented arguments rooted in science, both against evolution and the insistence of scientists that the world was billions, not thousands, of years old.[6]

Even many Orthodox Jews did not feel the need to follow the Rebbe's reasoning on this issue. They understood the Genesis account of Creation as not literally binding and were willing to believe in the overall truth of the biblical account, that it was God who created the world, and thus created nature (outside the world of monotheism, ancient man commonly worshipped aspects of nature, such as the sun, as deities), without feeling compelled to accept the literal chronology of the text.[7] People often reached this conclusion via the assumption that science had *proven* that the world is of a much greater age than six thousand years. Thus, fossils, which bear witness to ancient creatures such as dinosaurs, establish to the satisfaction of most modern people, including many Modern Orthodox Jews, that the world must be much older than the chronology offered in Genesis, chapter 1.

Yet countering the common belief that science *proves* something is the nub of the Rebbe's argument. Science, he argued, particularly speculative science, can never *prove* anything; it can only offer theories. Therefore, if there is a dispute between what scientists say about the world's origins and what the Torah says, a Jew—and all human beings, for that matter—should accept the teaching of the Torah.

Why was the Rebbe, a man who had studied science for eight years in universities in Berlin and in France, so willing to disregard conclusions reached by scientists? And how could he insist that science could not prove anything?

To understand this, one must understand that the Rebbe saw it as part of his mission to correct a common misconception about science, that it offers clear and definitive answers. Thus, people commonly use expressions such as "Science proves...." But science, the Rebbe argued, was never intended to prove things. Rather, what science offers are theories, hypotheses, and probabilities, "while the Torah deals with absolute truths."

"Basically, the 'problem' has its roots in a misconception of the scientific method, or simply what science is. Thus, when it comes to dating the universe, we are not dealing with empirical science, which describes and classifies observable phenomena (such as different species of trees), but we are dealing with speculative science. Speculative science deals with unknown phenomena, such as the age of the universe."[8]

Science, the Rebbe posits, has two general methods of reaching conclusions. In the first, interpolation, we start by knowing the reaction of a substance at two extremes and attempt to infer what the reaction of that substance might be at any point between the two. Thus, if we know the reaction of a substance to a temperature of 0 degrees (water freezes at 0 degrees centigrade) and 100 degrees (the temperature at which water boils), we can infer the reactions at any point between the two, and can do so with confidence that we can reach accurate conclusions.

The second method, extrapolation, in which inferences are made beyond a known range, is far less reliable: "For example, suppose we know the variables of a certain element within a temperature range of 0 and 100 and on the basis of this we estimate what the reaction might be at 101, 200, or 2000 degrees. Of the two methods, the second (extrapolation) is clearly the more uncertain. Moreover, the uncertainty increases with the distance away from the known range. . . . Thus, if the known range is between 0 and 100, our inference at 101 has a greater probability than at 1001 degrees. Let us note at once that all speculation regarding the origin and age of the world comes within the second and weaker method, that of extrapolation."

Further, in advancing theories as to the age of the universe, proponents of the view that the world is billions of years old "blithely disregard factors universally admitted by all scientists, namely that in the initial period of the 'birth' of the universe, conditions of temperature, atmospheric pressure, radioactivity, and a host of other cataclysmic factors were totally different from those existing in the present state of the universe."

The Rebbe then considers some of the arguments advanced on behalf of evolution, noting that evolutionary theory is "based on the assumption that the universe evolved out of existing atomic and subatomic particles, by an evolutionary process that combined to form the physical universe and our planet, on which organic life developed also by an evolutionary process, until 'homo-sapiens' emerged." But why, the Rebbe asks, does it make sense to accept the creation of atomic and subatomic particles and to accept an evolutionary process, and yet be reluctant to accept "the creation of planets, or organisms, or a human being as we know these to exist?"

If science cannot provide definitive answers to these questions, the Rebbe argued, then "from a scientific perspective, believing that G-d created billions of atoms, for which he established certain natural laws, and that these atoms later developed and evolved from stage to stage in accordance with these laws, is no different than believing—in accordance with the straightforward meaning of the book of Genesis—that G-d created the heavens and the earth on the first day, separated the waters on the second, etc., until on the sixth day He created man, who possesses an intellect, can talk, and is on a very high evolutionary level."

One reason, as the Rebbe acknowledged, that people generally assume that the world is thousands of times older than the Torah's chronology is the discovery of fossils, the remains of early creatures, many now extinct, which scientists date as hundreds of thousands, and sometimes millions, of years old. The Rebbe offered a number of possible explanations for fossils and their seeming great antiquity. Most important, he argued that there is no proof that temperatures, atmospheric pressure, ambient levels of radioactivity, or interactions between flora and fauna could not have radically changed during these last thousands of years. To cite just one example, the great difference in atmospheric pressure could easily make something appear to be millions of years old when it isn't.

"[In addition], even assuming that the period of time which the Torah allows for the age of the world is definitely too short for fossilization (although I do not see how one can be so categorical), we can still readily accept the possibility that God created fossils, bones, or skeletons (for reasons best known to Him), just as he could create ready living organisms, a complete man, and such ready products as oil, coal, or diamonds without any evolutionary process. As for the question . . . why did God have to create fossils in the first place? The answer is simple.

We cannot know the reason why God chose this manner of creation in preference to another.... The question, Why create a fossil? is no more valid than the question, Why create an atom? Certainly, such a question cannot serve as a sound argument, much less as a logical basis, for the evolutionary theory."[9]

Furthermore, "though scientists have monitored certain species of animals and plants that have a very short life span over thousands of generations, it has never been possible to establish a transmutation from one species into another, much less to turn a plant into an animal. Hence, such a theory can have no place in the arsenal of empirical science."

Rooting His Arguments in Science, Not Religion

One figure to challenge the Rebbe concerning his position on evolution was Dr. Herbert Goldstein, an American physicist and the author of a standard graduate textbook, *Classical Mechanics*. Goldstein received his PhD from the Massachusetts Institute of Technology (MIT), taught physics at Harvard and Brandeis, and later served as professor of nuclear science at Columbia University.

Although we do not have a copy of Dr. Goldstein's letter to the Rebbe, we do have a copy of the Rebbe's reply to him, in which he emphasizes that when he speaks of these issues with scientists, he roots his arguments in science, not Torah.

He opens his November 14, 1962, letter with a prefatory remark, intended to fend off Goldstein's assumption that the Rebbe might in some way be antiscience: "It should be self-evident that my letter does not imply a negation or rejection of science or of the scientific method.... I hope that I will not be suspected of trying to belittle the accomplishments of science."

He then addressed a comment that he had heard attributed to Goldstein, the thrust of which was that the Rebbe had no business issuing public statements on science-related matters: "Just as Rabbinic problems should be dealt with by someone who studies Rabbinics, so should scientific problems be left to those who study science."

The Rebbe acknowledged that he accepted the validity of this dismissive comment, but what he didn't accept was that it applied to him: "I studied science on the university level from 1928 to 1932 in Berlin, and from 1934 to 1938 in Paris, and I have tried to follow scientific developments in certain areas ever since."

The Rebbe also acknowledged that "scientific theories must be judged by the standards and criteria set up by the scientific method itself" and cannot be challenged as a result of rabbinic texts alone: "Hence I purposely omitted from my discussion any references to the Scriptures or the Talmud." (In yet another letter to a different correspondent, he returned to this same point: "I uphold the truth of the Creation account in *Bereishit* [Genesis] on scientific grounds.")[10]

What the Rebbe affirmed in his correspondence with Professor Goldstein became the substance of the challenge he posed to the scientific world. He did not tell scientists that they should accept the Torah's account of Creation; he knew that such an argument would fall on deaf ears. What he wanted from the scientific community was the acknowledgment that evolution is a theory, a theory that does not have any "[irrefutable] evidence to support it." Thus, the *theory* of evolution might well contradict the biblical account of Creation, but scientists should have the humility to acknowledge that it doesn't disprove it.

As the Rebbe assured one correspondent bothered by this issue: "If you are still troubled by the theory of evolution, I can tell you without fear of contradiction that it has not a shred of evidence to support it."[11]

What Mattered to the Rebbe Far More Than a Person's Beliefs About Evolution

Passionate as the Rebbe's views were on the universe's age, the revolving sun, and evolution, these were never "make-it-or-break-it" issues for him. What concerned him most was not that people found his views convincing but that they observed the commandments. Thus, in a letter dealing with the age of the universe, he related his unhappiness at having heard that because of the recipient's doubts about traditional Jewish teachings on this subject, the man was becoming less observant: "I sincerely hope that the impression conveyed to me is an erroneous one. For, as you know, the basic Jewish principle of *na'aseh* [actions first] and *v'nishma* [understanding second; see Exodus 19:8] makes it mandatory upon the Jew to fulfill God's commandments regardless of the degree of understanding, and obedience to the Divine Law can never be conditioned upon human approval." Therefore, while in his opinion a belief in evolution was wrong, it was irrelevant in the larger order of things. In the final analysis, as the Rebbe told Nathan Yellin-Mor. "Judaism is not about thinking, it's about doing" (see page 172).

Chapter 24

WHY PEOPLE SHOULDN'T GO TO COLLEGE, AND WHY THOSE WHO DO SHOULDN'T DROP OUT

"If, Heaven forbid, the report I heard concerning your desire [to study] in college is correct . . ."

"You must finish [your MA]. Otherwise, you've wasted the effort you've made until now."

Although the Rebbe studied at universities in Berlin and Paris for eight years,[1] he almost always opposed his followers doing so and offered many arguments against attending college, an attitude that shocks many contemporary American Jews. Yet despite this opposition, the Rebbe developed Chabad Houses that now engage in full-time outreach to Jewish students at just over 200 campuses (an additional 200 campuses have Chabad representatives as well). A skeptic might assume that these Chasidic outposts were established to encourage students to withdraw from the university and pursue religious study at Chabad or other Jewish institutions, but that is not the case. When university students would come to Brooklyn for encounters with Chabad and tell the Rebbe that they wished to leave their schools to study Torah full-time, he would generally instruct them to first finish the education they had started. On more than one occasion, he offered to lend students money to complete their degrees. In at least two instances, when students returned to the yeshiva after completing PhDs, the Rebbe specifically instructed them not to pursue a rabbinical degree.

One thing is certain: The Rebbe's attitude to university education was multifaceted.

In the 1950s, a nineteen-year-old student at the Lubavitch yeshiva came for a *yechidus* to discuss his intention of going to college. More than three decades later, the then middle-aged man related to Rabbi Simon Jacobson the story of the encounter he had that day with the Rebbe.

"I told the Rebbe that the reason I wanted to go to college was because I felt I had done my studies in Torah and I wanted to expand my horizons." He explained that he intended to remain a Chasid but hoped a secular education and a college degree would help prepare him for a future livelihood.

After the student concluded his presentation, the Rebbe responded, "Are you asking for an *eitzah* [advice] or a *bracha* [blessing]?"

The young man, perhaps sensing the response that was coming, answered, "I came in for a blessing."

"A blessing with advice is always better than one without advice." The Rebbe then proceeded to tell him, "In my opinion, you shouldn't go. You should continue your studies in yeshiva. You will be *matzliach* [successful] and you can be a leader in the Jewish community with that."

For the young man, the stakes were sufficiently high that he found it impossible simply to accept the Rebbe's veto of his plan. "How can the Rebbe tell me that when the Rebbe himself went to college?"

"Precisely because I went to university, I know what it's about. I know the environment, and I think it will have a detrimental effect on you instead of a positive one." Seeing that the young man was still unconvinced, the Rebbe tried another tack. "Can you draw a circle?" he asked.

"Yes," the young man answered, presumably perplexed by the question.

"Can you draw a perfect circle?"

"No, I can't, not on my own."

"What would you need to draw a perfect circle?" the Rebbe pressed.

"A compass."

The Rebbe, whose interest in and aptitude for mathematics was well known, continued. "Tell me the difference between the circle you would draw on your own and the circle you would draw with a compass."

"The circle I draw on my own won't have a sturdy center around which to draw the borders, but the compass's center creates a perfect circle."

The Rebbe then elaborated: "All knowledge you'll ever learn, every experience you'll have in life, are the circles. They're not the center. If you don't have a solid center, you'll have jagged circles, incomplete circles, many different circles. I sense that you need that center before you start building your circles."

When the man, then in his early fifties, related this story, he added, "I didn't listen. I went anyway." He then started to cry softly. "And I still don't have a complete circle. I have many circles, this one, that one, none complete."

"Just because one person goes into a fire and comes out unhurt, doesn't mean that everybody should go into a fire."

For American Jews, a larger percentage of whom attend university than fast on Yom Kippur,[2] the Rebbe's opposition to college studies seems unfathomable. To this day, Jews are associated in Jewish and non-Jewish minds alike with a passionate attraction to education and high levels of intellectual attainment. They are admitted to Ivy League colleges at a rate more than ten times their percentage of the American population and win Nobel Prizes at a rate some hundred times their percentage of the world population. It is therefore difficult for many people to accept that a rabbi, one who himself spent eight years in the university world, would oppose a student wishing to further his education. When I showed a draft of this chapter to a dear friend with a highly discerning literary taste, he said, "You can't begin the chapter with an incident in which the Rebbe tells a young man not to attend college. It makes him seem primitive and very unsympathetic."

The truth is, the Rebbe advocated education with even greater passion than do most American Jews, but the education he most espoused was religious education, the study, in particular, of the "three Ts": Torah, Talmud, and *Tanya* (the basic philosophical treatise of Chabad). Regarding college education, particularly when carried out during the late teens and early twenties, when most Americans attend university, the Rebbe's attitude was indeed negative, as this above story conveys.

Why?

In an article published in 1962, the Rebbe outlined several reasons for this opposition to attending college, most fundamentally that the secular atmosphere prevalent at universities will be injurious to a young student's religiosity: "I therefore state with the fullest measure of conviction and responsibility that he who sends his child to college *during his formative years* subjects him to shock and profound conflict and invites quite unforeseen circumstances" (emphasis added).

Although the Rebbe acknowledged that there are students who remain unaffected by the prevailing secular and often antireligious bias on most university campuses, this did not justify an endorsement of college education. "One may use the analogy of the shoeshine boy who becomes a millionaire and everyone talks about him. It is not because he was a shoeshine boy that he attained success, and no one will suggest that in order to become a millionaire one should start in the shoeshine business. The greater the exception . . . the greater is the proof of the rule."

Bernie Rader, a British follower of the Rebbe, recalls a *yechidus* he attended with his wife at which the Rebbe was expressing his opposition to university studies. Noticing a questioning look flickering across Mrs. Rader's face, the Rebbe said, "You could ask me, 'But you went to university?' So, I'll answer you before you ask, 'Just because one person goes into a fire and comes out unhurt, it doesn't mean that everybody should go into a fire.'"[3] The scientist Herman Branover cites the case of a mother who pushed the Rebbe to approve of her son's attending college. But the Rebbe remained unconvinced, noting rather the perils he foresaw: "If one is willing to jump from a high floor out the window, he is free to do it, but it is a great miracle if he jumps out and doesn't destroy himself. The same is with university."

In the comments cited, the analogies drawn by the Rebbe speak of physical dangers (such as jumping out of a window), but it is clear that he is using provocative language to catch people's attention; in actuality, it is the danger to the students' souls that concerns him. In a 1967 letter to a writer who had raised the seemingly compelling point that universities produce people such as physicians, who can take care of other people's life-threatening needs, the Rebbe turns the argument against his challenger: "I will use this same analogy in my answer to you. Indeed, as is customary among Jews, I will answer your question with a question of my own. Have you ever met a mother who tried to persuade her son to choose for his career the field of infectious diseases, ruling out everything else, when he himself wished to choose some other means of livelihood, one that would not be quite so fraught with danger? To make my point even stronger, what would you think of a mother who, pressing her son to pursue that dangerous career, insists upon his getting started right away, by having him mix and come into daily contact with people who have already come down with various infectious diseases, on the assumption that he will somehow stumble upon the measures necessary to protect himself from infection, and in this way develop into a specialist in the field, one able to bring relief and cure to the unfortunate sufferers? I believe that in such a case no mother would fail to realize that, whereas the danger is certain and immediate, the chances of her son becoming a specialist are, at best, years away."[4]

As for the frequently offered argument that a university education is a necessary prerequisite for financial stability, the Rebbe was fond of noting that "the majority of college graduates establish themselves in occupations and businesses not directly connected with their course of study in college." In instances in which a direct correlation existed between a person's area of study and potential livelihood, the Rebbe was far more open to college attendance. Martha Stock, a member of the community, recalls that she initially encountered opposition to her decision to attend City College of New York from the Rebbe, but he was assuaged when he learned that she was pursuing an accounting, not a liberal arts, degree. However, when no obvious connection between the course of study and future livelihood existed, as is frequently the case with those who concentrate in subjects such as history, sociology, and literature, the Rebbe opposed college attendance. Presumably, he felt that the students' minds would be far more nourished by expanding and deepening their Torah knowledge.[5]

Such is the approach advocated by the Alter Rebbe, Shneur Zalman of Liadi, in the *Tanya* (chapter 8). The Alter Rebbe makes it clear that the most important intellectual pursuit for Jews is the study of Torah and, ideally, nothing else: "[Regarding] one who occupies himself with the sciences of the nations of the world, this is considered as 'idle chatter' [a waste of time] insofar as the sin of neglecting the Torah is concerned."

However, the Alter Rebbe offers two justifications for pursuing secular studies:

- in order to attain a more affluent livelihood, "so as to be able to serve God";
- in order to learn how to apply the secular knowledge that has been gained to the service of God and Torah.

In the first instance, if a person can earn a better and less physically demanding livelihood through higher education than through performing strenuous or less skilled labor, he will in the end have additional time to devote to spiritual pursuits such as learning Torah (in addition, greater affluence will enable him to provide his children with a superior Jewish education).

Regarding the second case, applying one's secular knowledge "to the service of God and Torah," there are several ways in which this can be accomplished. One can, for example, become a physician and prolong and save lives, a Torah value so important that the Talmud rules that all Jewish laws with but three exceptions (the prohibitions against murder, certain forbidden sexual activities such as incest, and idolatry) are suspended when life is at stake. The Torah itself makes reference to the role of physicians in healing (see Exodus 21:19; see also *Bava Kamma* 85b). But even less obviously applicable forms of secular knowledge can be employed in the service of God, as Rabbi Adin Steinsaltz notes in his commentary to the *Tanya*: "If a person studies philosophy to clarify for himself the ways of serving God, if he studies astronomy to see how 'the heavens relate the glory of God' (Psalms 19:2) . . . his pursuit of these studies constitute a part of his service of God. . . . Maimonides' [writings on astronomy] made him think not of Ptolemy (as was said of Copernicus) but of God. His assumption is that the more one knows about creation, the more one knows about the Creator."[6]

Do these arguments offered by the Rebbe and the *Tanya* suffice to explain the reason that the Rebbe himself pursued university studies, yet generally opposed his followers emulating such behavior? Since the Rebbe generally remained quite unrevealing about the details of his own life, and never formally offered an explanation for his decision to study at universities in St. Petersburg, Berlin, and Paris, we are now in the realm of speculation.

One thing, though, is certain: His opposition to university education did not emanate out of any sort of hostility to the acquisition of secular knowledge per se. First, as noted, the Rebbe himself had pursued such study, and for many years. Second, there is no shortage of great sages in Jewish history who pursued secular studies, the most prominent being Maimonides (Rambam) in the twelfth century. In addition to producing several of Judaism's most important religious texts—one of which, the fourteen-volume legal code the *Mishneh Torah*, the Rebbe encouraged his followers to study through each year—Maimonides served as a physician in the royal Egyptian court and was regarded as one of the leading doctors of his age. Finally, how could there be any fundamental wrong in seeking to know how the world functions, since the world was created by God? Therefore, understanding biology, chemistry, and physics, understanding, for that matter, the nature of trees, all bring one to a deeper understanding of God's "Mind," and enable one, as it were, to enter into God's way of thinking.

While the above arguments might justify the study of natural sciences, it is clear that the Rebbe's appreciation of secular knowledge extended beyond the realm of the sciences, as illustrated in a 1968 letter he wrote to Jonathan Sacks, a Cambridge University student (and the future chief rabbi of Great Britain) whom the Rebbe had encouraged to become more religiously involved (see pages 104–105). Upon returning to college after his meeting with the Rebbe, Sacks found himself in turmoil. On the one hand, he felt the pull of Jewish spirituality much more strongly than before. On the other, he feared that such a commitment would confine him intellectually, aesthetically, and, in a certain sense, even spiritually. He wondered, "Could I really embrace this life, which seemed so narrow after the broad expanses of Western culture? Where in this world was there a place for Mozart and Milton, Beethoven and Shakespeare? . . . I wanted to live more fully as a Jew, but at the same time I was reluctant to give up my love of art and literature, music and poetry, most of which had been created by non-Jews and had nothing to do with Judaism." He wrote to the Rebbe and expressed his fears and his dilemma.

The Rebbe wrote back with an answer in the form of a parable. He asked the young Sacks to imagine two people, both of whom have spent their lives carting stones; one rocks, the other diamonds. One day, they are both asked to carry a consignment of emeralds. To the man whose life has been spent transporting rocks, these jewels are just another type of rock, a burden, a weight that has to be moved from one place to another. After a lifetime of such work, this is how he regards whatever he is asked to carry. But the man who has spent a lifetime carrying diamonds understands that emeralds, too, are precious stones, different from diamonds, but still items of value and beauty.

So it is with different civilizations and faiths, the Rebbe continued. To the person for whom his own faith is precious, so, too, are others. Because he cherishes his own, he can value someone else's. His may be diamonds, the other's emeralds, but he sees the beauty in each. Therefore, the Rebbe concluded, in most cases you will find that your attachment to Judaism will heighten your appreciation of the gifts of other cultures. In short, the more deeply you value what is yours, the more you will value the achievements of others.[7]

Might there have been any other reasons for the Rebbe's general opposition to college? Rabbi Simon Jacobson speculates that, in addition to the prevalence of secular and often antireligious attitudes among university professors, particularly in the liberal arts, the Rebbe's resistance to such studies might also have been shaped by the fact that there simply were not enough people teaching and spreading Judaism's holy writings. Thus, in a balanced world, one in which there were many learned Jews and many Jews devoted to teaching Judaism, it makes sense that a Jewish scholar or yeshiva student could verse himself in all areas of knowledge, from anatomy to zoology. But the world the Rebbe confronted in America was an unbalanced one, in which a disproportionately high percentage of Jews focused their intellectual efforts on worldly rather than divine wisdom. Thus, to use Jacobson's analogy, if there is a city with a thousand accountants, a thousand lawyers, and only ten doctors, it makes sense to encourage people to study medicine; that is what the city is in need of. In such a metropolis, one would certainly discourage a doctor who wanted to stop practicing medicine so as to study law from doing so. But if the city already has a thousand doctors, a thousand accountants, and a thousand lawyers, but is missing soul doctors, then educating people in spiritual and religious studies needs to become the central focus. When most of the population has enormous amounts of knowledge but is lacking knowledge in the purpose of life and what direction to take in life, then everyone who has this knowledge—what Jacobson calls "soul doctors"—must feel obligated to address this glaring vacuum.

Rabbi Shlomo Riskin, a non-Chabad devotee of the Rebbe, had a similar explanation for the Rebbe's particular opposition to his *shluchim* going to college. The Rebbe, as is commonly acknowledged, wanted to build a force of committed *shluchim* to spread Jewish teachings and practices throughout the world. If these young men and women suddenly took off years to study in college and perhaps graduate school, some, perhaps many, would opt to enter professions other than the rabbinate.

It is well known that at Yeshiva University, the bastion of Modern Orthodoxy, many of its finest students become rabbis in communities but a far larger number pursue non-rabbinic careers. It is their extensive secular education that enables them to pursue a secular profession rather than the rabbinate or work in Jewish education. Riskin, himself a YU graduate, conjectures that the Rebbe, by denying his most devoted followers the option of a higher secular education and profession, guaranteed that they had no choice but to dedicate their lives and earn their livelihood through the one highly developed skill they did have, the spreading of Judaism. A Jew with a medical or law degree, even if he has extensive Jewish knowledge, as do so many YU graduates, is unlikely to move—and certainly not to move permanently—to Des Moines, or Calgary, or Shanghai to expose unknowledgeable Jews to Shabbat. A Jew immersed in studying Judaism's holy writings and lacking these secular professional options will be much more open to doing so.

This speculation—and it is speculation, as the Rebbe never enunciated such a view—is in no way intended to sound cynical. Rather, the Rebbe saw himself in the manner in which a general sees himself; he is commanding an army and his responsibility is to send troops where they are needed. If this analysis is correct, the Rebbe's reasoning was pragmatic as much as it was ideological. For an army to succeed, it needs a cadre of professional soldiers fully dedicated to the cause and fully willing to be sent to any post to which their commander assigns them. Unquestionably, there was only one religious Jewish leader in the last century who produced such a cadre.

"Be sure to use your talents for your people."

"Soul doctors" can, of course, be either male or female. Bassie Garelik (then Posner), a native of Pittsburgh—her father had been sent there by the Frierdiker Rebbe—and a decades-long *shlucha* in Milan, Italy, graduated high school at sixteen and planned on attending college half-time while continuing her seminary studies on a half-time basis. With Garelik's agreement, her father wrote of her intention to the Rebbe, who responded at length with a letter on November 25, 1954, outlining his basic objections to college studies. This time, however, in addition to referring to the potential antireligious impact of universities, he invoked the special needs of the Jewish community in the wake of the Holocaust:

> *After so many Jews lost their lives in recent years, among them the best and choicest of our people, the responsibility of those whom G-d in His mercy has spared is increased many-fold. It is therefore more obvious than ever that no Jew has a right to give of his time, and even more so of his heart and mind, to matters which not only do not help, but are very likely to hinder in the fulfillment of his sacred task and purpose [to illuminate the world with the light of the commandments and of the Torah]. One*

of these matters would be to spend several years in college, and especially in a college environment. While it is true that in recent years, in certain colleges, especially in New York, there are groups of Orthodox Jewish students, young men and women— and may G-d help them to come out of it unharmed, at any rate not worse than they were when they entered college—we have a rule not to rely on miracles. It is certain, however, that . . . even at best [attending college] would be an irretrievable loss of time and energy. [emphasis added][8]

As strongly as the Rebbe felt about this matter, he did not want Garelik to accept his response as binding simply because he had said it; rather, he hoped that she would come to this conclusion on her own. Garelik did so, though for her the mere fact that the Rebbe issued such strongly worded advice was apparently sufficient to determine her behavior.

On the other hand, when a person of Chabad background had already started college and his or her commitment to continuing higher education was strong, the Rebbe could be quite flexible. As noted, when the Rebbe asked Chana Sharfstein (then Zuber) why she felt the need to go to college, Sharfstein said it was because she wanted to be a teacher. The Rebbe asked her if it was necessary to go to college to do so,[9] and she answered yes, that she was studying psychology and methods of teaching, because "I want to be a really good teacher." The Rebbe smiled and said, "Fine, but be sure to use your talents and abilities for your people."

Sharfstein's rationale for pursuing such studies was in line with the second justification offered by the *Tanya*: "if one knows how to apply the knowledge gained through secular studies to the service of God and Torah." She subsequently became the principal of a Beis Rivkah school, a Lubavitch educational institution for girls, but during her long career in education she taught in public schools as well (for a more extensive discussion of the Rebbe's advice to Sharfstein on this and other issues, see pages 62–73).

Clearly, however, the Rebbe did not want people to think of college as an option at the age when the overwhelming majority of Americans attend college, in their late teens and early twenties. This is the time when people's minds are still being shaped and formed, and he did not think liberal arts professors were the people best suited to exerting so profound an influence on young adults. A few years later, once a student had developed a mature religious outlook[10] and particularly if the student had married, and therefore was more focused on earning a livelihood and less subject to sexual and other lifestyle temptations that are common on campuses, then the likelihood of the student being adversely affected by a secular approach would be greatly diminished.

What of the Rebbe's own university experiences? How did they affect his outlook on studying at such institutions? It seems likely that his years at university, particularly in Germany during the late 1920s and early 1930s, might have soured him on the morality and sense of civility associated with the academic world.

Rabbi Dr. Moshe Berger of Cleveland's Siegal College of Judaic Studies recalls a Saturday-afternoon informal discussion in Brookline, Massachusetts, at which people were posing questions to Rabbi Soloveitchik. At one point, he remembers the Rav speaking of a class he had attended in Germany taught by Professor Martin Heidegger, widely regarded as the greatest German philosopher of the twentieth century. The Rav remembered Rabbi Menachem Mendel Schneerson also attending the sessions, and his surprise at seeing the future Rebbe studying *Tanya*, the basic Chabad philosophic text, while Heidegger was lecturing.[11] When the lecture concluded, the Rav asked the future Rebbe why he bothered coming to the class if he was going to spend his time studying a Jewish text instead of listening to the professor. Thereupon the Rebbe proceeded to repeat with full comprehension the major points the professor had made. So impressed was the Rav that at the following lecture, he brought with him a volume of the Mishnah and started to study it. He discovered, however, that he became so caught up in the Mishnaic text that he could not absorb any of what Heidegger was saying, and when he tried to focus on the philosopher's words, it was impossible for him to study the Mishnah. The Rav was obviously telling this story to underscore the Rebbe's very unusual and impressive ability to simultaneously focus on different intellectual disciplines, a trait attested to by different people over the course of his life (see, for example, page 239).[12]

But implicit in this story, too, is another message, one known to all students of Heidegger and to those familiar with modern intellectual history. Just a few years later, Heidegger, a man of powerful intellect, became a Nazi. In April 1933, when he assumed the rectorship of Freiburg University, he declared at his inaugural address: "The Führer himself and alone is today and in the future German reality and its law." Heidegger finished the speech with three "Heil Hitlers!" Several days later, on April 10, 1933 (by which time both Rabbis Soloveitchik and Schneerson had left Germany), Heidegger instructed his deans to dismiss all faculty members who professed the Jewish religion or were of Jewish background.

That great evil and stupidity can coexist in a person of immense intellectual capabilities is best illustrated by an incident recorded by the anti-Nazi philosopher Karl Jaspers. Shortly after Hitler's rise to power, Jaspers asked Heidegger, "How can a man as coarse as Hitler govern Germany?" Heidegger responded, "Culture is of no importance. Just look at his marvelous hands."

It is likely that the Rebbe's deep disappointment with the moral quality of so many of "Hitler's professors" (as pro-Nazi professors came to be known)[13] was one factor that inclined him to want to protect his followers from exposure to the world of academia, particularly during their formative years. As was noted in a different context and, as the Rebbe wrote to Professor Velvel Greene, "For it was precisely the nation which had excelled itself in the exact sciences, the humanities, and even in philosophy and ethics, that turned out to be the most depraved nation in the world" (see page 258).

However, this negative assessment of the university is not the whole story. Despite his general opposition to university studies, the Rebbe also was decidedly practical. He might personally prefer that young people not attend university, but what if the large majority of American Jewish parents disagreed with him and enrolled their children in such studies? If the Rebbe were to write such people off, he would be dismissing the large majority of young American Jews. That is something that the Rebbe, regarded by his followers as "the leader of the generation" (*manhig ha-dor*) and not just the leader of Chabad—and a man whose love for his fellow Jews extended to the entire Jewish community—would never do.

"What is the most vulnerable time [on the campus]? Not in the classroom."

Rabbi Efraim Sturm, the long-term executive vice president and chief executive officer of the National Council of Young Israel, a leading association of Orthodox synagogues, recalls his growing concern in the late 1950s and early 1960s with the rising number of students from yeshiva high schools who were attending out-of-town colleges. During the earlier history of the Jews in the United States, young Jewish men and women who pursued post–high school education generally attended local city colleges, in New York, for example, schools such as CCNY (the City College of New York), Brooklyn College, and Hunter College. These were institutions where a very high percentage of students were Jewish, and where students continued living at home with their parents. But as Jewish affluence increased in the postwar years, and as many American Jews, including many of those who were religiously committed, wished to more fully share in the American experience and achieve greater professional success, more graduates of Jewish day schools began attending colleges away from home.

Along with observing a declining level of religious observance among many of these students, Rabbi Sturm started to notice a rise in rates of intermarriage among Jews at out-of-town schools. Rabbi Sturm recalled: "I called together the officers of Young Israel and I said, 'We have a problem. The Jewish young men and women, particularly the young men, who spend twelve years in yeshiva, and then go to an out-of-town college, we lose [many of] them. All this *chinuch* [education] and all this *Yiddishkeit* that we try to develop gets lost on the college campus."

Sturm arranged for a number of colleagues and himself to meet with several of the foremost Orthodox rabbinic figures to solicit their opinions as to what could be done to reverse this decline in religious observance among students at out-of-town colleges. Decades later, he recalled the variety of responses they received. One rabbi said that the Jewish community had to make sure that there were more Orthodox professors on campus. Sturm thought this a good idea, but also knew that it was not within the power of either the yeshivas or the Young Israel movement to make this happen. Several others said that it was the responsibility of Jewish high schools to imbue their students with such deep feelings of religiosity that they would be able to withstand both the secular and the social pressures of the university campus. This, too, sounded good in theory, but clearly those students most committed to strict observance and most impervious to secular influences were least likely to attend out-of-town schools. Anyway, there was no guaranteed method of transmitting Judaism that would keep eighteen- and nineteen-year-olds in the fold. Several other rabbis urged Young Israel to issue a proclamation forbidding attendance at out-of-town colleges: Let all such students remain in city schools, where they would go home daily and be with their parents on Shabbat; this way, the family environment could offset the campuses' secular atmosphere. But this, too, Sturm knew, was not in Young Israel's power, particularly when many of the movement's parents were themselves eager for their children to attend the most prestigious out-of-town schools.

"And then we went to the Rebbe," Sturm explained. "The Rebbe had the ability to rip away a lot of the symptoms and penetrate to the heart of the problem. And so the Rebbe sat down and analyzed with us what's happening. He [explained to us that] in Berlin, if you were a religious Jew, or if you were a member of another religion, you would have to defend your religion, you would have to be able to meet challenges of other people who challenged your religion. You would have to know the philosophy, know the content, know the mysticism, and be able to defend your philosophy. But, he said, Americans are not interested in defending religious philosophies. They are interested basically in consistency. If a person is religiously consistent, the average American will respect him. The average American wants sincerity, honesty in religion, whatever religion you choose. The Rebbe said that we have found that people who are working among non-Jews and who are consistent with their Sabbath observance will be told by the non-Jew on Friday, 'Hey, you know, it's getting late, you better go home,' because they admire people who have principles. And so, what we need to give college students is consistency, not keep talking [to them] about the philosophy of Judaism, but rather offer them the consistency of observance. So, the Rebbe then said, let's look at how we can create consistency on campus life. He says a religious boy or girl goes to an out-of-town college, and says to his parents, 'Don't worry. I'll observe Shabbos and I'll keep kosher. I'll have cottage cheese every day for lunch, and I'll have salad every day for dinner, and I'll have Corn Flakes every day for breakfast, and I'll manage for four years.'

" 'Let's assume they mean it,' the Rebbe continued. *'But can they do it?* You sit in a college dining room and you're sitting next to a peer group, a girl, and you [plan on] putting on your yarmulke and eating cottage cheese every single day. . . . And what if she says, "Take a taste of this, it's delicious." How long can you deny it, and not take a taste?' The Rebbe continued, ruminating aloud, as he placed himself in the mind-set and circumstances of these young students. 'After a while, the peer group pressures you, not because they mean to pressure, not because they are opposed to what you are doing, but [because] colleges are known for their liberalism, and so, after a while, you yield to that pressure.'

"The Rebbe said, 'What we have to do is create an atmosphere in which all the Jewish men and women are together in one place at the most vulnerable time. And what is the most vulnerable time? Not in the classroom. In the classroom, each one is interested in his own notes, in his own grades, but in the non-classroom area, that is when the Jewish men and women have to be together.' After offering this analysis, the Rebbe then offered a suggestion that could immediately start to address this problem: 'The best thing to do is to establish kosher dining clubs on campuses.' " [14]

Following this meeting with the Rebbe, the Young Israel movement started to establish such clubs. Their flagship one was created at Cornell University in 1959, and over the next few years, a total of seventeen such programs were established.

As Rabbi Sturm notes, all this was the idea of the Rebbe, who was the first one to foresee the need for such clubs on campuses. "Of all the suggestions that were given to us [by the rabbinic figures with whom we consulted], the only one that we really could tackle, the only one that we could really relate to, was the kosher dining club."

To this day, the most consistently well attended events at Chabad Houses on college campuses are the Friday-night Shabbat dinners. A large percentage of attendees are young Jews from homes where Shabbat is not observed, and for these students Friday night would otherwise be, as the Rebbe put it, "a vulnerable time," a time for partying.

"So tell me, until October is it permissible to eat non-kosher food?"

Freddy Hager, a devotee of the Rebbe from England, recalled a *yechidus* he had in January 1970; at the time, he was a student at the University of London. Some months earlier, he had had an extended personal meeting with the Rebbe, but on this occasion he was part of a delegation of Jews visiting from England. Rabbi Leibel Groner, the Rebbe's secretary, had instructed the group to limit the meeting to no more than ten minutes, as there were hundreds of people at 770 that night waiting to see the Rebbe.

Hager recalled the meeting: "We were discussing various matters about university life and all of a sudden, out of the blue, the Rebbe said, 'What do the students at London University do about kosher food?' So I said, 'Well, they are rebuilding Hillel House, it will be finished in October [it was now January], and there will be kosher facilities.'

"The Rebbe looked at me, a piercing look, and he said, 'So tell me, until October is it permissible to eat non-kosher food?' I felt very stupid." The Rebbe's next comment surprised Hager greatly. Although he had never visited England, the Rebbe suddenly started to speak knowledgeably about the University of London's layout. The campus is not a typical one, in which all the school's divisions are on one site; rather, the various colleges are spread out and "dotted around"—Hager remembers the Rebbe using that expression. " 'So would I not be correct in saying that only a committed student who is specifically looking for kosher food will come to the Hillel House?'

"I nodded my agreement. The Rebbe said, 'So, what do we do about the other students?'

"I remained silent as the Rebbe continued: 'Wouldn't it be a good idea to make a meal service, and actively invite people to come and eat kosher food?' So I got very enthusiastic, and I warmed to the theme, and I said, 'That's a wonderful idea, and we could have lectures and guest speakers and be *mekarev*, bring the people closer to Judaism.'

344]REBBE

"The Rebbe held up his hand, and said, 'That's very nice, and it may be a good idea, but that's not what I have in mind. What I have in mind with this suggestion is purely that a Jewish boy should sit next to a Jewish girl, should sit eating a kosher meal next to a Jewish girl, rather than eating a non-kosher meal next to a non-Jewish girl.'[15]

"Anyway, to cut a long story short, we did it. I came back to London and talked to a friend of mine, a very enthusiastic young man, and we arranged a meal service. We collaborated with one of the then major kosher restaurants in London and they began delivering meals to three colleges: London School of Economics, Kings College, and Imperial College. And the service went on for many years, and was a tremendous success."

Discussing these events more than thirty years later, two things struck Hager as extraordinary. First, it all emerged out of a brief, ten-minute meeting and was, in fact, only part of the meeting, "yet it was a cataclysmic idea which changed many people's lives." In addition, there was another remarkable feature of the encounter, what it revealed about the Rebbe's unusual, broad-based understanding of *ahavat Yisrael*, love of all Jews. For "the Rebbe wasn't worrying in this case about his Chasidim [who were certainly not students at the University of London]. There are a number of Jewish leaders, Rebbes, rosh yeshivas, who worry about their communities, and that's very laudable, and that's wonderful, and we need more leaders like that. But the Rebbe had a breadth and was concerned about the wider world. He was concerned about people that he'd never met, that he might possibly never meet, but those people concerned him and their needs wouldn't let him rest until he did something about it."[16]

"Work with Only Seven People":
The Rebbe's Approach to Campus Outreach

As the Jewish population at out-of-town campuses exploded in the 1960s and 1970s, the Rebbe's commitment to reaching out to students on campus increased as well. When Rabbi Leibel Wolf, who had worked with university students in his native Australia, wrote to tell the Rebbe of his wish to switch to full-time religious studies at a Kollel, he received a sharply worded page-and-a-half response. "G-d forbid," the letter began, "that you should now go and study in a Kollel; this is a *zman milchamah* [a time of war], and at a time of war a good soldier doesn't leave the front line." Instead, the Rebbe exhorted Wolf to continue working "with academic youth." There were no Chabad Houses at the time, and when Wolf asked the Rebbe's secretaries how he should go about fulfilling the Rebbe's wishes, he was instructed to contact Hillel, the international organization devoted to Jewish students on campus.

Wolf wrote to Hillel and, to his surprise, was offered a position as assistant to the Hillel director, a Conservative rabbi, at the University of Wisconsin. Wolf was now perplexed, and he wrote to the Rebbe asking how he, an Orthodox Jew, could operate in a professional setting in which he would be the assistant to a Conservative rabbi. The Rebbe did not respond to Wolf's query but simply offered him a *bracha* on the work he was undertaking. Shortly thereafter, the Conservative rabbi took suddenly ill and Wolf found himself responsible for seven thousand Jewish students.

The number was daunting. Here he was, one person, needing to reach out to a group that was, in effect, the size of ten congregations. "How am I as a single individual to operate with 7,000 students?" Wolf wrote to the Rebbe. The Rebbe's answer was not one Wolf had anticipated. "[You] should work with only seven people, and they will find their seven, and those seven will find their seven." In other words, as Wolf understood the Rebbe's directive, "I was to work very specifically and particularly with individuals." Working like this would give Wolf a sense of accomplishment (instead of feeling overwhelmed), as he would find himself tangibly moving individuals from point A to point B; through such an approach, the number of people affected would gradually grow and grow. Certainly, as Wolf now appreciates, such an approach is far more effective than some all-encompassing approach of trying to work all at once—and, of necessity, much more superficially—with thousands.

Although a rabbi responsible for so many students must also work on the macro level (think of the large services that a Hillel rabbi needs to organize for the High Holidays, the Purim megillah reading, and the

Passover Seder), on a day-to-day basis the Rebbe's emphasis to Wolf was on working with individuals. "That focus became a very important message to me for the rest of my career as a *shliach*." [17]

"Finish your dissertation, finish your dissertation."

Although one might have expected that the Rebbe would have been particularly encouraging to those who wanted to drop out of university to study at Chabad, that was not the case. The Rebbe had an abiding belief that there was a divine reason why a person placed him- or herself in a given situation, and that as long as one was doing something legal and not forbidden by Jewish law (like working on Shabbat), a person should complete the task that he started.

At first, this attitude of the Rebbe was not widely known within the community. We mentioned earlier the incident with Yitzchak Block, who wanted to drop out of Harvard University and study full-time at the Lubavitch yeshiva. To Block's great surprise, the Rebbe did not approve of this decision at all; instead, he repeatedly affirmed to Block the importance of completing his degree.

Block returned to Harvard, but then, sometime later, when he failed the oral examination on the area of his doctoral dissertation, he wrote to the Rebbe, "I'm finished with the whole thing. I'm going back to the yeshiva." The Rebbe responded, "You'll try it again, you'll pass." Sure enough, Block retook the exam and passed the second time.

A short time later, Block started researching and writing his dissertation on Aristotle's theory of perception and found that the work was moving very slowly. Two years passed and he still was not near finishing his work. "The Rebbe kept nudging me: 'Finish your dissertation. Finish your dissertation.'" Finally, Block felt the motivation to get it done and started to work at it feverishly, sometimes twelve hours a day. Many nights, he remained at the Harvard library until ten o'clock. All along, he kept writing to the Rebbe about his progress, and the Rebbe kept encouraging him,

Finally, in 1958, Block completed the dissertation, which was approved. He printed three copies, one for the Harvard library, one for himself, and one for the Rebbe. At the next *farbrengen*, the Rebbe looked at him and smiled. He said, "*Yetz kenst du hubben menuchas ha-nefesh*" (now, you can relax).

Now that he had finally completed his doctoral studies, Block decided to study for *semicha*, rabbinical ordination, and wrote a letter to the Rebbe informing him of his decision. He assumed the Rebbe would be pleased to hear this, but he wasn't. To Block's surprise, he soon got back a four-word response: "*Lo mit an aleph*," which more or less translates as "No, with a capital N." Or, as Block has phrased it, "Under no circumstances should you become a rabbi." As Block understands it, it was clear to the Rebbe that what the world most needed from *him* was that he become Dr. Block or Professor Block, not Rabbi Block. This subsequently became clear to Block as well.

His first teaching position was at Brooklyn College. A large percentage of Block's early students came from the famed yeshiva Torah Vodaas; these young men attended the yeshiva during the day and took college courses at night. Seeing that Block was himself a religious Jew (he wore a yarmulke and had an untrimmed beard), many students would line up after class to talk to him. They wanted to know if he, with his extensive secular education, really believed in God, in the Torah's divinity, and in the binding nature of the *mitzvot* (commandments). Block assured them that he did. "They couldn't get over the fact that I had a PhD in philosophy from Harvard. And they would talk to me about these questions that they were afraid to talk to their rosh yeshiva about" (the term "rosh yeshiva" literally refers to the overall "head of a yeshiva," but is also used to denote the teacher of an advanced Talmud class).

Block was in shock. During the summers he had spent learning at 770, he had never encountered fellow students who were troubled by such fundamental questions, even doubts, about Judaism's core beliefs. From the perspective of half a century, Professor Block recounts, "Now I know why the Rebbe sent me to Harvard. That I should have influence on Jewish students; that's what he had in mind. You have no idea the influence that I'm able to have on a student by not even saying a word to him, just being a professor who has a PhD from Harvard and who is *frum*. All they have to do is look at me, and I've done more than a hundred rabbis could do. I understand that now, but I didn't understand that then."

The Rebbe, though, had larger ambitions for Block than simply inspiring those students who happened to take his classes: "The Rebbe
wanted me to become as important in the world of philosophy as I could
possibly become, because the more important I became in the world of
philosophy, the more the fact of my *Yiddishkeit* would have an influence
on students and other people." Shortly after completing his PhD, Block
submitted an article based upon his dissertation to a prestigious academic journal devoted to classical studies, and Professor Ludwig Edelstein, the journal's editor, quickly sent back a rejection letter without
even bothering to offer any explanation. Block, who by this point regarded the Rebbe as his adviser on all matters, sent a letter to the Rebbe
informing him of what happened, and asking, "What should I do now?"
Decades later, Block recalled, "The Rebbe told me something I would
never in my wildest imagination think to do. He said, 'Why don't you get
in touch with one of your Harvard professors and tell him the problem;
maybe he might be able to help you?' " [18] Block's first response was, "My
God, how can I do a thing like that? Here I wrote an article that disagreed
with the main scholarly opinion of the day, and true, one of my professors at Harvard liked it. But what could he do for me [after] the editor of
the journal rejected it? So how is this professor going to help me? Thank
God, however, I had a bit of faith. I said to myself, 'Look, the Rebbe said
to do it.' It seemed to me completely irrelevant and a somewhat embarrassing thing for me to have to do, but I did it." Block informed the professor of what had happened and, to Block's amazement, the professor
told him that he would call Edelstein and find out why he had rejected
the piece. It had never occurred to Block that his young Harvard professor might actually know the elderly Edelstein.

The professor soon recounted to Block the conversation he had with
Edelstein. " 'I said to him, you got a paper from a student of mine, Irving
Block, on Aristotle. I thought it was a good paper.' " Edelstein acknowledged that the paper may have been good, "but who is he to go and
criticize W. D. Ross, one of the greatest scholars on Aristotle in the past
150 years?" The professor, however, believing that Block's analysis and
critique were correct, didn't back off. Instead, he pressed Edelstein: "Just
tell me, was he right or wrong?" A short time later, Edelstein wrote

Block, telling him that he had changed his mind and that he was going to publish the paper.

Under the Rebbe's prodding, and by virtue of the quality of his work, Dr. Block went on to have a distinguished career as a professor of philosophy at the University of Western Ontario in London, Canada.

"You'll do more for Yiddishkeit *with three initials after your name."*

A decade after Block, graduate student Jacob Hanoka started spending time at Lubavitch and soon found himself an unexpected object of interest from the Rebbe. At the time, Hanoka was becoming very involved in Jewish religious life and was thinking of withdrawing from Penn State, where he had already finished an MA in ceramic technology and was enrolled in a PhD program in physics. The Hillel rabbi at Penn State contacted Chabad and was able to arrange that Hanoka meet the Rebbe. After Hanoka was ushered into the Rebbe's office at about one in the morning, the Rebbe spent an hour with him, encouraging him to open up about his entire life. At one point, when Hanoka expressed interest in starting to learn at the yeshiva immediately, the Rebbe insisted that he first finish the semester at school; then he could come and spend some time at the yeshiva. However, the Rebbe made it very clear that after this break in his secular studies, it was important that he return to Penn State and complete his PhD. Hanoka told the Rebbe that his preference was to learn at the yeshiva, become a rabbi, and work with Jewish students on campus. The Rebbe told him, "You'll do more for *Yiddishkeit* with three initials after your name." The Rebbe then offered Hanoka a loan to finish his studies.

In addition to making his intentions for Hanoka known to him, the Rebbe soon revealed them to everyone else. At a large *farbrengen*—with many hundreds of people present and at a time when the young Hanoka was still a graduate student—the Rebbe publicly referred to him as "*Professor* Jacob Hanoka" and blessed him that he should indeed become a professor and spread *Yiddishkeit* among professors.

Several years later, Hanoka completed his doctoral work and ended up taking, at the Rebbe's advice, a high-profile industrial position. For three decades Hanoka was involved in the field of solar energy, and he went on to develop an international reputation and a very successful career.

It is clear that the Rebbe's plans for Hanoka were similar to those he had for Block: to become recognized and esteemed in the wider world, in Hanoka's case, at a time when there were few religious scientists. In the early years after he finished his degree, Hanoka would attend conferences where he was the only one with a beard and a yarmulke. Obviously, this was what the Rebbe was thinking of when he first spoke to him about the importance of having the three initials after his name.

The Rebbe's belief was that people can use any experience from their lives, any body of knowledge they possess, to serve God. In Hanoka's case, the Rebbe wanted him to use secular studies for a Godly purpose. This in fact was Hanoka's mission, as the Rebbe understood it, and over the years he never discussed with Hanoka his Torah learning and his praying: "All he wanted to know was about my career. I don't think that 'What's going on in your career?' is the typical question that a Chasid is asked by the Rebbe." What the Rebbe wanted from Hanoka was that he pursue his career, publish academic papers, and become well known in his field.[19]

"What do you think the Rebbe advised me to do, which topic to choose [for my dissertation]?"

A decade later, Susan Handelman, an emerging literary scholar, found herself likewise receiving encouraging, and very practical, guidance from the Rebbe. Dr. Handelman, now a professor at Bar-Ilan University in Israel and formerly at the University of Maryland, first became involved with Chabad in the mid-1970s, during the time she was working on her PhD at the State University of New York in Buffalo. Handelman started attending services at the Chabad in Buffalo and was impressed with the hospitality and warm acceptance she encountered (at the time she was far from being an observant Jew), and the willingness of the local *shliach* to study with her both the *sichos* (talks) of the Rebbe and Chasidic *ma'amarim* (the more analytic discourses) as well: "I was just amazed at the depth of the Rebbe's Torah interpretations, and it influenced me a lot in my academic work, because I was working on literary theory, and on how to interpret texts. I began to be interested in the ways that the Rabbis interpreted texts. I saw that there was a rich tradition there." [20]

That December (the year was 1975), one of the Buffalo rabbis suggested she go to Chabad in Brooklyn for a weekend "Encounter." Handelman was so taken with the experience that she spent the following semester in Crown Heights, studying at a women's school, attending *farbrengens*, and starting to learn Chasidic philosophy in greater depth.

One major challenge to traditional Judaism that she struggled with during this time came from Handelman's feminist inclinations: "The issue of women in Judaism was very troublesome to me. I went to Smith College; I graduated in 1971. It was the height of the feminist movement. Gloria Steinem [a leading figure in American feminism] was our graduation speaker. She gave a rabble-rousing feminist speech, so when I came to Crown Heights to study in the mid-seventies, this was a big concern for me. And one of the profound things I learned through the Rebbe's *sichos* and through my learning in Crown Heights was the [positive] role of women in Chasidic philosophy and in kabbalah." Handelman started to write articles on this subject to help her work through her conflicts.

The first article Handelman wrote was titled "The Jewish Woman—Three Steps Behind?" It was accepted for publication by *Di Yiddishe Heim* (*The Jewish Home*), a half-Yiddish, half-English publication of N'shei Chabad, a Lubavitcher women's organization. At just about the time the article was to come out, a beloved uncle of Handelman became very ill. When she wrote to the Rebbe asking for a blessing for his recovery, "right away, I got a response from the Rebbe's secretary that the Rebbe would pray for my uncle's recovery. And then there was another interesting line in the response: 'I enjoyed your article in the forthcoming *Yiddishe Heim.*'"

Handelman was taken aback: "How did the Rebbe know that I wrote an article in the *Yiddishe Heim* about Judaism and feminism? The Rebbe, I understood from friends of mine who worked closely in his office, got so many letters a day, met with people till all hours of the night, and was overseeing Chabad *shluchim* all over the world. So how did he know that I wrote this article, which had not even been published yet, in the *Yiddishe Heim*?"

Handelman soon learned from the journal's editor that the Rebbe took particular interest in the magazine and in women's activities in Chabad. The Rebbe, she learned, so wanted to encourage these efforts that after she edited the articles, he reviewed and edited them as well. The editor returned to Handelman the manuscript she had submitted, along with the Rebbe's editing: "I was astonished. I taught writing, I taught freshman composition. He edited my English like an English professor, putting in apostrophes, changing words, taking out redundant words, the kind of editing that a copy editor would do. I was astounded at the quality of the editing and the care that he took. . . . I wish I could give the same attention to correcting my own students' papers as he did to my manuscript."

Two years later, when it was time for Handelman to choose her dissertation topic, "I had two possible topics: one was on Shakespeare and one was, as a result of my studies of Chasidus, on the relationship of rabbinic interpretation to literary theory, how the rabbinic manner of interpretation related to the new developments that were now taking place in literary theory."

Choosing a dissertation topic is perhaps the most significant decision a graduate student makes; it can determine the direction of his or her future academic career and will, at a minimum, commit the student to several years of research and writing. When Handelman found herself continuing to vacillate between these two very different areas, her Chabad friends suggested she write to the Rebbe for advice. Although her first inclination was not to do so, eventually, and after some additional prodding, she did write and ask the Rebbe which area he thought would be more fruitful for her to pursue.

"I like to tell this story, and I always like to ask people, 'What do you think the Rebbe advised me to do, which topic to choose?' So some people will say, 'He must have told you to write on Shakespeare.' I say, 'Well, why?' 'Because he wouldn't think that a woman should write on rabbinic subjects or that you shouldn't combine your Jewish studies with academic things.' Other people say, 'Oh, I'm sure he told you to write on rabbinic interpretation.' I say, 'Why?' They say, 'Because the Rebbe believed that we should spread Judaism everywhere and you should write, therefore, on that and fulfill that mission.' "

In actuality, the Rebbe's advice was of a far more practical—and decidedly nonideological—bent. He did not advise her to write on one topic or the other; rather, her decision should depend on who would be her adviser, and on who else would examine her on her dissertation: If her academic advisers were opposed to religion or if there was a suspicion that they might disturb her work, then she shouldn't choose a Jewish topic. Otherwise, by implication, she should feel free to do so.[21]

"This was very profound advice. It was extremely pragmatic and extremely faithful to my experience at the university. And it's advice that I give my own graduate students. I tell them that the most important thing of course is that 'you write on a topic that is really meaningful to you.' The Rebbe didn't tell me on which topic to write. And the second most important thing, I tell them, is that 'you have the right adviser.' "

Reflecting on this experience some thirty years later, Handelman remains quite astonished by the Rebbe's sophisticated practical grasp. "So the Rebbe, who had the deepest insights into Torah, who could discuss the deepest mystical ideas, was also able to give me the most concrete, effective, and practical advice. He wasn't saying, 'Use this opportunity to spread Torah,' and he wasn't saying, 'A woman should or shouldn't do that.' It was about making sure that whichever topic I chose, I had the right adviser—and to make sure, therefore, that if I chose to write on rabbinic thought that my advisor did not have an anti-religious bias."[22]

Handelman decided to write her thesis on rabbinic thought and literary theory and turned her dissertation into her first book, *The Slayers of Moses: The Emergence of Rabbinic Interpretation in Modern Literary Theory.* And, of course, she was careful to choose the right adviser.

"If, Heaven forbid, the report I heard concerning your desire [to study] in college is correct . . ."

"You must finish [your MA]. Otherwise, you've wasted the effort you've made until now."

There is no one summary statement that can be made regarding the Rebbe's attitude to college studies. On the one hand, when members of his community inquired about attending college, he almost always opposed their doing so. The opposition was strongest when the person making the inquiry was in his or her late teens or early twenties and if the person wanted to pursue a liberal arts education rather than a professional degree (such as accounting or medicine). At that age in particular, the Rebbe feared the alienating effect the largely secular universities, whose faculty members often have an antireligious bias, might have upon students. Shmuel Isaac Popack, a Chasid, had every intention of attending college, until the Rebbe convinced him not to do so. But this example of Popack and many others like it—though sometimes cited as definitive expressions of the Rebbe's view—are not the whole story. In contrast, for example, Professor Velvel Greene, of the University of Minnesota and later Ben-Gurion University in Israel, recalled several instances in which the Rebbe asked him to help arrange for certain Chasidim to be admitted into university programs. And Rabbi Dr. Norman Lamm, the longtime president of Yeshiva University, recollected an instance when a young man from a highly regarded Lubavitch family expressed a strong desire to become a doctor and was advised by the Rebbe to begin his college studies at YU.[23]

Furthermore, while the Rebbe might have generally opposed an individual's desire to seek a university education, his opposition frequently melted if the person had started the process. Bernie Rader recalls an instance in which a young man in London was working on his MA in mathematics and made it known to the Rebbe that he wished to give it up to go and learn in the Lubavitcher yeshiva. The Rebbe's response? "You must finish [your MA]. Otherwise, you've wasted the effort you've made until now."[24]

Similarly, when the Rebbe learned that Bentzion Bernstein, a young British Jew, had been studying law but was now thinking of pursuing a career in Jewish education instead, he urged him to carefully check into the steps necessary to qualify to practice law. The Rebbe told Bernstein that he wanted to build up a task force in the sciences and professions of people who could serve as models to others that there need be "no dichotomy between professional life and life as a *frum* [religious] Jew." Bernstein eventually became among the first lawyers in England to appear in court wearing a yarmulke. Even more remarkably, the Rebbe, knowing that Bernstein lacked sufficient funds to pay for the three additional years of training that would be needed, informed him of a scholarship fund he had available. In the end, Bernstein was paid through the offices of Chabad what was in effect a salary sufficient to cover family and all living expenses for three years (although Bernstein was not expected to repay this money, years later, when he achieved greater financial success, he did).[25]

These incidents demonstrate forcefully that the Rebbe did not regard the pursuit of a university education as something wrong in and of itself; otherwise, he would have wanted people, particularly those inclined as these young men were, to give it up at any stage. Certainly, the Rebbe would not have told someone who discovered in the middle of a meal that the food was unkosher to finish eating it, on the assumption that otherwise food would be wasted.

What the Rebbe did want ideally was that people not even think about attending college until they had mastered the major texts of Judaism. With their bellies, so to speak, filled with Jewish knowledge, the environment of college would, he hoped, be insufficient to challenge their faith.

But even in such cases, the Rebbe did not generally feel that college was necessary, certainly not for his Chasidim. One looks in vain for an example of a *shliach*—and the Rebbe sent out hundreds and hundreds of *shluchim*—whom the Rebbe counseled to seek a college education.[26] Just the opposite. There are a number of letters written by the Rebbe to *shluchim* who were considering going to college, and the attitude expressed by the Rebbe is akin to horror. In a letter posted to an unnamed *shliach* on 24 Elul 24 5710 (August 23, 1950; this was in the period after the Frierdiker Rebbe had died and before the Rebbe assumed the role as head of the movement), he writes: "If, Heaven forbid, the report I heard concerning your desire [to study] in college is correct . . ." The Rebbe goes on to note what he regards as several negative consequences of a *shliach* going to college, among them, that much of his time will be spent on his secular studies instead of his work in the community, that a portion of his time will be devoted to studying matters "that run contrary to your mission," and that the *shliach*'s behavior will be "noticed and followed" by others in the community. In characteristic fashion, the Rebbe then writes, "Nonetheless, the choice is yours."[27]

Clearly, the Rebbe believed that the work of bringing Jews to a more intense involvement in Jewish life, even in a largely secular society, could be performed without acquiring advanced secular knowledge. That *shluchim* devoid of post–high school secular education have achieved such success on hundreds of university campuses is perhaps the most powerful vindication of the Rebbe's position.

The Rebbe also understood that the world was not comprised only of Lubavitcher Chasidim and that one approach for all Jews would not work. Was the Rebbe unhappy with the many Jews who actively pursued university educations and advanced degrees? We have no absolute way of knowing, but as we have seen, he certainly did not encourage those who were studying at universities to drop out. Rather, the fact that he wanted people such as Professor Block and Dr. Hanoka to shine in their respective disciplines indicates that he deemed it important that there be Jews identified in the public consciousness as both religious and accomplished scholars.

In short—and perhaps some would regard this as an unanswerable question—would the Rebbe's attitude to university education have been different if the whole Jewish world were Chabad and open to following his recommendations? Would he then have almost always opposed a young man or woman attending college? Would he have wanted a world in which there were no Jewish physicians, lawyers, scientists, or professors?

I believe I can say with confidence, "No." The Rebbe never would have developed the excessive veneration for university education that many American Jews have.[28] And he would have wanted to make sure that all of these highly educated people first acquired a solid knowledge of

Judaism's holy texts before they pursued secular studies. If this meant that they would need to defer their university education until their mid-twenties, as he did, I think he would have regarded that as the right thing to do. Yet, even within these limitations, I believe the Rebbe would have continued to believe, as he told Jacob Hanoka, that there are people who can do more for the Jewish people and the world "with three initials after your name."

Part Seven

·❮❯·

The

REBBE

and

HIS FAMILY

·(⟵⟶)·

Chapter 25

MRS. SCHNEERSON FROM
PRESIDENT STREET

"They all feel that they have to show me special *kavod*
[honor], and that is not what I want."
—*Rebbetzin Chaya Mushka Schneerson*

Chaya Mushka Schneersohn was born on March 16, 1901, the second
of three daughters born to Rabbi Yosef Yitzchak and Nechama
Dina Schneersohn. At the time of her birth, her father was not yet the
Sixth Rebbe (he took the position in 1920), and it was her grandfather,
the Rebbe Rashab, who proposed that she be named Chaya Mushka,
after her great-great-grandmother, who was Chabad's third Rebbetzin.
Twenty-seven years later, she married her distant cousin, Menachem
Mendel Schneerson, who was himself named for the Third Rebbe.
Thus, the couple had precisely the same names as the Third Rebbe and
Rebbetzin, Menachem Mendel and Chaya Mushka Schneersohn.

From an early age, Chaya Mushka was recognized by her father as
possessing a great maturity of judgment. In a document dated December 4, 1924, when she was twenty-three, her father appointed her to serve
as his backup in financial matters involving the movement: "I hereby
empower citizen Chaya Moussia Yosepuvna [Russian for 'daughter of
Joseph'] Schneersohn, residing at Machovaya Street 12/22, apartment
10, to receive monies on my behalf or documents that are addressed to
me in all forms, from the government bank and all of its branches and
offices, and from other banks, government or communal, or from other
organizations of private persons or by telegraph."

Three years later, when her father was arrested and exiled to Kostroma, Russia, Chaya Mushka accompanied him into exile. Fortunately, international pressure forced the Soviet regime to terminate the supposed three-year exile after a little more than a week, and Chaya Mushka accompanied him back to Leningrad. Shortly thereafter, along with the rest of the family, they went to Latvia, then an independent country (it was later taken over by the Soviet Union).

Though deeply pious, Chaya Mushka led a more worldly existence than the previous six Rebbetzins; she attended university classes and lived with her husband for more than a decade in the Westernized cities of Berlin and Paris.

Regarded within Chabad as the personification of a loyal partner to her husband and an *aishet chayyil*, "a woman of valor," Chaya Mushka was a powerful spiritual and intellectual force in her own right. As Rabbi Zalman Gourary, who grew up in the Frierdiker Rebbe's house, put it: "She had the head of her father, and was similar to him. She [herself] was able to be a Rebbe...."

R ebbetzin Chaya Mushka Schneerson spent her entire life as either the granddaughter, daughter, or wife of a Rebbe (except for the one-year hiatus [1950–1951] between the death of her father and the succession of her husband). This means that her entire life was lived in the public eye. Yet, it seems safe to say that of the principal personalities involved in the Chabad hierarchy, it is she about whom we know the least. She was and has long been described as being a "private person." While her husband was by nature of a somewhat shy disposition, he quickly grew into his role as Rebbe. One who watches videos of *farbrengens* and sees him waving his arms to raise the volume of the singing might not guess at his shyness, but we know enough of his early years to know that his public, more exuberant persona was an acquired, not a natural, trait.

Unlike her husband, however, the Rebbetzin never felt compelled to become a public figure. Most notably, she did not play any sort of public role and did not attend *farbrengens*, even those at which there were many women in attendance. She was not present, for example, in 1980, at the very large public celebration of her husband's thirtieth anniversary as the movement's leader or even in less public settings. This private persona seems to have been her wish, and there is no indication that her husband wanted to influence her to act differently.

Above all, Rebbetzin Schneerson never pulled rank. When she called a store to order something, she never identified herself as Rebbetzin Schneerson, only as "Mrs. Schneerson from President Street." Sometimes, she even omitted the "Mrs."; a cousin remembers telephone calls from her typically beginning, *"Da redt Schneerson"* ("Schneerson speaking"). Dr. Elliot Udell, a podiatrist, recalled an incident during the period after he had stopped making house calls in the Crown Heights area; there had been an increase in crime in the neighborhood, and he feared walking alone in the area carrying his black doctor's bag. One day, he received a call from a Mrs. Schneerson who needed a doctor's care and felt too unwell to come in. As Schneerson is a relatively uncommon name, Udell suspected, but was by no means certain, that it was the Rebbetzin, and he agreed to come over. When his secretary expressed surprise at seeing him leaving the office to make a house call, he explained that if he practiced medicine in London, he'd go see Queen Elizabeth even if she was staying in a bad neighborhood.

When Udell arrived at 1304 President Street, he still wasn't certain if it was the Rebbetzin who had summoned him because, unlike her husband, her face was not widely known—certainly not to non-Lubavitchers. However, within a matter of minutes, he knew for sure that he was in the Rebbe's home, if only because it was the only Chabad household he had been in that didn't have a prominent photo of the Rebbe on display.

Chaya Mushka Schneerson knew that if she had identified herself on the phone as Rebbetzin Schneerson, Dr. Udell would have immediately agreed to come over, but that is exactly what she didn't want to do.[1] For the same reason, she generally refrained from shopping at local stores in Crown Heights—even though she confided to friends that she would have liked to—because of the fuss storekeepers and other shoppers would make over her. As she told a friend, "It's embarrassing, because they all feel that they have to show me special *kavod* [honor], and that is something I don't want."[2]

Her desire to avoid any excess attention was intense. On Rosh Hasha-nah, her husband used to blow the shofar for her at home. When a friend asked her why she didn't attend synagogue to hear the shofar, as the Rebbe blew it there as well, she is reported to have answered, "I couldn't bear the commotion that would be created around me."

One suspects, however, that there was another reason as well for her great reticence, one that had to do with family loyalty and family pain. The Rebbetzin was well aware that her older sister, Chana Gourary, had coveted the position of Rebbe for her husband, Shmaryahu. Though Chana Gourary's husband adjusted to the new reality and even grew close to the Rebbe, for Chana Gourary the pain of that lost dream lin-gered until her last years. One strongly suspects that Chaya Mushka refrained from presenting herself in public to avoid slighting her sister, "rubbing it in her face," so to speak, that it was she, not Chana, who was Chabad's First Lady.[3] If this was indeed her intention, and I know few people in Chabad who would dispute this suggestion, her strategy did not and could not fully succeed. Rebbetzin Gourary remained perma-nently embittered. Still, Chaya Mushka made every effort to minimize the pain and maintain family peace.

Despite refraining from public appearances, Rebbetzin Chaya Mushka assisted her husband in a variety of ways. Herself highly educated, she would read many academic and other journals, in several languages, and then share the information and sometimes the articles with the Rebbe. She also very much enjoyed hosting people, and became renowned for her graciousness as a hostess. "Even if there were ten or twelve people at the table," her cousin Hadassah Carlebach recalled, "she would give each one a turn to speak. Also, she would pour the tea herself. Although there was a teapot on the table and everybody could help themselves, she would pour in the tea herself, then hand the teacup to each person."[4]

The Rebbetzin's graciousness also extended to acquainting herself with subjects that she knew would be of interest to the people whom she was meeting. Dr. Ira Weiss, the Chicago cardiologist who started treating the Rebbe in the aftermath of his 1977 heart attack, subsequently also became one of the Rebbetzin's physicians. At a certain point in their relationship, the Rebbetzin learned that Weiss was an ardent Chicago Cubs baseball fan, and from then on, she would make it her business to check the news-papers to see how the Cubs were faring. Weiss grew accustomed to being greeted on the phone by the Rebbetzin with congratulations when the Cubs triumphed: "You must be happy today, Dr. Weiss." She also followed weather reports for Chicago and, knowing that Weiss was an avid biker, expressed concern for his well-being when the weather was bad.

In addition to being unusually hospitable to guests, the Rebbetzin showed great concern for the people who worked in her home and at-tended even to their minor needs. During the period Mendel Notik was performing periodic tasks there, the Rebbetzin learned that the young man loved rugelach (a traditional Jewish pastry), which was not at the time available in the Crown Heights area. She would periodically go down to the Lower East Side to get it for him, or she would ask someone else to go and get it for him. More significant, at a time when it was not common to do so, the Rebbetzin, meticulously honest, insisted on paying her employees on the books, thereby also ensuring that they would be eligible in their later years for Social Security; one of Notik's memories is of seeing an accountant at the home, filling out the paperwork.[5]

Living in what was in effect Chabad's White House (by odd coinci-dence, the Rebbe and Rebbetzin's home was on *President* Street), the Reb-betzin desired that the workers there feel at ease. She certainly did not want people to idolize her husband, though this was not easily achieved. On one occasion, when the Rebbe arrived home earlier than expected, Notik, who was eating a snack in the kitchen, started preparing to make a quick exit (it was a common feature of Chasidim to immediately leave when the Rebbe came home so as not to deprive the couple of the lim-ited time they had together).[6] His undisguised hurrying made the Reb-betzin uncomfortable. "Why are you running?" she said to him. "My husband doesn't bite." Yet despite her reassuring words, and the Rebbe himself greeting him, Notik simply waited until the Rebbe started to take off his coat and ran out the front door.

It would seem that the reverence in which Lubavitchers held the couple, the Rebbe in particular, limited the couple's ability to have easy-going, spontaneous interactions with others. Dr. Ira Weiss, though not a Chasid, was so anxious when the Rebbe and Rebbetzin invited him to join them for dinner that he remembers the experience—which one would think he would regard as a highlight in his life—as uncomfortable; he felt as if he was a tongue-tied intruder.[7]

Another story, one that reflects a different dimension of the Rebbetzin's good-heartedness, is quite unknown in Chabad and is more surprising, as it relates to an animal. In the winter of 1972, when this same cousin, Hadassah Carlebach, came to visit, she found to her shock that the Rebbetzin was wearing casts on both arms. The Rebbetzin explained that a short time earlier, she had opened her front door to get the mail but had not noticed a thin, virtually transparent, sheet of ice on the porch. She slipped and broke both her wrists. Because she couldn't support her arms, she was unable to stand up, and because the fall occurred on a part of the porch that was not easily seen from the street, there also were no passersby to come to her aid.

Then, a large dog appeared. This, however, was not entirely a coincidence; the Rebbetzin told Hadassah that it was a stray dog that had appeared in the neighborhood several weeks earlier and used to bark loudly and constantly. The Rebbetzin had felt sorry for the dog and would go out and feed it. This gesture may seem like nothing out of the ordinary, but it is well known that the most traditionally Orthodox Jews are not keen on domestic animals. In any case, this dog now walked onto her porch and, as Hadassah Carlebach recalls the Rebbetzin telling her, " 'I put my arms around the dog's neck, and he *schlepped* me into the house, and I managed to call for help.' "[8]

When Leadership Is Necessary: Three Episodes

"IF YOU DON'T BECOME REBBE, THIRTY YEARS OF MY FATHER'S LIFE WILL HAVE GONE TO WASTE."

As unobtrusive a figure as Chaya Mushka was in the movement's leadership during both her father's and her husband's years as Rebbe, she stepped forward on three occasions when the movement's future was at stake. The first occurred during 1950–1951, the year following her father's death. She was a primal force, and perhaps *the* primal force, in overcoming Menachem Mendel's opposition to becoming Rebbe. Although she paid a heavy price for her husband becoming Rebbe, knowing that it would be an utterly consuming job that left very limited time for anything else, she did not hold back. And well she might have. Several confidantes recall the warmth with which she would speak of their years in Paris. He was studying engineering and was deeply engrossed as well in Talmudic, halachic, and kabbalistic studies, and she was studying mathematics and architecture. This rare period in their lives when they were granted relative anonymity—Menachem Mendel was known to plead with friends not to make known to others that he was the Lubavitcher Rebbe's son-in-law—enabled them to live the private life of a young married couple. Still, putting herself last, she now chose what was good and right for the Chasidim and the movement. Well aware of her husband's scholarship and skills, she told him that he had no choice: "If you don't become Rebbe, thirty years of my father's life will have gone to waste."[9]

Once Menachem Mendel Schneerson assumed the *nesiut* (leadership role), the Rebbetzin remained in the background, emerging again when her husband's life and the movement's future were at stake. When the Rebbe suffered a massive heart attack in 1977 and made it known that he did not want to be hospitalized, an immediate crisis ensued. A number of physicians, some of whom had been present at the Shemini Atzeret holiday service at 770 when the heart attack occurred, and other nearby physicians who had been summoned, wanted to sedate the Rebbe and transfer him to a hospital. When the Rebbetzin learned of the doctors' plans, she refused to give her consent: "All the years that I have known my husband, I can't recall one instant that he was not in total control of himself, and I can't agree to do that, to give him any sedation against his will."[10] She also supported her husband in his decision not to be hospitalized; because the Rebbe was a man who was repeatedly called upon to counsel others on matters of life and death, the Rebbetzin was willing to rely on his own judgment as to whether or not he should be hospitalized.

The doctors left, explaining that they did not want to take responsibility for treating so ill a patient outside of a hospital (several of the
physicians who subsequently treated the Rebbe believed that it would
have been bad medical practice to dispatch a patient, particularly one
with as strong a will as the Rebbe, to a hospital against his wishes).

When the doctors departed, Rabbi Krinsky walked into his office and
sat down in his chair with his head in his hands, worried and perplexed.
"How do we get out of this conundrum?" he wondered. The Rebbetzin
soon came in and challenged him: "Rabbi Krinsky, you know so many
people. You can't find a doctor for my husband?" More than thirty years
later, Rabbi Krinsky recalls that the Rebbetzin's question triggered him
like a "bolt of lightning" to think of Dr. Ira Weiss, the Chicago cardiologist whom Krinsky knew and who now went on to play a key role in
the Rebbe's recovery. Once reached by phone, Dr. Weiss knew it would
take him hours to reach Crown Heights from Chicago, and he asked
Dr. Louis Teichholz to go there immediately. To this day, Weiss credits
Dr. Teichholz with stabilizing the Rebbe's condition and saving his life.[11]

The third occasion in which the Rebbetzin's involvement proved vital
to Chabad was in the court case involving the ownership of the Chabad
library. Her dramatic declaration that the "books belonged to the Chasidim because my father belonged to the Chasidim" visibly impressed
the judge and is generally regarded as the emotional high point of the
entire legal proceedings (see page 402).

During the last decade of the Rebbetzin's life, Dr. Weiss used to speak
to her on the telephone an average of five or six times a week, about both
her husband's health and, later, her own. He grew so impressed with the
Rebbetzin's astuteness and determination that he confided to me his
certainty that if the Rebbetzin had lived a few years longer, she would
have single-handedly stood up and stopped the movement to declare
the Rebbe the Messiah: "She would have put an end to it. She would
have made even a public appearance if it was necessary. She would have
put her fist down on it."

Along with assuming a leadership role when circumstances demanded it, the Rebbetzin herself was a spiritual force. When the
Lubavitch Women's Organization sent the Rebbetzin a bouquet of

flowers with a letter listing names of people for whom a *bracha* was requested, one of the Rebbe's secretaries sent the flowers to the Rebbetzin
and brought the sheet with the names to the Rebbe so that he could offer
the requested blessings. But when the Rebbe saw that the letter accompanying the flowers was addressed to his wife, he asked the secretary
to give the names to her: "She too is capable of giving blessings." On
another occasion he remarked, "Her father gave blessings which were
fulfilled. Her grandfather [the Fifth Rebbe] gave blessings which were
fulfilled. And her great-grandfather [the Fourth Rebbe] gave blessings
which were fulfilled." [12]

The Passing of the Rebbetzin

"IT SHOULD BE DONE THIS WAY BECAUSE THIS IS HOW THE REBBETZIN
WOULD HAVE WANTED IT TO BE. . . . THIS IS WHAT WOULD MAKE THE
REBBETZIN HAPPY."

The Rebbetzin was not a young woman when she died (she was
eighty-six), but when the end came, it happened so quickly and unex-
pectedly that it left those attending to her in shock. It started with her
feeling ill and very weak over a period of several days. Her physician,
Dr. Robert Feldman, suspected a bleeding ulcer, a serious but treatable
condition. The Rebbetzin's inclination, reminiscent of her husband's,
was not to be hospitalized. But when a group of physicians conferred
with Dr. Feldman and unanimously agreed that her condition required
hospitalization, and her husband assented, too, she consented.

At this point, there was a sense of great concern but not emergency;
perhaps this is why the Rebbe did not accompany her to the hospital,
as he had done on other occasions. The Rebbetzin in fact walked down
the steps of her house on her own and was taken to the hospital in a regular car, not an ambulance, driven by Rabbi Krinsky. The Rebbe came
down to escort his wife to the car and to say good-bye. Just before the
car pulled away, Rabbi Krinsky, speaking from the driver's seat, said to

the Rebbe, "I ask for a *bracha* that we should come back soon, and in good health." The Rebbe responded enigmatically, *"Gam atem"* ("You, too"). "I somehow felt very uncomfortable, to put it mildly" is how Krinsky later recalled the event, referring to the fact that the Rebbe did not reply directly to the blessing request.

Inside the car, everything seemed to quickly return to normal. With Rabbi Krinsky in the car were Rabbi Shneur Zalman Gourary, a prominent Chasid well connected with the medical establishment; Scholem Gansbourg, the longtime attendant in the Rebbe's house; and Dr. Feldman. Though the Rebbetzin was in considerable pain, she did not talk to the doctor about her condition. But she was not quiet, either.

Instead, she carried on a conversation with Dr. Feldman about his daughter Sarah, who had visited her just a few days earlier to give her advance notice of her soon-to-be-announced engagement to Levi Shemtov. The Rebbetzin had been particularly pleased by the match between the young woman and the grandson of the renowned Chasid Rabbi Bentzion Shemtov, commenting, "I am very happy because now I know that you will raise the children in Yiddish." Now, as the car was heading for the hospital, the Rebbetzin started asking Feldman about the engagement party being planned for Sarah. When the doctor told her they would be arranging a modest reception, the Rebbetzin urged him to prepare something more elaborate. She even questioned the doctor about the sort of dress he thought his daughter would buy for the occasion.

Shortly thereafter the car arrived at Cornell Medical Center in Manhattan. A room had been reserved in advance for the Rebbetzin, but it was not yet ready for occupancy and the Rebbetzin was seated in a chair near the room. Her conversations during the next moments were ordinary, with no indication of urgency. The Rebbetzin asked for a glass of water and made a blessing before she drank it. She requested that on the following morning a female aide bring her some clothing and other items from her house.

A doctor came over to ask her the standard litany of questions posed to a newly admitted patient. She easily answered them, but then suddenly she turned strikingly pale. The doctor asked her, "Are you with us?" and was reassured when she responded, "Yes." A few minutes later, she seemed very weak again, and the doctor asked her again, "Are you with us?" This time there was no response.

The Rebbetzin was interred at the Old Montefiore Cemetery next to her grandmother, Rebbetzin Shterna Sara, who is buried right next to Rebbetzin Nechama Dina, the Rebbetzin's mother; the Rebbetzin's grave is only a few yards from her father's. The Rebbe broke down several times during the graveyard service. "I regard the Rebbe as the loneliest man I knew," Rabbi Krinsky told me once. Everyone related to him as "Rebbe." For the Rebbe, therefore, to lose the person who related to him as a husband was singularly difficult. And as devastating as the death of a spouse is, it is even more devastating when there are no children or grandchildren and the spouse is the only person with whom one has an intimate relationship.

Per Chabad custom, no eulogies were delivered. A twenty-member motorcycle police guard escorted the procession from Crown Heights. Also accompanying the Rebbetzin was a ring given to her by her sister Sheina, who was murdered in Treblinka; the Rebbe instructed that the ring be interred with her. The last line on the Rebbetzin's *matzevah* (monument), after various honorifics about Chaya Mushka and her parents, mentions her sister, "the righteous Rebbetzin Sheina."

During the shiva, the Rebbe wrote a note to Rabbi Krinsky stating that since he was the sole inheritor of his wife's estate, he wanted to donate it in its entirety to Agudas Chasidei Chabad, the umbrella organization for worldwide Chabad-Lubavitch.

Among the first people the Rebbe arranged to see when shiva ended was Dr. Feldman, the last person to have had a sustained conversation with the Rebbetzin. During the meeting, he asked the doctor when the engagement party for his daughter would take place. Because of the Rebbetzin's death, the family was considering delaying it, but before Feldman could respond, the Rebbe continued: "The party should take place on the day it was originally scheduled to occur, and it should not be smaller than originally planned. In fact, it should be larger." In earlier years, the Rebbe had urged people to scale down engagement parties to hold down expenses. However, desiring now to honor his wife's last wishes, he urged Dr. Feldman to rent out a hall and hire musicians, something that in the normal order of events the Rebbe would never have proposed: "It should be done this way because this is how the Rebbetzin would have wanted it to be . . . and this is what would make the Rebbetzin happy."

Making the Rebbetzin happy had been one of the Rebbe's top priorities through the years of their marriage. The Rebbe once confided to Dr. Weiss how important it was for him to set aside time each day for a relaxed discussion with his wife over a cup of tea. He regarded this tea break as sacrosanct and said that it was "as important to him as putting on tefillin"—not a small acknowledgment from a man who transformed tefillin into the mitzvah most associated with Chabad.[13]

The Rebbetzin's devotion to him was no less intense. Even on the most demanding days, the Rebbetzin told several friends, she would never go to sleep until her husband returned home. And when he did return, and no matter what the hour, she would serve him the dinner she had prepared.[14] Danièle Gorlin Lassner, whose parents were friends of the Rebbetzin from her years in Paris, once had an extended afternoon meeting with the Rebbetzin, during which Gorlin Lassner related much information about the life she and husband were leading in South America. The Rebbetzin seemed fascinated by the details, then suddenly said, "You know, my husband comes home very late, sometimes two, three in the morning. When he comes home [tonight], I am going to have so much to say to him about this special visit."

Throughout their almost sixty years of marriage, they took great pride in each other. When Jules Lassner, Danièle's husband, subsequently had a brief encounter with the Rebbe, he told him, "After having met your wife, I understand the expression, 'Behind every great man, there must be a great woman,' and I met the great woman." As he said this, Lassner recalls, the Rebbe smiled from ear to ear.

Just as the Rebbe took pride in his wife's spiritual powers, the Rebbetzin took perhaps her greatest pride in her husband's steadfast faith and spirituality. In a discussion with a friend—shortly before the High Holidays—about the Rebbe's health, the Rebbetzin said, "My husband is not afraid of pain, my husband is afraid of Rosh Hashanah." [15]

As a postscript, Dr. Feldman's daughter, Sarah, and her husband, Levi Shemtov, did not have children for more than a decade. Objectively, the situation started to seem hopeless, but the couple never let go of the Rebbetzin's words about raising their children to speak Yiddish. The words had not been uttered as a blessing but as a simple statement, and spoke not of a single "child," but of "children." Finally, after twelve years, Sarah Shemtov become pregnant and gave birth in August 2001 to twins, a boy and a girl. The children were named Menachem Mendel and Chaya Mushka.

But sadly, the Rebbetzin and the Rebbe had always remained childless. Never spoken of in public, we can only imagine what a great tragedy and disappointment this was. In the early years of their marriage, one sees the blessing that they have children as an oft-recurring theme in the letters sent to them by both of their fathers. To cite but one example: On their first anniversary, the Sixth Rebbe sent them a *bracha* "from far in place but close in heart . . . that you be blessed with a generation of upright children who shall be blessed with all good." [16]

However, within a few years after they were married, these blessings were offered less frequently (in the case of the Rebbe's father, they went on a bit longer).

Among the most common blessings the Rebbe was called upon to dispense were for women to become pregnant. A story that has long circulated in Chabad relates that one of the movement's senior scholars, who was childless, repeatedly beseeched the Rebbe to bless him and his wife to have a child. The petitioner, convinced that God would accede to the Rebbe's demands, begged him to do so again and again. At one point, the Rebbe apparently said—according to some accounts, with tears in his eyes—"What can I do? I myself don't have."

While Chasidim shared in the unspoken pain of the childless Rebbe and Rebbetzin, the Rebbe's lack of children in no way seems to have shaken his followers' belief in the efficacy of his blessings. One can regard this, of course, as blind faith, or one can conclude, as does a

Jewish proverb based on a Talmudic teaching, that "a tzaddik can't give himself a blessing" but can give it to others.[17]

One Chasid, who insists on anonymity, relates that shortly after the birth of one of his sons in the early 1950s, he went to the Rebbe and, with the permission of his wife, offered their newborn child for adoption. The Rebbe waved off the suggestion and made it clear that he did not wish to pursue the matter.[18]

The blow of infertility was made more difficult by the fact that both the Rebbetzin and the Rebbe loved children. Many of the women who knew the Rebbetzin used to visit her with their children in tow. The Rebbetzin would make preparations for these special young guests and had appropriate games and child-friendly food available (Boston cream pie being a particular favorite). She would often ask children to call her *doda*, the Hebrew word for "aunt," and hold the young ones on her knees.

Few anecdotes suggest with such poignancy the desire she must have had for a child of her own as Louise Hager's recollection of the time she had sent her six-year-old son, Mechel, along with her husband on a visit to the Rebbetzin. Hager, who lived in London, was nervous the whole day, fearing that the young boy might break something in the Rebbetzin's house or that some other problem would occur.

That evening, when she spoke to the Rebbetzin, she was reassured and happy to learn that all had gone smoothly. In fact, as it was Chanukah, the Rebbetzin had gotten Mechel a dreidel filled with candy balls. And she didn't just give it to him as a gift, but also spun the dreidel with him. She repeatedly reassured Hager that nothing had been broken and that "it was just wonderful." She then said, "He was so adorable, and I just had to do something. I hope you don't mind." Hager's mind raced. What could the Rebbetzin have done that Hager could possibly have minded? The Rebbetzin continued: "I just had to put my arms around him and give him a kiss."

When Yosef Yitzchok Holtzman was a boy, he visited the Rebbe and Rebbetzin's house with his parents. In his youthful innocence, he asked the Rebbetzin, "Why do you and the Rebbe need such a big house if there aren't any children here?" Before the Rebbetzin could say anything, the boy reasoned aloud, "It must be that there were once children here and they grew up and got married. So now only you are left here."

The Rebbetzin answered, "That's right. All Chasidim are the Rebbe's children," a response that perhaps mystified the child, though not the parents.

Denied children of their own, the Rebbe and Rebbetzin invested their emotions in hundreds and hundreds of surrogate children, the *shluchim* who took the message of Chabad into the world. That the couple's perception of the *shluchim* as their children was very real came across most powerfully years later, on the night the Rebbetzin died. Instead of requesting Rabbi Krinsky to immediately prepare some kind of general statement announcing her death, the Rebbe's first request to Krinsky was, "We must tell the *shluchim*. We must tell the children."

Chapter 26

DEVOTION BEYOND MEASURE

"WE ARE TRYING TO USE ALL OUR STRATEGIES TO KEEP
[MY MOTHER] FROM LEARNING ABOUT THIS."

"MY SON HAS JUST LEFT MY HOME. HE VISITS ME DAILY AND TWICE
ON FRIDAY. HE MAKES MY LIFE MUCH BETTER, AND AS THEY SAY
HERE [IN AMERICA], MAKES ME FEEL BETTER. HIS VISITS GIVE ME
LIFE FOR THE TWENTY-FOUR HOURS UNTIL TOMORROW'S VISIT,
G-D WILLING."
—*Rebbetzin Chana Schneerson, writing in her diary
about her son, the Rebbe*

A most unusual event associated with the Rebbe was the manner in which he handled the news of the sudden death in 1952 of Yisrael Aryeh Leib, his younger brother (normally referred to as Aryeh Leib) and the youngest of his parents' three children. Aryeh Leib was only forty-five at the time of his death. He and the Rebbe had been very close growing up, and their bond had continued during the Rebbe's years in Berlin, where Aryeh Leib had come to study as well.

With the rise of the Nazis in Germany, Ramash and his wife moved to Paris, where he continued his university studies. Aryeh Leib moved to Tel Aviv, in what was then Palestine. At one point, he opened a clothing store, at another time he managed a lending library. We also find a number of letters in which the Rebbe asks Moshe Gourary, one of the leading Chabad Chasidim in Israel, to forward to his brother money, which he, Menachem Mendel (he was not yet Rebbe), would pay back.

Like his brother, Aryeh Leib had a powerful intellect, and in 1950 he left Israel and moved to Liverpool, England, to study for a doctorate in mathematics. He was in the final stages of completing his work when, on May 8, 1952, he died suddenly of a heart attack.

To the Rebbe, the death must have come as a great shock. His youngest brother, DovBer, had been murdered by the Nazis; now his only remaining sibling was dead. Well aware that such news could utterly devastate his mother, the Rebbe made a decision to conceal this information from her. Jewish tradition maintains that withholding such information when a person is ill or fragile is permitted, perhaps even mandated. The Rebbe seems to have concluded that finding out about the death of yet another of her three children, and having earlier lost her husband under very difficult circumstances, might trigger a physical or emotional collapse. As he wrote his aunt Rochel Schneerson a short time later, "My mother knows nothing of this matter and we are trying to use all stratagems to keep her from learning about this, because of her health." In yet another letter from the same period, he mentions that all of her acquaintances have been asked not to mention the death in any letters written to her.[1]

What is most unusual, though, is that the Rebbe maintained this concealment for the remaining twelve years of his mother's life. Doing so necessitated his carrying out a series of ruses that started immediately upon learning of his brother's death.

Because the Rebbe's brother had adopted the surname Gurari (when he fled the Soviet Union he used a false passport so as to conceal that he came from the prominent and persecuted Schneerson family), it was somewhat easier to conceal that it was the Rebbe's brother who had died. During shiva, the Rebbe observed the traditional week of mourning without publicizing that he was doing so. This was an audacious decision since it meant precluding his mother from observing shiva. During the week of mourning, the Rebbe continued his daily visits to his mother (throughout the seventeen years that she lived in the United States, the Rebbe visited his mother daily); we can imagine what a strain it must have been to act in a normal, upbeat manner during the very week that his brother had died. As Jewish law dictates not to wear leather shoes during shiva, a follower painted a pair of canvas shoes black so that the Rebbe's mother would not notice the casual and uncharacteristic footwear he was sporting.

Starting at the same time, the Rebbe had a copy made of his mother's mail key and arranged to have her mail checked daily before being redeposited in her mailbox. Any condolence cards or letters that made reference to his brother's death were withheld from her. The Rebbe even wrote a number of letters to his mother in his brother's handwriting. Meanwhile, those who were in contact with her by telephone were instructed not to make mention of what had happened. Just how difficult this concealment was for the Rebbetzin as well is reflected in a comment she made to Rabbi Bentzion Shemtov: "This was the only time in my life that I did not state the truth."

When reading of this, it becomes hard to imagine that the Rebbe had any notion at the outset that this concealment would go on for over a decade, until his mother's death in 1964. Perhaps he initially thought that his mother would live a shorter span of time and he did not want to so demoralize her final years. And perhaps he just reacted instinctively in choosing to withhold the information until a better time. However, such a time to inform her of this news never came.

Even with the Rebbe's occasional writing of letters in his brother's name, how could such concealment persist for so long? After all, in the early 1950s, it was possible, albeit very expensive, to make international phone calls, and certainly one might expect a son to come visit his mother every few years. Here, too, the Rebbe came up with a stratagem, accompanied by a letter to his mother that he wrote in his brother's name. Rabbi Chaskel Besser, who was friendly with the Rebbe's mother, learned of the stratagem while visiting her. He mentioned to Rebbetzin Chana that he would soon be traveling to Europe. In the past, she had always urged him to stop off in London and see Aryeh Leib, but this time she said, "You don't have to go anymore." Besser assumed at first that she had learned of her son's death, but she hadn't. Rather, she explained, "He wrote me that he got a position [in England] with the Atomic Energy Commission; nobody's allowed to see him. So you cannot see him anymore."[2]

Did Rebbetzin Chana ever suspect that something was awry? Most visitors thought not, but Hadassah Carlebach recalls that while Rebbetzin Chana never referred to Aryeh Leib as dead, at a certain point beginning shortly after his death, she simply stopped speaking of him. Hadassah Carlebach long remained quite certain that Chana was aware of what had happened to her son and was also aware of what the Rebbe was doing, but simply said nothing; remaining quiet was somehow less painful. Other visitors were equally convinced that the Rebbetzin really did believe her son to be alive. Although it seems highly unlikely that such a concealment could proceed undetected for so long, a recently discovered diary kept by Rebbetzin Chana until the end of her life makes it clear that though she felt deep sadness at not having seen her son for so long, she did in fact continue to believe that he was alive.[3]

However one assesses this story—and unlike other stories about the Rebbe, I know of no instances of Lubavitcher Chasidim who have tried to emulate this behavior of the Rebbe—it makes clear the depth of the Rebbe's devotion to his mother.

Just how difficult the act of hiding this news from his mother so as to spare her pain must have been for the Rebbe is reflected in a later incident. In 1975, a little over ten years after his mother's death, and well over twenty years since his brother's demise, the Rebbe solicited the assistance of Professor Paul Rosenbloom, a mathematician, in examining the writings his brother had left behind. He wanted Rosenbloom to assess the academic value of these writings and to determine whether they made a significant intellectual contribution. The Rebbe did not initially disclose to Rosenbloom the identity of the writer because he did not wish the professor to be influenced in any way. Only after Rosenbloom had read through the material, with which he was quite impressed (though he felt he needed to see more of the writings), did the Rebbe disclose the writer's identity. Rosenbloom was startled at learning this information. The Rebbe then twice made a remarkable statement, referring to the death of his brother some ten years earlier. But his brother had died more than twenty years earlier.

The misstatement seems to suggest that as long as he continued to invent strategies to convince his mother that Aryeh Leib was alive, he continued, at some level, to feel so himself.[4]

"Do this without publicizing the matter."

Rabbi Menachem Mendel, in the years just before he became Rebbe, adopted a similar strategy in a somewhat similar circumstance. On July 28, 1949 (2 Av 5709), he received a letter from a Mr. Mordechai Unrad, informing him that Unrad had been incarcerated in the Treblinka death camp with Mendel Horenstein, Menachem Mendel's brother-in-law and the husband of his wife's sister Sheina. In a letter he wrote the same day, he asked Unrad to supply him with as many details as he could about Mendel Horenstein and his wife (whom he refers to as Sonya) and Mendel's mother, "where they were located in their last days, what happened with them, the exact dates of their *yahrtzeits*, and what happened to Mendel's mother, and when they did arrive in Treblinka. The more comprehensive particular details you write to me, the more grateful I will be to you."[5]

Unrad turned out to be a fount of information, though all of it was tragic. On August 28, 1942, a *kapo* had passed to Mendel Horenstein a note from his wife, informing him that his mother had been taken a day earlier to the gas chambers. The same *kapo* informed Horenstein on September 14, 1942, that on the preceding day, the second day of Rosh Hashanah, his wife had been taken to the gas chambers. On October 5, 1942, when Unrad returned from his work detail, Menachem Mendel Horenstein was not in the barracks, and others who were in the same work detail as he reported that he had been taken from their place of work, along with other Jews, and sent directly to the gas chambers.[6]

Three and a half weeks after hearing this from Unrad, on August 22, 1949, Rabbi Menachem Mendel wrote to Rabbi Chanoch Hendel Havlin, a member of the Lubavitch community in Jerusalem and a man who had a close connection with Mendel Horenstein's sister, Rachel Landau. Menachem Mendel was convinced of the accuracy of the information supplied him by Unrad and felt that he could now establish accurately the day of death for all three Horensteins; Sheina, for example, had been murdered on the second day of Rosh Hashanah 1942, and from that point on Ramash recited Kaddish for her on that day.

He advised Havlin to exercise caution in telling Mendel Horenstein's sister of what had been learned, and to do so only if he thought her health would not be adversely affected. In any case, Havlin should arrange that *yahrtzeit* be observed for the three victims on the appropriate dates, but he then imposed the following caveat: "Do this without publicizing the matter because the household of my revered father-in-law, the Rebbe, Shlita, knows nothing about this."[7]

Did Menachem Mendel *ever* share this news with his father-in-law? It seems very unlikely. For one thing, if he withheld the news of his brother's death from his mother out of concern that it could be injurious to her health, he would certainly fear the same concerning his father-in-law, who was even more frail. Referring to the Frierdiker Rebbe's stroke and incapacitation, one Chasid of the time said, "The world has become so dark that we cannot hear the Rebbe's words."[8] Also, the Frierdiker Rebbe died less than a year and a half after the Rebbe learned this news, and it is difficult to imagine an appropriate time that the Rebbe would have found to tell the Frierdiker Rebbe this news.

Still, we know that the Rebbe shared the news with his wife and sister-in-law, and we can assume that he did so at some point with his mother-in-law (who survived her husband for more than two decades), though we don't know when.

Rabbi Krinsky commented to me on several occasions that the Rebbe had broad shoulders, a willingness to assume responsibility for actions that others would shirk. This was certainly manifest in many instances, for example, in the dangerous battle to keep Judaism alive in the Soviet Union, in the struggle to keep the Jewish community in Crown Heights from moving out, and in his willingness to take on virtually the entire organized Jewish community on the issue of school prayer. But when we see how he bore all the grief of his brother's loss to protect his mother— and he carried the same burden for his father-in-law—we understand just how far the Rebbe's broad shoulders could widen.

Part Eight

"It Is

THE BOOKS

That Were

VICTORIOUS"

Chapter 27

THE COURTROOM BATTLE THAT
TORE APART A FAMILY

"[The books] belonged to the Chasidim, because my father
belonged to the Chasidim."
—Rebbetzin Chaya Mushka Schneerson

24th of Adar I 5706 [February 25, 1946]

To the renowned scholar, Dr. Alexander Marx,

Greetings and blessings!

So began a letter from the Frierdiker Rebbe to Professor Alexander
Marx, head of the library at the Jewish Theological Seminary:

*After the Nazi occupation of Poland in [1939], the evildoers confiscated several
boxes full of aged manuscripts and valuable books which had been kept in my library
in Otwock [Poland].*

*Manuscripts: Three large boxes full of aged manuscripts were confiscated, as
mentioned, by the Nazis. Among these manuscripts are some from the author of the
Tanya and from the five generations of Chabad leaders coming after him, during
a period of about 150 years. These manuscripts are on the subject of Chasidism
and also halacha [Jewish law], among them many manuscripts—letters and
correspondence—which are a packed treasure-house on the subject of our people's
history in the land of Russia during the past two centuries.*

These manuscripts are registered under the names of the Rabbis, members of Agudas Chasidei Chabad, Rabbi Israel Jacobson, and his son-in-law Rabbi Shlomo Zalman Hecht, both American citizens [who are] the official owners of this property.

Books: Several thousand books, among them many ancient books of great value and very rare. These books are the property of Agudas Chasidei Chabad of America and Canada. . . . In order that the State Department should work energetically to locate these manuscripts and books in order to return them to their owners, the State Department needs to understand that these manuscripts and books are a great religious treasure, a possession of the nation, which have historical and scientific value.

Therefore, I turn to you with a great request, that as a renowned authority on the subject, you should please write a letter to the State Department to testify on the great value of these manuscripts and books for the Jewish people in general and particularly for the Jewish community of the United States to whom this great possession belongs.

The above letter makes quite clear just how precious the Frierdiker Rebbe's library was to him and, as he believed, to the whole Jewish people. Yet, in the years following his death in 1950, little attention had been paid to the library outside of very limited scholarly circles. (Rabbi Menachem Mendel had already begun assembling another library for Merkos in 1941.) The library itself consisted of forty thousand volumes and was set up in several rooms of the basement at 770. From the time of the Frierdiker Rebbe's arrival in the United States until the early 1980s, the library was supervised by Rabbi Chaim Lieberman, a man who had worked for decades as a top aide to the Sixth Rebbe and was a world-renowned expert on Jewish books. Due to old age, Rabbi Lieberman's day-to-day involvement in the administration of the library greatly decreased, and the direction of the library was assigned to Rabbi Yitzchak Wilhelm.

In early 1985, in the library's darkened rooms, Rabbi Wilhelm started to notice gaps appearing on the shelves containing the rarest and most valuable books. Over the coming weeks, the gaps increased and Wilhelm reported this to Shalom D. Levine, the director of the Rebbe's library. Reports also reached Chabad from Yehoshua Zirkind, a Chabad Chasid and rare-book dealer in Israel, that he had come across books from the Chabad library for sale. Since all books in the library at 770 were marked and stamped with the library's emblem, it was easy to tell their source. When efforts were made to try to determine the identity of the person behind the sales, they met with no success.

At the same time, Chaim Baruch Halberstam, a man of considerable technological sophistication (he was the mastermind behind the sophisticated worldwide telephone broadcasts of the Rebbe's *farbrengens*), was working on an extensive repair job then taking place in the library. When he heard reports about the missing books, he installed a buzzer system and arranged that it would alert him if anyone entered the library during the hours it was closed. The buzzer system was always turned off during Shabbat and on one weekend, by the time it was reactivated, more books had been taken.

Halberstam, who would often help the Rebbetzin with various matters related to her and her husband's house, told the Rebbetzin what he had heard, that there were reports of books going missing from the library and being sold overseas. The Rebbetzin advised him to set up a surveillance camera in the library, a procedure that was far less common in 1985 than it is today. Halberstam followed the Rebbetzin's advice, and for the first few weeks nobody appeared on the video. After some time, the day after the holiday of Shavuot, in late May 1985, a man was seen taking books off the shelves, examining them, and putting some into suitcases. Neither Wilhelm nor Levin recognized the man. They asked Halberstam to examine the video; he immediately identified the man as Barry Gourary, the Rebbe's nephew.

The three men were all shocked, and Halberstam informed the Rebbetzin (Barry was the son of her sister Chana). The Rebbetzin then told her husband. It is not known precisely what the Rebbe's response was when his wife informed him of what had occurred, but we do know that he called in Rabbi Gourary, Barry's father, and told him what had happened. Anxious to rectify the situation and to keep the matter private, the Rebbe asked Gourary (known in Chabad circles as Rashag) to approach his son and arrange to have the books returned. He warned Rashag that if the books were not returned by 12 Tammuz (June 30, 1985), he would be compelled to talk about the issue at a *farbrengen,* since it related to the entire community.[1] Rashag approached his son and attempted to convince him to return the books. We can assume that Rashag spoke about the issue to his wife, Chana, as well, in both cases without success. When the books were not returned, the Rebbe delivered the speech he had promised: "The Frierdiker Rebbe made a clear self-sacrifice [on behalf of his] Torah books and manuscripts which are his living legacy.[2] This applies to every single book and manuscript [in the library], some which he had written himself." The Rebbe continued speaking without mentioning Barry or any specific details of the case. "As time passes"—his voice was rising now—"the Frierdiker Rebbe becomes *more* connected, not *less*, to all his Torah books and manuscripts." Increasing in volume almost to a yell, the Rebbe's voice now cried out, "The books will remain my father-in-law's living legacy and his very essence to the End of Time."[3]

Except for a few select individuals (among them, those who worked in the library), no one in attendance knew what the Rebbe was referring to, though his ill-concealed unhappiness made it clear that he was speaking about a very serious offense.[4]

"Why does he come like a ganoff *[thief] in the middle of the night?"*

At one time, Barry Gourary and his uncle had been very close. When Barry was six, and his father and grandfather were away for an extended trip to Eretz Yisrael and the United States, Barry had lived with his mother and grandmother near Rabbi Menachem Mendel and his wife in Berlin. During those months, he saw a great deal of his uncle, and a close relationship developed between them. He commented on several occasions that over the coming decades, there were years he was closer to his uncle than to his father. He admired, among other things, Ramash's secular knowledge. Some older Chasidim recall seeing Ramash studying mathematics with his nephew; this was after they had both come to the United States. Barry eventually went on to do graduate work in physics.

But all this goodwill seems to have evaporated in the pivotal year following the Frierdiker Rebbe's death. Barry felt that his uncle had orchestrated a campaign to become Rebbe and that his father, who, in Barry's eyes, was definitely qualified to assume this role, had been slandered by the Rebbe's supporters. He seems to have suspected that this came about either at Ramash's instigation or, at the very least, that Ramash did not stop it.[5]

After Ramash's elevation to the leadership of the movement, relations between uncle and nephew deteriorated quickly. Two years later, in 1953, when Barry married, he did not invite his uncle to the wedding.[6]

In the early to mid-1980s, Gourary, a management consultant, found himself in need of money. He had had little income over the preceding years and was now in his early sixties, a difficult age at which to be caught in a cash crunch. Apparently, Chana Gourary told her son that there was a valuable asset in the family that could be tapped—the books in her father's library—which she regarded as her sister's and her legacy. Chana was well aware that Barry's selling books from the library could trigger controversy; however, she told her son, she had discussed this issue on several occasions with her sister Chaya Mushka, the Frierdiker Rebbe's only other living heir. She said that the Rebbetzin had told her that if Barry wanted to take books he should do so, but *bli pirsum*, without publicity. "Let him take as many as he wants" (we shall soon see that the Rebbetzin vehemently denied that she said such a thing). According to Barry, his mother told him that his aunt also said something to the effect that "I have no heirs. I myself will not study these books. Let Barry go ahead and take as many as he wants."[7]

Shortly after his speech at the *farbrengen*, the Rebbe convened a meeting of some of the leaders of Agudas Chasidei Chabad (the movement's umbrella organization, of which the Rebbe was president), among them Rabbi Yehuda Krinsky and Rabbi Avraham Shemtov, the two Chabad figures who emerged as the Rebbe's representatives on the case. The Rebbe at that point revealed the details of what had happened and Barry's refusal to return the books, insisting that half of them belonged to his mother, and through her to him. The Rebbe asked rhetorically: "Why [then] does he come like a *ganoff* [thief] in the middle of the night?" All those present were very upset, stunned by the revelation of what had happened and at the intensity of the Rebbe's distress. Despite the lateness of the hour, at 2:00 a.m. Rabbi Krinsky called Nat Lewin, one of America's most highly regarded attorneys, waking up the soundly sleeping lawyer. He informed Lewin of what had been discovered on the videotape and asked if he thought that the police should be called to stop further sale of the books.

Lewin, shocked by the account, responded: "What would you do?" Krinsky reiterated that Barry had no right to remove books, let alone sell them, and Lewin asked, "On what basis is he doing it?" Krinsky explained that Barry claimed partial ownership of the library. Lewin advised against calling in the police, which could turn into a major spectacle. Rather, he advised going to a *din Torah* (a hearing before a Jewish court) or to a secular court to establish ownership of the library. The call ended with the understanding that Rabbi Krinsky would come to Lewin's office in Washington, DC, the following day.

When Krinsky arrived, he brought with him the relevant passage from the *Shulchan Aruch*, the sixteenth-century Code of Jewish Law, and commentaries on it, outlining the instances in which it is permitted by Jewish law to go to a non-Jewish court; normally, Jewish law insists on disputes within the Jewish community being resolved by Jewish courts in accordance with Jewish law, and not by non-Jewish courts in accordance with non-Jewish law. Krinsky told Lewin that the Rebbe had insisted that he show Lewin the passages from the *Shulchan Aruch*; the Rebbe wanted the lawyer to understand that the decision to pursue redress in a secular court, and not a *beit din* (Jewish court), was not reached lightly.

The two dominant concerns were bringing the sale of the books to an immediate halt and then recovering the volumes that had been sold as well as those that were still in Barry's possession. Lewin understood that the first priority—stopping the sale of the books—could only be achieved by going to a secular court, for whatever a *beit din* might eventually conclude about the books' ownership, it would lack the power to *compel* Barry to stop selling the books before a verdict was reached. *Only* a secular court, which has at its disposal law enforcement agents to enforce its rulings, could immediately achieve this.

Lewin also learned at this meeting that Barry lived in Montclair, New Jersey, where he had brought the books after taking them from the library in Brooklyn. Crossing state lines with property that Chabad charged had been removed illegally raised the possibility of turning this into a federal case, a prospect Lewin welcomed: "I personally have much more confidence in the federal courts than I do in state courts, and they generally have better judges."[8]

Rabbi Krinsky authorized Lewin to prepare the papers as soon as possible and to go into federal court to secure a restraining order to stop Barry from selling any more books. Chabad's intention was to achieve this goal, have the books still in Barry's possession impounded, and to then let the ownership of the books be determined by a Jewish religious court.

Shortly after the meeting with Krinsky, Lewin heard from Rabbi Avraham Shemtov, who told him that the well-known Philadelphia attorney Jerome Shestack (a future president of the American Bar Association) would be working with him on the case, a welcome development. (Shestack had already worked with Shemtov some years earlier in securing the release of a large portion of the Frierdiker Rebbe's library that had been stuck in Poland during the war.) Lewin now selected Seth Waxman, an up-and-coming young lawyer from his own office, to help prepare the papers for submission to the court (some years later, during the Clinton administration, Waxman was appointed solicitor general of the United States). Within two days, a complaint was filed in the Federal District Court in Brooklyn.

Federal courts use a lottery system to choose judges to preside over cases; a clerk spins a wheel and pulls out the name of a judge. Under this procedure, Justice Charles Sifton was selected to serve in the case that now became known as *Agudas Chasidei Chabad v. Gourary*.

Because Chabad's first concern was to halt further sale of the books, Lewin immediately went to court to seek such a ruling. Sifton was on vacation, and Judge Leo Glasser was assigned to deal with the cases of judges not present. Glasser summoned the lawyers into his chambers and, after hearing the basic outline of the dispute, commented: "I don't understand why you folks are here. I think this ought to go to a rabbinic court." Lewin then outlined for Glasser the relevant issue at this point, the desire that the books still in Barry's possession be impounded, so that no more books could be sold until a legal ruling on the library's ownership was issued. Once this occurred, Lewin said, Chabad would be willing, indeed very much preferred, to take the case before a Jewish court.

At this point, Alvin Hellerstein, one of Barry's two attorneys, interjected that his client had no intention of having the case decided by a Jewish court (perhaps Barry feared that a court comprised of rabbis would be biased in favor of his uncle, who was so prominent a rabbi): "The case is now in court, and we want the court to make a decision on who owns the whole library. We claim that it belongs to the family, and not the community."[9] Hellerstein also announced that Barry's mother, Chana Gourary, was joining the case alongside her son.

Over the next months, the Chabad legal team developed the strategy they would employ throughout the case, at the heart of which was the contention that the library belonged to the Chabad movement, represented by the board of Agudas Chasidei Chabad, and not to the Frierdiker Rebbe (or, for that matter, the current Rebbe) individually.[10] The two lead lawyers, along with Rabbis Krinsky and Shemtov, met with the Rebbe to discuss their approach.

The Rebbe made known his belief that one of the documents unearthed at the library—a 1946 letter from his father-in-law to Alexander Marx, the chief librarian at the Jewish Theological Seminary library (and which appears at the start of this chapter)—should be treated by the legal team as the key document in proving that the Frierdiker Rebbe did not regard the books in the library as his personal property (the Rebbe by no means insisted that they follow his suggested strategy but that they consider it as they plotted their legal strategy).[11] Lewin was struck at the meeting by how carefully the Rebbe had read through every document that had been filed in the case. He also recalls learning around this time that when the Rebbe heard that some Lubavitchers were trying to influence Lewin, an observant Jew but not a Chabadnik, to become more involved in Chabad activities, such as attending *farbrengens*, he commented in annoyance: "Let the lawyer remain a lawyer and don't try to make a Chasid out of the lawyer" (*Luz der lawyer bleiben a lawyer un macht nisht a Chasid fun der lawyer*).

Judge Glasser granted Chabad's request and ordered that the books in Barry's possession be impounded until the case was resolved; some

450 books were taken from Barry's house and brought to a bonded ware-house. Barry subsequently revealed that prior to Judge Glasser's order, he had sold about 100 of the books, for which he had been paid $186,000. The most valuable was an illuminated eighteenth-century Haggadah, known as the Kittsee Haggadah, which Barry sold to a book dealer in Switzerland for $69,000. The dealer in turn sold it to a private collector in Zurich for almost $150,000.[12] In line with Barry's claim that he was in the legal right in all that he had done, he insisted on all sales being carried out in a manner that was totally aboveboard, payment by check, and no cash transactions.

Even before all of the details of Barry's transactions became known, the Rebbe instructed various individuals to locate and buy back all of the books that they could locate. Also, at the Rebbe's insistence, Chabad issued a standing offer to fully reimburse those who had purchased the books taken by Barry. In the end, it cost the movement $432,000 to buy back the books that had been sold (Chabad also had legal fees in excess of $200,000).

In preparation for the trial, various parties to the controversy were deposed, among them Barry Gourary, Chana Gourary, Chaim Lieberman,[13] and Rebbetzin Chaya Mushka Schneerson. Both Rabbis Krinsky and Shemtov were opposed to the idea of the Rebbetzin being deposed. They were aware that depositions, like courtroom testimony in general, can be unpleasant and were not always respectful. In consequence, Krinsky told the Rebbe that they would do all they could so that the Rebbetzin would not need to give a deposition.

To their surprise, the Rebbe was not worried over such a prospect: "No, we don't have to avoid it. She'll come through with flying colors. You'll see." Twenty-five years later, Krinsky still recalls his surprise at the Rebbe's mild reaction, but it was clear that he was completely confident in his wife's ability to face off against Barry's lawyers.

But then, Barry's legal team made it known that they intended to depose the Rebbe as well. This time, Krinsky and Shemtov found themselves even more upset. The thought of someone of the Rebbe's stature being subjected to a withering cross-examination, with lawyers looking to catch and magnify seeming or possible discrepancies, bothered them no end. But here, too, their anxieties exceeded those of the Rebbe: "You know, if they're so persistent, fine. I'll do it. Let them set up a date," the Rebbe told Krinsky. But this was a prospect Krinsky refused to countenance: "I said to the Rebbe with all the boldness I could muster, 'It's not going to happen.' I never said anything like that to the Rebbe, and would never speak like that to him in the normal course of events. But I just felt it. I just couldn't bear him consenting to be deposed and all the ramifications thereof. The Rebbe sort of looked at me, and it was left at that." Nat Lewin's recollections of the Rebbe's response to the prospect of being deposed differ somewhat from those of Rabbi Krinsky. He recalls the Rebbe as very strongly opposing the possibility of this happening. But Lewin's account is fully consistent with Krinsky's recollection that the Rebbe never for a moment considered dropping the suit to avoid a deposition.

Eventually, after some courtroom sparring, the request for the deposition was dropped by Barry's lawyers. One Chabad source has speculated that the request for the deposition was perhaps intended as a pressure point to force Chabad to make a deal with Barry. But this seems unlikely, since Barry's legal team never tried to negotiate a settlement. Rather, both sides argued that the battle was simply over who owned the library.

At the deposition of Chana Gourary on November 18, 1985, she was adamant in insisting that her father always regarded the library as his: "that I heard from him . . . several times. . . . He referred to the library as being his own property" (pages 50–51; the page citations here and following are all based on the official transcripts of the depositions). Nat Lewin continued pressing this issue from a variety of angles. "Did you discuss with Chaim Lieberman the ownership of the library at any time between the time your father died and the time that your mother died?" Chana Gourary responded: "There was nothing to talk about. It's my father's" (pages 62–63). And, a moment later, "It's clear that it's my father's library . . . an inheritance, belonging to my sister and me" (page 63). Consistent with her belief that half the library was hers, Chana Gourary also revealed that she had signed a document asserting: "By right, I own 50% of the library. I give all my interests in and my rights to the whole library to my son, Barry S. Gourary, as a gift" (page 87).

It was in the course of this deposition that Chana Gourary offered the rather shocking claim that her mother, Rebbetzin Nechama Dina, the mother as well of Rebbetzin Chaya Mushka, regarded herself as the *only* Lubavitcher Rebbetzin, and thereby, by implication, did not regard Menachem Mendel Schneerson as the Seventh Rebbe. Furthermore, Chana Gourary made it clear that she concurred in her mother's supposed self-assessment: "All I know is that she was the only Lubavitcher Rebbetzin" (page 34).

QUESTION: "And how about your sister, is she not a Lubavitcher Rebbetzin?"
CHANA GOURARY: "I don't know. . . ."
QUESTION: "Do you recognize that your brother-in-law is the Lubavitcher Rebbe?"
CHANA GOURARY: "I won't answer that."
QUESTION: "Do you consider yourself a Lubavitcher Chasidische [feminine for Chasid]?
CHANA GOURARY: "I held from my father" [i.e., I accepted my father as Rebbe].
QUESTION: "And the present Rebbe?"
CHANA GOURARY: "No" (pages 34–35).

Rebbetzin Gourary explained that in the years following the Frierdiker Rebbe's death, women used to confer with her mother "as they used to go in to my father. They used to go in the same way with my mother. She was a genuine Rebbetzin" (pages 37–38).

QUESTION: "So do I understand your testimony to be, Mrs. Gourary, that between 1950 and 1971, when your mother died, you viewed her as the authority for Lubavitch . . . in place of your father?"
CHANA GOURARY: "Yes" (page 38).

In light of Chana Gourary's testimony, one can understand the Rebbe's statement to a meeting of Agudas Chasidei Chabad that "this is a war against the Alter Rebbe and all the Rebbes. It should be understood that the conflict is not over the *seforim* but rather *oif'n benkel*" ("over the seat"). In other words, the great wrong that was done was not simply the taking of the books, but a desecration of the whole idea of *what* a Lubavitcher Rebbe is and *how* a Rebbe acts. Does a Rebbe's life and legacy come to an abrupt end with his physical demise, whereupon his possessions are divided and sold to the highest bidder? Do his writings and books no longer continue to play a key role for the movement beyond his death? And would a Rebbe lie by writing a letter asserting that his library was the possession of the Jewish people (see page 386), but then pass it on as a personal inheritance to his family members?[14]

The Rebbe knew firsthand of the Frierdiker Rebbe's extraordinarily high regard for the books he had acquired, and the Rebbe spoke of the effort to break up his library as a second funeral for his father-in-law. That, from the Rebbe's perspective, the issue was not the monetary value of the books but maintaining the integrity of his father-in-law's collection—which the Rebbe considered to be an extension of his father-in-law's very life on earth—is reflected in the fact that he wanted every book returned, even some that booksellers regarded as having little monetary value. The fact that it was part of his father-in-law's library, that it was a book the Frierdiker Rebbe might well have handled and studied, was sufficient to make the book invaluable. For the Rebbe, the Frierdiker Rebbe lived. As he said at the *farbrengen*, "God forbid that he be just a leader of the past. He is alive, and he and his children will remain alive until *moshiach tzeiten* (the Messiah comes)." Barry, by taking books of his grandfather and selling them, by breaking up his grandfather's library and bringing it to an end, was metaphorically killing the Frierdiker Rebbe.

While Barry did not see himself as engaged in such an assault, this was, I believe, the fundamental issue from the Rebbe's perspective far more than the fight "over the seat." In any case, by 1985, when the *seforim* case exploded, more than three decades had passed since the Ramash's ascension to Rebbe, and I am certain that the Gourarys were well aware that they had irrevocably lost the battle over the movement's leadership (within approximately a year of Rabbi Menachem Mendel becoming Rebbe, Rabbi Gourary fully acknowledged his leadership; it was his wife and son who seemed troubled by this). Although both Chana and Barry Gourary seem to have retained a sense of personal bitterness—refusing to acknowledge Menachem Mendel Schneerson as the Rebbe—they also knew that they had no hope of removing the wildly popular Rebbe from his position. What they apparently wanted now was the one thing they hoped they could still get—the money—that Barry apparently needed.

During the course of her testimony, Chana Gourary related her version of the conversation that had transpired between her sister and herself concerning the library's ownership. According to Gourary, she told her sister, "I must have money. I would like to sell some *seforim* from the library," and her sister responded that she could do so: "You may take as much as you'd like, whatever you'd like, and in the best of health. You can do whatever you like with it" (page 71).

Barry expressed his belief as well that the books were his, or rather half his. To Jerome Shestack's question: "Mr. Gourary, is it your contention that the entire library at 770 Eastern Parkway belongs to your mother and aunt?" Barry answered, "Yes."

"And the Lubavitch movement has absolutely no right to possession, title, or interest in the books in the library?"

"Yes."

"Is it your contention that the present Rebbe, Menachem Mendel Schneerson, also has no legitimate interest or right to these books?"

"That is right."

"And the entire library belongs to two old ladies in their eighties to do with as they wish, no matter what their whims may be?"

The sarcastic tone of this last question prompted Brian Cogan, one of Barry's two attorneys, to note his "objection to the form [of the question]," though he instructed Barry to answer.

"That is my understanding," Barry said.

"That is your contention?" Shestack pressed.

"Yes" (pages 3–5).

As Barry subsequently testified, he had a key to the library from the time he was a teenager and had been given one by his grandfather. The Frierdiker Rebbe's library was located at 770, the movement's headquarters and the building in which Barry's parents lived. Over a period of months, Barry would come to visit his parents and then, late at night, go into one or both of the two libraries; the larger was located in the basement and the smaller in the office of his late grandfather, a room that had been left untouched since his grandfather's death. He would bring suitcases or paper bags and fill them with books. Because his parents were the only ones then living at 770, and because he entered the library at night, the likelihood of his running into anyone while gathering the books was nil. Even if someone did see him leaving with packages, no one would suspect that Barry Gourary—whose father was head of the United Lubavitcher Yeshiva and whose uncle was the Rebbe—was doing anything wrong; people would likely assume that he was simply carrying items that were his or that had been given him by his parents. At times, in fact, he asked yeshiva students to help him carry some of these suitcases. The students, unaware of what they were carrying, eagerly agreed to assist Barry, the nephew and grandson of Rebbes.

Over the next months, Barry started having books appraised and sold. He offered several different accounts to the appraisers of how he had acquired what were clearly rare and valuable volumes. On some occasions, he said that he had acquired the books from the estate of an old man who had died in New Jersey; at other times, that the books belonged to his father-in-law. To an appraiser who seems to have been aware of his family background, he said that the books were a personal gift from his grandfather.

What is clear is that there must have been ambivalence in Barry regarding what he was doing. On the one hand, the fact that he came to take the books late at night, at a time when there was no chance anyone else would be in the library, suggests that he knew his activities might be regarded as thievery (even though he did not regard it as such). Chana Gourary seems to have anticipated the possibility of such an accusation by assuring Barry that his aunt had approved of his taking the books as long as he did so "without publicity." Still, the fact that his mother did not speak of this matter in the presence of her husband must have seemed odd. One would think that the "without publicity" restriction would not apply to Rabbi Gourary, Barry's father. But clearly it did.

Indeed, Rabbi Gourary only learned of the taking of the books much later, at which time he expressed strong opposition to his son having done so, and pleaded with him to return the volumes. The fact that his mother excluded her husband from the discussion concerning the books must have underscored to Barry that what he was doing was, at the very least, highly controversial.[15]

At another point in the deposition Shestack asked Barry: "Did you ever think that you might be accused of stealing these books?"

"No, remember we had a clear-cut agreement with my aunt." He shortly thereafter offered his own speculation as to what happened, that his aunt had been open to his taking the books "without publicity," but that once her husband learned of what happened, she changed her position: "What was happening apparently was my aunt was being put under pressure by my uncle" (page 240).

According to this explanation, Rebbetzin Schneerson had granted permission for Barry to take the books, on the assumption that her husband would never learn about it.

This explanation, however, defies credulity for a number of reasons; most obviously, how could the Rebbetzin think that Barry could take and sell books for large sums of money and her husband would never learn of it? In addition to this being the kind of deceptive behavior utterly inconsistent with all that we know of the Rebbetzin, it would also have been quite foolish; the sale of such books would be difficult, if not impossible, to keep a secret.

In his testimony, Barry emphasized that he avoided taking any books that were of particular significance to Chabad—"I took the things that had no emotional value for the movement"—and certainly did not take any of the items that were most holy, the *ketavim,* or manuscripts authored by the earlier Rebbes. While such behavior might reflect a certain sensitivity on Barry's part, it indicates prudence as well. Had he taken manuscripts of the earlier Chabad Rebbes, they would probably have been unsalable. No book dealer would have wanted to deal in such "hot items" any more than an art dealer would want to buy famous art works known to be in museums, and now, suddenly and inexplicably, being offered for sale by a private collector.[16]

The Rebbetzin's deposition took place on November 12, 1985, at her home on President Street. In addition to Nat Lewin, Jerome Shestack, and Seth Waxman, the three lawyers representing Chabad, and Alvin Hellerstein and Brian Cogan, Barry's lawyers (both of whom are now federal judges), present as well were Rabbi Krinsky and both Barry and Chana Gourary.[17] We can only imagine how uncomfortable it must have been for Rebbetzin Schneerson to offer her testimony in the presence of her sister.

Throughout the deposition, Rebbetzin Schneerson repeatedly denied that her father had granted any ownership in the library to his daughters—and often repeated her answer two or three times. When Lewin asked her, "After your father died, did you think you owned the library?" she answered, "Never. Never entered my mind. Never."

QUESTION: "Did you ever think you owned part of the library?"
REBBETZIN SCHNEERSON: "Never."
QUESTION: "Did your mother indicate to you that she thought she owned the library?"
REBBETZIN SCHNEERSON: "My mother never mentioned anything to me about the library."
QUESTION: "Did he [Chaim Lieberman] ever come to ask you about the library?"
REBBETZIN SCHNEERSON: "Never. Never. Never heard anything from him about the library."
QUESTION: "Your sister, Chana Gourary, did she claim to you, after your father died, that she owned the library?"
REBBETZIN SCHNEERSON: "I never heard anything like that from her" (pages 18–20).

There were two moments of high drama during the Rebbetzin's testimony, the first when she was questioned regarding her discussion with her sister about the books. Unlike Chana, who quoted her sister as inviting Barry to take as many books for himself as he wanted, Rebbetzin Schneerson's recollection of the conversation was very different: "My sister called me and said that Barry was in the study, my father's study, and he took a couple of books. . . . He didn't take any manuscripts, only a few books."

QUESTION: "And what did you understand when your sister said that Barry had taken a few books?"
REBBETZIN SCHNEERSON: "I assumed [that Barry] simply took a few books to look at, and would bring them back later" (page 35; the Frierdiker Rebbe's study had been preserved exactly as it was when he died and, as a general rule, nobody removed anything from the room).
QUESTION: "Did you ever in any conversation with your sister tell her that Barry could take all the books he wanted?"
REBBETZIN SCHNEERSON: "Never." Then, perhaps not wanting to brand her sister a liar, she added, "I definitely don't recall [saying] such a thing" (pages 35–36).

The sisters clearly spoke again when the news about Barry's nighttime withdrawals from the library came out. The Rebbetzin testified that she had said to her sister, " 'People saw Barry going into the library and he took out books.' She answered, 'My son is not a thief.' I said to her, 'He went in secretly.' Then we went on to discuss the matter. I said, 'If my father wanted to leave anything for the children . . . he could have designated it. He had time to reflect. . . . He would have written a note or something about the library. Since he didn't write anything, it certainly does not belong to me.' "

One can only imagine how unpleasant this conversation must have become. According to Rebbetzin Schneerson, she finally cried out in what seems to have been a combination of desperation and fury: "As far as I am concerned, we had a younger sister who died in the concentration camp. Just as she died and she is not here, so am I not here. It's as if I died. Do whatever you want" (page 33). At that point, the Rebbetzin testified, she hung up the phone.

These words, "do whatever you want," come across more in the nature of a cri de coeur, a cry from the heart, and certainly did not constitute, from the Rebbetzin's perspective, a mandate for either Chana or Barry to take possession of, let alone sell, the library books.

At the end of the deposition, when the Rebbetzin was pressed on the issue of what she thought her father's possessions were, and to whom her father's books belonged, she answered: "I think they belonged to the Chasidim, because my father belonged to the Chasidim." [18]

A little legal sparring then ensued between the attorneys Nat Lewin and Brian Cogan, and then Lewin concluded the deposition with one final query:

Question: "From knowing your father and from the knowledge you had with regard to your father, did that library belong to the Chasidim?"

"Oh yes."

At this point, the video camera was turned off, and the Rebbetzin said to Rabbi Krinsky, who was seated alongside her: "His *tallit* and tefillin [that was all my father owned]." [19]

These final exchanges, both the Rebbetzin's response that her father belonged to the Chasidim, and her concluding statement to Rabbi Krinsky about her father's total lack of material possessions, summarize what both the Rebbetzin and Rebbe wanted people to understand about Rabbi Yosef Yitzchak and about all of the Lubavitcher Rebbes; they had no interest in material possessions beyond their basic needs; [20] they were interested in serving and leading their followers to serve God and not in being enriched by them.

As is generally the case, it does not seem that anyone's opinions were altered by the depositions, though both sides now knew the intended legal strategy of the other.

Throughout this period, starting with the revelation of the taking of the books and leading up to the trial, the Rebbe was deeply disturbed over what he regarded as an act of robbery, made even more outrageous by the fact that the victim—his deceased father-in-law, whose spiritual legacy was invested in the books—was dead. In addition, Chana Gourary's assertion that the movement had ended with the death of her parents must have deeply hurt and angered the Rebbe (this presumably was Chana's rationale for why the library could now be divided up and disposed of). To the Rebbe, who felt that his father-in-law's legacy and inspiration would continue forever, nothing could be more offensive than her assertion that the movement had ended. This is likely why he refused to consider any compromise or out-of-court settlement with his nephew and sister-in-law,[21] as a settlement would suggest that ownership of the library was an open issue—maybe Barry was right, maybe the Chabad community was right—and such ambiguity was unacceptable.

During the summer of 1985, the Rebbe spoke repeatedly and with intense emotion regarding his horror at the violation of his father-in-law's books. On one of those occasions, he spoke of those who had bought any of the books as having "bombs" in their possession. On another occasion, he elaborated that the act of taking the books from the library and selling them was like extracting limbs from the body of his father-in-law. (He also announced that Chabad would reimburse the full purchase price to anyone who had bought one of the volumes.)

In August 1985, a mentally unbalanced Chabadnik knocked on Chana Gourary's door, gained entrance to her home, yelled at her for upsetting the Rebbe, and then proceeded to attack the eighty-six-year-old woman, leaving her badly hurt.[22]

Subsequent to this incident, the Rebbe never again spoke in public about the books with the same sense of raw emotion and betrayal.

The attacker quickly boarded a plane to Israel, where he has remained since. Not surprisingly, tensions between the Rebbe and his nephew escalated, as Barry Gourary blamed his uncle's rhetoric for having prompted the attack.

The Trial

Judge Charles Sifton presided over the trial, which he believed to be significant because of the underlying question it addressed: To whom do the possessions of a religious leader belong, to him or to the movement he heads? He also commented on several occasions that this might well have been the most interesting case he had had as a federal judge.

Sifton's interest in religion was real, reinforced by his former marriage to Elisabeth Niebuhr, the daughter of Reinhold Niebuhr, one of

America's most prominent Christian thinkers. He regarded this earlier connection—Sifton was now divorced—as so potentially significant that he met with both legal teams and offered to recuse himself from the case if either of them thought that this would make it impossible for him to preside over the case in an objective manner. Both sides raised no objection.

One unusual feature at the trial was the large daily attendance at the proceedings. Lewin recalls that "every seat in the courtroom was filled every day of the trial." As is common among highly Orthodox Jews, men and women sat separately, in different rows.

One of the most damaging admissions in the Gourary case emerged during Lewin's cross-examination of Rabbi Chaim Lieberman, during which Lieberman, who was supporting the claims of Barry and Chana Gourary, confessed to burning some pages pertinent to the case that could have helped establish Chabad's ownership of the library, as well as throwing other pages into the toilet. The pages included receipts for books the library had purchased with Chabad money after the Frierdiker Rebbe's death. In addition to the impropriety of using institutional money to purchase books for a privately owned library, the newly acquired books—which had been rescued from Europe after World War II—were intended to be sold only to communal libraries. Although Lieberman was in his nineties, he remained mentally acute and aware that these receipts constituted implicit acknowledgment that the library was the property of the movement; hence, his attempt to destroy them. Lieberman himself was in a painful quandary. A lifelong bachelor, the only "family" he had was the Gourarys, with whom he dined nightly.

The most moving testimony at the trial was offered by Elie Wiesel, the Romanian-born Nobel Peace Prize recipient and author of *Night*, which remains to this day the most widely read memoir of a Holocaust survivor. Wiesel testified as an expert witness on Chasidic life and, because of his great admiration for Chabad and the Rebbe, refused any fee. According to Wiesel's testimony, Chasidic tradition rejected the notion of a Rebbe amassing personal wealth through gifts tendered him by his followers. Rather, "the attitude of the Rebbe toward personal wealth was one of disdain. First, because he didn't have it. And if he had it, he never kept it."

He went on to speak of Rebbes who, whenever they received a ruble from a Chasid, would give it away. "Most Chasidic masters claimed that money never stayed in their house overnight. From the time they received it and the time they went to bed, they had already found the opportunity to give the money away to the poor."

While there have in fact been certain Chasidic dynasties whose leaders and families had achieved significant wealth deriving from gifts from their followers, this was never the case with Chabad, whose Rebbes were known for leading lives of great simplicity. The upshot of Wiesel's testimony was clear. It is inconceivable that the Frierdiker Rebbe would have intended his highly valuable book collection to pass out of the movement, let alone to an heir who would claim ownership of half of the books and try to sell them.[23]

At the trial's end, and after some final papers were submitted, Sifton announced that he would be serving as judge in a complex criminal case involving violent crimes and several defendants. He therefore noted that it might take three or four months until he could issue a definitive ruling. The criminal case was even more complex than he had anticipated, and a full nine months passed until Sifton's ruling was issued in January 1987. It comprised some forty pages and included a brief but surprisingly comprehensive overview of the significance of books and manuscripts within Chabad. He quoted, for example, a striking comment made by Chana Gourary: "Even my great-grandfather [the Maharash, the Fourth Rebbe], when they were burning the towns around [Lubavitch], had horses ready twenty-four hours around the clock to save the *ksovim* [manuscripts]."

Though Sifton acknowledged that in previous generations, the various Chabad Rebbes had been regarded as the owners of their libraries (for example, the Fifth Rebbe had stipulated that the library was to be inherited by his son, Joseph Isaac Schneersohn, who succeeded him), he maintained that one should not regard the libraries as property in the popular sense of the term, that is, that the Rebbe or his family could sell the books for their own personal gain. Rather, this was "property [intended to be] used to serve the purposes of Chabad Chasidism."

In addition, and even more significantly, though the Frierdiker Rebbe did own the library in the earlier years of his leadership, ownership of the library had passed out of his hands voluntarily because of the events of the Holocaust. Thus, in a number of letters sent by the Frierdiker Rebbe in 1939, he wrote to Agudas Chasidei Chabad in the United States asking them to exert all their efforts to get his library out of Europe, and referred to the books "as the property of Agudas Chabad." [24]

Sifton's ruling, therefore, was unequivocal: "I conclude that the library was not part of the estate of Rabbi Joseph Isaac Schneersohn at the time of his death." It was not, therefore, the Frierdiker Rebbe's possession to bequeath to his daughters, nor did Sifton believe it was his inclination to do so.

Sifton's ruling hinged in large measure on what he referred to as the "extraordinary letter" (which appears at the beginning of this chapter) that the Frierdiker Rebbe had written to Professor Alexander Marx, the head of the Jewish Theological Seminary library, the flagship institution of the Conservative movement.

Most important, this letter posits that the Frierdiker Rebbe regarded this library not as his personal possession but as a "treasure" of the Jewish people. How indeed did Barry Gourary, Chana Gourary, and their legal team explain the language employed in this letter by the Frierdiker Rebbe? They argued that the Frierdiker Rebbe was, to put it delicately, being less than forthright, or, as Judge Sifton characterized their argument, he was being "duplicitous." In short, they claimed the Previous Rebbe understood that if he asked Professor Marx to use whatever influence he had with the State Department to help him regain *personal* property, his request would likely fail; he therefore allegedly pretended that he was asking the help not for himself, but on behalf of the Jewish people for whom these books were a national treasure. However, his real intention was to retrieve the books for himself.

Indeed, it was this argument of the defendants that Judge Sifton dismissed with a certain seeming contempt: "Not only does the letter, even in translation, ring with feeling and sincerity, it does not make much sense that a man of the character of the Sixth Rebbe would, in the circumstances, mean something different from what he says, that [it was his intention that] the library was to be delivered to the plaintiff [Agudas Chasidei Chabad] for the benefit of the community." The court of appeals subsequently used even sharper language to characterize the defense's depiction of the Frierdiker Rebbe's intention with this letter: "It simply defies reason and common sense to believe that a religious leader of the [Previous] Rebbe's stature . . . would deliberately write letters of misrepresentation regarding the ownership of a valued and to him sacred national treasure in order to feather his own nest."

On the day that Judge Sifton issued his ruling, Rabbi Krinsky came to the courthouse and received a copy of the decision, which he immediately brought to the Rebbe at his office.

In Chabad, the verdict was met with great joy and festivity. Local schools closed and children came to 770 to dance with their teachers. Prayers were sung in traditional festival tunes, and the older yeshiva students celebrated and danced for a full week. The Rebbe gave a special talk each day of the celebration.[25]

But, as a baseball adage attributed to Yogi Berra teaches, "It ain't over till it's over." Barry appealed, and another ten months passed. However, his appeal was in vain; the ruling of the court of appeals on November 17, 1987, was as definitive as Judge Sifton's, and even more dismissive of Barry's claims. In addition to affirming Sifton's verdict, the court of appeals offered a number of commonsense proofs, among the most powerful being that the Frierdiker Rebbe's widow, Rebbetzin Nechama Dina, and her daughter, Chana Gourary, had never acted as if they regarded the library as belonging to them. For example, after her husband's death and during the remaining twenty years of her life, Rebbetzin Nechama Dina "never went to the library or asked about its condition. Nor did Chana Gourary." In addition, "Neither contributed to its maintenance."

This second point is critical: Did Rebbetzins Nechama Dina Schneer-sohn and Chana Gourary expect Chabad to pay for the library's upkeep even though it was they, and not Chabad, who owned it? How could they justify Chabad laying out these funds, which included paying a full-time librarian? Rather, as the court of appeals argued: "Their actions toward this collection strongly suggest that he [the Frierdiker Rebbe] must have told them during his lifetime that he no longer had an ownership in the library that they could claim at his death."[26]

The court of appeals then offered yet another, perhaps even more definitive, argument. When the Frierdiker Rebbe's estate was closed in 1958, Chana Gourary, along with Chaya Mushka Schneerson, executed a sworn "fiduciary release" declaring that they each had received "everything due me from said Estate." As if to reinforce this conclusion, when Rebbetzin Nechama Dina died in 1971, she, too, like her husband, died intestate, leaving behind no legal document either affirming her ownership of the library or her disposition of the library to her daughters.

The case was finally over. The courts had ruled that the library belonged to Chabad, that Barry Gourary had no right to take any of the books and certainly no right to sell them, and those books that had previously been impounded should be immediately returned to Chabad.

On November 23, 1987, an armored van was dispatched to the bonded warehouse, and the 450 impounded books were removed by Chabad in thirteen boxes. This time, the Rebbe was at the *Ohel*—earlier, during the trial, he would stand at the *Ohel* for several hours every day, a detail that offers us just a glimpse of the immense power the Rebbe drew from the Frierdiker Rebbe's spirit—and he requested that Rabbi Krinsky bring over three of the books from the several hundred that had been recovered. The Rebbe carefully examined the books and asked that one of them, *Derech Emunah (Path of Faith)*, by Rabbi Meir ibn Gabbai (published in Italy in 1562), be republished and reset with the addition of a biographical sketch of Rabbi Meir. Remarkably, within two days the book was available for sale at bookstores, and that Shabbat the Rebbe explained some passages from it in his *farbrengen*.[27]

Sadness Amidst the Joy

D *idan notzach* ("Our side won"), the Chasidim declared when the court ruling was issued. But victory is not incompatible with tragedy, though obviously it would have been more tragic had Chabad lost the suit and the precious library been disbanded. The family of the Frierdiker Rebbe was shattered. And this was not a large family to begin with. Of the Previous Rebbe's three daughters, one had died in the Holocaust; she had left behind no heirs. The two remaining sisters had long been close.[28] No more. This came out in a sad moment during the Rebbetzin's deposition: The opposing counsel, Brian Cogan, after first establishing that the two sisters used to speak a minimum of twice daily, asked, "Now, you know that she [Chana Gourary] was injured in August of this year, don't you?" [See page 403.]

REBBETZIN SCHNEERSON: "Oh, yes."
QUESTION: "Did you call her in the hospital to see—"
REBBETZIN SCHNEERSON: "No."

We do know from other sources that the Rebbetzin made inquiries to learn how her sister was doing and to receive regular updates, but there was no direct contact between them. Two years later, when the Rebbetzin died (the Rebbe believed that her life was shortened by the aggravation caused by the fight over the books), Chana Gourary did not attend the funeral.

Sad enough. But there was more. Rabbi Gourary sided fully on this issue with the Rebbe and the Lubavitch movement and opposed both his wife and his son. It was an act of heroic self-sacrifice that cost him dearly. During the last years of her life, Chana Gourary moved in with her son, while her husband continued living at 770. When Rabbi Gourary died on February 11, 1989, the final line in the *New York Times* obituary read: "he is survived by his wife Chana of Montclair [New Jersey]." During this period, Chana Gourary made provisions with the Munkatcher Cemetery in Deans, New Jersey, to be interred there after her death, whereas her husband was subsequently interred near the Frierdiker Rebbe at the Lubavitch cemetery. A false rumor was spread by opponents of Chabad that the Rebbe had forbidden Chana Gourary from being buried in the Chabad cemetery, where her mother and father are buried. This was not the case, and in the days following her death, a delegation of four prominent Lubavitchers, sent by the Rebbe, visited Barry at his home,[29] where he was observing shiva for his mother, and pleaded with him to allow his mother to be reinterred at the Chabad cemetery. Barry was polite, but he refused. The break was irrevocable. In death as in life.

A year later, on the first anniversary of Judge Sifton's decision, in a lengthy talk about the significance of the court's ruling, the Rebbe proclaimed, "How do we celebrate the victory of the books? It is the books that were victorious. So let us ask the books. Their clear answer is: to study them and live by their teachings."[30]

Part Nine

·❦·

The

WORLD

of

MESSIANISM

Chapter 28

·❦·

THE REBBE AND THE MESSIAH

"I BELIEVE WITH PERFECT FAITH IN THE COMING OF THE MESSIAH,
AND, THOUGH HE MAY TARRY, I WILL WAIT DAILY FOR HIS COMING."
—*Maimonides, Twelfth Principle of Jewish Faith*

This chapter examines one of the most common, and for many
Jews troubling, associations people have with Chabad, that its
adherents believe that Menachem Mendel Schneerson, the Seventh
Rebbe, was, or will be, the Messiah. The claim that the Rebbe was
the Messiah was made by large numbers of Chasidim during the last
years of the Rebbe's life, and continues to be proclaimed by some
Lubavitchers today.

Some people still recall hearing reports of a meeting convened in
1993 by the International Committee to Bring Moshiach to crown the
Rebbe as Messiah, and reading about posters inside the synagogue at
770 Eastern Parkway declaring of the Rebbe, "Long live our Master, our
Teacher, King Moshiach, forever and ever." Ads in secular newspapers
would sometimes appear speaking of the Rebbe as the Messiah. There
are still Chabadniks who speak of the Rebbe as the Messiah, and the
posters are still present inside the synagogue.[1]

Throughout the most active years of the Messianic campaign
(the early to mid-1990s) there were strong internal forces in Chabad
resisting this development. This resistance was associated in particular with the movement's official leadership, specifically Rabbi Yehuda
Krinsky, who had been designated by the Rebbe to be the executor of
his estate and who serves as Chabad's official spokesman, and Rabbi

Avraham Shemtov, the man appointed by the Rebbe to head the movement's umbrella organization, Agudas Chasidei Chabad.

As will become apparent in the course of this chapter, I have a definite
view on the subject of whether the Rebbe was the Messiah and it is not
an affirmative one, but I will try to present fairly the views of those with
whom I disagree. What I came to understand while researching this
issue is that when Lubavitchers use the word "Messiah" in referring to
the Rebbe, they do not mean what people think they mean. Perhaps the
most surprising conclusion I reached is that the Messiah issue is, in the
final analysis, a nonissue. I know this sounds shocking. Professor David
Berger has written a book (*The Rebbe, the Messiah, and the Scandal of Orthodox
Indifference*) arguing that Chabad, or at least, in his view, most of Chabad,
has moved itself so far from traditional Jewish beliefs that it should be
shunned, specifically because of the Messiah issue. Why I have come to
so opposite a conclusion will be explained in the following pages.

Whether or not Rabbi Menachem Mendel Schneerson was or is the
Messiah might seem to be the sort of issue that can be cleared up
in a few sentences. After all, there are specific criteria in Jewish sources
that define the traits and achievements a person has to possess and accomplish to be designated the Messiah. All these characteristics are set
forth in the final book of Maimonides's fourteen-volume code of Jewish
law (*Mishneh Torah*). In the work's two final chapters, Maimonides writes
of the Messiah and how we can recognize if he has arrived:

"In the future, King Messiah will arise and restore the kingdom of
David to its former state and original sovereignty. He will rebuild the
Temple [in Jerusalem] and gather the dispersed of Israel. . . . Do not
think that King Messiah will have to perform signs and wonders [i.e.,
miracles], bring anything new into being, revive the dead, or do similar
things. For we see that this is not the case. Rabbi Akiva was a very wise
man, a great sage of the Mishnah, yet he was [also] the armor-bearer of
Bar-Kochva.[2] He said that Bar-Kochva was the Messiah; he and all the
wise men of his generation shared this belief [3] until Bar-Kochva was slain

in his iniquities. Because he was killed, it became known to them that he was not [the Messiah]. Yet the Rabbis had not asked him for a sign or token" (Maimonides, *Mishneh Torah*, Laws of Kings and Wars, 11:1.3).

Maimonides then elaborates on additional achievements we should expect from the Messiah, tasks that largely concern the Jews, but which culminate in a universal mission as well: "If there arises a king from the House of David who studies the Torah and occupies himself with the commandments, like his ancestor David, in accordance with the Written and Oral Law, observes the precepts prescribed in the Written and the Oral Law, and compels all Israel to walk in the way of the Torah and strengthens it, and fights the battles of the Lord, *this man enjoys the presumption of being the Messiah* [emphasis added]. If he does these things and succeeds, if he builds the Temple on its site, and gathers the dispersed of Israel, *he is beyond all doubt the Messiah (Moshiach Vaddai)* [emphasis added]. And he will mend the whole world so that all serve the Lord together" (Laws of Kings and Wars, 11:4; this does not mean that there will be one universal religion, Judaism, but rather that there will be universal acceptance of one God).

And finally, a sign by which we can recognize that a person is *not* the Messiah: "But if he does not succeed to this degree or is slain,[4] it is obvious that he is not the one promised in the Torah. He is, rather, to be regarded like all the wholehearted and worthy kings of the House of David who died" (Laws of Kings and Wars, 11:4).

As one reads through the criteria Maimonides enumerates for identifying the Messiah, one thing is clear: The Seventh Rebbe was not, to use Maimonides's formulation, "beyond all doubt the Messiah," and it becomes impossible to imagine that any members of Chabad could believe that he was.

Did he succeed in rebuilding the Temple in Jerusalem? No. Did he restore the Kingdom of David to its former state? No.[5] Did he gather all the Jews back to Israel from the four corners of the earth? No. Did he successfully carry out the task of preparing the *whole* world to serve God with one accord and usher in an age of universal peace?[6] No.

In fact, the Rebbe himself made it clear that if a person assumed to be the Messiah does not fulfill *all* of the conditions laid down by Maimonides, then that person is not the Messiah. In one letter he wrote in 1971, he stated: "We see clearly that even after he induces all of the Jewish people to walk in the path of Torah, it may only be *assumed* [emphasis added] that he is the Messiah, but it is not yet certain, and it could in fact turn out that he is not. In other words, there is still the possibility that even this development will not necessarily spell the end of the *Galut* (Exile). . . .[7] Only when, as Rambam (Maimonides) says, he will build the Sanctuary [i.e., the Temple] in its place and will gather the dispersed of Israel, only then will it be certain that he is the Messiah beyond all doubt."[8]

If Rabbi Menachem Mendel Schneerson did not achieve *any* of these Messianic tasks, how then did so many Lubavitcher Chasidim hail him in the final stages of his life (and some still do today) as the Messiah?

The answer is that they both did and didn't.

In fact, this is the crux of the issue and one that has rarely been made clear to those who are not part of Chabad.

In general, when people use the term "Messiah," they are referring to the person identified by Maimonides as "beyond all doubt" the fully realized Messiah (*moshiach vaddai*), the flesh-and-blood figure who achieves all of the above-mentioned tasks.

But if that is the meaning of the word "Messiah," how, then, did Rabbi Akiva proclaim Bar Kochba to be the Messiah at a time when the great warrior had not fulfilled all these functions and indeed never did?

Readers of Maimonides often gloss over the fact that Maimonides provides *two* definitions of the Messiah. The first is the one just discussed, that is, the man who redeems the Jewish people and the whole world. The second, however, is the person whom Maimonides describes as the "presumed Messiah" (*chezkat moshiach*), one who greatly strengthens the observance of Torah and fights the battles of the Lord, but who has not yet realized, and who might never succeed in realizing, the more formidable tasks demanded of the Messiah (gathering all the Jews to Israel, rebuilding the Temple, and ushering in world peace). Thus, although Rabbi Akiva spoke of Bar Kochba as the Messiah, Maimonides makes it clear that it was a *presumed* Messiah to whom he was referring, and that when Bar Kochba was killed, it became clear that Rabbi Akiva's presumption was wrong.

In addition to Maimonides's formulation, there is also a third usage of the term, one that has great significance within Chabad.

A Potential Messiah in Each Generation

A number of Talmudic texts and post-Talmudic religious scholars advance the idea that in every generation there is one person who is worthy, and has the potential, to be the Messiah (*moshiach she'b'dor*).

This idea is found already in a fourth-century Talmudic discussion (that is, eight hundred years before Maimonides) in which Rabbi Nachman declares: "If he [the Messiah] is among the living, he is someone like me." In support of this position, Rabbi Nachman cites a verse in Jeremiah (30:21): "And their prince shall be one of their own, and their ruler shall emerge from their midst." Rabbi Nachman understands both "prince" and "ruler" as referring to the Messiah; hence he understands the verse to mean that the Messiah could well be "among the living" (*Sanhedrin* 98b).

At first blush, Rabbi Nachman's statement that the Messiah is someone like him sounds arrogant. But Rabbi Nachman's main concern seems to be establishing that the Messiah may well be alive—"if he is among the living"—while his citation from the prophet Jeremiah is intended to narrow down the possibilities as to who that person might be. Thus, to Rabbi Nachman, Jeremiah's words—"And their prince shall be one of their own and their ruler shall emerge from their midst"—suggest that the Messiah will be a powerful ruler who is a descendant of the House of David, the Jewish royal family. Since Rabbi Nachman possessed both these qualities—he held a position of authority within the Jewish community of Babylon, and he apparently traced his ancestry to David[9]—the Messiah could be one such as he.

The Talmud then cites the sage Rav: "If the Messiah is among the living, then he is someone like our holy Rabbi [i.e., Rabbi Judah, the editor of the Mishnah]." In other words, if the Messiah is currently alive, then he must be someone like Rabbi Judah, the leading rabbinic figure of his age, and a more noted scholar and leader than Rabbi Nachman.

As it turned out, the Messiah was neither Rabbi Nachman nor Rabbi Judah, but the fact that both rabbis begin their comment with the words "If the Messiah is among the living" suggests the possibility that in each generation there is a *potential* Messiah within the Jewish community.

Indeed, this was the conclusion reached more than fifteen hundred years later by the Chatam Sofer (the nineteenth-century Austrian-Hungarian rabbi known by the title of his most famous work, *Chatam Sofer*): "In every generation there is one righteous man [tzaddik] who merits to be the Messiah . . . and when the time comes, God will reveal Himself to him and send him."[10] The person himself will not know that he is destined to be the Messiah until this information is revealed to him, just as Moses did not know that he was destined by God to lead the Israelites out of Egypt until God revealed this to him at the Burning Bush[11] (Exodus 3:10).[12]

Among Chasidim, not just Chabad, the Rebbe of their group is often regarded as the most righteous person of the generation (*tzaddik ha-dor* or *nasi ha-dor*) and is not uncommonly thought of as the most likely candidate of the generation to be the Messiah (*moshiach she'b'dor*). The Rebbe himself also spoke of this concept, particularly regarding the Frierdiker Rebbe, asserting that he, as the generation's most righteous leader (*nasi ha-dor*) was also the generation's potential Messiah (*moshiach she'b'dor*). Faithful Chasidim of different Rebbes regularly express the wish that their generation merit that their righteous leader become the Messiah. Such was also the case with many of the Chasidim of Rabbi Menachem Mendel Schneerson. Because of the depth of his achievements and his great stature (recognized well beyond Chabad), Lubavitcher Chasidim saw him as a "potential Messiah," and, given that they already believed that a Messianic coming was imminent if God deemed the time right, urgently hoped that he'd be appointed by God to become the actual Messiah.

It is *this* sense of "Messiah" that many of the Lubavitchers intended when they spoke of Rabbi Menachem Mendel Schneerson as the Messiah. They were aware—how could they not be?—that he had not completed the tasks set forth in Maimonides and all of the traditional Jewish sources, but they were also sure that if there was anyone in this generation who could fulfill these tasks, it was the Rebbe. As Rabbi

Yehuda Krinsky[13] told the *New York Times* reporter Ari Goldman in 1988: "Our sages tell us that the Messiah is a man of flesh and blood who lives among us. . . . If I were asked in this generation who was the most suitable, beyond any question, in my mind, it would be the Rebbe."

What About Those in Chabad Who Continue to Believe, Even After the Rebbe's Death, That He Can Still Be the Messiah?

In addition to the views in the Talmud affirming a potential Messiah in each generation, two Talmudic texts offer another possibility, one that expands the net of candidates to include the possibility that the Messiah will come from the dead: "If he [the Messiah] is among the dead, he is someone like Daniel the Greatly Beloved" (as Daniel is referred to in the biblical book named for him [10:11]). A similar teaching, though it focuses on a different biblical hero, is conveyed in a passage in the Jerusalem Talmud: "King Messiah, if he is from the living, David is his name, if he is from the deceased, David is still his name [that is, it would seem, the original King David of the Bible]" (*Brachot* 2:4).

On the basis of these passages, Don Isaac Abarbanel (fifteenth century) suggests that belief in a resurrected righteous person becoming Messiah is acceptable, and the *Sedei Chemed* (nineteenth century) quotes the view of a rabbi, based upon this Talmudic passage, that it is possible, though not likely, that the Messiah will come from the dead.

However, in both instances, these views were presented almost as incidental comments, and few subsequent efforts were ever made in the Jewish tradition to identify the Messiah with one who died.

Indeed, in polemical discussions with Christian leaders over the centuries, prominent rabbis such as Nachmanides—who was forced into a Jewish-Christian debate in Barcelona, Spain, in 1267—aggressively asserted that Judaism did not believe that the Messiah would die and come back as a proof that from Judaism's perspective Jesus could not be the Messiah.

In mainstream Jewish theology, the Messiah won't die. If a person assumed to be the Messiah does die, then that means, as Maimonides wrote, that he isn't the actual Messiah (and was, at most, perhaps, a potential Messiah).

A story told about Rabbi Chaim Soloveitchik (popularly known as Reb Chaim Brisker), the brilliant Talmudist and grandfather of Rabbi Joseph Soloveitchik, is representative of traditional Jewish belief. The rabbi was once on a train in which a group of Jews were speaking to a man who turned out to be a Christian missionary. The man was trying to convince the group that Jesus was the Messiah. One Jew responded that it was sufficient for him that the rabbis of the Talmud rejected such claims on Jesus's behalf. The missionary responded: "But can you just simply rely on the judgment of your rabbis? After all, Rabbi Akiva, one of the greatest of the rabbis, believed that Bar Kochba was the Messiah." The Jews were dumbfounded and didn't know what to answer. At this point, Reb Chaim stepped in and asked the missionary: "But how do you know that Bar Kochba wasn't the Messiah?" "That's obvious," the man answered. "Bar Kochba died without bringing the redemption." Reb Chaim smiled and walked away.[14]

Yet, subsequent to the Rebbe's death in 1994, a number of people started to "resurrect" the relatively unknown notion of the Messiah coming from the dead. Some of them began proclaiming that although doctors at Beth Israel Hospital in New York reported the death of Menachem Mendel Schneerson on June 12, 1994, and thousands attended his funeral (described by Elie Wiesel as "the day when most of us who were there [thought] that the sky that was extinguished will never be lit again"), nonetheless, the Rebbe did not die.

Among religious Jews, reference to one who has died is followed by formulaic expressions, such as *alav ha-shalom* (peace be upon him), *zichrono livrakha* (may his memory be a blessing), *zechuto yagen aleiynu* (may his merit shield us), or *zeicher tzaddik livrakha* (may the memory of the righteous be a blessing). The Messianists, however, will not use such terms when writing of the Rebbe, and they have removed such terms from plaques mentioning him. They also adamantly refuse to visit his grave or observe his *yahrtzeit*.

In April 2011, I interviewed a man who served as one of the medics at the Rebbe's bedside during the final period of his illness. The man is not a Chabad Chasid, though he is a practicing Orthodox Jew.

Although he was not present at the moment of the Rebbe's death, he was one of those who escorted the Rebbe's body on a stretcher from Beth Israel Hospital to 770 Eastern Parkway, where the body was laid on the floor of his office and covered, in accordance with Jewish tradition. Before leaving the room, he raised the cover so that he could see the Rebbe's face. He wanted to be able to say with certainty that the man whose body he was helping carry was Menachem Mendel Schneerson and that he was dead. And indeed it was, of course, the Rebbe's face that he saw.

The medic's task that day was to be present as people passed by the Rebbe's room so as to assist those who fainted or collapsed (there were a few who did) or who might have overwrought emotional responses that required medical attention. He also assisted those who wished to perform *kria*, the Jewish ritual of making a rip in one's clothing upon the death of an immediate family member. In the case of a parent, the rip is made over the heart, and this was performed by many Chasidim that day, even though they were unrelated to the Rebbe (in line with the *Shulchan Aruch*'s ruling that a disciple should do so for his teacher).

The medic told me that a small, but not negligible, number of people who passed by the room that day refused to make a rip in their garments and insisted that they did not believe that the Rebbe had died. Several hours later, at the funeral, there were some Chasidim who drank *l'chaim* and danced during the funeral, providing cumulative hours of TV broadcasts and angering and wounding most Lubavitchers, while shocking and confusing many other non-Chabad admirers of the Rebbe.

Long representative of those who believed the Rebbe was the Messiah was one prominent Lubavitcher rabbi, chairman of the International Committee to Bring Moshiach, who declared in the aftermath of the Rebbe's death: "What happened on Sunday [the death of the Rebbe] was only a test. The Messiah is coming and the Rebbe is the Messiah. We don't know how it happens, but he is going to get up."

This had never been a significant idea among Chasidim, and I suspect that had anybody proposed, for example, in 1970, that the Rebbe would die and subsequently return from the dead as the Messiah, the person would likely have been dismissed, at best, as peculiar. I can find no records *prior* to the Rebbe's death of Chasidim speaking of such a possibility. Indeed, while the Rebbe was alive but very sick, they hoped that he would emerge from his illness, regain his strength, and be empowered by God to become the Messiah. They did not talk *during his lifetime* of the possibility that he would soon die, be resurrected, and only then reveal himself as the Messiah.

This, of course, is the point. When the Rebbe died, Rabbi Zalman Posner of Nashville opposed those who continued to claim that the Rebbe could still be the Messiah. He responded, "It's very hard to argue with mortality."

I remember discussing the issue of the Messianic claims made about the Rebbe with Rabbi Abraham Twerski, MD, a wide-ranging rabbinical and Chasidic scholar (though not a Chabadnik), the author of over sixty books, and a psychiatrist. Dr. Twerski had met personally with the Rebbe and held him in the highest regard. When I asked Rabbi Twerski what he thought of the discussion as to whether or not the Rebbe was the Messiah, he answered, "While he was alive I hoped he was the Messiah. He was certainly a worthy candidate. But when he died, I knew that he wasn't."

Rabbi Dr. Norman Lamm, too, said shortly after the Rebbe's death, "If [people] believe the Rebbe could have been Moshiach, fine, I agree. Many people could have been the Moshiach, and he had a far better chance than most. But to say he's Moshiach after he died?"

For those who reject the resurrected Messiah scenario, how then should the Rebbe be regarded? What happens if many hoped that someone would become the Messiah and it turns out that the person isn't? Does this mean that the person should be regarded as a false Messiah? By no means! In addition to the fact that people often forget that the Rebbe never said that he was the Messiah (see the following section), Maimonides makes it clear that if a person presumed to be the Messiah is otherwise righteous in his behavior and achieves a great deal of good, he is "to be regarded like all the other wholehearted and worthy kings of the House of David."

"Wholehearted and worthy kings." That is what they were, and for that they are to be esteemed.

Rabbi Aharon Lichtenstein, the longtime coleader of the Gush Etzion yeshiva, holder of a PhD in English literature from Harvard University, and son-in-law of Rabbi Joseph Soloveitchik, gave a eulogy at his yeshiva when the Rebbe died. Rabbi Lichtenstein began his assessment of the Rebbe with the words, "It never occurred to anyone to declare that Rabbi Moshe Feinstein, Rabbi Aharon Kotler, or the Rav was the Messiah. And did they not have followers? Did they not have a tradition? Were they not part of a long dynasty? They certainly did.

"It seems to me," said Lichtenstein, "that at the root of the matter, the concept of Messianism attached itself to the Rebbe because of his image and status.... The Rebbe embodied—and in a powerful way—a certain combination in which one who wished to, could see the reflection of a reflection of the Messiah King."[15]

How Did the Rebbe React to the Messianic Claims Being Made About Him?

In 1965, Rabbi Avraham Parizh, an elder Chasid who had been with the movement from the time of the Fifth Rebbe, printed letters stating: "With great joy, we can inform you that King Messiah, for whom we have waited so many years, is already among us. He is the holy Lubavitcher Rebbe, Rabbi Menachem Mendel Schneerson, the King Messiah. His address is 770 Eastern Parkway, Brooklyn, New York. He does not need us to choose him since God has chosen him." Rabbi Parizh printed up many of these letters and started handing them out in Israel. According to one account, Parizh also distributed these letters by dropping them out of a helicopter.

When the Rebbe learned of the letter, he instructed his secretariat to immediately dispatch a telegram to Parizh, dated June 24, 1965: "We were shocked by the letter [you wrote and handed out] and ask that you immediately cease distributing it. Gather and send to the secretariat all copies of the letter, every last one, and please confirm immediately that you have fulfilled this instruction." Chasidim tell how Parizh spent several weeks scrounging around the streets of Tel Aviv looking for every such sheet he could find.

But did the Rebbe continue to remain opposed to such declarations throughout his life? The answer apparently is yes, certainly as long as he possessed the ability to communicate clearly.

More than twenty-five years later, when Chasidim started talking of the Rebbe as a Messianic figure—though in a less extreme manner than had Parizh—the Rebbe's reaction was no less pointed. In 1991, Rabbi Aharon Dov Halprin, the editor of Chabad's Israeli magazine, *Kfar Chabad*, wanted to print an article explaining why the Rebbe was worthy of being considered the presumed Messiah. When the Rebbe learned of this he responded sharply, "If you, God forbid, [plan to write] anything even remotely similar, it is preferable that you shut down the periodical completely" (*kadima sheyisgor ha-michtav-et legamrei*).[16]

In an urgent audience to which the Rebbe summoned Chabad activist Rabbi Tuvia Peles, the Rebbe rebuked those who were making Messianic claims about him, saying, "They are taking a knife to my heart" and "they are tearing off parts of me." It is hard to imagine a more anguished and pained expression for a Chasid to hear from his Rebbe.

On one occasion in 1991, as the Rebbe was leaving the evening prayers, some Chasidim began singing one of the Rebbe's favorite songs, but with an added twist: They attached the words to *Yechi*—"Long live our master, our teacher, our Rebbe, King Moshiach"—clearly identifying "our Rebbe" as the Messiah. As the Rebbe continued walking, he signaled his encouragement of the singing—Chasidim would sing Chasidic melodies before and after each service—and the Messianists celebrated, thinking that they had finally received the Rebbe's acquiescence.

But they hadn't. The next morning, he refused to go down to the synagogue until he was assured by Rabbi Groner that there would be no such songs sung again. And, indeed, the song was never again sung in front of the Rebbe until some months after a stroke felled him and removed his ability to speak or write.

Several months later, however, and still before the stroke, a few people present at a *farbrengen* did start singing an older song that implied, without stating explicitly, that the Rebbe was the Messiah. The Rebbe heard the words and responded in a grave manner: "Really, I should get up and leave. Even if some people consider it disrespectful that I would need to [be the one to leave], I don't need to reckon with the views of a small number when [what they are singing] is the opposite of reality. Unfortunately, though [even if I leave], it will not help anyway. Further, it will disrupt the good feeling of brothers sitting together [*shevet achim gam yachad* (Psalms 133:1)], for if I were to leave, others will leave, too."[17]

Needless to say, this singing, too, was not repeated.

Perhaps the most poignant public pronouncement of the Rebbe on the Messiah issue was on April 11, 1991, less than a year before his first stroke (March 2, 1992): "What more can I do to motivate the entire Jewish people to cry out and demand that Moshiach should come? All that has been done until now has not helped. We are still in exile. . . . I have done everything I can. From now on you must do whatever you can. Now, all of you must do all you can to actually bring Moshiach here and now, immediately."

Whatever else one might say about this pronouncement, these words do not sound like the pronouncement of a man who feels that he himself is the Messiah.

Some months later, and shortly before the Rebbe's stroke, the Alaska-based *shliach*, Rabbi Yosef Greenberg (author of *Y'mei Bereishit*), brought a letter to be given to the Rebbe in which he referred to him as "King Messiah." Later that same day, Rabbi Groner told Greenberg that the Rebbe had looked at the letter, thrown it down in frustration, and then wrote on it, "Tell him that when the Moshiach comes, I will give him the letter."

An even more definitive statement of the Rebbe on this same issue occurred at around the same time. An Israeli journalist, Sarah Davidowitz of the *Kol Ha'ir* newspaper, approached the Rebbe and said, "We appreciate you very much, we want to see you in Israel; you said soon you will be in Israel, so when will you come?" The Rebbe responded: "I also want to be in Israel." The journalist insisted, "So when will you come?" The Rebbe responded, "That depends on the Moshiach, not on me."

The journalist persisted, "You are the Moshiach!," to which the Rebbe responded, "I am not."[18]

There is, in addition, one act of the Rebbe that would appear to be totally inconsistent with the idea that he thought that he was the Messiah, an act that he initiated the day after his wife, Rebbetzin Chaya Mushka, died (February 10, 1988). The following day, her funeral and burial were held, after which the Rebbe returned to his house on President Street to observe shiva.

In an interview in 2009 with Rabbi Yehuda Krinsky, he related: "[The first night of shiva, the Rebbe] called me up to his office [on the second floor of his house] and told me a number of things. One of the things he said was that he wanted to make a will. . . . This was very, very painful [for me to hear]. But you're a soldier, you've got to do what the commander in chief tells you to do. . . . He said he would like to have it done, if possible, during the week of shiva."

A distinguished probate lawyer, Nahum Gordon, was recommended by Nat Lewin, who had represented Chabad in the trial over the books, and the will was executed and signed by Menachem Mendel Schneerson on February 14, 1988 (the fourth day of shiva).

The will begins with the standard formulaic wording of most wills: "I, Menachem Mendel Schneerson, of Kings County, New York, hereby make, publish and declare this to be my Last Will and Testament."

In the next sentence, the Rebbe revoked any previous wills. This was a legal formality, given that he had never written any earlier will.

The will then specified what should be done at the time of his death: "I request that my debts, my funeral expenses (including, but not limited to the cost of a suitable monument), and my administrative expenses be paid as promptly as shall be practicable."

He then designated that any other assets he had (such as books and manuscripts) "at the time of my death" should be bequeathed to Agudas

Chasidei Chabad. He also appointed Rabbi Krinsky as "my executor," and noted that "in the event of Rabbi Krinsky's death or refusal to serve as executor for any reason," this role was to be assumed by "Rabbi Abraham I. Shemtov" and, if not by him, then by "Rabbi Sholom M. Simpson," who are each "to serve singly and in the order named, as alternate or successor executor."

The will, as the Rebbe directed, was witnessed and signed by Rabbis Krinsky, Leibel Groner, and Binyamin Klein, and notarized by Nahum Gordon.

Does anybody who reads this will feel that it sounds like it was written by a man who regarded himself as the Messiah?

Furthermore, for a Messianic figure to issue such a document without any acknowledgment of his special role in Jewish life strikes me as unlikely to the point of virtual impossibility. And, if one were to argue that perhaps the Rebbe did not come to acknowledge his Messianic role until a later date (he was almost eighty-six when this document was written), it makes no sense that he would never have revised this document to include some acknowledgment of just who the author of this will and testament was.

In short, there is a reason this document does not sound like it was authored by a person who thought he was the Messiah: because the Rebbe didn't think so.

If the above assessment is correct, that Rabbi Menachem Mendel Schneerson did not think that he was the Messiah, then why did he not issue a public statement explicitly denying it, particularly given that he knew that the number of Chasidim making such a claim was growing?

As the Rebbe rarely spoke of why he did or didn't do something, we are pretty much in the realm of speculation.

One possibility is that if the Rebbe entertained the thought that there was a person alive in his generation who was the potential Messiah, and if the thought had occurred to him that he might be that person, it would be odd for him to issue an unequivocal denial. Refusal to make such a statement does not mean, therefore, that he thought he was a potential Messiah but just that he might be, something that he would know if and when the time came and such information was revealed to him. In the meantime, he might have thought it peculiar to say, "As of now, I am not the Messiah."

Some might argue that thinking that one might be the Messiah would in itself be a sign of arrogance, but that need not be the case. Consider a somewhat, and I emphasize *somewhat*, similar circumstance involving Rabbi Moshe Feinstein, the great twentieth-century halachic scholar. A few years before Reb Moshe's death, he needed to have a pacemaker installed. "Quite uncharacteristically," his son-in-law, Rabbi Dr. Moshe Tendler, recalled, "he was reluctant to accede to the doctor's orders." When Tendler asked him to explain his hesitancy, given that a number of doctors agreed that the procedure was essential, Reb Moshe answered, "I know how unworthy I am. I know how little Torah I know, but I am also aware that if they are to pick seventy-one people to make up the Sanhedrin [the ancient Jewish High Court that tradition teaches will be reconstituted in the Messianic era], they most likely will pick me too. However, a *ba'al mum* (someone with a physical defect) cannot join the Sanhedrin. I am perturbed at the thought of doing something to myself that would make me unfit to join the Sanhedrin when the Moshiach comes." Only after Tendler showed Reb Moshe diagrams illustrating exactly what would be done did he realize that the procedure would not render him a *ba'al mum*, and he agreed to have the pacemaker put in. Though Rabbi Feinstein was known for being a particularly humble person, his humility did not preclude him from thinking that his knowledge made him a likely candidate, if the Messiah came, to be appointed to the Sanhedrin.[19]

Rabbi Leibel Groner, one of the Rebbe's secretaries, reports a conversation he had with the Rebbe in 1992. The Rebbe asked him one morning about the Messianic talk going on in the community. Groner responded that "the Rebbe certainly seems most suitable." The Rebbe, in turn, said, "The one who is the Messiah will have this revealed to him from Above. This has not been revealed to me."

The Rebbe might well have feared that if he repeated what he said to Groner in a public setting, it would only cause the Messianic zealots to further pressure him to "acknowledge" that he was the Messiah in the hope that it would then be revealed to him from Above that he was. This seems to be what he was alluding to months earlier when he said that if he left the *farbrengen* due to the Messianic singing going on, it would not help anyway: The Messianists would simply say what they wanted to say even against his wishes! Rabbi Sholom Wolpo, a leading Israeli Messianist and author of the Messianist handbooks *Yechi ha-Melech ha-Moshiach* and *Mevaser Tov* (both published after the Rebbe's stroke and inability to comment), went to great lengths to explain, in his books, "why everyone must still consider and proclaim the Rebbe as the Messiah despite the fact that he himself never said he was." Wolpo tries to explain the Rebbe's negative reactions to such claims being made on his behalf and insists that it is nevertheless incumbent upon everyone to proclaim the Rebbe as the Messiah. "Acceptance of the Messiah must be done by the people, and not by the King [Messiah]."

The Rebbe understood the mind-set of the Messianists, and he knew that whatever he would say would somehow be construed by them as further "proof" that he was the Messiah.

The Rebbe's Hope That the Subject of the Messiah Rises to the Top of the Jewish People's Agenda

There might have been yet another reason that the Rebbe did not more actively disavow the Messianic talk surrounding him, although he did, as noted, try to do so on several occasions. Though he was unhappy that people were identifying him as the Messiah, I believe he was even unhappier that the whole issue of the Messiah was irrelevant to the large majority of Jews. Although traditional Jews affirm belief in the Messiah, as Maimonides mandates, the subject has often been given little attention in the Orthodox world, and even less so in the non-Orthodox world. The Rebbe wanted to refocus Jewish attention on this issue. In not more actively and repeatedly disavowing assertions that he was the Messiah, he might well have been influenced by an incident involving his father-in-law. At one point during the 1940s, when the Frierdiker Rebbe learned, to his chagrin, that there were Chasidim speculating that he was the Messiah, he commented, "At least they are talking about the Messiah."[20]

The Rebbe likely concurred. What comes through very palpably from reading and listening to his talks on this subject is his passion and insistence that world redemption via the Messiah must happen soon and that people must do everything in their power to influence it to happen. He would speak about this time and again, often with tears and barely suppressed sobs.[21]

Beginning with his very first *farbrengen* in 1951, the Rebbe spoke of this generation's mission to complete the *dirah b'tachtonim* (making this world a dwelling place for God); he urged everyone to do all that they could to help the world reach its ultimate state of perfection, when Godliness and goodness will be apparent and prevalent and the Messiah will come and usher in the Final Redemption.[22]

The Rebbe would generally finish his public talks with a prayer for the imminent arrival of the Moshiach. In the 1970s he sought to raise awareness of the Messianic age by encouraging people to learn and become knowledgeable in the laws of the Holy Temple, laws that will apply when the Messiah comes, but not before. The Rebbe expressed the belief that learning about the Redemption would raise awareness of the Messiah and could actually bring the Messiah sooner.

In addition, the Rebbe did not want people to become accustomed to material wealth and forget that affluence is not the sign of the Messianic age. Instead, what he urged people to do was to infuse the Godly into the material and the spiritual into the mundane. Most of all, he wanted the world to be redeemed of its sorrows and to arrive at an era of universal peace. This hope, which dominated his life from his earliest years, was expressed in a letter he wrote to Yitzhak Ben-Zvi, Israel's second president, in which he apologizes for not addressing the president with the Hebrew title "*nasi*" (the word that is used in Hebrew for president) because that title is used in the Talmud for the Messiah: "From the time I was a child attending *cheder* [elementary school], and even before, the vision of the future Redemption began to take form in my imagination—the Redemption of the Jewish people from their final Exile, a redemption of such magnitude and grandeur through which the purpose of the suffering, the harsh decrees and annihilation of Exile will be understood." [23]

The Rebbe would frequently cite earlier rabbinic authorities who stated that the Redemption was imminent, and he liked to quote the Chaffetz Chaim (1838–1933), who stated that it is crucial for Jews to actively appeal to God for the Messiah's coming.

In 1981, a group of children at a Chabad summer camp composed a song with the words "*Am Yisrael* [nation of Israel] have no fear, / Moshiach will be here this year; / We want Moshiach now, / we don't want to wait." The Rebbe seems to have received great satisfaction from the children's initiative, and the song soon began to be sung at *farbrengens*.

The Rebbe was in no way intimidated by criticism expressed by some longtime Chabad opponents about the demanding tone of these words. The Rebbe explained that this "has always been the hope and yearning of the Jewish people—that the Messiah should come now, immediately. Therefore it is inappropriate for someone to say that . . . he is not comfortable with people declaring in an imploring voice, 'We want Moshiach now.' Each Jew clearly prays and pleads three times a day in the *Amida* [prayer] . . . that we 'hope for Your salvation [or redemption] the entire day [*ki li-y'shuatcha kivinu kol ha-yom*]." [24]

Though he remained aware of the mounting criticism directed at his passion on this issue, the Rebbe continued to urge people to do all they could to bring about the Redemption by adding to their observance of Torah and mitzvahs. On one occasion he remarked, "I have merited that the complaint people have against me is that I am passionate about the Moshiach." [25]

Twenty Years Later: The Mainstream Chabad View

Today, two decades after the Rebbe's death, the majority of Chabad Chasidim continue to see him as the leader of the generation (*nasi ha-dor*). They regard him as the most influential rabbinic leader of our time, whose influence continues to be wielded through his teachings (over two hundred volumes of his teachings have been published) and through the hundreds of stories that circulate about him (see chapter 29). These Chasidim acknowledge that he died, visit his grave, and observe his *yahrtzeit* (some fifty thousand to sixty thousand come to the cemetery each year on the anniversary of his death). They place little emphasis on whether or not he will one day come back as the Messiah, and focus instead on what they can do to hasten the Messiah's arrival, whoever he may be; they also yearn to be reunited with him during the Messianic age, when tradition says that all the dead will be resurrected. In addition, the Chabad leadership has been vocal against the shrinking Messianic movement. Agudas Chasidei Chabad, the official representative organization of the movement, took out an ad in the *New York Times* (February 9, 1996) to make its feelings clear to as large an audience as possible: "With regard to some recent statements and declarations by individuals and groups concerning the matter of Moshiach and the Lubavitcher Rebbe, Rabbi Menachem Mendel Schneerson, of sainted memory, let it be known that the views expressed in these notices are in no way a reflection of the movement's position . . . they are in fact misleading and a grave offense to the dignity and expressed desires of the Rebbe."

The mainstream members of the movement are aware of the Rebbe's reaction when people made Messianic claims about him, and they know that he felt there is no point trying to identify who the Messiah will be. They also are aware of the rabbinic writings that allow for the possibility that a righteous person may be resurrected to become the Messiah, as well as those who opine otherwise. Some of them interpret the sources as categorically ruling out the Rebbe ever becoming the Messiah, while others say that such a possibility cannot objectively be ruled out. But most of all they recognize that they have no way of knowing and it's all simply up to God.

In brief, as regards the identity of the Messiah, some Lubavitchers still hope and anticipate that the Rebbe will return from the dead to be the Messiah, but all Lubavitchers, including those who harbor that hope, also recall a story told by the Rebbe. During a public speech, he spoke of an incident in which the Alter Rebbe, Chabad's founder, was asked, "Will the Messiah be a Chasid or a non-Chasid?" The Alter Rebbe responded that the Messiah would not be a Chasid. When asked why, he explained: "If the Messiah comes and he is a Chasid, the non-Chasidim will not want to join him; if, however, the Messiah is a non-Chasid, the Chasidim will nevertheless accept him." [26]

The Rebbe, the Messiah, and the Rebbe's Place in Jewish History

One suspects that part of the problem for those in Chabad who believed—or still do—that the Rebbe is the Messiah is that if he isn't, who exactly is he? The Rebbe was so major a figure, it would seem that he needs a special appellation acknowledging his specialness. Abraham is known in Jewish tradition as *Avraham Avinu* (our Father Abraham), Sarah as *Sarah Imeinu* (our Mother Sarah), Joseph as *Yosef ha-Tzaddik* (Joseph the Righteous), and Moses as *Moshe Rabbeinu* (our Master Moses). Rabbi Judah, the editor of the Mishnah, is called *Rabbeinu ha-Kadosh* (the Holy Rabbi) or simply *Rebbe*, while the tenth- to eleventh-century German rabbi Gershom is known as *Rabbeinu Gershom me-Or ha-Golah* (Rabbi Gershom, the Light of the Exile). The eighteenth-century founder of Chasidism, Rabbi Israel ben Eliezer, is known as the *Baal Shem Tov* (Master of the Good Name) while Rabbi Elijah of Vilna is invariably referred to as the *Vilna Gaon* (the Genius of Vilna).

On the other hand, such appellations are not absolutely necessary to establish a person's uniqueness or greatness. The two greatest teachers of Jewry since the Talmud are known simply as Rashi and Rambam (Maimonides), not terms of adoration but acronyms (Rashi is an acronym for Rabbi Shlomo Yitzchaki [son of Isaac], and Rambam is an acronym for Rabbi Moses ben [son of] Maimon), and the Hebrew equivalent of referring to the thirty-fifth American president as JFK instead of calling him by his full name, John Fitzgerald Kennedy. In the case of the Rebbe, the fact that he is universally known as "the Rebbe" is a sufficient mark of distinction. In every generation, the leaders of Chasidic dynasties are called "Rebbe," but once they die, the title is transferred to their successor. However, one suspects that in the case of Menachem Mendel Schneerson, the title "Rebbe" will remain permanently attached to him by the whole Jewish world, that is—and this, indeed, is fitting—until the Messiah comes.

Why the Question of Whether or Not the Rebbe Was the Messiah Is Ultimately a Nonissue

All students of the Talmud are familiar with the rabbinic question, *L'mai nafka meena?* "What are the practical implications of the question you are raising?" In the spirit of *L'mai nafka meena?*, one may ask: Why ultimately does it matter whether or not there are Chasidim who consider the Rebbe to be the Messiah?[27] Will a contemporary Chabad rabbi, Messianist or not, issue different rulings on Jewish law as a result? No. All the laws of Judaism that a Jew is bound to observe remain binding whatever one's beliefs are about the Rebbe's Messiahship. Thus, while there are traditional Jewish sources that speculate that many of Judaism's ritual commandments will be suspended after the Messiah comes, no one within Chabad with whom I am familiar—even ardent Messianists—holds that any Jewish laws or holidays should be observed differently because he or she maintains that Menachem Mendel Schneerson is the Messiah. This, in itself, suggests, as argued earlier in this chapter, that in their hearts the Messianists do not see the Rebbe as the actual Messiah—despite the fact that they proclaim in loud voices that he is. There is a long-standing Jewish tradition (see, for example, Zechariah 8:19) that Jewish fast days will be abrogated in the days of the Messiah, a position not instituted by any Chabad Messianists.

So this big issue—Is the Rebbe the Messiah or not?—turns out to be a big nonissue. *Mai nafka meena?* What are the practical implications?

In the meantime, nothing has changed. Jews know what their obligations are, and they are continuing to fulfill them. And when the Messiah comes, evidenced by the ingathering of the exiles and the ushering in of world peace, it will be clear to everyone that the Redemption is upon them. One thing we know for certain: This was the yearning that propelled the Rebbe's life from a very young age.

More than five decades ago, in the early years of his leadership, the Rebbe visited Chabad's Camp Gan Israel in the Catskills. A few days later, Rabbi Aaron Soloveitchik came to visit his son who was a camper there and asked him what the Rebbe had spoken about during his visit. The boy answered that the Rebbe had talked about the importance of belief in the imminent arrival of the Messiah. Rabbi Soloveitchik, one of American Jewry's great rabbinic scholars, said to his son, "But all religious Jews believe that." The son replied, "But he really means it."

Part Ten

·❲W❳·

LEADERSHIP
AFTER LIFE

Chapter 29

LEADERSHIP AFTER LIFE

The Rebbe's Priorities as a Blueprint for Shaping the World

"WE MAY NO LONGER SEE THE REBBE WITH OUR EYES, BUT HIS
SPIRIT LIVES IN OUR HEARTS, IN OUR SOULS, AND IN OUR DEEDS."
—*Congressman John Lewis, 1995*

It is hard for me to say this, but I will say it nonetheless: We must follow the example of Chabad." These are the words of Rabbi Eric Yoffie, president of the Union for Reform Judaism, at the organization's biennial convention in November 2003. Yoffie went on to note that he disagreed with Chabad about practically everything but, as he acknowledged on yet another occasion, Chabad's commitment to welcoming all Jews and to seeking out Jews throughout the world "is a principle established by the Rebbe and has outlasted him." Rabbi Rick Jacobs, Yoffie's successor, spoke of Chabad in his inaugural speech: "We can learn important lessons from Chabad about creating non-judgmental opportunities to experience Jewish practice and build sacred relationships." It is fair to say that prior to Rabbi Menachem Mendel Schneerson's emergence on the Jewish scene, no leader in the Reform movement ever had occasion to note lessons that the Reform movement should learn from a Chasidic group.

Indeed, the Rebbe cast a wide net; he had to, because he wanted to reach every Jew. For him, there was no small or unimportant Jew (see page 204). There were no unimportant non-Jews either (see pages 156–57). As the Rebbe made clear, no human being created "in God's image" could ever be regarded as "small" or unimportant.

There were also no small commandments. Lao-tzu, the sixth-century BCE Chinese philosopher, wrote, "A journey of a thousand miles begins with a single step," a teaching President John F. Kennedy quoted when he announced an early success in the space program. The Rebbe intuited that any commandment, posting a mezuzah on the doorpost of one's home, donning tefillin on a city street, lighting a Shabbat candle even on a onetime basis, could be the very vehicle to a person establishing an ongoing relationship with God. But he understood something far deeper. The Chinese proverb implies that the importance of the first step is that it leads one closer to the second step and to the third step and eventually to the completion of the thousand-mile journey. For the Rebbe, every step a person took, every *mitzvah* a person performed, was important and of value in and of itself.

The Rebbe applied this insight to all righteous behavior, for both Jews and non-Jews. His focus on charitable giving—made known to the larger world by his weekly dispersing to thousands of people of a dollar bill to be given to charity—applied with equal force to non-Jews. To make this world a "dwelling place" for God (see pages 36–37), every human being created "in God's image" has to be reached. He urged all employers to add a dollar bill to the envelope containing their employees' salary checks to remind them both to think in terms of their moral obligation to help others. And even though he was already quite sick at the time, imagine the gratification the Rebbe had upon seeing a photograph of President Clinton, standing alongside Rabbi Avraham Shemtov, putting a dollar bill into a charity box at the White House.

The Rebbe devoted his life to making the world aware that there is a loving God Who demands loving behavior, and to encouraging Jews to practice the ritual commandments as well and thereby deepen their relationship to God. Again and again, he preached the practice of goodness, and *ahavat Yisrael*, the love of one's fellow. One reason, I suspect, had to do with the fact that he came to leadership less than a decade after the Holocaust. If the Holocaust had shown the evil of which human beings are capable—underscored, as the Rebbe noted, by occurring in what was arguably the world's most academically and culturally advanced country—the Rebbe wanted to remind human beings of the good of which they are capable. If the Nazis had murdered Jews with Zyklon B gas because it was cheap,[1] a few pennies for each person they suffocated, the Rebbe wanted to elevate the value of human life. He wanted the whole world to understand that in the absence of God human life becomes devalued. And in the aftermath of the Nazis who had done everything to devalue Jewish life, he wanted all Jews to appreciate that every life has infinite value. And what could illustrate this more dramatically than his commitment to reach every Jew and every Jewish community in the world? Every town. Every village. No matter how remote. No matter how minuscule. The infinite value of every life. In all of Jewish history, nothing of this magnitude had ever been attempted before.

He sent out emissaries, the *shluchim*. And when there were people he thought could reach those whom his *shluchim* might not, he sent them. At the Rebbe's request, Rabbi Benjamin Blech, a Modern Orthodox, decidedly non-Chasidic, rabbi, was sponsored by Chabad on a lecture tour to the small far-flung Jewish communities of Asia. When Rabbi Dudley Weinberg asked if he should leave his Reform pulpit, he guided him to stay within his movement and affect change from within (see pages 223–24). He urged JTS graduate Professor Dov Zlotnick to publish his sermon on the topic of *mikveh* so that Conservative Jews could be influenced to support building *mikvehs* and using them. And the same applied to secular Jewish leadership. When Frank Lautenberg, then serving as national chair of the United Jewish Appeal, came to meet him, the Rebbe encouraged a reorientation of UJA's focus toward Jewish education, and told him that the UJA should use their vast mailing list not only to fund-raise but to disseminate Jewish teachings.

The Rebbe involved himself in every area that was shaping the Jewish world. In the post–World War II years, the Jewish people united around the need for a Jewish state, and the creation of Israel was the greatest solace for the Jewish community during this period; a state whose first law offered citizenship and refuge to any Jew who requested it, thereby guaranteeing that never again could oppressed Jews find the doors of all countries closed to them. But the Rebbe also understood that Zionism and the State of Israel in and of themselves could not guarantee the

Jewish future. In a 1959 letter he wrote to Israeli prime minister David Ben-Gurion, he argued that without an exposure for young Israelis—many of whom were being raised in a totally secular environment—to Jewish religious practice, Israel was in danger of raising a generation of Israelis who would know Hebrew, even know the contents of the Bible, but who would nevertheless be "completely divorced form the past of our people and its eternal and essential values." The letter was in many ways prophetic, as many Israelis connected with a sense of Israeli identity but not with Judaism, the ultimate source of Jewish identity. In addition to the many *shluchim* working in Israel, the Rebbe himself established relations with many figures of significance in Israel, and particularly in the Israeli army and the medical, educational, and political worlds. He understood that a Jew could live in Israel and still assimilate, and early on he urged Ben-Gurion to confront this issue. At the time of this writing, twenty years after the Rebbe's death, this issue remains on Chabad's agenda, reaching out to Israelis and not just in Israel. In 2012, more than 1,800 young Israeli backpackers in Thailand, many of whom felt little connection to Jewish rituals or to traditional religiosity, found their way to Passover seders organized by Chabad throughout Thailand. Before these seders became available, many of these people might well have had no answer to the most fundamental question posed at the Passover seder, "Why is this night different from all other nights?" Now they did.

Jewish law rules that if a Torah scroll, even one written with perfect clarity, has one letter rubbed out or written incorrectly, it becomes *passul*, invalid. It cannot be used in a prayer service. It is unkosher. In a metaphorical sense, for the Rebbe, anytime a Jew goes missing from a Jewish community, the community becomes irretrievably diminished, in a sense *passul*. As he had said on the very night he became Rebbe, at a time when Chabad was still a very small movement: "One must go to a place where nothing is known of Godliness, nothing is known of Judaism, nothing is even known of the Hebrew alphabet, and while there, put one's own self aside and ensure that the other calls out to God!" No Jew must ever be left behind. The Rebbe's concern, though, extended beyond the Jewish world; he, who had lived in Russia under Communist oppression and in Germany during the rise of the Nazis, wanted to do what he could to ensure that nations would not devour other nations, and that human beings would not oppress and harm each other. And so be initiated an effort to prevail upon all of society to adhere to the Seven Noahide Laws (see page 160), a task he regarded as an absolute requirement of Jewish law.

Upon meeting Brigadier General Israel Drazin, assistant chief of chaplains of the U.S. Army, the Rebbe encouraged him to influence the military to observe the Seven Noahide Laws. Sensing Drazin's concern that non-Jews might not appreciate what might be considered an unwanted Jewish intrusion into other people's affairs, the Rebbe assured him that he need not fear speaking this way; the officers who would hear him would welcome it. Upon reporting to the Rebbe how widely and well his talks were being accepted, the Rebbe encouraged him to speak to wider circles and to publish his talks as well.

The Rebbe also passionately campaigned to allow all children a moment of silence at the beginning of each school day. His hope was that they would use this time to reflect upon the Creator, the God who brought into existence all of humankind ("Have we not all one Father? Did not one God create us?" [Malachi 2: 10]). Such reflection, the Rebbe believed, particularly if it occurred daily, could also be an important step in achieving peace and harmony among all people.

The Rebbe thought that the United States was the perfect place from which to export these efforts to other countries as well, for these values were already ingrained in the American ethos. He would frequently cite the statement on all U.S. currency, " In God We Trust." And, the effect of that, the Rebbe taught, could lead to the fulfillment of the other statement on the American currency: e pluribus unum. "From many—one."

During the previous decades, starting with the Rebbe's assumption of leadership in 1951, Chabad's enormous expansion was attributed largely to his charismatic influence on his followers. It therefore was not surprising that many people expected that the movement's growth would grind to a halt and likely contract—maybe even wither—in the aftermath of his disabling stroke in 1992 and his death a little over two years later. Probably, there were some Lubavitchers who feared this as well; this,

I believe, was an important reason why the Messianic fervor increased so substantially during the period between the first stroke and the Rebbe's death. I think many Lubavitchers could not envision a future without the Rebbe; hence, they believed that the Messiah must come immediately.

While many insiders were praying for an immediate Messianic revelation, most outsiders did not see a great future for a movement that seemed so dependent on one man's leadership. Notable among them was Professor Menachem Friedman, the well-known Israeli sociologist and observer of Orthodox life. Writing at a time when the Rebbe was already ill but still alive, Friedman raised a number of questions about the movement's future, the final one of which was whether Chabad could "continue to exist without the bonding cement of the Rebbe." Friedman's conclusion? "The answer to all such questions appears negative. Even if Chabad does remain part of the Jewish scene, it will have become an entirely different sect."[2]

In the meantime, and to the consternation of Lubavitchers, the Messiah was not destined to come before the Rebbe's death and has still not come. To the amazement of outsiders, however, the movement has more than doubled in size in the years since the Rebbe died, a phenomenon that no one, either inside or outside the movement, predicted. Chabad, as noted, at the time of the writing of this book, is represented in approximately eighty countries, and Chabad houses are present in forty-eight out of the fifty American states, and its influence reaches significantly beyond its own institutions. Speaking of the Rebbe and Lubavitch to the *New York Times* on the occasion of the fiftieth anniversary of the Rebbe's assumption of leadership, the Conservative rabbi and distinguished historian Rabbi Dr. Arthur Hertzberg explained that the Rebbe's movement "has made an enormous change in the Jewish world [that left him] absolutely staggered with admiration. . . . If almost all the branches of Judaism have gotten into outreach," Hertzberg continued, "Lubavitch is the reason. They have shamed all the rest of us" (January 22, 2000).

How did this happen? How did it come about that the Rebbe—who left behind no successor—bequeathed to his followers and to others the one sure sign of a leader's success: the continued expansion and influence of his or her movement and goals.

Five years of studying the Rebbe's life and leadership have led me to conclude that he constructed a blueprint for all his followers to emulate, so that even in the absence of a living leader, they possess a code of instruction for how to lead their lives and how to conduct the well over one thousand communities served by his *shluchim*. At a 1961 meeting between the Rebbe and Rivka Blau (then Teitz), Blau, a student at Barnard, was accompanied by a friend who had recently spent several weekends in the Chabad community and who posed a provocative question to the Rebbe: "I hear that you know better than the doctor whether there should be surgery or not. And you know better than the lawyer which way to proceed with the case. Do you know more medicine than the doctor? Do you know more law than the lawyer?"

The Rebbe, who was indeed known to offer advice on medical[3] and many other issues, was not thrown off by the question: "When a house is built, the architect draws up a blueprint. He gives the blueprint to the contractor, and then the contractor tells the plumber how to do the plumbing, the mason how to do the masonry, the electrician how to do the electrical work. It's not that the contractor can do it better than everybody, but he can read the blueprint and that's why he can give the instructions." The Rebbe then quoted from a midrash, " 'God looked into the Torah and created the world.' The blueprint of the world is the Torah, so if somebody can understand Torah, he can tell other people what they have to do even within their own métier [vocation]." He then concluded: "No, I don't know law better than lawyers, and I don't know medicine better than doctors, but based on what I learn from the Torah, that's how I can give people advice."[4]

Insofar as the Rebbe is concerned, the "blueprint" he left behind is both written and unwritten. The written part consists of some two hundred volumes comprised of transcripts of the Rebbe's speeches and well over ten thousand of his letters. In addition to the daily study enjoined by the Rebbe of his Chasidim, consisting of Torah, *Tehillim* (Psalms), *Tanya*, the weekly discourse on the Torah portion authored by the Alter Rebbe, at least two tractates of Talmud each year, and Maimonides's code of Jewish law (*Mishneh Torah*), most Chasidim study from a variety of the

Rebbe's teachings; the letters (*igrot*) in which he responded to questions addressed to him; the public lectures (*sichot*) in which he dealt with a variety of topics, ranging from the weekly Torah portion to current events, Chasidus; the talks on the mystical philosophy of the movement, which are found in the volumes containing the Rebbe's *ma'amarim*; and the numerous videos of *farbrengens*.

In addition, the Rebbe left an unwritten code, one that was shaped by the narrative arc of his life and by thousands of teachings and anecdotes told by him and about him through which his followers—and others as well—have learned how to reach out to Jews in an age of widespread assimilation. There exists a profound connection between the teachings and actions of the Rebbe as described in this book and the actions of his *shluchim*. They look to these writings and to the stories told about the Rebbe and, in the case of older Chasidim, to their own interactions with the Rebbe, for guidance on how to behave. The secret of Chabad's growth since the Rebbe's death is the secret of its growth during the Rebbe's life: the Rebbe himself. By studying his teachings *every day*, the Rebbe's followers see him as an ever-present force in their lives.

I received one indication of this ongoing impact of the Rebbe when speaking to Rabbi Avraham Berkowitz, who told me of an experience he had in Alaska when he was about twenty (at the time he was still a yeshiva student). For three summers in the mid-1990s, Berkowitz and a friend from Chabad went to Alaska, particularly to its more remote corners, to seek out Jews.

On one occasion, they came to a small city in the northwest part of the state. The mayor told them that he knew of no Jews in the city—the population was largely comprised of Native Americans—but invited them to give a talk to the students at the local school. The men shared with the fourth- to eighth-grade students some teachings about Judaism. The students in turn performed a few Eskimo dances for them, and the two Lubavitchers performed a Chasidic dance.

Knowing that the Rebbe wanted them to find Jews if they could, Berkowitz asked the students, "Did any of you ever meet a Jew?"

A young girl, of clear Eskimo appearance, raised her hand.

"Who ever did you meet?" Berkowitz asked her.

"My mother," the girl answered. "She's right there." She pointed to the school's fifth-grade teacher.

After the class, the mother was visibly moved and thanked him for coming. A native of the lower forty-eight, she had always loved nature and years earlier had come to Alaska and fallen in love with a native man.

"I must tell you that living here, I don't know if my daughter will ever meet another rabbi again. I ask you to give my daughter a message so that she will always be proud of her Jewish identity."

Berkowitz's mind began racing. He knew he only had these few minutes, that this was, as he told me, "a once-in-a-lifetime opportunity," but what should he say? Thinking back to the Rebbe's talks, he realized that one of the Rebbe's great strengths was his ability to personalize a mitzvah for the individual to whom he was speaking, and to thereby inspire and empower that person. He started to speak to the girl about the holiness of the Sabbath, the day that Jews dedicate to God: "And who ushers in Shabbat?" he continued. "It is mothers and daughters who light the Shabbat candles. They bring peace and light into the world."

He then asked her: "Where is the first place in the world where the sun sets?" The girl, who knew her geography, said, "Probably New Zealand or Australia."

And Berkowitz told her: "That's right. Jewish women in New Zealand and Australia are the first to usher in Shabbat. And then Shabbat is ushered in with lit candles in Asia, in Israel, in Europe, and then New York, Chicago, Seattle, Anchorage. And even then, there is one part of the world where the sun has not yet set. Here in the Yupik territory of Alaska. When mothers and daughters around the globe have welcomed the Shabbat, God and the Jewish people are still waiting for you, the last Jewish girl in the world, to light the Shabbat candles."[5]

In thinking about the incident, Berkowitz himself recognized that the answer he offered her was an inspired one—over the years, he has related this story in Jewish communities throughout the world, and it has influenced many Jews to start lighting Shabbat candles. Berkowitz attributes this inspiration to the one personal interaction he had had with the Rebbe, an incident that had occurred almost a decade earlier, and left Berkowitz with a particular mitzvah that he appropriated as his own in the same way he now wished the young girl in Alaska to appropriate candlelighting as her special mitzvah.

In Berkowitz's case, it all came about shortly before his bar mitzvah when he visited Crown Heights during Passover. Unlike other boys who came from well-established Chabad families and who knew many people in the area, Berkowitz was a child of parents who had become observant Jews as adults and who were not connected in the world of Chabad. When he came to Crown Heights, the one person whom he recognized was the Rebbe, who did not know him.

An emotional high point during the morning prayer services on holidays occurs when the *kohanim*, Jews of priestly descent (the most common last name for *kohanim* is "Cohen"), go to the front of the congregation, cover their heads with their *tallit*, and bless the congregation with the words of the priestly benediction recorded in the Torah ("May the Lord bless and protect you. May the Lord make His face shine upon you and be gracious to you. May the Lord lift up His countenance upon you and grant you peace." [Numbers 6:24–26]). Although only a small percentage of Jews are *kohanim*, because of the very large numbers of people in attendance at the central Chabad synagogue, a tradition had developed that only the elder *kohanim* stepped forward to the main platform to perform the *duchaning*, the blessing of the congregation, while the younger ones would do so from the floor. The young Berkowitz, who knew himself to be a *kohen*, was not aware of this tradition and he therefore acted as he did in his hometown congregation and stepped up to join his fellow *kohanim*. Yet, because of another tradition, that young men do not wear a *tallit* until they are married, Berkowitz, unlike all the other *kohanim* on the platform, found himself standing without a prayer shawl (which all the *kohanim* wear; in his home shul, he would stand under his father's *tallit*): "People were staring at me, because I was a short young kid alongside these much older figures, and I didn't have a *tallit* on me. Nobody from the crowd offered me one."

The young boy was embarrassed and bewildered, not knowing what to do. He glanced in the direction of the one person he did know in the congregation, the Rebbe, who, because he was not a *kohen*, was standing during this prayer with the rest of the congregation. Seeing the boy's discomfiture, the Rebbe immediately started to lift his own *tallit* off his shoulders to hand to him. Other Chasidim, seeing what the Rebbe was doing, rushed over to provide the young Berkowitz with a *tallit*: "At that moment I felt so loved by the Rebbe. Although the Rebbe never spoke during prayers, when the *kohanim* would come down, he would thank them for their blessings. As we came down, he said three times, '*Yasher koach, kohen. Yasher koach, kohen. Yasher koach, kohen*' (in effect, "Congratulations, *kohen*"; literally, "May your strength be firm"). The Rebbe endeared me to this mitzvah ever since, with the idea that as a *kohen* it is my duty to bless others.[6] He influenced me in that one moment of life."

Just as the Rebbe had cemented in the young Berkowitz's mind that as a *kohen* he should offer blessings to others, so during that moment in Alaska did he know that he should cement the blessing of Shabbat candles as the special mitzvah for this young girl: "God and the Jewish people are still waiting for you."

Stories like these—in this instance, rooted in the Rebbe's love and concern for every individual—became widely known in the world of Chabad, and the lessons the Rebbe modeled, along with his teachings, remain clear even when the Rebbe is not present, and later, even when the Rebbe was no longer alive.

Probably the best, and certainly the most popular, book written on the work performed by the Lubavitch *shluchim* is *The Rebbe's Army*, by Sue Fishkoff, a journalist. Though Fishkoff did not choose to become a Chabadnik, or in any way Orthodox, by the time she finished writing the book, the experience of immersing herself for a year within Chabad profoundly affected her. The changes were not because she witnessed public Chanukah candlelightings for thousands of Jews or saw otherwise secular men putting on tefillin, or nonobservant women lighting Shabbat candles. What most affected Fishkoff was a series of kind, loving acts directed both to others and to herself that she witnessed repeatedly over the year during which she was writing her book: "[These people] incorporate into their daily lives the Jewish values to which most of us give lip service: They visit the sick. They comfort the grieving. They take care to avoid embarrassing others."

On the day that Fishkoff completed a visit to Chabad in Minneapolis, Rabbi Moshe Feller, the city's head *shliach*, dropped her off at the airport for her trip home to California. Fishkoff recalls that as she was waiting for the flight, she looked over the sandwiches at the airport food stands and discovered that all that remained for sale that day were ham and cheese sandwiches, and "whereas ordinarily I wouldn't think twice, this time I hesitated. It felt wrong, somehow, after spending a weekend with Chabad, to eat *trayf* [unkosher food] so soon. Maybe that's silly, but I just couldn't do it."

Then, as Fishkoff, now anticipating a long trip without food, proceeded to the security checkpoint, she saw Rabbi Feller "running around the waiting area, clutching a small brown paper bag to his chest. Seeing me, he ran up and thrust the bag into my hand. 'I got home, and my wife couldn't believe I let you go without giving you lunch,' he apologized. 'Here, please, you shouldn't go hungry.' Inside the bag were neatly wrapped slices of kosher cheese, some bread, a cookie, and a bottle of juice. I almost cried."[7]

Yet another reason that Chabad has been able to continually expand its activities both during the Rebbe's lifetime and since his passing is its uncanny ability to generate donations from Jews who themselves are not Orthodox. This is unusual; most groups receive the lion's share of their donations from people who share the groups' denominational affiliation. I know of no breakdown of the religious affiliation of donors to Reform synagogues and to Hebrew Union College, but I would guess that they, particularly the largest donors, overwhelmingly are Reform; likewise with donors to the Conservative movement. This, however, is not the case with Chabad; the money needed to support Chabad Houses in over a thousand communities is largely (though not exclusively) donated by residents of those communities. From extensive anecdotal evidence, it is clear that many of these donors are not observant Jews in the conventional sense (e.g., observers of the Sabbath and kashrut laws).[8] Why then do they give to Chabad?

Chabad is one group that they are confident will perpetuate Jewish observances,[9] and therefore perpetuate Jewish survival, particularly in the Diaspora. That is the power, along with the humor, behind the special "January 1, 2100" front-page supplement that the *New York Times* published on January 1, 2000. Many articles portrayed on the front page depicted scenarios that made the future world seem a very unfamiliar place, particularly one that raised the issue of whether or not robots should be allowed to vote. Reading through the headlines could make a reader acutely uncomfortable; the future world seemed very alien. And then a familiar notice suddenly appeared, announcing to Jewish women the proper time for candlelighting that Friday evening (January 1, 2100, indeed falls on a Friday).

A number of years ago, I was speaking to the head of one of the largest Jewish federations in the United States (the man asked not to be identified) who mentioned in passing that even Reform Judaism sends people to Chabad. The remark was puzzling, and I asked him what he meant. He told me that upon assuming leadership of the federation, he made a dozen phone calls to a variety of synagogues, Reform, Reconstructionist, Conservative, and Orthodox. In each instance, he represented himself as a married man in his thirties with two children, and who had been unemployed for more than a year. His financial resources were now exhausted, but with the Jewish holidays approaching, he was seeking a High Holiday service the family could attend, along with an afternoon Hebrew school program in which his children could enroll.

In several instances, he was told that if he had already been a member of the congregation, some financial accommodation could be made. But given his previous noninvolvement, there was nothing that could be done for him. Several other congregations were more sympathetic, offering to put him in touch with a synagogue administrator, who could determine, following a detailed financial investigation, if some sort of partial scholarship could be arranged. The range of responses and the level of sympathy extended varied, but there was only one bit of advice that was uniformly offered by all twelve institutions:

"Call Chabad."

Part Eleven

·(❁❂❁)·

The

LIFE

of

RABBI

MENACHEM MENDEL

SCHNEERSON

Chapter 30

MAJOR EVENTS IN THE LIFE OF
THE REBBE

A Timeline Designed to Be Read

1902: April 18 (11 Nisan 5662):[1] Menachem Mendel Schneerson is born in the city of Nikolayev, in southern Ukraine. The oldest of three children, all boys, born to Rabbi Levi Yitzchak and Chana Schneerson, the future Rebbe is named for his great-great-great-grandfather, the Third Rebbe, Menachem Mendel Schneersohn.[2] The second son, DovBer (Beryl), who showed great brilliance in his early years, was diagnosed with schizophrenia as a teenager and was eventually institutionalized; he was later murdered by the Nazis. The youngest, Yisrael Aryeh Leib (Leibel), an accomplished Talmudist as a youth, subsequently studied for a PhD in mathematics in England and died while still in his forties (see chapter 26).

While yet a young child, Menachem Mendel revealed extraordinary capabilities in a wide range of traditional Jewish studies and stopped attending a local Jewish school at age eleven and a half;[3] he continued his studies with a private tutor (whose name is not known) until his bar mitzvah. From then on, he studied with his father, a Talmudic scholar and an equally renowned Kabbalist, and alone. He seems to have had an early fascination with astronomy, and a map of the universe hung in his bedroom (as regards the young Menachem Mendel's wide-ranging secular, as well as Jewish, knowledge, see page 119).

In addition, Menachem Mendel, from a remarkably young age, seems to have been passionate, even obsessed, with the problems of Jewish suffering and hopes for divine redemption. In a 1956 letter to Yitzhak Ben-Zvi, president of Israel, he noted: "From the day that I was a child attending cheder [Jewish elementary school], and even before, the vision of the future Redemption began to take form in my imagination—the Redemption of the Jewish people from their final Exile, a Redemption of such magnitude and grandeur through which the purpose of suffering, the harsh decrees and annihilations of Exile will be understood . . . with a full heart and cognizance."[4]

1909: Upon his father's appointment as chief rabbi, the young Menachem Mendel moves with his family to Yekaterinoslav, the fourth-largest city in the Ukraine (in 1926, the Soviet changed the city's name to Dnepropetrovsk), with a Jewish population of approximately seventy thousand. Rabbi Levi Yitzchak Schneerson serves in this post for thirty years.

1917: The Bolshevik revolution brings Russia and the countries it controls, including Ukraine, under Communist rule. The regime, aggressively atheistic in nature, has a particular animus against Judaism and succeeds in repressing most religious activity. Over the coming years, Rabbi Levi Yitzchak is outspoken about preserving Judaism in the face of Communist oppression and is frequently summoned by the Soviet authorities for questioning about his religious activities.

In a 1972 speech in Brooklyn, the Rebbe recalled, "My father was the chief rabbi of Yekaterinoslav. The fact that I was his eldest son and fluent in Russian meant that on a number of occasions I was called into the Yevsektsia [the Jewish section of the Communist Party; the Yevsektsia's members were infamous for their hatred of Judaism and of Zionism, and for their willingness to inform on both religious and Zionist-oriented Jews to Soviet authorities]. They would interrogate me, all the while screaming at me."[5] In one instance that we know of, he was pressured, unsuccessfully, to have his father certify as kosher for Passover matzah that was being produced by Communist-run bakeries and that did not meet proper specifications. The Rebbe also spoke of being mocked by his questioners and being forced to debate with them, with the threat of punishment hanging over his head if they were displeased with his responses.[6] In a speech three years later, the Rebbe suggested that these early encounters afforded him a lifetime of strength to face opposition and not be overwhelmed by criticisms and threats: "I grew up during the times of the Yevsektsia, and I was taught not to be afraid of them. This was despite the fact that they could not only threaten, but could also fulfill their threats and send you off to Siberia"[7]—which they often did. In 1939, eleven years after his son had left Russia, Rabbi Levi Yitzchak was arrested by the Soviet government and exiled to the tiny town of Chili in Kazakhstan, from which he never returned.

1923: Menachem Mendel Schneerson travels to Kislovodsk to meet his distant cousin, Yosef Yitzchak Schneersohn, the Sixth Lubavitcher Rebbe. The Sixth Rebbe seems to have been highly impressed with the reports he heard about the young scholar from Yekaterinoslav, and confides to his follower Rabbi Eliyahu (Elye) Chaim Althaus, his intention to give his "precious daughter" Chaya Mushka in marriage to him. Althaus is dispatched to Yekaterinoslav to arrange the introduction (i.e., speak to Menachem Mendel and his parents) and bring the young man to Kislovodsk, where the Sixth Rebbe is spending several weeks. The two men meet there, and a short time later the Sixth Rebbe hosts Menachem Mendel in Rostov for a week.

While it is uncertain whether Menachem Mendel and Chaya Mushka had already met, the Sixth Rebbe discusses Menachem Mendel with his daughter; at the end of the week in Rostov, he sends Chaya Mushka a letter that reveals his impressions of the young man: "My daughter, this week I studied *Hilchos Mendel* (the subject of Mendel), may he be well, almost every day, several hours each day. On Sunday, the three of us [including Shmaryahu Gourary, his son-in-law] spent the entire day together, and it was very pleasant."

While the young man's extensive Jewish knowledge was already well known, the Sixth Rebbe writes also of the pleasant hike they had taken (from the tone of the letter, it is possible to infer that Menachem Mendel and Chaya Mushka might also have gone hiking earlier). What is clear, and suggests that Chaya Mushka was very interested in seeing this relationship work out, is the tone of the Frierdiker Rebbe's letter; he is anxious for his daughter to know that Menachem Mendel went away with a "very pleasant impression of the reception he had received."[8]

A few months later, Menachem Mendel spends the High Holidays with the Sixth Rebbe, and over the coming year, the Rebbe increasingly draws him into his inner circle. Rabbi Shlomo Yosef Zevin, one of twentieth-century Jewry's great religious scholars and writers, spends a long train ride with Menachem Mendel and reports to the Sixth Rebbe that the young man's piety impressed him "even more than his deep Torah learning and vast knowledge," about which Zevin had "previously heard."[9]

1927: The arrest of the Sixth (Frierdiker) Rebbe in Leningrad (after Menachem Mendel becomes the Seventh Rebbe, the Sixth Rebbe becomes known as the Frierdiker Rebbe, the Previous Rebbe; today, Frierdiker Rebbe is the title by which he is most commonly referred to). The Yevsektsia had been pushing for years for the arrest of the Frierdiker Rebbe. Among other things, he had been maintaining a system of underground Jewish religious education and was receiving funds from the American-based Jewish Joint Distribution Committee to help finance his activities. Just after midnight on June 15, two men, quickly followed by a group of armed men, burst into the Frierdiker Rebbe's apartment, shouting, "We are from the GPU" (secret police). Leading the group was a man named Nachmanson, a son of a Lubavitcher Chasid; the second in command, Lulov, also came from a Chabad background and was the son of a prominent Jewish philanthropist. Though Jews by birth, both men had long since joined the Communist Party and repudiated Judaism.

Chaya Mushka was not with her family when the secret police entered the apartment. She had been out that evening with her now fiancé, Rabbi Menachem Mendel, and when they approached the building and saw lights on throughout the apartment, she warned him to stay outside and entered the apartment herself. According to the Rebbetzin's recollections, when she perceived what was going on, she peeked out a window and mouthed, "We have guests."[10] Menachem Mendel understood what had happened and immediately woke up Rabbi Elye Chaim Althaus, and together they went to the home of the Rebbe's secretary, Rabbi Chaim Lieberman. At that point, Lieberman started to burn papers, presumably documents pertaining to the Jewish schools and synagogues that Chabad was operating throughout the country. By the time the secret police came to Lieberman's house, he had succeeded in burning almost all of the relevant papers.[11]

The Frierdiker Rebbe was taken to the infamous Spalerno jail for political prisoners. While it appears that the Soviet authorities might have initially planned to execute him, thinking thereby to put an end to Chabad, an international outcry, organized in part by Jews in the United States, led them to relent. Nineteen days after his arrest, the Frierdiker Rebbe was told that he would be released and exiled for three years to the city of Kostroma, some four hundred miles from Leningrad (today, St. Petersburg). His daughter Chaya Mushka accompanied him into exile. During the exile to Kostroma, the pressure on the government mounted, and only nine days after his arrival in the city he was informed by the secret police that he was free to go.[12]

1927: The Frierdiker Rebbe—and shortly thereafter Menachem Mendel Schneerson—departs the Soviet Union. After his release from prison, it becomes clear that the Frierdiker Rebbe's position in the USSR is not viable; he is under surveillance and it is unsafe for Chasidim to meet with him.

International pressure on the Rebbe's behalf is again mounted, this time to allow him to leave the Soviet Union.[13] The Frierdiker Rebbe is granted permission to emigrate to Latvia, then an independent country (in 1940, it is annexed by the Soviet Union). He is allowed to take a number of people with him, mainly family members and a few close aides; he includes Menachem Mendel Schneerson in the group, though the young Schneerson and Chaya Mushka, the Rebbe's daughter, are not yet married. Government officials insist that the young Schneerson be deleted from the list; surely the Frierdiker Rebbe can find another husband for his daughter, one not already living in Russia. When the Rebbe refuses to back down, insisting, "A son-in-law like this is impossible to find," the government officials relent.

A late October date is set for their departure. Menachem Mendel returns to Dnepropetrovsk to spend a few days with his parents. Years later, Rebbetzin Chana Schneerson recalled those final days with her son: "No one, besides my husband and I, was aware that he was about to set out on his long journey. That Simchat Torah, we spent so much time together. We danced constantly. In order to hide our true feelings, we strove that holiday, with all our might, to be more lively and cheerful than always." The Rebbe never again sees his father, and will not see his mother for almost twenty years.

On October 20, 1927, the Frierdiker Rebbe leaves Russia by train for Riga, with his immediate family members; five days later, Menachem Mendel Schneerson, the future Rebbe, departs Leningrad for Riga.

After well over a century of Lubavitch in Russia, never again does a Lubavitcher Rebbe set foot in Russia.

1928: Menachem Mendel Schneerson begins his studies at the University of Berlin, where he remains until 1932. His academic forms for the spring semester in 1928 reveal that he takes courses in philosophy, analytical geometry, higher mathematics, and both experimental and theoretical physics. Among his professors that semester are one past and one future Nobel Prize winner: the German chemist and physicist Walther Nernst, who won a Nobel Prize in Chemistry in 1920, and Erwin Schrödinger, who received the Nobel Prize in Physics in 1933. Although the Rebbe rarely spoke of himself or his achievements, on occasion references to his university years came up in correspondence and private meetings, particularly when talking with academics. Columbia University professor Paul Rosenbloom recalls a discussion he had in the early 1960s with the Rebbe concerning Professor Schrödinger. Rosenbloom, who had been reading Schrödinger's book *What Is Life?*, noted to the Rebbe certain similarities between Schrödinger's notion of the "divine mind" and Maimonides's explanation of the "Godly soul." The Rebbe acknowledged the validity of the comparison and added that it would be worthwhile for Rosenbloom, and for rabbis as well, to share

Schrödinger's insights with university students: "When a rabbi tells a college student that there is a God and that everyone has a soul which is a portion of God, [the student feels that] the rabbi has to say this, that it's [his] livelihood [to say such things]! However, if a rabbi tells the student that Schrödinger [a Nobel Prize winner] wrote this, the student will believe him, since Schrödinger doesn't have an ulterior motive." [14]

Among the people the young Rabbi Schneerson befriends in Berlin is Rabbi Joseph Soloveitchik (later known as "the Rav"); the two men maintain an affectionate and mutually admiring—though sporadic—relationship for the rest of their lives (see chapter 17). [15]

1928: Menachem Mendel Schneerson and Chaya Mushka Schneersohn marry in Warsaw, the city with the largest Jewish population in Europe, on November 27 (the fourteenth of Kislev 5689). The waiting period of several years between their first meeting and their marriage is very unusual in Orthodox life, and understandably, given the highly private nature of both the Rebbe and his wife, no explanation is ever formally offered by either partner as to why this occurred. It most likely had something to do with the great persecutions Judaism and the Frierdiker Rebbe were encountering in the Soviet Union. As regards the year's delay between their arrival in Riga and marriage, two reasons have been suggested, and both likely are valid:

• Menachem Mendel's hope that Soviet authorities would allow his parents to leave Russia to attend the wedding; this is indicated in a letter written by the Frierdiker Rebbe to Shneur Zalman Kramer, a Chabad supporter in the United States. The Frierdiker Rebbe explained that he had not written to his followers in the United States with more precise information concerning the wedding "because we ourselves did not know the exact date. We waited, hoping that the government officials would grant the groom's father, Rabbi Levi Yitzchak, may he be well, permission to travel to the wedding. We waited from day to day, hoping for the good news that he would come. But to our heartfelt distress, he was not given permission, so we set the date of the wedding through an exchange of telegrams with him . . . and [only] then we immediately informed our friends."[16]

• Another significant reason had to do with the great poverty facing the court of Lubavitch at this time, and the inability of the Sixth Rebbe to mount a wedding of suitable dignity for his daughter. In another letter to the United States (indicating just how early the American Jewish community's financial support was becoming vital for Chabad in Europe), Rabbi Yechezkel Feigin, the Sixth Rebbe's secretary, described to Rabbi Israel Jacobson, the chairman of Agudas Chasidei Chabad in the United States, how desperate the financial situation was: "Eventually, whether a month earlier or a month later, the wedding will have to take place. But with what?" When a wedding date was finally set, Feigin sent Jacobson a more urgent appeal: "You surely understand that we do not even begin to have what is needed. . . . We must strategize and put together within a short time a respectable amount . . . which should be sent straight away by telegraph; there's no point in waiting until the final days" (written on October 14, 1928, six weeks before the wedding).

At the wedding reception, surrounded by other Chasidic Rebbes and rabbinical scholars, the Sixth Rebbe delivers a *ma'amar* (Chasidic discourse), which he introduces with a striking image: "It is a tradition that during a wedding, the souls of the ancestors of the bride and groom come from the World of Truth. . . . As an invitation to the souls of our righteous Rebbes who will come to the chuppah to bless the couple, I will now deliver a *ma'amar*, part of which has its source in the Alter Rebbe, the Mitteler Rebbe (the Second Rebbe), part in my great-grandfather, the Tzemach Tzedek [also, the great-great-great-grandfather of the groom], part in my grandfather, great-grandfather of the bride, the Rebbe Maharash (the Fourth Rebbe), and part in my father, grandfather of the bride (Rabbi Sholom DovBer, the Fifth Rebbe). As our sages have said, 'Whoever repeats a teaching should envision the author of the teaching standing before him' " (Jerusalem Talmud, *Shabbat* 1:2). The Frierdiker Rebbe then proceeds to cite teachings from each of his five predecessors.

Twenty-two years later, when Menachem Mendel becomes the Seventh Rebbe, his first *ma'amar* cites teachings from his six predecessors, and he continues this practice on key dates each year, including Rosh Hashana.

Later that evening, at the celebration, the Frierdiker Rebbe proudly introduces his son-in-law to the great Torah sages present, among them Rabbi Meir Shapiro, the originator of the *Daf Yomi* (the daily study cycle of a page of Talmud), and Rabbi Menachem Zemba, a towering rabbinic figure who tragically becomes even more famous for his later leadership inside the Warsaw Ghetto.

Because Menachem Mendel's parents are not permitted by Soviet authorities to attend the wedding and remain confined to Dnepropetrovsk, a celebration is organized in their home, with some three hundred people in attendance, a virtually unprecedented event in the totalitarian and antireligious Soviet Union. Eyewitness accounts report that the dancing went on through the night.

1929: The Frierdiker Rebbe, while in Baden Baden, Germany, writes a letter to his wife, Nechama Dina, describing the powerful impression their new son-in-law made on the philanthropist Mendel Rothstein. Rothstein, who spent many hours with Menachem Mendel over Shabbat, had come in to tell him: "This young man is extraordinary. He is a person with remarkably broad knowledge." Rothstein was a world traveler, which Menachem Mendel definitely was not, yet what particularly impressed the worldly philanthropist was that whenever he mentioned an important place he had visited, Mendel was familiar with it from having read about it, and asked him, 'And did you see this-and-this item there?' " On the preceding day, the Frierdiker Rebbe writes, Rothstein had started to speak about a trip he had made to Cairo and his visit there to the Third Pyramid. Soon, the two men got into a polite debate concerning some of the pyramid's contents; later, after Mendel reminded Rothstein that in the third room there was a certain mummy with a particular inscription on it, Rothstein acknowledged that Mendel was right. A short time later, the two men got into a discussion about Rothstein's visit to the Temple Mount in Jerusalem. The philanthropist reported that a particular tunnel there was a certain length, but Mendel, basing himself on a passage in the Talmud, said that it should be such-and-such a length. Rothstein, he correctly conjectured, "was recalling the length as it appeared when one entered from the other side, through the Nikanor Gate, as written by the chroniclers of the Roman period." Rothstein was flabbergasted by the young Schneerson's knowledge and his impressive ability to draw practical conclusions from it. The Frierdiker Rebbe, who could not suppress his pride, concluded, "And all this he [our son-in-law] states quietly and calmly."

1932: The Frierdiker Rebbe tasks Menachem Mendel, who is in Berlin, to work to release the Lubavitch library from Russia. Since its inception, the Chabad Rebbes held a collection of many thousands of books and manuscripts, which were in essence the "crown jewels" of the movement. The Fifth Rebbe, Rabbi Sholom DovBer, had lived in Lubavitch until 1915, when, due to the turmoil caused by the First World War, he moved to Rostov on the Don River. At the time, he stored his library for temporary safekeeping at a warehouse in Moscow, with the intent of retrieving the books and manuscripts after the war. However, in 1917, before the war ended, the Bolshevik Revolution occurred and the newly installed Communist government confiscated the books and relocated them to the state-owned Lenin Library. In 1920, the Fifth Rebbe died, and was succeeded by his son, the Frierdiker Rebbe. He too had no success in his efforts to regain the Chabad library from the government. In 1932, the Frierdiker Rebbe wrote to Menachem Mendel, who was then in Berlin: "You know that my books, the Lubavitch library, is still in Moscow. . . . This bothers me greatly but I'm sure that efforts [to release them] will only bring good." He asked Menachem Mendel to impress upon the chief rabbi of Berlin, Dr. Meier Hildesheimer, Dr. Oscar Kahn, a socialist deputy of the Bundestag, the German legislative body, and Hans Gaslar, a Jewish activist and press officer of the Prussian Ministry of State, to do all they could to help secure the release of the books. "You should meet him [in this instance referring to Gaslar] a few times and tell him how . . . this is truly a desecration of the name of G-d that the books from which the Holy Rebbes studied during their lives, including some which they wrote on, are now lying imprisoned. . . . Explain this to him with rabbinic passages and stories and in a way he can understand." [17]

With the Nazi takeover of Germany a year later, all efforts to enlist German support to recover the books ended. As of 2014, these books are still being held inside Russia and the government refuses to release them.

1932: Shortly before the rise of the Nazis to power in Germany (January 1933), Menachem Mendel and his wife, Chaya Mushka, leave Germany. They remain for an extended period with the Frierdiker Rebbe in Warsaw, during which Menachem Mendel is asked by his father-in-law to act as a spiritual mentor for yeshiva students. [18]

The couple subsequently emigrate to France, where he enrolls as an engineering student at the École Spéciale des Travaux Publics, du Bâtiment et d'Industrie (ESTP), one of the French *grandes écoles*, schools that were more selective in their admissions processes than the public French universities. He eventually graduates (1937) with a degree in mechanical and electrical engineering. Menachem Mendel also takes a number of classes at the Sorbonne, France's most famous university. Rebbetzin Chaya Mushka also takes university classes in Paris but is not known to have acquired a degree.

In later years, Rebbetzin Schneerson, in conversations with friends, used to speak with great joy of her and her husband's years in Paris. For the Rebbetzin, coming from a family of Rebbes, this period, in which she and her husband lived as private citizens, and not as famous and carefully monitored figures, seems to have been very special.

1932: The Frierdiker Rebbe, who already suffers from various illnesses, is diagnosed with multiple sclerosis and given only a few months to live. He requests Menachem Mendel's advice for his medical predicament, and has his doctors consult with the young man. From this point on, the Frierdiker Rebbe's increasing reliance on Menachem Mendel becomes increasingly apparent in his correspondence: "The doctor told me to [go to a sanatorium in] Vienna. I would like to know if you can come, it is important that you be there since you are familiar with everything that the doctors said" (March 25, 1934). On another occasion he writes to him, "The doctor [who treated me at Sanatorium Purkersdorf and in Paris] has now traveled to America. . . . I now have two options: either I can go to a doctor in Paris or [to a doctor] in Vienna. . . . I wish to know your opinion on the matter" (November 25, 1936).[19] The variety of medical treatments prove helpful, and though he suffers greatly, the Sixth Rebbe lives another seventeen years, until 1950.

1935: While in Paris, and in addition to his engineering studies, Rabbi Menachem Mendel prepares his father-in-law's teachings for publication. This includes his formal discourses (*ma'amarim*), the less formal speeches (*sichot*), and letters; these sources are regarded as the most important repositories of information about a Rebbe's thinking.[20]

Despite all the work he is doing on his father-in-law's behalf, Menachem Mendel himself prefers to remain very much in the background. Thus, during the years 1935 to 1938, the Chabad yeshiva publishes *Hatamim*, a scholarly and highly regarded rabbinic journal. Menachem Mendel's name does not show up in any issues of the journal, neither as the author of an article or as an editor. However, subsequent to his death, and among his papers, a letter from the Frierdiker Rebbe to his daughter Chaya Mushka surfaces in which he wrote: "Through the work and dedication of your honorable husband, my dear and beloved son-in-law . . . an important journal, *Hatamim*, will soon be printed. Although others' names will be printed as the authors, the entire work is really his."

1938: Menachem Mendel actively encourages the Jews he encounters in Paris to send their children to a local Jewish *cheder*. Efraim Steinmetz, then ten, remembers the future Rebbe coming to his father in an effort to enroll him in the local Jewish school.[21] Three decades later, when the Rebbe sent Rabbi Shmuel and Bassie Azimov as *shluchim* to open a school in Paris, the Rebbetzin, reflecting on the years she and her husband had lived in there, told Bassie Azimov, "We plowed and sowed; now you must go and harvest."[22]

1939: Throughout the Paris years, the Frierdiker Rebbe tries to push the retiring and somewhat shy Menachem Mendel into the public eye. At one point he writes to his daughter, Chaya Mushka, "I would really like him to become known, but this can be achieved only through his speaking up and not by remaining silent. Hiding from people won't lead to anything. I don't know why [Menachem Mendel does this]."[23] He asks his confidant Alexander Reinin to arrange for his son-in-law to be present at a certain class, for "surely, then, they will honor [Menachem Mendel by asking him] to give a *shiur* [class], which I greatly desire, and surely after the *shiur* he'll talk about topics related to awakening people to G-d, in which he has great talent."[24] In 1939, seizing on a response Menachem Mendel sent to a query from Rabbi Zalman Shmotkin, a Chasid in Warsaw, about an obscure area of Talmudic thought, the Frierdiker Rebbe insists that the Rebbe develop his scholarly insight into an advanced scholarly tract[25] (the text itself, however, remains unpublished until after the Rebbe's passing).

1939: September 1: Germany invades Poland. Almost immediately, both France and England declare war on Germany and World War II begins.

On the day of the German invasion, Menachem Mendel and Chaya Mushka are in Paris, at that point a safe city for Jews. However, the Frierdiker Rebbe is in Otwock, a Warsaw suburb where he had set up his headquarters and yeshiva in 1935.

A frenzied effort is undertaken by the Frierdiker Rebbe's devotees in the United States to secure his exit from Poland. Because America is not yet at war with the Germans, the Roosevelt administration intervenes with the German government, which, as a matter of goodwill, agrees to permit the Rebbe, along with his closest family members and aides, to leave.[26]

Improbable as it sounds, an officer in the Nazi army, Major Ernst Bloch, son of a Jewish father, is dispatched to war-torn Warsaw to find the Sixth Rebbe. Hearing reports that a Nazi soldier wearing a swastika is searching for the Rebbe, Lubavitchers inside Warsaw undertake an impassioned effort to hide him. On December 14, the Frierdiker Rebbe and his entourage are nevertheless located by Bloch and are put on a train for Berlin, with Bloch and other Nazi soldiers accompanying them. Inside the German capital, the group is handed over to Latvian diplomats, who bring them to safety in Riga (which is not under attack by the Nazis and where the Frierdiker Rebbe holds citizenship). Several months later, the entire group leaves Riga for Sweden, and from there they board a ship to the United States.

1940: March 19 (9 Adar II 5700): The Frierdiker Rebbe arrives in the United States. In the face of the catastrophe looming over European Jewry, he commits himself on the very day of his arrival to energizing Jewish life in America: "We whose steps have been directed here, have been so [directed] in order to . . . make America a place of Torah." To those who caution him that he will not be able to undertake the sort of religious activities in the United States that he carried out in Eastern Europe, he responds with what becomes one of his two most famous pronouncements, "America is not different,"[27] meaning that a religious Jewish life can flourish in the United States as it had in Europe. On this same day, he announces that he will be starting a Yeshivat Tomchei Temimim Lubavitch (the same name as that of the branch of Lubavitch yeshivot in Europe). The following day, ten students gather in New York to begin their studies and inaugurate the school.[28]

1940: June 14: The Nazis occupy Paris. Three days before the city falls, Menachem Mendel and Chaya Mushka flee to Vichy, capital of the French region that the Nazis do not occupy, but which is ruled by General Philippe Pétain and French officials sympathetic to the Nazis and hostile to the Jews. After a few months in Vichy, the future Rebbe and Rebbetzin relocate to Nice, in southern France.

The ensuing months are difficult and frightening, both because of fear of the advancing Nazis and great financial deprivation. Yet as evidenced by a letter the future Rebbe wrote in December 1944 to one who had shared with him the experience of exile in France, there were spiritual gains made during this period as well: "When a person is uprooted from his habitual environment . . . there come to light certain traits of his inner character. . . . Often, these traits reveal the hidden good in this person, of which perhaps he himself had been unaware.... Fortunate is the person who does not allow these traits to disappear when he subsequently settles down and finds tranquility."

While on the run, Menachem Mendel and his wife refuse to part with crates of Chasidic manuscripts, which they successfully take to safety. In subsequent decades, Menachem Mendel publishes many Chasidic volumes from these writings.

Meanwhile, in New York, the Frierdiker Rebbe and the court of Chabad exert great and ultimately successful efforts to procure American visas for the Rebbe's daughter and son-in-law. The future Rebbe and his wife escape France in June 1941; on June 12, they board the *Serpa Pinto* in Lisbon, bound for New York.

The Rebbe and the Rebbetzin lose close relatives, including his brother DovBer, her sister Sheina and brother-in-law Mendel Horenstein, his grandmother Zelda Rachel Yanovsky, and a number of cousins. Despite this, the Rebbe would later assert that no matter his personal pain, "life according to God's command must go on, and the sign of life is in growth and creativity." [29] Contrary to some noted Orthodox figures, the Rebbe asserted his belief that there was no explanation for the Holocaust: "To say that those very people were deserving of what transpired, that it was a punishment for sins, heaven forbid, is unthinkable. There is absolutely no explanation or understanding for the Holocaust.... Certainly not the explanation of a judgment and punishment" [30] (regarding nontheological explanations for the Germans' behavior, see the Rebbe's comments to Harvey Swados, pages 56–58). As to the question why did God permit the Holocaust, the only possible answer human beings can offer, the Rebbe writes, "is only God knows." [31]

1941: June 23: Rabbi Menachem Mendel and Chaya Mushka Schneerson arrive in the United States. The Frierdiker Rebbe is too ill to meet the boat, but he sends four of his leading Chasidim to form a welcoming committee. The emissaries are dispatched with an elaborate pronouncement concerning his son-in-law: "Let me reveal to you something of this man . . . he knows the Babylonian Talmud by heart, together with the commentaries of Rabbeinu Nissim, Rosh, and Rif; he knows the Jerusalem Talmud with all its commentaries, and Rambam [Maimonides], and *Likkutei Torah* [of the Alter Rebbe] with all its annotations. Now, go and greet him." [32]

1941: Menachem Mendel brings a new spirit to public communal activity. On Rosh Hashanah, he instructs those going to the traditional *Tashlich* service at the Brooklyn Botanic Garden that they not walk there as individuals or in small groups; rather, those attending the ritual (in which people symbolically throw their sins into a body of water) should go in one large group and parade down Eastern Parkway, singing. At a time when American Jews were very private about their religious behavior, yeshiva student Zalman Posner recalls the great discomfort he felt at the prospect of singing Jewish songs in public; in the end, Posner remained a block or two in back of the group, assisting a slow-walking elderly Chasid. Suddenly, a well-dressed man, by appearances a nonobservant Jew, approached him. "Why are they singing? Why are they singing?" he demanded. Before Posner—fearing from the man's insistent tone that he was offended—could respond, the man resumed: "Do you know that deep down I have a spark, and when I heard these people going down the street singing, [it was as if they were saying] 'Hurray, I'm a Jew' and that spark [inside me] burst into a flame."

This Rosh Hashanah march to the water was perhaps the first indication that Menachem Mendel wanted Judaism to be celebrated publicly and proudly. Over the coming years, he would initiate a Lag B'Omer procession as well, in which Jewish children from New York's public schools would gather at 770 for a rally, followed by a parade on Eastern Parkway. These parades, which still take place yearly in Crown Heights, mark, as far as is known, the first organized annual Jewish parades in the United States.

1942: The future Rebbe starts work at the Brooklyn Navy Yard, utilizing the engineering skills he acquired in France. Although he almost never speaks about details from his personal life, at a 1957 *yechidus* with Yaakov Hardof, an electrical engineer, the Rebbe starts reminiscing about his earlier work experience: "When I came to this country,

I wanted to contribute to the war effort . . . and I was a supervisor at the Brooklyn Navy Yard."

When Hardof asked him what sort of work he supervised, the Rebbe explained that many of the Liberty cargo ships constructed by the U.S. Navy[33] were produced at the Brooklyn Navy Yard, and all required electricians to wire them for lighting and electrical controls. The Rebbe told Hardof that his job was to take the ship's blueprints and to make sure that all the wiring was done according to their specifications. The Rebbe clearly took pride in the work he had done: "I at least did my share for the war effort of the United States, which gave me shelter," he told Hardof.[34]

1942: The Frierdiker Rebbe appoints Menachem Mendel, known among Chasidim as Ramash (an acronym for Rabbi Menachem Mendel Schneerson), as chairman of Machne Israel, Merkos L'inyonei Chinuch, and Kehot Publication Society, the social service, educational, and publication wings of the movement. Ramash quickly demonstrates an ability to reach out to American Jews on their own terms and in a manner not commonly found among rabbinic immigrants from Eastern Europe. One of the early projects he oversees is the children's magazine *Talks and Tales*. The Jewish artist Michel Schwartz—subsequently hailed by *Fortune* magazine (1970) as "a visionary of unobstructed and unparalleled foresight"—is only fifteen when Ramash hires him as a freelance illustrator for the magazine. At the time, Ramash is preparing to introduce a feature called "Curiosity Corner," a monthly column that would illustrate, in an entertaining style, several little-known facts about Jewish life and customs. Schwartz is startled when Ramash—whom he knows to be the son-in-law of the Sixth Rebbe—tells him that the column *"zol oys'zehn vee Ripley"* ("should look like Ripley"). At the time, the "Ripley's Believe It or Not" newspaper feature is an illustrated and syndicated column consisting of unusual facts and is printed in newspapers reaching tens of millions of Americans daily. Later, Ramash discusses with Schwartz his ideas for a cartoon character about whom adventure stories could be written, and tells him, "He should look like Dick Tracy"; Tracy, a crime fighter, is the most famous comic strip hero of the time, and a pop hero among American youth of all ages. In these seemingly minor events, modeling columns for young readers on artwork resembling that of Ripley's and Dick Tracy, we see an openness—not commonly found in the Chasidic world—to utilizing American culture as a vehicle for reaching out to American Jews.

The workload, though, is staggering. In addition to *Talks and Tales*, his primary responsibility at Kehot is supervising and editing publication of books extending from the most scholarly to the most basic sorts of texts geared toward less knowledgeable Jews. The range of his activities is reflected in a 1946 letter to Rabbi Menachem Zev Greenglass, a leader in the Chabad community in Montreal who had apparently expressed upset at not having heard for some time from Ramash: "I have not written you due to the many obligations especially in the area of publications. . . . Recently, I had to edit a booklet about Purim and Passover in French, one about Purim in English, volume 1 of *Our People* in English, a final editing of the Chasidic discourse *Mayim Rabbim*. I am also in the midst of editing an addendum to the *Tzemach Tzedek* (it will contain 125 responsa), a booklet entitled *The Tzemach Tzedek and the Enlightenment*, a collection of the [Fifth] Rebbe Rashab's talks," and on and on, culminating with "a book of questions and answers in English between a teacher and a child regarding Jewish religion and practice, a code of Jewish law for youth in English, and more." All this in addition to his other organizational responsibilities beyond publishing.

1943: Ramash publishes his first book, *Hayom Yom (Today Is the Day)*. The title is drawn from a daily prayer recited at the conclusion of the morning service that begins with the words, "Today is the day . . . on which the Levites recited at the Temple," followed by the psalm designated for that day of the week. The book's goal, as explained in its subtitle, is to provide "an anthology of aphorisms and customs arranged according to the days of the year, assembled from talks and letters of Rabbi Yosef Yitzchak Schneersohn." The book's objective, therefore, is to inspire readers in their daily behavior with a teaching drawn from the Sixth Rebbe, and its intended audience is all Jews, not just Torah scholars. The book has since been reprinted forty-nine times, translated into several languages, and is still widely used on a daily basis by thousands of Lubavitchers.

1943: Presents Judaism to Jewish public school children. One of the major innovations Ramash oversees is programming for Jewish children at public schools. Every Wednesday, during a federally mandated "Released Time" hour when children are permitted to leave school premises for religious instruction, Ramash sends yeshiva students to teach Jewish subjects to public school children, providing what is for many of them their only opportunity to learn about Judaism. At the behest of his father-in-law, he also arranges gatherings for Jewish public school children on Shabbat afternoons (known as *Mesibbas Shabbas*— Sabbath get-together) at which Torah stories are told, Jewish games and songs are played and sung, and refreshments are served. A young Chasid, Tzvi Fogelman, records in his diary how Menachem Mendel "ingrained in us the perspective that Lubavitch was not just a small and obscure Chasidic sect, but that it was a universal movement to 'transform the world.'" He writes that at one *farbrengen* Ramash proclaims, "The [Sixth] Rebbe began with *Mesibbas Shabbas*, and from *Mesibbas Shabbas* he will influence the entire world."

1943: Ramash creates the Merkos L'Inyonei Chinuch summer visitation program to deepen the connection of Jews in remote locations to the rest of the Jewish people and to assist them with their religious and educational needs. Beginning with ten cities in upstate New York, and subsequently expanding to California, the Deep South, and an ever wider international orbit, pairs of yeshiva students seek out Jews at their homes, farms, and businesses. In its first decades, Rabbi Menachem Mendel personally oversees the students' routes, and commissions from them detailed reports, which they send to him upon their return. In many locations, seeds are sown for the development of local communal institutions; in some instances, the students' visits eventually culminate in permanent Chabad-Lubavitch representation.

1944: August 9, 1944 (20 Av 5704): Rabbi Levi Yitzchak Schneerson, the Rebbe's father, dies in exile in the city of Alma-Ata, Kazakhstan. Starting with the rabbi's arrest in 1939, Rabbi Levi Yitzchak is not only cut off by the Soviet regime from all Jewish communal activities (there was no Jewish community in Chili, the tiny town to which he was exiled; shortly before his death, he was freed from exile and went to Alma-Ata, where there was a small Chabad community), but the Communist regime denies him access to ink, so he cannot write letters or record his Torah thoughts. His wife, Rebbetzin Chana, follows him into exile and manufactures ink for him from local herbs and plants. Three years after his death, Chana succeeds in smuggling some of his writings out of Russia, and they are edited and published decades later by their son.

Rabbi Schneerson, or Reb Leivik, as he was commonly called, apparently died from cancer, though he also suffered from extreme privation during his years in exile. Years later, when the Rebbe saw a photograph of his father during this period, he wrote on the back of the picture, "My father, of blessed memory?," the question mark signifying the difference between how his father looked in this picture and how he had looked earlier, "a difference so vast that it was difficult for anyone . . . even his own son, to identify him as the same person."[35]

1946: The future Rebbe publishes a Passover Haggadah with extensive explanations on the Haggadah's text and with a listing of specific Chabad customs. For example, though Jewish law dictates that a Jew not eat matzah on the day preceding the Seder—so that he or she will truly appreciate the taste of the matzah when it is consumed—the Rebbe notes that "it is our custom not to eat matzah during the thirty days preceding Pesach." Elsewhere, the Rebbe notes that prior to the recitation of the Mah Nishtana (known in English as "The Four Questions"), in which a young person directs a series of questions about the Seder to his or her father, the person reciting the questions should first say, "Father, I will ask you four questions." After listing this custom, the Rebbe then adds another, "This is said even if the father is no longer alive."[36]

Throughout the Haggadah, the Rebbe makes references to Minhag Beit Harav, the customs practiced in the household of the Chabad Rebbes (at the time the Haggadah is published, there had been six Rebbes since the movement's inception). It becomes clear that it is the Rebbe's desire to encourage all Chabad Chasidim to observe many of the customs carried out by the various Rebbes. For example, in writing about the search for *chametz* (leavened products) carried out the night before the holiday, the Rebbe describes the procedure: "Ten pieces of hard bread are placed in different places of the house, each one wrapped in paper to prevent crumbling. One searches by the light of a wax candle, and with a bird's feather." He then details the full nature of the search—one that involves the children of the house—in making sure that all *chametz* is removed from the house. The rabbinical scholar Rabbi Shlomo Yosef Zevin, struck both by the comprehensive nature of the footnotes and the book's extensive insights, commented that the Haggadah established the Rebbe as a "scientific researcher and scholar of the highest rank, and a philologist of note as well."

The commentary on the Haggadah is one of only a few books the Rebbe wrote (see also 1943, *Hayom Yom*), though some two hundred volumes have been published containing transcripts of his speeches (*sichot* and *ma'amarim*), copies of over ten thousand of his letters (*igrot*), and detailed notes and essays he wrote on a variety of subjects (*Reshimot*).

1946: November 14: Rabbi Menachem Mendel Schneerson becomes a U.S. citizen. This is the first time since leaving Russia eighteen years earlier that he has formal citizenship in any country.

1947: March 17 (25 Adar 5707): The Rebbe travels to Paris to see his mother, who has escaped from Russia and whom he has not seen since leaving Russia in 1928; he arranges to bring her to the United States. He remains in Paris for two months, arranging her papers so as to move her to the United States. During this time, he oversees the publication of a booklet in French about Judaism, is involved in finding housing for local Jewish refugees, establishes a Beis Rivkah School for girls, and conducts *farbrengens* for the local Chasidim.

1947–1948: Shortly before the November 1947 United Nations vote to partition Palestine and establish part of it as a Jewish state, Zalman Shazar, the Labor Party activist and future Israeli president, comes to the United States. Shazar, who comes from a devoted Chabad family, calls the Frierdiker Rebbe and expresses his fear that the UN will not

vote to approve Jewish statehood. The Frierdiker Rebbe expresses confidence that it will do so and asks Shazar to visit him in Brooklyn after
the vote. The resolution passes, and a few weeks later Shazar visits the
Frierdiker Rebbe, who asks his assistance in creating a village in Israel
to be comprised of Lubavitchers (most of them Holocaust survivors and
immigrants from the Soviet Union). The village, established in 1949, is
named Kfar Chabad and is one of the first villages established in the new
state. Shazar is pleased to help, though he is taken aback by the request;
the opposition of the Frierdiker Rebbe and the even more intense opposition of his father to Zionism was well known to him.

This incident, not well known (although Shazar's involvement with
the creation of Kfar Chabad is), represents a significant lessening of the
anti-Zionist fervor epitomized by the Fifth Rebbe, who had declared:
"If the Zionist plan to take possession of the land will, G-d forbid,
materialize, they will defile it and disgrace it with their abominations
and misdeeds, causing our exile to be lengthened, G-d forbid."

During his years of leadership, the Rebbe—consumed by a concern
for Israel's security and a fervent love for Israeli soldiers who, he often
repeated, daily risked their lives to safeguard Jews—moves Chabad from
an anti-Zionist position to a non-Zionist one.[37]

1949: A little over a month before his death, the Frierdiker Rebbe
sends out Rabbis Shlomo Carlebach and Zalman Schachter-Shalomi,
both in their twenties, instructing them to reach out to Jewish students
at American colleges. The two men go to Brandeis, a recently established
secular university under Jewish auspices (named for Louis Brandeis, the
first Jew appointed to the U.S. Supreme Court). Reb Shlomo teaches
students Jewish religious songs, while Reb Zalman instructs male students on how to put on tefillin, giving away thirteen pairs. However,
the school administration, uncomfortable with such explicit religious
activity on their campus, warns the two men not to come back.[38]

The experiences of Reb Shlomo and Reb Zalman represent, as far as is
known, the first systematic effort at outreach to Jewish college students
by Chabad, and Shlomo Carlebach later recalled how Rabbi Menachem
Mendel urged them to continue efforts at outreach in the months

following the Frierdiker Rebbe's death. In the 1960s, the Rebbe initiates a campaign to dispatch *shluchim*, eventually on a full-time basis, to university students throughout the United States and, later, the world. The first campus Chabad House is established at UCLA by Rabbi Shlomo Cunin. Today, there are Chabad Houses at 200 additional campuses, and Chabad representation at just over 200 campuses as well. In February 2012, to cite just one example, Chabad at Columbia University (directed by Rabbi Yonah and Keren Blum) celebrated its fifteenth anniversary at a dinner honoring, among others, Nobel laureate Dr. Eric Kandel. Kandel was introduced by the Nobel laureate Dr. Richard Axel, who spoke in his introductory comments of the Chabad values of *Chochmah, Binah, v'Daat* (wisdom, understanding, and knowledge) and their relationship to science and scientific inquiry. It occurred to me while sitting at the dinner that much had happened in American Jewish life and in the perception of Chabad since Rabbis Carlebach and Schachter-Shalomi were warned off the Brandeis campus. Indeed, Brandeis itself has had a Chabad House since 2001.

1950: January 28 (10 Shevat 5710): The Frierdiker Rebbe dies. Over the following weeks and months, Menachem Mendel regularly urges all Chasidim to feel even more responsible than before to fulfill the Frierdiker Rebbe's mission and teachings. He specifically asks Chasidim to discover inside themselves even more capabilities than they previously thought they had, capabilities that would enable them to carry out the tasks that the Frierdiker Rebbe no longer can. Menachem Mendel resolves of course to do the same. Within days of the completion of shiva, the seven-day mourning period for his father-in-law, Menachem Mendel appoints *shluchim* to the Jewish community of Morocco (he writes that he had previously discussed the appointment with his father-in-law). Over the course of the year, and prior to the various Jewish holidays, he issues public pastoral letters addressed to "All the Sons and Daughters of Our People Israel, Everywhere," in which he presents applicable life lessons drawn from the upcoming holiday. He also writes to synagogue rabbis, yeshiva heads, and rebbes of other Chasidic groups, imploring them to reach out to Jews who are less knowledgeable than they. Yet despite all these activities, Menachem Mendel rebuffs all attempts to influence him to assume the role of Rebbe. "What do you suppose? That Mendel Schneerson is a Rebbe?" he asks the first Chabadnik who solicits him during the week of mourning, and despite the increasingly energetic pressure exerted upon him, he repeats this sentiment in one form or another over and over. He insists, rather, that the Chasidim continue to be guided by the spirit and teachings of his father-in-law, a foreshadowing of what occurs forty-four years later, when the Rebbe dies and leaves no successor. The Chasidim are not dissuaded by Ramash's continued refusal to head the movement, and continue to pressure him to do so (see chapter 2).

1950 (and following years): Without leaving Brooklyn, the soon-to-be Rebbe becomes actively involved in a broad spectrum of Israeli activities, including encouraging business development in the new country and in setting up a school system, one that includes trade schools. In 1950, Ephraim Ilin, a security expert who soon emerges as one of Israel's foremost business leaders, comes to meet with Rabbi Menachem Mendel at 770. At the time, Ilin was considering establishing a car production company based in Israel, but had such grave trepidations about its chances for success that he couldn't bring himself to sign the $2 million contract to start the company. The two men enter into a prolonged discussion, and Ilin expresses amazement that "when I talked to him about cars, he knew more than I did." The soon-to-be Rebbe strongly encourages forming such a company, and assures Ilin that "the plant could be the foundation of all Israeli industry." Ilin has long acknowledged how encouraged he was by the Rebbe's words, and soon signs the contract and establishes Kaiser-Frazer, a company that produces 55,000 cars over the coming years; in 1956, Kaiser-Frazer accounts for 28 percent of Israel's exports.[39]

Over the coming years, Chabad establishes its own school system in Israel, and also sets up a series of trade schools geared toward immigrant youth, many of whom are intimidated by the more rigorously demanding academic high schools, and who are at risk of dropping out. Schools are established teaching carpentry and woodwork (1954), agriculture (1955), printing and publishing (1956), and textiles (1957).

Many of the activities that later come to typify Chabad are inaugurated during this period as well. The Rebbe directs the newly arrived Chasidim in Kfar Chabad to bring religious joy and observances both to the soldiers at army bases and to the nonreligious kibbutzim near them.

1951: In the lead-up to his father-in-law's *yahrtzeit* (the anniversary of his passing), Ramash urges every person to impact the religious lives of at least ten other people, and to effect a chain reaction.

1951 January 17 (10 Shevat 5711): On the first anniversary of his father-in-law's death, Rabbi Menachem Mendel assumes the role of Seventh Rebbe. He signals his acceptance of the position by initiating his first *ma'amar* (Chasidic discourse) with the words *"Bati le-gani"* ("I have come into my garden"), the topic sentence of his predecessor's final talk. In a statement that soon comes to characterize his leadership, the Rebbe urges the Chasidim present not to simply rely on him for leadership; rather, he puts power and responsibility into their hands: " 'Now listen, my fellow Jews! In Chabad, the Rebbes have always demanded of Chasidim to take action personally and not rely on the Rebbe. . . . So do not deceive yourselves. . . . One should not rely on anyone else to do their work for them. . . . Each of you on your own has to toil to transform the [darkness of impurity] and the passion of your own animal soul into great holiness."[40]

1951: The Rebbe establishes the Lubavitch Women's and Girls' Organization (Agudat N'shei U'bnot Chabad) and the Lubavitch Youth Organization (Tze'irei Agudat Chabad) in Israel. Their mission is to engage in outreach directed to women and teens, respectively.

1953: The Rebbe establishes the Lubavitch Women's Organization in the United States and several other countries. Several months earlier, as it was starting to become apparent to careful observers that the then new Rebbe was expanding the involvement of women in the movement, Chaya Tzirla Plotkin, who was having a private meeting with the Rebbe, noted that the Alter Rebbe, the movement's founder and himself an enormous scholar, showed how *gaonim*, brilliant people, could become Chasidim (opponents of the movement long thought it could only appeal to simple Jews); his son, the Second Rebbe, demonstrated how young people could become Chasidim; the Third Rebbe (Tzemach Tzedek) showed how rabbis, even of non-Chasidic background, could become Chasidim. She then indicated similar innovations detailing how the Fourth, Fifth, and Sixth Rebbes had expanded the scope of the movement. "But now," she said, "the Rebbe is turning the women into Chasidim." Mrs. Plotkin reported that the Rebbe smiled broadly, even laughed, as she got to her description of him and what he was doing. He seemed pleased to have been found out, that he was opening up the movement—perhaps the first Chasidic Rebbe to do so—to the active participation of women. Sixty years after this encounter and the founding of the Lubavitch Women's Organization, there are over four thousand *shluchot*, women serving as emissaries alongside their husbands in over a thousand communities and in some eighty countries.

1953–1954: The Rebbe initiates wide-scale efforts to increase observance of a number of Jewish laws that are frequently ignored by modern Jews. For Sukkot, he starts a campaign to get as many Jews as possible, men and women alike, to recite the blessing over the *lulav* and *etrog*.[41] A few months later, he starts sending out hand-baked *shmurah matzot* to individuals—some of them prominent figures—within the Jewish community (a tradition still followed by *shluchim*) and organizes a campaign to get as many Jews as possible to eat *shmurah matzo* over the holiday.[42] He also calls on all rabbis to arrange communal Passover Seders for their communities, and to provide necessary Passover foods to those incarcerated in jails.

Many of the recipients of the *matzot* sent out by the Rebbe, though in no way traditionally observant, are deeply moved by the gesture. Curt Leviant, who translated into English three novels by the esteemed Yiddish writer Chaim Grade, recalled visiting Grade (pronounced *Grad-a*) in his Bronx apartment shortly before Passover. To Leviant's surprise, Grade, who had grown up as a highly accomplished yeshiva student but was no longer traditionally observant, suddenly said to Leviant: "Wait, I want to show you something." He went into another room and soon returned with a flat cardboard box of *shmurah matzot*. "You know who sent it to me?" he asked Leviant, and then proceeded to answer his rhetorical question: "The Lubavitcher Rebbe. Every year at this time, he sends his personal *shliach* [messenger] to bring me a box of *shmurah matzot*. He's been doing this for years." [43]

1953: November 21 (14 Kislev 5714): This day is the twenty-fifth wedding anniversary of Rabbi Menachem Mendel and Chaya Mushka Schneerson. During an extended *farbrengen*, the Rebbe, who rarely speaks in public about himself, his wife, or his marriage, announces: "This is the day that bound me to you and you to me. You will press me, I will press you, and together we will squeeze out the complete and final Redemption."

1953: The Rebbe states that according to halacha (Jewish law), it is prohibited to travel on an Israeli, or any Jewish-owned, ship if part of the travel occurs on Shabbat. While it is uncharacteristic of the Rebbe to comment on Jewish legal issues—he generally directed questioners on matters of Jewish law to local rabbis—in this instance he felt compelled to speak out because he felt no one else was and, in addition, because of his special knowledge of the subject. As he noted in response to a questioner who wrote that he had booked passage to Israel on the SS *Israel*: "I can tell you, however, most emphatically, being myself an engineer and knowing the mechanical intricacies involved in navigating a modern ship, there is no question whatsoever that such a voyage is definitely forbidden by the Torah." [44]

When Zim, the Israeli shipping company, publicized an assurance to the Jewish community that its ships ran on automatic for all of Shabbat, the Rebbe did not back down. Rather, he compiled a series of questions directed to the ship's engineers and administrators questioning whether any ship could run without human intervention for twenty-four hours:

- "Does this mean . . . that the rudder of the ship operates automatically when the ship is in motion . . . ? And what happens when a change in the course, or a deviation is necessary (by reason of the proximity of another ship, etc.)? And if the steering has to be adjusted occasionally, at least by hand, is it not true that the rudder is connected with the engine room, and that a change in the position of the rudder influences the engines, increasing or decreasing the operation of the boilers?"

• "Is it not necessary for a ship on the high seas to send out periodic radio messages about its position [an activity forbidden on the Sabbath] and does it not receive in its own radio room similar messages from boats or ships in the proximity? Do not such messages have a bearing on the course of a ship? Is it permissible for a ship in motion to shut off its radio room for 24 hours?"

• "I would like to know as well, whether or not the ship's log, particularly with reference to the fire room and the engine room, can be suspended for 24 hours or must the entries be made immediately after the periodic [mandatory] inspection of the [ship's] machines?"

• "How are the commands and instructions relayed from one department of a ship to another?"

• "Can a ship be run for 24 hours without any need for adjustments, changes or repairs in any of its machinery or devices of any kind?"

The Rebbe concludes his letter with a request for a response to each of these questions, one he never received; as he explained in another letter: "I am sure that there will not be found anyone who will state that any of these enumerated items can be worked automatically, if he has any regard for the truth and does not want to be caught . . . making false statements."

What the Rebbe hoped to achieve was *not* the shutting down of the Israeli shipping line but rather that Jewish-operated ships schedule their voyages so as to be docked for Shabbat. Zim argued that doing so would lead to a vast and commercially unviable increase in travel time.[45] As the Rebbe did not wish to harm Israeli companies or to be perceived as doing so, he suggested to questioners to fly to Israel by El Al instead.[46] It was traveling on a Jewish-owned boat on Shabbat that struck him as both wrong and absurd. As he wrote to yet a third correspondent: "Would it not be ridiculous . . . for a person desirous of going to the land which is regarded as holy even by non-Jews, to choose a way of transportation which involves an open violation of one of the Ten Commandments." (The Fourth Commandment enjoins: "Keep the Sabbath day holy"; see chapters 19–24 for additional controversial opinions of the Rebbe.)

1955: The Rebbe establishes the Lubavitch Youth Organization in the United States and Canada to strengthen, in the Rebbe's words, "the observance of Torah al *Mitzvot*" in North America.

1956: Arab terrorists attack Kfar Chabad and murder five students and a teacher (ten other students are wounded in the attack).[47] The towns-people, most of whom have lost close family members to Nazi or Soviet violence and are finally restarting their lives, are in shock, as is a good part of the country. In response, the Rebbe urges Kfar Chabad's leaders to redouble their efforts, explaining that comfort will come only from rededications to their mission of Jewish outreach (as he writes in a tele-gram of condolence to the village: "*B'hemshech ha-binyan tinachamu*" ["By your continued building you will be comforted"]). The Rebbe specifically urges the villagers to create a vocational school focused on teaching the printing trade and geared toward children from disadvantaged back-grounds. Several weeks later, the Rebbe dispatches ten Lubavitchers from Brooklyn to Kfar Chabad to offer consolation and support (the trip makes a large impression in Israel, as in 1956 it was much less common than it is today for American Jews to visit Israel). Throughout this period, the Rebbe emphatically states that he refuses to venture any special "religious explanation" as to why this awful event happened, as it is unexplainable; he dwells instead only on the response to it.

1956: The Rebbe visits Camp Gan Israel, a newly established Chabad summer camp for boys, and Camp Emunah for girls, both in upstate New York, just before they open for the summer. This is one of only three times the Rebbe sets foot outside of New York City from the time he takes over leadership of the movement in 1951 until his death in 1994. All three trips are made to the Lubavitch youth camps; he returns for a second visit in 1957 and a third in 1960; at these visits, the Rebbe addresses the campers and staff as well.

1958: June 30 (12 Tammuz 5718): The Rebbe proclaims his *U'faratzta* campaign, to increase Jewish learning of all kinds and to significantly expand outreach worldwide. Ever since, this campaign has defined Chabad to the outside world (see chapter 4).

1959: The Rebbe tries to convince Israeli prime minister David Ben-Gurion to maintain the status quo about the suddenly volatile, and potentially divisive, issue of how to determine who is a Jew. Ben-Gurion writes to the Rebbe and other leading Jewish figures both in Israel and the Diaspora, questioning them as to how they believe Israel should determine who is a Jew; the problem has great resonance, as under Israel's Law of Return, any Jew is entitled to immediate citizenship. In response, the Rebbe strongly affirms that the definition of a Jew comes from traditional Jewish law and can apply to only a person born to a Jewish mother or converted according to halacha (Jewish law); no human being, he emphasizes, has the power to change that. The Rebbe further points out that this should not be regarded only as an internal Israeli matter, since altering the traditional definition of a Jew (such as by permitting anyone to declare himself to be a Jew, and thereby gaining Israeli recognition and citizenship) has the potential to "raise a barrier between the Jews of Israel and those of the Diaspora," which "no one" has a right to do. The Rebbe insists that the solution "must be one that is . . . capable of . . . strengthening the bonds between, and the unity of, all Jews, and certainly not . . . cause, even the remotest disunity and dissension." (For more on this issue, see pages 493–94.) The following day, the Rebbe, conscious of the secular environment in which most Israeli youth are being raised, sends a personal letter to Ben-Gurion urging him to utilize "the unique and most wonderful opportunity granted" to him to steer the ship of Israel in the direction of Jewish practice, so that the "new generation will [not] grow up [to] speak Hebrew, dwell in the land of the Patriarchs and wax enthusiastic over the Bible, [and still be] completely divorced from the past of our people and its eternal and essential values; and, moreover, hostile to it in its world outlook, its culture, and the content of its daily life." [48]

1959: Chabad starts offering lessons in the *Tanya*, the main text of Chabad teachings, on the radio; the classes are taught by Rabbi Yosef Weinberg. Though the movement has long been offering holiday messages and other programs on the radio, the *Tanya* classes inaugurate a new era in what subsequently becomes a characteristic feature of Chabad, the use of modern technology to transmit Judaism's ideas. In a 1966 talk, the Rebbe speaks of radio's outreach potential, in words that continue to apply to other, more recent forms, of electronic communication: "There is a special advantage in using radio to teach Torah. Even if a person is not sufficiently motivated to go and attend a class, or even if he only turned on the radio to hear something else, the words of Torah reach him." [49]

In 1970, Chabad inaugurates electronic broadcasts—via telephone hook-ups—of the Rebbe's *farbrengens* to Jews in London, Melbourne, and Israel. Still later, in 1980, the movement starts broadcasting the Rebbe's talks to television stations via satellite, particularly cable stations, throughout the country. As the talks are in Yiddish, a simultaneous English translation is offered. The wide distribution of these programs helps account for the increasing recognition of the Rebbe (perhaps the one rabbi so widely recognized) throughout the United States.

One person who tuned in to watch the Rebbe's *farbrengen* was the legendary theatrical producer and director Joe Papp, founder of the Public Theater. Papp later recalled that he listened to "this extraordinary man" speak for four hours "discussing ideas of such vast diversity and scope." Papp, who said that he "then felt there is a wise man left in the world" went on to personally host a pre-*farbrengen* broadcast honoring the Rebbe's eightieth birthday.

The radio (and later the television) broadcasts were initially met with criticism from some figures in the ultra-Orthodox *haredi* world for using radio, which they considered to be religiously forbidden and a source of evil (as it could be used to spread antireligious ideas or promote immodest behavior, through songs, for example). In a response that has influenced Chabad *shluchim* ever since to employ modern technology to spread Jewish teachings (television, videotapes, DVDs, the World Wide Web), the Rebbe noted that nothing created by God is evil in and of itself; it depends on the purpose for which it is used. Thus, radio, and all modern technology, can play a very positive role, particularly in an age when many American Jews cannot be reached by other means. This was one of the Rebbe's fundamental insights, an understanding that if Jews restrict the teaching of Torah, or in this case *Tanya*, to those who are willing to go to a class in a synagogue or school, the Jewish leadership will end up ignoring the large percentage of American Jews who will not do so. The years following the inauguration of the radio class witness an expanded use of technology to reach out to Jews who would otherwise not be reached, including an annual telethon organized by Rabbi Shlomo Cunin of Chabad of Los Angeles that, since its inception in 1980, has significantly raised Jewish consciousness in Southern California, along with tens of millions of dollars for local charitable and educational purposes.

The Rebbe's commitment to the use of the most modern technology to spread Jewish teachings continues to influence Chabad long after his passing. In 2005, Rabbi Gedaliah Shemtov, director of the Shluchim Office, founded the Nigri-Shluchim-Online-School for children of *shluchim* in cities where there are no full-time Jewish schools. Today, the Online School serves almost a thousand children of *shluchim* in six languages and in 343 cities on six continents.

1961: In a publicly released letter to an unnamed professor—which subsequently becomes among the most widely published of any of the Rebbe's English letters—the Rebbe makes the case for Jews continuing to accept as literal the biblical chronology of the world, according to which the universe is then 5,722 years old.[50] He argues that people mistakenly believe that science demands an acceptance of an age for the universe numbering in the billions of years, but this is simply not the case. The Rebbe distinguishes between "empirical science," which describes and classifies observable phenomena (e.g., the composition of a tree), and "speculative science," which offers theories dealing with unknown phenomena, such as what the world was like in the distant past (see chapter 22).

1961: On May 25, 1961, President John F. Kennedy addresses the American Congress, telling them that he is dedicated to America "landing a man on the moon" and to doing so "before this decade is out."

Within the Orthodox world, some religious leaders are dismayed by Kennedy's words (in segments of the Christian world as well), arguing that human beings were never intended by God to reach the moon and should not even try. In defense of this position, the biblical verse most often quoted is that of the Psalmist: "The heavens belong to the Lord, but the earth He gave over to man" (Psalms 115:16). Rabbi Menachem Mendel Kasher, a highly esteemed rabbinic scholar in Israel, publishes an extended essay, "Man on the Moon," in which he offers reasons why human beings going to the moon is forbidden by Jewish law.

The Rebbe's very different view becomes widely known in the aftermath of astronaut John Glenn becoming the first person to orbit the earth (in February 1962). Israeli journalist Shlomo Nakdimon questions the Rebbe about his views of Glenn's achievement and of the space exploration program. The Rebbe speaks enthusiastically and knowledgeably of the work being done by NASA (National Aeronautics and Space Administration), and Nakdimon publishes his views on March 16, 1962, in the Israeli newspaper *Herut*, under the title "Lubavitcher Rebbe: It's Possible to Reach the Moon."

Over the coming years, and in the aftermath of the various Apollo space missions, the Rebbe speaks on several occasions of lessons both spiritual and practical, to be learned from the space missions (see in particular his analysis of the 1969 moon landing, chapter 13).

1962: The Supreme Court issues a ruling outlawing all prayers in public schools, including those that simply affirm God but favor no specific religion. The American Jewish community overwhelmingly supports the Court's decision, while most Orthodox leaders, whose children attend private Jewish schools, remain silent. (It is unclear if their silence was dictated by a lack of concern with this issue or by tacit support of the Court ruling; perhaps they opposed the idea of Jewish children praying alongside non-Jews even if the prayer was nondenominational.) The Rebbe, concerned both that Jewish children who attend public schools might now not engage in any daily prayers whatsoever, and that non-Jews, no less than Jews, need to engage in a daily acknowledgment of a source of morality higher than human beings, critiques the Court's ruling and calls upon Jews to participate in legal efforts to have it overturned. In September 1967, the Catholic journal *Commonweal* republishes one of the Rebbe's letters on this issue. Several years later, when it becomes apparent that the ruling is unlikely to be altered, he shifts his efforts to the support of a proposal to start each school day with a "moment of silence" and reflection (see chapter 19).

1962: The "Encounters with Chabad" program is initiated in Crown Heights, during which college students are invited to spend Shabbat at 770 (participants are housed with local residents) and experience an exposure to a Chasidic lifestyle. Along with seminars and lectures, participants attend the Rebbe's Shabbat afternoon *farbrengens* (in keeping with the Rebbe's careful and optimistic choice of language [see chapter 7], he titles the program "Encounters with Chabad," and not "Retreats with Chabad," as the primary meaning of the word "retreat" is "to go backward" and has a negative connotation).

1964: September 12 (6 Tishrei 5725): Rebbetzin Chana Schneerson, the Rebbe's mother, dies during the *Aseret Y'mei Teshuvah* (the Ten Days of Repentance) between Rosh Hashanah and Yom Kippur. After being unable to see her for eighteen years, once she arrives in the United States, the Rebbe does not miss a day of visiting with her and, as his mother proudly pointed out, twice on Friday. In memory of his mother, the Rebbe initiates the explication of a teaching of the commentator Rashi at his weekly Shabbat *farbrengen,* and over the coming years he becomes known as one of the foremost expositors of Judaism's greatest biblical exegete. Professor Nehemia Polen of Boston's Hebrew College has noted that "the *sichot* trace Rashi's sources in Talmud and Midrash, noting how Rashi shapes and molds his material for his purposes. They draw upon the rich library of Rashi supercommentaries [commentaries on Rashi], and arrive at original conclusions regarding Rashi's intent. . . .

"In their richness, scope, sustained creativity, and vigor, they are a remarkable body of work."

In the years following his mother's death, the Rebbe establishes the Keren Chana Fund to provide financial assistance to young women who desire to continue their Torah studies.

1965: The Rebbe voices opposition to interfaith dialogues. Replying to a request by 250 Jewish leaders who had asked him for his views on interfaith dialogue, the Rebbe declared: "There is no need for us whatever to have any religious dialogues with non-Jews, nor any interfaith activities in the form of religious discussions, interchange of pulpits, and the like. The brotherhood of mankind is a positive concept only so long as it is confined to commerce, philanthropy, and civil and economic aspects of society. Unfortunately, brotherhood has been misconstrued to require members of one faith to explain their religious beliefs and practices to members of another faith." Noting the increase of intermarriage, the Rebbe said that interfaith dialogues have created confusion in the minds "of the young as well as of their parents."[51]

1966: Israel's third president, Zalman Shazar, visits the Rebbe. On Saturday night, July 30, while on his first official trip as Israel's president to the United States to meet with President Johnson, Shazar comes to 770 for a *yechidus* with the Rebbe. That a sitting head of state should travel to a non–head of state, let alone to a non-Israeli rabbi, is initially met with sharp criticism by some in Israel, including a number of Israeli newspapers.[52] Prime Minister Golda Meir is known to be unhappy as well with Shazar's behavior. Yet Shazar, who maintains a regular correspondence with the Rebbe, and is himself of Chabad background, is not dissuaded. One of those who comes out in defense of Shazar is Elie Wiesel, who writes of this encounter: "Shazar believes that a person can be both a president and a Chasid, and that the Chasid needs the Rebbe. This is Shazar's real greatness. . . . In my opinion, the people that are trying to make a fence between the two souls are doing a terrible thing."[53] When Shazar comes to 770, he and the Rebbe remain secluded for close to three hours, discussing matters of state.

1967: Six-Day War. In May 1967, as the armies of Egypt and Syria prepare to attack Israel, and Egyptian president Gamal Abdul Nasser announces, "Our basic objective will be the destruction of Israel," the Jewish world falls into a state of great anxiety, even panic, fearing massive Jewish deaths only twenty-two years after the Holocaust. Inside Israel, many Jews with foreign passports flee the country, but the Rebbe tells people to remain in Israel and to have no fear. On May 28, just over a week before the war begins, the Rebbe, speaking before an audience of many thousands, proclaims that Israel will soon emerge from the current situation with great success: "There is no reason to be afraid. I am displeased with the exaggerations being disseminated and the panicking of the citizens in Israel." His optimistic pronouncements are headlined in Israel's newspapers: "God Is Defending the Holy Land, and Victory Will Come Soon"(*Yediot Achronot*, May 31, 1967).

In the aftermath of the war, and referring to the great bravery exhibited by the Israeli army, the Rebbe speaks of "the advantage and greatness of those who go out to war [to protect the Jewish people] over those who study Torah."[54] (For more on the Rebbe and issues concerning Israeli security, see chapter 20.)

1967: During the tense period preceding the Six-Day War, the Rebbe initiates the Tefillin campaign, which is intended to safeguard and serve as an "extra merit" for the Jewish community, particularly Israel's soldiers, at this vulnerable time.[55] The operation sets out to influence Jewish men age thirteen and up to put on tefillin, particularly those who have never done so. Around the world, Lubavitcher Chasidim begin putting tefillin on Jewish men on street corners and in offices. In Israel, Lubavitchers also head to army bases, where they encourage Israeli soldiers to don tefillin and to recite the appropriate blessing when doing so.

After the war, the campaign shifts as well to the Western Wall (the *Kotel*); in the more than forty-five years since the Wall came under Israeli rule, Lubavitchers have been placing tefillin on the arms and heads of visitors. Among those who have put on tefillin at the *Kotel* are General Ariel Sharon (a subsequent prime minister), General Ezer Weizman (a future president), and the American songwriter and performer Bob Dylan. In more recent years, among those who have donned tefillin at the *Kotel* is Eric Cantor, a future House of Representatives majority leader. A November 24, 1967, article in the *Boston Globe* reported that over four hundred thousand men who did not previously observe this commandment had already put on tefillin at least once, and on May 7, 1968, the Jewish Telegraphic Agency reported that over one million people (the number presumably includes some who put on tefillin with *shluchim* more than once) had put on tefillin as a result of the campaign.

1967: In the aftermath of the Six-Day War, during which Israel increases its territory to four times the size of its prewar borders, the Rebbe launches an effort to stop Israel from returning any conquered lands to Arab rule. He argues that the overriding issue is not the sacredness of Eretz Yisrael (though this is of course strongly affirmed in the Jewish tradition) but *pikuach nefesh*, the saving of an endangered life; Israeli lives, the Rebbe insists, will be put in jeopardy as a result of Israel vacating any of the territories conquered during the war (see chapter 19).

The Rebbe orders the restoration of the Tzemach Tzedek synagogue, built by Chabad Chasidim in 1856 and the only synagogue found intact inside the Old City of Jerusalem following the Six-Day War.[56]

1969: On the final day of Pesach, the Rebbe addresses the problem of widespread Jewish emigration from Crown Heights, Brooklyn, the headquarters of Chabad since shortly after the Frierdiker Rebbe's arrival in the United States in 1940. As the neighborhood had started becoming more racially mixed in the 1950s, whites, many Jews among them, started moving out. The process accelerated greatly during the next decade; in 1960, Crown Heights was 71 percent white, by 1970, 27 percent.[57] In numeric terms, the white population declined from about

140,000 to a little over 50,000. In his speech, the Rebbe cites a series of Jewish legal rulings, the effect of which would be to forbid Jews from moving out of Crown Heights (or any Jewish neighborhood). Basing himself on these sources, the Rebbe argues that such flight undermines and destroys the neighborhood's Jewish institutions, particularly synagogues, schools, and kosher establishments. Also, Jews who lack the financial means to purchase homes in more affluent areas ("the poor, orphans, widows") are exposed to increased danger as crime in the old neighborhood rises with the departure of many of the old residents. The campaign to keep Jews in Crown Heights becomes the first successful attempt within the Jewish community to resist the phenomenon of "white flight," in which white residents flee an area when African Americans, particularly poor African Americans, move in. Subsequent to the Rebbe's speech and over the coming years, Lubavitcher Chasidim stop leaving Crown Heights. The impact of the Rebbe's speech is dramatic. "By 1991, the remaining white populations of great Crown Heights . . . consisted almost entirely of the area's twenty thousand Lubavitchers . . . and Crown Heights remained one of the very few American neighborhoods where a large and growing number of Jews lived as a minority side by side with blacks."[58]

1970: The completion of the writing of a most unusual Torah scroll. The belief in the Messiah's imminent arrival, a theme long associated with the Rebbe, was similarly emphasized by his predecessor and father-in-law, Rabbi Yosef Yitzchak, the Frierdiker Rebbe. In 1941, a year after his arrival in the United States, the Frierdiker Rebbe announces his intention to commission the writing of a Torah scroll with which to welcome the Messiah, and the writing commences in April 1942. Among those who purchase letters in this unique Torah scroll are the Israeli rabbi Yaakov Kanievsky, known as the Steipler Gaon (genius), and other non-Chasidic leaders. The Frierdiker Rebbe writes: "We must hold ourselves in readiness for the deliverance which is at hand, and in particular to write a *Sefer Torah* with which to welcome our righteous Messiah." For reasons that are not fully known, the scroll is never completed. Then, in 1970, shortly before the twentieth anniversary (*yahrtzeit*) of his father-in-law's death, the Rebbe announces his intention to complete the project in honor of the Frierdiker Rebbe's *yahrtzeit*. The Rebbe summons Rabbi Shmaryahu Factor, the original Torah scribe, to fill in the scroll's final letters, finally completing, almost thirty years after the project was first announced, a Torah scroll with which to greet the Messiah.

1970: The "Who is a Jew?" controversy. "The Law of Return," the first law enacted by the Israeli Knesset after Israel's creation, guarantees Israeli citizenship to any Jewish person. In 1970, the law is updated to read that a Jew is someone who was "born Jewish or who converted to Judaism." The Rebbe argues that these last words are inadequate, and insists that a word be added to this legislation "or who converts *ke-halacha*" ("according to Jewish law"; see page 134). In the absence of this addition, the Rebbe argues, the effect of the law will be to enshrine acceptance by Israel of non-Orthodox conversions, conversions the Rebbe regards as invalid. He argues that it is not the place of the State of Israel to be meddling and deciding who is a Jew. The Rebbe's proposed change would have the effect of invalidating for purposes of recognition by Israel the Jewishness of individuals converted by Reform and Conservative rabbis. The Rebbe's suggestion, backed by both Chasidic and non-Chasidic Orthodox rabbis, creates great ferment and provokes anger in much of the broader American Jewish community.

The Israeli government, not wishing to alienate large segments of Diaspora, particularly American, Jewry, does not pass the legislation as demanded by the Rebbe. The Rebbe in turn insists that the lack of uniform procedure for defining who is a Jew will eventually lead to a schism within the Jewish community and to Jews being unable to marry one another without conducting genealogical investigations to determine whether their intended partner is or is not Jewish.

Since the conversion issue was first raised by the Rebbe, it has remained a perennial bone of contention in the Jewish community, particularly in America, and has been exacerbated by several further developments in Jewish life. Thus, independent of the conversion issue, Jewish law (halacha) has long defined a Jew as a person born to a Jewish mother. However, in 1983, the Reform movement in the United States instituted a new definition, defining a Jew as one born to *either* a Jewish mother or a Jewish father and who is raised with an exclusively Jewish identity. During the coming years, this pronouncement impelled a further intensification in the Rebbe's efforts to have the Israeli Knesset accept the traditional definition of who is a Jew.

Much of Chabad and the Rebbe's popularity within American Jewish life was temporarily eroded during 1988–1989, at the height of the Rebbe's campaign. Indeed, in 1988, when it appeared that the Israeli Knesset might pass the Orthodox definition of "Who is a Jew?" (*haredi* political parties had recently won more seats in an Israeli election), Jewish federations in several American cities threatened to halt fundraising activities on behalf of the United Jewish Appeal if the legislation was enacted.

At the time, the Rebbe explained to the *shluchim* that it was not their role to debate anyone about the "Who is a Jew?" issue. Their focus needed to remain on helping people grow in their observance of Torah and commandments. The "Who is a Jew?" issue, the Rebbe insisted, should be handled by those in Israel who will be able to bring about benefits there.

Chabad continues, of course, to adhere to the Rebbe's view that only a non-Jew converted by an Orthodox rabbi is regarded as Jewish.

Today, given the high rates of intermarriage among American Jews, some of the college students who visit Chabad Houses on campus are not Jewish according to the traditional understanding of Jewish law (either because their mothers underwent no conversion to Judaism or had a non-halachic conversion). I have found no position by the Rebbe on whether children of Jewish fathers and non-Jewish mothers should be encouraged to convert to Judaism, though obviously those concerned with Jewish demographics realize that in the absence of conversions, the American-Jewish population will suffer a large decline in numbers.

1971: The Rebbe, known for his intense involvement with the Jews behind the Iron Curtain, criticizes the protest movement on behalf of Soviet Jewry. At a *farbrengen* in February, the Rebbe delivers his most explicit critique of the movement, arguing that anti-Soviet demonstrations in the West cause religious and other activist Jews inside the USSR to suffer and sometimes to be arrested and imprisoned. In addition, the Rebbe argues that such demonstrations have been responsible for Jews being denied visas to leave Russia. Behind the scenes, though, he does cooperate on certain projects with organizations that promote anti-Soviet demonstrations (see chapter 20).

1971: Calls by the Rebbe to transform the world through Torah learning. This emphasis by the Rebbe heralds a fundamental change in outreach that had focused until now primarily on performance of commandments, and expanding educational opportunities for the young. From here on in, Torah classes start springing up for adult, often uninitiated Jews, in Torah, Talmud, and Chasidic philosophy.

1972: The phenomenon, both earlier and later, of *farbrengens*. At a 1972 *farbrengen* attended by Elie Wiesel, Chaim Potok, and thousands of others, the Rebbe expounds upon the responsibility of every individual to utilize his or her God-given talents and abilities to help other people and, when possible, to bring them to a closer relationship to God and to the Torah's commandments. A *farbrengen* (literally "get-together") is the setting in which the Rebbe offers Torah and Chassidic discourses, along with insights into current events and how a Jew should react to them. At times, a *farbrengen* can last as long as eight hours, during which the Rebbe is seated on a dais, surrounded by the movement's elders and other prominent guest rabbis. Attendance often numbers several thousand. The Rebbe's speeches, delivered in Yiddish, generally last anywhere from thirty minutes to an hour and a half, and are delivered without any texts or notes. Following each speech, participants sing traditional melodies. It is also at these *farbrengens* that the Rebbe addresses the most pressing issues facing world Jewry at the time, such as territorial compromise by Israel, the release of Arab terrorists in exchange for captured Israeli soldiers, public demonstrations against the Soviet Union, and public school prayer. He also addresses world affairs of a broader scope and not directly connected to the Jewish community, such as the U.S.– Soviet space race, the hippie movement, the attempted assassination of

President Reagan, and the need for energy independence in the United States (see page 504).

A recurring theme the Rebbe touches on at almost every *farbrengen* is that the Torah is not simply a code of laws and narratives handed down more than 3,000 years ago, but is a "living Torah" that provides ongoing daily lessons on how people should lead their lives. "Live with the times" is an expression the Rebbe commonly uses; for him "the times" mean the weekly Torah portion, and the specific lessons it can yield for a person's behavior over the following days. Another observation the Rebbe frequently cites at *farbrengens* is the Baal Shem Tov's teaching that everything that occurs is by Divine Providence, and therefore anything we see or hear, whether good or not good, can instruct us in how to conduct our lives and how to serve God. To that end, at almost every *arbrengen*, in addition to a talk on a teaching of Rashi, of Maimonides, a talk based on a teaching of his father, Rabbi Levi Yitzchak, on the Zohar, and a talk on an aspect of Chasidic philosophy, the Rebbe invariably devotes one talk to the weekly Torah portion, and finds ways to relate it to the personal lives of those present. Frequently, he also ties in a Torah teaching to world events, and sometimes his teachings relate simultaneously to both world events and people's personal lives (see, for example, the Rebbe's talk in the aftermath of the 1969 moon landing; page 181).

In the early years of the Rebbe's leadership, a typical *farbrengen* can have as few as thirty people in attendance. But as the years pass and the community grows, more and more people start coming, not just from nearby neighborhoods in Brooklyn, but from across the tristate area, and later from throughout the country.

Since most *farbrengens* occur on Shabbat and Jewish festivals, when Jewish law prohibits videotaping and recording, most of the Rebbe's talks cannot be recorded. A group of talented people with trained memories gather after the Rebbe concludes his talks and repeat among themselves the Rebbe's words, writing them down immediately after Shabbat ends. The Rebbe himself later edits many of these transcripts. The edited speeches have been published under the title *Likutei Sichot* and comprise thirty-nine volumes (along with another ten volumes titled *Sefer Ha-Sichot*). In addition, there are more than a hundred published volumes of transcripts not edited by the Rebbe. All these volumes, along with the hundreds of hours of speeches recorded at weekly *farbrengens,* continue to be studied assiduously by Chasidim, many of whom routinely spend an hour a day or more studying the Rebbe's teachings.

1972: The Rebbe turns seventy. In line with his passionate opposition to retirement for people of any age (see pages 128–29) and his commitment to looking forward and not focusing on past achievements, he requests of his Chasidim—who wish to pay him homage on this special occasion—that, in honor of his entering the seventy-first year of his life, they establish seventy-one new Chabad outreach and educational institutions during the coming year. This wish is met, and among the cities in which new Chabad Houses are established are the Old City of Jerusalem, the Israeli cities Nazareth and Afula, Houston, Seattle, Berkeley (on the campus of the University of California–Berkeley), as well as cities in England, Australia, and Italy. In Los Angeles, Chabad *shliach* Rabbi Shlomo Cunin opens the Chabad Residential Treatment Center, a facility to treat people with drug addictions. In the past four decades, the center has treated several thousand people and has worked with both Jews and non-Jews. Early on in the center's history, Rabbi Cunin consulted the Rebbe concerning a problem. While the laws of Shabbat were of course observed inside the facility, including, for example, a ban on smoking on the Sabbath, Cunin had received complaints about residents of the facility standing on the street smoking on Shabbat. He asked the Rebbe's advice as to what he should do about this. The Rebbe replied that he should first take care of the residents' physical well-being [by getting them off drugs], and then their spiritual well-being.[59]

In a rare newspaper interview in honor of his birthday, conducted by *New York Times* reporter Israel Shenker, the Rebbe offers his views on a wide range of subjects, among them:

His followers' reverential view of him: "I am not a *tzaddik.* I have never given a reason for a cult of personality, and I do all in my power to dissuade them [my followers] from making it that." A poignant example of the Rebbe's attempt to discourage magical thinking about him is reflected in a letter he wrote on November 22, 1973, to an infertile couple who asked why his blessing for children had not proven effective. Though he could not, for obvious reasons, offer a definitive response, he does suggest that it was "because the couple forgot that it is God Who is the source of blessing and the One who gives it. [Instead], they placed their trust in a man of flesh and blood alone—in me."[60]

On the Rebbe's willingness to offer opinions and advice on a large range of issues, including theology, business, family affairs, and even medical questions: "[First] I am not afraid to answer that I don't know. If I know, then I have no right not to answer. When someone comes to you for help and you can help him to the best of your knowledge, and you refuse him this help, you become a cause of his suffering."

God, the big bang, and the supposed challenge posed by science to religion: "It is much easier to accept one human being, two human beings [created by God], than to accept billions of disordered atoms whirling around without any concept, any pattern, and then with a big bang or a small bang the universe is created."

The enduring relevance of Torah: "Everything that happens in 1972 . . . must be evaluated from the point of view of Torah, even if it happened for the first time in March of 1972."

Who will be the eighth Lubavitcher Rebbe?: "The Messiah will come and he will take [away] all these troubles and doubts. He could come while I am here. Why postpone his coming?"

His understanding of his role in life: "Awakening in everyone the potential he [or she] has."

The birthday gift he wants from his followers: "An additional portion of study and devotion to the cause of spreading goodness and kindness" (the *Times* headlines the article, "Lubavitcher Rebbe Marks His 70th Year with Call for Kindness").[61]

1973: The Rebbe launches a worldwide Chanukah campaign, urging that every Jew be given the opportunity to light his or her own Chanukah menorah, and to bring about global awareness of the Chanukah lights' story of miraculous salvation. After a run on all extant tin menorahs, and with only a few days left till Chanukah, Lubavitch obtains the services of a military manufacturer that churns out tens of thousands of additional menorahs for worldwide distribution. The Rebbe blesses the manufacturer that his own life be illuminated in merit of illuminating so many others'. The following year senior Chabad *shliach* Rabbi Avraham Shemtov of Philadelphia institutes a public lighting of a Chanukah menorah at the foot of the Liberty Bell, and from year to year lightings of menorahs on public grounds spread to dozens of American cities and then overseas.

In 1979, five years after the campaign's inauguration, Stuart Eizenstat, President Jimmy Carter's chief domestic policy adviser, lights a menorah at Lafayette Park, in front of the White House, with President Jimmy Carter standing beside him and Rabbi Avraham Shemtov as well. Despite this White House precedent, several Jewish groups, among them the American Jewish Congress, legally challenge the candlelightings on public properties, which are now spreading from city to city, and which they claim violate the constitutional principle of separation of church and state. Some groups also argue that the enormous menorahs that Chabad is setting up might well generate antisemitism. The Rebbe, a proponent of Jews being highly public, when appropriate, about their religious observances, writes to one communal leader: "It is difficult to imagine that after what happened in Hitler's Germany, some Jews still entertain the idea that by making themselves as inconspicuous as possible [and] concealing their Jewishness, they will gain favor with their gentile neighbors." The legal challenges eventually reach the Supreme Court, and Chabad's position—that such lightings do not violate American law—prevails. Currently, public lightings of the menorah are conducted in thousands of locations throughout the world.

1974: The Mitzvah Tanks (also known as Mitzvah Mobiles) and the Ten Campaigns. Repurposed mobile homes start appearing in Manhattan with bright signs proclaiming, Identify! and Help Israel, Help Yourself. The trucks are parked, their back doors open, and Chasidim welcome passersby to come inside: "Are you Jewish?" "Come, put on tefillin," or "Here are some Shabbos candles for you." The "tanks," in essence a Chabad House on wheels, signify an escalation in Chabad's efforts to reach out to all Jews, men and women alike, including those who rarely come to synagogue (see chapter 4).

1976: The Rebbe arranges a meeting with a group of disabled Israeli war veterans who have been brought to the United States by the Israeli Defense Ministry. Breaking with his tradition of giving his public speeches in Yiddish, the Rebbe addresses the soldiers in Hebrew (see page 111).

1977: The Rebbe emphasizes the need for American society to pro-mote moral education. In a talk delivered on his seventy-fifth birthday, the Rebbe declares, "Education should not be limited to the acquisition of knowledge and preparation for a career, or, in common parlance, 'to make a better living.'" At a time when Americans are debating the propriety of schools trying to inculcate moral values (as opposed to offering a neutral, value-free education), the Rebbe makes clear his belief that great evils can result in a society when a society glorifies intellectual achievement over goodness: "Need one be reminded of what happened in our lifetime in a country that ranked among the foremost in science, technology [and] philosophy? Education must put greater emphasis on the promotion of human rights and obligations of justice and morality, the basis of any human society, if it is to be truly human and not turn into a jungle." Some months later, President Jimmy Carter issues a proc-lamation in which he notes the Rebbe's seventy-fifth birthday and desig-nates the coming year "A Year of Education." The president announces that in honor of the Rebbe's upcoming seventy-sixth birthday in April 1978, he will designate the day "Education Day, U.S.A."

Every year for the more than thirty years since, every American pres-ident has designated the anniversary of the Rebbe's birth as a day dedi-cated by the United States to educational awareness and to an emphasis on moral education.

1977: The newly elected prime minister of Israel, Menachem Begin, visits the Rebbe at Chabad headquarters in Crown Heights, the first sit-ting Israeli prime minister to do so. When reporters question Begin as to the reason for his visit, the prime minister, preparing for a meeting with

American president Jimmy Carter, responds: "Rabbi Schneerson's ... status is unique among our people. So I am certain his blessings will strengthen me as I embark on a mission of acute importance for our future." After the meeting, when Begin is asked what he and the Rebbe spoke about, the prime minister responds: "This is not the first time I am meeting with Rabbi Schneerson. I have met him many times before, while I was still serving in the opposition. We have a long-standing agreement, myself and the Rebbe, that whatever we say remains between us" (see page 281).

1977: Rebbe's heart attack. On the holiday of Shemini Atzeret (the eighth day of the holiday of Sukkot), the Rebbe suffers a massive heart attack while dancing during the *hakafot*, the celebratory carrying around of the Torah scrolls. Dr. Ira Weiss, the chief cardiologist treating the Rebbe (among the other doctors involved are Louis Teichholz, Bernard Lown, and Lawrence Resnick), later reveals that this was the most serious heart attack he had ever treated from which the patient experienced recovery and was able to resume a full workload. In other such instances, Weiss stated, a heart attack of such magnitude generally led to death or, at best, disability and enforced retirement. In a letter to a well-wisher in the weeks following the heart attack, the Rebbe wrote, "Your warm expressions of concern for my health, and your good wishes, are sincerely appreciated. With the help of G-d—the 'Healer of all flesh who works wondrously' (as we praise Him in our daily prayers)—my recovery has been most satisfactory, and I have already been able to resume my duties."

1979: The Iranian Revolution (also known as the Islamic Revolution), during which the shah, who was supported by, among others, the United States, is overthrown and is replaced with radical Islamic dictator Ayatollah Khomeini. shortly after the shah's exile from Iran in April 1979, the Ayatollah Khomeini arrived in Teheran and was greeted by several million Iranian supporters. On April 1, 1979, Iranians voted by national referendum to become an Islamic Republic, and Khomeini soon emerged as supreme leader of the country. Realizing the highly intolerant nature of the form of Islam espoused by Khomeini, the Rebbe works to arrange passage out of Iran for approximately three thousand

Iranian youth between the ages of twelve and nineteen. Israeli diplomat Yehuda Avner recalls meeting with the Rebbe during the early days of Khomeini's rule, and the Rebbe predicting, at a time when nobody else was doing so, that the emergence of an Islamic Iran would carry with it "the seeds of jihadism that will spread across the Middle East, threaten Europe, and ultimately the whole of Western civilization." Speaking in 2008 of this three-decade-old encounter with the Rebbe, Avner labeled the Rebbe's insights as being "almost in the realm of prophecy, or, if you will—as a political scientist, in the realm of strategic analysis."

1980: Drawing on the very first commandment in the Bible, God's injunction to "be fruitful and multiply, fill the earth and conquer it" (Genesis 1:28), the Rebbe strongly encourages married couples to have large families. Speaking at a Chabad convention before three thousand women, the Rebbe sharply critiques the common use of various methods of family planning, and argues that "the greatest blessing God bestows upon a married couple is children." The Rebbe also declares that many couples, particularly later in life, "very often deeply regret that they limited the size of their families, and thereby deprived themselves of so much potential joy." His encouragement of large families is not confined to the Jewish community; he supports the Israeli government granting financial stipends to large Arab families, no less than to Jewish (see page 563). On the basis of anecdotal evidence, it is clear that the average size of Chabad families starts to grow in the years following the Rebbe's 1980 talk, and subsequent talks, addressing this issue.

1980: The Rebbe establishes Tzivos Hashem (Soldiers of Hashem), a children's organization for youth under the age of bar and bat mitzvah (thirteen for boys and twelve for girls). Despite the organization's name, it is in no way militaristic; rather, the children are divided into levels and, as they advance in performance of the commandments (*mitzvot*), their ranks eventually move up to captain, major, general, and eventually even five-star general. When questioned by one correspondent concerning the organization's name and her fear that it could lead to "the glorification of the military and an aggrandizement of arms, wars and battlefields," the Rebbe replies that after having "thought long and hard" he "came to the conclusion" that the best way to induce "an American child to get used to the idea of subordination to a higher authority, despite all the influences to the contrary—in the school, in the street, and even at home, where [many] parents . . . have all too often abdicated their authority and left it to others to deal with truancy, juvenile delinquency, etc.," was by setting up the Tzivos Hashem children's program.[62] The Rebbe regularly speaks at rallies comprised entirely of young boys and girls; he personally distributes two, sometimes more, coins to each child and asks the recipient to donate one to charity and to use the other for his or her pleasure. At the end of one children's parade, when the emcee thanks the individuals who coordinated the event, the Rebbe asks for the microphone and adds, "and especially let us thank the children, the children of Abraham, Isaac, Jacob, Sarah, Rebecca, Rachel, and Leah."

An unexpected consequence of the organization's formation and of the magazine it publishes is the raising of the status of young women within the Orthodox world (see pages 215–17).

1980: The *Sheva Mitzvot* (Seven Commandments) campaign. The Rebbe initiates a campaign to make known among non-Jews "The Seven Noahide Laws,"[63] the ordinances Judaism believes to be the prerequisites for a just society. Six of the laws are prohibitions, outlawing murder, stealing, forbidden sexual activities, cruelty to animals (epitomized by the act of cutting off a limb of a living animal), denying God (as expressed, for example, through idolatry), and blaspheming God. The seventh is a positive injunction to establish a judicial system to ensure compliance with the other laws.[64]

As a result of the Rebbe's campaign, the preamble to the 1986 congressional bill commemorating the annual Education Day (starting in 1978 and observed each year on the Rebbe's birthday) formally recognizes the Seven Laws of Noah: "Whereas [Congress recognizes that] these ethical values and principles have been the bedrock of society from the dawn of civilization, when they were known as the Seven Noahide Laws" (see chapter 11).

1982: At a public speech during a *farbrengen*, the Rebbe declares that unless America, the world's most powerful nation, achieves energy independence, it risks losing its superpower status and instead runs the risk of becoming financially and politically dependent on non-democratic governments that possess oil but oppose American values. To help ensure that the United States averts such a fate, the country must "fully develop [its] own resources and strength, so that [it] need not be dependent on other nations." Sounding more like a hardheaded political analyst than a Chasidic Rebbe, the Rebbe proclaims, "When this country depends on others for oil and other resources, then it is forced to obey the agenda of others in ways which distort justice, morality, and goodness."

The Rebbe declares his opposition to the approach of those "who, for various reasons, oppose the development of domestic resources, whether it be oil, coal, etc." In the same talk, he also speaks of the importance of aggressively pushing for the development and expansion of the use of solar energy. "The southern regions of this country receive abundant sunlight, intense heat from the sun. It is quite easy to harness the energy from the heat of the sun's rays, and transport it for use throughout the country. And this can be achieved, with God's help."

If America develops all its resources, he declares, then "in a relatively short time the country will be freed from its subservience to small states who have oil in their lands; their production capabilities, parenthetically, were developed by Americans, in the first place. It was Americans who helped them develop the ability to pump oil to supply the entire world."

1982: The Rebbe's special relationship with President Ronald Reagan. A joint resolution of both houses of Congress designates April 4, 1982, the Rebbe's eightieth birthday, as a "National Day of Reflection," a time intended to focus on character education. The resolution is signed by President Ronald Reagan, who also sends the Rebbe a warm birthday letter.

In response, the Rebbe writes to the president about the need for Americans to undertake commitment to the "universal moral code of the Ten Commandments. Indeed, it is this commitment to the same

Divine truths and values that . . . unites all Americans in the true sense of *E pluribus Unum*" (from the many, one).

On the night of the Rebbe's eightieth birthday, he conducts a five-hour *farbrengen*. It concludes in the early-morning hours, at which point the Rebbe remains in the synagogue hall for an additional three hours and personally hands to each of several thousand participants copies of the *Tanya*.

1984: The Rebbe calls for a campaign of Jewish unity to be fostered by Jews throughout the world learning the one Jewish legal code that encompasses all the laws of the Torah. He suggests that all Jews, men, women, and children, study a daily portion of Maimonides's fourteen-volume legal code, the *Mishneh Torah*. To enable both scholarly and less knowledgeable people to participate, the Rebbe offers three systems of daily study. The most comprehensive involves a commitment to study three chapters per day, and thereby learn through the whole work in a year. Alternatively, one can study one chapter each day and complete the cycle in three years. For those for whom neither of the above arrangements is feasible, the Rebbe suggests a daily study schedule based on Maimonides's *Sefer Hamitzvot*, the *Book of the Commandments,* in which he lists and briefly explains the 613 commandments of the Torah.

Commenting on the significance of this global program, Rabbi Adin Steinsaltz observes that "prior to the Rebbe's initiative, people did not learn Maimonides's [*Mishneh Torah*] as one continuum; rather, it was learned together with the Talmud in bits and pieces. A new era in learning has begun where we can learn the entire span of Torah, via Maimonides, in one continuous fashion."[65] In addition to local celebrations throughout the world each year upon concluding the learning cycle, a completion ceremony is observed annually at the Maimonides Synagogue, in Cairo, Egypt.

1985: The court fight over the Frierdiker Rebbe's library takes place, during which it becomes apparent that defending the Frierdiker Rebbe's books and legacy is, for the Rebbe, a matter of the gravest significance. A legal battle ensues when it is discovered that Barry Gourary, the Rebbe's nephew, has been taking valuable books from the Frierdiker

Rebbe's library and selling them. When Gourary is asked to return the books, he and his mother argue that the Frierdiker Rebbe intended the books to be bequeathed to his descendants, while his uncle and aunt, the Rebbe and Rebbetzin, insist that the Frierdiker Rebbe intended his library to remain within the movement. The case ends up in federal court, and Judge Charles Sifton rules (and his decision is later reaffirmed by the court of appeals) that the books belong to Chabad. The Hebrew date of the court ruling, *Hei Tevet* (the fifth of the month of Tevet), is still celebrated annually as a holiday within Chabad (see chapter 26).

1986: Dollars. The Rebbe initiates the practice on Sundays (starting in the late morning) of handing out dollar bills to visitors to be distributed to the charity of each person's choice. He quotes his father-in-law, the Frierdiker Rebbe, who said, "When two people meet, something good should result for a third." As the Rebbe had stopped conducting private meetings (*yechidusen*) shortly before his eightieth birthday, the Dollars line enables people to meet with the Rebbe very briefly and receive a blessing in addition to a dollar.

Gordon Zacks, an American Jewish communal leader and philan-thropist, had not seen the Rebbe since early 1970, when they had met to discuss the state of Jewish education in the United States. Though that visit had been their sole encounter, in 1987, when Zacks was visiting New York and learned that his daughter was heading for the Dollars line, he joined her. When the Rebbe saw Zacks, he greeted him and his daughter and then, without skipping a beat, returned to the subject of his earlier conversation with Zacks about the pressing needs of Jewish education. Zacks, flabbergasted that the Rebbe remembered both him and the topic of their previous discussion from among the tens of thou-sands of people he had encountered in the preceding *seventeen* years, said, "You are amazing." Rather than acknowledging the compliment, the Rebbe asked, "What will be the benefit for the community that 'I am amazing'?" and extracted from Zacks an assurance that he would make a renewed effort in this area.[66]

Rabbi Yehuda Krinsky told me that between six thousand to eight thousand dollar bills were prepared for each Sunday, all new bills drawn from a bank. The Rebbe would stand during the entire time he distributed the bills, sometimes as long as six or seven hours. When an older woman, who had found the process of waiting in line for a much shorter period tiring, said to him, "Rebbe, how can you do it? How is it that you do not tire?" he responded: "Every soul is like a diamond. Who grows tired from counting diamonds?"

Most recipients of dollars would keep the actual bill the Rebbe handed them and then donate other money to charity (the Rebbe expressed the wish that it be for far more than a dollar), but not in all cases. David Luchins, a longtime aide to Senator Daniel Patrick Moynihan, recalls an encounter he and the senator had with the Rebbe, at the end of which the Rebbe gave each of them money and gave a bill as well to Moynihan's driver, a police detective named Chuck Bennett. On the drive back into the city, Bennett, a religious Catholic, stopped the car in front of St. Patrick's Cathedral and rushed inside. Neither Moynihan nor Luchins knew why he had stopped there, and when the driver returned, Senator Moynihan asked him, "What happened, Chuck?" The driver explained: "I put the dollar bill in the charity plate right away. The Rabbi said to do it; I didn't want to take any chances."[67]

The practice of distributing dollars on Sunday continued for six years—by then the Rebbe was almost ninety, yet he remained standing the whole time—until his stroke in March 1992. Because of the extraordinary number of dollars distributed, reflecting the large number of people who came to "Sunday Dollars" (often, in cases of special need or some unusual request, the Rebbe would give a recipient two or more dollar bills; in the case cited above, Luchins recalls that the Rebbe gave him three dollars), Dollars remains one of the Rebbe's most widely known activities.

When one of the Rebbe's secretaries suggested putting a large *tzedaka* box outside 770 to recoup some of the thousands of dollars distributed each week, the Rebbe vetoed the idea. He did not want dollar recipients to think that it was his intention to influence people to donate money to Chabad; rather, he wanted it known that he was pleased if people simply increased their charitable giving, whether it was to Chabad or to any other worthy cause.

1988: Rebbetzin Chaya Mushka Schneerson dies at the age of eighty-six. The daughter of the Previous Rebbe and a powerful figure in her own right (her husband was known to tell people that she could bestow blessings), Rebbetzin Chaya Mushka Schneerson was a highly private person, a characteristic epitomized by the fact that, although she was the movement's First Lady for over forty years, there are *very* few extant photographs of her (unlike the countless photographs and videos of her husband), and the most widely distributed picture of her was taken some two years before she became Chabad's Rebbetzin. Reflecting her retiring nature and avoidance of the limelight, the Chasidic poet Zvi Yair wrote a poem about her shortly after her death, titled "On the Day on Which the Hidden Was Revealed"; the poem's opening line conveys an emotion many within the movement felt: "When you were with us, we did not know you."

Since her death, the name Chaya Mushka has become the most common name given to newborn baby girls. On the first anniversary of her passing, the Rebbe was "presented with an album of namesakes born during the previous year, 324 Chaya Mushkas from around the world."[68] (For a more comprehensive assessment of the Rebbetzin, see chapter 25.)

1988: Preparation for transition. Starting in 1988, and continuing over the next four years until his stroke, the Rebbe initiated a process that, in retrospect, seems to have been preparation for Chabad's next stage, one in which the movement might be without one central leader. He called upon every Chasid to find a personal spiritual mentor, known as a *mashpia*, who could help guide without bias and serve as a role model. Additionally, he repeatedly expressed his directive that for certain spiritual or other Jewish legal issues people should turn to local rabbinic authorities who could help them determine how to lead their lives according to Chabad tradition. Should individuals need advice on more mundane matters, he encouraged them to discuss these issues with *yedidim mevinim*, devoted friends and ones who have an understanding of the matter at hand. For medical issues, he counseled people to turn to *rof'im mumchim*, highly competent physicians, and when medical dilemmas arise, they should also consult with *rof'im yedidim*, doctors who are also one's friends. In instances in which one consults with several physicians, the Rebbe advocated following the majority opinion.

As regards Chabad-Lubavitch institutional policy, the Rebbe designated Agudas Chasidei Chabad as the movement's umbrella organization with movement-wide oversight and policy-making responsibility; he designated Merkos L'Inyonei Chinuch to direct the movement's vast outreach efforts; and specified Vaad Rabbonei Lubavitch (Committee of Chabad-Lubavitch Rabbis) as the judicial branch to adjudicate in cases of institutional and other disputes.

1988: The Rebbe calls for an increase in charitable giving and in all acts of kindness. He urges everyone to install charity boxes in their homes, thereby turning their physical abode into a holy place. He asks people to make daily contributions to the boxes and when the money accumulates to donate it to a charity of their choice. He also suggests that charity boxes be present in workplaces, and he asks employers to add an additional dollar to the paychecks of their workers, to serve as a reminder of the importance of charity. The giving of charity, the Rebbe emphasizes, is important for all humankind, not just Jews. Among those who responded to this request from the Rebbe was President Bill Clinton, who, standing alongside Rabbi Avraham Shemtov at the White House, deposited a bill into a *tzedaka* box.

1989: Chanukah Live. The first international Chanukah menorah satellite hookups, featuring simultaneous lightings on all six continents, are initiated. As the menorah has eight candles, the screens show a different one being lit in each of the participating cities. The Rebbe himself participates in these hookups, and his speech is broadcast live to all locations. Over the coming years, Chanukah Live expands, and features live events from and to Jerusalem, New York, London, Paris, Hong Kong, Melbourne, Moscow, Buenos Aires, Sydney, Johannesburg, Cape Town, and Montreal. In Jerusalem, the two chief rabbis of Israel participate and light the candle at the Western Wall. At the 1990 Chanukah Live hookup, it was a child from Chernobyl who had recently been rescued by Chabad and brought to Israel who personally thanked the Rebbe (see following entry). The 1991 Chanukah Live features a live broadcast of a menorah lighting inside the Kremlin, where six thousand Russian Jews are gathered (communism in Russia had just recently fallen). In Paris, thousands gather at the foot of the Eiffel Tower, where a large menorah is kindled and broadcast worldwide. In Manhattan, New York mayor David Dinkins participates, and from Canada, Prime Minister Brian Mulroney speaks about the lessons to be learned from the menorah (for more on the Rebbe and Chanukah celebrations, see pages 261–70).

1990: On April 26, 1986, a nuclear reactor in the Ukrainian city of Chernobyl explodes, releasing four hundred times more radioactive material than had been released during the atomic bombing of Hiroshima. Over the following years, cancer rates and birth defects begin to skyrocket, and the impact of the nuclear meltdown causes people in the region to suffer physically, mentally, and financially. As the children of the Chernobyl region start to mature, the effects of the radiation on so many of them become increasingly apparent. By 1990, the radiation from the explosion reaches epidemic proportions, and that same year, the Rebbe asks Chabadniks to "take upon yourselves the responsibility for the well-being of these children and bring them to Israel." On August 3, 1990, Chabad successfully arranges the first rescue flight, and 196 children are brought to Israel, where they are provided with housing, education, and medical care. As of 2013, Chabad has arranged ninety-nine rescue flights, bringing 2,863 children to Israel. Chabad's Children of Chernobyl (CCOC) maintains a collaborative relationship with the World Health Organization, UNESCO, and the United Nations Department of Humanitarian Affairs. Both Jewish and non-Jewish children are served. For those children who cannot leave the Chernobyl region, CCOC sends medical equipment, medicine, and other necessary supplies to the contaminated area. In April 1997, the organization's work is recognized by twenty-one countries that issue postage stamps honoring Children of Chernobyl's vital relief work.

1991: The Gulf War. Following Iraq's invasion and takeover of Kuwait (August 2, 1990), Iraqi dictator Saddam Hussein publicly threatens that if Iraq is attacked, it will retaliate by firing Scud missiles at Israel.

The following months prove extremely stressful for the Western and Arab worlds and for Israel in particular. Some thirty countries provide troops for an international force to remove Iraq from Kuwait. Israel, though the strongest Middle Eastern power, is asked by the American government *not* to be involved in the war effort as Israel's participation will preclude Arab countries such as Syria, Egypt, and Saudi Arabia from participating. Out of a commitment to maintain good relations with the United States, Israel agrees. Over the coming months, and in an attempt to garner support in the Arab world, Saddam Hussein repeatedly threatens that if the United States attacks Iraq, "then Tel Aviv will receive the next attack, whether or not Israel takes part."[69]

Israel regards the threats from Hussein with the utmost seriousness, particularly given that a little over a decade earlier, Hussein had initiated the construction of a nuclear reactor with the intention of building an atom bomb and dropping it on Israel. At that time, and in an action Prime Minister Menachem Begin regarded as among the most important of his life, he ordered the Israeli air force to fly into Iraq and destroy the Osirak nuclear complex (twelve days later, on June 19, 1981, the United Nations Security Council unanimously condemned the raid). Now, ten years later, Iraq, frustrated by Israel's earlier attack, seems poised to exact revenge. The Israeli government starts distributing gas masks to the entire populace, Jews and Arabs alike.

The Rebbe repeatedly declares that Israel has no reason to be afraid, that it is, indeed, "the safest place on earth."[70] During the weeks before the January 17 American-led attack on Iraqi forces—the event that soon triggers the Scud attacks on Israel—people standing on the Sunday Dollars line, particularly those with family members in Israel or those contemplating visits there, keep asking the Rebbe about the threat posed by Iraq. What follows are three representative examples, all recorded on video:[71]

- A man reports that his son's upcoming bar mitzvah is scheduled to be celebrated in Israel, but that his wife is very afraid to travel there for the event. What should the family do? The Rebbe replies: "God says that he watches over the land of Israel, and there is no reason for concern at all."

• An older gentleman informs the Rebbe that he has two married children with children of their own in Israel; he asks if he should bring them all back to America until the crisis passes. "God forbid," the Rebbe answers, "they must stay there. If one always needs to be there, now even more so."

• A mother tells the Rebbe that her daughter is studying at a girls' seminary in Jerusalem and that she is thinking of flying her back to safety in the United States. The Rebbe's response is definitive and reproving: "G-d forbid! And don't tell anyone you even considered leaving."

Shortly before being deployed to Iraq, Rabbi Jacob Goldstein, a chaplain in the U.S. Army, asks the Rebbe if he should take a megillah (the book of Esther written by a scribe) with him, as it appears that he will most probably be in Iraq during Purim. The Rebbe tells him that there is no reason to take a megillah as the war will be over before the holiday.

The holiday of Purim comes up in another discussion as well. When Dr. Elliot Udell, one of the Rebbe's physicians, suggests that the Rebbe make a special prayer that the war be brought to an end on the holiday of Purim—then only a week away—so that "we can celebrate two *smachot* [happy events] on the same day," the Rebbe gives Udell a piercing look and says, "I don't want to wait a week until Purim for this to happen. People are contacting me from Israel and they are in terror, absolute terror, and I fear for their lives. I'm praying that it ends right now."

The war ends the day before Purim.[72]

1991: The Rebbe reminds the Chasidim in a most forceful manner of their responsibility to hasten the Messiah's coming. At an April 1991 speech, he stuns the assembled with a dramatic announcement: "I have done everything I can. . . . What more can I do to motivate the entire

Jewish people to cry out and demand that Moshiach should come?... All that I can possibly do is to give the matter over to you. Now, do everything you can to bring Moshiach, here and now, immediately. I have done whatever I can; from now on, you must do whatever you can" (see page 425).

1992: On March 2, while at the *Ohel*—the site where the Frierdiker Rebbe is buried and where the Rebbe goes several times a week to offer prayers, meditate, and read through letters and requests—he suffers a sudden and debilitating stroke, never to walk or talk again. Rabbi Krinsky, the one person with him at the time, recalled years later: "I was standing right next to him. He seemed to be finishing with the letters and getting ready to leave. And then, he just collapsed. I tried to pick him up... his eyes were open, but I couldn't get any response from him." As Krinsky does not have a cell phone (cell phones did not come into popular use until later in the nineties), he lays his coat under the Rebbe's head and runs out to the car in which he brought the Rebbe; it is parked right outside the cemetery and has a phone. Krinsky calls the Chabad office in Brooklyn and informs them of what has happened; it is now 5:40 p.m. A series of mishaps follow, culminating in a delay of almost two hours until an ambulance arrives at the cemetery. Throughout this excruciating wait, the Rebbe remains, in Rabbi Krinsky's words, "totally nonresponsive." When the ambulance arrives, Krinsky wants the Rebbe taken immediately to a hospital, but others, recalling the Rebbe's refusal to be hospitalized for his heart attack in 1977, insist on bringing him back to 770.

Dr. Ira Weiss, who flies in from Chicago when he hears about the stroke, is displeased when he learns that the Rebbe has not been hospitalized; perhaps inside the hospital the doctors could have dissolved the clot in his brain. Weiss acknowledges that this is far from certain; too much time might have elapsed from the time of the stroke to his admission to a hospital for the procedure to be effective; also, as it was a new and very potent procedure, hospital personnel might have been averse to using it on a ninety-year-old man, out of fear that it would kill him. Nonetheless, he deeply regrets that it was not attempted.

After the stroke, the Rebbe's right side remains paralyzed and he is never again able to speak. In Dr. Weiss's assessment, and based on his interactions with the Rebbe, the Rebbe recovered partial intellectual cognition. On the other hand, the neurologists who were treating him, including Dr. Jay P. Mohr and Dr. Louis Kaplan, did feel that he could understand and follow all that was being said to him.

Ironically, it is during this period of terrible illness when the Rebbe could not speak that the Messianic movement reaches its greatest fervor (see chapter 28).

The debilitation from the stroke continues for two years, until March 10, 1994, when the Rebbe suffers a second, far more incapacitating, stroke, at which point he is admitted to Beth Israel Medical Center in Manhattan, where he remains hospitalized for the remaining three months of his life.

1994: June 12 (3 Tammuz 5754): The Rebbe dies early Sunday morning, just before 2:00 a.m. In the preceding weeks, increasingly somber reports are being released by the movement concerning the Rebbe's medical condition, and sometimes one can hear a sob in the announcer's voice on the tape-recorded messages. Those who have been following the reports are aware that nothing short of a miracle can restore the Rebbe to health, yet many Lubavitchers, and non-Lubavitchers as well, continue to hold out hope and to even expect that such a miracle will happen. His death, therefore, shocks a great many Chasidim, even though it has been clear for the preceding weeks that the Rebbe's medical prognosis is very grim and declining.

President Bill Clinton pens a condolence letter "to the Lubavitch community and to world Jewry" referring to the Rebbe as "a monumental man [who] . . . as much as any other individual, was responsible over the last half century for advancing the instruction of ethics and morality to our young people." Israeli prime minister Yitzhak Rabin, citing the Rebbe's great scholarship and contribution to the entire Jewish people, proclaims, "The Rebbe's loss is a loss for all of the Jewish people." Foreign Minister Shimon Peres cites words from the prophet Malachi as applying with particular force to the Rebbe: "He brought back many from iniquity. For a priest's lips shall guard knowledge, and teaching should be sought from his mouth, for he is a messenger of the Lord."

El Al airlines adds a special Jumbo Jet flight for Israelis who wish to make it to the funeral on time. A small number of Chasidim, convinced that the Rebbe will now arise and the Redemption will begin, dance and even toast "L'Chaim" in the streets of Crown Heights, but the large majority walk about in shock. During the hours preceding the funeral, thousands of Chasidim walk by the *tallit*-covered body of the Rebbe and make a rip in their garments (*kria*) over their hearts.

At the cemetery, the Rebbe is buried in a wooden casket constructed from his desk and lectern. As the casket is being lowered, Rabbi Shlomo Cunin, the head *shliach* from California, calls out, "Rebbe, in the name of the *shluchim*, I promise that we will continue our work as *shluchim*, we will preserve the Rebbe's institutions, and we will develop and expand them."

Outside of the Jewish world, there is enormous attention paid as well, and the world's media devote an enormous number of articles and many hours of broadcast time to the Rebbe's passing. The *New York Times* reports the Rebbe's death on the front page, and the extended obituary by Ari Goldman is headlined: "Rabbi Schneerson Led a Small Sect to World Prominence." Over the following week, the *Times* publishes an additional six stories and editorials and op-ed pieces about the Rebbe. Four days after the Rebbe's passing, in an article by Chaim Potok in the *Philadelphia Inquirer*, the widely read novelist notes that the Rebbe's death has headed the news in many unexpected places, and he poses the question: "When was the last time the death of a rabbi made front-page news and network television?"

Since the Rebbe's death, the number of *shluchim* has tripled to some four thousand couples in over one thousand communities, and there are now Chabad Houses in forty-eight American states and in some eighty countries (see page 444).

GLOSSARY

Alter Rebbe. Rabbi Shneur Zalman of Liadi, the founding Rebbe of Chabad. Alter Rebbe literally means "the old Rebbe."

Chuppah. "Chuppah" literally means "wedding canopy," but it is also used colloquially to refer to a wedding ceremony (e.g., "I attended a chuppah").

Etrog. A fruit known in English as a citron, it is one of the four species used by Jews in a biblically ordained ritual carried out during the holiday of Sukkot (see *lulav*).

Frierdiker Rebbe. Literally, "the previous Rebbe," this term refers to Rabbi Yosef Yitzchak Schneersohn, the Sixth Rebbe of Chabad, and the father-in-law of Rabbi Menachem Mendel Schneerson, the Seventh Rebbe (also known as the Rebbe).

Halacha. Jewish law.

Haredi. Usually translated as "ultra-Orthodox," the term "*haredi*" applies to the most theologically conservative Orthodox Jews. Feeling, as do many in the Orthodox community, that the word "ultra" unfairly connotes that *haredi* Jews are by definition extremists, Rabbi Motti Seligson of Chabad .org has launched a campaign to encourage journalists to define *haredi* as "traditional Orthodox."

Israel Baal Shem Tov. The eighteenth-century founder of Chasidism.

Ksovim (alternatively, *ketavim*). Manuscripts authored by the seven Lubavitcher Rebbes.

Lulav. A closed frond of the date palm tree, it is one of the four species used during the Sukkot holiday; it is bound together with an *arava* (willow), and *hadas* (myrtle), and blessed along with an *etrog*.

Ma'amar. A Chasidic discourse, one delivered only by a Rebbe. Such talks are usually rooted in kabbalah and Chasidic teachings, and it is customary for Chasidim to stand when a Rebbe is delivering a *ma'amar*.

Mezuzah (plural, mezuzot; also mezuzahs). The commandment of mezuzah is ordained in the Torah: "And you shall inscribe them [these words from the Torah] upon the doorposts (mezuzot) of your house and upon your gates," immediately followed by the words, "that your days may be lengthened and the days of your children" (Deuteronomy 11:20–21). Jewish law ordains that mezuzot be installed on the doorposts of Jewish homes and on the doorposts of the rooms inside the house. Inside each mezuzah is a small scroll that contains the biblical verse ordaining the mezuzah.

Mikveh. A bath consisting of natural water, built according to very precise regulations, that is used for ritual immersion.

Minyan. According to traditional Jewish law, a full public prayer service can only be conducted in the presence of ten adult (over the age of thirteen) male Jews; such a group is known as a minyan.

Mitzvah (plural, *mitzvot*). Commandment, as in, "There are 613 *mitzvot* in the Torah."

Mivtzah (plural, *mivtza'im*). Campaign. Refers to various campaigns initiated by the Rebbe to encourage the observance of a variety of *mitzvot*. For example, the *Neshek* campaign was started to influence Jewish women, from the age of three and up, to light Shabbat candles.

Niggun. The Hebrew word for "melody," often used to refer to a Chasidic melody. A *niggun* is usually wordless. It is intended to stir the soul, and is often sung over and over.

Ohel. Literally, "tent," the *Ohel* refers to the open-air structure at the Old Montefiore Cemetery in Brooklyn in which both the Frierdiker Rebbe and the Seventh Rebbe, Rabbi Menachem Mendel Schneerson, are buried. Tens of thousands of people come to pray at the *Ohel* throughout the year, and on the day of the Rebbe's *yahrtzeit* as many as fifty to sixty thousand people come.

Ramash. The name by which Menachem Mendel Schneerson was generally called by Lubavitcher Chasidim following his marriage to Chaya Mushka, the Sixth Rebbe's daughter, in 1928, and until the time he became Rebbe in 1951. Ramash is an acronym for Rabbi Menachem Mendel Schneerson.

Rashag. The acronym for Rabbi Shmaryahu Gourary, the son-in-law of the Frierdiker Rebbe and the brother-in-law of the Rebbe. Rabbi Gourary was the longtime administrative director of the Lubavitch yeshiva.

Rebbe. In Hebrew, the word "Rebbe" has two meanings: leader of a Chasidic group (which is what it refers to in this book), and a teacher of Judaism's holy texts (a student might say of his teacher, "He's my rebbe"). In Hebrew, the plural of Rebbe is Rebbe'im; in this book, I have used the word "Rebbes," the term American Jews generally use when referring to more than one Rebbe.

Satmar. A large Chasidic sect that originated in the Transylvanian city of Satu Mare, Satmar in Yiddish. Following World War II, it was reestablished in Brooklyn, in the Williamsburg neighborhood. It was long headed by Rabbi Yoel Teitelbaum, a rabbinic scholar who was known in the broader community for his very strong anti-Zionist views.

Sichot (alternatively, *Sichos*). Refers to a talk given by the Rebbe on a variety of religious topics, but one that could encompass newsworthy events as well; for a different sort of speech, see *Ma'amar.*

Sixth Rebbe. Rabbi Yosef Yitzchak Schneersohn, more commonly referred to as the Frierdiker Rebbe.

Sukkot. A weeklong biblically ordained holiday (observed for eight days outside of Israel) in which Jews are commanded to build a booth (sukkah), and in which meals are eaten throughout the holiday. The other well-known Sukkot ritual involves the blessing of the *lulav* and *etrog.*

Tahara. The ritual cleansing of the body of one who has died.

Tefillin. A set of two black leather boxes (one is placed on the head, the other on an arm) containing scrolls of parchment inscribed by a scribe and containing verses from the Torah. Tefillin is one of the *mitzvot* most commonly associated with Chabad, and it was the subject of the first *mivtzah* by the Rebbe, a campaign to encourage Jewish men over the age of thirteen to put on tefillin. The Torah commands that tefillin be worn as a "sign" and "remembrance" of God bringing the "children of Israel" out of Egyptian slavery. They are worn during the weekday morning prayer service.

Tisha Be'Av. The ninth day of the Hebrew month of Av. Tisha Be'Av is a fast day that commemorates the destruction of both the First Temple (586 BCE) and the Second Temple (70 CE), and is generally regarded as the saddest day on the Jewish calendar.

Tzemach Tzedek. A commonly used name for the Third Rebbe, Menachem Mendel Schneersohn, and the man for whom the Seventh Rebbe was named. The term *"Tzemach Tzedek"* refers to a series of scholarly books he authored.

Yechidus (plural, *yechidusen*). A private meeting with a Rebbe; see chapter 3 for a description of what transpired at such meetings.

ENDNOTES

Chapter 1: A Rebbe for the New World

1. Since then, clergy recipients have included, among others, Mother Teresa, Pope John Paul II, Reverend Billy Graham, and the Dalai Lama.

2. While researching this book, I learned in an interview with Gary Bauer, an adviser on domestic policy to President Reagan, that the president would take the letters he received from the Rebbe upstairs from the Oval Office to his residence and personally draft his responses. See the Rebbe's correspondence with President Reagan at Chabad.org/142535.

3. Peggy Noonan, *What I Saw at the Revolution: A Political Life in the Reagan Era* (New York: Ballantine Books, 2003), 358. Noonan's reference underscores the Rebbe's significance in yet another way. When she mentions "the pope" as a source of moral teaching, it could be any pope to whom she is referring; it is the position of which she is speaking (the leader of the world's 1.2 billion Catholics), not a specific pope. The same applies to the Archbishop of Canterbury. In the case of the Rebbe, it is a very specific individual to whom she is referring, Rabbi Menachem Mendel Schneerson; such a reference to the Lubavitcher Rebbe alongside the pope and the archbishop would not have occurred to any non-Jew to make prior to the Seventh Rebbe.

4. The term "Rebbe" refers to a teacher of Judaism's holy texts, and to a leader of a Chasidic dynasty. "Lubavitcher" derives from the White Russian city of Lubavitch, the town in which the movement was headquartered between 1815 and 1917. Today the terms "Lubavitch" and "Chabad" are used interchangeably to refer to the movement. The word "Chabad" is an acronym for three Hebrew words, *Chochmah, Binah, Da'at* (wisdom, understanding, knowledge), the three intellectual underpinnings of the movement.

5. For example, religious Zionists are all familiar with Rabbi Abraham Isaac Kook, the former chief rabbi of Israel (then British Mandatory Palestine), and a man whose influence continues to be profound in religious Zionist circles. But mention Rabbi Kook's name to contemporary non-Orthodox Jews in the United States, Russia, or France and you will likely draw blank stares, and maybe an occasional flicker of recognition.

Similarly, in the first half of the twentieth century, the most famous rabbi in the United States was Stephen S. Wise, a Reform spiritual leader known for his fervent Zionism, powerful speaking abilities, and the warm relationship he had with

President Franklin Delano Roosevelt. Today, if Wise's name is recognized, it is generally because of the Stephen S. Wise Synagogue in Los Angeles and the Stephen Wise Free Synagogue in New York, two prominent American Reform congregations. Mention Rabbi Wise's name to Israeli or Russian Jews and probably less than one in a hundred could identify who he was.

In the world of religious scholarship and leadership, there are numerous figures who have lived since Maimonides and who have achieved great heights in Jewish learning. Rabbi Joseph Karo (sixteenth century) is the author of the *Shulchan Aruch*, the standard code of Jewish law; to this day, mastery of sections of this work is a requirement for Orthodox rabbinical ordination. Is his name well known? Very, but primarily in religiously observant circles where his work is consulted for legal rulings. Yet while Orthodox Jews are familiar with Rabbi Karo, a decidedly smaller number of Conservative Jews know who he is, and only a small number of Reform Jews can tell you anything about him at all.

6.   One visitor to Morocco who noted this was New York's Senator Daniel Patrick Moynihan: "When I met with Jewish leaders in Morocco and toured several of their synagogues and civic centers, I discovered two pictures in every building— His Majesty King Hassan II and the Lubavitcher Rebbe, Rabbi Menachem Mendel Schneerson" (cited in obituaries for the Rebbe, June 13, 1994).

7.   The Rebbe's precise wish to Lacalle was that he "use his influence for the benefit of the many" and that he give the dollar to charity, "a commandment accepted by all the people of the world." The Rebbe thanked Lacalle for "giving me the opportunity to meet with you and wish you all good things." Lacalle in turn showed the Rebbe a book he had been reading, *The Path of the Righteous Gentile*, a book about the Noahide laws (see chapter 11).

8.   Walesa had not been given the dollar personally by the Rebbe, but had been given it by David Chase who had received it directly from the Rebbe (on the Rebbe's distribution of dollars and his reason for doing so, see pages 506–7).

9.   See Chase's firsthand account, "Lech Walesa and the Rebbe's Dollar," available at Chabad.org/1023840. Chase, who was first introduced to the Rebbe by Rabbi Moshe Herson, enjoyed a very warm relationship with the Rebbe for many years.

10. As Rabbi Krinsky noted, the man didn't say, "Rabbi Schneerson," but said, "the Lubavitcher Rebbe." Rabbi Krinsky recalls another occasion when some hard-hat workers were doing construction work near the Chabad headquarters. As the Rebbe walked by, one of the men, pneumatic drill in hand, called out to him and said, "Hey, I saw you on television last night."

11. Just two weeks after the attempted assassination, the president wrote a warm seventy-ninth birthday message to the Rebbe, and the Rebbe wrote back condemning "the demented attempt on your life," and concluded with the wish that God bless the president: "with the Divine promise to our Patriarch Abraham, 'I will bless those that bless you'" (Genesis 12:3).

12. Jewish men are required to place one box on their head and tie the other on their arm each weekday morning. The text inside the boxes is handwritten by a scribe and drawn from the biblical verses of the *Sh'ma*, in which Jews are commanded, among other things, to love God, to pass on their traditions to their children, and to wear tefillin (Deuteronomy 6:5–8). One reason the Rebbe might have chosen to focus on tefillin is that unlike the Sabbath, which occurs once a week, the commandment of tefillin is observed each weekday.

13. Miriam Fellig was interviewed on March 22, 2011, by JEM.

14. In the first century BCE, Rabbi Hillel was approached by a non-Jew, a would-be convert, who asked that he be taught the nature of Judaism while standing on one foot. Hillel responded with a negative formulation of the Golden Rule, "What is hateful unto you, don't do unto your neighbor. This is the whole Torah. The rest is commentary. Now, go and study" (*Shabbat* 31a). A century later, the great Rabbi Akiva (first–second century) taught, " 'Love your neighbor as yourself.' This is the great principle of the Torah" (Jerusalem Talmud, *Nedarim* 9:4).

15. One stark statistic: All the moderate leaders who headed the Jewish community at the revolt's beginning in the year 66 were dead within two years, and not one had died at the hands of a Roman; all had been killed by fellow Jews. Having noted this, it is also true that the Roman military might at the time was so great that the Jews would likely have lost the revolt even if they had been more unified; nonetheless, the lack of unity magnified Jewish losses by the tens, perhaps hundreds, of thousands.

16. The Dominican Order had been appointed by Pope Gregory to head the Inquisition, which was intended to be directed only against Catholic heretics. It was French rabbis who involved the Dominicans in ferreting out supposed Jewish heresies.

17. Eliyahu Stern, *The Genius: Elijah of Vilna and the Making of Modern Judaism* (New Haven: Yale University Press, 2013) , 87.

18. The impact of the Rebbe's teachings on his followers in this regard was profound. Lis Harris, a writer for the *New Yorker* and the author of *Holy Days*, an in-depth look at the life of a Chasidic family, notes a comment she heard from Sheina Konigsberg (a pseudonym), a member of the Lubavitch community in Brooklyn: "These labels—Orthodox, Conservative, Reform—have no real meaning to us. As far as we're concerned, a Jew is a Jew; nobody's relationship to God can be conveyed by a label." See also the Rebbe's letter to Donna Halper, assistant professor of communication at Lesley University, dated 13 Iyar 5737 (May 1, 1977): "I must first point out that the division of Judaism into 'Orthodox, Conservative, Reform,' etc. is a purely artificial one, for all Jews have one and the same Torah, given by the One and same G-d, though there are more observant Jews and less observant Jews. To tag on a 'label' does not, of course, change the reality." The letter is available at Chabad.org/887542.

19. See the online edition of *The Atlantic*, "1,100 Pounds of Matzo in Kathmandu: Welcome to the World's Largest Seder," April 12, 2012.

20. For an explanation of Rabbi Yossi Ben Kisma's words in line with the Rebbe's teachings, see Israel Rubin's *Small Town Jewry* at Chabad.org/281336.

21. The description of this incident concerning the Rebbe and Representative Chisholm is based on an interview I conducted with Professor David Luchins, who was present when Chisholm spoke of her meeting with the Rebbe and its impact on her work. See also Professor Luchins's interview conducted by JEM (May 8, 2007), available at Chabad.org.548435.

Chapter 2: 1950–1951

1. Rabbi Raphael Nemotin, who shared a room with the young Schneerson in Leningrad in the 1920s—the future Rebbe was then in his early twenties and boarding in the Nemotin house—reports that it "was very difficult to converse with the Rebbe during this period that we were living together in the same room. He was always a very inward, closed person, and one who minimized his speech." While Nemotin's account of the young Schneerson is very laudatory (he didn't waste time, he was the last to enter the room at night and the first to leave in the morning), what is also clear is that he was not a "people person"; in Nemotin's recollection, "he didn't speak almost at all with anyone" (interview with Nemotin in Chaim Rapoport, *The Afterlife of Scholarship* [Oporto Press, 2011], 133n339).

2. Menachem M. Schneerson, *Igrot Kodesh*, 3:155 (Brooklyn, NY: Kehot Publication Society, 1985–2013).

3. Although the Second Rebbe had two sons, neither one succeeded him. Rather, his oldest daughter, Chaya Mushka, married her cousin, Menachem Mendel Schneerson, who subsequently became the Third Rebbe, known as the Tzemach Tzedek. Interestingly, the Seventh Rebbe, a direct descendant of the Tzemach Tzedek, was also named Menachem Mendel Schneerson, was also married to a Chaya Mushka, and, like his ancestor, was the only other Rebbe to be a son-in-law and not a son.

4. More than two decades earlier, in 1928, Rabbi Eliyahu Chaim Althaus, who was assigned to be Ramash's guardian (*shomer*) on the day of the wedding, wrote in a letter to his family in the aftermath of the wedding: "Do I not yet know that upon the path of this . . . young man are also dependent the paths and the futures of our children and their children?" This is likely the first prediction that Menachem Mendel Schneerson would subsequently become a Rebbe.

5. The theme of Menachem Mendel's shy manner was noted by his father-in-law as well, and was something he regretted. Already on the Frierdiker Rebbe's visit to the United States in 1930, he wrote to his wife, Nechama Dina, that—given Menachem Mendel's great scholarship—"if he would only study public speaking, and not be overwhelmed by large crowds, he would win over the hearts of rabbis and lay people alike" (unpublished letter in Library of Agudas Chasidei Chabad). This frustration about Menachem Mendel's shyness and inwardness was an ongoing one; it greatly bothered his father-in-law that Menachem Mendel was "concealing

his vast knowledge of Torah" (Yosef Y. Schneersohn, *Igrot Kodesh* [Brooklyn, NY: Kehot Publication Society, 1983–2013], 9:134. The Sixth Rebbe spelled the name Schneersohn with an *h* as the next-to-last letter. The Rebbe simplified the spelling by deleting the *h*).

6.   Two of the most important documents about the Rebbe's life during his Berlin and Paris years have both come out since his death, the five volumes of journals published under the title *Reshimot* (in which we learn about the Frierdiker Rebbe advising him to put on the additional pairs of tefillin), and volume 15 of the Frierdiker Rebbe's *Igrot Kodesh*, consisting of 378 pages of letters between the Frierdiker Rebbe, Menachem Mendel, and Chaya Mushka. In addition, there is also a volume, *Likutei Levi Yitzchak*, vol. 3 (Brooklyn, NY: Kehot Publishing Society, 1972) of letters from the Rebbe's father to Menachem Mendel and Chaya Mushka.

7.   See, for example, *Reshimot ha-Yoman* (Brooklyn, NY: Kehot Publication Society, 2006–2012), in which Menachem Mendel records a conversation his father-in-law had with him in Berlin on 8 Av 5690 (August 2, 1930), during which the Frierdiker Rebbe confided in him a custom that had been followed only by the Rebbes, of wearing tefillin at the morning Shacharit service on Tisha Be'Av, though the Jewish tradition on that day is to wear tefillin at the afternoon Mincha service. The Frierdiker Rebbe tells Menachem Mendel to do the same, but to make sure to do so secretly (page 155). On another occasion, Menachem Mendel records that on the eve of Sukkot of 5691 (October 6, 1930), while in Riga, Latvia, his father-in-law gifted him two *etrogim* to use in succession during the Sukkot holiday, one from Calabria, Italy, and another one from Israel. At that time the Frierdiker Rebbe disclosed to him an unknown custom handed down by each of his forebears dating back to the Alter Rebbe, declaring that he is giving them to him "just as they [the Fifth and Fourth Rebbes] gave me." The Frierdiker Rebbe instructed Menachem Mendel to first make the blessing on the Italian *etrog*, and then use the Israeli one for the traditional shaking as well, and concluded with his wish that this remain confidential between the two of them. See *Reshimot Ha-Yoman*, page 161.

8.   See, for example, *Reshimot*, sec. 127, pp. 149–56, where Menachem Mendel transcribes his analysis of *Kuntrus Pinui Atzmot Metim* by Rabbi Yechiel Yaakov Weinberg. Menachem Mendel's own style of Talmudic and Maimonidean study was modeled in many ways on that of Rabbi Joseph Rosen, known as the Rogatchover Gaon. Although Rosen was more than forty years his senior, the Rebbe and Rosen held a scholarly correspondence during the 1920s and 1930s, concentrating on a number of areas, some of them quite obscure, of Talmudic and halachic law. The young Menachem Mendel Schneerson also spent time with Rosen in both Leningrad and Dvinsk. And while Rabbi Weinberg definitely ordained Menachem Mendel Schneerson, Rabbi Rosen reportedly did so as well. Some of the correspondence between the young Menachem Mendel and Rabbi Rosen has been published in the *Reshimot*.

9.   See *Reshimot ha-Yoman*, xi–xxxix, for a timetable of Menachem Mendel and Chaya Mushka's visits to the Frierdiker Rebbe during the years 1928–1938. Menachem Mendel and Chaya Mushka were also with the Frierdiker Rebbe during much of 1933.

10. See, for example, *Reshimot*, vol. 1, sec. 7, pp. 159–233, where Menachem Mendel transcribed his lengthy 1931 Sukkot *farbrengen*.

11. See Rapoport, *The Afterlife of Scholarship*, 62–64. See examples in Yosef Y. Schneersohn, *Igrot Kodesh*, 15:123, 125–28.

12. There are a number of letters in the Frierdiker Rebbe's *Igrot Kodesh* and in unpublished letters as well signed by Mendel Schneerson, Secretary, or Secretary, M.S. In addition, at rabbinical conferences in Berlin and Paris, he represented his father-in-law and the movement (see Yosef Y. Schneersohn, *Igrot Kodesh*, 15:96–97).

13. See, for example, Yosef Y. Schneersohn, *Igrot Kodesh*, 15:134, 150, 216–19, 235.

14. See *Reshimot ha-Yoman*, 296, where Menachem Mendel records a 1933 conversation in which his father-in-law advised that he begin laying four pairs of tefillin. "I will order them for you so that no one else will know. All I have to give you [at the moment] are the tefillin my father, the Fifth Rebbe, would wear. I don't think you will want to use them, just as I am afraid to use them myself." Traditionally all Jews don one pair of tefillin, that is, tefillin that have been written in accordance with the universally accepted position of Rashi (the eleventh-century scholar). In addition, there are another three opinions regarding the order of the parchment scrolls contained within the tefillin; the opinions of Rabbeinu Tam (twelfth century), Ra'avad (twelfth century), and Shimusha Rabba (thirteenth century). These three tefillin, however, are not worn by all Jews (a significant number, but definitely a minority, wear the tefillin written in accordance with the views of Rabbeinu Tam), and have traditionally been reserved for only the most pious and spiritually inclined. Also, one does not decide to put them on on one's own. Thus, the Rebbe did not don these additional pairs of tefillin until told to do so by his father-in-law.

15. Such a belief was by no means unique to the Frierdiker Rebbe. The Chaffetz Chaim was known to say, "Even a blind man can see that we are the generation of the Messiah. All signs indicate that he is not far off." And Rabbi Moshe Feinstein, the outstanding scholar of Jewish law in the second half of the twentieth century, wrote that "we are obligated to anticipate the arrival of the Messiah on any given day as a near certainty."

16. Five of his other sons, though not the oldest, became Rebbes in other cities. Rabbi Shmuel, the Fourth Rebbe, was in turn succeeded by his second son, Shalom DovBer, who was subsequently succeeded by his oldest son, the Sixth Rebbe, Yosef Yitzchak. This, however, proves little, as Yosef Yitzchak was his *only* child.

17. Yosef Y. Schneersohn, *Igrot Kodesh*, 4:368. Ironically, this complimentary letter about Rashag was written in response to a critical letter that had been sent to him about his son-in-law.

18. See, for example, Rabbi Yosef Y. Schneersohn, *Igrot Kodesh*, 4:288; see also Shalom D. Levine, *Mibeis HaGenozim: Treasures from the Chabad Library* (Brooklyn, NY: Kehot Publication Society, 2009), 62; see also Rapoport, *The Afterlife of Scholarship*, 82, for a list of such examples where both brothers-in-law are mentioned in tandem.

19. Similarly, Rabbi Yossi Goldstein, who was in periodic correspondence and contact with the Frierdiker Rebbe, recalls that at one point in the late 1940s, the Frierdiker Rebbe said to him: "From now on, give over your questions to my son-in-law, Menachem Mendel, and he will surely answer all of your questions." Goldstein recalls the thought that these words prompted in him: "It's like . . . he [was] appointing me to take his son-in-law as my Rebbe from then on." It is significant to note that starting even before Ramash's marriage to Chaya Mushka, the Frierdiker Rebbe referred many scholarly inquiries to him. In his later years, this tendency became even more apparent. In a 1948 letter to Rabbi Yisroel Noah Belinsky, he writes: "I have handed these [questions] to my son-in-law, the rabbinic genius and pious Chasid, Rabbi Menachem Mendel. . . . He has shown me his detailed response which addresses all aspects of your inquiry. I trust that his written response will be studied with the attention it deserves" (Yosef Y. Schneersohn, *Igrot Kodesh,* 14:405). There are many other such instances of the Frierdiker Rebbe referring questions to his erudite younger son-in-law, while there are no instances with which I am familiar of these sorts of questions being directed to his older son-in-law. This observation is by no means a criticism of Rabbi Gourary; he simply was not the intellectual equal of his brother-in-law, but then again, who else in Chabad was?

20. Both Rabbis Berel Shemtov and Shalom Feldman report having heard this story directly from Rabbi Kazarnowsky. Kazarnowsky himself reported that subsequent to this event, Ramash never again answered his questions until he became Rebbe. See also letter of Yoel Kahan, 3 Iyar 5710 (July 20, 1950).

21. As one careful student of this period put it to me, Chana Gourary seemed to fear that if she did not become the movement's Rebbetzin after her father's death, she would fade away and be regarded as peripheral.

22. See these words of Rebbetzin Nechama Dina in a letter dated 17 Adar II 5711 (March 25, 1951) written and signed by eight of the leading Chabad rabbis of the time, several of whom had been present at the meeting at which Nechama Dina uttered these words.

In the months after the Frierdiker Rebbe's death, even as many Chasidim began rallying around Ramash, Rashag, who was anxious to become Rebbe, tried to mobilize whatever support he could. He began holding *farbrengens* and speaking to various lay leaders of the movement in an attempt to gain support. When these efforts didn't seem to bear fruit (his *farbrengens* do not seem to have been successful in attracting followers, and some of the diaries written during that period spoke of them in a disparaging way), he and Chana enlisted the assistance of his bereaved and deaf mother-in-law, the Frierdiker Rebbe's widow, Nechama Dina.

Nechama Dina herself held her younger son-in-law, Rabbi Menachem Mendel, in very high esteem; she liked to relate the story of the occasion when her husband, seeing Ramash walking by, exclaimed to those nearby, "There goes the Tzemach Tzedek." But under the influence of her eldest daughter and son-in-law, who complained bitterly of being completely disrespected by so many Chasidim, she soured on those campaigning for the Rebbe, sometimes screaming at them that they were hurting the older son-in-law. Of the Rebbe she said, "He's a Gaon [Torah genius], he'll be successful [as a leader] no matter what. Even during the time of the Alter Rebbe he would have been reckoned with" (letter of Yoel Kahan, 26 Adar II 5711 [April 3, 1951]).

In an effort to help Rashag during what was for him a difficult period, she demanded from the movement's elders that Rashag should take the place of the Frierdiker Rebbe as president of the yeshivot. Given the significance of the yeshivot, such an appointment would have created, in effect, a sort of partnership between Rashag and Ramash. Though the elders to whom she presented this proposal were sympathetic to the personal quandary she was in because of the pressure being exerted by her oldest daughter and son-in-law (at the meeting with the elders, Nechama Dina was reading from a sheet that seems to have been prepared for her by Rashag), they told her that such a request was untenable. The tradition in Chabad had always been that the Rebbe was the head of all Chabad institutions; leadership could not be shared. But they also reassured her that Rashag should and would continue to serve as chairman of the yeshivot, the same position he held under his father-in-law. Indeed, over the coming decades the Rebbe always supported Rashag in this highly prestigious and significant position.

Throughout the remaining decades of her life, Rebbetzin Nechama Dina always was concerned to fully safeguard Rabbi Gourary's dignity when he was at her house. Thus, at holiday meals, she made sure that he and the Rebbe were served simultaneously, even though Chasidim would have served the Rebbe first. In her will, she asked that Rashag be the one to recite Kaddish for her. Some have cited this as an indication that she felt a personal preference for him. This is, of course, possible, but Rebbetzin Hadassah Carlebach, the Frierdiker Rebbetzin's cousin who had a relationship with her and with both of her daughters, told me that she felt this gesture had less to do with a preference on Nechama Dina's part and was in effect a "sort of lollipop for her older daughter," who had never gotten over her disappointment at her husband not becoming Rebbe.

23. Documents chronicling the period following the Frierdiker Rebbe's death include personal diaries, primary among them those of Eli Gross, an American student at the Lubavitch yeshiva, and letters to parents and friends in other countries apprising them of the goings-on. Among the latter, the lengthy correspondence from yeshiva student Yoel Kahan stands out. Kahan, a Russian-born prodigy who had arrived from Israel to study at Chabad's flagship yeshiva, later emerged as the movement's deepest thinker and author. He also became the Rebbe's chief oral scribe—training scores of students to memorize the Rebbe's talks on Sabbath and holidays and to later record them in writing—and the head *mashpia*, or spiritual guide, in the Lubavitch central yeshiva, Tomchei Temimim.

24. One of the queries that Reb Zalman recalled: Before re-dressing the body of the Frierdiker Rebbe, which had just been ritually cleansed, a question arose among those performing the *tahara* (purification) as to which garment should be put on first, the pants or the shirt. One of the men emerged from the room and

posed the question to Ramash, who answered: "As I recall, Rambam rules that in the case of the High Priest, the pants are put on first, and afterward the shirt. If such is the ruling concerning the High Priest, that is how we should now act" (see Maimonides, *Hilchot Klei ha-Mikdash*, 10:1; also, Leviticus 6:3, and *Yoma* 23b; this incident is recounted as well in Yosef Greenberg, *Y'mei Bereishit* [Brooklyn, NY: Kehot Publication Society, 1993], a path-breaking account of the Rebbe's rise to leadership in the year following his father-in-law's death; see p. 75).

25. Detailed research into documents, diaries, and correspondence written during 1950–1951, along with two well-researched and documented overviews of the events leading up to the appointment a year later of Menachem Mendel Schneerson as the Seventh Rebbe—Rabbi Yosef Greenberg's *Y'mei Bereishit*, and more recently Chaim Rapoport's *The Afterlife of Scholarship*—have demonstrated that the move to secure the leadership role for him began in the days immediately following his father-in-law's death, and that the efforts were undertaken not at his behest but in defiance of his wishes. Rabbi Rapoport has written an unconventional and very important book on the Rebbe, unconventional because the book originated as an extended unfavorable review of a critical biography of Rabbi Schneerson, *The Rebbe: The Life and Afterlife of Menachem Mendel Schneerson*, by Samuel Heilman and Menachem Friedman (Princeton: Princeton University Press, 2010). Rapoport's original review of Professors Heilman and Friedman's work focused on a number of factual errors they made, which in turn led to errors in interpretation and to a somewhat mean-spirited analysis of the Rebbe's rise to leadership. Rapoport's book, an expanded version of his review, is particularly detailed in its account of the events of 1950–1951 and Ramash's rise to leadership. I am indebted to this book for many of the incidents cited in this and in other chapters. I am indebted as well to Rabbi Yosef Greenberg's previously cited *Y'mei Bereishit* (see previous footnote), in which he has reproduced hundreds of documents from that period.

26. Zalman Posner, *Think Jewish* (Nashville: Kesher Press, 2002) 79. Thus, Beryl Weiss, a wealthy Los Angeles businessman, once consulted with the Rebbe about taking his business public; selling a substantial stake in his business, he explained to the Rebbe, would bring him a considerable amount of money, and he promised that as soon as this took place, he would donate a million dollars to Chabad, money the movement obviously needed. The Rebbe challenged Weiss: "Why do you want to give away so much control of your business to others?" and strongly advised him against doing so. At the moment the Rebbe was advising the man, he had to be thinking only of what was best for the person in front of him; as devoted as the Rebbe was to Chabad, his job at that moment was not to procure a large donation for Lubavitch, but to help this man decide on a course of action most suitable for him.

27. Ibid., 80.

28. Rapoport, *The Afterlife of Scholarship*, 159 and 160, and Greenberg, *Y'mei Bereishit*, 84.

29. The Rebbe's letter is published in Menachem M. Schneerson, *Igrot Kodesh*, 21:99.

30. Ibid., 21:161.

31. During this period, my grandfather, Rabbi Nissen Telushkin, received an international phone call from Rabbi Zevin in Israel (such calls were rare and highly expensive in 1950), trying to clarify if Ramash was indeed going to be appointed as successor. My grandfather, who also hoped for the appointment of Ramash, was impressed by how concerned Rabbi Zevin was that this happen, and by his desire to do whatever he could to help bring it about.

32. See Rapoport, *The Afterlife of Scholarship*, 164 and 212, where a facsimile of Zalmanov's handwritten letter is published.

33. Rabbi Dubov's words proved prophetic. Rabbi Gourary eventually came to fully accept his brother-in-law as Rebbe and remained for the rest of his life in the highest echelons of Chabad. His wife and son, however, deeply resented Ramash's appointment and subsequently broke with the movement in a particularly public and painful manner (see chapter 26).

34. The letter was published in part in Rapoport, *The Afterlife of Scholarship*. The entire letter, including the somewhat provocative final sentence, has not previously been published.

35. Rabbi Schachter-Shalomi told me that one reason he so wanted Ramash to be the Rebbe was that he had studied at universities and knew the outside world, and Schacter-Shalomi believed that this would be a very valuable asset for a Rebbe for our time.

36. This is one of only three instances I have come across in which a person made direct reference to the Rebbe about his childlessness. As is clear from Reb Zalman's recollection, Ramash did not want to engage this subject, though Reb Zalman has always felt that the tears that sprang to Ramash's eyes had to do with the reference he had made to his childlessness. Yet he said nothing about it. Indeed, given how significant this issue must have been in his and the Rebbetzin's life, one wonders if—subsequent to his father-in-law's and mother's deaths—there was anyone other than his wife to whom the Rebbe could speak openly about his personal life (regarding the other two instances, see pages 206–7 and 374). Reb Zalman also shared with me the contents of yet another remarkable conversation he had with Ramash during the period following the Frierdiker Rebbe's death. Reb Zalman, who has had a lifelong interest in alternative forms of spirituality, asked Ramash if he wanted him (Zalman) to study channeling techniques, by which one transmits messages from the dead, so that he could bring Ramash messages from his father-in-law. When Reb Zalman told me this, I was shocked, since communing with the dead is explicitly forbidden in the Torah (Deuteronomy 18:10–11 legislates: "Let no one be found among you . . . who inquires of the dead. For anyone who does such things is abhorrent to the Lord"). In response, Reb Zalman cited the Talmudic teaching (*Brachot* 18a) that speaks of the righteous (*tzaddikim*) "who even after their death are still called living." Therefore, the effort to receive a message from a deceased *tzaddik* is permitted. I asked him how Ramash responded. He told Reb Zalman, "If my father-in-law wants to transmit a message, he will find a way to do so without any dancing tables" (*ohn di tantzedike*

tishlach; films depicting séances in which dead spirits are raised frequently show tables moving, and the Rebbe's ironic response shows his awareness of such depictions).

37. See Yosef. Y. Schneersohn, *Igrot Kodesh*, 2:8–10, in which Rabbi Yechezkel Feigin, the Frierdiker Rebbe's secretary, writes to Israel Jacobson in the United States: "I am writing to you in great secrecy, to [describe to] what extent [the financial situation has deteriorated] . . . a wedding must take place, but with what?"

38. Menachem M. Schneerson, *Igrot Kodesh*, 3:91.

39. The Frierdiker Rebbe was himself aware of the great financial and organizational burdens Menachem Mendel was facing as head of the three major Chabad institutions. Thus, in 1946, he wrote to Alexander Cowen that "My dear son-in-law, the Gaon, Rabbi Menachem Mendel Schneerson, experienced great hardships from the institution . . . for reasons of financial strains we had to hold back [on carrying out a variety of activities]." See Yosef Y. Schneersohn, *Igrot Kodesh*, 9:101.

40. It is hard to find almost any rabbinic figures supporting the candidacy of Rabbi Shmaryahu Gourary; his brother-in-law Rabbi Chaim Yosef Rosenblum is perhaps the most notable exception. Another supporter was Rabbi Yitzchak (Irving) Feldman.

41. See diary of Eli Gross, 4 Iyar 5710 (July 21, 1950).

42. During the *shloshim* (the thirty days following his father-in-law's death), Ramash donned rabbinic garments, but when the thirty days concluded, he returned to his usual gray suit, except for Shabbat and holidays.

43. Letter of Yoel Kahan, 3 Iyar 5710 (July 20, 1950).

44. Greenberg, *Y'mei Bereishit*, 103.

45. Letter of Yoel Kahan, 24 Tishrei 5711 (October 5, 1950). It should be noted that Ramash had already been called up with this title for several months in the weekday yeshiva minyan.

46. Rabbi Yosef Weinberg, in an interview on June 24, 2008, conducted by JEM.

47. For more on this subject, see also the *New York Times* interview, March 27, 1972.

48. In the course of researching his article, Rabbi Weiner asked Rabbi Gourary the method by which a new Rebbe was chosen when the deceased Rebbe had no sons, obviously a more sensitive question to direct to Gourary, who did not get the position, than to the Rebbe, who did. "Gourary looked at me sharply for a moment," Weiner later wrote. Then, obviously concluding that Weiner had not asked the question to be provocative, Rabbi Gourary simply stated: "If the Rebbe leaves a will, his instructions are followed. Otherwise, the elders of the movement decide." Weiner posed to Gourary as well the question that he had earlier asked the Rebbe about offering advice on areas presumably outside his expertise, such as medicine. That Gourary had by this point fully reconciled himself to his brother-in-law being Rebbe is suggested by his response: "Chasidim believe in the Rebbe's blessing. A Chasid believes in higher destiny, what you call luck. But what is luck, after all,

but higher destiny? Chasidim believe in the power of the Rebbe to influence that destiny" (Herbert Weiner, *9½ Mystics* [New York: Touchstone, 1969], 183).

49. See introduction to Menachem M. Schneerson, *Igrot Kodesh*, 3:15–16.

50. From the diary of Eli Gross as cited in Greenberg, *Y'mei Bereishit*.

51. Greenberg, *Y'mei Bereishit*, 376.

52. Two weeks earlier, on the occasion of the anniversary of the *yahrtzeit* of the Alter Rebbe, the elders of the movement placed prominent notices in the leading Jewish newspapers announcing that Ramash had been chosen to succeed his father-in-law as Rebbe, and that on the first *yahrtzeit* of the Frierdiker Rebbe, Ramash would formally accept the role. When Ramash heard of this, he demanded that the Chasidim place a "denial" in the newspaper saying that no such appointment had been made, and even threatened that if they wouldn't, he would have no choice but to write to the newspapers himself. Rabbi Shmuel Levitin, known as one of the wittier Chasidim, told Ramash, "We didn't write that you accepted the position of Rebbe. We wrote that we accepted you as our Rebbe" (see Greenberg, *Y'mei Bereishit*, 348–51, and Rapoport, *The Afterlife of Scholarship*, 174).

53. A recording of the Rebbe's *ma'amar* can be heard at Chabad.org/550378.

54. I heard this story from Rabbi Shlomo Zarchi, a dean at the Central Lubavitch Yeshiva, who heard it directly from Rabbi Moshe Groner; Zarchi is renowned for his extraordinary memory.

55. The Rebbe sourced his last words to the Midrash (*Numbers Rabbah* 19:13), which states that God assured Moses before his death that although he and his generation were denied the privilege of entering Israel before their passing, during the future redemption led by the Messiah they would go together into the Holy Land. The Rebbe thus expressed his yearning that when the Messiah came, he and his fellow Chasidim would be reunited with their Rebbe—the Frierdiker Rebbe—and go together with him into the Redemption, a period in which people's connection to the essence of Godliness would be readily visible to the naked eye. The words "he will redeem us" thus do not mean that *he* is the Redeemer. Rather, that when the Messiah comes, the Jewish people, certainly those who were the Rebbe's followers, will be redeemed with him. Just as Moses will be redeemed with his people and lead them, so will the Frierdiker Rebbe lead his followers when the Messiah comes. In a talk delivered three days later, on 13 Shevat 5711 (January 20, 1951), the Rebbe mentioned that he had been asked by people about his concluding statement. He then proceeded to offer greater explanation. See Menachem M. Schneerson, *Likutei Sichot* (Brooklyn, NY: Kehot Publication Society, 1959–2013), 2:577–78; and *Torat Menachem Hitvaaduyot* (Brooklyn, NY: Lahak Hanochas, 1981–2013), 2:228.

Chapter 3: Connecting to Individuals

1. Cited in Mendel Kalmenson, *Seeds of Wisdom* (New York: Jewish Educational Media, 2013), 129.

2. Israel Shenker, "Lubavitch Rabbi Marks His 70th Year with Call for 'Kindness,'" *New York Times*, March 27, 1972.

3.   This was characteristic advice of the Rebbe, in essence, "Stay where you are and do good there." It is similar to the advice he gave Rabbi Dudley Weinberg, a Reform rabbi who was so taken with the Rebbe and his philosophy that he asked him if he should leave his Reform pulpit (see pages 223–24).

4.   Professor Block taught me a great deal about the Rebbe and their discussions during an interview. I was also aided by a transcript of an interview with Professor Block conducted by JEM.

5.   Rabbi Herbert Bomzer, a great admirer of the Rebbe, told him that he used to identify himself to others by saying, "I am a Chasid of the Lubavitcher Rebbe." After he had mentioned this to the Rebbe several times, the Rebbe said, "*Shoin gekumin tzeit*"—"The time has come you should say already you're a Lubavitcher Chasid." Since then, Bomzer reports, he tells others, "I'm a Lubavitcher Chasid." The case of Bomzer is similar to but subtly different from that of Yehuda Avner. Bomzer had long identified himself as the Rebbe's Chasid, so that the step to formally declaring himself a Lubavitcher Chasid was not a large one. On the other hand, prior to the Rebbe's request of Avner to become a Lubavitcher, he had never indicated any particular attachment, other than affection and admiration, to the Rebbe and to Chabad.

6.   He was also committed to the Palestinians having a homeland, not a fully independent state but one linked to Jordan. From the perspective of 2011, this would be viewed as a moderate policy, and very acceptable to Israel, but it was not regarded as moderate by Israel in 1977, when the PLO, and the rest of the Arab world, were committed to Israel's destruction, and Egyptian president Sadat had not yet made his famous visit to Jerusalem.

7.   Similar questions were directed to Israeli president Zalman Shazar when he would come to meet with the Rebbe. There were those in Israel who felt that it was beneath the dignity of an Israeli president to go the court of a Chasidic Rebbe; rather, the Rebbe should come to him. To such criticism, offered by, among others, Prime Minister Golda Meir, Shazar responded: "What can I do? I am a Chasid and a Chasid goes to his Rebbe."

8.   A video of Prime Minister Begin's meeting with the Rebbe is available at Chabad.org/132942.

9.   In Avner's seven-hundred-page memoir, *The Prime Ministers: An Intimate Narrative of Israeli Leadership* (New Milford, CT: Toby Press, 2010), the Rebbe is the only nonpolitical and non-family figure of whom he writes at considerable length.

10.   This remarkable encounter is described in Avner, *The Prime Ministers*, 406–7, 443–46. See also 409–41 for a detailed account of Begin's meetings at the White House. In 2010 and again in 2012, I spoke with Avner in Jerusalem of his encounters with the Rebbe. Avner remains to this day a great admirer of the Rebbe and the work of Chabad, but he has never chosen to become a Lubavitcher Chasid. In 2008, he was invited to be the guest speaker at the annual convention of the Chabad *shluchim*; he told there the story of the Rebbe's request of him.

11. Swados apparently set down his recollections of the meeting a short time later but never published them. After his death, the article lay for years in the Swados archives at the University of Massachusetts in Amherst. It was subsequently found, and a section of it was published by the *New York Times* (op-ed, June 14, 1994) at the time of the Rebbe's death. The citations from the interview cited here are based on the manuscript at the University of Massachusetts archives.

12. Gordon Zacks recalls, "He looked at me in such a penetrating way that I felt like I was being X-rayed" (for more on a later encounter between Zacks and the Rebbe, see page 506).

13. It is a striking feature of Chabad headquarters that both during the Rebbe's lifetime and until today, as little money as possible is spent on the building, enough to keep it functional, but not enough to make it physically attractive. Whether this was the Rebbe's explicit wish or the natural inclination of the staff, which has continued to work there since his death, I haven't been able to ascertain, though it certainly seems consistent with the Rebbe's emphasis on simplicity and on spending money on the most pressing causes.

14. As the Rebbe wrote in 1964: "Anyone who knows how insignificant was the minority of Germans who opposed the Hitler regime, realizes that the German cult was not something which was practiced by a few individuals, but had [been] embraced [by] the vast majority of the nation"; see page 258).

15. See the posthumously published op-ed piece by Swados in the *New York Times*, June 14, 1994.

16. More than seven decades later, Rebbetzin Sharfstein recalled the event to me, noting her belief that a person's Hebrew name represents the person's essence. During her college years, Sharfstein stopped using her secular name entirely, believing that when a person utilizes both a secular and a Hebrew name, the person becomes compartmentalized. She looks back upon her childhood encounter with the Frierdiker Rebbe as the first step in guiding her to use her Hebrew name exclusively.

17. The Rebbe's goal was to bring his mother either to the United States, where he lived, or to Eretz Yisrael (then Palestine), where his brother Aryeh Leib lived. But when writing to Rabbi Zuber, his most pressing desire was to get her out of Stalinist Russia as soon as possible. Since the immigration process both for the United States and Palestine "require[s] an extended period of time," he wanted Zuber to find out if a visa to Sweden could be procured more quickly. If so, Rebbetzin Schneerson should be brought to Sweden, where she could stay while waiting for a visa to either the United States or Palestine. He asked Zuber to be discreet in his efforts, and that all initiatives should come from the outside, as it would endanger his mother if she was seen as, in any way, instigating the process. Finally, because of Sweden's proximity to Russia, he asked the rabbi to send his mother, "on my account," matzah and other food for the upcoming Passover holiday (*Igrot Kodesh*, 2:111). As far as we know, Rabbi Zuber had no success in helping to bring the Rebbe's mother out. However, that same year, Rebbetzin Schneerson was smuggled out of the Soviet

Union into Poland, then into Germany (to the Pocking refugee camp) and from there to Paris, where the Rebbe met her and brought her to the United States.

18. "Death ends a life, but not a relationship" is the opening sentence of Mitch Albom's *Tuesdays with Morrie* (New York: Doubleday, 1997), one of the best-selling nonfiction books in the United States in the last fifty years.

19. *Apikores* literally means a "heretic," and the term has a very serious connotation in Jewish law. Maimonides rules that one should do what one can to bring about an *apikores*'s death (Laws of Murderers 4:10). The Rebbe, it is obvious, did not think that the professor's words rose to the level of heresy (if he did, he probably would have instructed Sharfstein not to participate in the class). Rather, *"apikores"* is the sort of term commonly used to describe someone who offers antireligious arguments (a person might say to a friend expressing a very critical comment about some aspect of Judaism, "You sound like a real *apikores*").

20. See also Chana Sharfstein's memoir, *Beyond the Dollar Line* (Brooklyn, NY: Merkos Publications, 2010). I have also relied on my interview with Mrs. Sharfstein on September 5, 2012, as well as a transcript of a JEM interview.

Chapter 4: The Ten Campaigns

1. Other forms of the word do occur.

2. The Moroccan Jewish community was different in that it was largely obser-vant; still, this rather poor North African country provided a very different social environment from that of the Chabad community. When the Lipskers arrived, an estimated 250,000 Jews lived in Morocco, but starting in the late 1950s, a large migration of Jews from the country started, and today there are an estimated 5,000 Jews left in the country.

3. Menachem M. Schneerson, *Igrot Kodesh,* 17:52.

4. Rabbi Berel Shemtov, then a young student at the yeshiva, recalls the Rebbe speaking in 1952 of Chabad's mission to change the Jewish world. Shemtov noted that this grandiose vision was stated at a *farbrengen* at which fewer than thirty people were present, a typical attendance at a *farbrengen* in those days. The Rebbe's com-ment, and Chabad's subsequent growth, puts one in mind of the words of the noted anthropologist Margaret Mead: "Never doubt that a small group of thoughtful committed citizens can change the world; indeed, it's the only thing that ever has."

5. Genesis 45:18; Pharaoh instructs Joseph to invite his family, then living in famine-desolated Canaan, to come to Egypt and to "live off the fat of the land."

6. A JEM video of the Rebbe's talk of Purim 5721 (March 2, 1961) is available at Chabad.org/ 878371.

7. It was a characteristic feature of the Rebbe, who believed that everything was by Divine Providence, to derive life lessons for individuals and for people in general from world events. On occasion, he would similarly utilize secular, non-Jewish holidays as well, holidays that were otherwise ignored by traditional Jews. Peter Kalms recalls

a *yechidus* he had with the Rebbe on January 2, 1977, which concluded with the Rebbe offering him a special *bracha* (blessing), and then explaining: "Rabbi Levi Yitzchak of Berditshev was always searching for an occasion to give a *bracha*. Once he did so on the New Year of the gentiles. People said to him, 'How can you, a rabbi, do this on the special time of the gentiles?' He said, 'To make a *bracha*, all occasions are okay. Now," the Rebbe concluded to Kalms, "it is also a day or two ago the New Year of the gentiles." (Peter Kalms, *Guidance from the Rebbe* [Jerusalem: Shamir Publishing House, 2001], 83.)

8.   See Chabad.org, "1974: The Mitzvah Tank," 1.

9.   The word "*neshek*," which is the Hebrew for "weapon," is an acronym for *neirot Shabbat kodesh* (candles of the holy Shabbat).

10.   For example, when Chasidim from other Chasidic courts chose to join Chabad, he asked them to continue to wear the clothing of their distinctive group, presumably to minimize the hurt to the parents.

11.   Menachem M. Schneerson, *Likutei Sichot*, 21:382. In the characteristic formal manner in which the Rebbe wrote and spoke, he phrased his comment to the questioner in the third person (i.e., "it was the custom of the women in her family not to read newspapers . . .") but I have rephrased it in the second person ("It was the custom of the women in your family") as it was intended to be understood.

12.   The Rebbe's letter of Chanukah 5735 (December 1974) is available at Chabad .org/1943030.

13.   Senator Lieberman spoke of this at the annual Chabad Kinus, the gathering of Chabad *shluchim* from around the world, on November 3, 2013. A video of Lieberman's speech is available at Chabad.org/2376576.

14.   Among them, that everyone purchase a letter in a *sefer* Torah. According to Jewish law, the final commandment of the 613 Torah laws is a directive to every Jew to write a Torah scroll for himself (see Deuteronomy 31:19). The medieval *Sefer ha-Chinuch* (which lists and explains the Torah commandments in order of appearance) explains: "Whoever does not find it possible to write it with his own hand should hire someone to write it for him." Chabad popularized the campaign of asking Jews to contribute a dollar to "buy" a letter in a Torah, whose writing Chabad commissioned. Chabad also commissioned the writing of Torah scrolls with dollars collected from children. Another campaign, initiated at the Rebbe's behest, was to make available to Jews *shmurah matzoh* (matzah that is specially watched to make sure it does not come into contact with water; see page 480 for the story of a prominent Jewish writer who was proud to receive each year a package of *shmurah matzoh* from the Rebbe). Another campaign involved *shluchim* going out in public on Sukkot with a *lulav* and *etrog* and enabling Jews who did not acquire them for the holiday to make the mandated blessing over them.

Chapter 5: Love Your Neighbor

1.   The Rebbe explained that he heard from his father-in-law the details that he was now relating. For the account of that conversation with his father-in-law, see *Reshimot ha-Yoman*, 361; the conversation occurred in Vienna in 1935.

2.   Such reasoning would be in line with Maimonides's ruling that when an issue involving endangerment of life occurs, the carrying out of normally prohibited acts such as chopping wood should be performed by "adult and scholarly Israelites" in order to demonstrate to everyone that the purpose of Jewish laws is "to bring mercy, kindness and peace to the world" (Laws of Shabbat 2:3).

3.   The Rebbe spoke of this incident at a *farbrengen* on 19 Kislev 5743 (November 25, 1983). A video of the speech is available at Chabad.org/1663535.

4.   Unfortunately, Kaplan does not have a copy of the Rebbe's response, but what follows is the gist of his answer.

5.   In July 2012, some thirty-five years after this event, Rabbi Kaplan told me that he was still in touch with this woman, who is now a grandmother and whose life has turned out well.

6.   This story was related to me by Rabbi Efraim Mintz, the executive director of the Rohr Jewish Learning Institute (JLI).

7.   This story was related to me by Rabbi Lipskar in an interview I conducted with him on June 12, 2013.

8.   He even spoke of this in a public talk, saying that if people didn't stop staring at him during prayers, he would *daven* (pray) alone (*Hitva'aduyot*, 5744 [Brooklyn, NY: Lahak Hanochas, 1981–2013] 1:484–87).

9.   During my five years of working on this book, Rabbi Shemtov gave very generously of his time to me, relating many of his first-person experiences with the Rebbe, including this story, along with much additional information and insight that I incorporated into the book.

Chapter 6: Creating Fearlessness, Creating Leaders

1.   Rabbi Groner told me of this incident in an interview with him in 2008. As a general rule, the Rebbe directed questions posed to him on matters of Jewish law to local rabbis; he did not wish to undercut the authority of rabbis. Rabbi Groner told me that in this instance, the Rebbe had first told him to ask his question of my grandfather, Rabbi Nissen Telushkin. However, my grandfather felt self-conscious about answering a question that had been posed to the Rebbe and sent Groner back to the Rebbe. It was at that point that the Rebbe told Groner that he should search out the answer himself.

2.   Mrs. Hager was interviewed by JEM on August 9, 2007.

3.   Rabbi Dr. Weinreb related this incident to me in a conversation I had with him. I also relied on a transcript of an interview with Rabbi Weinreb conducted by JEM.

4.   Jonathan Sacks, *To Heal a Fractured World* (New York: Schocken/Random House, 2005), 255.

5.   Menachem M. Schneerson, *Igrot Kodesh*, 6:245.

6.   Rabbi Nachman Sudak, who directs Chabad-Lubavitch in the United Kingdom, in an interview I conducted with him on November 22, 2005.

7.   Rabbi Moshe Feller, who directs Chabad-Lubavitch of the Upper Midwest, in an interview I conducted with him on November 8, 2010.

8.   Rabbi Berel Shemtov, who directs Chabad-Lubavitch in Michigan, in an interview I conducted with him on June 11, 2013.

9.   Rabbi Yitzchak Meir Gourary, in an interview on January 18, 2011, conducted by JEM.

10.   Based on an interview I conducted with Rabbi Zev Katz in June 2013. Katz eventually went on to succeed his father as *gabbai* of the main Lubavitch Synagogue at 770 Eastern Parkway.

11.   Mrs. Sternberg, in an interview I conducted with her at her home on September 5, 2012.

Chapter 7: Optimism and the Careful Choosing of Words

1.   The Hebrew word "*dvarim*" means both "things" and "words."

2.   Jewish law permits speaking ill of another in an instance when the person to whom you are speaking needs the information (for example, it is permitted to inform a person if someone is going about besmirching his or her reputation).

3.   So deeply rooted is the tendency to associate hospitals with the word "sick" that the term for "maternity hospital" in Hebrew is *beit cholim le-yoldot*, which literally means "home of the sick for those giving birth" (for the variety of terms associated with *beit cholim*, see Reuben Alcalay, *The Complete Hebrew-English Dictionary* [Brooklyn, NY: P Shalom Publications, 1996], 233).

4.   I cannot state with certainty that the Rebbe is the one who coined this term, but I have never seen it in a dictionary.

5.   In Samuel Rosenblatt's biography of his father, *Yossele Rosenblatt: The Immortal Cantor*, Rosenblatt relates how his father, the most famous cantor in American Jewish history, was approached by the philanthropist Jacob Schiff to sing at a public event for the Montefiore Home for the Incurables, of which Schiff was president. In Schiff's subsequent letter of thanks to Cantor Rosenblatt for his performance, he wrote that Rosenblatt's presentation had been "dignified to the audience and cheering to the inmates." Given that Schiff was a man of great generosity, it becomes clear both from the name of the institution he headed and the reference to hospital patients as "inmates" that words regarding the sick were used less sensitively in 1913, when this event happened (Samuel Rosenblatt, *Yossele Rosenblatt: The Immortal Cantor* [New York: Cantors Assembly, 2004], 119).

6.   The Rebbe's talk of August 19, 1976, is published in Menachem M. Schneerson, *Sichot Kodesh 5736*, 2:633–38. A JEM video of the Rebbe's talk is available at Chabad .org/1076652. An interview, conducted by JEM, with Yosef Lautenberg, a founder of the IDF Disabled Veterans Organization and leader of the delegation to the Rebbe in 1976, is available at Chabad.org/2349213. Lautenberg was injured in the battle for Jerusalem in 1948.

7. I read of this incident with the disabled army veteran many years ago, but subsequently lost the information and have not been able to identify him.

8. The same applied to less severe handicaps. A man I know, who today is a noted rabbi and community leader, was dyslexic as a child and recalled being summoned, along with his parents, for a meeting with his principal, who informed the parents, in my friend's presence, that "your son is mildly retarded." Because of a learning disability, he was taught to think of himself as stupid.

9. From a conversation between the Rebbe and Cantor Malovany on Sunday, December 10, 1989. A video of this encounter is available at Chabad.org/1744438.

10. The initial impetus for the Rebbe's refusal to use less refined language was a passage in the Torah that describes the animals Noah brought on to the Ark: "Of clean beasts and of beasts that are not clean . . . there went two and two with Noah into the Ark" (Genesis 7:8–9). Based on this verse, the Talmudic sage Rabbi Joshua ben Levi concluded: "Let a man never permit offensive speech to issue from his mouth, for the Torah resorted to an [additional] eight-letter circumlocution to avoid an offensive statement ['unclean beast'; see *Pesachim* 3a]." Although the Torah normally is terse in its use of words, on this occasion, the additional words, "of beasts that are not clean," were added simply to avoid using the word "unclean."

11. I was inclined to see such concern about how words could affect a person's psyche as excessive, until I recalled an incident I had personally witnessed that, in retrospect, confirmed for me the notion that people often hear negative associations even when not intended. At the time, my daughter Naomi was two and a half and had a cold. She heard me telling someone on the telephone that "Naomi has a bad cough." Unaware that she was even listening, I suddenly heard her call out, "Naomi has a *good* cough."

12. Menachem M. Schneerson, *Igrot Kodesh*, 6:175–76.

13. Just today (October 26, 2012), while writing this section, I met an elderly Jewish woman, a self-proclaimed atheist, who told me that she thought Jews who went on identifying as Jews after the Holocaust were crazy, particularly if they were not religious, for by doing so, they exposed their descendants to all the horrors of antisemitism.

14. Not convincing is the argument sometimes offered that trying to assimilate won't help since the Nazis checked into a person's ancestral background and murdered people with Jewish parents and grandparents, since Nazism was the only antisemitic movement in history that targeted for death all people who had Jewish ancestry. Only if one believes that a Nazi-type movement is likely to occur in the United States will a Jew assume that assimilation won't help him or his children avoid antisemitism.

15. In addition, as a by-product of these other behaviors, such Jews will generally concern themselves with issues affecting the well-being of the Jewish people, such as supporting Israel, fighting antisemitism, and encouraging the availability of Jewish education for all Jewish youth.

Chapter 8: "I'm Also Tired. So What?"

1.   See the introduction to Menachem Mendel Schneerson, *The Letter and the Spirit: Letters by the Lubavitcher Rebbe*, selected and arranged by Nissan Mindel (Brooklyn, NY: Kehot Publication Society, 1998–), xvii.

2.   Even Moses, the Torah tells us, was stymied when the five daughters of the recently deceased Tzelafchad, who had no sons, challenged the inheritance laws that would have made it impossible for them to hold on to their father's land. Caught between the anguished appeal of the daughters—"Let not our father's name be lost to the clan"—and the competing claims of the tribal chiefs of Menashe that when these daughters would marry men from other tribes, the land would pass into the possession of those tribes, Moses was perplexed and had no answer to offer until God spoke to him: "The plea of Tzelafchad's daughters is just; you should give them a hereditary holding among their father's kinsmen; transfer their father's share to them." To maintain the territorial integrity of each tribe, the daughters married cousins who were members of the same tribe (see Numbers 27:1–11 and 36:1–12). Moses, as the biblical account conveys, did not always answer on the spot. In the case of the Rebbe, he sometimes answered very difficult questions on the spot, but he frequently postponed doing so until he had spent time considering the question at his father-in-law's grave.

3.   Drawn from an interview with Yona Kessa that was televised in Israel. A video of Kessa's interview is available at Chabad.org/295126. See also Rapoport, *The Afterlife of Scholarship*, 24n63; Rapoport does not, however, include the material about the Rebbe's wide-ranging secular knowledge.

4.   As a rule, the primary witnesses to these achievements are the child's immediate family members, whose objectivity cannot necessarily be relied upon. Yet most details of the Rebbe's childhood are known from the written or recorded memoirs of tutors, neighbors, friends, and classmates, some of whom went on to play leadership roles in Israeli society, among them cabinet minister Yisrael Bar-Yehuda (formerly Idelson) of the Labor Party, Knesset member Yona Kessa (Labor), poet Zelda Schneersohn Mishkovsky (recipient of the Bialik Prize for literature), poet Avraham Shlonsky, composer Verdina Shlonsky (the last three were cousins of the Rebbe), Yeshayahu Shar (one of the founders of Kfar Bilu), as well as his *cheder* peer Rabbi Nochum Goldschmidt.

5.   This statement sounds so extreme that it is important to state that it is meant literally; none of the Rebbe's secretaries can recall the Rebbe ever taking a vacation or not coming to work during his forty years as Rebbe because he was "taking the day off." The Rebbetzin once told Zalmon and Roselyn Jaffe that her husband would be taking a few days' "vacation" during the coming week. When Jaffe inquired as to where they would be going, the Rebbetzin answered without a trace of irony, "Oh, he is not going anywhere. Instead of retiring at three or four in the morning he will do so at one a.m." (Zalmon Jaffe, *My Encounter with the Rebbe* [Brooklyn, NY: PCL Publishing, 2009], 2:248.)

6.   In contrast, one certainly imagines that many people who stayed up with the Rebbe till three in the morning felt quite justified in sleeping late the following day. But the Rebbe, it would seem, came in the following morning and was at his desk.

7.   Rabbi Herbert Bomzer, in an interview on June 2, 2009, conducted by JEM.

8.   Rabbi Zev Segal, in a speech delivered on Monday, July 11, 1994, at Congregation Ahavat Achim of West Orange, New Jersey. A transcript of the speech is available at Chabad.org/395797.

9.   When reading accounts of the Rebbe's advice to individuals, it is important to keep in mind what he told Professor Block and many others: "What I say to one individual is not necessarily for everybody."

10.   This statement from Steinsaltz's speech is reprinted in Arthur Kurzweil, *On the Road with Rabbi Steinsaltz* (San Francisco: Jossey-Bass/Wiley, 2006), 72–73.

11.   Hindy Lew, in an interview on August 8, 2007, conducted by JEM.

12.   Menachem M. Schneerson, *Sichot Kodesh 5730* (Brooklyn, NY: Hanochas Ha-Temimim, 1981–1991), 1:469–70; recorded in *Reshimot ha-Yoman*, 266–67.

13.   Rabbi David Hollander, in an interview on February 23, 2006, conducted by JEM.

14.   This seems to have been a characteristic response of the Rebbe. When he asked Chana Sharfstein about her uncle, Rabbi Noteh Zuber of New Jersey, and Sharfstein responded that he had just retired, the Rebbe said: "Retired, what does that mean?" Sharfstein started to explain that his congregation had dwindled greatly in size, and the Rebbe simply reiterated that just because a situation arises that necessitates changes, one should make appropriate adjustments, but not retire. He immediately started outlining alternative options for Rabbi Zuber, involving scholarly pursuits, and other ways in which he could continue to contribute to the Jewish community. The Rebbe's words later inspired Sharfstein, even after she reached retirement age, to continue to conduct workshops and lectures and serve as a docent (a guide at a museum). For Sharfstein, the Rebbe remained the model: "The last period of his life saw the most fruitful expansion of Chabad Houses throughout the world."

15.   Rabbi Shemtov told me this in an interview I conducted with him (June 11, 2013).

Chapter 9: Expressing Disagreement Without Being Disagreeable

1.   Despite his own personal resistance to some of the Rebbe's arguments, Shlonsky also felt that "the Lubavitcher Rebbe, and he alone, is capable of turning a heretic into a believing Jew and into one who observes Torah and *mitzvot*" (*Yediot Achronot*, March 24, 1972).

2.   President Shimon Peres, in an interview I conducted with him at his residence in Israel on April 3, 2012.

3.   The letter from the Rebbe to Shimon Peres is published in Shlomo Haski, *Maidanchik: Haketer Shel Chabad* (Tel Aviv: Israel, 2013), 329.

4.   The Rebbe had the ability to maintain a warm manner even with those with whom he had profound disagreements. A 1985 New Year's letter from the Rebbe to Yossi Sarid, the Israeli left-wing parliamentarian whose views on the Israel-Palestine issue differed greatly from those of the Rebbe, was itself written in a response to a letter by Sarid asking for the Rebbe's blessing. The Rebbe blesses Sarid with spiritual and material blessings and wishes him "success in his position of importance for the true good of many." There is nothing particularly unusual about the Rebbe's letter, only that few people would have imagined such a correspondence between Yossi Sarid and the Lubavitcher Rebbe. In a similar manner, at a *farbrengen* on Tuesday, November 5, 1974, the Rebbe spoke in praise of Shulamit Aloni for standing strong to her principles. What is particularly fascinating about this talk is that Aloni, who identified as an atheist, had long been a left-leaning politician, the founder of the Ratz Party and leader of the Meretz Party, secular parties whose views on political as well as religious issues were very different from those of the Rebbe. Yet the Rebbe felt comfortable to suggest that others had things to learn from her. Years later, in an interview with the Israeli newspaper *Maariv* (October 4, 2009), Aloni proudly stated that her door was adorned with a mezuzah she received from Chabad.

5.   Howard Fine, the well-known acting coach in Los Angeles, told me that a problem commonly faced by actors is how to cultivate affection for an actor whom they dislike, but with whom they need to maintain a warm relationship onstage. In such circumstances, he has them perform an exercise in which they focus on at least one aspect of the other person for which they can feel genuine admiration and affection (when we dislike another, most of us repeatedly focus on those features of the other we dislike). It was a form of this technique that the Rebbe seems to have practiced naturally.

6.   Begin relied heavily on Dayan's advice in matters of security and would not have agreed to the return of all of the Sinai had Dayan not assured him that it would not endanger Israel. Henry Kissinger said of Dayan, "History will record him as a principal architect of the peace treaty with Egypt."

7.   It is evident from Yael Dayan's bittersweet memoir of her relationship with her father, *My Father, His Daughter*, that one of Dayan's two sons did not intend to say Kaddish at all, and the other only on the thirtieth day after his death (*shloshim*) and on his *yahrtzeit*, the anniversary of the death (Yael Dayan, *My Father, His Daughter* [New York: Farrar, Straus and Giroux, 1985], 279–89).

8.   Though the dimensions of the surprise attack had been prepared before Dayan's appointment as defense minister, he was the one who ordered the attack to commence and received much of the credit both at home and abroad for Israel's remarkable victory.

9.   The Satmar Rebbe was opposed to the Rebbe on many issues. Some years after the interview with Swados, the Rebbe started a campaign to encourage all Jewish men to put on tefillin. The campaign was initiated during the tense period preceding the Six-Day War of 1967, when Israel's existence seemed in great danger and, at

the Rebbe's behest, a particular effort was made to influence nonobservant Jews, particularly soldiers in the Israeli military, to put on tefillin. This effort, which became widely known as the Tefillin Campaign, was strongly opposed by the Satmar Rebbe, Rabbi Yoel Teitelbaum. In an adulatory biography of Rabbi Teitelbaum, *The Rebbe: The Extraordinary Life and Worldview of Rabbeinu Yoel Teitelbaum, the Satmar Rebbe*, by Rabbi Dovid Meisels, the author explains that the Satmar Rebbe's opposition to the campaign was rooted in his belief that real sinners—as the Satmar Rebbe regarded the large majority of Israeli soldiers—should not don tefillin. The Talmud speaks of the requirement that those who put on tefillin should have a "clean body" (*Shabbat* 49a; in context the Talmud speaks of not falling asleep while wearing tefillin, but the Satmar Rebbe, in line with the medieval Talmud commentator Rabbi Menachem Meiri, understood the edict concerning a "clean body" as meaning clean of sin; therefore, Jews not clean of sin should neither put on tefillin nor be encouraged to do so (see Dovid Meisels, *The Rebbe: The Extraordinary Life and Worldview of Rabbeinu Yoel Teitelbaum, the Satmar Rebbe* [Lakewood, NJ: Israel Book Shop, 2010], 515–16). Obviously, dismissing Israeli soldiers, who were risking their lives on a daily basis to protect the lives of Israel's population as unworthy of putting on tefillin was a way of thinking very far removed from that of the Rebbe.

10. Weiner, *9½ Mystics*, 174.

11. *Commentary* magazine opined that *Tales of the Hasidim* had "had a greater impact on non-Jewish writers—whether theologically inclined or theologically indifferent—than any other Jewish book of recent times" and that it "worked an even more powerful fascination on Jewish writers and intellectuals, and particularly those who stand outside the organized Jewish community." In December 1962, the magazine inaugurated a bimonthly column on *Tales of the Hasidim* by Norman Mailer, one of the most highly regarded American writers of his time.

12. There is no one way, Buber believed, to hallow God. Some do it by eating, others by fasting; some by learning Torah, others by praying. The Orthodox, of course, responded that one person can do all four, eating luxuriously and reciting the blessings on the Sabbath, fasting on Yom Kippur and other fast days, learning Torah, and praying three times a day.

13. It was not only Orthodox Jews who felt that Buber was misrepresenting Chasidism, at least in part. Gershon Scholem, the twentieth century's greatest scholar of kabbalah and not a traditionally observant Jew, offered a similar critique of Buber's writings on Chasidism.

14. Rabbi Zalman Schachter-Shalomi (widely known as Reb Zalman) prepared a booklet on meditation and Chasidism and sent it to the Rebbe, who approved it. In the bibliography, Reb Zalman cited additional books and articles dealing with these subjects, and among the authors whose works were cited were Rabbi Abraham Joshua Heschel, who taught at the Conservative movement's Jewish Theological Seminary, and Martin Buber. The Rebbe asked Reb Zalman to delete Buber because he regarded Buber's writings on Chasidism as misleading, but he did not ask him to delete Heschel.

15. Levanon's recollection of his meeting with the Rebbe was written in as respectful a manner as the Rebbe had spoken of him.

16. Both Begin's quote about Ben-Gurion and Ben-Gurion's comment about Begin are cited in Tom Segev, *The Seventh Million: The Israelis and the Holocaust* (New York: Henry Holt, 1991), 220 and 375n. Many years after these events, the two reconciled, and Ben-Gurion even wrote to Begin that while he had been strongly opposed to several of his positions in the past, "on a personal level, I have never had anything against you." But obviously, when one has no personal animus against another, one doesn't compare the person to Hitler, the most offensive comparison one Jew can make about another. Unfortunately, though, their reconciliation could not undo the fact that for many years, throughout the 1950s and most of the 1960s, Ben-Gurion and Begin's enmity kept them and their parties from working together on all issues, and not just issues on which they disagreed; the State and the people of Israel ended up paying the price for this lack of cooperation. It was this type of enmity that the Rebbe sought to avoid by refraining from personal invective even when he strongly disapproved of another's views.

17. I find that most people, when hearing this story, assume that the Rebbe's final words will be, "You're not there to tell them who they are, but to tell them who they can become." But such an approach (which can also come across as patronizing) so implies the superiority of the speaker to his listeners—the case, too, with harsh criticism—that it may well have an alienating effect and build the impenetrable wall against which the Rebbe warned. Instead, simply let people know what the teachings of Torah can offer them.

18. Rabbi Shach's statement was cited on December 29, 1990, in *Yated Ne'eman*, a newspaper that he cofounded. A fuller transcript of his remarks can be found in *Mussar Eruai Ha-Tekufah* (Bnai Brak, Israel: 2011), 35–38.

19. That Shabbat (March 30, 1990), the Rebbe responded to the substance of Rabbi Shach's remarks (without mentioning any names): "All Jewish people are one single unified entity. . . . We must appreciate the importance of speaking positively and the detrimental effects of speaking negatively. . . . Criticizing or speaking unfavorably about any portion of the Jewish people is like making such statements against G-d Himself. It is like one who strikes G-d in the eye. An attack against any Jews, heaven forbid, is an attack against Him. When one speaks, his motives are irrelevant, what matters is how people understood his words. This is certainly the case when such statements are made in public, with great publicity, to the extent that they are publicized even by the secular press. In particular, when the person making the statements is a public figure who has influence on others. If a person has stumbled and made such statements in public, he must repent in a manner that all of those who heard the negative statements hear how he regrets making them. Have we anyone greater than the prophet Isaiah, who after speaking in a way that was opposite of respect of Jews [see, for example, Isaiah 6:5]—even though he had a good reason to do so—he was punished. The reason the Bible relates this incident is to 'open the way for repentance,' so that should anyone ever make such statements, they should realize the need to correct their behavior. Those who were spoken negatively of should know that these words will have no effect on them. On the

contrary, G-d will bless them in both material and spiritual matters with good health and long life" (Menachem M. Schneerson, *Hitva'aduyot 5750*, 2:480–88).

20. Most of these examples concerning the reactions to Rabbi Shach's speech are drawn from David Landau, *Piety and Power: The World of Jewish Fundamentalism* (New York: Hill and Wang, 1992), 114–18.

21. Cited in M. Avrum Ehrlich, *The Messiah of Brooklyn: Understanding Lubavitch Hasidism Past and Present* (Brooklyn, NY: Ktav, 2005), 110n15.

22. Speech of 10 Tevet 5751 (December 27, 1990); see *Sefer Ha-Sichot* for 5751 (Brooklyn, NY: Kehot Publishing Society, 1987–2013), 229n55.

23. As I understand this, because Jews were the ones who proclaimed God to the world, it made demonic sense that Hitler, who declared that his mission in life was to "destroy the tyrannical God of the Jews" and His "life-denying Ten Commandments," would seek to annihilate the Jews. Hitler made these comments to Hermann Rauschning, a member of the Nazi Party and an admirer of Hitler, who subsequently broke with him. These comments of Hitler are cited in Rauschning's preface to Armin Robinson, ed., *The Ten Commandments* (New York: Simon and Schuster, 1944), ix–xiii. In the same preface, Rauschning also records Hitler's boast that "we are fighting against the most ancient curse that humanity has brought upon itself. Against the so-called Ten Commandments, against them we are fighting."

24 The Rebbe's letter is dated January 28, 1984, and is available on Chabad .org/2188391.

25. As regards the efforts to explain the Holocaust as punishment for Jewish sins, I have found an observation of Rabbi Irving Greenberg to be particularly pertinent: "Now that [the victims of the Holocaust] have been cruelly tortured and killed . . . their hair made into pillows, and their bones into fertilizer, their unknown graves and the very fact of their death denied to them [by Holocaust deniers], the theologian would inflict on them the only indignity left; that is, an insistence that it was done because of their sins" ("Cloud of Smoke, Pillar of Fire: Judaism, Christianity and Modernity After the Holocaust," in *Auschwitz: Beginning of a New Era* [New York: published jointly by Ktav Publishing, the Cathedral of St. John the Divine, and the Anti-Defamation League, 1977], 25).

26. Two of the figures most identified with the view of the Holocaust as punishment for Jewish sins were Rabbi Yoel Teitelbaum, the Satmar Rebbe (see page 56), and Rabbi Shach, both of whom were also sharp critics of Chabad.

Chapter 10: Anything Worth Doing Is Worth Doing Now

1. Because tefillin are expensive, stores often don't keep them in stock but wait for them to be ordered.

2. Mr. Bernie Rader in an interview on August 6, 2007, conducted by JEM.

3. I confirmed these details with Rabbi Sholom Lipskar, the world-renowned Chabad emissary to Bal Harbour, Florida, who founded the Aleph Institute, which

is dedicated to addressing the needs of Jewish individuals in the military and institutional environments.

4.   Rebbetzin Jill Katz, in an interview on December 11, 2008, conducted by JEM; a segment of the interview is available at Chabad.org/1052371. I have based this account on Rebbetzin Katz's extended interview and on Rabbi Eliyahu and Malka Touger, *To Know and to Care* (Brooklyn, NY: Sichos in English, 1996), 95–99.

5.   The extant hour and forty minutes of the conversation between the Rebbe and Frank Lautenberg (which Lautenberg recorded) is available at Chabad.org/551695.

6.   Esther Sternberg, in an interview I conducted with her at her home on September 5, 2012.

Chapter 11: Judaism's Mission to the World

1.   Geoffrey Davis, in an interview on March 21, 2012, conducted by JEM, and available at Chabad.org/2139959.

2.   See Menachem M. Schneerson, *The Letter and the Spirit*, 17. Mindel was the secretary in charge of the Rebbe's English-language correspondence, and therefore in a position to know the Rebbe's priorities in responding to mail.

3.   From a conversation between the Rebbe and Mayor David Dinkins on Sunday, September 1, 1989. A video of this encounter is available at Chabad.org/604940.

4.   Rabbi Moshe Herson, who directs Chabad-Lubavitch institutions in New Jersey, had also informed the Rebbe about Chase's experience on his yacht.

5.   The Rebbe's talk of March 25, 1983, and April 6, 1983, during which he related the incident of David Chase and his prayers on the yacht, are published in Menachem M. Schneerson, *Torat Menachem Hitvaaduyot 5743*, 3:1207–16 and 1335–42.

6.   There is one unusual, and hardly typical, story in which the Alter Rebbe offered a lesson in biblical ethics to a non-Jew. There are several versions of the story, in all of which the basic facts are the same. While the Alter Rebbe was in prison, facing a possible death sentence, an official in the prison, possibly the head of the prison guards, approached the Rebbe, whom he had been informed was a religious scholar, with a question about the Bible: "Why is it," he wanted to know, "that after Adam sins by eating of the Tree of Knowledge of Good and Evil, and he hides in the Garden of Eden, God calls out to him, 'Where are you?' [*ayekah*; Genesis 3:9]. God is all-knowing. How could he not know where Adam was?" The Alter Rebbe answered: "This is God's question to man in every generation: 'Where are you? What are you doing with your life? Where do you stand and what do you stand for?'"

7.   The Rebbe's recognition that America was vastly different from other nations in which Jews had lived was in no way a repudiation of his father-in-law's oft-cited aphorism, "America is not different." What the Frierdiker Rebbe meant by that statement—which he coined upon arriving in the United States in 1940—was that even though people had been warning him that strict observance of Jewish laws was alien to American Jews, and would not catch on here, America and American

Jews, in his view, were no different from all other Jews, and there would be openness among American Jews to leading a life of Jewish commitment. It was in this regard that he believed "American is not different." However, what became increasingly apparent to the Rebbe and to Lubavitchers in general was that in terms of openness to Jews, America was very different from Europe; in recent years, it has become even more so. To cite just one example: In 2012, both the Democratic and Republican parties invited rabbis to deliver prayer invocations at their conventions, an act that would have been quite inconceivable in Eastern Europe, Germany, and the Arab world, the three societies from which the large majority of American Jews descend.

8. See Todd S. Purdum, "Dinkins Calls for Healing in Brooklyn," *New York Times*, August 26, 1991.

9. The laws actually come to far more than seven, as they include entire categories of prohibited acts. Thus, the ban on robbery, for example, includes prohibitions of theft, extortion, and withholding or delaying payment of an employee's wages. It is estimated that the laws come to about sixty in number, perhaps more.

10. Cited in Menachem M. Schneerson, *The Letter and the Spirit*, 2:21.

11. For the history of the establishment of Education Day, see Chabad.org/816546.

Chapter 12: "It Is a Commandment to Tell the Story"

1. Cited in Shaul Shimon Deutsch, *Larger Than Life* (Brooklyn, NY: Chasidic Historical Productions Ltd, 1997), 2:133.

2. Rabbi Zeilingold in a February 1, 2011, interview conducted by JEM.

3. Pre–World War II Warsaw had a large Jewish population, and the Frierdiker Rebbe was aware that there were many more Yiddish newspapers serving the Jewish community.

4. This is the language used in the Haggadah and is based upon the biblical precept recorded in Exodus 13:8; this verse constitutes the twenty-first of the 613 commandments, as recorded in the medieval *Sefer ha-Chinuch*.

5. Moshe Ishon, in an interview on August 5, 2009, conducted by JEM; available at Chabad.org/1367241.

6. Major General Yehoshua Saguy, in an interview on March 3, 2010, conducted by JEM, available at Chabad.org/1720338.

7. Chaim Dalfin, *Conversations with the Rebbe, Menachem Mendel Schneerson* (Los Angeles: JEC Publications Company, 1996), 31.

Chapter 13: Chess, Thieves, Astronauts, and Atoms

1. Bible scholars identify the ants in this passage as harvester ants, tiny insects that settle near grain fields and carry seed after seed into their storehouses. When winter comes, the stored-up food feeds them until the next harvest. Such ants have much to teach the *atzeil*, the lazybones, to whom this passage is addressed.

2.   *Commentary on Mishnah Sanhedrin* 3:3. Maimonides believed that a person's primary activities should be gaining wisdom, particularly Torah wisdom, and promoting one's livelihood, a position reminiscent of the eighth chapter of the *Tanya*, in which the Alter Rebbe asserts that the only justification for pursuing secular studies is so one can utilize such studies as a means to achieve a more affluent livelihood so as to better serve God, or if one can directly apply such studies in the service of God and Torah (see page 332).

3.   See Greenberg, *Y'mei Bereishit*, 337.

4.   Menachem M. Schneerson, *Sichot Kodesh 5729* (Brooklyn, NY: Ha-Temimim, 1981–1991), 1:252–54. A translation and adaptation are available at Chabad.org/71930.

5.   The book that Kalms subsequently wrote, *Guidance from the Rebbe*, remains what is probably the most systematic and accurate presentation of what transpired at a *yechidus*. A well-known *shliach* said to me: "I was born into a Chasidic family, and was always a Chasid. But Kalms's book records how the Rebbe transformed a regular, non-Chasidic Jew into a Chasid."

6.   For almost fifty years, my father, Shlomo Telushkin, served as the accountant for both the Frierdiker Rebbe and the Rebbe, as well as for Merkos (the Center for Education) and the Lubavitch Yeshiva. As I well knew from the one summer when I assisted my father, he was very precise in his work. When the monthly bank statement arrived for any of these institutions, my father would reconcile the statement with his own records and would not stop until every dollar had been accounted for. (If the bank records indicated that there was $12,341 in the account and my father's records showed $12,417, he would go over every entry from the preceding month—sometimes there were many hundreds—until he found what had led to the $76 disparity.) When Rabbi Shmaryahu Gourary, the Rebbe's brother-in-law and head of the yeshiva, once asked my father why he went to such great lengths each month, particularly when the amount being tracked was small, my father answered: "If you wait many months, and then suddenly discover a gap between what the bank says you have and your own records, it will involve much more work to try to figure out who is right, what is missing, and where the error, or errors, was made." Rabbi Gourary nodded his head, and said, "There is a lesson to be learned from this about making a *cheshbon ha-nefesh* [an accounting of the soul]. If you examine your deeds carefully on a regular basis, and you discover something wrong, it can still be easy to correct. But if you continue to do a wrongful act for a long time, and only then try to correct it, it will be much harder to do so."

7.   Letter number 1493, published in the *Igrot Kodesh* of the Frierdiker Rebbe, 5:437.

8.   I have tried unsuccessfully to track down the origins of this story, published in the *Kfar Chabad* magazine and attributed to Yossi ben Eliezer; the name might be a pseudonym.

9.   Published in *Commentary* magazine (March and April 1957) and later incorporated into Weiner's book *9½ Mystics*, 155–96.

10.   The young Shemtov's arguments were in consonance with the Rebbe's position on Reform Judaism: "The very word 'reform' denotes something that has been reformed and changed, so that it is no longer the authentic original" (see the Rebbe's

1969 letter at Chabad.org/2387494). In another letter, the Rebbe wrote, "The very term 'reform' indicates that it is something which has been reformed by humans, and consequently it can no longer be considered divine. For what is divine cannot be reformed by man" (see the Rebbe's letter, also from 1969, at Chabad.org/2387459). On the other hand, the Rebbe once expounded on a number of lessons that all Jews can learn from the behavior of Reform and Conservative Jews (see chapter 15).

11.   Years later, Weiner, under the impact of the Rebbe's influence, came to a much more traditional understanding and practice of Judaism, but at the time, the argument from the atom simply left him bewildered: "I had the feeling which often came to me while speaking to the students of the Yeshiva: a sense of walking along together and coming suddenly to a door of the mind, through which only a Chasid could pass, while others were left outside, bewildered" (*9½ Mystics*, 162).

12.   Polter, *Listening to Life's Messages* (Brooklyn, NY: Sichos in English, 2004), attributes this teaching to a letter of the Rebbe cited in *Igrot Kodesh*, 13:311.

Chapter 14: Going to the Poolroom with the Rebbe's Blessings

1.   I confirmed this incident with Rabbi Vilenkin's great-grandson and namesake, Rabbi Zalman Vilenkin. The Rebbe's behavior is reminiscent of a text in the Jerusalem Talmud (*Bava Mezia* 2:11) that records that when the great rabbinic scholar Rav (2nd–3rd century) learned that his childhood teacher had died, he tore his garments as a sign of mourning.

2.   Meir Harlig, in an interview on December 12, 2009, conducted by JEM.

3.   Though the Rebbe cited no biblical or Talmudic references in his brief response to Mr. Jaffe's offer, his desire to keep the objects with which he practiced Jewish rituals as simple as possible was likely influenced by a Talmudic passage in which the Rabbis urge that all Jews, particularly the more affluent, refrain from practicing rituals in a manner that might make poorer Jews feel self-conscious. The Talmud records: "Formerly, people used to bring food to the house of mourning, rich people in baskets of silver and gold, poor people in baskets of peeled willow twigs, and the poor felt ashamed. Therefore, a regulation was made that everybody should bring food in baskets of willow twigs out of concern for the honor of the poor. . . . Formerly, when they would serve drinks in a house of mourning, the rich would serve in white glasses and the poor in colored glasses [which were less expensive], and the poor felt ashamed. Therefore, a regulation was made that everyone should serve drinks in colored glasses, out of concern for the honor of the poor" (*Moed Kattan* 27a).

4.   See the gift he solicited from several thousand people on his seventieth birthday (page 497).

5.   Letter of 12 Nisan 5741 (April 16, 1981); see Chabad.org/1911307.

6.   I base this recounting on a November 11, 2013, conversation with Rabbi Krinsky.

7.   In the United States, the birthday itself used to be celebrated (Washington's on February 22, and Lincoln's on February 12), but now, in order to extend people's

vacation times, Presidents' Day is celebrated on the third Monday in February. Dr. Martin Luther King's birthday is celebrated as a national holiday on the third Monday in January (King was born on January 15).

8.   Although the Rebbe and Rebbetzin's wedding contract (*ketuba*) was written on the fourteenth of Kislev, the wedding was celebrated the night of the fifteenth, the same day as Rabbi Krinsky's birthday.

9.   As regards the significance of birthdays in the Rebbe's thought, see Chabad .org/481233 and Chabad.org/481238.

10.   Interview of Baila Olidort with Dr. Ira Weiss, March 22, 2013.

11.   From Diane Schulder Abram's speech to the International Conference of *shluchot* on February 19, 2006.

12.   Rabbi Boteach's recollection of this life-transforming meeting is found in his book, *Judaism for Everyone: Renewing Your Life Through the Vibrant Lessons of the Jewish Faith* (New York: Basic Books, 2002), xii.

13.   The term "tzaddikim without tefillin," to refer to members of Bricha, apparently was first coined by Rabbi Israel Jacobson, the leader of Chabad in the United States prior to the Frierdiker Rebbe's arrival. The Rebbe's comments about the great merit of Israeli soldiers is found in an article by Gershon Jacobson, "The Lubavitcher Rebbe: 'Greater Is the Merit of the Fighters of the Army Than of Those Who Study Torah' " (*Yediot Achronot*, July 24, 1967).

14.   The Rebbe's oft-expressed willingness to rely on guidelines offered by his father-in-law, the single human being whom the Rebbe most revered, is reminiscent of Moses, who established a system of justice in the Sinai Desert based on the advice offered him by his father-in-law, Yitro (Exodus 18:13–26; see also the advice the Rebbe offered Rabbi Dov Zlotnick; page 224).

15.   Yisroel Katzover, in an interview on March 4, 2010, conducted by JEM.

16.   Zalman Schachter-Shalomi, *The Geologist of the Soul* (Boulder, CO: Albion-Andalus Books, 2012), xi. For the Rebbe's response to questions that were subtly similar to the above, see the incidents with Yehuda Avner (page 51) and Rivka Blau (page 445).

Chapter 15: "There Also Needs to Be a Girl"

1.   As if to underscore the association of *tzadkaniot* (saintly women) with acts of self-sacrifice, a recent Chabad publication retold this story, concluding that through Dvorah Leah's "self-sacrifice . . . she preserved the Tree of Life, the teachings of Chasidus" (see Yosef Kaminetzky, *Days in Chabad: Historic Events in the Dynasty of Chabad-Lubavitch* [Brooklyn, NY: Kehot Publication Society, 2005], 4–6).

2.   As a general rule, images of women are less apt to appear in *haredi* publications. A recent example of such exclusion is so strange, it's hard to know whether to treat it as funny or sad, perhaps both. In May 2011, the United States succeeded in tracking down Osama bin Laden, the terrorist mastermind of the 9/11 attacks on

New York City and Washington, DC. At the time, the government released a photograph of the country's leadership, starting with President Barack Obama, gathered in the White House Situation Room to watch the CIA operation that killed Bin Laden. Prominent in the photograph was Secretary of State Hillary Clinton. While this picture was published in thousands of newspapers and magazines, a doctored version appeared in an ultra-Orthodox publication, *Der Zeitung*, in which Clinton's image was excised because, as the newspaper later explained, it is the paper's policy never to print a woman's photograph. If the death of a prominent woman needs to be reported, either no photograph is printed or the paper prints a picture of the deceased woman's husband.

3.　The episode concerning women dancing with the Torah is recounted in Shlomo Riskin, *Listening to God* (New Milford, CT: Maggid, 2010), 193–96.

4.　A third great American Jewish rabbinic leader, Rabbi Moshe Feinstein, the preeminent twentieth-century decisor of Jewish law, similarly told Riskin that if there were women who would leave Orthodoxy if Riskin withdrew permission to continue having the special women's *hakafot*, he should definitely not stop such services.

Chapter 16: Reform Jews, Conservative Jews, and the Rebbe's Open Door

1.　The Rebbe was referring to these movements' departures from traditional halachic observance, and to the nontraditional views of many of their leaders on the divine authorship of the Torah.

2.　Zvi Hirsh Gansbourg, *Portrait of a Chassid: The Life and Legacy of Rabbi Zvi Hirsh Gansbourg* (Brooklyn, NY: GJCF, 2008), 187. The Rebbe's talk is found in *Torat Menachem Hitvaaduyot* (Brooklyn, NY: Lahak Hanochas, 1981–2001), 23:168.

3.　Rabbi David Hollander, in an interview on February 23, 2006, conducted by JEM.

4.　Weiner, *9½ Mystics*, 176.

5.　This material is based both on an interview I conducted with Rabbi Dov and Alice Zlotnick in November 2013, and on interviews conducted with both Zlotnicks on December 26, 2009, by JEM.

6.　For Weiner's recounting of this event, see his article, "Remembering the Rebbe," in the *Jerusalem Post*, June 24, 2004.

7.　Maimonides based this teaching on a passage in the Talmud (*Kiddushin* 40b).

Chapter 17: No One Is Beyond the Possibility of Repentance

1.　Israel Singer, in an interview on January 18, 2010, conducted by JEM.

2.　Robert Conquest, *The Great Terror: A Reassessment* (New York: Oxford University Press, 1990), 13. In the years following Stalin's death in 1953, Soviet prime minister Nikita Khrushchev stripped Kaganovich of his power and status. "The town of

Kubany [in which Kaganovich was born], once known as Kaganovich, is now officially known as Novo Kashirsk. Lazar Kaganovich had eight towns and villages named in his honor. All have had their former names restored. The Kaganovich Subway is now known as the Lenin Subway" (*New York Times*, October 7, 1957).

3.   When Stalin first voiced his "suspicion" to Kaganovich about Mikhail, Kaganovich, apparently afraid to antagonize Stalin (one assumes that he did not think his brother was a Nazi collaborator or that Hitler, for that matter, would choose a Jew as his collaborator), answered, "If it's necessary to arrest him, arrest him." Mikhail was almost immediately arrested, at which point Mikhail's wife, Anya, appealed to Kaganovich in the name of their mutual father—"He is the son of Moisev, as are you"—to intervene on his brother's behalf. Kaganovich immediately wrote back: "I have only one brother, Josef Stalin, and forget about the voice of blood." See Stuart Kahan, *The Wolf of the Kremlin* (New York: William Morrow, 1987), 223; for a slightly different account of this event, see Alan Bullock, *Hitler and Stalin: Parallel Lives* (New York: Alfred A. Knopf, 1993), 114.

4.   For a unique perspective on Kaganovich, see Kahan, *The Wolf of the Kremlin*. Kahan, an American Jew and Kaganovich's great-nephew, met with and interviewed Kaganovich in Russia.

5.   There is some reason to believe that Fischer's biological father might have been a different man, Paul Nemenyi, a Hungarian-Jewish physicist, though this is by no means certain.

6.   The best biography on Fischer is Frank Brady, *Endgame: Bobby Fischer's Remarkable Rise and Fall—From America's Brightest Prodigy to the Edge of Madness* (New York: Broadway Paperbacks/Random House, 2010). There are over thirty listings in the book's index under the heading "anti-Semitism of Fischer."

Chapter 18: Differences That Don't Affect a Friendship

1.   Members of a different Chasidic court, such as Bobov, Satmar, or Bostoner, also refer to their leader as "the Rebbe." Thus, a recent biography of Rabbi Yoel Teitelbaum, the late leader of Satmar, is titled *The Rebbe*. Outside the Satmar community, few if any Jews would assume from the title alone that the book was about the Satmar Rebbe. During the past several years, when I told people that I was writing a book about the Rebbe, they invariably understood that it was a book about the Lubavitcher Rebbe.

2.   To cite just one example, Professor David Luchins, who long worked for the late New York senator Daniel Patrick Moynihan, notes that Moynihan would routinely refer to Rabbi Schneerson as "the Rebbe." That the Rebbe was the one Chasidic leader widely known outside the Jewish world is reflected in a large variety of incidents.

3.   In Shulamith Meiselman's memoir of the Soloveitchik dynasty (Meiselman is Rabbi Soloveitchik's sister), she writes of her grandfather Rabbi Chaim Soloveitchik's antagonism to secular studies, that he sheltered his children from

non-Jewish studies and culture, "banning library books from the house." According to Meiselman, her father, Reb Moshe, "was not exposed to any form of secular learning, with the exception of mathematics. He did not learn any of the fundamentals of the Polish language, the tongue of the country where he lived, until his own children began to study Polish and taught it to him" (Shulamith Soloveitchik Meiselman, *The Soloveitchik Heritage* [Hoboken, NJ: Ktav, 1995], 109). When Reb Moshe, at his wife's urging, proposed moving to America, his father, Reb Chaim, expressed bitter opposition: "What America? Secular education is compulsory there. You'll have to send your children to public schools. Under no circumstances will I permit it." His pressure kept the couple from leaving Europe till decades later (p. 116).

4.   Rabbi Soloveitchik was speaking in this instance to Julius Berman, a former student and a prominent leader in the American Jewish community. Soloveitchik related his recollections of this first encounter with the Rebbe to several people; the basic details were always the same.

5.   Rabbi Bomzer's informant was Rabbi Feivel Reese, who had, in turn, been told this detail by Rabbi Soloveitchik himself.

6.   Professor Moshe Berger recalls Rabbi Soloveitchik reminiscing about a series of lectures (possibly in the context of a class) that both he and the young Rabbi Schneerson attended (see page 338).

7.   Yosef Y. Schneersohn, *Igrot Kodesh,* 5:368.

8.   Menachem M. Schneerson, *Igrot Kodesh,* 27:110.

9.   About ten years after the elementary school's founding, Maimonides—which remains to this day a vibrant and highly popular school—also established a high school.

10. Rabbi Soloveitchik was the oldest of five children. His brother Shmuel went on to become a professor of chemistry at Yeshiva University, and his much younger brother Aaron became a distinguished Talmud scholar as well, who taught at Yeshiva University, later headed the Skokie yeshiva in Chicago, and subsequently established Yeshivas Brisk in Chicago. Rabbi Soloveitchik had two sisters, Anne Gerber and Shulamith Meiselman, the latter of whom authored *The Soloveitchik Heritage: A Daughter's Memoir.*

11. I am basing this in part on a conversation I had with Professor Haym Soloveitchik in December 2012. To this day, the Frierdiker Rebbe's intervention on behalf of Rabbi Soloveitchik is not widely known but, in my view, might reflect a somewhat more open attitude to secular education than is usually attributed to him. The prevailing assumption about the Frierdiker Rebbe's attitude toward such studies is typified by the recollection of Professor Yitzchak Block, who recalls that when he started to learn at Chabad, there were two positions associated with the recently deceased Rebbe: the need for all Chabad students to grow beards, and a ban on college education (see, for example, a letter written by the Frierdiker Rebbe during the last weeks of his life, in which he answers a questioner: "In response to your letter about registering for college, [my answer is] completely negative"

(Yosef Y. Schneersohn, *Igrot Kodesh,* 10:325). This ban, Block recalls, applied not only to attending university classes at night while studying at a yeshiva during the day (as was commonly done by students at Yeshiva Torah Vodaas), but an absolute prohibition on such studies, even after a student had completed his course of studies at the yeshiva.

However, this letter of the Frierdiker Rebbe, which wholeheartedly advocated the candidacy of Rabbi Soloveitchik, holder of a PhD in philosophy from the University of Berlin, to assume the role of rosh yeshiva—coupled with the financial support the Frierdiker Rebbe extended for so many years for his son-in-law's university studies—might indicate a more open attitude to secular studies, at least in instances in which the student had first acquired a mastery of Jewish studies.

One additional incident: Rabbi Abraham Twerski, a psychiatrist from a highly learned Chasidic, though not a Chabad, background, recalls that one of his older brothers who was considering going to college went to consult with the Frierdiker Rebbe in 1944 or 1945. He asked the Rebbe directly his opinion as to whether he should attend university. The Frierdiker Rebbe said, "*Ir hut ah Tatten*—You have a father." In other words, as Twerski explains, "He wouldn't tell him to go or not to go. He says, go and ask your father. Do what your father says" (Rabbi Abraham Twerski, M.D., in an interview on January 17, 2012, conducted by JEM).

12.   They had previously seen each other at events such as a Chabad dinner in the 1940s, which Rabbi Soloveitchik attended, but I am referring to instances in which one specifically sought out the other.

13.   Sholem Kowalsky, *From My Zaidy's House* (Lakewood, NJ: Israel Book Shop, 2003), 275. Rabbi Kowalsky was the Rav's driver that day.

14.   Rabbi Shlomo Riskin, during one of the many interviews I conducted with him during my five years of research on this book. Rabbi Riskin was very generous with his time and shared much important information with me.

15.   Rabbi Soloveitchik presumed that the young Rabbi Schneerson was observing the custom of Behab, which involves fasting at the beginning of the Hebrew months of Cheshvan and Iyar. The custom is to fast on the first Monday, then Thursday, and the following Monday of each of these months. The Rebbe, though, likely fasted on additional days as well, as is evident from his father beseeching him for health reasons to fast less often.

16.   Rabbi Avraham Shemtov, interview with this author. See also Rabbi Hershel Schachter in *MiPninei HaRav* (Brooklyn, NY: Flatbush Beth Hamedrosh, 2001), 187.

17.   "*Gaon*" is usually translated into English as "genius," but Schachter remembers that when the Rav repeated his comment in English, he used a synonym for "genius," but he doesn't recall precisely which word.

18.   Another striking description is offered by Rabbi Israel Meir Lau, who attended a *farbrengen* with his father-in-law, Rabbi Yitzchak Yedidya Frankel. "As the Rebbe strode quickly into the hall, a small book of Maimonides under his arm,

the atmosphere was electric. The Rebbe gave a class that lasted four hours, without using notes or opening a book, not even one. In his class, he referred to both classic and esoteric sources, early and late authorities, from all periods. He cited entire sections by heart." Lau went on to describe the considerable impression the Rebbe's scholarship made on Frankel, who told him: "I witnessed the magnificence of Polish Jewry; I had the honor of visiting Rabbi Kook, who gave me a personal letter [of recommendation]; and I have known more of the great scholars of recent generations. But I have never seen such a command of the material. That is genius" (Israel Meir Lau, *Out of the Depths*, 201–2).

19. I have found no better description of the Rebbe's style of study and delivery than that of Rabbi Lord Jonathan Sacks, who himself authored an anthology of the Rebbe's earliest talks. "Time and again a talk will be set in motion by a seemingly microscopic tension—a question on a comment by Rashi, perhaps, or a problem in understanding a halacha, a practical provision of Jewish law. Once in motion, however, the argument leads us into fresh perspectives. . . . Thus a problem in the laws of divorce leads us to consider the concepts of separation and unity and to a radical reinterpretation of the nature of exile. A passage relating to the fruit of trees in their fifth year takes us through the levels of spiritual reality, an examination of the Baal Shem Tov's life, and a reversal of our normal understanding of holiness and sanctification. A meditation on the name of a Sidra [a Torah portion] passes through the subjects of leprosy, repentance, and personal identity. Each talk moves from the specific to the general, the finite to the infinite, and back again. . . . The very form of the talks—their intellectual rhythms of question and answer, their reasoning and rigor—mirrors a central feature of Chabad, that through a mental journey we affect both emotion and action. A truth grasped first by the mind then shapes heart and limb, and in perceiving reality we become our real selves.

These talks, then, are addressed with relentless clarity to the contemporary Jewish condition. Their implicit starting point is the darkness of a post-Holocaust world in which spirituality, moral conviction, and the divine purpose of creation seem almost beyond reach. Their tacit faith is that step by step we can be led from the present moment of confusion to the timeless lucidity of Torah, beyond the low clouds to the Infinite Light (Jonathan Sacks, *Torah Studies: Discourses by the Lubavitch Rebbe, Rabbi Menachem M. Schneerson* [Brooklyn, NY: Kehot Publication Society, 2001], vii–ix. Available at Chabad.org/110249).

20. "We are therefore opposed to any public debate, dialogue, or symposium concerning the doctrinal, dogmatic, or ritual aspects of our faith vis-à-vis 'similar' aspects of another faith community" (see Joseph B. Soloveitchik, *Community, Covenant, and Commitment: Selected Letters and Communications*, edited by Nathaniel Helfgot (Jersey City, NJ: Published for the Toras HoRav Foundation by Ktav, 2004), 260. Among the ten topics that Rabbi Soloveitchik enumerates as forbidden to be discussed in a public dialogue are monotheism and the trinity, the Messianic idea, the Jewish attitude toward Jesus, and the idea of the covenant. In discussing the above ruling of Soloveitchik, Professor Gerald Blidstein, a student of his, comments: "Without

making too much of it, it seems to me that his use of the word 'public' is not co-incidental" (Gerald Blidstein, *Society and Self: On the Writings of Rabbi Joseph Soloveitchik* [New York: Ktav, 2012], 49n17).

21. Among other issues, Pope John wanted to, and did, remove references to Jews as killers of Jesus from the Catholic liturgy.

22. The text of the letter can be found in Soloveitchik, *Community, Covenant and Commitment*, 249–52.

23. *Ma'ariv*, October 28, 1977. Cited in Aaron Rakeffet-Rothkoff, *The Rav: The World of Rabbi Joseph B. Soloveitchik*, edited by Joseph Epstein (Hoboken, NJ: Ktav, 1999), 1:158–59.

24. Norman Lamm, "The Rav: Public Giant, Private Mentsch," in Zev Eleff, ed., *Mentor of Generations: Reflections on Rabbi Joseph B. Soloveitchik* (Jersey City, NJ: Ktav, 2008), 40.

25. Some years later, Riskin was teaching Talmud at YU when the school started to construct a very tall science building, the Belfer Physics Center. The building, filled with labs, dwarfed in size the *Beit Midrash*, the Talmud study hall, and Riskin, along with some of the other younger rabbis at the school, was upset: "Wouldn't such a science center negatively impact upon the Torah mission of Yeshiva University [particularly as there might be some heretical views and classes taught there]?" The young rabbis went to Rabbi Soloveitchik to express their concern, and he told them that he would think about their objections and get back to them. The next morning, though, when Soloveitchik saw Riskin, he said to him: "Riskin, I don't understand you. What are you afraid of and why are you an againstnik? Maimonides includes the study of science and philosophy [*ma'asei bereishit* and *ma'asei merkava*, the physics and metaphysics of Aristotle] under the rubric of Gemara, within the structure of our Oral Law. Ultimately, all of true science and wisdom can only deepen our understanding of the One Creator of the Universe and validate our sacred Torah. Never be afraid of knowledge and don't be against intellectual inquiry and discovery." Riskin recalls: "I sheepishly left the presence of my rebbe, who had once again taught an invaluable lesson" (see Shlomo Riskin, *Listening to God: Inspirational Stories for My Grandchildren* [New Milford, CT: Maggid Books, 2010], 78–79).

26. Ibid., 222.

27. These positions of the Rav can be found in Joseph B. Soloveitchik, *Community, Covenant and Commitment*, 235, 236, 242.

28. Saul Berman, "The Approaches of the Rav to Psak and Public Policy," in Zev Eleff, ed., *Mentor of Generations: Reflections on Rabbi Joseph B. Soloveitchik* (Jersey City, NJ: Ktav, 2008), 63.

Chapter 19: United States

1. Amicus curiae, "friend of the court," refers to an individual or a group that, though not directly involved in a legal proceeding, volunteers information to assist

a court in deciding a case before it. Usually such briefs offer an opinion supporting one party in the suit.

2.　As a rule, only the more liberally Orthodox rabbis joined the Synagogue Council of America. More right-wing Orthodox rabbis generally avoid joining rabbinical organizations in which non-Orthodox rabbis are members. Chabad rabbis avoid joining such groups as well. The SCA dissolved in 1994.

3.　Now called the Jewish Council on Public Affairs.

4.　Although the Jewish groups acknowledged that the prayer was voluntary and that any student was free to leave the room or simply remain silent when it was recited, they argued that children who did so would run the risk of being ostracized or ridiculed. Thus, they might end up feeling emotionally coerced to recite a prayer in which they did not believe.

5.　"Lubavitcher Rebbe Urges Reversal of Supreme Court Ban on Prayer," Jewish Telegraphic Agency, November 26, 1962. Another noted rabbinic figure, Rabbi Immanuel Jakobovits, who several years later was appointed chief rabbi of England, publicly debated the school prayer issue with Will Maslow, executive director of the American Jewish Congress and a major supporter of the prayer ban. Jakobovits argued that the Jewish organizations in pushing for the ban "have added dangerous fuel to the flames of antisemitism. . . . By allying themselves with the rampant forces of atheism and secularism, these organizations were bound to expose the Jewish community to the charge of undermining the religious foundations of our society." Maslow responded with the argument commonly espoused within the broader Jewish community, and with which the Rebbe disagreed, that "no other religious group in the United States has as great a stake in the separation of church and state as the Jewish community" (see Jewish Telegraphic Agency, October 31, 1962).

6.　The presumption that a relationship between belief in God and moral behavior is as significant for non-Jews as for Jews is reflected in an oft-told story about Rabbi Israel Baal Shem Tov (1700–1760), the founder of Chasidism. He hired a wagon driver to take him to another town, but early in the trip, when the driver passed a church and didn't cross himself, the Baal Shem Tov stopped the wagon, paid the driver, and got off. He explained that if the driver had no fear of God (and by implication of a moral authority above him), then he would have no scruples about robbing or killing him. Similarly, the Torah records the patriarch Abraham explaining to King Abimelech why he had instructed his wife Sarah to tell people that she was his sister, and not his wife: "I thought surely there is no fear of God in this place, and they will kill me because of my wife" (Genesis 20:11).

During the decades following the Supreme Court ruling, the Rebbe came to put ever greater emphasis on encouraging belief in God among non-Jews; he felt a particular affection for President Reagan, who often spoke of God as the source of morality and decency.

7.　Letter to Professor Velvel Greene, January 30, 1964. Available at Chabad .org/1899565.

8.   Letter written April 18, 1964. Available at Chabad.org/2051611.

9.   The Rebbe's talk on these issues of 10 Shevat 5743 (January 24, 1983) is published in Menachem M. Schneerson, *Hitvaaduyot* 2:899–904. A video of the talk is available at Chabad.org/433702 (part 1), Chabad.org/433707 (part 2), and Chabad.org/443372 (part 3).

10.   The most significant non-rabbinic figure on the American Jewish scene to make a strong case for prayer in public schools was the nondenominational theologian Will Herberg. Although there is no record of the Rebbe and Herberg meeting, they had quite similar thoughts on the role religion should play in public life.

Fearful of dangers posed by an exclusively secular education, Herberg was therefore critical of American Jewry's reflexive opposition to anything smacking of religion in the public schools. In arguments reminiscent of those offered by the Rebbe, he argued that Jews want schools to inculcate " 'basic moral principles,' and 'social ideals' without recognizing that the moral principles they want to see transmitted emanate from religion." Herberg argued that it is impossible to rely upon secular culture to transmit these values, for secular values, even those that are noble, are like cut flowers. Such flowers may look beautiful but, cut off from their roots, cannot reproduce. Only ethics rooted in transcendental religious teachings offer an intellectually and spiritually nourishing basis to maintain the moral values Americans hold sacred. Therefore, "whatever the 'neutrality' of the state in matters of religion may be, it cannot be a neutrality between religion and no-religion, any more than . . . it could be a neutrality between morality and no-morality."

11.   Unfortunately, most contemporary American Jews are not even familiar with the word "Shavuot" or with the obscure English word sometimes assigned to it, "Pentecost." In actuality, Shavuot means "weeks" and refers to the seven weeks between the Exodus and the Revelation at Sinai—the forty-nine days of the Omer (see Leviticus 23:15–16). .

12.   Jenna Weissman Joselit, *The Wonders of America: Reinventing Jewish Culture 1880–1950* (New York: Henry Holt, 1994), 239–40.

13.   I doubt if any of the Rebbe's predecessors were ever involved in such exchanges (Reform Judaism came into existence shortly before the Alter Rebbe's death in 1812). Thus, for example, we know of no letters between the Frierdiker Rebbe or his father, the Rebbe Rashab (who died in 1920), and the leadership of the Reform movement. On the other hand, we have records of the Rebbe meeting with individual Reform rabbis starting in the mid-1950s, only a few years into his leadership (regarding the Rebbe's essential critique of Reform, see page 223). The first Reform rabbi whom we know of the Rebbe speaking with at length was Herbert Weiner, who went on to write of his two encounters with the Rebbe, and with the Chabad movement, in *Commentary* magazine (March and April 1957); these articles brought Chabad to the attention of *Time* magazine, and an article there (March 25, 1957) led to Chabad becoming more widely known in the American Jewish community). In the following years, other Reform rabbis, sometimes as part of small groups (such as Hillel rabbis), met with the Rebbe at 770 Eastern Parkway.

14. Crèches, also called "Nativity scenes," are three-dimensional models of the scene described in the New Testament of Jesus's birth in a stable in Bethlehem. The three individuals always portrayed in crèches are Jesus, Mary, and Joseph. Such displays frequently include the "three wise men," who, according to Christian tradition, visited the stable after Jesus's birth.

15. Pesach fell unusually late that year, and Rabbi Glaser's letter was written during *Chol ha-Moed*, in the middle of the holiday.

16. A year earlier, in April 1977, Rabbi Arthur Lelyveld, a leading Reform rabbi and former president of the Central Conference of American Rabbis, had called Chabad a "cult" and compared it to Hare Krishna, Scientology, and the "Moonies." Lelyveld depicted four attributes these groups supposedly had in common: surrendering to the authority of a charismatic leader, irrationality in their approach to religion, driving a wedge between parents and children, and removing those "who have been captured from the mainstream of society so that they are lost not only to their parents, but to Jewish life in the form which we have come to cherish. . . . All the evils that I have mentioned are present in contemporary Chabad." To cite just one, and in my view, highly unfair example from Lelyveld's critique: In his denunciation, Lelyveld placed significant emphasis on his accusation that Chabad tried to separate children from parents, a charge that was fully inaccurate, given the Rebbe's well-known encouragement to children *never* to break ties with nonobservant parents, and his similar demand that parents *never* break ties with children who had become nonobservant.

17. The term "loosely affiliated" likely refers to the phenomenon of Jews who maintain synagogue membership, but who essentially restrict attendance to two or three services a year, generally on Rosh Hashanah and Yom Kippur.

18. The correspondence between Rabbi Glaser and the Rebbe is found in Jonathan Sarna and David G. Dalin, *Religion and State in the American Jewish Experience* (Notre Dame, IN: Notre Dame University Press, 1997), 288–300.

19. Jonathan Sarna, "How Hannukah Came to the White House," *Forward*, December 11, 2009.

20. Joshua Eli Plaut, *A Kosher Christmas: 'Tis the Season to Be Jewish* (New Brunswick, NJ: Rutgers University Press, 2012), 167.

21. A video of the Rebbe's talk on December 1, 1991, is available at Chabad.org/1052374.

Chapter 20: Israel

1. The first pages in this chapter draw on material from my earlier book, *Jewish Literacy* (New York: William Morrow, revised edition 2008), 329–32.

2. Menachem M. Schneerson, *Igrot Kodesh*, 27:332.

3. Articles about the telegram appeared in *Yediot Achronot*, *Ma'ariv*, *Haaretz*, and *Davar* as well.

4.   The mood in Israel further deteriorated when Prime Minister Levi Eshkol delivered a speech during which he stumbled and stuttered over some unexpected handwritten words that the speechwriter had inserted into his speech at the last minute. The speech became known as the "stuttering speech" and exacerbated the level of fear in the country as it seemed, unjustly, that even the prime minister was lacking confidence in Israel's ability to defend itself.

5.   Menachem M. Schneerson, *Igrot Kodesh,* 27:232. Like the aforementioned telegram, the Rebbe's response to the yeshiva students was likewise publicized in Israeli newspapers.

6.   Quoted in *Yediot Achronot* (May 25, 1967) under the headline, "Lubavitcher Rebbe Calls on His Followers to Help Israel." The article reported that "the Rebbe instructed the student to remain in Israel and assist with the war efforts."

7.   Menachem M. Schneerson, *Sichot Kodesh 5727,* 2:111–13. A video is available at Chabad.org/397220.

8.   It is estimated that approximately twenty thousand soldiers from Egypt, Jordan, and Syria were killed.

9.   My father also had rabbinical ordination, but because he did not work professionally as a rabbi, he always requested that he be referred to without the title "Rabbi."

10.   Israeli journalist Ari Shavit, in his no-holds-barred and by no means flattering account of the Israeli conquest of the city of Lydda in 1948 (a city that contained both Jewish and Arab residents), relates that when the Israelis defeated the Arabs, the Arab elders asked to leave the city "with their one condition being the release of all prisoners detained in the Great Mosque." When the Israeli military commander, Shmaryahu Gutman, didn't immediately respond, the elders pressed him, "What will become of the prisoners detained in the mosque?"

Gutman, who had summoned two young Israeli officers to witness the conversation, answered, "We shall do to the prisoners what you would do had you imprisoned us."

The Arab leaders responded, "No, no, please don't do that."

"Why, what did I say?" Gutman asked. "All I said is that we will do to you what you would do to us."

"Please, no, master. We beg you not to do such a thing."

Gutman then said, "No, we shall not do that. Ten minutes from now the prisoners will be free to leave the mosque and leave their homes and leave Lydda along with all of you and the entire [Arab] population of Lydda."

The Arab leaders responded, "Thank you, master. God bless you" (Ari Shavit, *My Promised Land: The Triumph and Tragedy of Israel* [New York: Spiegel and Grau, 2014], 121–22).

11.   Yehuda Avner (see pages 51–55) told me that he recalls seeing a letter expressing a similar thought sent by the Rebbe to Israeli president Zalman Shazar. For an elaboration of the Rebbe's views, see Schneerson, *Sichot Kodesh 5731,* 1:86.

12. Menachem M. Schneerson, *Sichot Kodesh 5731*, 1:186.

13. Menachem M. Schneerson, *Sichot Kodesh 5739*, 3:363, 460–61. See also *Hitvaaduyot 5752*, 2:376–79.

14. See the Rebbe's conversation with Israeli attorney general Elyakim Rubenstein on November 12, 1989; available at Chabad.org/408959.

15. Menachem M. Schneerson, *Hitvaaduyot 5746*, 2:233.

16. The Rebbe argued that it was only the "politicians who want to hold their seats," and those "who want to please the United States" who were advocating return of the captured lands. This was less a critique than a realization that politicians do not only take into account, as do generals, security issues. The Rebbe also said that the opinions of retired military figures could not be relied upon any more than one can rely on the medical diagnosis of a retired physician; in both instances, certainly when one is dealing with an issue that is of life-and-death significance, one needs to listen to the views of those who have access to the most current and relevant information.

17. *Likutei Sichot* 15:489–90. See also *Sichot Kodesh 5738*, 1:226–31.

18. The Palestine Liberation Organization, headed by Yasser Arafat, committed ongoing acts of terror against Israel, among them the Munich Massacre of nine Israeli Olympic athletes (1972); the 1974 attack in which members of the DFLP (Democratic Front for the Liberation of Palestine), a member organization of the PLO, seized a school in the Israeli city of Maalot and murdered twenty-six students and adults and wounded seventy others; and the 1978 Coastal Road massacre in which the PLO killed thirty-seven Israelis and wounded seventy-six more.

19. Menachem M. Schneerson, *Sichot Kodesh 5739*, 3:460–61. I am indebted to Ambassador Dore Gold for conveying to me the historical background of the events of which the Rebbe was speaking, and the grave significance of the Egyptian army's violation of the 1970 agreement.

20. See Menachem M. Schneerson, *The Letter and the Spirit*, 307–13; available at Chabad.org/2387552.

21. Even when life is at stake, it is forbidden to murder, practice idolatry, or engage in certain forbidden sexual acts, such as incest (*Pesachim* 25a-b).

22. The *Shulchan Aruch* ruling is based on the Talmudic discussion in *Eruvin* 45a; for the Talmud's rationale, see ArtScroll commentary on *Eruvin* 45a, n21.

23. The *Shulchan Aruch* records the view that "nowadays" we desecrate the Sabbath even if the attackers are only coming for the sake of possessions, "for if a Jew will not allow a non-Jew to plunder and pillage his property, the non-Jew will kill him, and one must therefore treat the attack as being for the sake of taking Jewish life [unless one is certain that there is no danger of life being at risk]" (*Orach Chayyim* 329:7).

24. Interview with General Piron conducted by Israeli journalist Yitzchak Yehuda, August 29, 2013; I am grateful to Mr. Yehuda for making the audio recording of this interview available to me.

25. Preservation of life is so high a value in Jewish law that except for the three exceptions cited in note 21 above, all Jewish laws are suspended when human life is at stake. For instance, although Jewish law forbids driving on the Sabbath, a Jew who refuses to drive a very sick person to the hospital on that day violates Jewish law.

The basis for mandating such violations is Leviticus 18:5, which teaches, "You shall, therefore, keep My laws and My rules, by the observance of which a person shall live." The Rabbis understood these final words to mean, " 'a person shall live' and not die because of them" (*Yoma* 85b).

26. Menachem M. Schneerson, *Sichot Kodesh 5740*, 3:421.

27. Menachem M. Schneerson, *Sichot Kodesh 5738*, 1:226–27.

28. In Israeli prime minister Golda Meir's autobiography, *My Life*, she writes that the morning of the war, hours before the joint Egyptian-Syrian attack, army chief of staff David "Dado" Eliezer argued in favor of a preemptive strike: "I want you to know," he told Meir and the leading members of her cabinet, "that our air force can be ready to strike at noon, but you must give me the green light now. If we can make the first strike, it will be greatly to our advantage." Meir acknowledges that she had already made up her mind not to authorize such a strike; her reasoning was rooted in the belief that while it would cost Israeli lives in the short run, it might well save many more lives in the long run: "Dado," she told General Eliezer, "I know all the arguments in favor of a preemptive strike, but I am against it. We don't know now, any of us, what the future will hold, but there is always the possibility that we will need help, and if we strike first, we will get nothing from anyone. I would like to say yes because I know what it would mean, but with a heavy heart I am going to say no." Earlier at the same meeting, Minister of Defense Moshe Dayan had insisted on mobilizing only two divisions of Israel's army (Eliezer had wanted a much larger mobilization), arguing that if Israel ordered a full mobilization before any shots had been fired, the world would have an excuse for calling Israel the "aggressor" (see Golda Meir, *My Life* [New York: G. P. Putnam's Sons, 1975], 426–27). To the Rebbe's mind, Meir's recollections illustrated his central point, that on an issue like this, military figures such as General Eliezer could think fully clearly, while the political leaders' thinking was adversely impacted by an exaggerated sensitivity to external factors (such as possible American disapproval) and this caused them to adopt a policy that led to many needless deaths and made Israel less secure.

29. Golda Meir wrote that on the day before the war, Israeli intelligence officers and the country's foremost military figures repeatedly assured her that no war was looming. In her heart, though, Meir didn't trust these assurances. One item uncovered by intelligence—the report that families of the Russian advisers in Syria were packing up and leaving the country in a hurry—convinced her that war was indeed imminent. "Why the haste?" Meir asked herself. "What did those Russian families know that we didn't know? Was it possible they were being evacuated?"

Despite her inner conviction that war would come very soon, Meir found that the people around her—who were far more knowledgeable about military matters—

remained unperturbed about this detail. Meir could never forgive herself for not acting on her belief: "Today I know what I should have done. I should have overcome my hesitation [and ordered a full-scale mobilization, which in itself might have frightened Egypt and Syria and caused them to back off]. I shall live with that terrible knowledge for the rest of my life. I will never again be the person I was before the Yom Kippur War" (Meir, *My Life*, 425). It was this sentiment to which the Rebbe was alluding in his statement about the prime minister.

30. For the record, this was eleven years after the Rebbe's death, so we have no way of definitely knowing how he would have reacted. As regards the growing Arab population, the Rebbe did not seem overly concerned by this issue. Thus, the Rebbe supported the Israeli government granting financial stipends to families that had large numbers of children, and when another Chasidic Rebbe (the Sadigura Rebbe, Avrohom Yaakov Friedman) suggested to him that such subsidies be limited to Jews, the Rebbe vehemently opposed him, noting both that Israel would be regarded as "racist" if it did so, and that, in any case, Jewish law encourages all human beings, Jews and non-Jews alike, to have many children (Genesis 1:28).

31. Two years earlier, the Rebbe made an exception and advised Chabad Chasidim in Israel to vote for Agudat Yisrael, an Orthodox party.

32. A series of letters from the Rebbe strictly warning against any Chabad involvement in Israeli politics, and stating his (and Chabad's) nonpartisan policy, is published in Shlomi Haski, *Maidanchik: Haketer Shel Chabad*, 230–35. See also Menachem M. Schneerson, *Hitvaaduyot 5750* 2:503. When asked by the Washington-based Kol Yisrael correspondent, "Does the Rebbe want Mr. Shamir to be prime minister?" the Rebbe responded, "I don't interfere in politics." A video of the Rebbe's conversation with the Kol Yisrael correspondent is available at Chabad.org/498519.

33. In a different context, Ariel Sharon was known to have commented in amused irony that the Rebbe, living in Brooklyn, could give an order to his Chasidim in Israel and it would be carried out more punctiliously that an army order he gave in Israel.

34. Israel Meir Lau, *Do Not Raise Your Hand Against the Boy* (Hebrew) (Tel Aviv: Miskal-Yediot Achronot, 2005), 194. There was an amused quality to Savir's words; he was certainly aware that the Rebbe was not acting to influence the choice of Israeli chief rabbi.

35. In a letter of August 20, 1970, the Rebbe wrote Sharon, who had asked his advice about retiring from the military: "As we discussed when you were here, it is my opinion that your proper place is in the IDF, and it is there that with G-d's assistance you are successful and will continue to be so.... You must certainly continue to serve in this very important capacity and role." Explaining why he felt it crucial that Sharon remain at his post, the Rebbe continued: "Although in general I am not a pessimist, one cannot ignore the reality of what will emerge if, G-d forbid, things continue along their current natural course. The enemy continues to strengthen and fortify itself on the other side of the Suez Canal. Despite all of Israel's official protestations,

the enemy utilizes each day to strengthen its military might, acquiring the best weapons, etc. . . . the path being followed is one that leads directly to renewed war, G-d forbid." Sharon went on to serve in his position for another three years. When the Yom Kippur War erupted only weeks after he retired, he was summoned back to active duty, and his service during the war was considered vital toward Israel's victory (the Rebbe's letter is available at Chabad.org/2458367).

36. Years later, long after Moshe Levi had retired from the army, he was sick and Ben-Hanan went to visit him. Levi recalled their conversation about the Rebbe and said to Ben-Hanan, "You were right and I was wrong." A video of Major General Yossi Ben-Hanan speaking of this episode is available at Chabad.org/1076660.

37. Menachem M. Schneerson, *Sichot Kodesh 5767,* 2:299.

38. Menachem M. Schneerson, *Sichot Kodesh 5734,* 1:136–38.

39. On July 20, 1967, he wrote to Rabbi Yisrael Leibov: "I am curious to know if among those killed in battle are men who left behind widows or orphans. If there are, how many are there and what are the ages? Who is taking care of them now?" A few weeks later, he returned to this theme: "We need this information . . . to be able to arrange for them a Bar Mitzvah celebration . . . to be able to give them free subscriptions to our publications . . . most importantly to be able to think in detail about the needs of each boy and girl and what can best be done for them" (letter dated August 11, 1967).

40. Noach Blasbalg in a January 21, 2009, interview conducted by JEM.

41. For Prime Minister Sharon talking about his encounters with the Rebbe, as well as the Bar-Lev episode, see Chabad.org/1038748 (at 3:40); see also Chabad .org/1900554, Chabad.org/133687, and Chabad.org/527537.

42. See Ariel Sharon with David Chanoff in *Warrior* (New York: Simon & Schuster, 1989–2001), 236; and Ariel Sharon in a January 21, 2000, interview conducted by JEM.

43. Netanyahu apologized in advance to those "capable and decent people" at the UN before quoting the Rebbe's potentially offensive words. Prime Minister Netanyahu's speech at the UN can be viewed at Chabad.org/1632210. A video of Netanyahu meeting with the Rebbe on April 19, 1988, can be seen at Chabad .org/1001699; a meeting on November 18, 1990, at Chabad.org/1161514, and Netanyahu's recollections of these encounters can be seen at Chabad.org/471241.

Chapter 21: Soviet Jewry

1. Menachem M. Schneerson, *Sichot Kodesh 5731,* 1:466–77.

2. The group whose activities the Rebbe most ardently opposed was the Jewish Defense League, the organization founded by the late Rabbi Meir Kahane, which advocated violence against Soviet officials in the West.

3. In an interview Dennis Prager and I conducted in 1978 with Abba Eban, the longtime Israeli foreign minister and earlier an ambassador to the United States and to the United Nations. Eban recalled that during his tenure in the United

States, the event that prompted the greatest outpouring of support for Israel was the publication of *Exodus*, which Eban dismissed as "poor literature," but which, he acknowledged, had evoked great admiration and love for Israel. Regarding *Exodus* and the Soviet Union, a former Russian Jewish dissident, Rabbi Leonid Feldman, told me that he was entrusted with a copy of *Exodus*, and instructed that he had twenty-four hours in which to read it. By the time he returned the book the following day, he had decided to leave Russia and go live in Israel.

4.　In a 1972 *yechidus* with Peter Kalms, the Rebbe emphasized the importance of influencing Russian Jews to engage in Jewish activities daily: "Do something every day, *Modeh Ani* [the one-sentence prayer to be recited upon waking up, thanking God for life], not higher philosophy." Then the Rebbe continued: "I am not a Zionist, but even [singing] *Am Yisrael Chai*" ["the people of Israel live"; see Kalms, *Guidance from the Rebbe*, 73]. "Am Yisrael Chai" was composed by Rabbi Shlomo Carlebach for performance at a Soviet Jewry rally, and became a theme song of the Student Struggle for Soviet Jewry. Within years, the song had become a sort of worldwide Jewish anthem.

5.　See *Dyedushka: The Lubavitcher Rebbe and Russian Jewry* (Kfar Chabad: Israel, 2009), 366–67. For some details of the episodes involving Chabad's work inside Russia, see also Aryeh "Lova" Eliav in an interview on January 14, 2007, conducted by JEM.

6.　Menachem M. Schneerson, *Igrot Kodesh*, 12:446.

7.　Menachem M. Schneerson, *Igrot Kodesh*, 21:356–57.

8.　Was such thinking paranoid? Not at all. As I recall from a trip I made to Russia (with Richard Stone, the future chairman of the Conference of Presidents of Major Jewish Organizations) to meet with dissidents in Siberia and Moscow in 1973, the realization that the government had informers everywhere—there was a person on each floor of hotels in Russia, recording when guests arrived and left their rooms—made me, and all visitors meeting with dissidents, extremely cautious about what we said. As a general rule, we did not speak of significant matters inside people's apartments; rather we walked and talked in a low voice in a park or other public place. While this trip lasted only eighteen days, I recall that on the plane ride home, during which I was planning meetings with people for whom I had been entrusted with messages, my first thought was, Should I have the person meet me in a park, or could we speak in their home or office? So quickly can a person who has spent time in a totalitarian society become frightened and overly cautious!

9.　Velvel Greene, *Professor Greene, Shalom U'bracha* (Beersheba, Israel: Beit Chabad Ha-Mercazi Beersheba, 2012), 42–43.

10.　The episode with Rabbi Israel Miller and the unused Torah scrolls in Russia was told to me by Rabbi David Miller and Debbie Kram, two of Rabbi Miller's children (February 15, 2014).

11.　A total of 26,000 left Russia in 1988, 185,000 in 1990, 148,000 in 1991, and over 60,000 each year in 1992, 1993, and 1994.

12. Reagan kept a placard on his desk that read: "There is no limit to the amount of good you can do if you don't care who gets the credit." Thus, Reagan was very open to using "quiet diplomacy" when it seemed the best way to achieve his intended goal. In early 1983, Reagan convened a meeting with Anatoly Dobrynin, the Soviet ambassador to the United States, at which he raised the issues of human rights in the Soviet Union, including the status of dissidents and Prisoners of Zion (Jewish activists who had been imprisoned for their efforts to leave for Israel). Reagan was also determined at that time to settle the issue of seven Pentecostal Christians who had been living in the basement of the American embassy since they had rushed past guards and sought refuge there in 1978. The president asked Dobrynin if something could be done for these people, and promised in exchange that he would not take any credit if they were allowed to leave the Soviet Union. A few weeks after the meeting with Dobrynin, the seven Christians received exit visas to leave Russia (see Gal Beckerman, *When They Come for Us, We'll be Gone* [New York: Mariner Books, reprinted 2011], 452).

One further note: The great tragedy of Reagan's later years was the onset of Alzheimer's. He was likely in the disease's early stage when he met Hecht in the Bahamas, and this probably accounts for why it was Mrs. Reagan, and not her husband, who related the details of Reagan's meeting with Gorbachev.

13. See article by Senator Chic Hecht, June 2004, available at Chabad.org/523711.

14. See Natan Sharansky with Ron Dermer, *The Case for Democracy* (New York: Public Affairs, 2006), 139–40.

15. Interview in November 2013 with Professor David Luchins, a senior adviser to Senator Moynihan, who was present at the meeting with the Rebbe.

16. Israel Meir Lau, *Out of the Depths* (New York: Sterling, 2011), 193. Aryeh Eliav similarly commented: "If there is one Jew to whom we all owe a debt of gratitude that there still remains a Jewish community in Russia, it is the Lubavitcher Rebbe." Shimon Peres, in the aftermath of the Rebbe's death, wrote: "It is in his merit that the flame of Judaism [in Russia] has been preserved."

Chapter 22: When It Is Wrong to Make Aliyah

1. The Rebbe's question was reminiscent of his response to a Chabad yeshiva student who came to inform him that he had decided to attend college. "Are you asking for an *eitzah* (advice) or a *bracha*?" (see page 328).

2. See Peter Kalms, *Guidance from the Rebbe* (Jerusalem: Shamir Publishing House, 2001), 21–28.

3. Menachem M. Schneerson, *The Letter and the Spirit*, 323–29. The Rebbe's letter is available at Chabad.org/2387581.

4. Greene was an influential figure in the local Jewish community, and while the Rebbe could understand the lure of a larger university, he didn't think that the gain justified the harm that might result to Jewish life in Minneapolis if Greene left.

When Greene persisted and asked the Rebbe if he would at least give him a *bracha* if he chose to take the new position, the Rebbe responded: "I have already given you a *bracha* [referring to a blessing for children that he had bestowed on the Greenes years earlier]. What other *bracha* do you need?" Greene chose to remain. Years later, when the Jewish community in Minneapolis had grown, and an opportunity presented itself to Greene at the University of the Negev in Beersheba, Israel, the Rebbe encouraged Greene to take the position.

5.   Rabbi Shmuel Isaac Popack, in an interview on June 10, 2009, conducted by JEM.

6.   This theme, of Jews walking about proudly displaying their Jewishness (by wearing a beard, for example), was very important to the Rebbe. In a 1977 letter (Erev Purim 5737), the Rebbe wrote of a senior Lubavitch student who had spent his summer vacation visiting small Jewish communities, and who later expressed his disappointment at one community in particular where he felt he had made no impact. "But several months later," the Rebbe wrote, "Merkos L'Inyonei Chinuch, which sponsors this program [of sending out students], received a letter from one of the families in that town. The writer, a woman, related that one summer day she happened to stand by her front window when she saw a bearded young man, wearing a dark hat, his *tzitzis* showing, approaching her door. She confessed that when she admitted the young man and learned of the purpose of his visit, she was not responsive, for she and her family were not prepared at that moment to change their life style. Yet for a long time after that encounter, the appearance of the young man haunted her. He reminded her of her grandfather and it refreshed her memories of the beautiful Jewish life she had seen in her grandparents' home, though the material circumstances were incomparably more modest than she had come to know in her married life. Finally—the letter went on—she decided to make the change. She made her home kosher, and the family began to observe Shabbos and Yom Tov [holidays such as Passover and Sukkot], and she is raising the children in a Torah way." The Rebbe went on to make several observations, among them that although the young *shliach* truly thought he was making no impact in the town, unbeknownst to him, his beard and tzitzis were making a great impact.

7.   The Rebbe believed that the Soviet Union was intentionally letting the most active Jews emigrate in the hope that those left behind would then assimilate. However, when one Jew who had left Russia was moved by remorse and wished to return to work on behalf of the Jewish community, the Rebbe dissuaded him: "You are now *persona non grata* [there]. Everyone who comes in contact with you is a consignment for Siberia. You will be watched, there is no benefit now."

8.   Efraim Halevy, in an interview on August 13, 2009, conducted by JEM.

9.   Among those who agreed with the Rebbe was America's most famous religious Zionist, Rabbi Joseph B. Soloveitchik. A strong supporter of Israel and of Jews going to live there, Soloveitchik also argued that "a man should . . . live in a place where he can accomplish the most for *yahadus* [Judaism]. If a man can accomplish the most for *yahadus* in New York, then he's got to stay in New York." Rabbi Soloveitchik liked

to cite the case of Rabbi Judah Halevi (1075–1141), the medieval Jewish poet and philosopher, "who accomplished in the Diaspora more than he did in *Eretz Yisrael.*" In short, he believed that if one can influence more Jews toward Jewish commitment in America than in Israel, one should remain in America. Regarding his view of aliyah, Rabbi Soloveitchik told David Holzer, "In this regard, I subscribe to the opinion of the Lubavitcher Rebbe. He said it and he's right." (See David Holzer, *Thinking Aloud: Transcripts of Personal Conversations with Rabbi Joseph B. Soloveitchik* [New York: HolzerSeforim, 2009], 221 and 239).

Chapter 23: The Revolving Sun, Evolution, and the Age of the World

1.   The Jewish laws that ordain that a man refrain from sexual, indeed any physical, contact with his wife during her period and for a week afterward. Relations are permitted only after the wife immerses herself in a *mikveh*.

2.   See the Rebbe's letter of November 5, 1975, available at Chabad.org/73253.

3.   Ibid.

4.   The Rebbe continues: "In discussing this question with another scientist, he expressed surprise that there should be an individual in the twentieth century who could still think that the earth stood still and the sun revolved around it. When I protested that from the viewpoint of modern science this could be as valid as the opposite theory, he could not refute it" (letter to Velvel Greene, August 24, 1964 [15 Elul 5724], reprinted in Greene, *Professor Greene, Shalom U'bracha* [Hebrew], 84. The Rebbe also noted that some of the arguments presented as definitive proofs of the earth's rotation around the sun are nothing more than opinions presented in scientific terminology that mislead readers into thinking that irrefutable scientific truths are being offered. On one occasion, he sent a letter to the editor of a journal that had critiqued his position on this issue: "I read with great surprise the view cited in the editor's note to the effect that the fact that we can calculate beforehand the time of the eclipse of the moon and of the sun, as well as calculate the orbits of space flights, support the theory that the earth is moving around the sun and not vice versa. This is a most amazing argument, especially and inasmuch as it is well known that the calculations relating to the eclipses of the moon and the sun were made thousands of years before Copernicus. Moreover, one of the tables used in the calculations was that of Ptolemy, whose theory was that the sun was revolving around the earth" (letter of May 14, 1964; printed in Menachem M. Schneerson, *The Letter and the Spirit*, 242).

5.   Menachem M. Schneerson, *Sichot Kodesh 5731*, 1:267–68.

6.   David Bezborodko, in an interview on November 1, 1998, conducted by JEM; a segment of the interview is available at Chabad.org/691380.

7.   Chief Rabbi (of what was then British Mandatory Palestine) Abraham Isaac Kook, for example, did not see a belief in evolution as a challenge to religious belief: "Evolution itself, moving upwards coordinately and undeviatingly from the lowest to the highest, demonstrates most clearly a prevision from afar, a

preset purpose for all existence. Divine greatness is thereby enhanced and all the goals of faith confirmed, and trust and service of the Divine is all the more justified" (*Orot ha-Kodesh*, 565). Great Britain's chief rabbi Jonathan Sacks, a great devotee of the Rebbe but one who accepts the likelihood of evolution, comments on this passage of Rabbi Kook: "The idea that evolution shows that life emerged by chance does not impress the religious mind, which knows from many biblical examples that what appears to be random is in fact providential. The Book of Esther, like the story of Joseph, is a providential narrative in which everything happens at the right time in the right way to bring about the fated end, yet the word 'God' does not appear in the book, and the festival to which it gave rise, Purim, means lotteries or chance." Rabbi Sacks cites a teaching of Malbim, the nineteenth-century Bible commentator, "There are things that appear [to have arisen] by chance but are actually providentially determined by God" (commentary on Proverbs 16:33). In the same book, Rabbi Kook argued that there is no difficulty "in reconciling the verses of Torah or other traditional texts with an evolutionary standpoint" (*Orot ha-Kodesh*, 559). In making this assertion, Kook seems to have relied, at least in part, on a teaching of Maimonides, that "the account given in Scripture of the creation is not, as is generally believed, intended to be in all its parts literal" (see *The Guide for the Perplexed*, Book II, chapter 29 [Chicago: University of Chicago Press, 1974]; for a more comprehensive discussion of these issues, see also Jonathan Sacks, *The Great Partnership: Science, Religion, and the Search for Meaning*, 351–68, particularly 354 and 362–63 [New York: Schocken/Random House, 2011], from which the citations of Rabbi Kook are drawn).

8.   The Rebbe's letter of 18 Tevet 5722 (December 25, 1961) is available at Chabad .org/60946.

9.   See Menachem Mendel Schneerson, *Mind over Matter: The Lubavitcher Rebbe on Science, Technology and Medicine*, compiled by Joseph Ginsburg and Herman Branover and translated into English by Arnie Gotfryd (Jerusalem: Shamir, 2003), 34–35. In recent years, Rabbi Natan Slifkin, who has written widely on issues of Judaism, animals, and the origins of the universe, has offered a commonsensical objection to the Rebbe's statement that the question "Why create a fossil?" is no more valid than the question "Why create an atom?" Slifkin argues that the two questions are quite dissimilar. "Asking 'why create an atom' is a pointless philosophical speculation, but asking 'why create a fossil which appears to be a dead dinosaur [from millions of years ago] if no such creature ever lived' is a very reasonable and obvious question" (Natan Slifkin, *The Challenge of Creation* [New York: Zoo Torah/Geffen Books, 2012], 159). While the Rebbe did not deny, as the above statement suggests, that dinosaurs might have once existed ("one cannot exclude the possibility that dinosaurs existed 5722 years ago, and became fossilized under terrific natural cataclysms in the course of a few years, rather than in millions of years"), the force of Slifkin's challenge remains: while the existence of atoms poses no challenge to a literal understanding of the biblical chronology and account of Creation, the existence of fossils that appear to be millions of years old does. Since Slifkin's book was written twelve years after the Rebbe's death, it is obviously impossible to know

how the Rebbe would have responded to Slifkin's critique. I assume he would have reiterated his objection to giving up the biblical version of Creation for the sake of theories that have never been proven.

10. The Rebbe's letter, dated 15 Elul 5724 (August 23, 1964), is available at Chabad .org/1899567.

11. The Rebbe's letters of 18 Tevet 5722 (December 25, 1961) and 17 Cheshvan 5723 (November 14, 1962) are available at Chabad.org/112083.

Chapter 24: Why People Shouldn't Go to College, and Why Those Who Do Shouldn't Drop Out

1. "I studied science on the university level from 1928 to 1932 in Berlin, and from 1934 to 1938 in Paris" (letter written November 14, 1962; see Schneerson, *Mind over Matter*, 39). In addition, prior to attending university in Berlin, the Rebbe had taken courses at the University of St. Petersburg in Russia (the Rebbe remarks in the same letter, "I received my scientific training . . . in German and French, and previously in Russian"; Schneerson, *Mind over Matter*, 41).

2. Professor Steven Cohen, the foremost sociologist of American Jewish life, estimates that over 80 percent (perhaps well over) of American Jews attend college, while approximately 55 percent fast on Yom Kippur (conversation with the author, April 13, 2012).

3. Some years later, when the Raders were preparing to bring out an anthology, *Woman of Valor*, the book's projected cover had a drawing illustrating women of different age groups, one of whom was wearing a mortarboard (a square-topped cap with a tassel that is characteristically worn at university graduation ceremonies). The Rebbe asked to have the mortarboard removed from the cover so that people would not think that to be a woman of valor, one had to go to college.

4. See Menachem M. Schneerson, *The Letter and the Spirit*, 1:194–95.

5. Martha Stock, in an interview on August 31, 2006, conducted by JEM.

6. *Opening the Tanya*, translation and commentary by Adin Steinsaltz (San Francisco: Jossey-Bass/Wiley, 2003), 216–17.

7. Jonathan Sacks, *A Letter in the Scroll* (New York: Free Press/Simon and Schuster, 2000), 210–11. Shortly after receiving the letter, Sacks gave it to a Chabad friend to whom he had shown it. The friend no longer has the letter, but Sacks is certain, as he told me, that his recollection of its contents is absolutely accurate.

8. The letter to Bassie Garelick, dated 28 Cheshvan 5715 (November 24, 1954), can be found at Chabad.org/2391352.

9. Presumably, the Rebbe was referring to a Jewish studies teacher, as one does require a college degree to be a certified secular studies teacher.

10. What does it mean, however, to have a "mature religious outlook"? Israel Singer recalls a conversation his father, a learned Jew, told him he had had with

the Rebbe. The Rebbe had expressed the view that "before you learn secular subjects, you have to learn *kol ha-Torah kula* [the entire Torah and rabbinic literature], and it has to be *shagurim b'ficha*" (fluent on your tongue; i.e., internalized). This helps explain the Rebbe's own intensive study of secular subject starting in his mid-twenties, only after he had first developed a wide-ranging knowledge of Judaism's major texts.

11. It is worth noting that the Rav is the only source we have that specifically places the Rebbe in Heidegger's classroom during their years at the University of Berlin. Rabbi Soloveitchik's studies with Heidegger are referenced in a 1968 lecture he gave before the Rabbinical Council of America: "I have also known some really great philosophers of international renown. I was in [Martin] Heidegger's class. I was a good student. He continually spoke about human destiny, spiritual perceptions, and the events of that time. Nevertheless, when Hitler came to power, the first to join the ranks of the Nazis were Heidegger and many other philosophers. . . . Only a few of the secular philosophers resisted the Nazi onslaught." (See Rakeffet-Rothkoff, *The Rav*, 1:195.) As there are no other sources indicating that the Rebbe studied with Heidegger, it is possible that Rabbi Soloveitchik's recollection was of a different course he attended with the Rebbe. The essential point, though, would be the same, that the Rebbe was well aware of the attraction of many Germans, including those with great intellectual attainments, to Nazism.

12. Professor Moshe Berger related this incident to me in an interview I conducted with him in January 2014.

13. *Hitler's Professors* is the title of Max Weinreich's book on this subject (New York: YIVO, 1946).

14. Rabbi Ephraim Sturm, in an interview on October 20, 2007, conducted by JEM; segments of the interview are available at Chabad.org/702101.

15. Efraim Sturm similarly recalled that the Rebbe did not initially push anything beyond the dining clubs. When others stressed to Sturm the need for lectures, he summarized the Rebbe's position by saying, " 'By all means, have your lectures, have Young Israel rabbis go there and speak to the students, but the fundamental idea, the foundation, the bread and butter must be bread and butter.' That was basically it."

16. Related to this aspect of the Rebbe was yet another characteristic, one that particularly endeared him to Hager: the fact that the Rebbe took his ideas, but not himself, very seriously. Hager remembers an occasion when the Rebbe was stressing to him some activity that he should carry out for fellow students, "and you can tell people in my name [that I want to see this done]." Then the Rebbe suddenly chuckled and added, "But if you think it will be more effective [if the people don't know that the idea came from me], then tell them to do it but *davka* don't tell them in my name." It was not only the Rebbe's words that struck Hager—that he cared only that the goal be achieved, not that he get credit for it—but that he chuckled when he made this comment. Freddy Hager in an August 9, 2007, interview conducted by JEM.

17. This approach of the Rebbe brings to mind a Talmudic passage that describes Rabbi Chiyya (late second century CE) going to a village that had no teachers or educational system in place. The first thing he did was to write out the Torah on five scrolls of parchment. Then, he taught each of the Torah's five books to five different students, and went on to teach each of six other students a different volume of the six sections of the Mishnah by heart. Then he told the students, "During the time that I go back to my home and return here, teach Torah to one another and teach Mishnah to one another." In this way, Rabbi Chiyya explained to a colleague, "I made sure that the Torah is never forgotten by the Jewish people" (*Bava Metzia* 85b). Leibl Wolf in a November 16, 2008, interview conducted by JEM.

18. The Rebbe's advice to Professor Block brings to mind his commonly offered advice to people who received a disturbing medical diagnosis: "Consult with a second doctor who is also a friend."

19. Professor Block similarly recalls: "From 1965 on, when the Rebbe started telling me to write a book on Aristotle, the only thing the Rebbe ever talked to me about was, 'When are you going to write your book on Aristotle?' " Years after the Rebbe's death, Block was still troubled by this recollection: "You would think I'm a big Chasid, I would do it. I couldn't do it." It is clear that Block regrets that he hasn't been able—at least not yet—to fulfill this request of the Rebbe. But the Rebbe's agenda was as clear to Block as it was to Hanoka: to produce an academic work that would reflect well on the accomplishments and capabilities of religious Jews.

20. Based both on an interview I conducted with Professor Susan Handelman in Jerusalem in April 2012 and an interview with Handelman on March 20, 2007, conducted by JEM; segments of the JEM interview are available at Chabad.org/574988.

21. In the Rebbe's precise words: "It depends on what could be surmised about the attitude toward religion and Judaism of those who will be examining [your] Ph.D. work (that they should not be anti-religious, for then there would be some apprehension that they would disturb [you] and be opposed)." The material in parentheses is in parentheses in the Rebbe's note.

22. Footnote Handelman's article Chabad.org/161694, where examples of the Rebbe's edits can be found.

23. The young man enrolled at Yeshiva College and later went on to study medicine at the university's Albert Einstein College of Medicine.

24. Bentzion Bernstein, in an interview on February 11, 2010, conducted by JEM.

25. Bernie Rader, in an interview on August 6, 2007, conducted by JEM.

26. When Rabbi Zalman Schachter-Shalomi asked for permission to study for a BA at Boston University, the Rebbe approved. But at the time, Schachter-Shalomi, though ordained by Chabad, was not functioning as a *shliach*; rather, he was serving as an Orthodox rabbi at a non-Lubavitch synagogue in New Bedford, Massachusetts. Some years later, Schachter-Shalomi told the Rebbe that he wished to study for a doctorate in pastoral psychology at Hebrew Union College, the headquarters

of the Reform movement. He explained that he expected to write his dissertation on the subject of the *yechidus*, the private meetings between a Chasid and a Rebbe (the dissertation was subsequently turned into a book, *Spiritual Intimacy: A Study in Counseling in Hasidism* [Lanham, MD: Jason Aronson, 1990]). The Rebbe blessed Schachter-Shalomi on his undertaking. At an interview with him in 2010, I asked him what he would have done if the Rebbe had opposed his studying for the BA or opposed his studying at Hebrew Union College: In both instances, Schachter-Shalomi told me, he would have withdrawn his application: "I wouldn't have gone."

Schachter-Shalomi feels that one factor influencing the Rebbe's approval in both cases was that he took into account the background of the person making the request. Thus, although Schachter-Shalomi had been involved in Chabad since his teen years, he had grown up in a religiously observant household that was very open to secular education. He himself had attended a secular high school in Austria, so the idea of attending a school such as Boston University was less foreign to him than to a person who had been raised his entire life in Chabad.

27. Menachem M. Schneerson, *Igrot Kodesh*, 3:472–74.

28. Dennis Prager has noted that it seems to be a cultural phenomenon of American Jews to make known even to strangers—and often within just a few minutes of meeting them—the college which their child attends, particularly if it is an Ivy League school.

Chapter 25: Mrs. Schneerson from President Street

1. Dr. Elliot Udell, in an interview on January 6, 2009, conducted by JEM.

2. Daniele Gorlin Lassner, in an interview on January 25, 1999, conducted by JEM, available at Chabad.org/471236.

3. Before 1950, the Rebbetzin attended weddings. Subsequent to becoming Rebbetzin, she stopped doing so, likely because she knew that it would be painful for her sister to witness the great honor bestowed on her. She herself was also uncomfortable with the great honor and fuss people made over her.

4. Yet one other feature another visitor recalled: "When she had guests, the phone could be ringing and it didn't exist. You were the focus."

5. For understandable reasons, this detail resonated for me, as I presume it was my father, Shlomo Telushkin, the Rebbe's accountant, who was the one filling out the paperwork.

6. In addition, because of the veneration Chasidim felt for the Rebbe, many were uncomfortable being with him in the less formal environment of his home.

7. Dr. Ira Weiss, in an interview I conducted with him at his home in Chicago in 2010. Dr. Weiss, who enjoyed a very close relationship with both the Rebbe and Rebbetzin, shared much valuable information about their private lives with me, which is incorporated throughout this book.

8.   As my daughter Shira Telushkin once expressed it, "When was the last time you saw a Chasid walking a dog?" So pronounced is this discomfort with dogs in much of the *haredi* world that some people in Chabad have told me that they find it hard to believe that this incident with the Rebbetzin, particularly her putting her arms around the dog's neck, ever happened. However, Hadassah Carlebach has assured me that she heard this story directly from the Rebbetzin shortly after it happened. It is not widely known that Jewish law has a large series of regulations going back to the Torah that outlaw the mistreatment of animals; there are more direct regulations in the Torah concerning the compassionate treatment of animals than there are concerning the Sabbath.

9.   Rabbi Yosef Weinberg, in an interview on June 24, 2008, conducted by JEM.

10.   These quotes and the ones that follow about the Rebbe's 1977 heart attack are drawn from a series of interviews I had with Rabbi Krinsky, who was an eyewitness to these events.

11.   Dr. Weiss also gives particular credit, among others, to Dr. Bernard Lown and Dr. Lawrence Resnick.

12.   Menachem Kaminker, *Harabanit* (Brooklyn, NY: Vaad Talmidei Hatemimim, 2003), 103.

13.   One senses that in Chabad tefillin was a touchstone used by the Rebbes to underscore the importance of an activity. In the Rebbe's first book, *Hayom Yom*, a collection of teachings gathered from the words of his father-in-law, he cites this extract from the Frierdiker Rebbe: "My revered father, the Rebbe [Rashab] once declared in a *farbrengen*, 'Just as putting on *tefillin* every day is a biblical commandment incumbent on every Jew, regardless of whether he is a great Torah scholar or a simple person, so, too, it is an absolute obligation for every Jew to dedicate half an hour every day to thinking about his children's education, and to do everything in his power, to see to it that they follow the path in which they are being guided'" (see *Hayom Yom*, 22 Tevet, 51). Given that educating one's children is, like tefillin, ordained in the Torah (Deuteronomy 6:7), what is striking is that the Rebbe used the analogy of tefillin not to refer to another biblical ordinance but rather to the importance of staying close in one's heart to one's children and to their Torah education.

14.   Preparing meals was in itself something of an acquired skill. Having been raised in the court of Chabad, the Rebbetzin once lamented that as a young girl, neither she nor her sisters were ever taught cooking and other basic household skills (JEM interview with Frieda Kugel).

15.   Kaminker, *Harabanit*, 98.

16.   Yosef Y. Schneersohn, *Igrot Kodesh*, 15:70.

17.   The proverb is based on an incident in the Talmud in which Rabbi Yochanan, who is ill, cannot revive himself, but his colleague, Rabbi Hanina, can—leading the Talmud to cite a folk maxim, "A captive cannot release himself from prison" (*Brachot*

5b), which became the basis for the proverb, "A tzaddik can't give himself a blessing." Others outside the world of Chabad sometimes commented on the oddity of couples seeking a blessing for children from a man who was childless. In one instance, the London *Jewish Chronicle* published a letter in which a woman identified with Chabad advised a childless couple to seek both a blessing and advice from the Rebbe. A columnist for the paper, Ben Azai (the pseudonym for the well-known Anglo Jewish writer Chaim Bermant) noted his incredulity at the thought of sending someone to the Lubavitcher Rebbe for a blessing for children. "[Doesn't] she know that the Rebbe himself is childless?" Ben Azai in turn received a response from Chana Sudak, age eleven, who pointed out her incredulity at his response: "Doesn't Ben Azai know that a tzaddik can't give himself a blessing?" Though the young Sudak was only eleven, her response captured the sense of how Lubavitchers felt.

18. The Chasid requested that the story remain anonymous, since he has never spoken of this episode to his son and does not want his son to realize that his father had offered him for adoption.

Chapter 26: Devotion Beyond Measure

1. Menachem M. Schneerson, *Igrot Kodesh*, 6:183 and 236.

2. Rabbi Besser, in an interview on May 13, 2005, conducted by JEM.

3. In addition, Aryeh Leib's daughter—Rebbetzin Chana Schneerson's only grandchild—did not come to visit her as it was feared that something would be said that would betray news of her father's death.

4. The discussion with Professor Rosenbloom, which was videotaped, occurred during a *farbrengen* on January 22, 1975, and can be viewed at Chabad.org/498524.

5. Menachem M. Schneerson, *Igrot Kodesh*, 3:161.

6. Introduction by the Rebbe to *Sefer Ma'amarim 1951* (Brooklyn, NY: Kehot Publication Society, 1942–2012), 106. Part of the Rebbe's introduction is translated in Yosef Kaminetzky (and Yosef Cohen, translator), *Events in the Dynasty of Chabad-Lubavitch* (Brooklyn, NY: Kehot Publication Society, revised edition 2005), 3.

7. Menachem M. Schneerson, *Igrot Kodesh*, 3:173–74.

8. See Menachem M. Schneerson, *I Will Write It in Their Hearts: A Treasury of Letters from the Lubavitcher Rebbe, Rabbi Menachem Mendel Schneerson*, translated by Rabbi Eliyahu Touger (Brooklyn, NY: Sichos in English, 2008), 4:ix.

Chapter 27: The Courtroom Battle That Tore Apart a Family

1. At a subsequent *farbrengen* later that summer, the Rebbe said that before he addressed the issue publicly, he had tried three times to take care of it privately. It was only when he did not succeed, he explained, that he felt that he had no choice but to speak publicly.

2. The Frierdiker Rebbe had refused to leave Russia in 1927, and risked being arrested yet again by the Soviet police, unless he was allowed to take the boxes of

books that the Russians had confiscated. The Soviet authorities finally agreed and permitted him to take the books.

3. A video of the Rebbe's talk of 15 Tammuz 5745 (July 4, 1985) is available at Chabad.org/796358.

4. For a comprehensive overview of the *seforim* case, see Shalom D. Levine, *Mishpat HaSeforim—Didan Notzach* (Kfar Chabad: Israel, 2008). Rabbi Levine is the chief librarian of the Agudas Chasidei Chabad Library at 770 and played an active role in the *seforim* case. His book reproduces many documents pertaining to the case and contains much valuable information, which I have incorporated into this chapter.

5. In point of fact, when some uncomplimentary documents (consisting of a number of critical comments that the Frierdiker Rebbe had made about Rashag in his diary [comments he obviously intended not to be seen by others) surfaced, the Rebbe warned Chasidim not to read and certainly not to spread such material.

6. Then, too, Barry refused the entreaties of his father to invite his uncle. Despite this, the Rebbetzin helped with the wedding preparations (preparing food), and the Rebbe devoted a number of talks to the spiritual significance of a wedding, during which he commented, "It is a *simcha* (celebration) for my father-in-law."

7. What strains credulity in these words—"Let Barry take as many [books] as he wants"—is that even if the Rebbetzin did not study from these books, she knew her husband might well do so, and she also knew how important these books, which had belonged to her father, were to him, and how important they had been to her father.

8. Mr. Lewin, in an interview I conducted with him on February 27, 2013, at Columbia University.

9. See Moshe Bogomilsky, *Hei Teves, Didan Notzach: The Victory of the Seforim* (Brooklyn, NY: Self-published, 2007), 57.

10. This assertion prompted criticism from other Chasidic courts in which it is generally assumed that all property of the court belongs to the Rebbe and his family. Lewin soon found himself fielding angry phone calls from prominent members of Chasidic families: "What you're doing is very harmful to us personally because it's recognized that all property belongs to the Rebbe and the Rebbe's family. How are you going around and trying to take it away from us and give it to the community?" Lewin, not wishing to provoke further ire, simply explained that different Chasidic communities have different views regarding the property the Rebbe receives from his followers, but that the tradition in Chabad is that the property is the possession of the community.

11. Both Nat Lewin and Jerome Shestack later recalled that the Rebbe said to them, "Look, the key document is this one which he wrote Professor Marx." That comment, Lewin later noted, "turned out to be one hundred percent accurate" (see page 385 for the text of the letter).

12. Rabbi Menashe Klein, a legal scholar who consulted on the case, was amazed at such a high price being paid for a Haggadah and commented jokingly: "What?

$150,000 for a Haggadah? Undoubtedly, Pharaoh autographed it personally" (see Bogomilsky, *Hei Teves*, 45).

13. Many in Chabad were shocked when it came out that Lieberman sided with Barry and his mother against the Rebbe, but, as noted, Lieberman, then in his nineties, had eaten daily at the Gourarys for decades, and this might well have made it harder for him to oppose this family, which had treated him so well. Rebbetzin Gourary noted that she had known Rabbi Lieberman for seventy-five years, maybe longer. It also came out in Lieberman's deposition that he had designated Barry Gourary as the beneficiary of his estate.

14. This is also reminiscent of something the Rebbe had implied at the earlier *farbrengen*, that Barry and his mother—he did not mention them by name—were claiming that as the Frierdiker Rebbe had died thirty-five years earlier, it was time to divide his estate. In other words, in their eyes the movement was finished, so divide up whatever assets remain. The Rebbe in turn countered that during the past thirty-five years, the movement had continued to grow and expand; indeed, it was thriving, so there was no reason whatsoever to divide up the estate.

15. Rebbetzin Gourary subsequently argued that because her husband was a son-in-law, and not a direct descendant, of the Frierdiker Rebbe, he had no tangible stake in the library, and therefore no need to know what she was advising Barry to do. When asked at the deposition, "Did you think that . . . [both your husband and your brother-in-law] did not have any rights in the library?" she answered, "No. Not my husband, not my brother-in-law" (p. 65). Nonetheless, her behavior remains quite odd, given that she and Rabbi Gourary had been married for more than sixty years.

16. When Barry approached Christie's, the renowned auction house, about auctioning the Judaica he had assembled, they demurred, apparently not satisfied with his insistence that the books were his to sell (see Bogomilsky, *Hei Teves*, 14). That Barry approached Christie's about conducting what would have been a public auctioning of the books indicates his strong belief that the books were his to do with as he wished. Subsequent to this rebuff, Barry seems to have sold most of the volumes to overseas book dealers.

17. Also present were Chaim Baruch Halberstam, who was videotaping the testimony; Yehoshua Leiman, a Yiddish translator; and Dr. Robert Feldman, the Rebbetzin's physician.

18. In a talk following Rebbetzin Chaya Mushka's death, the Rebbe quoted this sentence in her name, noting that it had made a great impact on the court's subsequent ruling.

19. Earlier in the deposition she had said something similar: "I don't recall his [that is, my father] having anything personal except his clothing . . . his tallit and his *tefillin*." After her father's death, her mother gave Rebbetzin Schneerson her father's *kittel* and *tallit kattan* (the small *tallit* worn under one's shirt throughout the day, unlike the large *tallit*, which is wrapped over one's shoulders and is worn during morning prayers).

20. As a teenager, I was once looking for something in one of my father's drawers and came across a tax return with the name Menachem Mendel Schneerson on it. If I recall correctly, the Rebbe received a salary of some $6,000 a year, a small sum even in the early to mid-1960s when this happened. I commented about this to my father, who acknowledged that the Rebbe drew a very low salary and then noted that I should not be looking at other people's tax returns; it was privileged information.

21. Barry claimed that an offer was broached by the Rebbe for $25,000 to each of the Frierdiker Rebbe's daughters, but that when Barry requested a meeting with his uncle to discuss the offer, the Rebbe refused to meet with him and, in effect, said, "Take it or leave it." As far as I can ascertain, Barry's lawyers never raised the issue of settlement, and Barry never encouraged them to do so, and both Rabbis Krinsky and Shemtov deny that the movement ever offered a settlement.

22. See Jerome Mintz, *Hasidic People* (Cambridge, MA: Harvard University Press, 1992), 286.

23. Another expert witness brought in on behalf of Chabad was Rabbi Louis Jacobs, the London-based founder of Britain's Masorti (Conservative) movement, and an expert on Chasidic literature and tradition. Despite differing views from the Rebbe on a number of fundamental religious issues (such as the divine authorship of all of the Torah), Jacobs was willing to testify on behalf of Chabad and Chabad was willing to summon him as a witness. Jacobs's testimony played an important role in convincing Judge Sifton that the Chabad library as acquired and expanded by the Frierdiker Rebbe was intended to be a research library and not a private collection for himself and his family. This accounts for the library containing antisemitic and Communist books, along with volumes the Frierdiker Rebbe regarded as heretical, the sort of works that would be useful for scholars doing research. As Jacobs concluded: "I can't [otherwise] imagine a Rebbe acquiring this kind of library, which . . . contains material which by no stretch of the imagination could be considered a personal library for the Rebbe's personal use." Based on Jacobs's conclusions, and other testimony as well, including that of Chaim Lieberman, Sifton concluded: "The community purpose for the library is confirmed by the nature of the books collected" (see Sifton decision of January 6, 1987, 5–6).

24. There are a number of letters from the Frierdiker Rebbe in this context, written from Riga during December 1939; see Yosef Y. Schneersohn, *Igrot Kodesh*, 5:5–7, and more. To make matters a little more confusing, the Frierdiker Rebbe did on occasion speak of the collection as "my library." However, the preponderance of his comments reflect a belief that the library was now the property of Agudas Chasidei Chabad. Furthermore, even if one believes that the Frierdiker Rebbe still regarded the library as his personal possession, it seems fair to assume that he regarded himself as owning the library on behalf of Chabad. In other words, even if one argues that he didn't formally transfer ownership to the movement (which Judge Sifton and the appeals court believed he did), I think it's clear that if he had envisaged that one day his grandson would start selling books from the library, he would have

formally made provision for transferring ownership. The analogy that comes to mind is the British crown jewels. Even if the queen formally owns these jewels, it is inconceivable that she, or a descendant of hers, would sell them for personal gain.

25. See a section of the Rebbe's talk, as well as the Chasidim's reaction to the verdict and Nat Lewin speaking at an event celebrating the victory, at Chabad .org/454550. See also the Rebbe's talk on the last day of the weeklong celebration at Chabad.org/454549.

26. Bogomilsky, *Hei Teves*, 96.

27. Ibid., 47.

28. Even in their periods of closeness, there might have been some tension, not exactly an unknown phenomenon among siblings. Hadassah Carlebach, who had a highly affectionate relationship with her cousin, Rebbetzin Schneerson, recalls that at one point she attempted to deepen her friendship with Chana Gourary as well. Rebbetzin Gourary discouraged the effort. "You belong to my sister," she told her, rather inelegantly.

29. Concerning the meeting at Barry's home, Rabbi Moshe Bogomilsky writes that Barry received the delegation "cordially and spoke very respectfully. . . . In the course of our conversation, he referred numerous times to the Rebbe as '*der feter*' (the uncle) or '*ir Rebbe*' (your Rebbe), and carefully avoided saying 'the Rebbe' " (Bogomilsky, *Hei Teves*, 6n). The Bogomilsky book is an overview of the whole episode of the books, and contains much valuable information, some of which I have incorporated into this chapter. Rabbi Bogomilsky himself played a pivotal role in recovering many of the books.

30. See Menachem M. Schneerson, *Sefer HaSichot* (Brooklyn, NY: Kehot Publication Society, 1987–2013), 1:184.

Chapter 28: The Rebbe and the Messiah

1. The leadership of the movement, represented by Rabbis Yehuda Krinsky and Avraham Shemtov, has gone to court and prevailed in an effort to win back control of the synagogue from the Messianists. The Messianists have appealed the case.

2. Maimonides calls him Ben Koziba, as does the Talmud, but it is Bar Kochba who led the Jews in revolt against the Romans in 132–135 CE, to whom he is referring and by which name he is today known.

3. Not quite all the wise men. Rabbi Yochanan ben Torta, a colleague of Akiva's, warned him when he made his Messianic pronouncement: "Akiva, grass will grow from where your jaw now is, and still the Son of David [the Messiah] will not have arrived" (Jerusalem Talmud, *Ta'anit* 4:8).

4. It is an interesting question why Maimonides writes "or is slain" rather than "dies." It would seem that since Maimonides saw the Messiah as possibly being a military figure (as Rabbi Akiva seemed to believe) as well as a spiritual one ("fights the battles of the Lord"), it made sense to see his death in battle as proof that he

was not the Messiah. In any case, it would appear that an incomplete fulfillment of the Messianic mission during one's lifetime disqualifies one from being Messiah, however one dies.

5.   Although the Rebbe was very supportive of Israel during its wars with the Arab countries surrounding it, he did not lead the community there in the battles that extended the country's borders, most notably in the Six-Day War of 1967. Indeed, he did not set foot in Israel during his lifetime (see page 314).

6.   Among the Bible's most famous prophecies of the Messianic days are the words of Isaiah: "And they [the nations of the world] shall beat their swords into plowshares and their spears into pruning hooks. Nation shall not lift up sword against nation; they shall never again know war" (Isaiah 2:4). There were continuing and repeated wars throughout the Rebbe's lifetime.

7.   One of the Messiah's achievements is that he will gather Jews from throughout the world and bring them to Israel.

8.   Menachem M. Schneerson, *The Letter and the Spirit*, 273; available as well at Chabad.org/2387519.

9.   See the ArtScroll commentary on *Sanhedrin* 98b, n40.

10.   This would seem to explain how Rabbi Akiva made so grievous an error in thinking that his contemporary, Simon bar Kochba, was the Messiah. According to this explanation, Rabbi Akiva might have been right in recognizing Bar Kochba as the *potential* Messiah of his generation; however, if God does not feel that the time for redemption has come, the potential Messiah will remain just that, "potential."

11.   Maimonides opposed all speculative attempts to identify a Messiah in advance: "The Messiah is not a person concerning whom it may be predicted that he will be the son of so-and-so, or of the family of so-and-so" ("Epistle to Yemen," in *Crisis and Leadership: Epistles of Maimonides*, translated by Abraham Halkin, discussions with David Hartman [Philadelphia: Jewish Publication Society, 2009], 125).

12.   See Chatam Sofer, responsa *Choshen Mishpat, Likutim* 6, chap. 98. Other rabbinic authorities who mention the idea of a potential Messiah in each generation include the fifteenth-century rabbi Obadiah ben Abraham of Bartenura and Rabbi Zadok HaCohen Rabinowitz of Lublin. The *Sedei Chemed* (nineteenth century), a highly regarded encyclopedic work of halacha by Rabbi Chaim Hezekiah Medini, claims that not only is there a potential Messiah in each generation, but that this figure is sometimes openly spoken about by the Jews of the time; he cites five examples, among them Rabbi Judah the Prince and the Arizal (the sixteenth-century kabbalist Isaac Luria).

13.   Even now (2013), almost twenty years since the Rebbe's passing, Rabbi Krinsky is routinely designated in an annual compilation in *Newsweek* magazine as one of the four most influential rabbis in the United States. Rabbi Krinsky's deserved prominence ultimately derives, as he himself would acknowledge, from his close relationship to the Rebbe and from the Rebbe's accomplishments.

14. I came across this story, and several other citations, in David Berger, *The Rebbe, the Messiah, and the Scandal of Orthodox Indifference* (Oxford, UK: Littman Library of Jewish Civilization, 2008), 11. While Professor Berger's book is regarded as anathema in many Chabad circles, I have consistently found his citation of Jewish sources concerning the Messiah to be accurate. This is not surprising, given Berger's noted achievements as a historian, particularly in the areas of medieval Jewish-Christian relations and disputations. My disagreements with Professor Berger have to do with what I believe is an intemperate and very unfortunate response to Chabad, rooted in his fear that Chabad, by and large, is distorting Judaism and should therefore be delegitimized.

15. Rabbi Lichtenstein went on to say: "To the best of my knowledge, no one in this generation compares to the Rebbe—or even comes close—in terms of applying his vision, implementing it, building the Chabad 'empire' and managing its 'kingdom.'" Regarding the Tefillin campaign, which some regarded as pointless—why put tefillin on the head of someone who has no intention of becoming an observant Jew?—Lichtenstein noted that even if such a person eats unkosher food and violates Shabbat, "you're helping him maintain a certain level, and preventing him from assimilating completely."

16. See Binyamin Lipkin, *Reckoning of the Universe* (Hebrew: *Cheshbono shel olam*) (Lod, Israel: Machon Hasefer, 2000), 185.

17. Menachem M. Schneerson, *Sichot Kodesh 5751*, 1:259.

18. The conversation took place on January 12, 1992 (7 Shevat 5752).

19. See Rabbi Moshe David Tendler's introduction to *The Responsa of Rav Moshe Feinstein* (Jersey City, NJ: Ktav Publishing, 2001), 1:20–21..

20. Menachem M. Schneerson, *Torat Menachem Hitva'aduyot 5720*, 2:129–130.

21. See, for example, the Rebbe's impassioned talk on September 28, 1983; a video recording is available at Chabad.org/712298.

22. Speaking of the Rebbe's Messianic fervor, Professor Elliot Wolfson of New York University, a careful scholar of the Rebbe's teachings, has noted that the frequency of the Rebbe's invoking the motto "forthwith to redemption" during the 1940s "indicates the intensity of his hope for the imminent arrival of the Messianic age, and this should put to rest those who maintain that the apocalyptic fervor was an outcome of his old age combined with despair over the death of his wife" (Elliot Wolfson, *Open Secret* [New York: Columbia University Press, 2009], 304–5n18).

23. Menachem M. Schneerson, *Igrot Kodesh, 12*:404.

24. Menachem M. Schneerson, *Likutei Sichot* (Brooklyn, NY: Kehot Publication Society, 1959–2013), 20:458–59.

25. Menachem M. Schneerson, *Torat Menachem Hitva'aduyot 5742*, 2:674.

26. Menachem M. Schneerson, *Torat Menachem Hitva'aduyot 5712*, 1:53.

27. While reading a draft of this chapter, my friend Ari Goldman (who authored the *New York Times* obituary of the Rebbe) challenged me on this point: "How can you say,

'Why ultimately does it matter whether or not there are Chasidim who consider the Rebbe to be the Messiah?' " Goldman pressed the point: "If you're going to say that, then what about Messianic Jews (Jews for Jesus)—Would you also say their beliefs should be ignored because *L'mai nafka meena?*—because what does it matter?" In truth, the two cases are totally different. For one thing, Messianic Jews do not only believe Jesus is the Messiah, they also believe he is God. Second, the religion they practice is not Judaism, at least as Jews have understood their religion throughout history, but Christianity (given their beliefs about Jesus, they have, for understandable reasons, dropped the requirement to observe the Torah's laws). The reason Jews find them so offensive is that they refuse to call themselves Christians, label themselves with names such as "Jews for Jesus," and list their houses of worship in phone books as synagogues. Regarding Jews for Jesus and Messianic Jews, Dennis Prager has noted: "If a Catholic were to embrace Muhammad as his greatest prophet and regard the Quran as his bible, Catholics would call this person a Muslim, even if he went to Mass and still felt Catholic" (*Ultimate Issues* [January–March 1990]: 7–8). As I indicate above, there is no practical upshot in the halachic behavior of those who believe that the Rebbe is the Messiah (a belief that I obviously think is erroneous), which makes this totally unlike the case of Jews who believe that Jesus is the Messiah, let alone that he is God.

Chapter 29: Leadership After Life

1.   Rabbi Irving Greenberg is the one who first called my attention to this fact.

2.   Menachem Friedman, "Habad as Messianic Fundamentalism," in Martin Marty and R. Scott Applesby, eds., *Accounting for Fundamentalism* (Chicago: University of Chicago Press, 1994), 354.

3.   There are many instances in which the Rebbe advised people not to have an operation, even when a doctor—and sometimes more than one—strongly advised it; there was also one instance when he advised family members to make a big fuss at a hospital so that the doctor and nurses would realize they were making a major error in treatment. Most commonly, however, when people consulted him about a course of treatment concerning which they were uncertain, the Rebbe would advise them, "Consult with a doctor who is also a friend."

4.   The above is a recapitulation of Rebbetzin Teitz Blau's recollection of a meeting that occurred more than four decades earlier. Hence, the words cited are not verbatim but represent a clear approximation of both the question posed and the Rebbe's response.

5.   Rabbi Berkowitz mentioned to me the name of the Alaskan town and the girl's name but requested that I mention neither; he has remained in touch with the young woman and does not want to expose her to unwanted attention.

6.   That Rabbi Berkowitz blesses others does not in any way derive from an arrogant belief in his own self-importance. The Talmud teaches that we all have the ability to bless others and that we should all take blessings offered us seriously: "A blessing given by an ordinary person (*hedyot*) should never be unimportant in

your eyes" (*Megillah* 15a). Priests (*kohanim*), though, have a particularly high status in Jewish life because they were the ones who supervised the service at the Great Temple (*Beit ha-Mikdash*) in Jerusalem. The highest status of all devolved upon the high priest (*kohen gadol*) who, on Yom Kippur, while standing alone in the "Holy of Holies" (*Kodesh Kodashim*), beseeched God on behalf of the entire Jewish people.

7.   Sue Fishkoff, *The Rebbe's Army: Inside the World of Chabad-Lubavitch* (New York: Schocken, 2005), 6.

8.   I am relying on anecdotal evidence because I know of no research study that has been done of donors to Chabad.

9.   They might feel this to be true of certain other Orthodox groups as well, such as Satmar Chasidim, but since these groups do not generally engage in outreach, they usually do not come in contact with them or feel a special affection for them (Chabad has been quite brilliant in stimulating affection from many nonobservant Jews). Modern Orthodox synagogues such as those affiliated with Yeshiva University and Yeshivat Chovevei Torah also have achieved some real success in attracting previously nonobservant Jews into their ranks, but because they are much smaller in numbers (and less outreach-oriented than Chabad), their reach is not nearly as extensive. The same applies to emissaries dispatched by yeshivot, such as the Jerusalem-based Aish Hatorah, and to the extraordinary work of the National Jewish Outreach Program (NJOP), headed for over twenty-five years by Rabbi Ephraim Buchwald. Quite frankly, though, no one has a comparable clout to an army consisting of over eight thousand people.

Chapter 30: Major Events in the Life of the Rebbe

1.   Because of the Julian, as opposed to Gregorian, calendar then in use in Russia (but not in the rest of the Western world), the secular date recorded on his Russian birth certificate was April 5. After the Revolution of 1917, Russia changed to the Gregorian calendar.

2.   More commonly referred to as the *Tzemach Tzedek*, the title of a series of volumes he wrote.

3.   One sometimes hears it said that he ceased studying in the local school at age nine, but eleven seems to be more accurate. His early childhood teacher was Rabbi Shneur Zalman Vilenkin, toward whom the Rebbe maintained a lifelong sense of gratitude (see page 191).

4.   Menachem M. Schneerson, *Igrot Kodesh*, 12:414.

5.   Menachem M. Schneerson, *Sichot Kodesh 5732*, 1:593.

6.   On another occasion, he recalls being told words to the effect that "if your conscience pulls you in another direction [in opposition to Marxist theories], then you'll be jailed or sent to Siberia" (*Hitva'aduyot 5746*, 2:234; see also *Igrot Kodesh*, 26:419–20, where he writes of how as a young man in the Soviet Union he became used to being sharply attacked for his views by Communists). The sessions with the

Yevsektsia were in some ways reminiscent of medieval Christian-Jewish debates, in which Jews were challenged to justify why they insisted on remaining Jewish, while being forbidden to say anything that could be regarded as offensive to Christianity, with the priests serving as judges of what was offensive.

7.   Menachem M. Schneerson, *Sichot Kodesh 5735*, 1:378.

8.   Yosef Y. Schneersohn, *Igrot Kodesh*, 15:31.

9.   Preface to Shlomo Yosef Zevin, *Ishim Veshitot* (Jerusalem: Kol Mevaser, 2007 edition), 23.

10.   I am basing this on what the Rebbetzin told DovBer Junik in 1977 (see *Kfar Chabad*, no. 843 [18 Shevat 5759; English sec.]: 16). As the Rebbetzin's conversation with Junik occurred fifty years after the event, and given the grave risk that would be involved in speaking—even in a low voice—through an open window with police present throughout the apartment, it is worth recording Rephael Nachman Kahan's recollection of what he heard from Chaim Lieberman in 1927, immediately after the event. Lieberman's version (which he presumably heard from Menachem Mendel) is virtually the same as Chaya Mushka's except for one detail: When returning home that evening, Chaya Mushka, upon seeing the lights and suspecting a police presence in the house, told her fiancé, the future Rebbe, that if the secret police were in the house, she would signal him by opening a particular window. A few minutes later, she did so, and Menachem Mendel immediately ran to Lieberman's house (*Shmuot Vesippurim*, 3:220; I am indebted for these sources to Rabbi Elkanah Shmotkin).

11.   One of the best-known stories the Frierdiker Rebbe relates about this period is that when he handed the bag containing his personal belongings to one of the soldiers, Lulov snatched the bag from the soldier and said words to the effect that "Chasidim remain Chasidim. My grandfather carried the bags of your grandfather and I will carry your belongings."

The Frierdiker Rebbe defiantly grabbed the bag out of Lulov's hands and said, "Your grandfather was a Chasid, a disciple of my grandfather, and therefore privileged to carry those bags to places where my grandfather chose to go. However, your desire is to carry my bag to a destination that I did not choose." He then returned the bag to the soldier who had been holding it.

12.   A well-known and often recounted incident within Chabad relates to the months preceding the Sixth Rebbe's arrest, when he was being regularly harassed and questioned by the Yevsektsia. On one occasion, when he repeatedly emphasized to the three officials questioning him that he would under no conditions give up his religious practices, one pointed a gun at him and said, "This little toy has made many a man change his mind." The Rebbe replied: "This toy impresses only one who has but a single world and many gods, but not one who has but a single God and two worlds."

13.   The leading advocate was Mordechai Dubin, a religious Jew and member of the Latvian parliament. In Germany, the two leading advocates for the Rebbe were an

unlikely pair: Rabbi Dr. Meir Hildesheimer, a community leader and a member of one of Germany's most prominent Orthodox families, and Leo Baeck, the country's leading Reform rabbi. These men, supported by other Jews in Germany, pressured the German government to exert pressure on the Soviet government to let the Rebbe leave.

14.   On occasion, the Rebbe's recollections were of a more humorous nature. Dr. Jacob Hanoka recalled a *yechidus* in the early 1960s at which the Rebbe made reference to the introductory course he had taken more than thirty years earlier with Professor Nernst. He told Hanoka that, at first, he couldn't understand why Nernst, a Nobel Prize winner, was teaching an introductory class. But, as he explained to Hanoka, "with a big smile on his face," he soon learned "that a teacher [at the university was] paid according to the number of students he had, and there were many more students that took the introductory courses than the advanced ones." In any case, the Rebbe's reasoning that an academic's arguments can sometimes make a greater impression upon students than a rabbi's helps explain why the Rebbe did not permit the Harvard-trained philosopher Yitzchak Block to pursue rabbinical ordination after receiving his PhD. He believed that Block would exert a greater spiritual impact on students if he spoke to them as Professor Block rather than as Rabbi Block. In a 1979 letter to a professor, the Rebbe returned to this point yet again: "People in the world of science, and young students especially, are impressed by the fact that one can be a scientist of the highest caliber and at the same time a strictly observant Jew and a Chasid, and it makes them more responsive to the actual fulfillment of *mitzvot* when the subject comes up" (2 Adar 5939 [March 1, 1979]); see Schneerson, *Letters from the Rebbe*, 4:156.

15.   Interestingly, the Rebbe's father had received rabbinical ordination from Rabbi Chayim Brisker, Rabbi Soloveitchik's grandfather, while the Rebbe's father-in-law, the Sixth Rebbe, later played an important role in bringing about Rabbi Soloveitchik's appointment as the successor to his father, Rabbi Moshe Soloveitchik, at Yeshiva University (see page 237).

16.   Yosef Y. Schneersohn, *Igrot Kodesh*, 16:304–5.

17.   Ibid., *Igrot Kodesh*, 15:116–19.

18.   Rabbi Yitzchak Hendel, in an interview on May 11, 2006, and Rabbi Yosef Weinberg, in an interview on June 24, 2008. The interviews were conducted by JEM, and both Rabbis Weinberg and Hendel were students at the yeshiva during that time.

19.   See Yosef Y. Schneersohn, *Igrot Kodesh*, 15:184–85 and 236–37. See also 15:130–31 (letter dated January 22, 1933). There, the Frierdiker Rebbe writes to his daughter Chaya Mushka about her husband, Menachem Mendel: "I am very pleased with his relationship with all the doctors and [medical] professors."

20.   As of 2013, some thirty volumes of the Seventh Rebbe's letters have been published under the editorial direction of Rabbi Sholom DovBer Levine.

21.   Efraim Steinmetz, in an interview on October 28, 1999, conducted by JEM; available at Chabad.org/666135.

22. The comment from the Rebbetzin is cited in Menachem M. Schneerson, *Sefer Ha-Sichot 5752*, 1:182n43.

23. Yosef Y. Schneersohn, *Igrot Kodesh*, 15:171–72.

24. Ibid., *Igrot Kodesh*, 17:86.

25. Ibid., *Igrot Kodesh*, 15:345–46.

26. Larry Price, director of the documentary *The Chabad Rebbe and the German Officer*, has noted that the operation to save the Rebbe "came about as a result of back-channel diplomatic efforts by the Germans to try and convince the Americans not to enter the war with the British and French against Germany." Eliezer Zak-likovsky, *Out of the Inferno* (Brooklyn, NY: Kehot Publication Society, 2002) reproduces dozens of documents and telegrams relating to the Frierdiker Rebbe's escape from Europe and arrival in America.

27. The other pronouncement was "immediate repentance, immediate salvation" (*l'alter l'teshuvah, l'alter l'geulah*).

28. Despite the Sixth Rebbe's optimistic statements about his hopes for Jewish life in the United States, he himself was emotionally quite shattered upon his arrival in New York; he had witnessed the Nazi bombings and then takeover of Warsaw and the sufferings of the Jewish community there. His second daughter and son-in-law, Chaya Mushka and Menachem Mendel, were still trapped in Europe, as were his third daughter, Sheina, and her husband, Menachem Mendel Horenstein, both of whom were later murdered in Treblinka. Regarding his emotional state upon his arrival in the United States, my grandfather, Rabbi Nissen Telushkin, recalled in a talk he gave in Palestine in June 1947: "At the reception made for the [Sixth] Rebbe when he came to America, the Rebbe said: 'When Moses returned from [his father-in-law] Jethro's home to Egypt, God told him that Aaron will "see you and be glad within his heart" [*ve-samach be-libo*; Exodus 4:14].' Now, why was Aaron only happy 'within his heart' to see his brother, but did not show any outward signs of happiness? Because he was broken and crushed by the suffering undergone by the Jews in exile." After offering this explanation of the Torah verse, the Sixth Rebbe then commented, "Although I am happy to see my brethren here in America, I am broken and crushed by the suffering of the Jews of Europe" (quoted in Gansbourg, *Portrait of a Chassid*, 81).

29. See letter from the Rebbe, January 28, 1984, available at Chabad.org/2188391.

30. Speech of December 27, 1990; see Menachem M. Schneerson, *Sefer Ha-Sichot 5751*, 1:225–39.

31. Ibid., note 485.

32. The statement about the future Rebbe's great scholarship is cited in Rapoport, *The Afterlife of Scholarship*, 74; the comment the Frierdiker Rebbe made in 1941 when sending the four men to pick up the Schneersons, who were arriving by ship from Europe, is found in Kaminetzky, *Days in Chabad*, 203–4.

33. During World War II, 2,752 such ships were built in navy shipyards around the country.

34. Yaakov Hardof, in an interview conducted by JEM.

35. Shalom D. Levine, *Mibeis HaGenozim—Treasures from the Chabad Library*, 74.

36 Dr. Isaac Herschkopf, a psychiatrist, comments: "The father might no longer be alive, but his presence is still felt at the Seder, since undoubtedly his children are emulating the manner in which he led the Seder."

37. In contrast, the well-known Satmar Rebbe, Rabbi Yoel Teitelbaum, remained a lifelong opponent of Zionism and routinely urged his followers not to vote in Israeli elections or to engage in any behavior that signified acceptance of Israel as a legitimate state. In the aftermath of the Six-Day War, during which Israel captured the Old City of Jerusalem, the Satmar Rebbe instructed his followers not to pray at the *Kotel* (Western Wall), lest they experience a feeling of gratitude to the Zionists for restoring it to the Jewish people. When figures such as the Lubavitcher Rebbe spoke of God having performed miracles for the Jewish people during the war, the Satmar Rebbe acknowledged that miracles might indeed have been performed, but he regarded them as a test conceived by Satan to attract Jews to heresy, similar to the miracles performed by a false prophet, against which the Torah warns Jews (see Deuteronomy 13:2–4). The Satmar Rebbe wrote that everything built by the Zionists would have to be destroyed during the Messianic age, for just as Jewish law wishes to see a Torah scroll written by a heretic burned, so that the heretic's name be erased and forgotten, so must the buildings and institutions the Zionists erected be destroyed, so that their memory might also be erased. Though one might assume that the above comments were compiled by an opponent of the Satmar Rebbe, in fact, all of these citations are culled from a highly admiring biography of him (Meisels, *The Rebbe*, 504–5 and 513).

38. See Schachter-Shalomi, *The Geologist of the Soul*, 70–73.

39. Ephraim Ilin, in an interview on September 23, 2009, conducted by JEM, available at Chabad.org/2336308. For an assessment of some of Ilin's accomplishments, see Israel's Ministry of Transport website.

40. The extant two-and-a-half-minute tape of this talk can be heard at Chabad .org/550379.

41. Sukkot also is an agricultural holiday (Leviticus 23:29) that celebrates the harvest in the land of Israel. Special prayers are recited during which Jews are commanded to hold four varieties of plants in their hands (Leviticus 23:40). The largest of these plants is the *lulav* (palm branch), which is bound together with two willow twigs and three myrtle twigs. The fourth plant is the *etrog* (citron), which looks like a large, somewhat elongated lemon. Jews traditionally try to acquire beautiful *etrogim*, ones that have no blotches, spots, or other discoloration.

42. Matzah is the flat, unleavened bread that Jews eat during Passover. Many of the more strictly observant Jews eat a special type of matzah during the holiday,

particularly during the Seder. This unleavened bread is called *shmurah matzah* (guarded matzah). From the time the wheat used in *shmurah matzah* is harvested, it is kept under guard to ensure that no water or leavening agents come in contact with it. The Rebbe's campaign and his sending *shmurah matzot* to many people is an important factor responsible for the increase in recent decades in the number of Jews who eat *shmurah matzah* during the Seder.

43. See Curt Leviant, "Translating and Remembering Chaim Grade," *Jewish Review of Books*, no. 4 (Winter 2011).

44. See Schneerson, *Letters from the Rebbe*, 4:7. Three letters from the Rebbe on this subject appear in this volume on pp. 6–8, 11–13, and 13–18. In the third letter, he notes as well that he had studied "marine mechanics." Also, as is discussed above, during World War II, the Rebbe worked at the Brooklyn Navy Yard (see pages 470–71).

45. Extending well beyond twenty-four hours, since the ships would have to arrive some hours before the Sabbath began so as to avoid the risk of being late, and would not be able to commence travel immediately upon the Sabbath's conclusion, since all preparations for travel cannot commence until the Sabbath has ended.

46. He wrote the first questioner: "If you want to go to the Holy Land very much, you can go by El Al, or by a non-Jewish boat and the like, or even not go at all. At any rate your planned voyage [on an Israeli boat] is absolutely contradictory to the Torah. . . . I trust that you will be able to inform me with the good news that you have cancelled your reservation on the above-named ship" (Schneerson, *Letters from the Rebbe*, 4:7–8).

47. This followed a series of earlier attacks inside Israel, and in response, according to Mordechai Bar-On, the biographer of Moshe Dayan, Prime Minister Ben-Gurion instructed the Israeli army to prepare for war (see Mordechai Bar-On, *Moshe Dayan: Israel's Controversial Hero* (New Haven: Yale University Press, 2012), 74. Fearing, it appears, war with Israel, Egypt temporarily stopped the actions of the fedayeen attackers, and the war with Egypt, prompted by these terrorist attacks, did not take place until October 1956.

48. The Rebbe's letter was written on February 17, 1959, and is available at Chabad .org/2391337.

49. Cited in Fishkoff, *The Rebbe's Army*, 281.

50. The letter was written on 18 Tevet 5722, corresponding to December 25, 1961. As of Rosh Hashanah 2014, the Jewish year is 5775.

51. See Jewish Telegraphic Agency (JTA) article of March 30, 1965, "Lubavitcher Rebbe Voices Opposition to Interfaith Dialogues."

52. *New York Times*, August 1, 1966.

53. Furthermore, Wiesel wrote: "Imagine President Lyndon Johnson showing up in the home of a famous composer or artist. Is there anyone who would have lessened respect for him and his position as president? Absolutely not. On the contrary. People would appreciate that he puts aside all political interests to visit a friend. He would be hailed as a fabulous, dedicated and real leader."

54. See also *Yediot Achronot*, June 24, 1967.

55. The Rebbe quotes the Talmud, which applies the Torah verse (Deuteronomy 28:10), "And the nations of the world will see God's name upon you and they will fear you," as referring to tefillin, which are worn on the head.

56. During the nineteen years the Old City had been under Jordanian rule, the Jordanians had destroyed or badly damaged all of the synagogues there.

57. Henry Goldschmidt, *Race and Religion: Among the Chosen Peoples of Crown Heights* (New Brunswick, NJ: Rutgers University Press, 2006), 14.

58. Edward Shapiro, *Crown Heights: Blacks, Jews, and the 1991 Brooklyn Riot* (Waltham, MA: Brandeis University Press, 2006), 82, 89–90. The Rebbe's talk is published in *Likutei Sichot*, 6:350–58.

59. Interview I conducted with Rabbi Cunin, November 2013.

60. Menachem M. Schneerson, *Igrot Kodesh*, 29:19, presents a facsimile of the Rebbe's letter, in which the observation about the couple having placed their trust in the Rebbe rather than in God is presented in a handwritten comment inserted by the Rebbe as an addition to the original version of the letter.

61. *New York Times*, March 27, 1972. Given that the interview was directed to *Times* readers, one suspects that the Rebbe might have deemed it pretentious-sounding to record here the wish he expressed at the birthday *farbrengen*, that his Chasidim establish seventy-one new institutions over the coming year.

62. Letter of the Rebbe, January 21, 1982; available at Chabad.org/1237192.

63. "Children of Noah" (*B'nai Noach*) is a generic name for non-Jews in the Jewish tradition, while "Children of Abraham" (*B'nai Avraham*) or "Children of Israel" (*B'nai Yisrael*; "*Yisrael*") is a term for Jews.

64. In actuality, these commandments establish categories, and there are in fact some sixty specific laws encompassed within them. Thus, in the enumeration of the 613 laws commanded in the Torah, there are many forms of dishonesty that are specified in addition to the ban on stealing—and Jewish law understands these prohibitions as applying to non-Jews as well, for example, not paying a worker his salary, denying a debt that one has incurred, preventing a laborer from eating of the fruit in a field in which he is working, kidnapping, and using false weights and measures (in *The Seven Laws of Noah*, Aaron Lichtenstein documents that the prohibition against stealing, just one of the seven Noahide laws, expands into sixteen prohibited acts [pp. 19–27]).

65. For more on this campaign, see Chabad.org/maimonides.

66. From a conversation between the Rebbe and Gordon Zacks. A video of this encounter is available at Chabad.org/640806. See also Gordon Zacks, in an interview on August 23, 2007, conducted by JEM, available at Chabad.org/640802.

67. David Luchins, in an interview on May 8, 2007, conducted by JEM.

68. Paul Berger, "Chaya Mushka, Again and Again," *Forward*, December 23, 2011.

69. See Reuters, December 26, 1990.

70. See the Rebbe's conversation with directors of the Jewish Federation of Central New Jersey on January 6, 1991; available at Chabad.org/839509.

71. See JEM's "Peace Upon the Land," available at Chabad.org/132979.

72. When the Rebbe issued his assurances about Israel being safe even in the face of Saddam Hussein's threats, many Chasidim understood his words as a guarantee that no Scud missiles would fall on Israel. The Rebbe, of course, issued no such promise but only stated his certainty that Israel would remain safe even in the face of such attacks. In the end, thirty-nine Scuds hit Israel. Two Israelis died in direct hits, and four more died from suffocation in gas masks. In addition, the Scuds damaged or destroyed some 3,300 apartments in the Tel Aviv and Haifa areas—a sobering statistic that only underscored the relatively low, but nonetheless tragic, loss of life.

ACKNOWLEDGMENTS

A s has often been the case throughout my writing career, the acknowledgments are a sort of public love letter to people who have provided me with assistance in the writing of this book. Gratitude, as my friend Dennis Prager likes to say, is the prerequisite trait for being a happy person, and the people mentioned here have brought great joy into my life.

There is one person in particular who played an indispensable role in helping to bring this book about, Rabbi Zalman Shmotkin, spokesman for the Chabad-Lubavitch movement and one of the most knowledgeable authorities on the Rebbe. For a number of years, Reb Zalman patiently and persistently urged me to write an article about the Rebbe and his impact on Jewish life. The article I wrote on the Rebbe's twelfth *yahrtzeit* (anniversary of his death) and published in the *Forward* was what first brought me to the realization that here was a man in whose life I might well want to immerse myself. Upon my discussing it with Reb Zalman, he willingly opened door after door for me within Chabad, no door more important than that of his brother Rabbi Elkanah Shmotkin, director of JEM, an organization devoted to chronicling the life of Rabbi Menachem Mendel Schneerson. JEM houses and curates the audio- and videotapes, along with many thousands of photographs, of the Rebbe's public appearances (except for those that occurred on the Sabbath and those festivals on which Jewish law does not permit either taping or the taking of photographs), and has also embarked on an ambitious project to document the Rebbe's life. So far they have conducted almost 900 intensive and videotaped interviews with different individuals about their encounters with the Rebbe, brief segments of which they release on DVD, mobile apps, and on Chabad.org. Reb Elkanah bestowed on me the greatest of favors and acts of trust by allowing me to read through the unedited transcripts of these interviews (I once computed that at the time it must have come to some 10,000 single-spaced pages, and more by now). I cannot overstate how the content of these interviews enriched the manuscript and also provided me with leads.

I am particularly indebted as well to Rabbi Motti Seligson in the Chabad.org office and Rabbi Yechiel Cagen in the JEM office, for their generosity of time and spirit. Both Motti and Yechiel are very kind, very bright people, the most blessed of combinations, and their patience in putting up with my questions and insistence on documentation was exemplary. Many others at both organizations, too numerous to enumerate, were very helpful as well, and I regard their work as crucial to maintaining the vitality of Jewish life in the coming decades.

Another person whose help was invaluable in tracking down certain historical details and to whom I am extraordinarily grateful is Rabbi Shalom D. Levine, librarian of the movement's Library of Agudas Chasidei Chabad-Lubavitch. I would also like to thank the Jewish Theological Seminary Library and its director and professor of Talmud, Dr. David Kraemer.

I want to acknowledge as well Rabbi Baruch Oberlander, chief Chabad-Lubavitch emissary of Hungary, who is co-authoring with Rabbi Elkanah Shmotkin, aided by Rabbi Levi Greisman, a book on the Rebbe's early years. The trove of documents they have amassed has already served as a priceless resource for many scholars and authors, myself included, particularly since so little has been known about that time until now.

I also want to thank my friend J. J. Goldberg, the former editor in chief, and now editor-at-large of the *Forward*, whose publication of my article on the Rebbe in 2006 helped inaugurate this whole project.

As this was not an authorized biography, everyone with whom I consulted at Chabad respected that all editorial decisions were mine, and no one ever tried to cross that line. Given the great veneration for the Rebbe felt by all these people, I am very grateful for that as well. To have given me such access without asking for any editorial control was an act of trust, one I hope I have never abused. I also hope that these people and all the Rebbe's followers will come to appreciate some of the conclusions I have reached, even if different from their own.

I feel privileged to have been greatly assisted by Rabbi Mendel Alperowitz, a young man whose wide-ranging knowledge is exceeded only by his kindness and calm, unflappable demeanor. Mendel is, God willing, at the start of what I believe will be a very accomplished career, and the assistance he provided me, in locating sources (including periodically tracking down some rather obscure data and uncovering sources of which I was unaware until he directed me to them), and in both challenging and supporting conclusions I reached, has helped make this book much better than it would otherwise have been. I bless every writer, particularly one working on so extensive a project, with such help.

Early in the project, Rabbi Simon Jacobson, himself the author of an important book on the Rebbe, *Toward a Meaningful Life,* spent several full days in conversation with me, both sharing with me from his extraordinary knowledge of the Rebbe and of Chabad, and directing me to others with whom I should speak. Simon's influence is felt in many sections of this book, none more so than in the chapter on the Rebbe and journalism (chapter 12). This is perhaps not surprising, as Simon is the publisher of the *Algemeiner Journal,* the newspaper founded by this father, Gershon Jacobson, of blessed memory.

I am of course indebted and grateful to all people who took the time to speak with me one on one about their interactions with the Rebbe, and their own assessments and understandings of the Rebbe, his persona, his teachings, and his role in their lives, in the lives of the Jewish people, and in the world. I was touched by how many people entrusted me with some of their most personal feelings and experiences; there were instances in which people cried during our discussions. Talmudic law has strict regulations concerning a *shomer,* a guardian, and I hope I have always treated the memories with which I was entrusted with the appropriate sensitivity.

Concerning many of the people I interviewed, I have so much I would like to say, but acknowledgments, I am aware, should not turn into a full-length chapter, so I regretfully will confine myself to listing the people who met with me. Some of these people did not know the Rebbe but simply offered me guidance and help in my work (I very sincerely apologize in advance to anyone whom I have inadvertently omitted).

President Shimon Peres, Ambassador Yehuda Avner, Rabbi Yehuda Krinsky, Rabbi Avraham Shemtov, Rabbi Leibel Groner, Rabbi Binyamin Klein, Rabbi Sholom Mendel Simpson, Rabbi Zalman Schachter-Shalomi, Diane Abrams, Robert (Bob) Abrams, Yanky Ascher, Gary Bauer, Rabbi Dr. Moshe Berger, Rabbi Avraham Berkowitz, Rabbi Yirmiyahu Berkowitz, Rabbi Saul Berman, Rebbetzin Rivkah Blau, Rabbi Benjamin Blech, Professor Yitzchak (Irving) Block, Rabbi Yonah Blum, Rabbi Shmuley Boteach, Rabbi Chaim Shaul Brook, Rabbi Moshe Bryski, Rebbetzin Hadassah Carlebach, Rabbi Naftali Citron, Professor Steven Cohen, Rabbi Shlomo Cunin, Rabbi Mendel Feller, Rabbi Moshe Feller, Rabbi Hirsch Fox z'l, Rabbi Tzvi Freeman, Rabbi Manis Friedman, Rabbi Menachem Genack, Ambassador Dore Gold, Professor Ari Goldman, Rabbi Yosef Greenberg, Rabbi Chaim Baruch Halberstam, Professor Susan Handelman, Rabbi Shmully Hecht, Judge Alvin Hellerstein, Malcolm Hoenlein, Yitzchak Yehuda Holtzman, Rabbi Shimshon Junik, Rabbi Yoel Kahan, Rabbi Nochem Kaplan, Rabbi Shmuel Kaplan, Rabbi Zev Katz, Rabbi Moshe Kotlarsky, Rabbi Dr. Norman Lamm, Rabbi Berel Lazar, Rabbi Moshe Lazar, Rabbi Shmuel Lew, Nathan (Nat) Lewin, Rabbi Mendel Lipskar, Rabbi Sholom Lipskar, Professor Naftali Loewenthal, Professor David Luchins, Rabbi David Miller, Rabbi Efraim Mintz, Dr. Susanna Mintz Morgenthau, Rabbi Mendel Pewsner, Rebbetzin Sara Pewsner, Rabbi Zalman Posner, Rebbetzin Risa Posner z'l, Dennis Prager, Rabbi Chaim Rapoport, Rabbi Shlomo Riskin, George Rohr, Sami Rohr z'l, Rabbi Eli Rubin, Rabbi Lord Jonathan Sacks, Rabbi Michoel Seligson, Rebbetzin Chana Sharfstein, Rabbi Berel Shemtov, Rabbi Eliezer Shemtov, Rabbi Levi Shemtov (of Washington), Rabbi Levi Shemtov (of Riverdale), Rebbetzin Rochel Shemtov, Rabbi Yisroel Shmotkin, Rebbetzin Esther Sternberg, Rabbi Nachman Sudak, Ambassador Daniel Taub, Rabbi Marvin (Moshe)

Tokayer, Rabbi Abraham Twerski, M.D., Rabbi Dr. Tzvi Hersh Weinreb, Dr. Ira Weiss, Rabbi Dovid Zaklikowski, Rabbi Shlomo Zarchi, Mrs. Alice Zlotnick, and Professor Dov Zlotnick.

Richard Pine of Inkwell Management has been my agent and friend for more than thirty years, and his involvement in my life has blessed my writing career since its earliest days. Richard has shown a great interest in this project about the Rebbe since its beginning and he, along with his editorial assistant, Eliza Rothstein, carefully read through earlier versions of this manuscript and shepherded it till it found its home at HarperCollins; there, I have had the pleasure of working with publisher Karen Rinaldi and editor Jake Zebede. At a time when I thought I had pretty much brought the book to completion, they showed me where there was still room, quite a bit of room, for improvement. They have taken this book so seriously, and Jake's dedication and skilled editing have inspired me to work further on and deepen chapters I thought I had completed. I would also like to thank my superb and methodical copy editor, Muriel Jorgensen.

Carolyn Hessel, executive director of the Jewish Book Council, has been a great booster, and careful reader of this book from the beginning. In addition to the instrumental work Carolyn plays in promoting the reading of Jewish books throughout the United States and beyond, she is, as far as I am concerned, most of all a friend. And of that I am very proud.

David Szonyi has worked with me for many years, since the writing of *Jewish Literacy*. His editing makes my writing clearer, his Jewish knowledge is broad, and I am very thankful for his help. He is a gifted freelance editor.

I did not have the chutzpah to ask any of my friends to read through the whole of this lengthy manuscript, but many friends read through a variety of chapters, and offered editorial suggestions. Unfortunately, I do not have the space to elaborate on each person's contributions, but I am profoundly grateful to all of them: Rabbi Saul Berman, David Brandes, Rebbetzin Hadassah Carlebach, Allen Estrin, Rabbi Leonid Feldman, David Friedman, Ambassador Dore Gold, Atarah Hazzan, Carolyn Starman Hessel, Rabbi Irwin Kula, Dr. Steven Marmer, Robert

Mass, Rebecca Menashe, Dennis Prager, Zalman Rothschild, Christine Silk, Roger Silk, Ambassador Daniel Taub, Benjamin Telushkin, Naomi Telushkin, Shira Telushkin, Ron Temkin, David Wohlberg, Rabbi David Woznica, and Richard Zaretsky.

It is customary for authors to thank their spouses and acknowledge their emotional support and patience. In this instance, I have far more than emotional support and patience to acknowledge. Dvorah has been my full partner in the writing of this book. Throughout these past years, I would consistently share with her what I uncovered in my research and wait to hear her reactions and assessments. She became as fascinated by the Rebbe as I, and in the last months of the writing of the book, she put aside all of her own projects, often staying up with me until three in the morning, and sometimes even later, to help me finish this manuscript. Dvorah, a gifted writer, has a particular skill in organizing material in a manner that maximizes dramatic impact while remaining fully accurate and true to the story. If this book manages not only to teach you things you might not have known about Rabbi Menachem Mendel Schneerson, but to hold your interest while doing so, much of that accomplishment is due to her. And of course along with all this, came her great emotional support and patience as well—all necessary features on those long nights when I feared that I had undertaken something so much bigger than I—and it was she who helped me cross the finish line.

Finally, and I hope this does not sound presumptuous, I thank Rabbi Menachem Mendel Schneerson. The Jewish people are different and better today because of him. I am confident that future authors will have more to write about the Rebbe and his life accomplishments; he was a man whose story can fill far more than one volume. I only hope that I have fairly and accurately conveyed at least a part of his essence. If I have, then of one thing I am confident: you will become a better person as a result of reading and learning about him, *zeicher tzaddik l'vracha* (may the memory of the righteous be for a blessing).

INDEX

ABOUT THE AUTHOR

Joseph Telushkin is the author of nineteen books, including *Jewish Literacy*, *The Book of Jewish Values*, and two volumes of *A Code of Jewish Ethics*, the first volume of which received the National Jewish Book Award in 2006. His most recent book, *Hillel: If Not Now, When?*, is a study of the enduring significance of the great Talmudic sage. He is a senior associate of CLAL, serves on the board of the Jewish Book Council, and represented HIAS at the United Nations in Geneva in December 2012. He lectures throughout the United States and lives in New York City.